Pauline Frommer's

ALASKA

SPEND LESS ★ SEE MORE™

1st Edition

W9-BUP-998

by David Thompson

Series Editor: Pauline Frommer

WILEY

Wiley Publishing, Inc.

Published by:

Wiley Publishing, Inc.

111 River St.
Hoboken, NJ 07030-5774

ISBN: 978-0-470-08957-6

Editor: Jennifer Reilly
Production Editor: Lindsay Conner
Cartographer: Andy Dolan
Photo Editor: Richard Fox
Interior Design: Lissa Auciello-Brogan
Production by Wiley Indianapolis Composition Services

For information on our other products and services or to obtain technical support,
please contact our Customer Care Department within the U.S. at 800/762-2974,
outside the U.S. at 317/572-3993 or fax 317/572-4002.

Wiley also publishes its books in a variety of electronic formats. Some content that
appears in print may not be available in electronic formats.

Manufactured in the United States of America

5   4   3   2   1

Contents

List of Maps.................................... vii

A Note from Pauline 1

1 Alaska, from Folly to Fantastic 2

The Regions of Alaska 3
Top Experiences 4
Suggested Itineraries........................... 8

2 Cruising Alaska's Coast..................... 15

Weighing Your Cruise Options 16
The Best Cruise Experiences in Alaska 19
Booking Your Cruise............................. 19
Cruise Lines Profiles 22

3 Anchorage & Environs..................... 28

Don't Leave Anchorage Without 29
A Brief History 29
Lay of the Land 30
Getting to & Around Anchorage................... 31
Accommodations, Both Standard & Not 33
Dining for All Tastes 40
Why You're Here: The Top Sights & Attractions..... 45
The Other Anchorage 49
Active Anchorage 51
Attention, Shoppers! 54
Nightlife in Anchorage......................... 56
Get Out of Town 58

4 Southcentral Alaska 79

Don't Leave Southcentral Alaska Without 79

Lay of the Land 80

Getting to & Around Southcentral Alaska 84

Valdez 84

Whittier 94

Cordova 97

Seward 108

Soldotna/Kenai 122

Homer 128

Kodiak 142

5 Southeast Alaska 152

Don't Leave Southeast Alaska Without 153

Lay of the Land 154

Getting to & Around Southeast Alaska 156

Ketchikan 157

Wrangell 172

Petersburg 181

Sitka 189

Juneau 206

Glacier Bay National Park 227

Tracy Arm-Fords Terror Wilderness 231

Admiralty Island 232

Skagway 233

Haines 247

6 Alaska's Interior 258

Don't Leave Interior Alaska Without 259

Lay of the Land 259

Getting to & Around Inner Alaska 261

Fairbanks 261

Interior Driving Tour #1: The Steese Highway 291

Interior Driving Tour #2: The Elliott Highway. 296

Interior Driving Tour #3: The Dalton Highway 297

7 Denali National Park & Preserve 306

A Brief History 307

Lay of the Land. 307

Getting to & Around Denali. 308

Accommodations, Both Standard & Not. 310

Dining for All Tastes 317

Why You're Here: The Top Sights & Attractions. 319

Active Denali 327

Nightlife in Denali. 328

Talkeetna: Back Door to Denali 328

8 The Bush 333

Don't Leave Bush Alaska Without 334

Lay of the Land. 334

Getting to & Around the Bush. 335

Unalaska & Dutch Harbor 335

Nome. 342

Barrow. 351

9 The Essentials of Planning. 359

When to Visit 359

Entry Requirements 365

Customs Regulations for International Visitors. 366

Getting to & Around Alaska. 367

Saving Money on Accommodations. 371

Outdoor Adventures/Tours. 373

Travel Insurance—Do You Need It? 376

Money Matters 377

Health & Safety. 377

Tips on Packing. 379

Specialized Travel Resources 380

Staying Wired 384

Recommended Reading. 384

Appendix: Alaska on the Wild Side. 389

Whale Spotting 101. 393

Index 397

List of Maps

Anchorage 35

Downtown Anchorage 37

The Kenai Peninsula & Prince
   William Sound 83

Valdez 87

Whittier 95

Cordova 101

Seward 111

Homer 131

Kodiak 145

Ketchikan 159

Wrangell 175

Petersburg 183

Sitka 193

Juneau Beyond Downtown 209

Downtown Juneau 211

Glacier Bay National Park 229

Skagway 237

Haines 251

Greater Fairbanks 265

Downtown Fairbanks 267

Denali National Park 311

Unalaska 337

Nome 343

Barrow 353

About the Author

Freelance writer **David Thompson** lives in the Hawaiian Islands. He is one of the authors of the *Pauline Frommer's Hawaii* guide.

Additional contributions by: Charles Wohlforth, Jerry Brown & Fran Wenograd Golden.

An Invitation to the Reader

In researching this book, we discovered many wonderful places—hotels, restaurants, shops, and more. We're sure you'll find others. Please tell us about them, so we can share the information with your fellow travelers in upcoming editions. If you were disappointed with a recommendation, we'd love to know that, too. Please write to:

Pauline Frommer's Alaska, 1st Edition
Wiley Publishing, Inc. • 111 River St. • Hoboken, NJ 07030-5774

An Additional Note

Please be advised that travel information is subject to change at any time—and this is especially true of prices. We therefore suggest that you write or call ahead for confirmation when making your travel plans. The authors, editors, and publisher cannot be held responsible for the experiences of readers while traveling. Your safety is important to us, however, so we encourage you to stay alert and be aware of your surroundings. Keep a close eye on cameras, purses, and wallets, all favorite targets of thieves and pickpockets.

Star Ratings, Icons & Abbreviations

Every restaurant, hotel, and attraction is rated with stars ★, indicating our opinion of that facility's desirability; this relates not to price, but to the value you receive for the price you pay. The stars mean:

No stars: Good
★ Very good
★★ Great
★★★ Outstanding! A must!

Accommodations within each neighborhood are listed in ascending order of cost, starting with the cheapest and increasing to the occasional "splurge." Each hotel review is preceded by one, two, three, or four dollar signs, indicating the price range per double room. Restaurants work on a similar system, with dollar signs indicating the price range per three-course meal.

Accommodations
$ Up to $100/night
$$ $101–$135
$$$ $136–$175
$$$$ Over $176 per night

Dining
$ Meals for $7 or less
$$ $8–$12
$$$ $12–$17
$$$$ $18 and up

In addition, we've included a kids icon 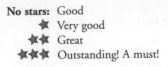 to denote attractions, restaurants, and lodgings that are particularly child friendly.

Frommers.com

Now that you have this guidebook to help you plan a great trip, visit our website at www.frommers.com for additional travel information on more than 3,600 destinations. We update features regularly to give you instant access to the most current trip-planning information available. At Frommers.com, you'll find scoops on the best airfares, lodging rates, and car rental bargains. You can even book your travel online through our reliable travel booking partners. Other popular features include:

* Online updates of our most popular guidebooks
* Vacation sweepstakes and contest giveaways
* Newsletters highlighting the hottest travel trends
* Online travel message boards with featured travel discussions

A Note from Pauline

I STARTED TRAVELING WITH MY GUIDEBOOK-WRITING PARENTS, ARTHUR Frommer and Hope Arthur, when I was just 4 months old. To avoid lugging around a crib, they would simply swaddle me and stick me in an open drawer for the night. For half of my childhood, my home was a succession of hotels and B&Bs throughout Europe, as we dashed around every year to update *Europe on $5 a Day* (and then $10 a day, and then $20 . . .).

We always traveled on a budget, staying at the mom-and-pop joints Dad featured in the guide, getting around by public transportation, eating where the locals ate. And that's still the way I travel today because I learned—from the master—that these types of vacations not only save you money, but they also give you a richer, deeper experience of the culture. You spend time in local neighborhoods, and you meet and talk with the people who live there. For me, making friends and having meaningful exchanges is always the highlight of my trip—and the main reason I decided to become a travel writer and editor as well.

I've conceived these books as budget guides for a new generation. They have all the outspoken commentary and detailed pricing information that you've come to expect from the Frommer's guides, but they take bargain hunting into the 21st century, with more information on how you can effectively use the Internet and air/hotel packages to save money. Most importantly, these guides stress the availability of "alternative accommodations," not simply to save you money but also to give you a more authentic experience in the places you visit.

In this Alaska book, for example, we tell you about an Art Deco–era lighthouse where you and up to 10 of your buddies can bunk for free near Cordova (p. 102); cozy waterfront apartments rented to sportsfishermen (or anyone in the know) in Kodiak for as little as $85 a night (p. 145); and public use cabins in the middle of the wilderness, where you'll be able to pick berries in your backyard and watch glaciers calving from your porch for as little as $50 a night (p. 373).

The individual chapter sections on "The Other Anchorage," "The Other Juneau," and so on immerse you in the life that residents of a particular place enjoy: the courses they take, the work they do, the crafts they practice. Page through this guide and you'll find classes in the odd sport of curling (p. 280), opportunities to volunteer on an archaeological dig in Unalaska (p. 342), and cooking classes led by a Homer local celebrity teaching you the best way to cook up the salmon you just caught (p. 138).

The result, I hope, is a valuable new addition to the world of guidebooks. Please let us know how we've done! I encourage you to e-mail me at editor@ frommers.com or write to me, care of Frommer's, 111 River St., Hoboken, NJ, 07030.

Happy traveling!

Pauline Frommer

Pauline Frommer

1 Alaska, from Folly to Fantastic

The top sights and experiences, plus recommended itineraries

WHEN U.S. SECRETARY OF STATE WILLIAM HENRY SEWARD NEGOTIATED the purchase of Alaska for 2¢ an acre in 1867, skeptics branded Seward a colossal sucker. He had just spent a walloping $7.2 million on an inhospitable, frozen wasteland as immense as it was useless. The only thing "Russian America," as it was then known, ever had going for it was fur. But the rapacious Russians, after a century of peeling the pelts from every sea otter and fur seal they would trap, shoot, stab, or club to death, had pushed the animals to the verge of extinction. No wonder the tsar wanted to dump the place on the United States. And Seward was his patsy.

It took a few decades before Americans realized that Seward had, in fact, negotiated one of the dirt-dog-cheapest land deals of all time. Sure, the 9 punishing months of winter were a bit much, but Alaska was anything but a wasteland. First, people discovered that Alaska was rich in gold, and with the succession of gold rushes in the late-19th and early-20th centuries, references to Walrussia, Icebergia, and Seward's Icebox went out the window. In the public's imagination, Alaska became The Last Frontier. Or simply The Great Land, using the translation of the Native word for Alaska. The gold rush was followed by rushes to mine copper, can salmon, cut timber, and drill for oil. In the annals of natural resource extraction, Alaska is a land that just keeps giving and giving.

Yet despite the constant drive to reap wealth from the wild, Alaska has remained remarkably pristine. To visit Alaska today is to immerse yourself in a land where civilization is a string of tiny footprints across a wild, untrammeled, and extreme landscape. In fact, Alaska has more land protected in national parks, preserves, wilderness areas, and state parks than all of the other states combined. Huge parts of Alaska are heaved upward into dazzling mountains. There are three major ranges and 30 smaller ones. Alaska's great mountains are so immense and remote that thousands of peaks have neither been climbed nor named.

The one thing that Seward's critics had right about Alaska was its enormity. Just to give you an idea of that scope, consider that it has:

- 3,000 rivers
- Three million lakes
- 100,000 glaciers

- 47,000 miles of coastline
- 17 of the 20 highest peaks in the nation, including McKinley, the tallest mountain on the continent
- And a wildlife population that rivals Africa's (the sea otters and fur seals have sprung back!)

Alaska is really more like a small continent than a single state. Transpose it on a map of the Lower 48, and Alaska would stretch from Mexico to Canada, and from the Atlantic to the Pacific. The easternmost city in the state, Ketchikan, would overlap Charleston, South Carolina, while the westernmost island, Attu, would fall in Los Angeles County. From north to south, Alaska would poke up around Winnipeg and drop down below Tijuana. If you could see 1 million acres of Alaska each day for a year, you still wouldn't quite get through the entire 375-million-acre state.

So how on earth do you begin to plan a vacation to the state so ridiculously big? Selectively. Very, very selectively. Advanced planning is important on all vacations, but for Alaska it will make or break your holiday. I'd suggest either zeroing in on one of the broad regions described below, or following one of the suggested itineraries you'll see later in the chapter. Those on a budget—and I assume that means you since you've picked up this budget guide—are well advised to calculate transportation costs before setting an itinerary (see p. 367 in "The Essentials of Planning" chapter for more on that) as that, more than any other element of the trip, will rip your wallet to shreds.

THE REGIONS OF ALASKA

SOUTHCENTRAL ALASKA

You can think of the Southcentral part of the state as a generous Alaskan sampler platter. It's got at least a little of what the rest of the state has to offer—from wilderness and wildlife, to salmon and halibut fishing, to calving glaciers, to sea kayaking and white-water rafting, to Native culture, to gold mines, to old Russian churches. It also has Anchorage, which has the distinction of housing half of the state's population within its metropolitan area, making Southcentral Alaska the state's most populous region by far. Don't get the wrong idea, though. It's not crowded. But it does have good roads for easy access to all the fun.

SOUTHEAST ALASKA

This long strip of Alaska, wedged between Canada and the Pacific Ocean, is what you'll visit if you choose a cruise vacation (though it can also be visited independently, by hopping on and off the ferries of the Alaskan Marine Highway System). Home to the state capital, Juneau, it's more akin to the Pacific Northwestern region of the United States, in ambience and weather, than the rest of Alaska (milder temps, more rain, and a hip, politically savvy populace). That being said, it still boasts many of the sights and experiences that have drawn you to Alaska in the first place. You'll witness mighty blue glaciers calving into the sea as eagles soar overhead, and on shore, bears shuffling by. There are alpine meadows and cedar forests to explore, and jagged mountain peaks to climb. You'll find all of that in the Alaskan Panhandle, as it's called, with living Native culture (think totem poles—lots of 'em) and a good measure of Russian and gold rush history thrown into the mix, as well.

THE INTERIOR

The Alaskan Heartland's greatest draw is the 6-million-acre Denali National Park, home to the tallest mountain on the continent. It's arguably the state's easiest wilderness area to tour thanks to a fleet of old school buses that shuttle visitors deep, deep into the wild. But the Interior is far more than just Mt. McKinley and its backyard. It's here where Alaska's extremes are lived and celebrated. In the "Golden Heart City" of Fairbanks, for example, baseball is played beneath the midnight sun in the summer and enormous ice sculptures are carved under the northern lights in the winter. Head to more rural areas and you'll find folks who enjoy hot springing in sub-zero temperatures, rafting down raging rapids, and crisscrossing the Arctic Circle just to say they did it.

THE BUSH

The sweeping stretches of Alaska that are inaccessible by road—which is really most of the state—make up the Alaskan Bush. Most of the Bush is simply too wild and remote for casual visitors, but there are communities you can visit without the help of a dog sled or bush pilot. They include: Barrow, where Eskimos still hunt for bowhead whales on the Arctic Ocean, as they've done for generations; Nome, a gold-rush boomtown on the Bering Sea where gold still turns up in beach sand; and the windblown Aleutian Island community of Unalaska/Dutch Harbor, home to the storied Bering Sea king crab fishing fleet.

TOP EXPERIENCES

BEST PLACES TO SEE GLACIERS

GLACIER BAY NATIONAL PARK   This is simply the largest concentration of tidewater glaciers on the planet. At Glacier Bay, 16 glaciers creep out of the snowy St. Elias and Fairweather mountains to the sea; there are even more glaciers in the alpine valleys overhead. See p. 227.

PRINCE WILLIAM SOUND   The dozens of glaciers here are scattered around the vast inland sea called Prince William Sound, including the sprawling Columbia Glacier, one of the most massive glaciers you'll ever see. It's so big, it could nearly cover Los Angeles. The face of the Columbia is 3 miles wide, and you have to keep your distance because of the enormous slabs of ice—some as big as shopping malls—that split off from the face and crash into the sea. See p. 80.

KENAI FJORDS NATIONAL PARK   All but one of the several glaciers you can visit in Kenai Fjords National Park are only accessible by boat. The exception is Exit Glacier, which is that rarest of glaciers: a drive-up glacier. Here, you can climb to the top of the mountain along the trail bordering Exit Glacier and look out across the Harding Icefield, a sea of ice the size of Rhode Island. See p. 109.

CHILDS GLACIER   The Childs Glacier keeps visitors on their toes. The Childs' 20-story face can send icebergs crashing into the river below it that are so huge, they create tidal waves that rush up the opposite bank, where visitors gather. Either be prepared to hightail it, or enjoy the ice show from the elevated viewing platform that will keep you out of the tsunami inundation area. See p. 105.

BEST PLACES TO SEE BEARS

PACK CREEK   The Alaska Natives' name for Admiralty Island, near Juneau, is Kootznoowoo, or "fortress of the bears." It is a bruin stronghold—home of the largest concentration of brown bears in the world. From a viewing tower and platform safely off to the side, you can watch hungry bears swipe swimming salmon out of the creek with their claws or snatch jumping salmon out of mid-air with their teeth. See p. 232.

KODIAK ISLAND   The brown bears of Kodiak Island have been isolated from their mainland brethren for so long, they've evolved into a separate subspecies, the Kodiak Bear. They are the biggest, baddest bears on the planet, and the Kodiak National Wildlife Refuge, accessible by floatplane, is the place to see them. See p. 143.

DENALI NATIONAL PARK   Alaska's most accessible—and affordable— wilderness is the easiest place to encounter brown bears, and a host of other wildlife. While there's no guarantee that you'll spot bears, passengers on the park shuttle who ride at least 60 miles into the park typically see at least a few. See p. 306.

ANAN CREEK WILDLIFE OBSERVATORY   The black bears feasting on the salmon in Anan Creek have to share their seafood smorgasbord with hungry harbor seals and bald eagles. Viewing platforms off to the side give you a front-seat view on the summer wildlife feeding frenzy. See p. 180.

BEST FISHING

HOMER   Halibut fishing is the name of the game in Homer, the "The Halibut Fishing Capital of the World" and home of Alaska's largest charter fishing fleet. Every day throughout the summer, fishermen land halibut larger than third-graders. See p. 139.

KENAI RIVER   The king salmon in the Kenai river are so big they're in a trophy class all by themselves. Land a 50-pound king in any other Alaskan river and the state Department of Fish and Game certifies it as trophy. On the Kenai River, you've got to muscle in a 75-pounder before you're in the trophy class. See p. 127.

BEST WHALE-WATCHING WATERS

FREDERICK SOUND   Humpback whales fatten up for the summer in the nutrient-rich waters near Petersburg, and small mom-and-pop-operated tour boats carry passengers out to have a look. See p. 188.

SITKA SOUND   Humpback whales are so common in the waters around Sitka, you can see them right from shore at Whale Park (tour boats can also take you out for a closer look). A local radio station with a hydrophone in the sound broadcasts the songs of the whales live, 24 hours a day. See p. 200.

KENAI FJORDS NATIONAL PARK   Visitors riding tour boats to see the tidewater glaciers in the park often spot humpback whales and sometimes killer whales en route. The killer whales live there year-round; humpbacks just visit for the summer. See p. 122.

BEST MUSEUMS

THE MUSEUM OF THE NORTH   Housed in a spectacular "concept" building that's all swoops, curves, and silvery skin, the University of Alaska Fairbanks' Museum of the North will bring you up to speed on the last 11,000 years of human history in Alaska, and the past few million years of natural history. Thousands of years of Alaskan art are also on display. Modern works are placed side-by-side with ancient ivory carvings. See p. 277.

ANCHORAGE MUSEUM AT RASMUSON CENTER   This big metropolitan museum boasts seven galleries packed with Alaskan history and art. Artifacts in the cavernous Alaska Gallery are displayed in life-size dioramas, and cover a span of time stretching from the days when Alaskans built the Trans-Alaska Pipeline back to when they were hunting woolly mammoths. See p. 45.

THE PRATT MUSEUM   The Pratt is a little powerhouse of a museum, packed from floor to ceiling with hands-on activities and surprises. Pull out a drawer and examine the remains of an ancient midden, a Native garbage dump that reveals what the locals had for dinner 2,000 years ago. Pick up a ship's receiver and listen to Captain Joseph Hazelwood explain to the Coast Guard that he just ran aground in his oil tanker, the *Exxon Valdez*. Pull a survival suit out of a bin and see if you can struggle into it in 30 seconds, which is how much time you'd get if your fishing trawler were to suddenly sink. See p. 137.

THE ALASKA STATE MUSEUM   Here, the rich history of Alaska is revealed largely through everyday objects, including the crisply pressed wool cape worn by William Henry Seward, who brokered the purchase of Alaska from Russia for the U.S., and a pair of caribou skin diapers lined with downy soft, disposable moss, which an Athabascan infant might have worn. See p. 217.

BEST PLACES TO LEARN ABOUT NATIVE CULTURE

KETCHIKAN   Totem poles can be thought of as books—very tall, very heavy, very well-illustrated books. They tell stories, record histories, trace genealogies, ridicule those in need of ridiculing, and do all sorts of other booklike things. Nowhere can you get a sense of the incredible versatility of totem poles quite like you can in Ketchikan, home of the largest collection of totem poles in the world. There you'll see ancient poles carefully preserved in a climate-controlled museum, old poles slowly weathering in the woods as their makers expected, and the next generation of poles emerging from freshly cut logs at the hands of modern Native artisans. See p. 157.

SITKA   You'll also see impressive Totem Poles in Sitka, which houses the older poles in a high-ceilinged gallery (you'll simply stumble upon the newer ones, slowly aging in the misty woods). The folks that make these poles and practice other Native arts and crafts have studios at the Southeast Alaska Indian Cultural Center, and a visit here will certainly be a highlight of your trip. For a touch of history, head to the Sitka National Historical Park; the Battle of Sitka, the last major fight between the Tlingit and the Russians, took place in the woods here. And you can chat with Native artisans in their studios at the Southeast Alaska Indian Cultural Center. See p. 189.

ALASKA NATIVE HERITAGE CENTER   Both a tourist attraction and a gathering place for Alaskan Natives from throughout the state, the Heritage Center features traditional Native dwellings from the Aleutians to the Arctic, as well as dance performances, storytelling, and exhibitions by Native athletes. See p. 47.

BARROW   The northernmost community in the United States is also the largest Eskimo village in Alaska. During April and May, Native hunters pursue giant bowhead whales, as their ancestors have done for thousands of years. If you're around when they land one, you might get to participate in their celebratory blanket toss and try a bite of muktuk, or whale blubber, the local delicacy. See p. 351.

BEST KAYAKING

PRINCE WILLIAM SOUND   Protected waters, a multitude of islands, hidden coves and beaches, and an abundance of wildlife and tidewater glaciers make for some awesome paddling here. See p. 53.

KACHEMAK BAY STATE PARK   This marine wilderness at the foot of the snow-capped Kenai Mountains, and just across the bay from Homer, is both easy to get to and easy to lose yourself in, on single- or multiday kayaking trips. See p. 140.

GLACIER BAY NATIONAL PARK   You can camp along the shoreline of this 65-mile-long, Y-shaped bay as you explore the many glaciers and hike in the surrounding area. See p. 227.

BEST "OTHER" ALASKA

DIG INTO THE NATIVE PAST   Lend a hand to the archaeologists from the Alutiiq Museum as they unearth tools, hearths, fish bones, and other remains from ancient Native villages on Kodiak Island. See p. 148.

BEND AN ELBOW WITH ALASKAN BREWERS   The same rich, malty, long-on-the-palate alt-style beer that Juneau's gold miners slaked their thirst on is still made in Juneau today. Visit the city's Alaskan Brewing Company and you can see how it's made and how it tastes. See p. 224.

RESEARCH IN THE FAR NORTH   Take a behind the scenes tour of the high-latitude research facilities at the University of Alaska at Fairbanks, and get current on global warming, Alaskan volcanoes, the aurora borealis, and other fields of geophysical interest. Immerse yourself in virtual reality in the Arctic Region Supercomputing Center, where scientists use huge stereoscopic screens and some of the world's fastest computers to bring their boring data sets to life. See p. 279.

HOBNOB WITH THE CURLERS   Scottish gold miners brought the ancient winter sport of curling (that curious intersection of ice skating, shuffleboard, and street sweeping) to Fairbanks in the early–20th century, playing on the frozen Chena River. Today you can watch the members of the Fairbanks Curling Club compete in their very own ice arena. Ask nicely and you can even get a lesson. See p. 281.

BEST THINGS TO DO IN WINTER

VISIT ALYESKA SKI RESORT   Deep snow, great views, a long season, and remarkably short lift lines make for fantastic downhill skiing at Alaska's only ski resort. See p. 67.

FLOAT BENEATH AURORA BOREALIS   Visit Chena Hot Springs outside of Fairbanks, strip down to your swim suit, and watch the colorful northern lights dance in the starry winter sky while you soak in steamy mineral water. See p. 290.

POLAR BEAR VIEWING IN BARROW   When the Arctic Ocean freezes, the polar bears come ashore, and tour guides out of Barrow will help you find them—safely. See p. 357.

CATCH THE IDITAROD   The longest dog sled race in the world starts in Anchorage and ends 1,000 miles later in Nome. There's a big party at either end and a grueling endurance race across a huge swath of frozen Alaska in between. See p. 76.

SUGGESTED ITINERARIES
A WEEK OF HIGH ADVENTURE

Scaling a mountain, paragliding, hiking and camping in the wilderness, white-water rafting, sea kayaking, and possibly an urban moose and whale hunt: This itinerary packs a slew of adventures into a short and busy week and is perfect for the vacationer with energy to burn, who gets antsy sitting in one place for very long. Bring whatever camping gear you can, and rent what you can't in Anchorage on Day 1.

Day 1   Hike, Paraglide

Head from Anchorage into the Chugach Mountains, which bump up to the edge of the city, and hike to the top of 3,550-foot Flattop Mountain (p. 52). Be sure to leave time for Girdwood (p. 68), where, if your courage holds, you'll take a tandem paragliding flight from the top of Mount Alyeska back down to sea level strapped to the body of an experienced instructor. Spend the night in Girdwood or camp at Bird Creek (p. 40) along beautiful Turnagain Arm.

Day 2   Buzz the Roof of the Continent

Set out early for the half-day drive to Denali National Park (p. 306), and check in at the park's Back Country Information Center to get a backcountry hiking permit (permits can be reserved no more than a day in advance). After consulting with the park rangers on your trip plan (and getting the required wildlife safety briefing), use the rest of the day for a flightseeing trip around 20,320-foot Mount McKinley, North America's tallest mountain. Since the mountain is obscured in clouds most of the time, getting up in a plane is the surest way to get a good look at The High One.

Days 3 & 4   Wander in the Wilderness

Spend Days 3 and 4 hiking, camping, and mingling with Denali's moose, caribou, bears, and other resident wildlife. There are no trails in the park, so it's up to you to find your way. It's not as hard as it sounds. Much of the landscape is wide-open tundra with long views.

Day 5   White-Water Rafting

Shoot the rapids on the icy Nenana River (p. 327) bordering the park. It has enough class III and IV thrills to give you an adrenaline buzz that should get you through the long afternoon drive back to Anchorage, where you'll spend the night.

Day 6   Sea Kayaking

From Anchorage, head to Whittier (p. 97) for a guided sea kayaking tour among the tidewater glaciers, icebergs, seals, and sea lions of Prince William Sound. No experience is necessary and the waters are as calm as can be, except when icebergs crash into the sea and kick up rollercoaster-like waves. Return to Anchorage that night.

Day 7   Urban Moose & Whale Hunt

Before your late flight home, rent bikes in downtown Anchorage for a ride along the Tony Knowles Coastal Trail (p. 51), which runs along the edge of the city and is the best place in town to catch a glimpse of Cook Inlet's resident population of beluga whales. Watch for moose along the way, and give them a wide berth if you come upon one—they have a John McEnroe vs. the umpire mentality when it comes to cyclists. If you pedal far enough, you'll come to the end of the airport runway, an area especially popular among moose, for some reason.

A SCENIC DRIVING TOUR

This driving tour begins and ends in Anchorage and takes you through a broad cross-section of Alaska without backtracking. It's a giant triangle of a drive that crosses one mountain range, dips in and out of another, and takes time for some Alaska history, Native culture, glaciers, wildlife, and sled dogs along the way.

Day 1   Turnagain Arm

Arrive in Anchorage, rent a car, and set off on the scenic Seward Highway along Turnagain Arm. Watch for mountain goats, rock climbers, and waterfalls at the edge of the mountains to your left, and beluga whales, bore tides, and windsurfers in the long narrow fjord to your right. Make time for a hike at one of the many trails along the way. Spend the night at the ski resort community of Girdwood (p. 63), where you can ride a tram to the top of Mount Alyeska for alpine hiking and sublime views.

Day 2   Ferry Across Prince William Sound to Valdez

Head to the oddball town of Whittier (where most of the residents live in a single high-rise) to hop aboard a tour boat for a visit to the tidewater glaciers on Prince William Sound (p. 96). When you return, put your car on one of the ferries of the Alaska Marine Highway System and cross the sound to Valdez, where you'll spend the night.

Day 3   Into the Chugach Range

The spectacular Richardson Highway traverses the Chugach Mountains, the next trek along your itinerary (you can motor quickly through much of it, but you'll want to take in the view from 2,678 ft. Thompson Pass and inspect Worthington Glacier). The Richardson Highway goes all the way to Fairbanks, paralleling the Trans-Alaska Pipeline, which carries crude oil from the Arctic oilfields at Prudhoe Bay to oil tankers in Valdez Harbor. You'll turn off on the Glenn Highway, and spend the night at Sheep Mountain Lodge (p. 71), where the moving dots speckling the nearby mountainside are actually wild sheep.

Day 4   Head to Palmer

Visit the Matanuska Glacier (p. 73), the only glacier in Alaska you can safely wander around on without special training or a guide. Then continue on the Glenn Highway to Palmer, an agricultural town founded by Midwestern farmers during the Great Depression. Make a pit stop at the Palmer Musk Ox Farm (p. 72), where a herd of shaggy arctic ungulates is raised for a fine, ultra-warm wool (Native weavers make garments from it).

Day 5   Into the Talkeetna Mountains

Today you head into the Talkeetna Mountains to explore the ruins and restored buildings of the Independence Gold Mine (p. 74), once Alaska's most productive hard-rock gold mine and now a historical park. Hike the high alpine tundra, or borrow a gold pan from the visitor center and try your luck panning for gold in the creek. Flecks of gold that work their way out of the mountain are still found there.

Day 6   Back to Anchorage

On your drive back to Anchorage, detour through Wasilla to visit the headquarters of the Iditarod Trail Sled Dog Race (p. 75). You'll get to pretend you're a contender in the race with a ride in a dog cart pulled by a yelping, slobbering team of sled dogs. Another worthy stop on the way back to Anchorage is the Alaska Native Heritage Center (p. 47), where Native storytellers, athletes, and dancers put on impressive performances and demonstrations.

Day 7   A Farewell Hike

Get up early and hike to the top of Flattop Mountain (p. 52) above the city for a final, phenomenal look at Alaska before heading to the airport for your flight home.

A WEEK WITH KIDS

With kids in tow, you want to limit the distances you have to travel and maximize the amount of time you spend loafing in and exploring interesting places. The Kenai Peninsula is the place to do it. It's within easy reach of Anchorage, and it's loaded with mountains, glaciers, fjords, and wildlife galore—it also boasts good campsites. Camping makes good sense for families: Kids won't feel cooped up in hotel rooms, parents won't need to enforce indoor voices in restaurants, and everybody will get in touch with Alaska's great outdoors. Plus, you'll save a ton of money.

Day 1   Arrive into Anchorage

Pick up your rental car, stock up on groceries, and head out of town on the Seward Highway along scenic Turnagain Arm. Make camp at Bird Creek Campground (p. 40), then head to Girdwood to pan for gold in the river at Crow Creek Gold Mine (p. 68), an amazingly well-preserved mining camp dating to the 1890s.

Day 2   Drive to Seward

Enjoy the scenic drive to Seward, then head to the Alaska SeaLife Center (p. 117). Put the family on the big digital scale by the sea lion's tank and see how you stack up, pound for pound, against Woody, the 2,000-pound resident Steller sea lion. Stay at Primrose Campground (p. 113), on the edge of Kenai Lake, not far out of town.

Day 3   Tidewater Glaciers

Hop aboard a boat for a trip to Kenai Fjords National Park (p. 118) to see tidewater glaciers and some of the large marine mammals you spotted at the SeaLife Center, only in the wild. Make sure everybody takes seasickness medicine before embarking. A segment of the trip crosses the Gulf of Alaska, which can be rough.

Day 4   Head to Homer

Stop in Soldotna or Kenai along the way (to break up the 4-hr. drive) to eat, and maybe stroll along the beach at the mouth of the Kenai River. In Homer, stop at the Islands and Ocean Visitor Center (p. 137) for a grounding in the area's cultural and natural history. Let the kids run around on Bishop's Beach for a while, or take in the Pratt Museum (p. 137) to learn about the area's natural history. Camp on Homer Spit (p. 135).

Day 5   Kachemak Bay State Park

If your kids are old enough for sea kayaking, go for a guided tour across the bay from Homer at Kachemak Bay State Park (p. 140). The park's sheltered waters, at the foot of the towering, snow-capped Kenai Mountains, are safe enough for raw beginners but awe-inspiring enough to hold the attention of even the most jaded 'tweens. Watch for marine life, including sea otters, seals, porpoises, and sometimes whales. On shore you might spot moose, black bear, coyotes, mountain goats, and wolves. If your kids are too young to sea kayak, take them to Bishop's Beach (p. 138) instead, for beachcombing and sand castle building.

Day 6   Return to Anchorage

Stop at the Alaska Wildlife Conservation Center (p. 61) on the drive back to Anchorage and see the resident elk, musk ox, bison, caribou, owls, and eagles. The enclosures are large enough to give the animals room to roam, but there's no guarantee of up-close sightings, which may frustrate young kids (under age 6 or so) who have trouble picking the animals out at a distance. If that looks like it might be the case, go instead to the Alaska Zoo (p. 48) in Anchorage, where you'll have guaranteed face time with the critters. Give yourselves a night in a hotel (and hot showers before you get on the plane!).

Day 7   A Day in Anchorage

Visit the Alaska Native Heritage Center (p. 47) and spend the morning listening to the age-old tales of Alaska Native storytellers, watching Native dancers and athletes perform, and exploring the traditional dwellings used by Natives from different parts of the state. After lunch, take in the Imaginarium Science Discovery Center (p. 47) to study frogs, solve puzzles, fire an air cannon, test the aerodynamics of an aircraft wing, examine plankton through a microscope, touch a meteorite, and stand inside a giant soap bubble, among other things.

CLASSIC ALASKA IN 2 WEEKS

As I've said before, Alaska is a huge state, and this tour covers an enormous chunk of it. It will give you a good taste of the drizzly Southeast, richly diverse Southcentral Alaska, the wildly popular Denali National Park wilderness, and the boreal forests and rolling gold hills of the immense Alaskan Interior. It's a fast-paced, whirlwind trip that will keep you on the move by ferry, mountain tram, tour boat, white-water raft, old school bus (the Denali shuttles), rent-a-car, and possibly riverboat, with a very relaxing treat at the end.

Day 1   Sitka: An Introduction

Sitka, once the capital of Russian America, is one of the most gorgeously situated cities in Alaska. For your first day here, take in the city's Slavic sights, visiting St. Michael's Cathedral (p. 201) to inspect age-old Russian Orthodox icons and religious treasures, taking a tour of the Russian Bishop's House (p. 196), whose original occupant was later named a saint, and climbing to the top of Castle Hill (p. 198), where Russia transferred Alaska to the U.S.

Day 2   Sitka: Native History & Wildlife

For your second day, concentrate on Sitka's Native and natural wonders, starting with the Sitka National Historical Park (p. 195) where ancient totem poles are displayed in a high-ceilinged gallery while latter-day totem poles slowly weather outdoors in the mossy woods. Chat with modern Tlingit artisans in their workshops, then stroll the battleground where the Tlingit made their last stand against the Russians. Pay a visit to the Alaska Raptor Center (p. 199), where injured bald eagles learn to fly again. Then get out onto the water to see seals, otters, sea lions, and humpback whales on a boat tour to the St. Lazaria Island National Wildlife Refuge (p. 200).

Day 3   Ferry to Juneau

Hop the all-day trip to Juneau aboard an Alaska Marine Highway System ferry (p. 208), as thrilling an experience as any of the state's more expensive nature cruises. Keep your eyes peeled for bears, whales, and other wildlife as you thread your way through the islands of the Inside Passage. In downtown Juneau, ride Mount Roberts Tramway (p. 216) to the top of a nearly vertical mountain looming over the city and take in the view from 1,800 feet.

Day 4   Juneau

Head out to the suburbs to poke around Mendenhall Glacier, then take a flight-seeing tour of the Juneau Icefield (p. 222), from which dozens of glaciers, including the Mendenhall, spring. If the weather grounds your flight (it happens in Juneau), head to the Alaska State Museum (p. 217), or go for a self-guided walking tour of downtown to see the state capitol, the governor's mansion, and other sites. Hop the 4:30 p.m. boat to Glacier Bay National Park, where you'll spend the night at Glacier Bay Lodge (p. 230). Watch for humpback whales along the way.

Day 5   Glacier Bay National Park

Board the boat docked out in front of Glacier Bay Lodge for a day-long tour of Glacier Bay (p. 229), which boasts the largest cluster of tidewater glaciers on earth. Bring warm clothing—you'll need it around glaciers, even in the summer. Ride back to Juneau that evening.

Day 6   Anchorage

Hop a flight to Anchorage and then rent a car to explore Alaska's largest city. Stop at the Alaska Native Heritage Center (p. 47), to get up to speed on Alaska's 11 distinct Native cultures and to see Native storytellers, athletes, and dancers perform. If you have time, pop over to the Anchorage Museum at Rasmuson Center (p. 45) as well. Then head up to Flattop Mountain (p. 52) for a hike with a sweeping view of the city, the mountains, and Cook Inlet.

Day 7   Day Trip Along Turnagain Arm

Drive the scenic Seward Highway (p. 58) between the edge of the Chugach Mountains and the turbulent waters of a long, narrow fjord called Turnagain Arm. Watch for waterfalls, rock climbers, Dall sheep, mountain goats, beluga whales, and—if you're lucky—the bore tide (a literal tidal wave) along the way. Trailheads and picnic areas dot the route. Poke around the funky ski town of Girdwood (p. 63) and take a tour of the rapidly retreating Portage Glacier (p. 63) before returning to Anchorage.

Day 8   Anchorage to Talkeetna

Head up the Parks Highway toward Denali National Park to spend the night in Talkeetna (p. 328), an old riverside supply town for trappers and gold prospectors which has become the staging ground for international mountain climbers preparing to ascend nearby Mount McKinley. On the way to Talkeetna, stop in Palmer to see the Musk Ox Farm (p. 72), then drive up into the Talkeetna

Mountains to explore the Independence Gold Mine (p. 74), once Alaska's most productive hard-rock gold mine and now a historical park.

Day 9   Talkeetna to Denali

Continue your road trip to Denali National Park (p. 306). Outside the entrance to the park, take a refreshing white-water rafting ride on the swift, icy waters of the Nenana River. It's filled with class III and IV rapids, as well as slower sections for the less bold. Because you made reservations for the shuttle that carries visitors into the park long before you got to Alaska, you don't need to worry about it today (but if you didn't, then you might have to skip rafting and stand in line at the visitor center to be sure you have a ticket on an early bus for tomorrow).

Days 10 & 11   Explore the Park

Spend 2 full days in Denali National Park, a completely intact sub-Arctic ecosystem. Plan to get an early start. The wildlife is most active in the morning. You may spot bear, moose, caribou, and wolves, which are among the 39 species of mammals inhabiting the park. On a clear day, you might even see the High One itself—20,320-foot Mount McKinley (p. 320). Alaskans prefer to use the mountain's Native name, Denali.

Day 12   Denali to Fairbanks

Drive to Fairbanks for the night. The winters may be 40 below, but the summers are the warmest in the state. Make a beeline for the University of Alaska campus to see a 36,000-year-old mummified steppe bison, an ancient piece of carved ivory known as the Okvik Madonna, Alaska's largest display of gold, and the other wonders and curiosities on display at the Museum of the North (p. 277). Then stop by the Large Animal Research Station (p. 277) and get face to face with musk ox, reindeer, and caribou. If you're up for some entertainment, take in The Golden Heart Revue (p. 288), a stage show exploring the central question regarding Fairbanks' existence: Why?

Day 13   Fairbanks to Chena Hot Springs

Drive out to Chena Hot Springs (p. 290), get a room or a campsite for the night, and soak in the 104°F (40°C) waters of an Olympic-swimming-pool-size, boulder-lined hot spring. Stop along the way for a hike in the rolling hills of the Alaskan Interior in the Chena River Recreation Area (p. 285).

Day 14   Back to Fairbanks

Head back to Fairbanks. Leave time before your flight for a 3½-hour trip on the Chena River aboard the *Riverboat Discovery* (p. 276), run by an old Alaska family that's been in the riverboating business since the Klondike gold rush.

2

Cruising Alaska's Coast

The lowdown on Alaska's most popular type of vacation

by Jerry Brown & Fran Wenograd Golden

ALASKA'S POPULARITY AS A TOP SUMMER CRUISE DESTINATION IS PARTLY the result of its own natural splendor and partly because of its unavailability for most of the year. Inclement weather dictates that the 49th state is of interest to cruise lines and their passengers essentially only from mid-May to mid-September. Each year during this brief period, more than 950,000 people take a cruise along the state's vast and rugged coastline (in fact, in 2008 the number could for the first time hit one million). Cruise passengers visit the towns and wilderness areas of the Southeast (the Inside Passage, also known as the Panhandle) or the Gulf of Alaska by day, and burrow into their ships for effortless travel by night.

The lack of roads between towns makes the waters of the Inside Passage the region's de facto highway. Your options are, basically, taking cruise ships or the Alaska Marine Highway System (the state ferries). You'd have to be willing to invest more time—both for the actual traveling and for the planning—to utilize the ferries. And you'd have to be willing to give up the comforts and diversions of the average cruise ship. (On the other hand, the ferry *does* give you unlimited stops along the way and a chance to meet Alaskan residents, not only in major cruise ports but in smaller, less-visited communities as well.) For many people, the ease of cruise travel is preferable to the rough-and-ready nature of ferry transportation.

But no matter how much revenue cruise passengers (and ships' crews) generate for merchants in the ports visited, some locals aren't as welcoming as they might be. Alaskans are known for their hospitality, but they have their limits (don't we all?). The presence of too many cruise passengers has unquestionably spoiled some of Alaska's quaint places. Once-charming streets are transformed into virtual carnival midways jammed wall-to-wall with vacationers from simultaneous ship landings. As a result, no matter what residents may say, service standards suffer somewhat—especially toward the end of the season when Alaskans have been subjected to a steady stream of strange faces for several months, and can get, ahem, a little grumpy.

Some communities feel that the cultural bulldozing brought by cruise ships is not worth the economic benefit, and have placed limits on the number of ships that can come into port or levied new taxes based on the number of people the ships bring.

So strident has much of the opposition become that the State Legislature in 2006—after a "yes" vote by the populace on a ballot sponsored by a citizen group called Responsible Cruising for Alaska—imposed a $50 head tax on every passenger carried by the cruise lines. The money is intended to offset the costs incurred by the ports in essential services used by visitors—police, sewage, roadways, and the like. It will be divvied up to the ports proportionately based on the number of ships visiting and passengers carried.

At the same time and as a direct result of the same ballot initiative, the state levied a 33% tax on shipboard casino profits (now *that* really hurts the cruise lines!) and insisted that each ship provide a cabin for a state employee to monitor the ship's pollution abatement practices. It also contained a clause that required cruise lines to disclose to passengers the commissions they earn from selling the shore excursions provided by local operators.

So get ready to pay a bit more than you would have in the past.

As a visitor, you can avoid much of the human congestion caused by ships by choosing an early season cruise—say, the last couple of weeks in May. One other option: You can always travel independently after the cruise to the real Alaska, inland from the cruise ports. In this chapter, we'll go through the affordable cruise options available in the state, focusing primarily on those that provide a true in-depth experience.

WEIGHING YOUR CRUISE OPTIONS

Your three main questions in choosing a cruise in Alaska are "When should I go?," "Where do I want to go?," and "Which ship/cruise line?"

WHEN TO GO?

As we said before, Alaska is very much a seasonal, as opposed to a year-round, cruise destination, so it's generally only open to cruising from May through September (although some smaller ships start up in late Apr).

May and September are considered the shoulder seasons, and lower brochure rates are offered during these months (and more aggressive discounts as well; watch your local newspaper and check the Internet). Cruising in May can be extremely pleasant—the real, near gridlock-inducing crowds have yet to arrive. Locals, coming off what is usually a fairly isolated winter, are friendlier than they are later in the season, when they're tired and, frankly, pretty much ready to see the tourists go home. May in the Inside Passage ports also happens to be one of the driest months in the season. Late September, though, offers the advantage of fewer fellow tourists clogging the ports.

If you are considering traveling in a shoulder month, keep in mind that some shops don't open until Memorial Day, and the visitor season is generally considered over on Labor Day (although cruise lines operate well into Sept).

INSIDE PASSAGE OR THE GULF OF ALASKA?

The Inside Passage runs through the area of Alaska known as Southeast (which the locals also call "the Panhandle"), that narrow strip of the state—islands, mainland coastal communities, and mountains—that runs from the Canadian border in the south to the start of the Gulf in the north, just above the Juneau/Haines/Skagway area. The islands on the western side of the area afford cruise ships a welcome degree of protection from the sea and its attendant rough waters (hence the name "Inside Passage"). Because of that shelter, such ports as Ketchikan, Wrangell, Petersburg, and others are reached with less rocking and rolling, and thus less risk of seasickness. Sitka is not on the Inside Passage (it's on the ocean side of Baranof Island) but that beautiful little community, with its Russian heritage, is included in most Inside Passage cruise itineraries.

Southeast encompasses the capital city, **Juneau,** and townships influenced by the former Russian presence in the state (**Sitka,** for instance), the Tlingit and Haida Native cultures (**Ketchikan**), and the great gold rush of 1898 (**Skagway**). It is a land of rainforests, mountains, inlets, and glaciers (including Margerie, Johns Hopkins, Muir, and the others contained within the boundaries of **Glacier Bay National Park**). The region is rich in wildlife, especially of the marine variety. It is a scenic delight. But then, what part of Alaska isn't?

The other major cruising area is the **Southcentral** region's Gulf of Alaska, usually referred to by the cruise lines as the "Glacier Discovery Route" or the "Voyage of the Glaciers," or some such catchy title. "Gulf of Alaska," after all, sounds pretty bland.

The coastline of the Gulf is that arc of land from just north of Glacier Bay to the Kenai Peninsula. Southcentral also takes in the truly spectacular **Prince William Sound;** the **Cook Inlet,** on the northern side of the peninsula; **Anchorage,** Alaska's biggest city; the year-round **Alyeska Resort** at Girdwood, 40 miles from Anchorage; the **Matanuska** and **Susitna** valleys (the "Mat-Su"), a fertile agricultural region renowned for the record size of some of its produce; and part of the Alaska Mountain Range.

The principal Southcentral terminus ports are **Seward** or **Whittier** for Anchorage. No ships abiding by the regular Alaska pattern actually head for Anchorage proper, instead carrying passengers from Seward or Whittier to Anchorage by bus or train. (Getting all the way around the peninsula to Anchorage would add a day to the cruise.) Let us stress that going on a Gulf cruise does not mean that you don't visit any of the Inside Passage. The big difference is that, whereas the more popular Inside Passage cruise itineraries run round-trip to and from Vancouver or Seattle, the Gulf routing is one-way—northbound and southbound—between Vancouver and Seward or Vancouver and Whittier. A typical Gulf itinerary also visits such Inside Passage ports as **Ketchikan, Juneau, Sitka,** and/or **Skagway.**

The Gulf's glaciers are quite dazzling and every bit as spectacular as their counterparts to the south. **College Fjord,** for instance, is lined with glaciers—16 of them, each one grander than the last. On a 2005 cruise, Fran saw incredible calving at **Harvard Glacier** with chunks of 400- and 500-year-old ice falling off and crashing into the water to thunderous sounds every few minutes (worries about global warming aside, the sight was spectacular). Another favorite part of a Gulf cruise, though, is the visit to the gigantic **Hubbard Glacier**—at 6 miles, Alaska's longest—at the head of Yakutat Bay (our all-time favorite, by the way!).

Not to raise again the specter of global warming but, sadly, most of Alaska's glaciers are in retreat, with some receding quite rapidly. On a visit to Sawyer Glacier last year, it appeared that the ice face had gone so far back that the ship was unable to get closer than a mile or so. Not the best way to view a glacier.

Cruisetours combine a cruise with a land tour, either before or after the cruise. Typical packages link the cruise with a 3- to 5-night Anchorage/Denali/Fairbanks tour, a 4- to 7-night Yukon tour (which visits Anchorage, Denali, and

Sick Ships

Every year, hundreds of cruise-ship passengers and plenty of visitors on shore come down with vomiting and diarrhea caused by a bug now known as the norovirus. The good news is it's rarer in summer than winter. Still, the illness is no fun. It lasts a day or two and is rarely serious, although some passengers do end up in the hospital because of dehydration. The virus is extremely contagious from the first symptoms until at least 3 days and up to 2 weeks after it clears up. Touching a contaminated handrail and then your face is enough to catch it. To minimize your chances of contracting the virus, wash hands frequently, drink bottled water, and avoid eating raw food on board, especially shellfish. The Centers for Disease Control also recommended in 1998 that passengers 65 and older or those with chronic illnesses check with their doctors before taking a cruise. The CDC website (www.cdc.gov/nceh/vsp) posts sanitation inspection scores for each ship. Type "norovirus" into their search page to find a fact sheet.

Fairbanks on the way), or a 5- to 7-night tour of the Canadian Rockies. Holland America, Princess, and Royal Caribbean/Celebrity lead the big ship cruisetour market. Even if you book with another cruise line, chances are that at least some portions of your land tour will be bought from one of these operators.

WHICH SHIP?

The **major ships** in the Alaska market fall generally into two categories: midsize ships and megaships. Carrying as many as 2,670 passengers, the **megaships** look and feel like floating resorts. Big on glitz, they offer loads of activities, attract many families and (especially in Alaska) seniors, offer a large number of public rooms (including fancy casinos and fully equipped gyms), and provide a wide variety of meal and entertainment options. And though they may feature 1 or 2 formal nights per trip, the ambience is generally casual. The Alaska vessels of the Carnival, Celebrity, Princess, and Royal Caribbean fleets all fit in this category, as do Norwegian Cruise Line's *Spirit, Sun,* and *Star* and Holland America's *Oosterdam* and *Westerdam*. **Midsize ships** in Alaska fall into two segments: the ultra-expensive Regent *Seven Seas Mariner* and *Silver Shadow,* and the modern midsize *Veendam, Ryndam, Amsterdam, Volendam, Zaandam,* and *Statendam* of Holland America Line, and *Tahitian Princess* of Princess Cruises. In general, the size of these ships is less significant than the general onboard atmosphere. Both the midsize ships and the megaships have a great range of facilities for passengers. Cabins on these ships range from cubbyholes to large suites, depending on the ship and the type of cabin you book. Big dining rooms and a tremendous variety of cuisines are the norm. These ships carry a lot of people and can, at times, feel crowded.

The sizes of these big ships also come with **three major drawbacks** for passengers: (1) They can't sail into narrow passages or shallow-water ports, (2) their size and inflexible schedules limit their ability to stop or even slow down when wildlife is spotted, and (3) when their passengers disembark in a town, they tend to overwhelm it, limiting your ability to get insight into the real Alaska communities (to be fair, shore excursions will whisk you well away from the crowds on out of town adventures). Your alternative therefore is either the Alaskan Marine Highway system, or, if you have $400 to $600 a night to spend, the elite, expensive smaller ships. Since this is a budget guidebook, we're not covering these smaller cruisers, but you can find information on them in the book *Frommer's Alaska Cruises & Ports of Call* (Wiley Publishing, Inc.).

THE BEST CRUISE EXPERIENCES IN ALASKA

Cruise lines are in the business of giving their guests a good time, so they've all got something going for them. Here are our picks for Alaska's best, in a few different categories.

- ◆ **The Handsomest of the Mainstream Ships:** Every line's most recent ships are beautiful, but **Celebrity's** *Infinity* is a true stunner, as is sister ship *Millennium.* These modern vessels, with their extensive art collections, cushy public rooms, and expanded spa areas, give Celebrity a formidable presence in Alaska. And the late-model *Sapphire Princess* and *Diamond Princess* have raised the art of building big ships to new heights. Both of these vessels will again be in Inside Passage service this year from Vancouver.
- ◆ **The Best Ships for Families:** All the major lines have well-established kids' programs. **Holland America** and **Norwegian Cruise Line** win points in Alaska for their special shore excursions for kids and teens, and **Carnival** gets a nod for offering shore excursions for teens.
- ◆ **The Best Ships for Onboard Activities:** The ships operated by **Carnival** and **Royal Caribbean** offer a very full roster of onboard activities that range from the sublime (lectures) to the ridiculous (contests designed to get passengers to do or say outrageous things). **Princess's** ScholarShip@Sea program is a real winner, with excitingly packaged classes in such diverse subjects as photography, personal computers, cooking, and pottery.
- ◆ **The Best Ships for Entertainment:** Look to the big ships here. **Carnival** and **Royal Caribbean** are tops when it comes to an overall package of show productions, nightclub acts, lounge performances, and audience-participation entertainment. **Princess** also offers particularly well-done—if somewhat less lavishly staged—shows. **Holland America** has not, historically, been noted for its entertainment package, but the company has improved considerably in that department in recent years.

BOOKING YOUR CRUISE

Every cruise line has a brochure full of beautiful glossy photos but often they feature published rates that are nothing more than a pie-in-the-sky wish (most customers will pay less). There are ways to save. We strongly suggest you look at the early-bird savings column and book your cruise early (by mid-Feb for average savings of 25%–30% and sometimes as much as 50%). In reality, you may be able to get the cruise for 40% or 50% off at the last minute. But here's the problem with waiting: Alaska right now is hot, hot, hot. Sure, you may be able to save by taking your chances, but if you don't reserve space early, you may also be left out in the cold. Keep in mind that the most expensive and the cheapest cabins tend to sell out first. The mid-range rooms are by and large the last to go. And increasingly aggressive marketing by the cruise lines to previous passengers is only contributing to the rising number of early bookings.

Should you book through a travel agent or the Internet? The answer can be both. If you're computer savvy, have a good handle on all the elements that go into a cruise, and have narrowed down the choices to a few cruise lines that appeal to you, websites are a great way to trawl the seas at your own pace and check out last-minute deals, which can be dramatic. There are also websites like Cruisecompete.com that take the "Lending Tree" paradigm for cruising: You say which cruise you want, date and ship, and different travel agents compete for your business. You need to be savvy to use these methods, as you'll barely get a stitch of personalized service searching for and booking a cruise online. If you need help getting a refund or arranging special meals or other matters, or deciding which cabin to choose, you may be on your own. So the best bet, according to our way of thinking, is to do your research electronically and, once you're better informed, then visit a travel agent to make the reservation.

If you don't know a good travel agent already, try to find one through your friends, preferably those who have cruised before. For the most personal service, look for an agent in your local area, and for the most knowledgeable service, look for an agent at a **cruise-only agency** (meaning that the whole agency specializes in cruises) or find somebody in a more conventional agency who is a **cruise specialist** (meaning he or she handles that agency's cruise business). If you are calling a full-service travel agency, ask for the **cruise desk,** which is where you'll find these specialists. If the agency doesn't have a cruise desk, per se, it might be wise to check elsewhere.

A good and easy rule of thumb to maximize your chances of finding an agent who has cruise experience and who won't rip you off is to book with agencies that are members of the **Cruise Lines International Association** (CLIA; ☎ 212/921-0066; www.cruising.org) or the **National Association of Cruise Oriented Agencies** (NACOA; ☎ 305/663-5626; www.nacoaonline.com). Member agencies of both groups are comprised either entirely of cruise specialists, or employ at least some cruise-specialists. Membership in the **American Society of Travel Agents** (ASTA; ☎ 800/275-2782; www.astanet.com) assures that the agency is monitored for ethical practices, although it does not designate cruise experience.

You can tap into the Internet sites of these organizations for easy access to agents in your area.

THE COST: WHAT'S INCLUDED & WHAT'S NOT

However you arrange to buy your cruise, what you basically have in hand at the end is a contract for transportation, lodging, dining, entertainment, housekeeping, and assorted other miscellaneous services that will be provided to you over the course of your vacation. It's important, though, to remember what extras are *not* included in your cruise fare. Are you getting a price that includes port charges, taxes, fees, and insurance, or are you getting a cruise-only fare? Are airfare and airport transfers included, or do you have to book them separately (either as an add-on to the cruise fare or on your own)? Make sure you're comparing apples with apples when making price comparisons. Read the fine print!

Aside from **airfare,** which is usually not included in your cruise fare, the priciest addition to your cruise fare, particularly in Alaska, will likely be **shore excursions.** Ranging from about $30 for a bus tour to $299 and up (sometimes as high as $600) for a lengthy helicopter or seaplane flightseeing excursion, these sightseeing tours are designed to help cruise passengers make the most of their time at the ports the ship visits, but they can add a hefty sum to your vacation costs. *Note from Pauline Frommer:* Budget conscious travelers may wish to arrange their own shore excursions through the outfitters listed in this book. The costs will be lower and the excursions just as exciting. In doing this, however, you take the responsibility for getting yourself back to the ship on time. If a cruise line–sponsored shore excursion runs late, the ship will wait for it; that's not so with personally planned ones (that being said, most outfitters are well aware of the ship's schedules and reliable about keeping to them).

You'll also want to add to your calculations **tips for the ship's crew.** Tips are given at the end of the cruise, and passengers should reserve at least $10 per passenger per day for tips for the room steward, waiter, and busperson. (In practice, we find that most people tend to give a little more.) Additional tips to other personnel, such as the head waiter or maitre d', are at your discretion.

Most ships charge extra for **alcoholic beverages** (including wine at dinner) and for soda. Non-bubbly soft drinks, such as lemonade and iced tea, are included in your cruise fare. You'll also want to set some money aside for optional offerings such as spa treatments, fancy dinners in your ship's alternative dining room (which may carry a price tag of up to $30 per person), shipboard photos, Internet access, and other temptations.

MONEY-SAVING STRATEGIES

Cruise pricing is a fluid medium, and there are a number of strategies you can use to save money off the booking price.

Early & Late Booking

The best way to save on an Alaska cruise is to **book in advance.** In a typical year, lines offer early-bird rates, usually 25% to 30% off the brochure rate, to those who book their Alaska cruise by mid- to late February of the year of the cruise. If the cabins do not fill up by the cutoff date, the early-bird rate may be extended, but it may be slightly lower—say, a 15% or 20% savings. Starting prices we've seen for 2008 are around $699 for an inside cabin on an early season weeklong cruise.

If the cabins are still not full as the cruise season begins, cruise lines typically start marketing special deals, usually through their top-producing travel agents. It's our feeling that in 2008, these last-minute discounts, which can run as high as 50%, will be less common than in some previous years. And keep in mind that last-minute deals are usually for a very limited selection of cabins. Planning your Alaska cruise vacation well in advance and taking advantage of early booking discounts is still the best way to go.

Shoulder Season Discounts

You can save by booking a cruise in the **shoulder months of May or September,** when cruise pricing is lower than during the high summer months. Typically, Alaska cruises are divided into budget, low, economy, value, standard, and peak seasons, but since these overlap quite a bit from cruise line to cruise line, we can lump them into three basic periods:

1. **Budget/Low/Economy Season:** May and September
2. **Value/Standard Season:** Early June and late August
3. **Peak Season:** Late June, July, and early to mid-August

Discounts for Third & Fourth Passengers & Groups

Most ships offer highly discounted rates for third and fourth passengers sharing a cabin with two full-fare passengers, even if those two have booked at a discounted rate. It may mean a tight squeeze, but it'll save you a bundle. Some lines offer **special rates for kids,** usually on a seasonal or select-sailings basis, that may include free or discounted airfare.

One of the best ways to get a cruise deal is to book as a **group** of at least 16 people in at least eight cabins. The savings include a discounted rate, and at least the cruise portion of the 16th ticket will be free. Ask your travel agent about any group deals they may offer.

Senior Discounts

Seniors may be able to get extra savings on their cruise. Some lines will take 5% off the top for those 55 and up, and the senior rate applies even if the second person in the cabin is younger. Membership in groups such as AARP is not required, but such membership may bring additional savings.

CHOOSING YOUR CABIN

Cruise-ship cabins run from tiny rooms with accordion doors and bunk beds to palatial multi-room suites with hot tubs on the balcony. Which is right for you? Price will be a big factor here, but so should the vacation style you prefer. If, for instance, you plan to spend a lot of quiet time in your cabin, you should probably consider booking the biggest room you can afford. If, conversely, you plan to be out on deck all the time checking out the glaciers and wildlife, you'll probably be just as happy with a smaller (and cheaper) cabin to crash in at the end of the day. Cabins are either **inside** (without a window or porthole) or **outside** (with), the latter being more expensive. On the big ships, the more deluxe outside cabins may also come with **private verandas.** The cabins are usually described by price (highest to lowest), category (suite, deluxe, superior, standard, economy, and others), and furniture configuration ("sitting area with two lower beds," for example).

SPECIAL MENU REQUESTS

The cruise line should be informed at the time you make your reservations about any special dietary requests you have. Some lines offer kosher menus, and all will have vegetarian, low-fat, low-salt, vegan, and sugar-free options available.

CRUISE LINES PROFILES

The ships featured in this section vary in size, age, and offerings, but share the common thread of having more activities and entertainment options than any one person can possibly take in over the course of a cruise. You'll find swimming pools, health clubs, spas, nightclubs, movie theaters, shops, casinos, multiple restaurants, bars, and special kids' playrooms, and, in some cases, sports decks, virtual golf, computer rooms, martini bars, and cigar clubs, as well as quiet spaces where you can get away from it all. In most cases, you'll find lots and lots of onboard activities, including games, contests, classes, and lectures, plus a variety of entertainment options and show productions, some very sophisticated.

CARNIVAL CRUISE LINES

Carnival Place, 3655 NW 87th Ave., Miami, FL 33178-2428. ☎ 800/CARNIVAL. Fax 305/471-4740. www.carnival.com.

Translating this line's warm-weather experience to Alaska has meant combining its standard "24-hour orgy of good times" philosophy to include natural wonders, so you may find yourself bellying up to the rail with a multicolored party drink to gawk at a glacier. Drinking and R-rated comedians are part of the scene, as are "hairy-chest contests" and the like.

Entertainment options are among the industry's best, with each ship boasting a dozen dancers, a 10-piece orchestra, comedians, jugglers, and numerous live bands, as well as a big casino. Activity is nonstop. Cocktails begin to flow before lunch, and through the course of the day you can learn to country line-dance or ballroom dance, take cooking lessons, learn to play bridge, watch first-run movies, practice your golf swing by smashing balls into a net, or just eat, drink, shop, and then eat again. Alaska-specific naturalist lectures are delivered daily. In port, Carnival offers **120 shore excursions,** divided into categories of easy, moderate, and adventure. For kids, the line offers Camp Carnival, an expertly run children's program with activities that include Native arts and crafts sessions, lectures conducted by wildlife experts, and special shore excursions for teens.

Carnival's ship in Alaska cruises the Gulf of Alaska route. In May and September, Inside Passage cruises that visit Glacier Bay are offered.

PASSENGER PROFILE Overall, Carnival has some of the youngest demographics in the industry: mostly under 50, including couples, lots and lots of singles, and a good share of families. It's the same Middle America crowd that can be found in Las Vegas and Atlantic City and at Florida's megaresorts. This is not a sedate, bird-watching crowd. They may want to see whales and icebergs, but they will also dance the Macarena on cue.

SHIPS The 2,124-passenger megaship *Carnival Spirit* returns to Alaska in 2008. It offers plenty of activities, great pool and hot-tub spaces (some covered for use in chillier weather), a big oceanview gym and spa, and more dining options than your doctor would say is advisable. **Sample rates per person:** Lowest-price inside cabins are $115, lowest outside $159, lowest suite $180 per night for an Inside Passage cruise.

CELEBRITY CRUISES

1050 Caribbean Way, Miami, FL 33132. ☎ 800/437-3111 or 305/262-8322. Fax 800/437-5111. www.celebritycruises.com.

Celebrity Cruises offers a great combination: a classy, tasteful, and luxurious cruise experience at a moderate price—it's definitely the best in the midpriced category. The line's ships are real works of art; the cuisine is above the norm although the line has ended an agreement with famed French chef Michel Roux; the service first-class, friendly, and unobtrusive; and its spa facilities among the best in the business.

A typical day might offer bridge, darts, a culinary art demonstration, a trap-shooting competition, a fitness-fashion show, an art auction, a volleyball tournament, and a not-too-shabby stage show. Resident experts give lectures on the various ports of call, the Alaskan environment, glaciers, and Alaskan culture. For children, Celebrity ships employ a group of counselors who direct and supervise a camp-style children's program. Activities are geared toward different age groups. There's an impressive kids' play area and a lounge area for teens.

Celebrity, like sister company Royal Caribbean, visits the tiny port of Icy Straight Point between Juneau and Glacier Bay; the port offers a prime vantage point for whale- and wildlife-watching and easier access to the Alaskan wilderness.

The company offers 7-night Inside Passage and 7-night Gulf of Alaska itineraries.

PASSENGER PROFILE   The typical Celebrity guest is one who prefers to pursue his or her R&R at a relatively relaxed pace, with a minimum of aggressively promoted group activities. The overall impression leans more toward sophistication and less to the kind of orgiastic Technicolor whoopee that you'll find, say, aboard a Carnival ship. You'll find everyone from kids to retirees.

SHIPS   Sleek, modern, and stunningly designed, the 1,896-passenger *Mercury* and the larger, 1,950-passenger *Infinity* and *Millennium* have a lot of open deck space and lots of large windows that provide access to the wide skies and the grand Alaskan vistas. All the ships (but especially *Mercury*) feature incredible spas with hydrotherapy pools, steam rooms, and saunas, plus health and beauty services and exceptionally large fitness areas. **Sample rates per person:** Lowest-price inside cabins $115, lowest outside $136, lowest suite $279 per night for a 7-night cruise.

HOLLAND AMERICA LINE
300 Elliott Ave. W., Seattle, WA 98119. ☎ 800/426-0327 or 206/281-3535. Fax 206/286-7110. www.hollandamerica.com.

Holland America can be summed up in one word: *tradition.* The company was formed way back in 1873 as the Netherlands-America Steamship Company, and its ships today strive to present an aura of history and dignity, like a European hotel where they never let rock stars register. And thanks to its acquisition over the years of numerous land-based tour operators, Holland America has positioned itself as Alaska's most experienced and comprehensive cruise company.

Though most of the line's Alaskan fleet is relatively young, the ships are designed with a decidedly "classic" feel—no flashing neon lights here. Similarly, Holland America's ships are heavy on more mature, less frenetic kinds of activities. You'll find good bridge programs and music to dance (or just listen) to in the bars and lounges, plus health spas and the other amenities found on most large ships. The line has improved its nightly show-lounge entertainment. Its Artists in Residence Program, arranged through the Alaska Native Heritage Center in Anchorage, has Alaska Native artists accompanying all 7-night cruises and demonstrating traditional art forms such as ivory and soapstone carving, basket weaving, and mask making. Club HAL is one of the industry's more creative children's programs, though the small children's playrooms are no match for what you find on the latest Princess or Celebrity megaships.

Alaska itineraries include 7-night Inside Passage cruises and 7-night Gulf of Alaska cruises.

PASSENGER PROFILE   Holland America's passenger profile used to reflect a much older crowd. Now the average age is dropping, thanks to an increased emphasis on its Club HAL program for children and some updating of its onboard entertainment. Still, HAL's passengers in Alaska include a large percentage of middle-aged-and-up vacationers.

SHIPS   The 1,258-passenger *Ryndam, Statendam,* and *Veendam* are more or less identical. All cabins have a sitting area and lots of closet and drawer space, and even the least expensive inside cabins run almost 190 square feet, quite large by industry standards. Outside doubles have either picture windows or verandas. The striking dining rooms, two-tiered showrooms, and Crow's Nest forward bar/lounges are among these ships' best features. The newer 1,432-passenger *Volendam* and *Zaandam* and 1,380-passenger *Amsterdam* are larger and fancier, with triple-decked oval atriums, nearly 200 suites and deluxe staterooms with private verandas, five showrooms and lounges, and an alternative restaurant designed as an artist's bistro, featuring drawings and etchings. The smallest cabin is a comfortable 190 square feet. The *Oosterdam* and *Westerdam,* the newest vessels in the fleet, weigh 85,000 tons and carry 1,848 passengers. These are sophisticated, spacious yet intimate ships well equipped to support HAL's position as a force in the Alaska market. **Sample rates per person:** Lowest-price inside cabins $114 per diem, lowest outside $157, lowest suite $242 for a 7-night cruise.

NORWEGIAN CRUISE LINE

7665 Corporate Center Dr., Miami, FL 33126. ☎ **800/327-7030** or 305/436-4000. Fax 305/436-4120. www.ncl.com.

Norwegian Cruise Line (NCL) offers an informal and upbeat onboard atmosphere on the *Norwegian Sun,* sailing from Vancouver, and the *Norwegian Sky* and *Norwegian Star,* both sailing from Seattle. The line excels at activities, and its recreational and fitness programs are among the best in the industry. Though the onboard food has been described as unmemorable, NCL does boast a very popular casual-dining policy that allows passengers to dine when they want pretty much any time between 5:30pm and midnight, with whomever they want, dressed however they want.

In Alaska, NCL offers an Alaskan lecturer, wine tastings, art auctions, trapshooting, cooking demonstrations, craft and dance classes, an incentive fitness program, and bingo, among other activities. Passengers can choose from a good selection of soft-adventure shore excursions, including hiking, biking, and kayaking. Entertainment is generally strong and includes Vegas-style musical productions. The top-notch kids' program includes an activity room, video games, an ice-cream bar, and guaranteed babysitting aboard, plus sessions with park rangers and escorted shore excursions.

The line offers 7-night Inside Passage cruises.

PASSENGER PROFILE   In Alaska, the demographic tends more toward retirees than on the line's warmer-climate sailings, but you'll find families as well, including grandparents bringing along the grandkids.

SHIPS   The 2,050-passenger *Norwegian Sun* is the first ship built with NCL's "freestyle" dining policy in mind, as evidenced by the nine separate onboard restaurants. An airy eight-story glass atrium welcomes visitors in the lobby. More than two-thirds of the guest rooms (about 650 in all) have ocean views, and closet space is more generous than on other NCL ships. The 2,240-passenger *Norwegian Star* has no fewer than 11 rooms in which people can eat—depending on the time of day. The *Star* is well equipped for the sports-minded and active vacationer—in addition to the fitness center, there are three heated pools, a jogging/walking track, and a wide array of sports facilities. The 2,466-passenger *Norwegian Pearl* is getting lots of attention from the company, and it shows. **Sample rates per person:** Lowest-price inside cabins $100 a night, lowest outside $122, lowest suite from $243 for a 7-night cruise.

PRINCESS CRUISES

24305 Town Center Dr., Santa Clarita, CA 91355. ☎ **800/LOVE-BOAT** or 661/753-0000. Fax 661/753-1535. www.princess.com.

Consistency is Princess's strength. With new ships joining its fleet like so many cars off a Detroit assembly line, you'd think that maintaining acceptable service standards could be a problem. All things considered, though, Princess accomplishes this rather well. Throughout the fleet, the service in all areas—dining room, lounge, cabin maintenance, and so on—tends to be of consistently high quality. Aboard Princess, you get a lot of bang for your buck, and it's all attractively packaged and well executed. Although its ships serve every corner of the globe, nowhere is the Princess presence more visible than in Alaska. Through its affiliate, Princess Tours, it owns wilderness lodges, motorcoaches, and railcars in the 49th state, making it one of the major players in the Alaska cruise market, alongside Holland America.

Princess passengers can expect enough onboard activities to keep them going morning to night, if they've a mind to, and enough nooks and crannies to allow them to do absolutely nothing, if that's their thing. Kids are well taken care of, with especially large children's playrooms. Princess offers 7-night Inside Passage cruises, 7-night Gulf of Alaska cruises, and 10-night Inside Passages cruises from San Francisco, and the new and smaller Tahitian Princess is doing 14-night cruises out of Vancouver to less-visited places including Kodiak and Valdez.

PASSENGER PROFILE   Typical Princess passengers are likely to be between 50 and 65, and are experienced cruisers who know what they want and are prepared to pay for it. Recent additional emphasis on its youth and children's facilities has begun to attract a bigger share of the family market.

SHIPS   Princess's diverse fleet in Alaska essentially comprises eight ships, five of which have entered service since the millennium. The fleet includes the *Diamond* and *Sapphire,* which were completed in 2004; the *Coral* and *Island,* of 2003 vintage; and the *Golden* (2001) and *Star* (2002), not to mention the *Tahitian*

Princess, which was built in 1999 and extensively refurbished in 2002 when it was purchased from Renaissance Cruises. The ships generally are pretty but not stunning, bright but not gaudy, spacious but not overwhelmingly so, and decorated in a comfortable, restrained style that's a combination of classic and modern. They're a great choice when you want a step up from Carnival, Royal Caribbean, and NCL but aren't interested in the slightly more chic ambience of Celebrity or the luxury of Seven Seas. **Sample rates per person:** Lowest-price inside cabins $107 per diem, lowest outside $122, lowest suite $207 for a 7-night cruise.

ROYAL CARIBBEAN INTERNATIONAL
1050 Caribbean Way, Miami, FL 33132. ☎ **800/327-6700** or 305/379-2601. www.royalcaribbean.com.

Royal Caribbean sells a mass-market style of cruising that's reasonably priced and offered aboard informal, well-run ships with nearly every diversion imaginable—craft classes, horse racing, bingo, shuffleboard, deck games, line-dancing lessons, wine-and-cheese tastings, cooking demonstrations, art auctions, and the like—plus elaborate health clubs and spas, covered swimming pools, large open sun deck areas, and innumerable bars, lounges, and other entertainment centers. The Viking Crown Lounge and other glassed-in areas make excellent observation rooms from which to see the Alaska sights. Royal Caribbean spends big bucks on entertainment, which includes high-tech show productions. Headliners are often featured. Port lectures are offered on topics such as Alaska wildlife, and the line offers some 65 shore excursions. The line's children's activities are some of the most extensive afloat.

The line offers 7-night Inside Passage and Gulf of Alaska cruises.

PASSENGER PROFILE   The crowd on Royal Caribbean ships, like the decor, rates pretty high on the party scale, though not quite at the Carnival level. Passengers represent an age mix from 30 to 60, and a good number of families are attracted by the line's well-established and fine-tuned kids' programs. In Alaska, Royal Caribbean is focusing more on international sales than the entrenched market leaders, Princess and Holland America, which often results in sailings populated by a good many international passengers, especially travelers from Asia and Europe.

SHIPS   Royal Caribbean owns the largest ships in the world: the new *Liberty of the Seas* at 160,000 tons, and four 142,000-ton Voyager-class vessels. Although these 3,000-plus-passenger ships—which introduced such cruise-ship design features as ice-skating rinks, rock-climbing walls, and cabins overlooking interior atrium areas—are not in Alaska this year, Royal Caribbean does offer the very up-to-date 2,500-passenger *Radiance of the Seas.* The ship is joined in Alaska by its sister ship, the similarly dimensioned *Serenade of the Seas.* The *Radiance* is in Gulf of Alaska service between Vancouver, B.C., and Seward, the *Serenade* in Inside Passage service out of Vancouver. Also returning to Alaska in 2008 is the older (1997), but still up-to-date 2,435-passenger *Rhapsody of the Seas,* a Vision-class ship. **Sample rates per person:** Lowest-price inside cabins on the *Rhapsody,* RCL's least expensive ship, is $95 per diem, lowest outside $122, lowest suite $207 for a 7-night cruise.

3 Anchorage & Environs

Straddling the line between urban & wild in the state's largest city

ANCHORAGE IS SQUARELY IN THE MIDDLE OF CIVILIZATION AND RIGHT ON the edge of it at the same time. The wild Chugach Mountains wrap around the eastern side of the city like a jagged, 8,000-foot backyard fence filled with holes. An extensive network of alpine trails lets city dwellers slip easily into the wilderness, while within the city a well-developed system of greenways, bike paths, and parks serve as cross-town expressways for large wildlife. Bears amble through quiet urban neighborhoods, knocking over garbage cans, breaking into kitchens, and sometimes getting shot dead like burglars caught in the act by irate homeowners. Moose trample summer gardens as they snack on peonies and delphinium, or they stand dumbly in the middle of the popular Tony Knowles Coastal Trail staring down bicyclists, joggers, and rollerbladers.

On its other sides Anchorage fronts Cook Inlet, a long reach of sea connecting the city with the Pacific Ocean. Here, too, it's "Wild Kingdom," as the inlet is home to a small population of beluga whales, which feed on the salmon that congregate offshore in summer, waiting for favorable tides before dashing up their home streams to spawn. Salmon streams cut right through the heart of the city, making life good for urban fishermen. In fact, one of the most popular fishing spots is beneath a freeway bridge near downtown, where anglers regularly land 40-pounders. (There's a little bait shop there [p. 53] where you can rent the gear necessary to try to land one yourself.)

All is not Edenic in this urban city, of course. The municipality of Anchorage (which is as large as Delaware) has some 300,000 residents—or 42% of the state's population. Along with all those people comes traffic, high-rises, gang problems, and all sorts of other distinctly un-Alaskan features more typical of a midsize American city. The rest of Alaska generally loathes Anchorage. "Los Anchorage," they call it, likening it to Los Angeles. Anchorage isn't *in* Alaska, they joke, but you can *see* Alaska from there (when you're stuck in an Anchorage traffic jam, staring at the raw mountains that fill half the sky, the joke seems pretty funny).

Anchorage is about more than just wildlife and urban woes, though. For visitors, it's Alaska's primary transportation hub, so there's a good chance you'll pass through town on your way to somewhere else. But the city is worthy of a few days of exploration in its own right, with all of its museums and galleries, theaters, crazy bars, fantastic restaurants, great shopping, and a premier Native cultural center. And the fact is, you don't have to go far from Anchorage to find the real

Alaska. Day trips abound. You can wake up in the city, spend the day climbing mountains, shooing the rapids of an icy river, or tramping around a glacier, then be back in town in time for dinner at a nice restaurant and a good night's sleep in a comfortable bed.

DON'T LEAVE ANCHORAGE WITHOUT . . .

Catching up on the last 10,000 years of Alaskan history and art. You'll find a treasure trove of artifacts and artworks, expertly exhibited at the **Anchorage Museum at Rasmuson Center.** See p. 45.

Meeting Eskimos, Aleuts, Tlingits, and other long-time Alaskans. Listen to Native storytellers, applaud Native dancers, cheer Native athletes, and visit a most unusual Native village at the **Alaska Native Heritage Center.** See p. 47.

Taking in the view. You'll get a God's-eye view of Anchorage from high atop **Flattop Mountain.** See p. 52.

Walking on the wild side. Hiking Girdwood's trails can be an adventure, especially if you decide to haul yourself across a roaring gorge in a hand tram. See p. 68.

Staring deep into the eyes of Alaska's Pleistocene past. Stop at the **Musk Ox Farm** in Palmer for face time with shaggy holdouts from the Ice Age, whose prized wool is one of the warmest natural fibers on earth. See p. 72.

A BRIEF HISTORY

The Anchorage area's original human occupants were Eskimos, but sometime between A.D. 500 and A.D. 1650, they were displaced by Athabascan Indians. Today about 20,000 Alaska Natives from every group, including Eskimo and Athabascan, live in Anchorage, earning it the nickname "Alaska's largest native village." The heart of this massive, loosely knit village is the Alaska Native Heritage Center. It's both a tribal gathering place and one of the city's top visitor attractions. Pay a visit and you'll see Native dancers and athletes on stage, you'll get to inspect the inside of a Tlingit longhouse, an Aleut sod house, and other traditional dwellings, and you might even learn how to smoke fish or tan a moose hide (see p. 47 for more on its attractions).

Anchorage got its start as a town in 1914, after Congress decided Alaska should have a railroad linking the river shipping routes of the Interior with the Pacific Ocean. A construction camp was built along Ship Creek, at the bottom of the bluff where downtown Anchorage is today, and by the summer of 1915 there were 2,000 souls there, looking for work and adventure. Before long, lots were laid out and auctioned off atop the bluff, and log cabins and clapboard homes began appearing. A new town had been born in the wilderness, but its inhabitants couldn't agree on what to call it. "Ship Creek," "Spenard," "Woodrow," and "Knik Anchorage" all had proponents. Finally, the U.S. Post Office Department settled things, declaring that the mail would be delivered to "Anchorage."

By the 1930s Anchorage had settled into a life as a quiet railroad town. That changed in the 1940s; with the world at war and imperial Japan occupying two

Aleutian islands, thousands of U.S. troops were posted to Anchorage. The soldiers and airmen doubled the city's population, turbo boosted its economy, and turned the sleepy railroad stop into a booming war-time city. Anchorage retained its strategic importance through the Cold War, as the U.S. warily kept watch on the Soviets from Alaska for a surprise over-the-North-Pole nuclear missile attack on the Lower 48.

On March 27, 1964, Good Friday, the ground began shaking and heaving so violently and for so long that people feared the Soviet Union had launched a nuclear attack. It was actually an earthquake that registered 9.2 on the Richter scale, the largest ever recorded in North America. Streets buckled, hillsides slid away, buildings cracked open, and people spilled out into the snowy streets. One side of 4th Avenue sank 20 feet, taking pawn shops, restaurants, bars, and liquor stores with it. The other side of the street got off with minor damage. Walk down 4th Avenue today, and you'll notice everything's newer on one side of the street.

A massive rebuilding campaign followed. Right on its heels came a second building boom in the 1970s, this one accompanying construction of the 900-mile-long Trans-Alaska Pipeline, which carries crude oil from Prudhoe Bay on the Arctic Ocean to Valdez on the Pacific Ocean. Anchorage became a staging area for pipeline construction and the home base for oil companies, whose new headquarters became the first high-rises in the city. Take a look at the skyline today and you'll see it's inscribed with the logos of British Petroleum, ConocoPhillips, and other fossil fuel giants.

With the state awash in oil revenues in the 1980s, Anchorage launched several big public building projects, including the expansion of the Anchorage Museum at Rasmuson Center (a top visitor attraction), and the construction of the Alaska Center for the Performing Arts, home of the Anchorage Symphony Orchestra, and a venue for hundreds of performances a year, from rock bands, to operas, to Broadway shows. During the summer there's a great multimedia show on the aurora borealis there.

LAY OF THE LAND

DOWNTOWN   Most visitors stick around downtown Anchorage, where the majority of the city's visitor attractions are. Downtown is easy to navigate on foot. There are few hills, and the streets are laid out in a grid, with lettered streets running north-south, and numbered avenues running east-west. Though it's easy to navigate downtown intuitively, I wouldn't stray far into the rest of the city without a good map—one more detailed than I could squeeze onto the pages of *Pauline Frommer's Alaska*. You won't find much west of downtown besides the railroad yard, a popular urban salmon fishing spot called Ship Creek, and the upper reach of Cook Inlet called Knik Arm. East of downtown is the city's broad Midtown midsection, which has some good restaurants and nightspots, and lodging that's close to the airport.

TO THE NORTH   North of Anchorage, across the mountains, are two enormous river valleys, the Matanuska and the Susitna. Alaskans think of the two as one 23,000-square-mile mega-valley, which they call, simply, the **Mat-Su Valley.** The rich alluvial soil combined with the long, long days of summer sunshine have made the Mat-Su Valley the breadbasket of Alaska, one where vegetables—exposed

Visitor Info

The **Anchorage Convention and Visitor Bureau,** 524 W. 4th Ave., Anchorage, AK 99501-2212 (☎ 907/276-4118; fax 907/278-5559; www.anchorage.net), offers information on the city and the entire state at its centers and extensive website. The main location is the **Log Cabin Visitor Information Center,** downtown at 4th Avenue and F Street (☎ 907/274-3531; daily June–Aug 7:30am–7pm, May and Sept 8am–6pm, Oct–Apr 9am–4pm). If it's crowded, go to the storefront office right behind it. You'll also find visitor information desks at the airport: there's one in the baggage-claim area in the C concourse and one in the international terminal.

to so much sunlight—grow freakishly large. If you're driving north to Denali National Park or Fairbanks, or if you're driving to Canada from Anchorage, you'll have to pass through the Mat-Su Valley. For visitors, the valley offers more than just highways and 75-pound rutabagas. There are glaciers to see, whitewater rapids to run, and a hard-rock gold mine, the headquarters of the Iditarod, a musk ox farm, and a farm community rooted in one of the U.S. government's more unusual social experiments (p. 73) to visit. From Anchorage, it's also less than an hour drive to the neighboring Mat-Su communities of **Palmer** and **Wasilla,** which started as farm towns but now function more as bedroom communities for the big city.

TO THE SOUTH South of Anchorage, the road runs along the narrow strip of shoreline wedged between the Chugach Mountains and a long extension of Cook Inlet called **Turnagain Arm.** The 37-mile drive along Turnagain Arm from Anchorage to **Portage Glacier** is one of the most scenic routes in the U.S. In addition to the exhilarating meeting of mountains and sea, there's wildlife to see, trails to hike, and the funky little ski resort town of **Girdwood** to visit. This is the way to go if you're headed to **Whittier,** gateway to Prince William Sound and its glaciers, and to the vast outdoor playground of the Kenai Peninsula, both covered in chapter 4.

GETTING TO & AROUND ANCHORAGE
BY AIR

Most Alaska visitors arrive into **Ted Stevens Anchorage International Airport.** (The airport is named for Alaska's powerful senior senator, who survived a Lear Jet crash at this airfield in 1978 that killed five, including his wife.) Stuffed bears, musk ox, and other wildlife greet you in the terminal, leaving no doubt you've landed in the right state. As the fourth busiest cargo airport in the world, Anchorage International is a major re-fueling stop for trans-Pacific freight carriers, as well as passenger airlines taking the polar route between Asia and the East Coast of the U.S. Most domestic flights to Anchorage originate or stop in Seattle, meaning you'll probably change planes there. **Alaska Airlines** (☎ 800/252-7522;

www.alaskaair.com) is the dominant carrier, with about 20 flights a day from Seattle (which is 1,644 nautical miles, or about 3 hr. flying time, away). Average airfares on the route can run anywhere from $350 to $450 round-trip. Alaska Airlines is also the only airline with jets that fly within the state. It has flights to Ketchikan in the far south (about $380), Barrow in the far north (about $380), and to most communities in between with airfields long enough for jet aircraft; the airlines work with various smaller airlines with prop-driven aircraft, such as **Era Aviation** (☎ 800/866-8394 or 907/266-8394; www.FlyEra.com), to get passengers to communities where it doesn't fly.

A taxi ride from the airport to downtown costs about $30. Among the cab companies to try are **Alaska Cab** (☎ 907/563-3535) and **Yellow Cab** (☎ 907/272-2422). But I recommend planning ahead and making a reservation with **Shuttleman** (☎ 907/677-8537) instead. From the airport to downtown, Shuttleman charges just $12 for one person, and $2 for each extra person (up to four, in the same party), in a van with room for seven; plus, they'll drop you off right at your door, just like a cab. Shuttleman just has one van, so you have to arrange for a pick-up before you arrive. You can also get downtown from the airport via the city bus, called the **People Mover** (Downtown Transit Center, 6th Ave. and H St.; ☎ 907/343-6543; www.peoplemover.org; $1.75 adults, 50¢ seniors, $1 children 5–18, day pass $4 adults, $1.25 seniors), but it's a slow, miserable way to travel.

BY CAR

Public transportation and taxi service in Anchorage is lousy, so it's best to have a car there. While you can walk everywhere downtown, to get anywhere else in this sprawling city—and more importantly to get out of town to explore the land—you need wheels. Rental car rates vary with the season. In May you might get a compact car for as low as $49 per day, before taxes and fees. By July, when prices peak, the same car might cost you $89. Most of the major car rental firms have desks at the airport, but you can save a lot by renting elsewhere, where the 11% airport tax and the $4.30-per-day facility tax don't apply. (There's no getting around the 10% state tax and the 8% municipal tax.) In downtown you can rent a car without the extra charges from **Avis** (5th Ave. and B St.; ☎ 800/230-4898 or 907/277-4567; www.avis.com). **Budget Rent A Car** (802 Gambell; ☎ 907/274-1002) and **Enterprise Rent-A-Car** (926 E. 4th Ave.; ☎ 907/277-1600) are also options, but Avis is the most convenient thanks to its central location.

BY RAIL

Hopping a train is a surprisingly pricey way to get around Alaska. That said, it provides a stress-free, highly scenic, and just plain fun way to see the region. Much of the **Alaska Railroad** (☎ 800/544-0552 or 907/265-2494; www.alaskarailroad.com) route is far from the highway system, cutting through mountains and running along rivers that the casual sightseer would never otherwise get to see. From Anchorage you can ride the rail south to Seward, where glacier cruises are the big thing, or you can ride north to Denali National Park and Fairbanks. A round-trip ticket from Anchorage to Seward during the summer high season (June 1–Sept 3) costs $109 (or $55 for children 2–11), while it runs $135 ($68 for children) to Denali and $189 ($95 for children) to Fairbanks.

BY SEA

Although Anchorage is on Cook Inlet, accessible by sea, it does not have a deep-water port. Cruise ships can't dock there, and the nearest terminal of **The Alaska Marine Highway System** (☎ 800/642-0066; www.ferryalaska.com) is in Whittier, 60 miles away. Cruise-ship passengers who arrive and depart from either Whittier or Seward, the city's other deep-water port, get to and from Anchorage by bus or train.

ACCOMMODATIONS, BOTH STANDARD & NOT

As in the rest of the state, accommodation rates here fluctuate drastically by season. Wintertime, with the exception of March when the Iditarod comes to town, is bargain season with prices dropping by as much as 50%. In the summer months, hotel rates go through the roof, making the city a particularly good candidate for bed-and-breakfast stays. Not only do B&B rates tend to be more reasonable than hotel rates, but you'll get a completely different take on the city by staying with people who live there. (***One note:*** With both types of stays you'll be stuck paying Anchorage's appallingly high 12% lodgings tax.)

DOWNTOWN

Bed & Breakfasts

There are more than 250 Anchorage B&Bs altogether, including some real gems where you'll feel right at home and fall in love with the hosts. But be warned, there are some real dogs too. A sure way to *avoid* them is to search through the **Anchorage Bed-and-Breakfast Association** (☎ 888/584-5147 or 907/272-5909). It's a cooperative of about 60 of the better B&Bs in town. Each member gets an annual inspection, conducted by a committee of their peers, for basics like cleanliness and security. There's even an ethics committee that listens to any beefs that arise and boots offending B&Bs.

Some members of the association offer homestay-style experiences, where you stay as you would in a relative's home—you get your own bedroom, but share a living room and sometimes a bathroom. Others offer apartments with private entrances and private facilities. But in every case the hosts live under the same roof as the guests. That's a plus if something goes wrong or you need advice about sightseeing or transportation, but can make privacy-seeking guests a bit squeamish. So before you book, be sure to ask how separate the guest's quarters are from the host's living space (usually the less privacy there is, the lower the cost, so you'll also have to weigh in budgetary considerations). The hosts run the gamut from downtown yuppies to retirees living in the foothills above the city. At one place the hosts are fluent in Swiss and German, at another they speak French and Hebrew, at yet another they can talk your ear off about hunting, fishing, and quilting. For a few examples of Anchorage Bed-and-Breakfast Association members, read the reviews that follow for the Wildflower Inn, Jewel Lake B&B, and Lake Hood Inn. There are plenty of other fine B&Bs in Anchorage, and I've reviewed some of them, too.

All B&Bs offer breakfasts of some sort, whether it's a full sit-down meal with sourdough pancakes and reindeer sausage, a continental breakfast of fruit and muffins, or a minifridge stocked with milk, cheese, and eggs. Prices range from a low of $95 a night (very good for Anchorage in summer) up to $200.

$–$$$ A good example of those B&Bs on the lower end of the rate scale, the 15-room **Caribou Inn Bed & Breakfast** (kids) (501 L St.; ☎ 800/272-5878 or 907/ 272-0444; www.cariboubnb.com; AE, DISC, MC, V) sits smack in the heart of the city, close to the start of the coastal trail running along the urban shoreline (p. 51), and within walking distance of downtown's shops, restaurants, and attractions. The rooms are plain and filled with inexpensive, slightly musty dressers, end tables, and lamps, but they all have phones and cable TV, and the rates are great for the neighborhood: $99 for rooms with shared baths in summer, $109 for digs with private baths, and $139 for family suites with two double beds, kitchenettes, and private baths. Included with the price of the room is a ride to and from the airport, and a meal of pancakes, eggs, toast, and breakfast meat prepared by the inn's Korean owners.

$$–$$$$ From the outside, **Susitna Place** (727 N St.; ☎ 907/274-3344; www. susitnaplace.com; AE, DISC, MC, V) doesn't look like much—an anonymous flat-roofed home hiding behind a broad carport. From the inside it's a different story. A roomy, cool-gray living room greets guests, filled with leather couches and dining tables. It boasts a wall of windows with a view across the constantly changing waters of Cook Inlet. On clear days you can see a string of mountain peaks ranging from Denali in the north to the sharp cones of the Aleutian range to the south. Built in the 1960s as a triplex, this spacious B&B has seven rooms and two suites decorated with a mixture of contemporary and antique furnishings. They range in high season from $100 for a small room with shared baths (winter rates go as low as $60 a night), up to $180 for a commodious two-room suite with a Jacuzzi tub, private deck, and the same long views the living room enjoys. You're welcome to squeeze extra people into the suites, but it will cost you $15 each for those over the age of 15, and $10 for children 6 to 12 (it's free for anyone under 6). The amiable hostess lives on-site and lays out big continental breakfasts in the morning.

A Hostel Option

$ **The Anchorage International Hostel** (700 H St.; ☎ 907/276-3635; www. anchorageinternationalhostel.org; MC, V) is the dirt cheap choice in town, with dorm beds going for just $20 a night and private rooms for $55. That being said, it's showing its age and can be rather dingy. It used to rent out rooms in an annex called **The Amundsen House,** a two-story log cabin that has served both as the chief of police's house and a brothel (not at the same time, obviously). Private rooms there were also $55 but had a lot more character than those at the hostel. Inquire to see if they've reopened the annex.

BEYOND DOWNTOWN
Hotels & Bed & Breakfasts

The area around Ted Stevens International Airport has the densest cluster of accommodations outside of downtown. Most are along Spenard Road. The nicest and priciest are closest to the airport, with prices dropping and sketchiness increasing as Spenard moves north.

Anchorage

ACCOMMODATIONS ■
Jewel Lake B&B **11**
Lake Hood Inn **6**
Microtel Inn & Suites **8**
Wild Flower Inn **2**

DINING ◆
Gwennie's Old Alaska
   Restaurant **7**
Organic Oasis Restaurant &
   Juice Bar **3**
The Peanut Farm **10**

ATTRACTIONS ●
Alaska Aviation Heritage
   Museum **5**
Alaska Heritage Library Museum **4**
Alaska Native Heritage Center **1**
Alaska Native Medical Center **9**
The Alaska Zoo **12**

$$–$$$ My favorite airport area hotel, **Microtel Inn & Suites** (5205 Northwood Dr.; ☎ 907/245-5002; www.microtelanchorage.com; AE, DISC, MC, V) is about a mile from the airport and not really within walking distance of anything. But it has 24-hour airport shuttle service, and surprisingly, a hot tub. As with all Microtel Inns, it was built from scratch within the last decade, so you know everything's going to be spiffy, ultra-clean, and modern. Here the rooms are also quite spacious with cozy (by chain hotel standards) window seats. Another nice feature of the Microtel Inns is free calls within the United States and free Internet access. Prices average $107 during the high season, with suites starting at $149. Multi-day stays will sometimes drop the rate to just $70 a night, even in high season (you'll find these deals listed under "Internet specials" on their website, but also try discounters such as Hotels.com—they sometimes undercut Microtel's own rates).

$$–$$$ The homiest airport area option—one that's cheaper than a decent hotel, and with a good breakfast to boot—is **Jewel Lake B&B** (8125 Jewel Lake Rd.; ☎ 907/245-7321; www.jewellakebandb.com; AE, MC, V). It's just 3 miles from the airport and thus a sensible option for those arriving on a late-night flight or leaving early in the morning. The owner, a young guy who lives in an apartment upstairs, cooks up waffles, fresh-baked muffins, and blueberry sourdough pancakes until 9am (late risers get a continental breakfast). Guests are always welcome to use the kitchen and outdoor grill, too (laundry facilities are even conveniently on-site). Built in 1972, the inn was originally a model home for a cedar home manufacturer. It has five simple bedrooms, with either shared or private baths, for $125 to $135 in the high season, though prices may drop if you stay for longer than 4 nights (ask!). The place has a "Grizzly Adams" vibe, but an upscale one with lots of burnished, knotty wooden furniture, and plaid decor. Guests get the comfortable living room all to themselves, plus a deck screened from a busy street with brushy pines.

$$$ The most uniquely located place to stay in Anchorage is the **Lake Hood Inn** ✯✯✯ (4702 Lake Spenard Dr.; ☎ 866/663-9322 or 907/258-9321; www.lake hoodinn.com; AE, DISC, MC, V), which sits right on the edge of the Lake Hood Seaplane Base, the busiest seaplane base in the world. Seaplanes and floatplanes take off and land on the lake all day long. Guests can listen to the chatter between pilots and the air traffic controllers through headphones kept on the balcony. There are four spacious rooms here, with high season rates ranging from $139 for those without a lake view, to $159 with a view. Digs are spare but swankily appointed, with Berber carpets, high-thread-count sheets, and showers with seating for two. They occupy the upstairs addition of an airy, modernist-style home, owned by a pilot who keeps his two floatplanes docked in the front yard. An aviation theme prevails, with surprising touches in the common areas, like a row of passenger seats from an Ilyushin IL-62 Russian passenger liner, magazines stored in one of the skinny service carts that once rolled up and down the aisle of an Alaska Airlines jet, and a ceiling fan painted like a propeller and adorned with the nose cup from a Piper aircraft. The price isn't too bad when you consider that nearby hotels charge $149 to $179 for rooms with a whole lot less character. If you stay more than 2 nights, you get a 30% discount on the total.

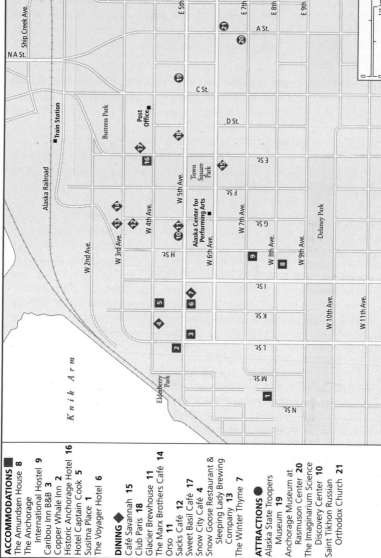
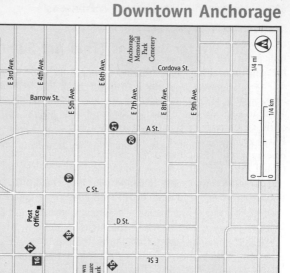

ACCOMMODATIONS ■
The Amundsen House **8**
The Anchorage
International Hostel **9**
Caribou Inn B&B **3**
Copper Whale Inn **2**
Historic Anchorage Hotel **16**
Hotel Captain Cook **5**
Susitna Place **1**
The Voyager Hotel **6**

DINING ◆
Café Savannah **15**
Club Paris **18**
Glacier Brewhouse **11**
The Marx Brothers Café **14**
Orso **11**
Sacks Café **12**
Sweet Basil Café **17**
Snow City Café **4**
Snow Goose Restaurant &
Sleeping Lady Brewing
Company **13**
The Winter Thyme **7**

ATTRACTIONS ●
Alaska State Troopers
Museum **19**
Anchorage Museum at
Rasmuson Center **20**
The Imaginarium Science
Discovery Center **10**
Saint Tikhon Russian
Orthodox Church **21**

Four Winter Bargains (That Are Summer Splurges)

The first thing many grizzled travelers do upon returning to Anchorage after roughing it in the wild is to check into one of the city's swankier hotels, take a long, hot shower, and gently acclimate themselves to the comforts of the civilized world. It's not a bad plan. While each of the below places is clearly a summer splurge, in the off season—when room rates throughout Alaska plummet—they transform from special treats into no-brainers.

$$–$$$ Your most romantic choice is the **Copper Whale Inn** ★ (440 L St.; ☎ 866/258-7999 or 907/258-7999; www.copperwhale.com; AE, DISC, MC, V), where, from some of the rooms, you can gaze across Cook Inlet at the snow-capped peaks of the Aleutian range without even lifting your head from your overstuffed pillow. The inn is essentially a small, boutique hotel with rooms in two buildings (an old doctor's home and a newer building that resembles the older one) separated by a water garden. Close to all the downtown attractions, it's just a block away from the coastal trail that runs along the Anchorage shoreline, convenient for long walks on bright summer nights. Each of the 14 rooms is shaped and decorated differently, but all have simple yet elegant mission-style furnishings and cushy beds. A few open onto a patio with a goldfish pond, and one has a fireplace. Most have private baths and go for $195 in summer, but drop to as little as $95 a night in winter. The budget options here are the two rooms that share a bath, and a third room that faces the street. Each of those go for $165, or a mere $75 when the temperature is low. None of these cheaper rooms are terribly large, but the whole place is so well-kept and refined you won't really care. Continental breakfast is included in the nightly rate.

$$$–$$$$ Next in line is a fabulous little four-story hotel where all 40 roomier-than-average rooms have sumptuous bedding and kitchenettes, and where three stay for the price of two. Although **The Voyager Hotel** ★ (501 K St.; ☎ 800/247-9070 or 907/277-9501; www.voyagerhotel.com; AE, DISC, MC, V) has no views to speak of, except for a parking lot ($6.50 a night per car), the staff is so friendly and professional, the housekeeping so impeccable, and the whole vibe of the place so pleasant, that the Voyager easily endears itself to guests. The high-season rate, which is for three people rather than the usual two, hovers around $179. That drops to about $89 in the off-season. If you check in late and there are still plenty of rooms available, you can usually talk the front desk into knocking 5% off—so give it a go. Tucked in the basement is a fine-dining restaurant called **Corsair** (☎ 907/278-4502; AE, DC, MC, V), which has a French and continental menu, a nautical decor, and very private booths that look like giant whiskey barrels that have been sliced open and then plushly upholstered.

$$$$ The grandest hotel in Anchorage is **Hotel Captain Cook** (939 W. 5th Ave.; ☎ 800/843-1950 or 907/276-6000; www.captaincook.com; AE, DISC, MC, V), which has more than 500 rooms in three towers that take up an entire downtown block. It's also got amenities galore: a shopping arcade, racquetball courts, gyms, Jacuzzis, saunas, massage services, yoga and pilates classes, around-the-clock room service, dry cleaning, concierges, three restaurants, and more. This place was built by Wally Hickel, a colorful Alaskan businessman and politician who was governor in the 1960s, then Secretary of the Interior for the Nixon Administration, then governor again in the 1990s. During the rebuilding of downtown following the 1964 Good Friday earthquake, the enterprising Hickel started building the first tower of this three-tower hotel, filling them with nautical decor and lavish teak interiors that include decking salvaged from a battleship. As the list of amenities mentioned above suggests, this is the place people go to for pampering in Anchorage. Rack rates are steep, starting at $245; however, you can often find better deals at Expedia.com—I've seen the starting rate drop to $160 and off-season specials can bring the rate as low as $99. When the temperatures are hovering in the teens and there's only five dim hours of daylight, being able to get a nice pedicure or take a good kick-boxing class in your hotel might very well justify the price.

$$$$ A smaller, more historic (it's the only Anchorage hotel on the National Register of Historic Places), and even more centrally located place to stay is the **Historic Anchorage Hotel** ★★ (330 E St.; ☎ 800/544-0988 or 907/272-4553; www.historicanchoragehotel.com; AE, DISC, MC, V). It was built in 1936 as an annex to the original and now defunct Anchorage Hotel, which was for years *the* place to stay in the city. After some hard times, new owners restored it in the 1980s, elegantly modernizing the 26 rooms and suites without scouring them of their sense of history. They all feature cushy beds with dark wood headboards; burgundy carpeting; and overstuffed chairs with silky upholstery. Suites have kitchenettes. During the summer high season, rooms go for $209, and suites for $249, with big discounts in the off season when the published rate drops to $149; web specials for around $79 are also often available—so definitely log on and check. Don't even think about trying to get a room here during the Iditarod in March. The hotel's located at the corner of 4th Avenue where the starting line is, and Iditarod people snap up every room well in advance.

$$-$$$ The **Wildflower Inn's** (1239 I St.; ☎ 907/274-1239; www.alaska-wild flower-inn.com; AE, MC, V) big bedroom suites and homey common area (guests get it all to themselves!) encourage lounging and languor. And as Martha Stewart would say, that's a good thing. Located in an old two-story home that keeps to a symmetrical floor plan, each of the inn's two suites is at the top of its own stairway. Both have plush beds with high-quality bedding in the bedrooms, and small living rooms with futon couches that convert into beds, meaning that groups or families can potentially bunk here (children under 6 share a room for free, older children and adults pay $15 more per night). The nightly rate in summer is $139. A third room, in the basement, goes for $129 in high season (just $79 in low season), and it's nicer and brighter than you'd expect. The two men who run the place live in their own private quarters in the house, and they whip up an unusual breakfast in the morning: Pannukakku, a Finish pancake that puffs up and then deflates, leaving a hole that you fill with cinnamon, berries, maple syrup, and other goodies. The inn is on a busy street corner, at least a 10-minute walk from the downtown core, but right across the street from New Sagaya Market, a neighborhood hang-out where people sit outside on nice days having coffee and Pad Thai.

Camping

Anchorage may be a big city, but it's a big *Alaskan* city, so there's camping in and around the urban area. The municipally owned **Centennial Park** (☎ 907/343-6986, or 907/343-4136 off season; www.muni.org/parks/camping.cfm) is on Boundary Road at the Muldoon Road exit from the Glenn Highway, just as you enter town from the north. It's near a run-down commercial strip, but many of the 88 sites are tucked away in a wooded area. The sites, which cost $20 per night, can accommodate tents or RVs. Hot showers are available.

South of town, **Bird Creek Campground** has an eye-candy location on the shore of Turnagain Arm. Nearby Bird Creek is a popular salmon fishing spot. There are 28 sites, and the fee is $15 per night. From Anchorage, drive 25 miles south on the Seward Highway to milepost 101.

The 57-site **Eagle River Campground** (☎ 800/952-8624 or 907/694-7982; www.lifetimeadventures.net) sits in a thickly wooded riverside spot, and it's well developed, with paved roads and large sites with lots of privacy. It costs $15 a night, and sites can be reserved up to a year in advance. The hosts also book rafting on the Eagle River. Take the Glenn Highway 12 miles north from Anchorage and exit at Hiland Road.

DINING FOR ALL TASTES

Anchorage's restaurant scene is vast, varied, and filled with halibut tacos, blackened salmon salads, knock-out microbrews, and the occasional stuffed grizzly bear. From cheap eats to fine-dining experiences, the city truly excels at meal time.

DOWNTOWN

$ Super fresh fruits and vegetables can be a rarity in Alaska, so it's not unusual to feel produce-deprived here. **Sweet Basil Café** (1021 W. Northern Lights Blvd.; ☎ 907/274-0070; Mon–Fri 8am–3pm, Sat 9am–3pm; AE, MC, V) offers perfect remedies: fresh-squeezed carrot juice in tall glasses, veggie-rich pasta specials, and vegetable soups. Everything somehow seems more nutritious here than the same foods would in the Lower 48. It's a strange phenomenon. Even the frozen blueberries and strawberries on the waffles and oatmeal seem more precious than frozen berries at home. There are wraps, hot sandwiches, and fish tacos too, all for under $10.

$ As a repeat winner of the *Anchorage Press*'s readers' choice award for best breakfast, it's safe to say that **Snow City Café** 🕵 (1024 W. 4th Ave.; ☎ 907/272-CITY; www.snowcitycafe.com; Mon–Fri 7am–3pm, Sat–Sun 7am–4pm; AE, DISC, MC, V) is Anchorage's favorite breakfast spot. The all-day breakfast menu is as generous to meat eaters as it is to vegetarians, with the build-your-own-omelet ($8.95) options including pork sausage, country bacon, or black forest ham, as well as baked tofu, Boca Burger, nuts, and seeds. Breakfast selections run from yogurt and granola parfait ($4.60), to tofu scramble ($8.95), to salmon cakes and eggs ($8.95), all the way to a Dungeness crab omelet with Swiss cheese and green onions ($13). Lunches feature soups ($3.25) and big, fat sandwiches ($9.95). A bright, cheerful waitstaff complements the bright, cheerful space. Weekends bring crowds and waits for tables.

$$–$$$ The married 20-somethings behind **The Winter Thyme** ★★ (930 W. 5th Ave.; ☎ 907/677-3843; Thurs–Mon 11am–midnight; MC, V) worked at some of Anchorage's best restaurants before opening their own place in a squat cinder block building in the cold shadow of the Captain Cook Hotel. They've dressed up this small, windowless dining room with cheerful orange walls and framed postcards, giving it the feel of a basement rumpus room. The servers are casual, reading the specials off the chalkboard. From the "Appetizer and Small Entrees" list—many of which are large enough for a meal, by the way—you can get salmon stuffed won-ton ($4), razor clam fritters ($7), or—best of all—two generous slices of pan-roasted trout propped up on a bed of sautéed greens and lightly dressed with red-wine caper sauce ($10). Entrees are just as creative, including venison bratwurst with cabbage, peppers, and onions braised in an Alaskan ale ($9); halibut parmesan, a breaded fish filet over spaghetti with marinara ($13); and buffalo meatloaf ($20), stuffed with fresh basil and melted goat cheese, wrapped in a puff pastry, and served with perfectly crunchy little asparagus segments and golden-brown red potatoes, stacked like gold doubloons.

$$$–$$$$ Standing on a bluff on the north edge of downtown, **Snow Goose Restaurant and Sleeping Lady Brewing Company** (717 W. 3rd Ave.; ☎ 907/277-7727; www.alaskabeers.com; daily 11:30am–midnight; AE, DISC, MC, V) looks toward the port across Ship Creek basin, where the tent city that grew into modern Anchorage sprang up in 1914. The downstairs dining room, second-floor pub with alfresco seating, and the rooftop beer-and-wine deck can handle a large, lively local drinking crowd. The menu reaches every which way—toward American with meat loaf and prime rib, toward Latin American with roast chicken with *pico de gallo*, toward Asian fusion with a wasabi-lime sauce halibut sandwich, and even toward French classic with the chicken *cordon bleu*. Yet it does best at home, with the simple stuffed halibut or the three preparations of salmon. Entrees run from $19 to $30. Better yet, stick to the well-crafted burgers ($11) and fish and chips ($14) on the pub menu, and enjoy the beers ($4.50 pints, $16 pitchers), the live music on summer Fridays and Saturdays, and the wonderful view. On a clear day you can see Denali.

$–$$$$ For better food and better beer, but no view, go to **Glacier Brewhouse** (737 W. 5th St., ☎ 907/274-BREW; www.glacierbrewhouse.com; Mon–Sat 11am–11pm, Sun noon–11pm; AE, DISC, MC, V). Its enormous, lodgelike dining room has an open kitchen, an open view of the brewing operations, and a menu that stretches from three-cheese pepperoni pizza ($9.95), to barbecue pork ribs with Jamaican jerk seasoning ($21), to a surf-and-turf featuring prime rib and a half pound of king crab ($37). This is a good place for lunch, when many of the same entrees served at dinner cost $6 or $7 less. The portions are a wee bit smaller, but that leaves room for more beer ($4.50 pints, $14 pitchers).

$$–$$$$ Sharing the same building, the same owners, and some of the same beers as Glacier Brewhouse is a nouvelle Italian restaurant called **Orso** (737 W. 5th Ave.; ☎ 907/222-3232; www.orsoalaska.com; Mon–Thurs 11:30am–4pm and 5–10pm, Fri–Sat 11:30am–4pm and 5–11pm, Sun 5–10pm; AE, DISC, MC, V). When you walk in, you're greeted by the friendly aromas of garlic and basil that emanate from the bright, busy kitchen and fill the unabashedly sensual dining room, done up in sexy, roasted-tomato-red. The place somehow succeeds at feeling elegant and homespun at the same time, with an attention to detail that extends all the way to the heated toilet seats. A global-fusion approach to Italian cooking prevails, though there's still room on the menu among all the polentas, pear sauces, and capers for good-old-fashioned spaghetti and meatballs. Orso, which means "bear" in Italian, has a thoroughly Alaskan side as well; the menu features halibut, salmon, and king crab. Most entrees run from $16 to $26.

$–$$$$ Dinner rushes at **Club Paris** ★ (417 W. 5th Ave.; ☎ 907/277-6332; www.clubparisrestaurant.com; Mon–Sat 11:30am–2:30pm and 5–11pm, Sun 5–10pm; AE, DISC, MC, V) come like the 6-foot bore tide that rushes up Turnagain Arm, only less predictably. The ebb and flow of meat eaters at this dark, narrow arm of a steakhouse is dictated by variables like bachelor parties, retirement send-offs, and the schedule of the nearby Alaska Center for the Performing Arts. One thing never changes: Club Paris is the place to go in Anchorage when the occasion, whatever it is, calls for red meat. Never mind the casual service or the slightly disreputable facade, with its smoked black windows, vintage '50s neon, and a faded cut-out of the Eiffel Tower leaning cockily toward the street. The char-broiled steaks here are as good as steaks can be. The 8-ounce petite filet ($25), the 16-ounce rib-eye ($29), the 14-once filet mignon ($34), and the rest are cut and aged on-site. There's seafood too, which isn't nearly as good as the meat, and at lunch, hamburgers ($9), which are quite delicious. Club Paris is as much a bar as it is a restaurant, and it has been since opening in 1957. "Before that it was a funeral home," the bartender said, pouring Scotch for a diner who had just inhaled a rib-eye. "They used to do the embalming where the kitchen is. Now we do it out here." Reservations are recommended.

$$$–$$$$ Younger, brighter, and more upscale than Club Paris, **Café Savannah** ★ (508 W. 6th Ave.; ☎ 907/646-9121; Mon–Thurs 11am–3pm and 5–10pm; Fri–Sat 11am–3pm and 5pm–midnight; MC, V) brings a little bit of Madrid to Anchorage in the forms of sautéed pimentos, poblano peppers, Manchego cheese, and other Spanish staples. The open kitchen, big oil and acrylic paintings, and silverware set into the decorative concrete tabletops and arranged into wall sculpture (fork tines curl like octopus tentacles, spoon handles undulate like the end of a certain reproductive cell) give the place a playful feel. Entrees range from $19 to $29, and include dishes like Catalonian pork with sherry glazed figs, and grilled salmon topped with orange saffron sauce and served with prosciutto-wrapped roasted asparagus. If you don't go overboard, you can save money and make a meal from the hot tapas, such as calamari a la Savannah (calamari with roasted peppers, Spanish olives, and shallots in a white wine and sherry reduction, $12), or the *hongo rellenos* (portobello caps stuffed with Spanish chorizo and Manchego cheese, $5.50). Since it's across the street from The Alaska Center for the Performing Arts (p. 56), this place is subject to rushes, and reservations are an especially good idea on Friday.

$$$$ The restaurant with the biggest buzz in Anchorage these days is a bright and airy bistro called **Sacks Café** ★★★ (328 G St.; ☎ 907/276-3546 or 907/274-4022; www.sackscafe.com; Mon–Thurs 11am–2:30pm and 5–9:30pm, Fri 11am–2:30pm and 5–10:30pm, Sat 11am–3pm and 5–10:30pm, Sun 10:30am–3pm and 5–9:30pm; AE, DISC, MC, V). Its downtown storefront location, small dining room, and reputation for adventurous cuisine mean that the place is always packed—though it gets especially crowded at lunch. Its imaginative, exquisitely presented dishes encourage repeat visits. Sacks is a place where people come to see and be seen, but more importantly, it's a place where everyone looks at what everyone else is having, and resolves to come back and try that next time. The salad with chèvre cheese, poached Bosc pears, and grape tomatoes ($7) couldn't be better—but oh my, doesn't the salad with the tiger prawns and polenta croutons ($14) look nice? The crab-and-scallop cakes with honey chipotle aioli ($10) are unbelievable, and the salmon tempura (market price) is outstanding—but hey, I think that table ordered the curried halibut (market price) and seared ostrich filet ($10) appetizers! Reservations are definitely recommended here.

BEYOND DOWNTOWN

$–$$ Alaska has precious few places where you'll find steamed quinoa, tabouli, or Veganaise—the vegan mayonnaise substitute. So when vegans, vegetarians, and their sympathizers discover **Organic Oasis Restaurant & Juice Bar** ★★ (2610 Spenard Rd.; ☎ 907/277-7882; www.organicoasis.com; Tues–Wed 11am–7pm, Thurs 11am–9pm, Fri–Sat 11am–10pm, Sun noon–5pm; no credit cards), they become instant devotees. This is no small health-food store deli, but rather a cavernous strip-mall space between a yoga studio and a comic book store, filled with plants, tables, racks of wheat grass, and reedy-looking waitresses with clear skin and bright eyes. There's also a stainless steel bar, where you can get a glass of organic beer or wine as you watch the chef prepare macrobiotic platters ($9.95, brown rice, baked tofu, and steamed veggies), big mixed green salads ($5.95, dressings include a vinaigrette made with apple cider vinegar and jewel yams), veggie pizzas ($11, topped with sprouts, of course), or veggie smoothies ($5.95, hydraulically pressed veggie juice, hemp oil, and spirulina). It's not all antioxidants and life-force though—dinner specials regularly feature salmon or halibut ($12–$15), burgers include free-range organic buffalo and lamb ($8.95) with melted Swiss, and the BLTs ($9.95) are made with turkey bacon and Veganaise (and they're delightful).

Harpo, Groucho, Chico & Zeppo Would Be Proud

The 1978 opening of a new restaurant in downtown Anchorage was accompanied by mayhem on the scale of *A Night at the Opera* (lots of alcohol and cops were involved), which led the owners to name the place the **Marx Bros. Café** ★★★ (627 W. 3rd Ave.; ☎ 907/278-2133; www.marxcafe.com; summer Tues–Sat 5:30–10pm, rest of year Tues–Thurs 6–9:30pm, Fri–Sat 5:30–10pm; AE, MC, V; reservations recommended; $$$$). It has since grown up and settled down to become the standard bearer for fine dining in Alaska, one with such a loyal following it puts out a newsletter, and one that's such an esteemed Anchorage institution it has an auxiliary branch serving lunch and dinner inside the **Anchorage Museum at Rasmuson Center** (p. 45). Photos from the madcap early days hang in one of the two snug little dining rooms of the original location, on the ground floor of an early Anchorage home. Of the four original partners (long-haired and bearded, and hamming it up in the old photos on the wall), two remain. One is the maitre d', moving from table to table distributing Caesar salads ($11) in a giant wooden bowl. The other partner holds down the kitchen, where meticulously prepared appetizers, such as a Neapolitan of seafood mousse (a $15 mix of lobster, smoked salmon, and halibut with a "yin-yang" of osetra and golden caviar), and main courses like the macadamia nut halibut ($34, with mango chutney, mild coconut curry, and steamed jasmine rice) originate.

The cuisine at the Café is, broadly, Alaskan-Asian-Italian fusion, and dinner is a slow, leisurely, and expensive (most entrees are $30 or more) affair. If a fine dining splurge isn't in your budget, you can get a taste of the Marx Bros. Café at its museum location and save a bundle. There you can try dishes like the open-faced, blackened salmon sandwich ($11) or some king crab niçoise ($15, but big enough to share).

$–$$$$ The most noteworthy thing about **The Peanut Farm** (5227 Old Seward Hwy.; ☎ 907/563-3283; Sun–Thurs 6am–2am, Fri–Sat 6am–3am; AE, DISC, MC, V) isn't that it looks like a log palace, or that sports are shown on a sea of video screens inside, including the flatscreen monitors anchored to every booth. The thing that most stands out is the creek out back where you can watch salmon spawn in the summer while you nibble on chicken wings. When I last visited, three enormous male kings thrashed about a gravel bar, jockeying for a favorable position on a single female who calmly held her ground just upstream. A similar contest was under way inside, where several men playing darts vied for the attention of three females, who sat at a tall table, calmly sipping mixed drinks. That's how it looked to me, anyway. The food is pretty good for pub grub, especially the wood-fired pizzas ($17), pastas ($12–$19), and—a pleasant surprise at a sports bar—salads ($10). The lengthy menu offers nearly as many choices at the satellite TV feed.

$$–$$$$ Gwennie's Old Alaska Restaurant (4333 Spenard Rd.; ☎ 907/243-2090; Mon–Sat 6am–10pm, Sun 8am–10pm; AE, DISC, MC, V) is a thoroughly Alaskan diner where big men with big appetites eat big plates of reindeer sausage and eggs ($10), enormous Monte Cristo sandwiches ($9) with shrimp cocktail chasers ($7), or heavy piles of deep-fried prawns ($19) and barbecue spareribs ($19). From its parking lot, Gwennie's looks like a cinder block monolith giving birth to a three-story Chinese restaurant. During the 1970s, when Anchorage was filled with construction workers building the Trans-Alaska Pipeline, Gwennie's actually was a Chinese restaurant, as well as an underground casino and a busy brothel. Today it's a hallowed and somewhat bizarre diner, with a bar that opens at 10am, a stuffed grizzly bear poised to take your head off at the door, and, when I was there anyway, an old waitress with a punk haircut, a severe limp, and six plates of food balanced on her arms. Things like that, along with the peculiar greenish cast of the light, give the place a delightful air of Alaskan unreality. It's on the road to the airport, so if you're flying out of town, it's a good stop for a fat, greasy meal and a final, concentrated dose of Alaska. Breakfasts range from $6 to $11, lunches from $7 to $11, and dinners from $15 to $29.

WHY YOU'RE HERE: THE TOP SIGHTS & ATTRACTIONS

Anchorage is often referred to as the "gateway to adventure," which is really a polite way of saying that it's not a destination in its own right. The truth is the city does have its share of worthwhile visitor attractions, though you may not want to devote much more than a day or two to explore them.

For example, you really don't expect a midsize, ugly-duckling city like Anchorage to have a world-class museum as big and beautiful as the **Anchorage Museum at Rasmuson Center** ★★★ (121 W. 7th Ave., corner of C St.; ☎ 907/343-4326; www.anchoragemuseum.org; $8 adults, children 17 and under free; Sept 16–May 14 Wed–Sat 10am–6pm, Sun noon–5pm; May 15–Sept 15 Fri–Wed 9am–6pm, Thurs 9am–9pm). But thanks largely to the state's flood of oil revenues, there it is. The museum has seven galleries filled with the art of Alaska and the rest of the circumpolar North; it gets more than 20 traveling exhibits a year; it has a full program of films, concerts, lectures, classes, and openings; it's got a kids' zone loaded with hands-on things to do; it lets artists and artisans sell their wares in its atrium during the summer; and it boasts an affordable gourmet restaurant (see the Marx Bros. Café review on p. 44). But the best thing about the Anchorage Museum is its cavernous Alaska Gallery. There you can examine woolly mammoth tusks, Eskimo harpoon tips, Russian samovars, and thousands of other objects pulled from a span of time stretching from the construction of the Trans-Alaska Pipeline back to the spearing of mastodons. The artifacts are exhibited with theatrical flair and a lot of help from faceless mannequins attired in some of the artifacts themselves, such as Iñupiat fur parkas, gold miner's dungarees, and bombardier jackets worn by WWII aviators. The exhibits are dominated by life-size dioramas—a Tlingit clan house, a Russian trapper's cabin, an underground Eskimo sod house—and the artifacts don't look like they're on display as much as they seem like they're still in use.

Alaska's Favorite Painter: Sydney Who?

The one artist every Alaskan knows, and no one else seems to have ever heard of, is **Sydney Laurence** (1865–1940), Painter of the North. Laurence's subdued-but-heroic images of Alaska—sailing ships crashing through heavy seas, lonely cabins sitting along frozen streams, totem poles standing in dark forests, Mount McKinley (aka Denali) looking enormous—turn up all over the state. Every boardroom, dentist's office, and postcard rack from Ketchikan to Kotzebue has its Sydney Laurences. The **Anchorage Museum at Rasmuson Center** (see above) has an entire gallery dedicated to the artist, the Sydney Laurence Gallery. It's dominated by a huge canvas of Mount McKinley, Laurence's trademark image. To keep up with demand, he painted McKinley over and over again, too many times, in fact. His later McKinleys, hastily done and one-dimensional, show how the subject wore on him. But the various McKinleys in the Sydney Laurence Gallery show a mountain that was still fresh and intriguing to the painter. In the foreground is the Tokositna River, which appears in nearly every McKinley Laurence did.

Laurence was born in Brooklyn and made a name for himself as a painter in New York City and Europe before coming to Alaska around 1904. As he explained to an interviewer in 1925: "I was attracted by the same thing that attracted all the other suckers—gold. I didn't find any appreciable quantity of the yellow metal, and then, like a lot of other fellows, I was broke and couldn't get away. So I resumed my painting. I found enough material to keep me busy the rest of my life, and I have stayed in Alaska ever since."

If you don't get enough Sydney Laurence at the Sydney Laurence Gallery, you can see more of his canvases in the lobby of the Wells Fargo Bank building in midtown, at what's known as the **Alaska Heritage Library Museum** (301 W. Northern Lights Blvd.; ☎ 907/265-2834; free admission; Mon–Fri noon–4pm). It's also got a nice collection of Native arts and crafts, 2,600 volumes on Alaska in its reference library, and a three-quarter size Wells Fargo stagecoach.

If you can get in on the docent tour of the Alaska Gallery, do it. It's a whirlwind 45-minute tour (starting at 10am, 11am, 1pm, and 2pm in the summer) that will give you a good grounding in the history and culture of Alaska, with incomparable visual aids. And if you can visit only one museum in town, make it this one. The admission fee is a small price to pay for the 10,000 years of Alaskan art and history you'll find there. If you have time for more, start here and ask for the "Alaska Cultural Pass," which gives you admission to the museum and the Alaska Native Heritage Center (p. 47) for $25, not much more than the walloping $24 adult admission to the heritage center alone. From the museum you can take a free shuttle to the heritage center, a few miles up the highway.

You could spend the whole morning at the Anchorage Museum and still come away bewildered by all of the different indigenous groups that fall into the category of "Alaska Native." There are at least 11 distinct cultures that speak 20 different languages, and not even all Alaska Natives agree on where the divisions lie. The best way to begin untangling the ethnographic lines (while still having an enjoyable vacation!) is to pay a visit to the **Alaska Native Heritage Center** ★★ kids (8800 Heritage Center Dr.; ☎ 800/315-6608 or 907/330-8000; www.alaska native.net; $24 adults, $22 seniors, $16 children 7–16, family passes also available; mid-May to mid-Sept daily 9am–5pm, rest of year Sat noon–4pm). There you can wander around an unusual Native village containing examples of the traditional dwellings of various groups from around the state. Natives stationed at each perform demonstrations and seem genuinely happy to talk about their cultures. You can't be sure who you'll meet, but you might find Tlingits at the clan house smoking fish, and Aleuts at the sod house weaving grass baskets or stretching seal skins over a kayak frame. In the cultural center's high-ceilinged main building, you can look around a gallery of Native art, watch a cultural film in a plush theater, and catch storytellers, dancers, and Native athletes on stage. Time your visit to catch one of the 30-minute stage presentations, which happen at 10am, noon, 2:15pm, and 4pm.

The thing I really like about the Alaska Native Heritage Center is that it's more than a checkmark on the mass tourism trail, although it's that too. The center's role as a visitor attraction is secondary to its mission to promote Native culture among Natives. Throughout the year there are all sorts of events that draw Alaska Natives from every group, such as intertribal gatherings, leadership conferences, CD releases, programs to honor elders, storytelling and drumming festivals, and celebrations of things like the arrival of winter or the return of spring.

Cop culture is the focus of the **Alaska State Troopers Museum** (320 W. 5th Ave.; ☎ 800/770-5050 or 907/279-5050; www.alaskatroopermuseum.com; free admission; Mon–Fri 10am–4pm, Sat noon–4pm), a small, downtown repository of mementos from the state's various law enforcement agencies, such as handcuffs and leg irons, early radios and walkie-talkies, and a shiny 1952 Hudson Hornet patrol car that any speeder would be proud to be pulled over by. As someone who prefers to minimize time spent with the local constabulary, I was in no particular hurry to see this museum. I wasn't especially impressed by all the badges and insignia on display, or by the goofy-looking Safety Bear costume. But I found myself getting caught up in seeing what cops find interesting, and I couldn't help but get sucked into the exhibits on early efforts to sabotage the Trans-Alaska Pipeline and on Alaska's first serial killer (he came to the territory with the U.S. Army during the Klondike gold rush, and unsuccessfully ran for a seat in the legislature in 1912). I wouldn't go out of my way to see the Troopers Museum, but it's worth a quick stop if you're passing by.

Got kids? Still have a few remaining shards of your own childlike curiosity? If you answered yes to either question, then head to **The Imaginarium Science Discovery Center** ★★★ kids (737 W. 5th Ave; ☎ 907/276-3179; www.imaginarium. org; $5.50 adults, $5 seniors and children 13 and under; Mon–Sat 10am–6pm, Sun noon–6pm). Located in the basement of the Glacier Brewhouse Mall, it seems a little out of place, like a public school classroom buried beneath artsy gift shops and noisy beer drinkers. If it's a classroom, though, it's one run by a brilliant and

Guided Tours & Visitor Help

The best **guided tour** of the historic downtown area is by **Anchorage Historic Properties,** 645 W. 3rd Ave. (☎ 907/274-3600), a preservation group, offering 2-hour, 2-mile walks from June to August Monday through Friday at 1pm. Meet at the lobby of Old City Hall, 524 W. 4th Ave., next door to the Log Cabin Visitor Information Center. Tickets cost $5 for adults, $1 for children.

Motorized city tours can get you beyond downtown to see what more of the town looks like. **Anchorage Trolley Tours** (☎ 907/276-5603) offers a 1-hour ride for $10 in a bus made up like a trolley car, taking in the downtown area, a Cook Inlet overlook near the airport, and the Lake Hood seaplane base. The operator has a fun outlook. Catch the trolley on 4th Avenue between F and G streets, across from the Alaska Public Land Information Center.

The people you see downtown on bikes and on foot in bright yellow-and-black outfits are the **Anchorage Downtown Partnership Security Ambassadors,** sometimes known as the "bumblebees" for their color scheme. They are funded by a self-imposed levy on downtown property owners in part to help visitors. Stop one to ask a question or report a problem, or call ☎ 907/277-7233 (www.anchorage downtown.org).

—*Charles Wohlforth*

maverick teacher who's always working on new contraptions to illustrate some principal of astronomy or physics, and who's constantly on the lookout for new creatures for her aquariums and terrariums. There's enough to do at the Imaginarium to happily fill a few hours, and should you tire of studying the frogs, solving puzzles, firing the air cannon, testing the aerodynamics of an aircraft wing in the wind tunnel, pondering the plankton under a microscope, running your fingers across the cold iron of the meteorite, and waiting for the boa constrictors to do something, you can always build a giant soap bubble around yourself and stand inside of it until it pops.

When you think of all the wildlife you might see in Alaska, an elephant on a treadmill is not the first thing that springs mind. **The Alaska Zoo** (4731 O'Malley Rd.; ☎ 907/346-3242; www.alaskazoo.org; $10 adults, $8 seniors, $6 children 3–17; daily 9am–6pm except in summer when closing hr. is 9pm Tues and Thurs) has one, though (the treadmill's for winter workouts), along with camels, tigers, and other exotic animals from around the world. At the time of writing, it was undergoing a huge transition, moving away from being a typical zoo and toward becoming a sanctuary for Alaskan animals that can't survive in the wild, rather than a menagerie of creatures from far-away places. For now, you can see moose, caribou, Dall sheep, and seals, as well as a brown bear and a polar bear (they were orphaned as cubs and grew up at the zoo together). Yes, you can see these same animals in the wild elsewhere in Alaska, but in most cases you'd need binoculars to get a good look at them. The zoo is way out on the east side of town. If you're not driving, a free downtown shuttle leaves from the Log Cabin Visitors Center (F St. and 4th Ave.) and from various hotels through the summer.

In a state with 16 times as many airplanes per capita as the entire Lower 48, and where one out of every 78 residents is a pilot, you know there's going to be a good aviation museum. For aviation buffs, the **Alaska Aviation Heritage Museum** (4721 Aircraft Dr.; ☎ 907/248-5325; www.alaskaairmuseum.com; $10 adults, $3 children 5–12, $8 children 13–18; summer daily 9am–5pm, rest of year Wed–Sun 9am–5pm) will be irresistible. For the rest of us, there's enough drama behind each of the aircraft to fill a good 45 minutes or so, not including the time you spend with the flight simulator taking off and landing (or crash landing, if you fly like I do). The museum's collection, housed in a couple of hangars, includes a plane known as "Old Patches" that was flown by one of Alaska's colorful governors; a WWII observation plane that could fly as slowly as 28 knots and then speed up to 108 knots; a plane that flew serum to the Arctic during a diphtheria epidemic; the wreckage of a plane that crashed; and the wreckage of a plane that used to search for downed planes before it too crashed. Naturally, the museum's out by the airport, right on the shores of Lake Hood Seaplane Base, the world's busiest seaplane base, which is itself a sight to see. If you're airport-bound on International Airport Drive, turn right toward Postmark Drive, then right again on Heliport Drive, then right once more on Aircraft Drive to reach the site.

THE OTHER ANCHORAGE

Why settle for a model of a Native village at the Alaska Native Heritage Center (p. 47), when there's an actual Native village 24 miles north of Anchorage on the Glenn Highway, at **Eklutna?** Athabascan Indians have lived there for more than a thousand years, which makes it the oldest continuously inhabited site in this part of Alaska. Some still maintain subsistence lifestyles, but don't expect to find people living in skin-covered shelters or sod houses. The 400 or so residents of Eklutna live in modern Alaskan homes, with kitchens, living rooms, and garages with snowmobiles in them.

I wouldn't recommend Eklutna to everyone, but if you're drawn to unusual cemeteries and old Russian churches—either out of historic curiosity or for purely photographic reasons—I bet you'll like it. In the **Russian Orthodox cemetery,** colorful little spirit houses, which look like a cross between dog houses and coffins, mark the graves instead of headstones or crosses. Beside the cemetery stands the **St. Nicholas Russian Orthodox Church,** which was built in the 1830s and is the oldest building in south-central Alaska. Nearby is a **Siberian-style prayer chapel,** an ancient little log structure that looks like an elaborately designed outhouse with a couple of rooftop onion domes tilting precariously. There's usually someone around the church between 8am and 6pm in the summer who will give you a 10-minute tour for $6. I recommend taking it so you can get inside the church and see the icons, which are hundreds of years old but are still used in worship services at the newer church next door.

Another way to immerse yourself in traditional Alaska Native culture is to go to the hospital. No, really. The **Alaska Native Medical Center** (4315 Diplomacy Dr.; ☎ 907/563-2662) is a tribally owned and operated hospital with 250 physicians serving Alaska natives and Native Americans in Anchorage (with satellite facilities throughout the state). I realize that going to a hospital to look at the patients might not sound like an appropriate vacation activity, but that's not what I'm suggesting. The reason you should go to the Medical Center is because it has one of the best displays of Native arts and crafts in the state, and it happens to be open to the general public. The arts and crafts are in showcases throughout the hospital, mainly around the elevators and in the stairwells. While you work your way from one to the another, incidentally, you will be among elders in wheelchairs, kids with balloons, men with braided pony tails, women in corporate attire—the whole broad cross section of humanity that you'd find on any given day in any big urban hospital anywhere, except just about everybody at this one has blood ties to the land stretching back 10,000 years or so. Another reason to go to the hospital is that the gift store there is one of the best places in Anchorage to buy Native crafts.

Remnants of Russian America can be found in little pockets and eddies all over the state. One is on the edge of downtown Anchorage, behind the avocado green walls of an otherwise nondescript corner building with a sign out front that reads **Saint Tikhon Russian Orthodox Church** (1539 Old Seward Hwy; ☎ 907/240-1888; www.sainttikhon.org). This is a great place to rub elbows with the locals—mostly Alaska Natives—and exchange pleasantries before or after the service. The highly ritualized services themselves are filled with chanting, singing, and burning incense, and they haven't changed a bit since Russian Orthodox missionaries began converting Natives in the 18th century. The church itself is nothing fancy, just a small room with an altar. There are no pews, because the congregation stands for the length of the 90-minute service (although chairs are offered to the sick). You don't have to stay for the whole thing, and even the regular parishioners sometimes leave early. The priest says he doesn't take premature departures personally, but he warns his parishioners that their spiritual development will suffer if they make a habit of it.

During the day when services aren't underway, you can stop by to look around the free, tiny, one-room museum, which has Russian Orthodox artifacts, and, more likely than not, an attendant or two fluent in Russian and more than happy to spend the morning with you recounting the 11th century rift in which the Catholic Church and Orthodox Church went their separate ways. There's also a miniature gift shop here, selling Russian nesting dolls and Polish jewelry boxes for next to nothing, as well as a little espresso bar.

Services are held every Saturday at 5pm and Sunday at 9am, and throughout the week on a schedule dictated by the busy calendar of the saints.

The University of Alaska's main campus is in Fairbanks, but its largest campus (17,000 students) is in Anchorage. Where there are big universities, there are free lecture series, and two are worth looking into while you're in Anchorage. **The Bartlett Lecture Series** (www.uaa.alaska.edu/campuslife/bartlett) aims to "promote a clearer vision of individual freedom and of the public good," and it does so with speakers like Noam Chomsky, Angela Davis, Native rights activist Ward Churchill, and other politically charged personalities who undoubtedly get under the skin of Alaska's Republican dominated legislature. Check the website for the current schedule. The other lecture series, and the more Alaskan one, is called **Science for Alaska** (☎ 907/786-1260; www.scienceforalaska.com). It brings to the podium a broad line-up of researchers. Past speakers have included a biologist who has traveled with Iñupiat hunters to study the impact of melting sea ice on Arctic seal populations, a hydrologist who discussed how the warming climate and melting permafrost are changing the state, and a wildlife biologist who gave

Birds of a Feather

More than 200 species of birds spend all or some of the year in the wetlands and woods around Anchorage, making the city a birding hot spot. You can meet local birders and compare life lists on free field trips organized by the **Anchorage Audubon Society** (☎ 907/338-2473; www.anchorage audubon.org). The experienced volunteer naturalists who lead the outings will have you spotting the red-breasted nuthatches, short-billed dowitchers, and wandering tattlers among the thrushes in nothing flat. The trips happen every weekend in May and June, and a couple of times a month from July through August. They last 2 to 4 hours. Call or check the website for specifics. Another way to meet birders in Anchorage, and other parts of Alaska, or other parts of the world for that matter, is through www.birdingpal.org, an international website that brings traveling and local birders together.

a scientific perspective on bear safety and showed gory slides from some high-profile bear attacks. Both lecture series are open to all, and they're excellent places to rub elbows with Anchorage's actual and would-be intelligentsia.

ACTIVE ANCHORAGE

Anchorage in the summer is a city that cries for you to get outdoors and have fun. Here are a few ways to do so:

BIKING & HIKING

Anchorage has plenty of trails, both urban and alpine, right in the city limits. There are 120 miles of paved trails alone, running along streams, following greenbelts, and cutting through nice little neighborhoods and parks. The most spectacular is the **Tony Knowles Coastal Trail** ★★, which runs along the Anchorage shoreline for 11 miles, from downtown, starting at the west end of 2nd Avenue, to Kincaid Park, way past the airport. The whole thing is paved and filled with walkers, runners, rollerbladers, bicyclists, dogs, children, the occasional moose or bear, and, during the winter, cross-country skiers.

In summer, biking is the most efficient way to take in all the changing terrain of this trail. Stop at **Earthquake Park** to view the hummocks and ponds that formed when the 1964 Good Friday earthquake liquefied the landscape here and flattened an upscale neighborhood (if you want to drive to the park, it's at the west end of Northern Lights Blvd.). Keep going about a mile and you'll come to Point Woronzof, a high bluff and the best viewpoint along the trail. It's at the end of the busy runway of Ted Stevens Anchorage International Airport, so you can do some jet-spotting—apparently a favorite sport among the moose and cows congregating along the fence that keeps them off the runway (give them plenty of room, especially if you see a cow with calves). The trail ends at Kincaid Park, a popular hiking and mountain biking spot. The best downtown entrance to the trail is at Elderberry Park, at the west end of 5th Avenue.

Stay Off the Mud Flats

The great tides of Cook Inlet leave broad, sometimes beautifully patterned mud flats along Anchorage's shoreline. They seem like natural places to explore, but don't do it. Each year the fire department has to rescue people who wandered past the keep-off-the-mud-flats signs and got stuck there. The colloidal mud can change from solid to liquid without warning, sucking people in up to the waist and holding them with a death grip. In 1988 the city watched with horror as the tide came in and drowned a woman whom the fire department was unable to free from the mud in time.

You can rent bikes at **Downtown Bicycle Rental** (333 W. 4th Ave.; ☎ 907/ 279-5293; www.alaska-bike-rentals.com; summer daily 8am–8pm). They've got hybrid bikes, mountain bikes, and road bikes ($16 for 4 hr. or $32 per day), plus kids' bikes, trailers, and bicycles built for two.

The most popular Anchorage hike is to the summit of a mountain that, unlike the dozens of sharply peaked mountains around the city, seems to have been lopped off at the top. The trail up **Flattop Mountain** begins in a busy parking lot 2,200 feet up in the Chugach State Park and climbs to a dizzying 3,550-foot plateau. On a clear day, the view from atop Flattop stretches far from Denali in the north and to the Aleutian Mountains in the south. It's a steep 3½-mile, 2- to 3-hour trip up and back, with a boulder scramble near the top, but it's not so difficult that you can't bring long-legged kids. Lots of parents do. Flattop can get packed on weekends. If you're out of shape, or just don't feel like a big hike, there's a short stroll on a paved path to an overlook, with a smashing view of its own. The Flattop parking lot, officially known as the **Chugach State Park Glen Alps Trailhead,** is the starting point for a network of trails that spread out across the dry alpine tundra, past alpine lakes and through rocky valleys of the Chugach Mountains. There's a $5 user fee, unless you're just there to use the overlook, which is free and has its own designated parking stalls. To see a full trail map of Chugach State Park, go to www.dnr.state.ak.us/parks/units/chugach/trails.htm or stop in at the park's headquarters (Mile 11.8 Seward Hwy., just south of town) for a hard copy.

Driving directions: Flattop is about 13 miles from downtown. Take New Seward Highway to O'Malley Road; go east on O'Malley about 4 miles to Hillside Drive; turn right on Hillside, then left on Upper Huffman Road, then right on Toilsome Hill Drive. **Shuttle:** The Downtown Bicycle Rental store runs the **Flattop Mountain Shuttle** (333 W. 4th Ave.; ☎ 907/279-5293; www.alaska-bike-rentals.com), which carries hikers from downtown or midtown to Flattop, for $22 for adults, $15 for children 6 to 12, and $5 for children under 6.

For a comprehensive rundown of Anchorage-area hikes, from casual 1-mile strolls to serious treks where you can disappear into the Chugach for days, stop in at the **Alaska Public Lands Information Center** (605 W. 4th Ave.; ☎ 907/271-2737; www.nps.gov/aplic).

Some of the most spectacular trails in Alaska are located along Turnagain Arm, and are described in the driving tour section, beginning on p. 58.

Looking for something a bit less strenuous? Try the pleasant, 1-mile stroll to **Thunderbird Falls** (25 miles north of Anchorage on the Glenn Hwy.; take Thunderbird Exit and follow signs to trailhead). The trail is wide, flat, and easy enough for even young kids, although there are steep cliffs along the trail in spots, so keep an eye on the little ones there. The trail forks near the end. Go right and you'll come across a viewing platform overlooking Thunderbird Falls, a small but Kodak-worthy cascade. Go left and the hike suddenly gets more difficult, dropping down a steep trail to the Thunderbird Creek.

FISHING

With a fishing license and the necessary tags, you can cast for salmon at historic **Ship Creek,** right in the heart of the city, where the original tent camp that would become Anchorage sprang up in 1915. Beneath the freeway bridge that crosses the creek is a **bait and tackle shop,** where you can get outfitted. Rods cost $5 per hour, boots $5 per hour, and nets $5 per hour. Don't bother with the net unless you've got backup. "The net only works with two people," says George, "Pete," Petry, the retired state trooper who runs the shop. "I've seen these guys catch a fish and try to hold the rod in one hand and the net in the other, and it just does not work."

KAYAKING & RAFTING

Although Anchorage sits right on the Pacific Ocean, the crazy tides that rush in and out of Cook Inlet and the treacherous mud flats along the shoreline make **sea kayaking** out of the question. The nearest place to set out in a sea kayak—with a good chance of returning—is Whittier on Prince William Sound, a far friendlier inland reach of the North Pacific, 59 miles away (p. 97). Anchorage doesn't have **white-water rafting** either, but you can find it just about an hour away. A company called **Nova Raft and Adventure Tours** ✦ (☎ 800/746-5753; www.alaskaone.com/nova) runs rafts down the rip-roaring Six Mile Creek on the Kenai Peninsula to the south (p. 74), costing $90 per person. Up north, in the Mat-Su Valley, Nova operates riverboats down the glacial-silt-filled Matanuska River, right past the tongue of the Matanuska Glacier (p. 73). Closer to town, a company called **Lifetime Adventures** kids (☎ 907/746-4644; www.lifetimeadventures.net) offers shorter, tamer, less expensive trips on the comparatively wimpy Eagle River, a few miles north of town. The 1-hour white water trip through a bit of class III rapids costs $30 for adults or children, while a 3-hour scenic float costs $75 for adults and $55 for children. These trips are slow and mellow—which makes them appropriate for young children. For an adrenaline rush, go with Nova instead.

ROCK CLIMBING

With mountains all around, it's no surprise that Anchorage is a hot bed for rock climbers. You can hang with the local climbing set (by the tips of your fingers, if they're strong enough) at the **Alaska Rock Gym** (4840 Fairbanks St.; ☎ 907/562-7265; www.alaskarockgym.com). If you're a climber, you already know what to do on the 5,500 square feet of climbing wall. If you've never climbed before, you can take a 90-minute class covering what you'll need to know to start scaling boulders and ascending rock chimneys on your own. Class is held every Monday at 7pm and costs $10. Get there at least half an hour early to do the paperwork and put on the climbing gear. Children 14 and older can sign up too.

ATTENTION, SHOPPERS!

Anchorage is Alaska's shopping capital for the simple reason that it has more stores than anywhere else in the state. The richest shopping grounds for gifts and souvenirs are downtown, between 3rd and 6th avenues. You'll see a lot of the same Native crafts, Russian curios, and smoked seafood gift packs that you'll find in other towns, but Anchorage has much more of it.

Some of the most useful and uniquely Alaskan native goods in the state are sold at the **Oomingmak Musk Ox Producers Co-op** ★★★ (604 H St.; ☎ 888/ 360-9665 outside Alaska or 907/272-9225; www.qiviut.com). In springtime Arctic musk ox, known as *oomingmak,* shed their fine undercoat, a wool called *qiviut,* which is as soft as cashmere and eight times warmer than sheep's wool by weight. About 200 native women from far-off coastal villages use qiviut to knit the downy garments on sale at the Oomingmak co-op. They make scarves, stoles, caps, tunics, and nachaqs, a seamless tubular thing that is worn around the neck and can be pulled up over the head like a hood. Each garment bears a pattern unique to the village it came from. They aren't cheap. A simple watchman's cap, for instance, runs $175. But there's another way to go: for $80 you can buy three cap patterns and a 2-ounce skein of qiviut. If you have the needles, the hours, and the skill, you can make your own cap. You might find a few qiviut garments for sale elsewhere in the state, but this is the main outlet.

Before you dive too deeply into the **Anchorage Market and Festival** ★★★ (3rd Ave. and E St.; ☎ 907/272-5634; www.anchoragemarkets.com), don't assume that you can breeze through it in a hurry. Perhaps you can simply grab a reindeer sausage, watch a teenage fiddling prodigy, and be on your way, but it's easy to get sucked in. The city's downtown, open-air bazaar (which runs Sat–Sun 10am–6pm, mid-May to mid-Sept) has the usual and easily bypassed panoply of souvenir Alaska baseball caps, T-shirts, and fleeces. But counted among the 300 or so vendors are also some unexpected finds. Some that I discovered were: Inuit women selling baleen baskets, carved whale vertebrates, and old trade beads that French trappers carried to Alaska long ago; a clear-eyed old cowboy hawking 19th- and early-20th-century pocket watches that still run, along with bargain-priced Japanese glass fishing floats that he finds at Cold Harbor; a woman with a barking lap dog who offered Eskimo dolls dressed in real fur; a dreadlocked fisherman selling cans of smoked salmon for a dollar off; a big man in khakis hawking *ulus*—indigenous cleavers with blades shaped like bells and handles made from materials of all sorts, including jade, antler, tusk, and even *oolik,* which is, as the ulu seller described it, "the fossilized private part of a male walrus."

"I think we are all bound by a common thread—regardless of race, creed, or color—that makes us one people, becoming one world, and I hope that in some way this store will prompt that oneness," says Trevor Rennie, the Trinidadian proprietor of a downtown gift shop called **One People One World** (425 D St.; ☎ 907/ 274-4063). Browsing here is like strolling though a global bazaar—the store stocks a little of everything from a lot of places, but Alaska Native arts and crafts are particularly well represented. Russia also makes a strong showing, with a broad

From the Depths to Your Doorsteps

There are plenty of places in Anchorage to buy souvenir gift packs with smoked salmon, smoked halibut, and canned crab. To bring home fresh Alaskan seafood—unprocessed and just hours out of the deep blue sea—head for **10th and M Seafoods** ★★ (1020 M St.; ☎ 907/272-3474; www.10thandmseafoods.com). This venerable Anchorage institution, doing business from the same downtown storefront since 1943, will take wild Alaskan seafood right off the fishing boat, pack it in ice, and FedEx it to your doorstep. Of course, if a 30-pound halibut or a king crab with a 6-foot leg span is more than you can handle, they've got souvenir-appropriate gifts too. For $53 you can get a small gift pack with cans of smoked king salmon, smoked red salmon, and smoked silver salmon, plus gourmet cheese and crackers, and a 14-ounce reindeer salami.

display of Russian nesting dolls and uncommon Russian clothing, such as Orenburg-style lace shawls with Cyrillic labels. The only part of the global village intentionally given short shrift is China, where the bulk of T-shirts, plastic moose, and cheap ulus that pass as Alaskan souvenirs in so many other gift shops come from. "Ninety-nine percent of this store is *not* made in China," Trevor says proudly. "We do have a few key rings and stuff, though. We can't get away from that."

A really good place to pick up affordable souvenirs you won't find sold anywhere but Alaska is at the **Iditarod Trail Store** (5th Ave. Mall; ☎ 800/545-6874 or 907/373-2710; www.iditarod.com). This is the official Anchorage outlet for all things Iditarod, and many of the goods sell for less than $10. Among the wares are Iditarod shot glasses, Iditarod Post-It Notes, Iditarod pencils, Iditarod rulers, Iditarod key chains, Iditarod rubber stamps, Iditarod ball caps, Iditarod T-shirts, and Iditarod bumper stickers. My favorite sticker has a sled dog saying "I'm the lead dog, and you're not." Proceeds from the store go right back to staging the 1,150-mile, Anchorage-to-Nome race.

Alaska Wild Berry Products (5225 Juneau St.; ☎ 907/562-8858; www.alaska wildberryproducts.com) is a sprawling gift store and candy factory, with life-size teddy bears sitting in the entryway, a chocolate waterfall (the chocolate's mixed with wax, so don't bother sneaking a taste), and a little shopping village nearby. With its boardwalks and copper-hooped barrels out front, the main store looks like a marketer's idea of an old-timey general store; it's the kind of place where visitors on package tours arrive by the busload and fill their shopping bags with T-shirts, toy moose, and wooden salad forks shaped like bear claws. Kitsch aside, the reason to go here is for the condiments and confections made with wild Alaskan berries. Alaskans across the state earn pocket money in the summer picking the berries that go into the store's 19 types of jam, six syrups and sauces, and its addictive Wild Berry Jelly Center Chocolates (take 'em up on the free samples!). The main store is in Midtown, off International Road between Old Seward Highway and New Seward Highway. There's also a downtown outlet at the

For Book Lovers

When new books about Alaska come out, the **Cook Inlet Book Co.** (415 W. 5th Ave.; ☎ 800/240-4148 or 907/248-4544; www.cookinlet.com) is generally where the authors go to do signings (though not always; see below). The store is the definitive Alaskan bookseller, with a vast collection of Alaskan titles and writings on the North. It includes new, used, out-of-print, and bargain-priced books. Just looking at all the categories the books are shelved by gets the mind reeling over the size and scope of Alaska.

Outside of the area where most tourists visit are a massive **Barnes & Noble** (200 E. Northern Lights Blvd.; ☎ 907/279-7323; www.bn.com) and a similarly well-stocked **Borders** (1100 E. Diamond Blvd.; ☎ 907/344-4099; www.bordersstores.com). If you can't find what you're looking for at these stores, it may not exist (both have very well stocked Alaska sections, as well).

Anchorage 5th Avenue Mall, with less cloying decor (and silly souvenirs) but the same wild berry products.

NIGHTLIFE IN ANCHORAGE

With a summer sun that sets far too late, and then pops right back up again, Anchorage nightlife can seem like a misnomer during tourist season. But whether you call it "nightlife" or "things to do in the twilight," there are plenty of choices. For a rundown of the current goings on about town, pick up a copy of the free weekly *Anchorage Press,* the city's alternative paper, available all over town. Or go to their website www.anchoragepress.com.

PERFORMING ARTS

If you're around on a Friday evening in June or July, you can count on finding a free outdoor community concert right downtown. The **Live at Five Concert Series** (Town Square, 5th Ave. and F St; www.anchoragedowntown.org/events) brings salsa, soul, blues, Cajun, and other danceable local bands, along with a beer garden, to the park beside the **Alaska Center for the Performing Arts** (621 W. 6th Ave.; www.alaskapac.org). The performing arts center, by the way, has a busy season during the fall and winter, but it's quiet during the summer.

What's better than hot popcorn and a good movie? The answer's easy—hot popcorn, cold beer, and a good, cheap movie. At Anchorage's most laid-back movie theater, the **Bear Tooth Theatrepub** ✫✫✫ (1230 W. 27th Ave.; ☎ 907/276-4200; www.beartooththeatre.net), the movies may be second-runs, but the popcorn's fresh, the beer's brewed on-site (that's right, you don't even have to sneak it in), and tickets are just $3. If all that isn't enough to make this the most happening movie house in town, there's a kitchen cranking out fat steak-and-guacamole burritos and hearty halibut tacos, and a confectionery counter stocked with hand-dipped bonbons. Every other row of seating (including the balcony seating) in this 400-seat movie house has been removed and replaced with tables, where you can set your frothy pints of Indian Pale Ale next to your grub.

For live theater, see what's playing at the **Cyrano's Off-Center Playhouse** (413 D St.; ☎ 907/274-2599; www.cyranos.org), a spirited little semi-professional theater company with a full summer stock season and a convenient downtown location. On the second Saturday of the month, an improv troupe called Scared Scriptless tests its powers of free association at 10pm (tickets are $7). Edgy **Out North Contemporary Art House** (1325 Primrose St.; ☎ 907/279-3800; www.out north.org) is the city's more experimental, and occasionally controversial, theater troupe. It features performance art, music, dance, puppetry, multimedia work, poetry and prose readings, films, photo expositions, art exhibits, and whatnot, with a bent toward social activism.

NIGHTCLUBS, BARS & BREWHOUSES

It may not have the best microbrews in Anchorage—that's a toss up between Moose's Tooth Grill and Glacier Brewhouse—but **Sleeping Lady Brewing Company** (717 W. 3rd Ave.; above the Snow Goose Restaurant; ☎ 907/277-7727; www.alaskabeers.com) has unparalleled summertime views. From either of its two rooftop decks, you can follow the barge traffic on Knik Arm, watch the glaring 8pm sun think about setting, and, on a clear day, see Denali. The cavernous but warmly designed **Glacier Brewhouse** ★★ (p. 42) is a bar and restaurant featuring gleaming stainless steel vats of the brewery behind a wall of glass. An amber, a blonde, an IPA, and an oatmeal stout are always on tap, and joined by brews off a long, seasonally changing roster. The **Moose's Tooth Pub and Pizzeria** ★★★ (1230 27th Ave.; ☎ 907/270-4200), located in midtown along Spenard, the main drag leading to the airport, has great beer from the Moose's Tooth Brewing Company and not nearly enough room at the bar. There is, fortunately, a whole restaurant where you can grab a table or a booth and order nothing but beer, if you like.

Humpy's Great Alaskan Alehouse (610 W. 6th Ave.; across from the Alaska Center for the Performing Arts; ☎ 907/276-2337; www.humpys.com) is the central hub in the downtown bar scene, located right across from the Alaska Center for the Performing Arts. It's a long, crowded, cheerful place with live acoustic rock, folk, and blues performances, more often than not. It's got dozens of beers on tap, and far better food than you'd expect. Mondays belong to the open-mic performers, for all the good and bad that implies. The place takes its name from pink salmon; when they're spawning, males develop a bulbous hump in their backs, which earned the species its nickname, "humpies."

Darwin's Theory (426 G St.; ☎ 907/277-5322; www.alaska.net/~thndrths) is a tightly packed little downtown bar with complimentary, very salty popcorn, a great jukebox, and absolutely nowhere to hide. Whoever you squeeze in next to will want to talk. But because this is Alaska, and everyone is a big character with an incredible story, you'll want to talk to them, too.

The city's most famous nightclub, **Chilkoot Charlie's** ★★★ (2435 Spenard Rd., corner of Spenard and Fireweed Lane; ☎ 907/272-1010; www.koots.com), takes the big-tent approach to being a bar. It's squeezed 10 bars under one roof, and put one bar on the roof. 'Koots has little bars and big bars, loud bars and quiet ones, bars with dance floors, and bars with stages; it has bars with padded beer kegs to sit on, and bars with patio furniture; a bar to get your groove on and a bar to watch the NFL in, a bar that does daiquiris, a bar that does martinis, a bar with a bar-top made of ice, a bar completely draped in ladies' lingerie, a bar dedicated to czarist Russia, a bar dedicated to Communist Russia, and more. It's the most extravagant bar in a state that puts a lot of emphasis on its watering holes. *Playboy* magazine once named it the best bar in America. It's a blast to walk through it even if you don't drink.

GAY NIGHTLIFE

With its supermarket-like selection of DJs, dance floors, and live bands, Chilkoot Charlie's is the perennial winner of *The Anchorage Press* readers' choice award for Best Place to Dance. But the downtown gay bar, **Mad Myrna's** (530 E. 5th Ave.; ☎ 907/276-9762; www.alaska.net/~madmyrna), runs a respectable second. It's got two dance floors and two DJs, as well as a Friday night drag show, and special events like the Fetish Ball. On Fridays and Saturdays, one dance floor is given over to techno and the other is dedicated to a mix of oldies and new hits. For other gay and lesbian events and bars around Anchorage, try the website www.out inanchorage.com (registration required).

GET OUT OF TOWN

The best thing to do in Anchorage is to get out of Anchorage—so strike out into the landscape and explore! Just two roads lead to and from the city, so there are only two ways you can go, either north or south. If you only have time for one day trip out of Anchorage, head south (well, southeast, actually). As soon as the city falls away, the spectacularly scenic drive along Turnagain Arm, which I describe next, begins.

A DRIVING TOUR ALONG TURNAGAIN ARM: HIKES, WILDLIFE, GLACIERS & OTHER ATTRACTIONS

The 127-mile Seward Highway, which leads to the Kenai Peninsula and links Anchorage with the deep-water port at Seward, is one of the most beautiful drives in the United States. The first 50 miles out of Anchorage runs between the edge of the Chugach Mountains and the turbulent waters of Turnagain Arm. Along the way, scenic turnouts and hiking trails lead into the half-million acre Chugach State Park, Anchorage's "backyard wilderness." Highlights here include the relaxed ski town of Girdwood (p. 63), and the rapidly retreating Portage Glacier. Depending on how much lingering you do, a round-trip could take between 2 hours and the entire day. The following driving tour starts in Anchorage and ends at Portage Glacier, with points of interest identified by the closest highway milepost.

The first stop comes up before you're even really out of town: **Potter Marsh** ★ (mile 117), inadvertent wetlands formed in 1917 when the Alaska Railroad put in an embankment that dammed a creek. Right on the east edge of Anchorage, it's popular with birds and thus birders, who come here to add bald eagles, Arctic terns, Canada geese, trumpeter swans, red-necked grebes, a variety of ducks, and the occasional Pacific loon to their "life lists." A boardwalk helps bird watchers keep their feet dry and prevents them from trampling the bird habitat. Not interested in our feathered friends? From mid-July to September, you can see salmon as they return to a nearby creek to spawn. Moose sometime wade into the marsh to feed on aquatic vegetation, and there are resident populations of muskrat and beavers. Bring binoculars if you can—the wildlife's not hard to spot, but it usually keeps its distance.

Farther along Seward Highway, at the south end of Potter Marsh, you'll come to the **Potter Section House** (mile 115; ☎ 907/345-5014; free admission; Mon–Fri 10am–4:30pm, closed noon–1pm), built in the 1920s to house the workers who maintained a 10-mile section of railroad track along Turnagain Arm. Section houses were once found all along the railroad. This is one of the few left. Today it's the headquarters for **Chugach State Park,** a half-million-acre mountain wilderness that stretches for 300 miles, from the edge of Anchorage almost to Canada. You can pick up hiking maps and parking passes here. There's also a small railroad museum and some old train cars to climb around on. One car has a wicked-looking, 9-foot-diameter rotary plow mounted to the front, used to blast snow off the tracks.

Four miles past Potter Section House, Seward Highway crosses rollicking little **McHugh Creek** (mile 111). There's a state wayside and a nice picnic area here, as well as a waterfall. The creek originates at Rabbit Lake, 5 miles and 3,000 vertical feet away. If you're up for a tough but glorious hike, you can climb up to the lake on **McHugh Trail** ✭. It begins its initial ascent in a spruce forest, which gives way to willow forest, and then changes to scrub and boulders. Finally, the trail reaches the lake, which is nestled in a magnificent mountain bowl and surrounded by alpine tundra. It's at least 6 hours up and back, but you don't have to go all the way before the views get good. There's a $5 day-use fee here. Signs warn of bears in the area (see p. 377 for info on bear safety).

There's no user fee at **Beluga Point** (mile 110) ✭, a mile away. There are no bears either, but if you're lucky, and the tides are right, you might spot belugas, small, white melon-headed whales with dolphinlike smiles. They swim into Turnagain Arm on salmon feeding forays, sometimes coming so close to shore that you can hear their clicks and squeals. Archaeologists have found the earliest traces of human life in the Anchorage area at Beluga Point, which has a sweeping view of Turnagain Arm. Ancient hunters used to camp there, leaving behind scraped and scorched bones from the many whales and Dall sheep they ate. Today, this is a good photo-op stop for the views of the snow-capped Kenai Mountains across the crazy waters, which often appear tortured with wind-whipped whitecaps, visible currents, and whirlpools. Picnic tables and benches, as well as interpretive signs galore, help make the site tourist friendly.

The cliffs along the highway for the next few miles rank up there with Denali National Park for mountain goat and Dall sheep sightings. Most often these animals appear as tiny white dots, moving slowly across the craggy cliffs, safe from wolves, bears, and highway traffic. Sometimes, though, they come all the way down to the road to nibble on greens and lick salt. Hitting one with your car is a possibility, but it's less of a risk than hitting someone breaking suddenly to look at sheep or goats high above the road. A safe place to stop is at **Windy Point** (mile 106), where you might also spot the handful of hard-core, cold-water windsurfers who brave the frigid glacial runoff, the deadly currents, and the scorn of the

Cook Inlet Belugas on the Decline

Beluga whale sightings in Cook Inlet are growing increasingly rare, and conservationists worry that the unique population of belugas there may be headed for extinction.

You can still see them, but not like you used to. In the 1970s scientists estimated that 1,300 belugas lived in Cook Inlet. By 2005 the number had dwindled to 300. Native subsistence hunters were initially blamed for the decline, but several years of strict limits on hunting haven't turned things around, and now greater attention is being paid to pollution.

The National Marine Fisheries Service is considering nominating the Cook Inlet belugas for federal protection under the Endangered Species Act, but there's not a lot of support for the idea among Alaska's congressional delegation, which is concerned about the impact this designation would have on the economic development of Cook Inlet. In the meantime, conservationists worry that one big catastrophe—an oil spill, a mass stranding—could push the animals over the edge.

The Cook Inlet belugas are a distinct population that has no contact with the healthier beluga populations in the Bering, Chukchi, and Beaufort seas. They've been isolated in Cook Inlet for so long (since the end of the last ice age, 10,000 years ago) that they've evolved into a subspecies.

The best times to spot belugas in Turnagain Arm, an upper branch of Cook Inlet, are during high tides from about mid-July through August, when the salmon move toward their home streams, and the whales make their moves on the salmon. You can sometimes see them in Anchorage too, from the Tony Knowles Coastal Trail.

To find out more about beluga conservation, contact the Alaska Beluga Whale Committee (www.fakr.noaa.gov).

---

un-stoked. People dismiss them as mad, but one windsurfer told me he'd *go* mad living in Alaska if he couldn't windsurf. Binoculars are helpful for studying both the wildlife and the windsurfers.

Six miles down the road, you'll come to the **Bird Ridge Trailhead** (mile 102). This 2½-mile round-trip hike starts off easily enough along a wheelchair-accessible path. That quickly changes as the route climbs steeply to a windy ridge with a sweeping view from about 3,000 feet. This is one of the first snow-free trails in the area to open up in the spring. Great views are to be had from just a few hundred feet up the trail. There's a $5 parking fee.

A mile farther down the road and just over the bridge, you'll come to part of the Chugach State Park called **Bird Creek** (mile 101). There's a (too) popular fishing stream here, a busy campground, and the beginning of a 10-mile-long bike trail to Girdwood, the **Bird-to-Gird Trail.** In July and August, you may witness "combat fishing," a variation on normal fishing in which so many anglers show up at one fishing spot, they end up standing elbow-to-elbow on the banks, trash-talking each other and getting their lines tangled. Adding to the tension at Bird Creek in recent times has been the nonchalant appearances of black bears and grizzlies, who've been walking off with backpacks and consuming the fish that frightened fishermen drop on the banks. Wildlife biologists implore fishermen to throw their catch back into the water rather than relinquish it to bears. Feeding the bears encourages them to come back again and again, which can turn out badly for the bears, who might ultimately get shot. Not all of the "combatants" on Bird Creek seem to have gotten the message, though.

For a less intense stop, keep going to the **Bird Point Scenic Overlook** (mile 96). Here you'll find a pleasant wayside with both a boardwalk leading to the seawater in Turnagain Arm, and a freshwater wetland with a beaver lodge. This is a good place to station yourself when the bore tide (p. 62) rolls through.

As you approach **Girdwood Junction** (mile 90), the turnoff for Alyeska Ski Resort and Crow Creek Mine (p. 68), the "ghost forest" will begin to appear. The 9.2 magnitude Good Friday earthquake in 1964 dropped this end of Turnagain Arm by as much as 12 feet in places. That put the roots of hundreds of trees in contact with saltwater, killing them. The trees' bleached trunks still stand, 40-some years later. The earthquake destroyed the little town of Portage, as well. If you look carefully, you can find the remnants of it at the **old Portage town site** (mile 80.1), a weathered ghost town that complements the ghost forest. It's about a half mile after **Twentymile River** (mile 80.7), where Native dip-netters catch hooligan, aka euchalon or candlefish, in the spring. When you pass the **Kenai Peninsula Visitor Information Center** (mile 80.3; ☎ 907/783-3001; Memorial Day–Labor Day daily 9am–6pm) on your left—stop if you want coupons for glacier cruises—start looking for the unmarked ghost town on your right.

Just before the turnoff to Portage Glacier, the final destination on this road trip, you'll come to a 140-acre drive-through wildlife park, the **Alaska Wildlife Conservation Center** ★★★ 🎒 (mile 79; ☎ 907/783-2025; www.alaskawildlife. org; Apr 5–May 10 daily 10am–6pm, May 11–Sept 17 daily 8am–8pm, Sept 18–Apr 5 daily 10am–5pm). It's well worth a stop. The nonprofit center takes in orphaned and injured animals that otherwise would die in the wild. It's like an orphanage for wildlife, and seriously, who can resist that? New animals are admitted all the time, such as lynx kittens whose mother was killed in a wildfire, a moose calf whose mother was killed by a car, and a Sitka black-tailed deer fawn whose mother was killed by a bear. Full-grown residents include elk, musk ox, bison, caribou, owls, and eagles. The animal enclosures are large, so you aren't guaranteed a close-up look at any of them, but the animals get more room, which they like. Bring binoculars. Admission is $7.50 for adults, $5 for seniors and children 5 through 12, with a maximum charge of $25 per vehicle.

A mile farther south you'll come to **Portage Valley Road** (mile 78), the turnoff for **Portage Glacier** and the tunnel to **Whittier** (p. 94). Drive 5.2 miles on Portage Valley Road to the **Begich-Boggs Visitor Center** 🎒 ★ (☎ 907/783-2326; late May to Oct 1 daily 9am–6pm, rest of year 10am–5pm), which sits on the edge of an 800-foot-deep lake carved by Portage Glacier. When the visitor center opened in 1986, it was dedicated to the glacier, which you could see across the iceberg-filled lake. The glacier has retreated more quickly than expected, and by 1995 it had disappeared around a corner, out of site from the visitor center, which is now dedicated to the Chugach National Forest as a whole, not just one finicky mountain of ice. There are plenty of excellent exhibits on Alaskan culture

Turnagain Arm's True Tidal Waves

Tsunamis aren't really tidal waves—bore tides are. Earthquakes, volcanic blasts, and large meteor impacts: Those are the sorts of things that cause tsunamis. Bore tides occur in constricted waterways with extreme tidal fluctuations. Long, narrow Turnagain Arm, where the difference between high tide and low tide can be as much as 41 feet, is just such a place. The bore tide here is one of the largest in the world, and a sight you must see if you're in the vicinity around the new or full moon. The bore tide floods the arm as a single wave that can stand anywhere from a half foot to 6 feet tall. It's a strange phenomenon—a slowly moving line of white water with low tide on one side and high tide on the other.

Occasionally you'll see harbor seals body surfing on the waves. During the bigger waves, they'll be joined by a handful of local surfers and kayakers (don't even think of trying it yourself unless you're an expert—the water is cold and dangerous). The seals can swim fast enough to catch the wave from behind over and over. The surfers and kayakers only get one shot at catching the wave. If they miss it or wipe out, the session's over. The bore tide travels at 10 to 15 miles per hour, slowly enough so that you can watch it go by, jump in your car, pass it, pull over, and watch it go by again.

There can be up to 10 good bore tides a month, especially in July around the summer solstice (if ice didn't choke the arm in Dec, there'd be good ones around winter solstice too).

Here's how to predict a good bore tide in Turnagain Arm: Get ahold of a local tide book (available at fishing stores) or click around at www.tidesandcurrents.noaa.gov. Look for low tides in Anchorage between −2 feet and −5 feet. Note the time, then make the following adjustments:

◆ For Beluga Point, add 1 hour and 15 minutes.
◆ For Bird Point, add 2 hours and 15 minutes.
◆ For Twentymile River, add 4 hours.

Try to get to your viewing point a half-hour early because all sorts of variables can foil the prediction. If you can't deal with tide tables, just ask about the bore tides at the **Alaska Public Lands Information Center** (605 W. 4th Ave.; ☎ 907/271-2737; www.nps.gov/aplic; summer daily 9am–5pm, rest of year Tues–Sat 10am–6pm). And stay well away from the water's edge when the tide comes through. You don't want to get swept along with it.

and natural history, aimed at both adults and children. And there's a film about glaciers shown every hour (tickets are $1 for adults, free for children under 16).

A short drive from the visitor center along the edge of Portage Lake brings you to the trailhead for 🧒 **Byron Glacier.** This path makes for a good hike for families with small kids. A well-maintained path less than a mile long leads to the snowfields at the base of a small glacier, where you can pick a slushy summer snowball fight, if you like. The trail leads along a rushing glacial stream into a glacial valley, and it costs nothing.

Keep going past the Byron Glacier trailhead and soon the road will dead-end at the dock of the MV *Ptarmigan,* a tour boat that bumps through the icebergs to within 300 yards of **Portage Glacier's** ★★★ blue-ice face. The 1-hour tours, run by **Gray Line of Alaska** (☎ 888/452-1737; www.graylinealaska.com), leave throughout the day. At $29 for adults and $15 for children, this is the cheapest glacier cruise in Alaska. Portage Glacier isn't as big or spectacular as, say, the glaciers in nearby Prince William Sound or at Glacier Bay National Park. If those aren't on your itinerary though, this one should do just fine.

GIRDWOOD

Girdwood is the ski capital of Alaska, but its original settlers weren't drawn there by the ungroomed double black diamonds. It was gold that brung 'em, and it was Girdwood's proximity to Crow Pass along the Iditarod Trail that made it a logical town site and supply point for miners. Taking Crow Creek Trail up to Crow Pass is one of the great summer hikes in the area today. At a weathered old gold camp on Crow Creek, you can poke around the log buildings where miners worked and lived, and try your hand at panning for gold in the creek.

When Girdwood was founded in the late–19th century, it was located along the shore of Turnagain Arm, not in the valley at the base of Alyeska Mountain where it is now. The town thrived around the turn of the century as a supply center for gold miners for awhile, then it settled into life as a quiet flag stop along the railroad.

The Good Friday earthquake of 1964 dropped the old Girdwood by about 10 feet, putting it below sea level at high tide. So the town moved into the valley. Already there was a small ski area there, which opened in 1950s with a Poma lift and a lodge. The ski operation grew over time into what is now Alyeska Ski Resort, the only ski resort in Alaska with more than a rope tow or a single chair lift.

Lay of the Land

Girdwood boasts about 2,000 residents scattered across the floor of a deep valley filled with wolf lichen and hemlocks, and with seven hanging glaciers tucked among its peaks. The turnoff into the valley is 37 miles from Anchorage along the Seward Highway, onto the Alyeska Highway. Along bumpy Crow Creek Road, 2 miles down the Alyeska Highway, you'll find some of Girdwood's restaurants and hiking trails, and a historic gold mining camp. Just past Crow Creek Road is Girdwood's small town center, with a restaurant, store, post office, and park. A mile further along, the Alyeska Highway ends at the foot of 3,939-foot Alyeska Mountain, an area called Olympic Circle. This is where the chairlifts begin, and where most of Girdwood's vacation-rental condos and some of its restaurants are. Most Girdwood residents live in unnumbered homes on unpaved streets laid out in the forest on either side of Alyeska Highway, between Olympic Circle and the town center.

Getting to & Around Girdwood

Driving is the only practical way to get to Girdwood in the summertime, and, because the town is so spread out, it's the most practical way to get around any time. In the winter, the **Alyeska Resort** (☎ 907/754-1111; www.alyeskaresort. com) operates a weekend ski shuttle from Anchorage that leaves in the morning and returns in the evening. Round-trips cost $14, one-way journeys $10. Call or check the website for details. In the summer you can rent bikes from **Girdwood Ski and Cyclery** (Mile 1.5 Alyeska Hwy.; ☎ 907/783-BIKE; $25 per day; Wed–Sun 10am–7pm) but you'll need a car to get there.

Accommodations, Both Standard & Not

The main game in town, when it comes to accommodations, is the Alyeska Ski Resort's big, dimly lit, slightly spooky **Hotel Alyeska.** The rooms are small and high-priced. Happily, the town brims with alternatives in the form of condos, cabins, chalets, and single-family homes available as vacation rentals. (It's also got bed-and-breakfasts, but I'll come back to those.) A lot of the Girdwood vacation rentals are owned by Anchorage residents, who escape to them when they can and try to fill them with visitors the rest of the time. The simplest way to find one of these places is through a property management company called **Alyeska Accommodations** (Olympic Circle Loop; ☎ 888/783-2001 or 907/783-2000; www.alyeskaaccommodations.com; DISC, MC, V), which lists about 50 such properties and offers substantial discounts on stays of 2 nights or longer. Efficiency condos—basically smallish, white walled, stucco ceilinged apartments—are the best deals, going for $110 for 1 night, $185 for 2 nights, and $560 for a week. Two-bedroom condos go for $175 1 night, $305 for 2, and $955 for a week. Since they're individually decorated by their owners, they have a hodge-podge of looks, but most tend towards the bland tan side of the scale, featuring easily cleaned carpets and stain-hiding furniture. If you'd prefer something with a porch, a yard, a hot tub, and a vaulted tongue-and-groove ceiling—in short, something with character—you might consider renting your own chalet. Much more spacious, with lots of privacy, these generally go for $172 for 1 night, $302 for 2, and $952 per week. Again, each property is different—I've seen ones with pretty quilts on imposing high wooden beds (kind of what you'd imagine the "Three Bears" of Goldilocks fame might have slept in) to others with furniture that looked so temporary it might have been a house someone was trying to "flip." But none can be termed "dumps" and some are quite nice. Photos of all the units are posted on the website, so study them carefully and ask a lot of questions. They'll help you decipher which units have enticing amenities like fireplaces, balconies, and chichi decor.

In addition to vacation rentals, Girdwood also has plenty of bed-and-breakfasts spread out along the unpaved streets of its wooded residential neighborhoods. Almost all of them are listed by at least one of Girdwood's two rival B&B associations, if not both of them. The older and smaller group, **The Girdwood Bed and Breakfast Association** (☎ 907/222-4858; www.gbba.org), limits its membership to bed-and-breakfasts where the owner sleeps under the same roof as the guests, in the fashion of a true B&B. As such, this is the place to turn to for a genuine homestay-style B&B experience.

A Mountain Cabin of Your Own

One of the most affordable, the most Alaskan, and definitely the most rustic places to stay around Girdwood is the U.S. Forest Service public use cabin high up in the Chugach National Forest near Crow Pass (see p. 373 for more on public use cabins). The **Crow Pass Cabin** (☎ 877/444-6777; www.reserveusa.com; AE, DC, MC, V; $) is a 16-foot A-frame with a sleeping loft on the open tundra at 3,500 feet. There's an alpine lake, a glacier, and the ruins of a gold mine in the neighborhood, not to mention black and brown bears, Dall sheep, mountain goats, and ptarmigans (the state bird) as your neighbors. It sleeps six and rents for just $35 a night, with a 3-night maximum. You have to hike 3 miles uphill to get there, and you have to bring all of your own supplies, including cooking utensils and bedding. There are no beds, in fact, so you'll be roughing it on un-padded plywood bunks, but there is an outhouse (if you were worried), and there's a glacial stream nearby to get water from (which you should boil for 5 minutes before drinking). The cabin is closed in the winter due to avalanche danger.

A bunch of the B&Bs in town that were excluded by the Girdwood B&B Association's membership policy got together and formed **The Alyeska/Girdwood Accommodations Association** (☎ 907/222-3226; www.agaa.biz). It has about 14 members (including half of the Girdwood B&B Associations' membership, and a few that are really just vacation rentals with no breakfast involved), so it's got the broader selection of properties. When calling either association, it helps to know how the phones work: Members take turns fielding calls, which gives them a rotating opportunity to book their places first. If you pick out promising places on the association's website before calling, you'll have more say in the matter.

Among the newer and larger group's members is **Alyeska Adventures** (314 Cortina Rd.; ☎ 907/754-2400; www.alyeskaadventures.com; MC, V). Its two rooms rent for $145 per night (non-advertised weekly discounts sometimes bring the price down, so don't be afraid to speak up). One of the owners spent time in Japan studying avalanche science, and he came home with a taste for the clean lines and Zen simplicity of Japanese interior design that's thoroughly incorporated into the two-level guest addition he's built onto his home. The two bedrooms— one on the upper level and one on the lower—have views of the dark green Chugach Mountains in the summertime and the solid white mountains in the winter, as well as cushy beds with high-quality sheets that invite you to put off getting up as long as possible. The bathrooms are destinations in themselves: One features a double-headed shower in a glass-enclosed steam chamber; the other has a *furo*, a Japanese soaking tub, large enough for two and constructed from cedar, which emits a woodsy aroma when filled with hot water.

Members of the rival homestay-only group include **Alyeska Hideaway** (last cabin on Dornin Lane; ☎ 907/783-0771; www.alyeskahideaway.com; MC, V), a charming little cabin that you get all to yourself, with a basket of fresh-baked blueberry or banana bread, and other breakfast goodies, left at the door each morning by the owner, who lives right next door. The woodsy cabin—think updated Little House on the Prairie—comes with a full kitchen, a sleeping loft, and a futon couch, which you can sit on while warming your feet before a wood-stove. It goes for $145 double occupancy, and it can sleep up to eight ($15 per additional person), if that many of you can get along with one bathroom and 640 square feet. There are 5% discounts on 4-night stays, and 10% discounts on week stays.

Just so you know: Although it's 40 miles away from the actual city of Anchorage, Girdwood falls within the long shadow of the Municipality of Anchorage and its punitive 12% room tax.

Dining for All Tastes

At the ski complex on top of the mountain, there's a dismal cafeteria and a ho-hum white-tablecloth restaurant with a view. Skip both of them and eat at one of these places in town:

$–$$$ Maxine's Glacier City Bistro ★ (Mile 0.3, Crow Creek Rd.; ☎ 907/783-1234; www.maxinesbistro.com; Wed–Mon 5pm–midnight; MC, V) is such a great all around bar and music venue (p. 69) that you'd still like the place even if the food sucked. Fortunately, the food's great. Maxine's calls it "American freestyle cuisine," which is another way of saying "vegetarian, Mediterranean, Californian, Italian, French, Asian, Alaskan, and everything else the cooks can do." On the so-called Small Plate side of the menu, you'll find inexpensive ($5–$11) and generously portioned tapas-style appetizers that you might piece together to make an inexpensive meal. The menu changes all the time, but the Small Plates might include the likes of Thai curry mussels ($13, with a tasty coconut rice), or wonton tacos (with carrot coriander slaw, turtle beans, and Thai curry sauce for $9). The portions are even more generous on the Large Plate side of the menu, where you could encounter entrees such as an ahi tuna steak (seared on the outside, sashimi on the inside, $18) or saffron risotto (smoked salmon, leeks, sweet peppers, spinach, and tomato, $15). One Large Plate fixture that two could easily split is Maxine's Meze (falafel, tabbouleh, hummus, pickled veggies, feta, tahini, and house-baked pita, $13), which comes in a dish big enough to be a wash basin.

$$–$$$$ In the winter, when the base of the mountain isn't covered with ice, you can ski right up to the front door of **Jack Sprat** ★★ (165 Mountain Loop; ☎ 907/783-4225; www.jacksprat.net; summer Mon–Thurs 5–10pm, Fri 5–11pm, Sat 9am–3pm and 5–11pm, Sun 9am–3pm and 5–10pm, rest of year Sun–Thurs 4–9pm, Fri–Sat 4–10pm; AE, MC, V), which serves what it calls, "fat and lean world cuisine," beneath the high-pitched A-frame roof of a small, usually crowded, chalet. If the restaurant's string bean–like nursery rhyme namesake and his corpulent wife were handed menus, there's no question about who would be eyeballing the black angus burger, topped with hickory smoked bacon ($12), or the grilled rib-eye served with horseradish whipped potatoes and onion rings ($31), and who would be weighing the pecan encrusted halibut ($27, served with wild rice) against the stuffed portobello mushroom ($21, filled with tomato, asparagus, spinach, and sweet pepper). As for who would order the yam fries ($5), served with jalapeño-arugula aioli in a dish that looks like a small pith helmet, that'd be a toss up. Dinners are priced between $12 and $31, and reservations aren't a bad idea.

The Other Girdwood

Every Sunday through the summer in Girdwood you can dance barefoot in the sunshine to live music, eat fat burritos, and meet local artists and artisans along Glacier Creek at the **Girdwood Market Place** (at Girdwood Lions Park, corner of Alyeska Hwy. and Hightower Rd.; Sun 11am–6pm). This outdoor arts and crafts fair is smaller and more pastoral than the Anchorage Market and Festival (p. 54), so you may find that the artists and artisans have more time to chat.

Really for aspiring mountaineers more than tourists **Glacier Travel Clinic** offers intense, exciting 8-hour seminars in glacier trekking. Most of the day is spent on Alyeska Glacier itself, where participants learn how to handle ice axes, rope up properly, get crampons on right, and learn that oh so important skill—trekking across the ice without falling into a crevasse (you also learn another important lesson in how to rig up a pulley to haul someone out of a crevasse if they do fall in). The clinic, limited to six people per session, is held every day in August and costs $249 per person. It's run by **The Ascending Path** (☎ 877/783-0505 or 907/783-0505; www.theascendingpath.com).

Active Girdwood

Alpine skiing and snowboarding is Girdwood's biggest attraction, and its long ski season usually starts in November and runs through April, with the highest and hairiest peaks often ski-able until Memorial Day. **Alyeska Resort** (☎ 800/880-3880 or 907/754-1111; www.alyeskaresort.com) runs the show on Alyeska Mountain, which has 1,000 ski-able acres, 27 lighted trails, and 10 lifts, including a 60-person aerial tram. It's a small resort by the standards of say, Colorado or Utah, but it includes some truly dazzling intermediate and expert runs. Mount Alyeska also gets plenty of snow—65 feet a year at the 3,939-foot summit, 40 feet midway up. Because the base of the mountain is virtually at sea level, that area gets only about 15 feet of snow a year, and it doesn't tend to stick (what's left is often too icy to ski), so this ain't the place to learn to ski (there's just one beginner's lift, along with a tubing park). But if you're a high powered schusser, you're going to love its un groomed double black diamond runs; if you're an intermediate skier, you'll like its broad, carve-able bowls. A 1-day lift ticket costs $48 for adults, $36 for children 14 to 17, $28 for children 8 to 13, and $10 for children 7 and younger. There are multiple day discounts available, too.

Just because there's no skiing on Mount Alyeska in the summer doesn't mean you shouldn't go up to the top anyway. Hop on the **aerial tram** from the resort hotel up to the mountain complex at 2,300 feet, wander the alpine tundra (try not to crush the tiny and delicate wildflowers), and take in the sublime views of the surrounding mountains, glaciers, and Turnagain Arm. The 7-minute tram ride is pricey—$16 adults, $14 seniors, $12 children 8 to 17, $7 those 7 and under—but you'll often spot coupons in local visitor publications. In the past, the resort has put a two-for-one discount coupon in the guidebook *The Milepost*. Another cost-cutting strategy is to hike to the top of the mountain from a trail that starts by chair 7, then ride the tram down for free. It's a steep, sweaty hike, but a well-maintained trail. There's a small glacier on Mount Alyeska, but don't try to trek across it without a guide, lest you wind up in deep trouble—possibly at the bottom of a deep crevasse. Guides are available through an outdoor adventure outfit based in a yurt at the bottom of the tramway called **The Ascending Path** (☎ 877/783-0505 or 907/783-0505; www.theascendingpath.com). It leads treks onto Alyeska Glacier two times a day for $139 per person (including a tram ride). Groups of no more than five hikers strap on their crampons, rope themselves together and to their guide, then set off onto the ice. The whole trip takes about 3 hours, and doubles as a glaciology class, filled with moats, moraines, bergschrunds, randklufts, firn lines, and nunataks. Ascending Path has a bunch of other outdoor activities, too, such as beginner **rock climbing** ($129 for 3 hours), and beginner **ice climbing** ($189 in the summer, $209 in the winter).

At just about a square mile, Alyeska Glacier is rather small, and there are other guided glacier treks in Alaska that are more exciting (such as a trek across Exit Glacier near Seward). But the ice formations are fascinating, and the view from 2,300 feet can't be beat. If you don't have time to do another glacier, this one will do just fine.

Or how about this for an adventure with a view: A skilled paraglider straps you to his chest, the two of you wait for just the right wind to lift your paragliding wing aloft like a kite, then you both run like hell until—suddenly—your feet no longer touch the mountain. You float peacefully above the valley riding the thermals, suspended from a colorful, rip-stop nylon wing that arches overhead like a surprised eyebrow. That's the experience you'll get with **Alaska Paragliding** ★ (☎ 907/301-1215; www.alaskaparagliding.com), which offers tandem rides for $195 a person (including a tram ticket; go before noon or after 8pm and get a $20 discount). Rides usually last 10 to 15 minutes, but can go longer if the thermals are really cooperative.

Back down in the valley, there are several worthwhile hikes. **Winner Creek Trail** ★★ is a long, easy stroll in the woods with an unforgettable payoff—a deep gorge that you cross by pulling yourself along in a hand tram, suspended by a cable high above roaring Glacier Creek. If nobody else is waiting, you can haul yourself out over the raging water and hang there as long as you like. There's a 400-pound weight limit, and people with acrophobia will not appreciate this part of the trail at all. There are two trailheads. From the trailhead beside the Hotel Alyeska it's a 4½-mile walk to the gorge and back. You can park for free at either end.

A more challenging hike climbs up the side of the valley for 7 miles to **Crow Pass** (Mile 7, Crow Creek Rd.), part of an old trade route used by Natives and miners. The trail is a segment of the original Iditarod Trail, which ran from Seward to Nome. Nowadays, this section of trail stretches from Girdwood all the way to Eagle River, 26 miles away. Near the top, there are the remains of a gold mine, as well as alpine glaciers, and a glacial lake, and usually lots of Dall sheep visible on the craggiest crags. There's also a public use cabin at 3,500 feet (see p. 373 for details), near Raven Glacier.

A few miles before the Crow Pass trailhead, you'll come to **Crow Creek Mine** ★★ (☎ 907/278-8060; www.akmining.com/mine/crow.htm; daily 9am–6pm), a remarkably intact mining camp founded in 1898. The buildings—a blacksmith shop, meat cache, bunkhouse, ice house, mess hall, barn, and so on—droop and lean and haven't lost a bit of their original character, the way old places that undergo elaborate historic restorations sometimes do. The prominent Alaskan Toohey family owns the place. One Toohey was a state legislator and another became an oil executive, but two Tooheys still live at the mine and continue to work the claim on a small scale. The real money isn't in gold anymore though, it's in the 20,000 or so tourists who come through each summer to see the historic camp and try their hand at placer mining. Admission is $3 for adults and free for children under 12; for an additional $10 per adult and $4 per child (under 12), you can get a shovel, a pan, some instruction, and the right to keep whatever gold you can find in the creek. For some reason, it's usually the kids who find the color, as the prospectors say.

Attention, Shoppers!

Girdwood has a standard assortment of gift shops and galleries concentrated around Olympic Circle. Yet my favorite shop is out on the highway, the **Alaska Candle Factory and Gift Shop** (along Alyeska Hwy. between the Seward Hwy. and town; ☎ 907/783-2354). The candles sold here are made with seal oil, which the factory buys from Eskimos in Unakleet, and which keep the candles burning longer than standard wax candles. They also come colored or uncolored; the brownish-black tint of the colored candles comes from an ugly but intriguing source: Prudhoe Bay crude oil. Besides everyday tapered candles, there are ones shaped like bears, wolves, beavers, moose, owls, otters, puffins, igloos, mukluks, and even a phallic Billiken, the early-20th-century good-luck charm. The teeny little husky puppy candles ($2) here are especially cute, though short lived; the polar bear head ($30) candle could burn all winter.

Nightlife in Girdwood

Ski bums like to party, and at a restaurant and watering hole called **Chair 5** (5 Linbald St.; ☎ 907/783-2500; www.chairfive.com) you can join them on any given night, summer or winter. The kitchen serves burgers, pastas, and pizza ($8–$20), while the bar pours microbrews (more than 60 on tap), and shots of Scotch (from the largest selection of single malt Scotch in Alaska). There's also a pool table.

For live music, head to **Maxine's Glacier City Bistro** ★ (see restaurant review on p. 66) on the weekend. Rock, reggae, dinner jazz, bluegrass, electronica, home-grown soloists, big-name out-of-staters—you never know what you'll find on stage. The ambience is sultry mountain chic, with low-slung couches, candlelight and confetti-glass track lighting, an art gallery's worth of original oils and pastels, and a well-worn wooden dance floor. Microbrews and sake cocktails flow at the horse-shoe-shaped bar, and there's a fire pit in the yard that crackles evocatively.

THE MATANUSKA-SUSITNA VALLEY & ENVIRONS

North of Anchorage, at the very top of the Cook Inlet, is the mighty Mat-Su, aka the Matanuska-Susitna Valley. Go there to ramble around the ruins of a hard-rock gold mine, to stare deep into the eyes of domesticated musk ox, to trek across a glacier, to ride in a cart pulled by sled dogs at Iditarod HQ, and—late in the short but intense summer growing season—to marvel at the giant vegetables (100 pound cabbages!). Parts of the Mat-Su can be seen in a reasonable day trip from Anchorage or during a detour on the drive north to Denali National Park or Fairbanks. But the Mat-Su is enormous—think the size of West Virginia—so you'll have to spend at least a night there to take in more than simply the highlights listed above (and there are plenty of other possibilities, especially for fishermen or hikers, in this area). Check with the **Mat-Su Visitors Center** (Mile 35.5 Parks Hwy., Palmer; ☎ 907/746-5000; www.alaskavisit.com; mid May–mid Sept daily 8:30 am–6:30 pm).

A Brief History

The Mat-Su Valley, Alaska's primary agricultural region, enjoys a growing season that is short but intense. Summer brings 90 frost-free days and up to 20 hours of daylight, which produce vegetables so big the farmers harvest them with forklifts. You won't find anybody boasting about the 75-pound rutabagas and half-ton pumpkins they're growing though, because everyone keeps mum about what they've got until fall's giant vegetable competition at the Alaska State Fair in Palmer. And then whoever rolls out the biggest chard, cabbage, or kohlrabi can brag all they like.

The agricultural development of the Mat-Su Valley started in Palmer in 1935 when 203 farm families arrived by train ready to participate in a government-sponsored farming cooperative. They were essentially colonists, sent to farm land that had not been farmed before, and the settlement they created was called the Matanuska Valley Colony. The foremost goal was to get farmers, hit hard by the Dust Bowl and then the Great Depression, off the dole and onto the land. A less talked about goal was to establish a source of food for U.S. troops, should Alaska ever become contested terrain in a war with Japan, which, as it turned out, it did. Each family was given 40 acres and low-interest home loans. Most of the colonists came from Michigan, Wisconsin, and Minnesota, under the government's theory that farmers of Scandinavian descent, so prevalent in those states, would be best suited to dealing with life in Alaska.

Like other New Deal programs, the colony was far too socialistic for the Roosevelt administration's conservative critics. The public was happy to declare it a failure the next summer, after half of the original colonists had decided Alaska was simply too much for them, notwithstanding the free land and giant vegetables. About 100 families stuck it out, though, and many of them thrived. Their farming cooperative survived until the farm crisis of the 1980s, when it became one of the thousands of casualties in the struggle between small farmers and big agribusiness. These days, farming is still big in the valley, and many current farmers are descendants of the original colonists. Reminders of colony days are all over Palmer, including the Colony Inn, which was originally the dormitory for the young women who came to teach the colony's children and is now one of the best places to stay in Palmer.

Getting to & Around Matanuska-Susitna Valley

Driving is the only practical way to get to and around the Mat-Su Valley. Two major highways cut through the region. The famously scenic **Glenn Highway** starts in Anchorage, skirts Palmer, 35 miles away, and ultimately leads to Tok, the last Alaskan town before Canada, 328 miles away.

The **Parks Highway** springs from the Glenn Highway just outside of Palmer, tears through Wasilla, and runs all the way to Fairbanks, 362 miles from end to end. But I'd advise you to also make a side trip along the **Hatcher Pass Road,** a scenic 49-mile alpine detour between the Glenn Highway and the Parks Highway, which runs through Hatcher Pass. To do the whole thing you should have a four-wheel-drive vehicle, since a good 22 miles is unpaved. But the 17-mile stretch from Palmer to the Independence Gold Mine—a sight I highly recommend—is an easy and beautiful mountain drive, with lovely roadside creeks to cool your heels in and sweeping high-altitude views of the Mat-Su Valley below.

Accommodations & Dining

There are fast-food places galore along the Parks Highway as it cuts through Wasilla, but precious few other options for eating. Palmer has one so-so Mexican restaurant, and a 24-hour coffee shop at The Valley Hotel (see below), that some-how gets away with charging $11 for a Western omelet. The best bets for dining are at the two lodges described below. Sheep Mountain Lodge has a full restaurant open from 7:30am to 9pm. Dinners there range in price from $7 for a deli sandwich to about $22 for the evening special, grilled salmon or halibut perhaps. The restaurant at Hatcher Pass Lodge, open from noon to 7pm, has a dinner menu that stretches from a fried egg sandwich for $7.25 to shrimp scampi for $24.

Add a 5% bed tax to any accommodations in the Mat-Su Borough.

$–$$$$ Palmer has all the trappings of a Midwestern farming community, complete with a main drag running parallel to the train tracks and a prominent steel water tower standing over the town. Only the sheer, jagged peaks of the Talkeetna and Chugach mountains off in the distance ruin the heartland illusion. If the mountains beckon, and I'm pretty sure they will, there are some alpine lodges where you can really get away from it all. **Sheep Mountain Lodge** ★★ (Mile 113.5 Glenn Hwy., north of Palmer; ☎ 877/645-5121; www.sheepmountain. com; MC, V) is a good choice if you plan to do a little ice trekking on the Matanuska Glacier, which is just 12 miles away, or rafting down the nearby Matanuksa River. The lodge has 11 quintessentially Alaskan log cabins, some with kitchens and all with private baths. Those with cooking facilities go for $189 while those without go for $149. Cheaper still is the eight-person bunkhouse, which four can take over for just $60, with $5 per head for each extra person. After coming back from a day on the ice or on the icy river, guests here warm back up in the lodge's wood-fired sauna. Looming above the lodge is 6,300-foot Sheep Mountain, which, as you might expect, is home to many sheep (you can peep at them through the lodge's telescope). The lodge is located along the Glenn Highway, about 2 hours from Anchorage.

$–$$$$ Closer to Anchorage (about 90 min. away) but seemingly even more remote is the **Hatcher Pass Lodge** (17 miles from Palmer on Hatcher Pass Rd.; ☎ 907/745-5897; www.hatcherpasslodge.com; AE, DISC, MC, V), nestled into a tranquil valley 3,000 feet up in the Talkeetna Mountains. In the winter you can cross-country ski beneath the northern lights or sweat in the sauna by the frozen creek. Hiking through tundra meadows, gobbling wild berries off the vine, and exploring the remains of Independence Gold Mine (right next door) are the big activities in summer. Or just sit quietly and watch eagles and falcons ride the thermals around the cool granite peaks. The nine cabins here aren't fancy, but they're comfy and cozy, with cheap-looking furnishings but great views. They average $169 for double occupancy, but the owner confessed to us that he will bargain (so why not give it a try?). Budgeteers may want to pick one of the three small rooms in the A-frame lodge, with similar decor if less privacy—they tend to go for $95 a night. The lodge serves surprisingly good meals (try the fondue hors d'oeuvre), and it has a tiny, much-frequented bar. Guests can get hot cakes and omelets for breakfast, and anybody can stop by for lunch or dinner. There is a slight element of roughing it here—there's a walk to the lodge building to use the showers and the bathroom area has chemical toilets. But these minor hardships feel less like deficiencies and more like little challenges that make the place seem even more like a high mountain summer camp than it already does.

$$ There's really only one decent place to stay in the town of Palmer itself: the **Colony Inn** (325 East Elmwood; ☎ 800/478-ROOM or 907/745-3330; AE, DISC, MC, V). This is where all of the VIPs who come to Palmer stay, such as the band Jefferson Airplane, which performed at the state fair here, and movie director Sean Penn, who shot scenes for the film *Into the Wild* nearby. Not only is the Colony Inn the cushiest best to stay in Palmer, it compares favorably with anything Anchorage has to offer. The lovely double occupancy rooms—with quilts on the beds, antique desks and armoires against the walls, and Jacuzzi tubs in most of the bathrooms—go for $110. An identical room in Anchorage, 40 minutes down the road, would fetch $150 or more. The inn was originally the Matanuska Valley Colony's teacher's dormitory, and downstairs, in the well-preserved sitting room, you can practically hear the ghosts of bachelor farmers discussing the merits of their giant cabbages with the young schoolmarms. Check-in for the Colony Inn is handled at **The Valley Hotel** (606 South Alaska St.; ☎ 800/478-ROOM or 907/745-3330; AE, DC, MC, V), which is less expensive, but not nearly as nice. It's got security cameras in the hallways and small scuffed-up rooms starting at $79 (if you're an AAA member, ask for a 10% discount). It's also got a coffee house, open all day long, which is a little pricier than it ought to be.

Why You're Here: The Top Sights & Attractions

At the **Musk Ox Farm** ★★ (☎ 907/745-4151; www.muskoxfarm.org; $8.50 adults, $7 seniors, $6 children 5–12; Mother's Day–Oct 1 daily 9am–6pm) just outside of Palmer you can get face-to-face with a shaggy herd of Arctic ungulates straight from Alaska's Pleistocene-era past. Unlike saber tooth tigers, woolly mammoths, and other less hardy species that went belly up in the last ice age, musk ox are survivors. Part of their secret is their ultra-warm undercoating of fur, which produces a cashmerelike wool called *qiviut*. All of the qiviut combed from the animals at the musk ox farm goes to the **Oomingmak Musk Ox Producers Co-op** in Anchorage (p. 54), a knitting cooperative made up of about 200 Native women in remote villages. It's fun to hang out with the herd at the Musk Ox Farm and get to know the animals' personalities, which fall into the narrow spectrum between mournful and disagreeable. They seem to wear their feelings on their long faces, which are framed by horns that drop from the tops of their heads below their big brown eyes, then turn up at the ends, like Mary Tyler Moore's hair

A Step Back in Time

The feeling you get of stepping back in time when you enter the **Colony House Museum** (316 E. Elmwood St., across from the Colony Inn; ☎ 745-1935; $2 adults, $1 children 12 and under; May 1–Aug 31 only Tues–Sat 10am–4pm) is more acute than it is at most museums. That's because everything there—not just the artifacts, but also the building itself . . . and even the docents—is linked directly to the Matanuska Valley Colony. As part of the deal (or rather, as part of the New Deal), the Roosevelt Administration gave the colonists 40 acres of land to farm, a low-interest home loan of $3,500, and a choice among five styles of homes. The Colony House Museum is one of those original homes, and it still feels very much like the Depression-era farmhouse that it is. It's filled with such an array of everyday items from the period—pots and pans, a washboard and laundry wringer, a milking pail, a child's wagon—it could double as a showroom for a 1935 Sears, Roebuck and Co. catalog, which is where a lot of the stuff originated. The volunteers who staff the museum are descendents of the original colonists, and though they're lifelong Alaskans, they've still got the pleasant faces and matter-of-fact tones typical of Midwestern farmers. And if you've got the time to listen, they've got the stories to tell. To track down more of the colony's original buildings, pick up a free walking-tour map at the **Greater Palmer Chamber of Commerce** (723 S. Valley Way; ☎ 907/745-2880; www.palmerchamber.org; May 1–Sept 30 9am–6pm).

once did. This gives them a perfectly ridiculous and utterly endearing look. Farm tours are given regularly throughout the day in the summer.

When reindeer turn up in movies or advertisements, there's a good chance they came from **The Williams Reindeer Farm** 🧒 (125 Bodenburg Rd.; 8½ miles south of Palmer on Old Glenn Hwy.; ☎ 907/745-4000; www.reindeerfarm.com; $5 adults, $4 seniors, $3 children 3–11; daily 10am–6pm). The farm's animals have appeared in publications such as *Vogue,* in Hollywood movies such as *Leaving Normal* with Meg Tilly and Christine Lahti, and in TV commercials, including one by Chevrolet in which the entire herd runs across the screen with a Silverado pickup truck in the background. Show biz, of course, is ruthless, but so is reindeer farming. When the farm isn't supplying talent to Hollywood, it's supplying reindeer meat to supermarkets and reindeer hides to fur dealers. (In Chinese medicine, reindeer antler is an aphrodisiac, and the farm used to be an antler supplier too. But Viagra killed that market.) In any case, the farm is a fun, quick stop, and is especially good for kids, who get to pet and feed the animals.

If Palmer had existed 18,000 years ago, it would have been beneath hundreds of feet of ice from the **Matanuska Glacier** ★. The glacier is now about 60 miles from Palmer, having receded considerably since the last Ice Age. Despite its reduced circumstances, it's still an impressive site, 27 miles long and 4 miles wide at the base. It's also the largest glacier you can drive to in Alaska. There are two ways to view it—from afar or from right on top of it. At the **Matanuska Glacier State Recreation Area** (Mile 101 Glenn Hwy.), a little over a mile away, you can get the big-picture view of the glacier, which is slowly flowing into the Matanuska Valley (it takes about 250 years for ice to make the trip from top to bottom). There's a nice 1-mile nature walk here, and a campground with a dozen sites ($15 per night). There's no charge to stop and look. To see Matanuska Glacier up close, you have to go through privately owned **Glacier Park** (Mile 102 Glenn Hwy.; ☎ 800/253-4480 or 907/745-2534; www.matanuskaglacier.com). The owner charges $15 for adults, $10 for students, and $5 for children 6 to 12. From the parking lot, it's a 15- or 20-minute hike to the ice, where a variety of marked trails are laid out.

A couple of companies lead guided hikes onto the glacier, which take you beyond the marked trails. A fun way to fill a day is to combine a trek across Matanuska Glacier with a trip down the **Matanuska River.** At one point the river squeezes between a massive rock wall and the face of the glacier. A company called **Nova** (☎ 800/746-5753; www.novalaska.com) bundles a 2½-hour hike on the ice with a 3½-hour river trip for $149. The glacier trek alone costs $80 and the river trip costs $99, so you save $30 with the package. Nova offers rafting trips of various thrill levels, but the most popular one passes through 14 miles of class III rapids and a few miles of class IV rapids. Calling it white water wouldn't be accurate since there's so much glacial silt in the Matanuska River that even the white water is gray. You can choose to go in either an oar boat steered by a guide, or in an inflatable raft paddled by the passengers. Around summer solstice, the company runs a midnight river run, under the bright Alaskan evening sun. Evening is when the river crests, and the thrill level is at its highest. Nova does not accept passengers under the age of 12.

Back in the days when the Matanuska colonists were farming in the valley, men with lights on their heads were blasting tunnels into the Talkeetna Mountains and extracting gold. The mountains had plenty of gold, but they never drew stampeders like the gold rushes of Nome and the Klondike did, because Talkeetna gold was simply too hard to reach. Mining there was a sober, industrial endeavor, but a highly lucrative one. At its peak in 1941, the **Independence Mine** was the most productive in Alaska, producing $1.2 million in gold (which would be worth $17.2 million today). More than 200 men worked there in round-the-clock shifts, breaking only for Christmas and the Fourth of July. Today the mine is a state historical park, the **Independence Mine State Historical Park** ★★★ (Hatcher Pass Rd.; ☎ 907/745-2827; www.dnr.state.ak.us/parks/units/indmine.htm;

The Weather Hole

Even if the weather's miserable throughout the rest of the Mat-Su Valley, you may find sunshine at the Matanuska Glacier. Through an odd meteorological phenomenon known as a weather hole, the glacier has the power to deflect or dissipate inclement weather above it.

A Memorable Drive . . . But Not for the Faint of Heart

If you're on you're way to Denali National Park or Fairbanks, and you've got four-wheel-drive and a sense of adventure, drive through **Hatcher Pass.** Shortly after Independence Mine, Hatcher Pass Road sheds its blacktop and ascends steeply through a 3,886-foot mountain pass. From there it bumps and winds for 20 unpaved miles, through spectacular alpine scenery, past Summit Lake (with a nice hike along the shore, just after the pass), by "Nixon's Nose" (a popular paragliding launch, just after the lake), two gold mines (the Lucky Shot mine on the left and the War Baby mine on the right, visible on the mountainside about 3½ miles after the lake), and wild berry patches (blackberries and strawberries), and all sorts of wildlife (bears and sheep) along the way, if you're lucky. The whole road makes a 49-mile loop around a humdrum stretch of the Parks Highway, starting just north of Palmer and coming out just north of Willow.

$5 per car use fee; summer daily 10am–7pm), and it's well worth a visit—the drive itself is gorgeous. At the complex, half of the two dozen or so old wooden structures have been carefully restored, while the others are in shambles. Stop in first at the nice one with the red roof. It's the old manager's house, and now the visitor center. You can get a free map for a self-guided tour there, or sign up for the $5 guided tour. Guided tours are offered daily at 1:30pm and 3:30pm, with an additional tour at 4:30pm on weekends. If you take the tour, you'll get inside the mess hall, the bunkhouse, and some of the other buildings that are locked the rest of the time. If you wander around on your own, there's still plenty to see. Don't overlook the water tunnel portal, the main conduit for transporting ore and materials out of the mountain. You can't go in, but you can stand at the mouth and feel the cold air from inside the mountain blow across your face. It's a bit of a climb, but there are nearly 12 miles of tunnels in the mountain that you can't go into, and this will give you a taste of what they're like.

Six million dollars in gold was taken from the ground here from the time the mine opened in the 1930s until it closed in 1951, with an intermission for World War II, when gold mining was deemed nonessential to the war effort. Government price controls on gold—$35 per ounce, take it or leave it—did in the Independence Mine, along with all the other big gold mines in Alaska. The mother lode has yet to be tapped out, and flecks and flakes of gold still turn up in the bug-clouded creek. For $6 you can buy a pan at the visitor center and try your hand at placer mining in the stream, or you can leave a deposit and borrow a pan. Bring bug spray, or better yet, mosquito-net clothing, because I'm not kidding about the bug-clouded creek. The historical park is closed in the winter, but the valley is wide open to cross-country skiers.

The biggest draw for visitors in Wasilla, otherwise an unremarkable bedroom community for Anchorage, is the **Iditarod Trail Sled Dog Race Headquarters**

(Mile 2.2 Knik Rd.; ☎ 907/376-5155; www.iditarod.com; summer daily 8am–7pm, rest of year Mon–Fri 8am–5pm). This is the nerve center, as well as the actual starting point, of Alaska's foremost athletic competition. The 1,150-mile Iditarod Trail

The Iditarod

The Iditarod Trail Sled Dog Race is the biggest event of Alaska's year, not only in terms of sports, but also culturally and as a unifying event. The race is big news—TV anchors speculate on the mushers' strategies at the top of the evening news and break away live to cover the top finishers, regardless of the time of day or night. School children plot the progress of their favorite teams on maps and over the Internet. Increasingly, the world is joining in. Visitors, especially Europeans, fill hotels in Anchorage and Nome for the Iditarod. Voices speaking French and German waft through the restaurants. It's a wonderful time of year to visit, with light skies, excellent late-season skiing, and winter festivals enlivening many towns. Nome goes crazy when the mushers hit. Even if the first team crosses the finish line at 3am in –30°F (–34°C) weather, a huge crowd turns out to congratulate the winner. And crowds keep turning out for the also-rans, too.

Given all this, it's difficult for me to report objectively on the activities of a Miami, Florida–based animal-rights activist group that opposes the race—but my editors insist that I try. The Sled Dog Action Coalition contends the race is cruel to the dogs, with some suffering and dying on the trail or inhumanely tethered in dog lots. The group has organized boycotts against race sponsors. While the campaign doesn't seem to be affecting the race, which grows every year, it has sparked occasional media coverage and angry debate. Iditarod supporters—the universal view in Alaska—claim the coalition exaggerates and distorts its charges. Iditarod mushers insist that the dogs, which are worth thousands of dollars, receive veterinary care superior to the doctoring that most people get. Mushers who abuse dogs are kicked out of the sport.

Harmful practices probably do occur in the lower ranks of mushing. For example, uncontrolled breeding can produce too many pups and some may end up being killed—sadly, that problem is common with pets in cities all over the U.S. At least sled dogs get the regular exercise they need.

To find out more about both sides of the issue, check out the websites of the Sled Dog Action Coalition (www.helpsleddogs.org) and of an Iditarod supporter responding to the coalition's charges (www.sunhusky.com). If you want to plan your trip to coincide with the race in March, plan well in advance because the event is extremely popular and hotels (particularly in Nome) fill up quickly. For information, contact the Iditarod Trail Committee (☎ **907/376-5155;** www.iditarod.com).

—*Charles Wohlforth*

Where Giant Vegetables Compete

To see what fertile river valley soil and 20 hours a day of Alaskan summer sunlight will do for a vegetable, pay a visit to the **Alaska State Fair** (2075 Glenn Hwy; ☎ 800/850-FAIR or 907/745-4827; www.alaskastatefair.org). This is your best bet for ogling the Baby Hueys of the Vegetable Kingdom that come from the Mat-Su valley, where the brief but hyperkinetic growing season produces some freakin' big produce. We're talking zucchinis bigger than kindergartners, single kohlrabies that weigh more than a half dozen bowling balls, and pumpkins that could crush you like an SUV in a rollover accident. These titans of the vegetable kingdom aren't easy to find before the fair, because the farmers growing them keep a tight lid on what they've got until showtime at the fair's "large vegetable competition." It's been like that every year since the original Mat-Su valley farmers rolled their giant cabbages into the display tent of the first fair in 1936.

The fair itself is a pretty big deal in its own right. Spread across 11 days, and always concluding on Labor Day, it draws some 250,000 people. Among the multitude of attractions are monster truck races, a rodeo, a lumberjack show, a Spam cooking contest, and a home brewing competition. But the gargantuan vegetables always get the most attention. Some have even traveled to New York to appear on *The David Letterman Show*. To give you an idea of the scope of things, here are some of the winners from the large vegetable competition in 2006: Biggest **celery:** 63.3 pounds; biggest **chard:** 71.75 pounds; biggest **rutabaga:** 75.75 pounds; biggest **kohlrabi:** 96.95 pounds; biggest **cabbage (green):** 105.6 pounds; biggest **cabbage (red):** 45.25 pounds; biggest **pumpkin:** 1,019 pounds; longest **bean:** 22.75 inches; tallest **dill weed:** 7 feet, 10 inches.

Sled Dog Race begins ceremonially on the first Saturday of March in downtown Anchorage. After a few blocks, the mushers pack up their sleds and dogs and drive to race headquarters for the actual start of the race, the next day. It's called The Restart. The headquarters, made from enormous white spruce logs, is filled with memorabilia like dog sleds, parkas worn by legendary mushers, that sort of thing. It's the sled dog rides you can take that make the visit really worthwhile. In the summer, for $10, you can sit in a cart pulled by a slobber-happy team of Iditarod-class athletes. No matter how much you enjoy the trip, it seems, the dogs enjoy it even more. (For more on this, see the Iditarod box above.)

Note that you can volunteer at the start and the finish line of the dog race; check out the Iditarod website for details.

River rafting is another top draw in the Mat-Su Valley. It's covered on p. 74.

The Other Mat-Su

The Mat-Su Valley's annual **"Running of the Bulls"** at the **Musk Ox Farm** (p. 72) is a 5K run and an uncommon opportunity to romp with the shaggy Arctic ungulates, bedecked with fine, cashmerelike wool, that are raised there. Unlike the better-known Running of the Bulls in Pamplona, Spain, there's no danger of being trampled or gored here, as the course is laid in the fenced-in chutes between musk ox enclosures. Some of the animals, especially the bulls, run along with the racers, but they remain safely on their side of the fence. They don't seem to want to kill anyone, just to play, but then again there's really no telling what's going through their minds. The event is held in August (call for the exact date) and the entry fee is $20 for adults, $15 for children 12 and under. Walkers are welcome too.

Southcentral Alaska

WHEN ALASKANS HIKE, FISH, HUNT, CAMP, BOAT, OR TROMP ACROSS GLACIERS, more often than not, they do it in the great wilds of Southcentral Alaska. This rugged, multifaceted region is Alaska's principal playground. For visitors, it's the most accessible and diverse part of the state. It encompasses the sheltered waters, 3,000 miles of coastline, and 20 tidewater glaciers of Prince William Sound. It takes in the majestic mountains, icy salmon streams, and funky seaside towns of the Kenai Peninsula, home of Kenai Fjords National Park and Kachemak Bay State Park. And it includes the wind-swept emerald islands of the Kodiak Archipelago, where 3,000 of the biggest, baddest bears on earth hold sway.

This monumental swath of The Great Land—nestled into the apex of the Northern Pacific Ocean—also includes Anchorage and two-thirds of the state's population, which helps to account for its popularity. But don't get the wrong idea, it's not overrun with people. With the exception of Anchorage (which is so big it gets its own chapter in this book), small, friendly communities of a few thousand people at most are the norm here. Some Southcentral towns, like Homer and Cordova, are downright enchanting. Others, like Whittier and Valdez, are gritty, unlovely places. But all of them act as easily reachable gateways to a spectacular region that has a little bit of just about everything Alaska has to offer.

DON'T LEAVE SOUTHCENTRAL ALASKA WITHOUT . . .

Feeling the chill on your cheeks from an icy glacial breeze. Southcentral Alaska has glaciers that you can hike to, drive to, kayak around, or visit aboard a glacier tour boat, including those in **Kenai Fjords National Park.** When you stand (or bob) before one of these slow-moving rivers of ice, the cold air hits you like someone left the door of the walk-in freezer open. See p. 82.

Scaling an alpine peak. The Kenai and Chugach mountains are loaded with trails, many with trailheads that you can walk to from your hotel or B&B, and all offering hours of outdoor adventure, for absolutely free.

Ogling enormous wildlife. From the humpback whales in and around Prince William Sound, to the bears in the salmon streams on Kodiak Island packing on as many pounds as they can before winter, to the moose you must take care not to run into when driving down the Kenai Peninsula, Southcentral Alaska is crawling with plus-size critters.

Reeling in dinner. Homer is the Halibut Fishing Capital of the World, and the Kenai River is home of the world's largest king salmon, as well as hefty silvers and reds. You need a charter boat to go after the halibut, but to try your luck with the salmon, all you need is a rod, a reel, and a fishing license—although hiring a drift boat is an option too.

LAY OF THE LAND
PRINCE WILLIAM SOUND

With its misty spruce and hemlock forests, its glacier-filled mountains, and its myriad islands and waterways to explore, Prince William Sound is like a smaller, more accessible version of the watery world of Southeast Alaska. To the north, west, and east, it's bordered by the tall, deeply glaciated folds of the Chugach Mountains. To the south, 50-mile-long Montague Island and several small islands shelter the sound from the stormy seas of the Gulf of Alaska. In between are 10,000 square miles of inlets, fjords, and forested islands—a wet dreamland for sea kayakers. Although wildlife in the sound was devastated by the *Exxon Valdez* oil spill in 1989, it's recovered to the point that today you'll view a fair number of otters, seals, sea lions, and even whales there. One of the marquee attractions is the 3-mile-wide Columbia Glacier, but it's only one of 20 glaciers dropping icebergs into the sound and keeping its waters well chilled.

Of the three principal communities on Prince William Sound, Valdez and Whittier are both accessible by car. Cordova is accessible only by air or boat.

VALDEZ   Because it's Prince William Sound's most easily accessible point by car, Valdez, in the northeast corner of the sound, is the area's most popular base for launching expeditions onto the water or into the mountains. The town itself isn't much of a looker—it's vintage 1970s ugly, and it's got the utilitarian soul of an oil tanker port (Valdez is the end of the line for the Trans-Alaska Pipeline). But the surrounding snowy peaks of the saw-toothed mountains and the sparkly waters of deep, dark Valdez Bay more than make up for the town's homeliness.

WHITTIER   Whittier, in the northwest corner of the sound, is another ugly duckling. It's a port town dominated by parking lots, fuel silos, rusting junk, and a single high-rise, cinder-block apartment building where 80% of the population resides. But nobody goes to Whittier for Whittier. They go there because it's Anchorage's nearest portal to Prince William Sound. On a day trip out of Anchorage through Whittier, you can get out onto the sound to see glaciers and wildlife, then beat it back to the city for dinner. Or you can hop a ferry in Whittier and head to more picturesque Cordova.

CORDOVA   In the sound's southeast corner, near the Gulf of Alaska, Cordova is the most charming community on Prince William Sound, a genuinely old-fashioned town that the modern world has, more or less, overlooked. Adjacent to the enormous, shimmering wetlands of Copper River Delta, it's a key stop for both migratory waterfowl and the flocks of birders they attract. Originally a shipping port for copper ore, Cordova now leads a slow, peaceful life as a fishing town. It's unconnected to the rest of the state by road, which makes it both harder to get to, and all the more worthwhile. A must-see attraction here is Childs Glacier, which calves icebergs from its 20-story face straight into the swift-moving Copper River.

KENAI PENINSULA

The Kenai Peninsula is a land of concentrated diversity. It has the coastal rain-forests, estuaries, bays, coves and salmon streams, snow-capped mountains, alpine tundra, and glaciers that you'll find in the rest of the state, only they're all squeezed within a relatively small, 9,050-square-mile area (about the size of Delaware, Connecticut, and Rhode Island, plus a little bit of New Hampshire).

Dominating the eastern side of the Peninsula are the Kenai Mountains, which run for 120 miles from north to south. Dozens of glaciers spill from two ice fields cradled in the mountain peaks toward the fjord-indented coastline. The mountains mainly drain into the western part of the peninsula, creating hundreds of lakes and ponds and world-class salmon runs like the Kenai River.

The Seward Highway heads from Anchorage down the east side of the Peninsula to a long deep fjord called Resurrection Bay and the town of Seward. The Sterling Highway springs from the Seward Highway early on, crosses the peninsula from east to west, then runs down its western shore along Cook Inlet (check out the views of the volcanic trio of mounts Iliamna, Redoubt, and Spurr across the inlet). The road ends at Kachemak Bay and the lively town of Homer.

There are several Kenai Peninsula communities—such as Ninilchik, Sterling, Cooper Landing, Moose Pass, and Hope—that really don't have much to offer visitors besides fishing (although Ninilchik does have an old Russian Orthodox Church by the sea that's quite photogenic). In this chapter I'll concentrate on the Kenai Peninsula's four main communities and visitor destinations: Seward, Soldotna, Kenai, and Homer.

SEWARD   On the east side of the Kenai Peninsula, Seward is neatly laid out on a small fan of land between the towering Kenai Mountains and a gorgeous, deep-water fjord called Resurrection Bay. This busy little seaside town, with its pictur-esque fishing harbor, tidy little downtown, and world-class aquarium, is a lovely place to spend a few days in its own right. But the bigger draw is the surrounding wilderness, especially Kenai Fjords National Park.

Via kayak or tour boat you can view the park's tidewater glaciers. Along the way you may have an up-close meeting with humpback whales, Steller sea lions, or other wildlife. Just out of town you can drive to Exit Glacier and—if your legs and lungs are up for it—climb a trail alongside the glacier for a look at the Harding Icefield, an unbroken sea of ice that's so big, it could cover Rhode Island.

SOLDOTNA & KENAI   The Kenai River, renowned for its seriously sizable salmon, cuts through the neighboring towns of Soldotna and Kenai. Fishing is the name of the game in these twin cities. Kenai, the more attractive of the two, sits on the shore of Cook Inlet, at the mouth of the river. It boasts a long beach to stroll and a bit of Russian history to explore. Soldotna was built at the intersection of the

Kenai Fjords Glaciers: Where Wildlife Comes with No Extra Charge

Alaska has dozens of tidewater glaciers spread across three regions: Southeast Alaska, Prince William Sound, and along the eastern Kenai Peninsula in Kenai Fjords National Park. So which is best? I think you get the most bang for your glacier tour buck in Kenai Fjords National Park. It's not that the glaciers there are any more spectacular than the glaciers out of Whittier or Valdez in Prince William Sound. But the Sound is a relative dead zone compared to the waters around Kenai Fjords, which teem with seals, Steller sea lions, Dall's porpoises, and whales, not to mention enormous colonies of seabirds. Tour boat captains have plenty of time to linger when something big pops up, so glacier cruises here really double as wildlife tours. Sure, Glacier Bay National Park in Southeast Alaska might trump Kenai Fjords National Park in its number of glaciers, but the two are neck-and-neck in wildlife, and a trip to Kenai Fjords is several times more affordable than a trip to Glacier Bay (see p. 227 for more on that area).

One caveat I have to add to this recommendation, however, is that a trip to the park requires a jaunt through the notoriously stormy Gulf of Alaska. When the seas pick up, the massive swells here inevitably send dozens of miserable, green-tinted passengers heaving over the rails. Seasickness preventives such as Bonine or pressure-therapy wrist bands are one solution, but if you're the type who gets seasick easily, the calmer waters of Prince William Sound might be a better option.

Kenai River and the Sterling Highway, roughly half way between Anchorage and Homer. If fishing isn't your thing, Soldotna has little to offer you besides a pit stop during the long drive to other parts of this region.

HOMER   Located at the bottom of the Kenai Peninsula and at the end of the Sterling Highway, the funky seaside town of Homer is known as both the Halibut Fishing Capital of the World and the artiest place in Alaska. Homer's museums, galleries, restaurants, huge charter fishing fleet, and ravishing natural beauty make it one of Alaska's most alluring destinations. The 4½-mile Homer Spit, which protrudes half way across Kachemak Bay, is the focal point of the festive summer scene. Across the water, roadless Kachemak Bay State Park offers sea kayaking, hiking, camping, and wilderness peace and quiet at the foot of the Kenai Mountains.

KODIAK ISLAND   Kodiak Island is the second largest island in the United States (after the Big Island of Hawaii). At its heart is the city of Kodiak, a bustling commercial fishing port, rich in Russian and Native history. Fishermen dominate the town, but it's an extra-large variety of brown bear that holds sway over the rest of the island. Kodiak bears, as they're called, have been isolated from their mainland cousins for so long that they've evolved into a distinct sub-species.

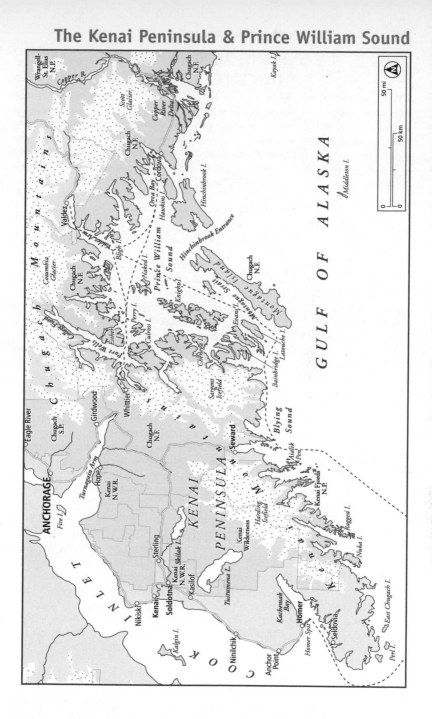

GETTING TO & AROUND SOUTHCENTRAL ALASKA

Driving makes the most sense if you're headed anywhere on the Kenai Peninsula, or if you're bound for one of the two gateway communities of Prince William Sound (Valdez and Whittier). Not only is it convenient and relatively quick, but the area abounds with scenic highways and byways. The only two towns in this chapter that you can't drive to are Kodiak and Cordova. **Alaska Airlines** (☎ 800/252-7522; www.alaskaair.com) flies out of Anchorage to both (but to no other towns covered in this chapter), and it usually has the best fares (round-trip fares start at about $126 to Kodiak and $270 to Cordova). **ERA Aviation** (☎ 800/866-8394 or 907/266-8394; www.FlyEra.com), which operates smaller, prop-driven aircraft, flies from Anchorage to all the towns in this chapter except for Whittier and Seward (prices range from about $126 and up round-trip to Kodiak, to as much as $330 round-trip to Cordova).

Ferries also serve Kodiak Island and Cordova, and you'll know from my other mentions of the **Alaska Marine Highway Ferry System** (☎ 800/642-0066; www.ferryalaska.com) that I think this method of travel is primo. The boats are well maintained and in the summer carry naturalists charged with expounding upon the natural wonders you'll be passing. In general, rates are reasonable. Ferries run between Homer and Kodiak three or four times a week during the summer, and between Whittier, Cordova, and Valdez on Prince William Sound almost every day in the summer. Travel times range from 3 hours on the fast ferry (there's a slow one, too) from Whittier to Valdez, to 10 hours on the boat from Homer to Kodiak.

A final and fun way to hop around the peninsula is via the **Alaska Railroad** (☎ 800/544-0552; www.akrr.com). The scenery—especially on the route to Seward—can't be beat (it's spectacular). The ride, however, isn't cost efficient; if more than one of you is traveling, renting a car will be cheaper.

Glacier tour companies sell day trips from Anchorage to both Whittier and Seward that include train fare. But I think it's folly to try to take the trip in 1 day. It takes 16 hours, which is just too long (you're supposed to be on vacation, right?).

VALDEZ

What Valdez lacks in charm—which is plenty—it makes up for in location. A homely little low-rise oil town of about 4,500 residents, it sits along the deep, dark waters of an exquisite fjord surrounded by jagged, snowy mountain peaks. While its most important economic role is as the terminus of the Trans-Alaska Pipeline (where crude oil pumped 800 miles from Prudhoe Bay in the Arctic is loaded aboard supertankers for shipment to West Coast refineries), tourists visit because it's a principal gateway to Prince William Sound. The city also works as a base camp for hiking or river rafting adventures in the Chugach Mountains that surround it.

A BRIEF HISTORY

Valdez was founded on high hopes and misinformation during the Klondike gold rush of the 1890s. The town's earliest boosters, angling to make fortunes by getting in on the ground floor of a boomtown, spread exaggerated reports of an easy trail from Valdez through the mountains to the gold fields of the Interior. The thousands of prospectors they lured to their muddy tent camp were livid when they discovered that this supposedly easy route involved climbing a glacier into the mountains, crossing an ice field, and descending along another glacier. Many who embarked upon the treacherous route lost their lives or were gravely injured. Eventually the U.S. Army, with pick axes and dynamite, blazed a safer and saner way through the Chugach. Only then did Valdez become what its founders had said it was: a year-round ice-free port offering a practical route to the Interior.

In 1964, Valdez was destroyed when a Good Friday earthquake flattened much of the town and dropped the original town site below the high-tide mark. The town was rebuilt nearby on firmer, drier ground, which is why Valdez is dominated by the characteristically awful architecture of the 1960s and early 1970s. In the 1970s, the town hitched its fortunes to the oil industry's and became the terminus of the Trans-Alaska Pipeline, where supertankers fill up with North Slope crude bound for West Coast refineries. In 1989, Valdez went down in infamy when one of these tankers, the *Exxon Valdez,* ran onto the rocks a few miles from port and caused the worst oil spill in American history. You won't see any obvious signs of the oil spill today, but wildlife in the sound is still recovering.

LAY OF THE LAND

Located in the northeast corner of Prince William Sound, Valdez sits along the north shore of a fjord that's 12 miles long, 2½ miles wide, and 750 feet deep. The town itself is small and flat. You can walk from one end to the other in 20 minutes. Though Valdez lacks a downtown, it makes up for it with a lively waterfront along its small boat harbor. On the opposite shore of the fjord, with 18 enormous holding tanks dug into the mountainside, is the terminus of the Trans-Alaska Pipeline, where tankers dock. You used to be able to tour the facility, but a post September 11, 2001, terrorist attacks security clamp-down ended that.

The Richardson Highway crosses the Chugach Mountains and links Valdez to the outside world by land. The first 30 miles or so out of Valdez are incredibly scenic. Highlights include: Keystone Canyon, about 13 miles from Valdez; 2,678-foot Thompson Pass, 26 miles from town; and Worthington Glacier, a drive-up glacier that's 28 miles away.

Valdez is known as the Little Switzerland of Alaska because its mountains get 350 inches of snow a year. That translates into 3,000-foot mountain peaks covered in 30 feet of snow all around, and a thriving heli-skiing business in the winter. Extreme powder hounds hitch helicopter rides to the tops of otherwise unreachable mountaintops, then jump out and carve huge lines through nearly vertical oceans of snow.

The Valdez Convention and Visitors Bureau maintains a **Visitor Information Center** at 200 Fairbanks Dr., a block off Egan Drive (P.O. Box 1603), Valdez, AK 99686 (☎ 907/835-4636; www.valdezalaska.org) where you can pick up a free town map and useful *Vacation Planner.* They're open in summer daily 8am to 7pm and the rest of the year Monday through Friday 8am to 5pm.

GETTING TO & AROUND VALDEZ
By Land

From Anchorage, it's a 304-mile drive to Valdez (it takes about 6 hr.), along the Glenn and Richardson highways. From Fairbanks, drivers head straight down the Richardson Highway for 366 miles (which can be accomplished in approximately 7 hr.). The road parallels the Trans-Alaska Pipeline the whole way. You'll probably end up renting a car in Anchorage or Fairbanks, but if you somehow end up in Valdez without one, you can get wheels at the airport through **Valdez U-Drive** (☎ 907/835-4402; www.valdezudrive.com) for about $60 a day for a compact car, $360 a week for the same.

By Sea

The **Alaska Marine Highway System** (☎ 800/642-0066; www.ferryalaska.com) connects Valdez, Whittier, and Cordova. The trip from Whittier, the closest port to Anchorage, takes about 3 hours on the new fast ferry, and costs $86 per adult, $43 for those 6 to 11, and is free for those 5 and under. The older, slower ferry takes almost 7 hours to make the trip (same price). The advantage of the slow ferry, which chugs along between 12 and 18 knots, is that you see more wildlife (the fast ferry scoots so quickly by any seals, whales, and whatnot that you won't get a good look, if you spot them at all). Taking a small car on the ferry costs an additional $102, and reservations are a must for that.

By Air

ERA Aviation (☎ 800/868-8394; www.flyera.com) offers daily flights to Valdez from Anchorage, year-round. It's a 35-minute flight, and costs about $200 round trip.

ACCOMMODATIONS, BOTH STANDARD & NOT

Most of Valdez's summer visitors bring their own places to stay. The town is a mecca for recreational vehicle owners, a place where RV spaces outnumber hotel rooms by two to one. Assuming you're not coming to town pulling a fifth-wheeler (and you can't rent one in Valdez), you'll likely stay at one of Valdez's seven hotels or 25 (or so) bed-and-breakfasts (B&Bs).

Bed & Breakfasts

I wish I could tell you that Valdez had a super helpful B&B association that rigorously scrutinized its members and sorted out the good from the bad. But it doesn't. Instead, it's got the **Valdez Bed and Breakfast Association** (www.valdez bnb.com), which isn't a group so much as a very basic website with links to 14 of Valdez's 21 B&Bs. It's true that all members have to comply with the standards of the Bed & Breakfast Association of Alaska, but since those standards aren't especially rigorous—all a B&B needs to do to comply is fill out a *self-inspection* form every 3 years—don't put too much weight on that. Still, the Valdez Bed and Breakfast Association is a fine starting point for researching the town's B&B offerings.

You'll find the remainder of Valdez B&Bs (and some already listed on the B&B Association sites) on the website of the **Valdez Convention and Visitors Bureau** (☎ 907/835-2984; www.valdezalaska.org; see p. 85 for more info). To get the full picture, check both. One helpful thing about the visitor bureau is that

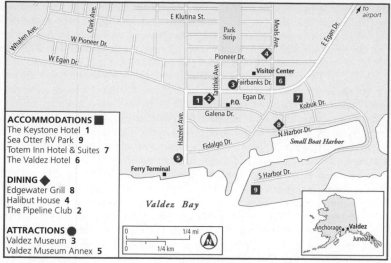

ACCOMMODATIONS ■
The Keystone Hotel **1**
Sea Otter RV Park **9**
Totem Inn Hotel & Suites **7**
The Valdez Hotel **6**

DINING ◆
Edgewater Grill **8**
Halibut House **4**
The Pipeline Club **2**

ATTRACTIONS ●
Valdez Museum **3**
Valdez Museum Annex **5**

an actual person answers the phone to field general questions (an advantage over the website-only Bed and Breakfast association). If you show up without reservations, head directly to the visitor bureau, which keeps a dry erase board in front of its offices listing the vacancies of its member B&Bs. Next to the dry erase board is a telephone hotline that rings directly to the members of the Valdez Bed and Breakfast Association. Both the hotline and the dry erase board are located outside the building, so you can use them even after hours.

If this all sounds like too much homework for you, consider one of the following two excellent Valdez B&Bs. These are my faves in town, and you'll find them listed on both the visitor bureau and the B&B association websites:

$$–$$$ Lake House B&B ★★★ (Mile 6, Richardson Hwy.; ☎ 907/835-4752; www.geocities.com/lakehousevaldez; MC, V) is grandly situated on a high hill, with a long, blue lake below it and 3,000-foot Chugach Mountain peaks above it—an unbeatable view. It's a boxy, two-story home plastered with balconies that take full advantage of the vistas. Five of the rooms (four with queens, and one with a king and a twin) go for $120, and a two-bedroom suite usually runs $135. All are furnished with comely antiques, have private baths, and feature colorful quilts on the beds. One special perk is that each room is supplied with a complimentary bottle of Lake House wine, which the owner (Dan Devans) makes himself. Common areas are also packed with antiques, Alaskana, and quirky local artifacts, like a jukebox in the dark downstairs living room and a player piano in the sunny upstairs library (feel free to play either of them). The Coast Guard officers in charge of cleaning up the *Exxon Valdez* mess were quartered here in 1989, and the house has another oil spill connection too—Devans was mayor of Valdez at the time of the accident. Want an insider's take on it all? Stay here.

$$–$$$$ Most of the buildings at the original Valdez town site were destroyed by the 1964 earthquake, but a few survived to be jacked up and hauled off to safer locations. One two-story home was taken to a peaceful spot along a brook between the old town site and the new one, and it's now the **Brookside Inn B&B** ✦✦ (1465 Richardson Hwy.; ☎ 866/316-9130 or 907/835-9130; www.brooksideinn. com; MC, V). The owners live in a small addition, giving guests the run of the older part of the house. It's just as nice as the Lake House B&B, but a bit closer to town. Four bedrooms upstairs, which go for $115 each, have various configurations of queens or twin beds, all of which have firm mattresses and extremely pretty bedspreads, linens, and pillows. All have private baths. Downstairs are several sitting rooms and a bright sun room, where breakfasts of salmon omelets, waffles, and quiche are served. The owners did a great job of restoring the interior's early-20th-century character while embracing the cleaner lines and less cluttered look of the 21st century. Two suites, in a newer building next door, go for $140 and $160 and have more room but not the historic appeal of the rooms in the main house. In the backyard pavilion are a hot tub, strawberry bushes (you can actually pick the berries), and a shallow brook where you can watch salmon reproduce. Bears sometimes come by for the easy pickings and, helpfully, mash down the vegetation by the gravel bars so—when you come by later—you can usually find an easy spot to stand and watch the fish.

Hotels

$–$$ Among Valdez's hotels, the most affordable, the most unusual, and in one sense the most Alaskan is **The Keystone Hotel** 🧒 (401 W. Egan Dr.; ☎ 907/835-3851; www.keystonehotel.com; AE, MC, V). I say it's the most Alaskan because it's constructed from ATCO structures, the Alaska oil industry's prefabricated, modular building unit of choice. Virtually all of the old Trans-Alaska Pipeline construction camps, and many of the dwellings at the oil fields of Prudhoe Bay today, consist of these units. They are oblong, Arctic-proofed structures that can be arranged like Legos in countless configurations. In the case of the Keystone Hotel, they're stacked two high and laid out like an "H." Exxon Corporation built the place as the command center for its clean-up effort following the *Exxon Valdez* oil spill. Most of the 100 tiny rooms have one double and one single bed, and a full bath. They start at $95 per night for doubles. Big families can get a "king room," which is exactly twice the size of a standard room. Kings have one king bed, two double beds, and two full baths, for $115. If you're a member of AAA, flash that card as it will net you a 10% discount; children share their parent's room for free. The Keystone isn't for everyone, but if you want a true taste of a bona fide contemporary Alaskan lodging—at a really good price for the area—the Keystone's got it.

$$–$$$$ The Keystone may be regionally authentic, but the **Totem Inn Hotel & Suites** ✦✦ (144 Egan Dr.; ☎ 907/834-4443; www.toteminn.com; AE, DISC, MC, V) has a moose head over the mantle place, darn it. Hence it offers a more classically Alaskan ambience, along with its cushier rooms and steep Web discounts that nearly match the Keystone's rates. With its plank siding and twin totem poles planted on the roof like goal posts, the main building looks like a roadside lodge. The front desk doubles as the register for the in-house restaurant, which itself doubles as a natural history museum of sorts, where you'll see stuffed wildlife, carved walrus tusks, and fossilized woolly mammoth parts. A wing attached to the restaurant has several dark, standard motel rooms, with queen-size beds, burgundy carpeting, and cherrywood furnishings. Better than the motel rooms are the 10 little cabins. Despite the blandness of their weathered plywood exteriors, they're cozy, bright, and comfortable inside, with queen beds, pull-out sofas, and tiny kitchenettes (oddly, it's an extra $10 if you want use of the dishes). The rack rate for either the rooms or the cabins is $129, but book on the Totem Inn's website (or on a discounter site such as cheaptickets.com) and the rate drops to $109. In what appear to be a pair of neighboring apartment buildings, the inn has several roomy, modern suites, with full kitchens and one- or two-bedroom units, great for families. The rack rate is $179, but again there's a steep discount if you book online—just $149.

$$$–$$$$ The Valdez Hotel 🧒 (100 Meals Ave.; ☎ 800/478-4445 or 907/835-4445; www.aspenhotelsak.com; AE, DISC, MC, V) has the pine-air freshened ambience of a national chain hotel, but it's actually part of a homegrown Alaskan hotel chain. Its spacious rooms, swimming pool (the only one in Valdez), and occasional discounts make it worth a look, especially if you've got kids in tow. The little ones will have lots of company here—the Valdez is typically frequented by incoming Coast Guardsmen and their families who've yet to find housing, as well as by oil company employees and travelers on package tours. Because of that, rates are a moving target, depending on which tour's in town; still, the average price for a double occupancy room hovers around $159, while a family suite that sleeps up to six is $170. E-mail discounts sent to return guests drop prices even more (to as low as $99 for a standard room). Sign up for these bulletins at the website and see what happens; or check one of the various hotel discounter sites before booking, as they sometimes drop rates to as little as $139 in summer.

Camping

In town there are $12 tent sites on a grassy patch near the boat harbor breakwater at **Sea Otter RV Park** (☎ 907/835-2787). High up in the mountains 24 miles out of town on the Richardson Highway is a more spectacular spot, the **Blueberry Lake Campground.** Campsites cost $12, and they're first come, first serve. This spot is above the tree line, and both the views and hiking there are outstanding.

DINING FOR ALL TASTES

The restaurants in Valdez tend to be simple, affordable, and genuinely interested in good service. It's hard to go wrong there. There's a lot of variety, but these are my favorites:

$ The halibut is caught locally, batter-fried, and decadently delicious at **Halibut House** (208 Meals Ave.; ☎ 907/835-2788; daily 11am–10pm; MC, V). Expect a no-frills, fish-and-chips shack staffed by local high-schoolers (and well-stocked with a fab do-it-yourself condiment bar). A basket loaded with four generous pieces of fish and a crispy gaggle of fries costs just $9.95. But a half order ($6.50) will be filling enough for most. This is a good breakfast spot, too, but sadly, there's no fish on the morning menu.

$$-$$$ Halibut's also the thing to get at the **Edgewater Grill** ★★ (107 N. Harbor Dr.; ☎ 907/835-3212; daily 6am–10pm; MC, V), though here it's a bit more healthily prepared—fish is usually grilled and served over a mess of wilted spinach or other greens. All entrees are simply constructed and generously portioned (carnivores may want to go for the giant pork chop, sautéed with garlic, mushrooms, and sauerkraut, for $15). The dining room is country-cute, with matching blue-checked tablecloths and curtains, but if it's sunny, request a table on the big outdoor deck so that you can watch the seagulls and sailboats glide by.

$$$-$$$$ For some reason, steak and crude oil seem to go hand-in-hand, or perhaps hand-in-hoof (is it because they have Texas in common?). A favorite haunt of the oilmen working in Valdez, **The Pipeline Club** ★ (112 Egan Dr.; ☎ 907/835-4444; Sun–Thurs 5:30–11pm, Fri–Sat 5:30pm–midnight; AE, DISC, MC, V) is one of the most celebrated steakhouses in the state and the town's major nightlife destination after hours. New York strips ($26), butterflied filet mignon with béarnaise ($25), and other bloody pleasures are given due respect, though you can also get quality fish like shrimp scampi ($25) and grilled Copper River red salmon ($31). (Or if you're a real killjoy, get the spaghetti, for $13). The Pipeline Club is divided between a dark, smoky dining room and a dark, smoky bar (which remains open until 4am daily in summer, 2am the rest of the year). The bar lives in infamy as the watering hole where Joseph Hazelwood, captain of the *Exxon Valdez,* downed vodka before then setting off on the ill-fated voyage that spilled 11 million gallons of crude oil into the sea.

WHY YOU'RE HERE: THE TOP SIGHTS & ATTRACTIONS

Most of Valdez's main attractions—the mountains, the glaciers, the wildlife—are out of town. In town, there's the **Valdez Museum** (217 Egan Dr.; ☎ 907/835-2764; www.valdezmuseum.org; $5 adults, $4.50 seniors, $4 children 14–17; children 13 and under free; Memorial Day–Labor Day daily 9am–6pm; rest of year Mon–Fri 1–5pm, Sat noon–4pm), which, at first glance, looks like the kind of small community museum you can breeze through. Once you get inside, it's another story. The exhibits on the destruction wrought by the 1964 Good Friday earthquake and the environmental catastrophe caused by the *Exxon Valdez* oil spill (you can actually view a jagged chunk of the ship's punctured hull) will suck you in for longer than you might have thought. And there's plenty more to get hung up on, including a re-created 19th-century saloon with an ornate bar salvaged from the original town site and an informative exhibit on glaciers, which usually features a little chunk of the Columbia Glacier in a cooler. If you somehow get through the museum with extra time on your hands, there's even an annex where you can study a scale model of the original Valdez before it was destroyed.

THE OTHER VALDEZ

Do like a Valdez local in search of free fun and check the summer happenings at the **Valdez Museum** (217 Egan Dr.; ☎ 907/835-2764; www.valdezmuseum.org; see above for pricing and hour info). The flagship program is a lecture series that pretty loosely interprets the meaning of lecturing. Past "lectures" have included performances by Native dancers, Russian folk dancers, Irish musicians, and the Anchorage Opera (scaled down), as well as actual talks by mountaineers, gold rush historians, and bear safety experts. Lectures are usually held on Thursdays at 7pm at the museum. Other museum-sponsored programs come and go. A lunch-hour drum circle on the museum lawn has been one of the more popular, especially among local kids and office workers (drums are provided and all are welcome to bang away on them). But if the drum master (who brings all the drums, clackers, shakers, cymbals, and other noise makers) decides to move on with his life, the program will go with him. Something will replace it, though. Check with the museum for the latest goings-on during your visit.

ACTIVE VALDEZ

With glaciers, rivers, fjords, and 5,000-foot Chugach Mountain peaks all around, homely little Valdez has spectacular hiking terrain. Both easy and challenging trails start right from town. Here's a sampling that includes a quickie, an overnighter, and an agreeable day trip. For free maps and information about all Valdez area hikes, stop at the Valdez Convention and Visitors Bureau (p. 85).

- ◆ **Dock Point Trail,** a .75-mile loop on a peninsula by the small boat harbor, is more of a nature walk than a bona fide hike. Still, it's a lovely walk, through spruce trees, dogwoods, and wildflowers, and right in the thick of Valdez's port. The dominant form of wildlife here is squirrels.
- ◆ **Shoup Glacier Trail** ★★ is a far more ambitious jaunt, beginning at the edge of town and running 12 miles along Valdez Bay to a tidewater glacier. Really gung-ho hikers go out and back in a day, but why rush it? Spend a night or two camping at the end of the trail, or try your luck at reserving the public use cabin there (p. 102). The trail traverses spruce and alder forest, grasslands, wetlands, and fields of wildflowers. It climbs up and down steep terrain, passes a waterfall (an excellent place to cool off), and finally comes out at Shoup Glacier. Stop at the Valdez Convention and Visitors Bureau for the low down on the campgrounds.
- ◆ **Solomon Gulch Trail** ★ is a 3.8-mile round-trip hike with nifty views and a spot to take a mountain dip. It starts across from the fish hatchery on Dayville Road, climbs steeply through a coastal spruce forest, parallels the Trans-Alaska Pipeline for a while, crosses beneath to surplus sections of the pipeline used to carry water to a power plant, then comes out at Solomon Lake, where locals sunbathe and swim. It's a worthy day hike, but with the hardware around, and with part of the trail following a gravel road, you may not feel like you're deep in the wild.

ATTENTION, SHOPPERS!

Valdez is not the place to load up on Alaskan souvenirs. If you're determined, though, your best bet is to check the small gift shop in the restaurant lobby of the **Totem Inn Hotel & Suites** (144 Egan Dr.; ☎ 907/834-4443; www.toteminn.com), which has a small stock of Native handicrafts.

On the other hand, Valdez has lots of competitively priced places to outfit yourself before setting out on a camping trip or overnight kayaking voyage. My favorite of the outdoor stores is **The Prospector** ★ (11 Galena St.; ☎ 907/835-3858; www.prospectoroutfitters.com), which has colossal moose and bear heads on the walls, every camping essential you can imagine, boots piled up to the ceiling, and racks of outdoor wear that span a century—everything from modern synthetic fleece to 19th-century tin cloth. Before entering The Prospector, I'd never seen actual tin cloth before, though I'd seen it worn in countless old photographs of railroad laborers and hard-rock miners. Impregnated with a paraffin-based oil finish, a tin cloth garment really is as stiff as tin until it's broken in, and then it lasts for decades. While dressing yourself in a pair of Hal Filson tin cloth pants ($110) with a matching tin cloth coat ($162) and original tin cloth hat ($35) may be a deeper step into Alaska than you care to take, it's good to know where to find the authentic stuff if you want it.

GET OUT OF TOWN

The mountains surrounding Valdez are streaked with impressive glaciers. So heading to the hills to look at some of these slow-moving rivers of ice should be high on your to-do list. You have plenty to choose from, including some you can't get to without a tour boat, some you can hike or kayak to, and one drive-up glacier along the highway to town.

The area's least expensive glacier expeditions, in that you don't have to take a pricey tour to view the ice, are the **Worthington Glacier** ★ (Mile 28, Richardson Hwy.; free admission) and **Shoup Glacier** (in Shoup Bay Marine Park). The first is a drive-up option, isolated high up in the Chugach Mountains, at the mountain's crest, 28 miles from town (park in the paved lot along the road and walk down the short path behind the little visitor center). Worthington isn't especially big or spectacular, but you can get a good close look at it, unlike a lot of the area's other glaciers (which you need to keep a safe distance from, so you don't get crushed by a calving iceberg). In fact, you can hike on Worthington Glacier, but unless you've got the experience and the necessary gear, don't try it without a guide, lest you end up at the bottom of a deep crevasse. Instead, sign up for a glacier trek with a Valdez outfit called **Pangaea** (☎ 800/660-9637 or 907/835-8442; www.alaska summer.com), which leads half-day trips onto the ice for $99 per person, ice axe and crampons included. For an additional $20, you can spend the rest of the day learning the basics of ice climbing on Worthington's face. There are some other glaciers you can hike to from spur roads along the Richardson Highway, and the **Valdez Convention and Visitors Bureau** (p. 85) has free maps showing their location.

Shoup Glacier is accessible by foot (it's a 12-mile hike from Valdez; see p. 91), sea kayak, or water taxi (about $35 per person). Since icebergs regularly crack off it and drop into the lagoon, you won't be able to get as close as you can at Worthington, but it's another affordable option (there are even three public use cabins nearby with lodgings; see p. 373 for more on how to rent those).

Though Worthington and Shoup are worthy introductory glaciers for those who've never seen a glacier, and great bargains—since you can visit both of them on your own at no charge—really, they're just oversize ice cube trays in comparison to Prince William Sound's most spectacular glacier, **Columbia Glacier** ★★★. At 400,000 square miles—an area nearly the size of Los Angeles—Columbia is the largest tidewater glacier in Alaska. Its face is a breathtaking 3 miles wide, and it moves at the rapid (by glacial standards) rate of 4 feet a day. With that much face and speed, it's no wonder the Columbia is also one of the most active glaciers in the state. Giant slabs of ice—some as big as Wal-Marts—crack from its face and crash into Columbia Bay, sending waves coursing through the ice floe and clogging the waters for several miles in front of it.

Unlike the Shoup or the Worthington glaciers, you'll need some help to get out to the Columbia Glacier. Two Valdez area companies offer tours. One is slightly cheaper for adults, the other is significantly less expensive for families with kids under 12. Both make side trips along the way to a sea lion rookery and puffin nesting area at Glacier Island. With either of them, you have an equally good chance (though no guarantee) of encountering humpback whales, orcas, and other large marine mammals while en route. But if I had to pick one, I'd pick **Lu-Lu Belle Glacier Wildlife Cruises** ★★★ (☎ 800/411-0090; www.lulubelletours. com; $95 per person) simply because the on-board experience is superior. The trusty old *Lu-Lu Belle* is a 75-foot motor yacht outfitted with oriental rugs and teak and mahogany trim. The owner, a veteran seaman and natural showman, pilots the boat and narrates the tour with flair. Since trips last anywhere from 5 to 7 hours, the captain has plenty of flexibility to indulge in whale-watching along the way, steering his craft towards his sightseeing prey like the experienced Ahab he is. The crew members even bake muffins and brownies while underway, which you can buy at the snack bar, along with bowls of clam chowder. *Money-saving tip:* Pay for your tickets with cash or travelers or personal checks for a $5 discount.

The better deal for families with young kids is **Stan Stephens Cruises** ★★ (☎ 866/867-1297; www.stanstephenscruises.com; $95 adults, $48 children 12 and under), which charges the little ones half the adult rate (and there's also no extra charge for the chowder). Its vessels are less yachty and its captains not as charismatic, but other than that, there's not much difference between it and Lu-Lu Belle Glacier Wildlife Cruises. Stephens also offers a two-glacier tour, for $130, which visits the Columbia Glacier and the even more remote **Meares Glacier,** the only glacier in the sound that's still advancing (no one's sure why). Meares is less active than Columbia, so the tour boat can get up closer to it (ice-choked waters keep vessels a good 3 miles from the face of the Columbia Glacier).

A more adrenaline-pumping yet intimate way to see Columbia Glacier is to do so while bobbing among its icebergs and harbor seals in a kayak. This is only recommended for experienced sea kayakers, of course, who can easily rent a boat through one of two harborfront outfitters, **Anadyr Adventures** (225 N. Harbor Dr.; ☎ 800/865-2925 or 907/835-2814; www.anadyradventures.com; $45 single, $65 double) or **Pangaea** (☎ 800/660-9637 or 907/835-8442; www.alaskasummer. com; call for rates). The water taxi ride to Columbia for you and your kayak costs about $110 per person, each way.

Both Anadyr Adventures and Pangaea offer guided kayaking tours of Columbia Glacier, as well as **kayaking/camping trips.** Go with Anadyr, as it has more experienced guides and has been involved in fewer mishaps over the years. It charges $199 for a full-day guided kayaking tour of Columbia Glacier, which includes paddling instructions and training in iceberg safety (beautiful blue icebergs the size of brownstone apartments look harmless enough—until they split in half and do 180-degree *el rollos* beside your boat). In the course of the tour, it ferries participants out to the ice, dropping them and a guide into the water for 6 hours of paddling through the ice floe and hiking through the rainforest and along wild beaches. Hot beverages and snacks (but not lunch) are included in the cost.

WHITTIER

Whittier is more than just the weirdest town in Alaska. It may just be the weirdest town anywhere. Since it was created during World War II as a secret military base, the town has very limited access to the outside world via land. Entry is limited to a single-lane, 2½-mile-long tunnel bored through the Chugach Mountains. Incoming and outgoing traffic take turns using the tunnel, and both yield when the train comes through. Most of the town—including city hall, the bakery, the grocery store, a church, and 80% of the population of 290 (along with all of its small town gossip and intrigue)—is contained beneath the roof of a single 15-story apartment building. People go to Whittier because it's the Prince William Sound entry point that's closest to Anchorage. Most people pass through and do not linger.

A BRIEF HISTORY

During World War II, the U.S. Army needed an ice-free, year-round port close to Anchorage but well-hidden from the Japanese. It picked a narrow fjord on Prince William Sound obscured by clouds most of the time and hemmed in tightly by mountains on three sides. Docks were built, a tunnel was blasted through the mountains, rail tracks were laid connecting the base to Anchorage, and Whittier as we know it today was created. The town became a key staging area for shipping troops and material to the Aleutian Islands, where the only ground battles of the war on U.S. soil took place.

After the Army pulled out of Whittier in 1960, the town eked out an existence as a tiny fishing port. When the tunnel was modified so that cars could use it in the 1990s, Whittier became more accessible. Today, many Anchorage residents keep boats there, cruise ships and the state ferry pick up and drop off passengers, and tourists rent kayaks or go on glacier cruises on the sound from it.

LAY OF THE LAND

The town of Whittier is dominated by its harbor, around which are boatyards, a train yard, a fuel tank farm, and a handful of buildings. Along the waterfront are a few dozen seasonal restaurants, shops, charter operators, and other businesses. A small green yurt serves as the **Forest Service Backcountry Information Center** (Glacier Ranger District; ☎ 907/783-3242); head here for maps and advice on hiking and camping around Prince William Sound. Whittier has no official visitor center, but the rangers in the yurt can field most Whittier questions.

Whittier has a 3% sales tax from April 1 through September 30.

GETTING TO & AROUND WHITTIER
By Car

It's about a 2½-hour drive from Anchorage to Whittier, first along the Seward Highway, then, at mile 78.9, on the Portage Glacier Road. Actually, it's a 2½-hour drive from Anchorage to the Whittier tunnel, where you might have to wait more than an hour if you don't time it right. The tunnel has just one lane, not to mention a train passing through twice a day, so you have to wait your turn. Check the schedule ahead of time at the tunnel's website, **www.dot.state.ak.us**, and click "Travel Information" or call the tunnel hot line (☎ 877/611-2586 or 907/566-2244). You can also tune your radio to 1610AM (if you're trying to get into

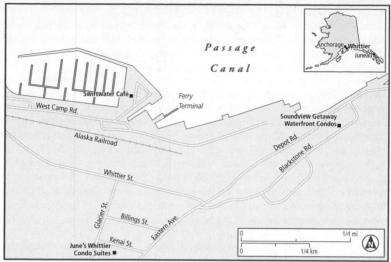

Whittier) and 530AM (if you're trying to get out) to hear traffic updates. In the summer, the tunnel opens at 5:30am and closes at 11:15pm. During peak times, especially weekends in the early evening, there may be more cars lined up than can get through the tunnel in one opening. Avoid rush hour if you can. The toll is $12 for cars to get into Whittier, but nothing to get out. Once you get to Whittier, there's a $10 fee to park.

By Train or Motorcoach

The **Alaska Railroad** runs from Anchorage to Whittier and back once a day. The round-trip fare is $72, or $36 for children. The large glacier tour boat companies time their trips to sync up with the train schedule, and all of them sell packages that include train or bus transportation between Whittier and Anchorage. The buses follow essentially the same route as the train, but cost around $15 to $20 less per passenger. If there are more than two of you traveling, it will be cheaper to rent a car in Anchorage (p. 32) for the day than to take either the bus or the train.

By Ferry

The **Alaska Marine Highway System** (☎ 800/642-0066; www.ferryalaska.com) connects Whittier, Valdez, and Cordova. The trip to Valdez takes about 3 hours on the new fast ferry, and costs $86 per adult, $43 for those age 6 to 11, and is free for those 5 and under. The older, slower ferry takes almost 7 hours to make the trip (for the same price). Take the fast ferry if you must to save time, a more leisurely trip across the sound offers better opportunities to spot wildlife. Bringing a small car on the ferry costs an additional $102, and reservations for that are a must.

ACCOMMODATIONS, BOTH STANDARD & NOT

To stay in Whittier is to experience, if just for a night, what it's like to be a Whittiot, as some Whittier residents refer to themselves. Except for the handful of souls living aboard their boats, the townsfolk all reside in one of two apartment buildings. And both of them have units that rent by the night.

$$–$$$ Twenty percent of Whittier lives in old Bachelor's Officers Quarters, a long, two-story apartment complex built during World War II. Four of the units have been set aside for visitors, and are rented through **Soundview Getaway Waterfront Condos** (☎ 800/515-2358 or 907/472-2358; www.soundviewalaska. com; MC, V). Efficiencies go for $120, and one-bedrooms go for $145. All have kitchens, some with original metal cabinetry and other fixtures from the war, and all are clean and spiffy—like dorm rooms at the beginning of the semester. The two harborside rooms look out on the barge dock, where gigantic forklifts move shipping containers about, and, every so often, tip over. This noisy activity can either be annoying or amusing, depending on your point of view.

$$$ The other 80% of the city lives in Begich Towers, a 15-story apartment building erected after the 1964 earthquake damaged the existing apartment complex beyond repair. It's a city within a city. Not only does it contain the city offices, the post office, the police station, a second-hand store, a bakery, a Western Union agent, and a notary public, it also boasts eleven condominium units on the top two floors that are rented out by the night through **June's Whittier Condo Suites** (☎ 888/472-2396 or 907/472-2396; www.breadnbuttercharters.com; AE, MC, V). Each unit has a different owner, so they're all decorated differently. But I have to say, each is surprisingly comfortable, considering the low expectations you have walking into the building, which features the cinder block walls and narrow hallways of a public housing project. The mountain-side units for $145 look out on a little waterfall (as well as junk cars and long-forgotten marine hardware), and the harborside rooms for $155 have views of the fjord, the berths of the fishing fleet, the gritty railroad yard, and a reindeer pen.

DINING FOR ALL TASTES

$$ Fish and chips is the way to go for a meal in Whittier, and a dark dockside eatery called **Swiftwater Café** (8 Triangle Way; ☎ 907/472-2550; April 28–Sept Sun–Thurs 11:30am–9pm, Fri and Sat 11:30am–10pm; MC, V) is the place to get it (at just $11 for a basket). The french fries themselves are nothing out of the ordinary, but the fish—halibut all the time and specials such as red snapper and rock fish, depending on what's biting—is all locally caught and super-fresh. The pasta salad ($3) makes for a tasty side dish, the Manhattan-style clam chowder ($5) is loaded with clams, and the walls are adorned with netting and a gallery of shipwreck photos—exactly the way a weathered fish-and-chips shack in a gritty little sea port should be.

GET OUT OF TOWN

Prince William Sound has the state's largest collection of tidewater glaciers, the most exciting kind of glacier to see. They're the ones that reach sea level and, with mighty cracks and booms, calve icebergs into the ocean. Three large tour boat operators, with offices in Anchorage but boats in Whittier, offer the most afford-able option for seeing the sound. They are Native-owned **Prince William Sound Cruises & Tours** (509 W. 4th Ave., Anchorage; ☎ 877/777-4054; www.princewilliam sound.com), **Major Marine Tours** (411 W. 4th Ave., Anchorage; ☎ 800/764-7300 or 907/274-7300; www.majormarine.com), and **Phillips' Cruises and Tours** (519 W. 4th Ave., Anchorage; ☎ 800/544-0529 or 907/276-8023; www.26glaciers. com) and there are major differences between the three. Prince William's most popular tour parks in front of two massive glaciers in Blackstone Bay and lingers quietly in the ice floe as passengers ooh and ahh over the sea lions and the crash of icebergs into the bay. Its 4-hour glacier tour is $99 for adults ($50 for kids 11 and younger), including a tasty hot crab cake lunch (its 6-hr. jaunt costs $129 adults, $65 kids, and includes a tour of a salmon hatchery). Book either of these tours online, and you'll get a free pass to the **Alaska Wildlife Conservation Center** (p. 61), which you pass on your way to Whittier.

Major Marine tours also charges $99 ($49 for kids), but its tours last 5 hours, include visits to 10 glaciers, and boast the advantage of having a uniformed National Park Ranger aboard to narrate and answer questions (both competitors use crew members to narrate). Of the three big tour operators, Major Marine puts the most emphasis on its food, a salmon and prime rib lunch in this case. Unfortunately, lunch costs an extra $15 ($7 kids), though you're free to save some bucks by packing your own.

The most gimmicky of the big boat glacier tours is Phillips' Cruises and Tours, which offers a 4½-hour, whirlwind tour of 26 named glaciers for $129 adults ($79 kids). It uses a fast, comfortable, triple-decker catamaran that whizzes along at 28 knots as a crew member counts off the glaciers you come to. The first two decks are enclosed and heated, and the top deck is wide open. Choose this tour if patience isn't one of your virtues and you think you might get bored floating around in front of one glacier waiting for it to calve. Pack your own lunch, or you'll be stuck at the over-priced snack bar.

The big boat glacier tours are definitely group experiences, with more than 100 passengers packed aboard each vessel. A far more intimate, if expensive, way to get acquainted with the local tidewater glaciers is from the seat of a sea kayak. **Alaska Sea-Kayakers** (offices at each end of Whittier Harbor; ☎ 877/472-2534 or 907/472-2534; www.alaskaseakayakers.com) offers 1-day kayaking tours of the glaciers at Blackstone Bay for $300 per person, with a four-person minimum. **Prince William Sound Sea Kayak Center** (☎ 977/472-2452 or 907/472-2452; www.pwskayakcenter.com) does similar tours, but with a price structure that drops as the number of paddlers rises. Rates range from $290 per person for four pad-dlers, to $210 per person for six paddlers. Both companies also offer classes, and the Sea Kayak Center rents boats to experienced paddlers ($50 per day for a sin-gle seater, $80 for a double).

CORDOVA

Cordova isn't exactly The Town that Time Forgot. It's more like The Town that Time Just Hasn't Spent a Lot of Time Thinking About. This is largely because there's no road to Cordova, so Cordova's pre–Automobile Age scale and charm has been pretty well preserved. It's a lovely fishing village way, way off the beaten tourist path. It's also as thoroughly old-fashioned of a town as you'll find, a place where people make honest livings off the sea or in the cannery, where festivals are thrown to celebrate shore birds and glacial worms, and where total strangers are welcomed warmly. Anglers are drawn to Cordova for the salmon fishing, and birders are drawn by the millions of waterfowl that make pit stops at the Copper River Delta, the largest contiguous wetlands on the Pacific Coast of North America. Other attractions include the Childs Glacier and the Bridge to Nowhere.

A BRIEF HISTORY

Cordova originated as a Native village, inhabited by Eyak Indians, and, today, the Eyak culture retains a strong presence in town. (You can meet some Eyaks and learn about their culture on the harborfront—at the Llanka Cultural Center, p. 104.) In 1884, a group of prospectors set up camp near Cordova and used it as a base for exploring the area. Nobody found any gold in the area, but copper was discovered far up the Copper River, in Kennicott. Cordova remained a sleepy little backwater until 1906, when the construction of the Copper River Kennicott Railroad got underway. Then Cordova boomed as the port from which the copper ore was shipped to the state of Washington for smelting. When the Kennicott mines closed in 1938, the railroad shut down too, and fishing became Cordova's economic mainstay. Cordova's fishermen are famous for netting the Copper River red salmon, which chefs from New York to Tokyo pay top dollar for when it runs in the spring.

LAY OF THE LAND

Cordova is scenically situated on the southwest edge of Prince William Sound, where the jagged Chugach Mountains meet placid Orca Inlet. The town has a population of 3,500 and a small boat harbor with 850 slips. First Street, 2 blocks uphill from the small boat harbor, is the main commercial area. Towering over the town are the jagged peaks of the Chugach Mountains (including Mount Eyak, which offers winter skiing and summer hiking). Just east of town is Lake Eyak, and east of that is the **Copper River Delta,** the largest contiguous wetlands on the Pacific Coast of North America. The **Copper River Highway** crosses the delta, following the old railroad route that once led to copper mines at Kennicott. The highway eventually leads to a spectacular glacier, the **Childs Glacier,** then dead ends after it crosses an old railroad bridge, known as **The Million Dollar Bridge,** aka **The Bridge to Nowhere.**

The 700,000-acre delta supports the largest population of migratory shorebirds in the Western Hemisphere, who fly in to rest and feast on fly larvae, tiny clams and fish, and a smorgasbord of other avian delights. Bird-watchers flock there themselves during the peak season, which is late April to early May. Not so coincidentally, that's also when Cordova throws its 4-day Copper River Delta Shorebird Festival (see p. 363 in "The Essentials of Planning" for info).

Cordova has a 6% sales tax, and an additional 6% tax on car rentals and accommodations.

The **Cordova Chamber of Commerce Visitor Center** (☎ 907/424-7260; www.cordovachamber.com) is at 404 1st St., north of Council Avenue (P.O. Box 99, Cordova, AK 99574). They're open Monday to Saturday 10am to 3pm in summer, the rest of the year Monday to Saturday noon to 4pm. Besides the usual information,

The Delta from Up High

An aerial view of the Copper River Delta is like a microscopic view of a beating heart. From up high, you see thousands of watery concourses snake through miles of mud and glacial silt like capillaries through blood-rich soft tissue. It's an awe-inspiring sight. If you come or go from Cordova by air on a clear day, you'll see it for yourself from the airplane window. The big satellite photos on display at the **Chugach National Forest Cordova Ranger District** (612 2nd St.; ☎ 907/424-7661; daily 8am–5pm) are nearly as impressive, and a lot cheaper to view. The highlight is the giant satellite photo of Prince William Sound that has been turned into a relief map and stuck up on the wall. You can run your fingers over it as you study how all of the glaciers, wetlands, islands, and little towns fit together. Besides the Ranger District's maps and photos, you'll find information on hiking, camping, fishing, and hunting, along with friendly biologists and forest service officials who seem eager to talk. "It's not that we're friendly," one told me. "We're just bored."

the center has a 60-minute recorded walking tour that you can listen to as it guides you around town.

GETTING TO & AROUND CORDOVA

You can get to Cordova by ferry or by air. The most fun, leisurely, and cheapest way to go is by ferry. The fare from either Whittier or Valdez to Cordova is $86 (half price for children under 12). From Whittier it takes 7 hours, and from Valdez it takes about 5 hours to get to Cordova on the older, slower ferry. A newer fast-ferry cuts the travel times in half, and costs the same. Why might you want to choose the slow boat? You'll see more wildlife along the way. The fast ferry is just too darned fast to get a good look at any whales, seals, or other wildlife you encounter along the way.

Guided tours are available of the Copper River Delta, but it's really an area best explored at your own pace and in your own vehicle. In most cases, it's cheaper to rent a car in Cordova than to rent a car elsewhere and take it to Cordova on the ferry. For a small car, the cost is a whopping $73 each way for ferry passage from Whittier, and $56 from Valdez. Compare that carefully with the 1-day rental cost at **Chinook Auto Rentals** (in the red caboose at Mudhole Smith Airport; ☎ 907/424-5279)—economy cars are $55 a day, and big Ford Expeditions are $85 a day. Keep in mind that state and local taxes up the cost by a walloping 26%.

If you choose to fly, you'll probably find the best fares with **Alaska Airlines** (☎ 800/426-0333; www.alaskaair.com), which has round-trip fares starting at around $270 from Anchorage. Occasionally you'll match that rate with **ERA Aviation** (☎ 800/866-8394; www.flyera.com), which flies smaller planes between Anchorage and Cordova, but on most flights it's a good $30 to $60 more expensive.

ACCOMMODATIONS, BOTH STANDARD & NOT

Cordova has a fine assortment of reasonably priced and authentically Alaskan places to stay. Vacancies rise and fall with the salmon fishing and bird-watching seasons. Rooms are tightest from the end of August through September, when the silver salmon spawn. The **Cordova Chamber of Commerce Visitor Center** (p. 98) keeps a list of just about all local lodging options, if the ones below are fully booked when you call.

Hotels

$ Of all the interesting places to stay in Cordova, there is one that I will recommend only to the most adventuresome and open-minded of budget travelers. To appreciate **The Alaskan Hotel** ★ (600 1st St.; ☎ 907/424-3299; desk open noon–midnight; DISC, MC, V) you must firmly embrace the notion that sometimes you have to step out of your comfort zone to truly experience Alaska. In this case, that means stepping into the dark, creaky hallways of a hulking three-story hotel built in 1908. This is no gussied-up historic site quaintly recalling the days of yore, but rather a living relic where people have been staying since Cordova's boomtown birth. The century it has stood on its downtown corner overlooking the harbor hasn't been kind, and without the help of the unpainted 2-by-12s shoring up its old timber framing, it probably would have blown over in a gale by now. The 10 rooms have high ceilings, bare light bulbs, exposed plumbing, and a few scuffed up furnishings, including firm, well-worn mattresses on the queen and twin beds. A big, noisy fishermen's bar (with shuffleboard and darts) takes up most of the ground floor. A little liquor store, which serves as the hotel's front desk, takes up the rest. If the Alaskan Hotel were in a big city, it would be filled with junkies and hookers. Here it's filled with people looking for work on the docks and backpackers looking for hot showers. It's seedy, but safe. And it's the best deal in Cordova—the rooms with shared baths (his-and-hers water closets, with a separate room where you can shower in a claw-foot tub) go for just $44. Slightly larger rooms with private baths go for $66.

$ A railroad magnate built the house that's now **The Northern Nights Inn** ★★★ 🧒 (500 3rd St.; ☎ 907/424-5356; www.northernnightsinn.com; AE, DISC, MC, V) in 1910, and it was once the finest residence in town. It had fallen into disrepair by the time the current owner discovered it while working as a meter reader for the electric company. To her surprise, the low-ball offer she made on the house was accepted. She's been fixing the place up nicely ever since. The outside still needs a little work, but the inside is drop dead gorgeous. Perhaps it's that odd disparity that keeps the prices low: As I write this, $65 buys you a night in the bright, third-floor sleeping room with turn-of-the-20th-century antiques, a plush queen bed, a private bath, and a harbor view. For $90, you score a large suite with two queen beds, and paying just $100 nets either a four-room suite or an entire ground-floor apartment, all with full kitchens, private bathrooms, and a bedroom that can sleep a large family or a small fishing party.

$$–$$$ The **Reluctant Fisherman Inn** (407 Railroad Ave.; ☎ 800/770-3272 or 907/424-3272; www.reluctantfisherman.com; AE, MC, V) sits right on the edge of Cordova's small boat harbor, offering the best seat in town to witness the

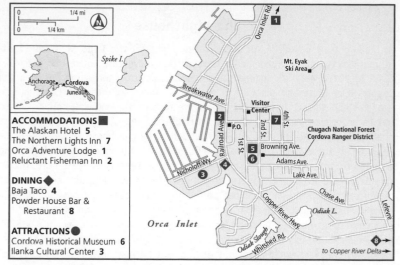

to Copper River Delta→

comings and goings of the fishing fleet. Location is its strong point. A general state of shabbiness is the tradeoff, although that's gradually changing. New owners—a married couple who gave up crab fishing in the Bering Sea to become hoteliers—are refurbishing the place room by room, hauling off the musty carpeting, tiling the bathrooms, putting in wainscoting and new furnishings, adding sliding doors and Juliet balconies to the harborside rooms, and giving the whole place a seaside nautical theme. "If we can make the building deserve the view it has, we will have done what we set out to do," says one of the owners, Sylvia Meyer. In the meantime, there's no distinction between the decrepit rooms and the nice ones, as far as the rates are concerned (so ask to change if you're not happy with the one you're assigned). From May through July, rooms go for $115 to $140, depending on the view. Through August and September, when the silver salmon run and the sport fishermen take over the town, prices rise by $15 at both ends of the scale. In the off season, you can expect to pay between $105 and $125. Even if you don't end up staying here, drop by the Reluctant Fisherman's bar to enjoy the view.

$$$–$$$$ The reasonably priced package deals and an unusual waterfront setting draw both sport fishers and non-fishers alike to **Orca Adventure Lodge** (2500 Orca Rd.; ☎ 866/424-ORCA or 907/424-7249; www.orcaadventurelodge. com; AE, DISC, MC, V), 2 miles north of Cordova. The lodge occupies a fish cannery that opened in 1886 and stayed in business until the *Exxon Valdez* oil spill wiped out the fishery. The place hasn't been spruced up much on the outside, but its insides have had tasteful makeovers. The old bunkhouses where the cannery's fishermen lived now hold cozy little motel rooms ($145 per night double occupancy, down to $95 off season) and two-story, two-bedroom suites ($175 per night double occupancy, $125 off season). Large families and groups traveling together fit nicely into the old four-bedroom dormitory where the cannery's women workers

To the Lighthouse

To *really* get away from it all, spend a few nights at the **Cape St. Elias Lighthouse** ★★★ (make arrangements through Orca Adventure Lodge; ☎ 866/424-ORCA or 907/424-7249), located on an uninhabited barrier island between the Copper River Delta and the Gulf of Alaska, 68 miles southeast of Cordova. The island, Kayak Island, is believed to be the first North American soil on which the early Russian explorers set foot. This 55-foot-tall, Art Deco style concrete lighthouse was built in 1916 and was tended to by lighthouse keepers until the Coast Guard automated it in 1974. The Coast Guard still maintains the light, and a nonprofit group called Cape St. Elias Lighthouse Keepers does its best to take care of the old structures. The group has renovated the boathouse, and up to 10 of you can sleep there in rustic but perfectly comfortable conditions. You have to bring everything you need, from bedding to food and water, but there's actually no charge to stay there. You don't get this scot-free, of course, as you'll pay $250 per person round-trip for the flight, and a $50 donation to the Cape St. Elias Lighthouse Keepers wouldn't be out of line. But for beachcombing, birding, and bear watching on a splendidly secluded island, this place can't be beat.

---

used to bunk. It's a sprawling, two-story, mossy-roofed bungalow, which goes for $250 per night but can sleep up to eight (though it's not available off season). Three meals a day are served at long, communal tables in the old mess hall, under the direction of a talented young chef who returns to his job as an instructor at the New England Culinary Institute in the winter. In addition to charter fishing tours, the lodge offers guided kayaking, hiking, brown bear photography, and rafting trips (past Childs Glacier), priced between $45 and $150. The "adventure package" is a good value—for $155 per person, you get a room, three meals, and the use of canoes, kayaks, and fishing gear.

In addition to the hotels I've listed, there are 17 **U.S. Forest Service public use cabins** (www.recreation.gov) in and around Prince William Sound that rent for less than $50 night. There's a catch, though: Most of them are on remote islands or stuck way off in the wilderness, and the bush planes you hire to take you there charge about $200 per person one-way, wiping out any savings on lodgings. There are, however, a few public use cabins that you can get to from Cordova by car, including the Forest Service's **McKinley Trail Cabin** (trailhead at Mile 21.6 Copper River Hwy.), a rough-hewn dwelling built in 1918 and historically used as a shelter for trappers and hunters. Like all public use cabins in Alaska, you have to bring everything you need with you, from bedding to toilet paper, but if you can do so, it offers very good value for this pricey state. (See p. 373 for more information on public use cabins.)

Camping

In a wooded area 13 miles from town off Copper River Highway, there are a dozen campsites at the **Alaska River Expedition Campground** (☎ 800/766-1864). They cost $15.

DINING FOR ALL TASTES

Cordova isn't much of a restaurant town. It is, however, a town where every restaurant, including the local taco stand, serves Copper River red salmon, a fish highly regarded by gourmets around the world. One of the Cordova fishing fleet's main targets, Copper River reds spend the oceanic part of their lives bulking up for their arduous spawning run home, up the long, swift, silty, ice-filled Copper River. It's a tougher swim than most salmon have to make, so the Copper River reds carry more Omega-3 oil—that heart-friendly unsaturated fat that makes salmon taste so good—in their flesh than other wild salmon.

$ Baja Taco ★★★ (no. 1 Harbor Loop; ☎ 907/424-5599; mid-Apr to Oct only daily 8am–8pm; no credit cards) serves gigantic fish tacos stuffed with either halibut or Copper River red salmon ($10). The kitchen and counter are inside an old red school bus, parked alongside a cedar-sided cabin that serves as the dining room. The owners (who retire to Baja California each winter, which is where they've picked up most of their recipes, as well as the sombreros and saddle blankets adorning the place) trade for much of their fresh fish, so there's always a chance that the guy in Xtratuf boots and a sweatshirt sitting next to you is the fisherman who netted your taco filling. This is my favorite place in town for breakfast, lunch, or dinner. (If you're in need of a big breakfast, the $8 huevos rancheros or the $10 breakfast burritos with reindeer or salmon sausage really hit the spot.) With its free Wi-Fi and home-baked muffins and biscotti, it's a great coffee nook, too.

$–$$$$ Those coming back into town from one kind of arduous outdoor adventure or another can regain their strength with the comfort food on offer at **Powder House Bar and Restaurant ★** (Mile 1.5 Copper River Hwy.; ☎ 907/424-3529; daily 11am–10pm but hours vary; AE, DISC, MC, V). It's got burgers galore ($7.50–11), including salmon burgers, halibut burgers, and a monster of a burger called The Blaster, which has two patties, ham, egg, cheese, and bacon ($11)—if you're hungry and reckless enough to eat two Blasters, the third one's free. Entrees at the upper end of the menu ($24–$29) include grilled razor clams, breaded and deep-fried scalloped Dungeness crab, a big rib-eye steak (cut on the premises and cooked with a tasty teriyaki glaze), and the ubiquitous Copper River red and king salmon. While the Powder House—so named because explosives used to build the railroad were stored here—doesn't have a dramatic harbor view, it does have a pretty impressive view of Lake Eyak and the surrounding Chugach peaks.

WHY YOU'RE HERE: THE TOP SIGHTS & ATTRACTIONS

Most of Cordova's attractions are of the outdoors variety, but you should save a little time to rummage around the town's past at the **Cordova Historical Museum ★★** (622 1st St.; ☎ 907/424-6655; free admission; summer Mon–Sat 10am–6pm, Sun 2–4pm; rest of year Tues–Fri 10am–5pm, Sat 1–5pm). This colorful little community museum, sharing the same building as city hall, has surprising depth for its size. A random sampling of its idiosyncratic collection includes: an old nickel slot machine that you can still play (bring nickels); a rare, three-man, skin bidarka (aka, a kayak), blackened with age like a mummy; and the peephole from Gloria's Box Car, a famous local box car of ill repute. The people of Cordova bring things to the museum when they don't know what else to do with them. That's why it's got the taxidermied remains of a 600-pound leatherback turtle, a tropical species that made some serious navigational errors and wound up in a fisherman's net in Prince William Sound. Jars filled with foul-smelling oil from the *Exxon Valdez* keep showing up, too. "Every time someone digs at the beach and finds that layer of oil down there, they bring us some," said a Coast Guard wife volunteering at the museum when I visited. "They're still furious and they just want to let someone know." You can buy postcards and sign them with an oily brown thumb print from the worst oil spill in U.S. history.

To delve into Cordova's local Native culture, visit the **Ilanka Cultural Center** (110 Nicholoff Way, across from Fishermen's Memorial at the harbor; ☎ 907/424-7903; www.nveyak.com; free admission; summer only Mon–Fri 10am–4pm). It's got a small museum with Native artwork and artifacts, and a big skeleton of a killer whale hanging from the ceiling. The museum's collection isn't as impressive at the Cordova Historical Museum's, but here you'll have the chance to meet living Eyak Indians, part of a small group that's culturally and linguistically distinct from other Alaska Natives. The cultural center is their community gathering place.

ACTIVE CORDOVA

For a complete run-down of the multitude of local hiking trails, I refer you once again to the **Chugach National Forest Cordova Ranger District** (p. 107). Here's my short list of personal favorites:

Stupendous mountain views are what recommend the **Heney Ridge Trail** (trailhead at Mile 5.1 Whitshed Rd.) just south of town. The first 2 miles of this 3.5-mile-long trail make for an easy stroll through the rainforest. At the tree line, you come to a wildflower meadow with a long view of Prince William Sound. From there the trail changes from a piece of cake to a calf-crampingly-steep challenge. Don't give up! Huff and puff to the top and you'll get an even better view from the crest of the ridge.

An even more impressive view of Prince William Sound, with tiny Cordova far below, is available from the 1,225-foot top of Tripod Mountain, which you'll get to via the **Tripod Mountain Trail.** The trail starts right in town, at the end of 6th Street. This hike is a calf-burner from bottom to top.

THE OTHER CORDOVA

Enroll in one of the 3-day adult education summer workshops offered by the **William Sound Science Center** (☎ 907/424-5800, ext. 231; www.pwssc.gen.ak. us) and you may end up flying to a remote island to count shorebirds, or paddling around the sound to gather edible sea weed. Or you may end up doing something entirely different. Whatever you do, though, you'll be under the tutelage of one of the researchers at the science center, who, each summer, lead crash courses for the general public on topics near and dear to their hearts and research grants. The offerings change all the time, and the cost ranges from around $150 to $300, depending on the expenses involved (a workshop that flies to a barrier island to study shorebirds, for instance, costs more than a workshop in the waters nearby the science center). Enrollment tends to be dominated by Alaskans, and particularly Alaskan school teachers, who attend to fulfill their continuing education requirements. So for you, taking one of the weekend workshops wouldn't just be a good way to get to know the natural world better, it would be a good way to get to know real Alaskans. Throughout the year, the center holds quickie workshops as well. They're usually for all ages, and have included investigations into tide pools, mudflats, toads, frogs, salamanders, crabs, eels, anemones, sea stars, and Native herbs, among other topics. The center also runs overnight youth camps for kids. See the website for more information.

Have you ever looked at one of the U.S. Coast Guard's broad-beamed, low-slung buoy tenders and thought, "Now there's a ship I wouldn't mind touring." Well, it just so happens that the 225-foot USGS buoy tender *Sycamore* is based in Cordova. Although there are no formal tours of the vessel, you might be able to arrange an informal **tour of the *Sycamore*** if the crew isn't exceptionally busy, and if you ask nicely. Go to the U.S. Coast Guard station north of the small boat harbor and inquire at the Quarterdeck shack on the North Fill Dock, off Seafood Lane. How much of a tour you get really depends on who gives it, but at a minimum you'll get to see the hefty cranes on the foredeck that pluck buoys from the water. You might also get to see the mess hall where the crew eat, poke your head into the engine room (the most spic-and-span engine room you've probably ever seen), and possibly take a look at the wheelhouse, where the captain works.

ATTENTION, SHOPPERS!

Stick around Cordova for more than a day and you'll start running into the same people over and over again. You'll also notice that many of them are wearing the same fleece jackets, fleece vests, and fleece hats featuring distinctive Tlingit designs. It's as if the whole town shops at **Copper River Fleece** (504 1st St.; ☎ 907/ 424-4304; www.copperriverfleece.com), the town's homegrown fleece maker. Off-the-rack items include fleece ski hats ($26–$32) and fleece vests and jackets in various degrees of wind-proofing ($118–$168). For those who take pride in recycling, there's even a handsome pumpkin colored zippered fleece jacket made from 100% plastic soda pop bottles ($109).

NIGHTLIFE IN CORDOVA

What nightlife Cordova has exists entirely within the fishing bars. They'll either be loud and packed or quiet and dead, depending on whether the fishing boats are in or out that night. The bars right on the harbor are too small, bright, and rowdy for me, but **The Alaskan** ★ (600 1st St.; ☎ 907/424-3288), which is on the ground floor of The Alaskan Hotel, is different. It's dark, cavernous, and rowdy. The drinks are cheap, and there's shuffleboard (a brilliant alternative to the more usual offering of darts).

GET OUT OF TOWN

Cordova's two biggest attractions are the 700,000-acre **Copper River Delta** ★★★, and a 20-story-tall wall of ice known as **Childs Glacier** ★★★ (see below). The Copper River Delta is a vast and beautiful outlet of the mighty Copper River, which tears through the Wrangell and Chugach mountains, carrying 2 million tons of glacial silt per day toward the sea. A watery nether world, it's a half step between the solid ground of the continent and the swirling currents in the Gulf of Alaska, and is composed of a complex, ever-changing patchwork of marshes, ponds, forested hills, stagnant backwaters, and coursing waterways. In spring, the delta hosts the largest gathering of migratory shorebirds in the Western Hemisphere. Millions of birds across dozens of species make annual appearances, including ducks from Baja California, song birds from South America, and 80% of the world's population of Western sandpipers. Naturally birders can't resist getting in on the action, and they flock to the delta during the peak season, in late April and early May. Year-round you'll see species like bald eagles and trumpeter swans. The delta also teems with wolves, lynx, mink, beavers, and other critters.

At the end of the 49-mile-long Copper River Highway, which traverses the delta, is the spectacular Childs Glacier. Its face is 3 miles wide and 300 feet tall, and it ceaselessly calves icebergs straight into the Copper River. By glacial standards, the Childs Glacier is hyperactive, flowing at a rate of about 500 feet a year. The swift-moving waters of the Copper River hold it at bay, undercutting its face and sending massive slabs of ice crashing into the water. When the bigger icebergs calve, they can send actual tsunamis smashing into the opposite bank of the river, where visitors gather. Three times a year or so, a 5-foot wave washes up the shore. A 10-foot wave hits every 2 years, on average. Once in a while, a box-store-size slab of ice will slam into the river and kick up a really big wave. In 1993, a 30-footer swept over the shore, carrying icebergs, boulders, and two terrified women several hundred yards inland.

You're free to sit on the bank and watch the show, as long as you're ready to high-tail it when you see a wave coming. Or you can retreat to an elevated viewing area that's been built to keep visitors out of harm's way. Bring something warm to wear, because the glacier generates a frigid wind that sweeps across the river, even in summer.

Among the delta's other highlights are:

◆ **The Million Dollar Bridge** (Mile 48.1 Copper River Hwy.). Shortly before you get to Childs Glacier, you'll come to the Million Dollar Bridge, so named because of its $1.4-million price tag. That figure wouldn't raise any eyebrows for a bridge today, but it was a staggering sum when the bridge was built in the winter of 1909–1910. Constructed as part of the railroad connecting the Kennicott copper mines with the port of Cordova, this bridge across the Copper River was an engineering marvel in its day. Take a look at the interpretive plaques along the road that explain the bridge builders' epic feat in constructing a four-span truss bridge across a frozen river, and why they had to work through the dead of winter (a federal tax incentive was involved). Then take a stroll on the rusting old thing and watch the river rush by through wooden planking laid out for cars to pass (if you're afraid of heights, you might just want to appreciate the bridge from a distance). You can drive across the bridge, but there's nowhere to go once you get to the other side, which is why the Million Dollar Bridge is also known as the Bridge to Nowhere.

◆ **Alganik Slough** (Mile 17 Copper River Hwy.). At several points around the delta, the U.S. Forest Service has set up spots to watch birds and spy on other wildlife. This is the one you want to visit. It's got a 1,000-foot boardwalk reaching out over the marsh, with blinds set up along the way so that you can ogle the waterfowl without them spotting you. Even if you've missed peak birding season, you should still spot trumpeter swans—awesomely impressive birds with 8-foot wingspans. Alganik Sough is 5 miles off the

Onto the Copper River Delta

The easiest way to get out on the delta is to **drive.** Rent a car in town (p. 99), and road trip out along the 49-mile-long **Copper River Highway.** There are plenty of stops along the way, where you can hike, picnic, or bird watch. Give yourself a full day to explore, and be sure to pack lunch: The delta may be a smorgasbord of fly larvae, tiny clams, and tasty worms for shorebirds, but there's nowhere for people to buy food.

Exploring by **bike** is another way to see the delta, but only if you're pretty serious about cycling. The road is flat enough, but cars speeding by can kick up dust, and the wicked headwinds that blast across the delta can make it feel as though you're trying to bike through wet mudflats. **Cordova Coastal Outfitters** (☎ 800/357-5145 or 907/424-7424; www.cordova coastal.com) rents bikes for $18 per day. Give yourself 2 days or more if you're biking, and camp along the way (check with the **Chugach National Forest Cordova Ranger District;** 612 2nd St.; ☎ 907/424-7661, for camp-grounds). Camp gear can also be rented at Cordova Coastal Outfitters.

Yet another way to explore the delta is by **canoe or kayak,** and again, Cordova Coastal Outfitters are the go-to guys. The company's guided kayak trips start at $75, or you can have the company plan a route for you and paddle yourself (if you've done this kind of thing before). Alternatively, you can simply bike out to a prearranged spot on the highway, pick up a canoe there, and spend the rest of the day paddling.

Rafting down the Copper River is still another option. **Alaska River Rafting** (☎ 800/776-1864 or 907/424-7238; www.alaskarafters.com) has trips ranging from easy half-day floats to wild, multi-day, white-water runs. Four-and-a-half-hour trips start at $95, or $75 for children ages 6 to 12 (children under 6 aren't accepted).

Copper River Highway. Nearby is the 1-mile-long **Fisherman's Trail,** good for a quick jaunt through the rushes.

◆ **Haystack Trail** (Mile 19 Copper River Hwy.). The walk to choose if you're more of an ambler than hiker, the .8-mile Haystack Trail climbs up a small knoll sporting a mossy spruce and hemlock forest. At the top of the knoll, on a clear day, you can see across the delta to the Gulf of Alaska and maybe catch a glimpse of Kayak Island, where the first Russian explorers are believed to have set foot in Alaska. The trail is lined with boardwalks for much of the way.

There's a lot more out on the delta than I have room to get into here, so before heading off to explore, stop by the **Chugach National Forest Cordova Ranger District** (612 2nd St.; ☎ 907/424-7661; daily 8am–5pm) in town and grab the free brochure entitled "The Copper River Delta." It includes a good map and details on all the attractions and hiking trails along the way, as well as camp-grounds and public use cabins.

SEWARD

Clinging to its smidgen of buildable land between mountain and sea, in a long, deep fjord with more saw-toothed mountain peaks than level ground, Seward is a booming little summer vacation town on the edge of a vast maritime wilderness. It's a neat and orderly place that slumbers deeply in the off season, then explodes with life in the summer. Anchorage residents drive down to fish, camp, and go on weekend benders. Thousands of tourists come and go by cruise ship or the Alaska Railroad, and RVers settle in for extended stays. Athletes train for a grueling Fourth of July foot race to the top of the mountain looming over town. Cyclists and skateboarders roll along a paved waterfront stretch of the historic Iditarod Trail. Young Europeans and Americans toil in the seafood processing plant by day and shake off the slime in the dive bars at night. And everybody goes to the Alaska SeaLife Center to see Woody, the resident Steller sea lion. From Seward, it's a short step into the wild, where there are calving glaciers to see, whales and other wildlife to encounter, and the spectacular Kenai Fjords National Park to explore.

A BRIEF HISTORY

Seward was founded in 1902 by the Alaska Central Railway Company, which laid out the neat grid of the town, brought in a steamship filled with townspeople to inhabit it, and set about building a railroad. Construction lasted 20 years, and when it was finally completed, you could ride the rails all the way from Seward to Fairbanks, 470 miles away. The railroad, along with a deep-water port that doesn't freeze in the winter, made Seward a transportation hub for Alaska. It still holds that distinction today, with thousands of summer visitors coming and going by cruise ship, train, and automobile.

In 1910 surveyors laid out a mail delivery route for dog sleds between Seward and Nome, the Iditarod Trail. Although the famous Iditarod Trail Sled Dog Race begins in Anchorage, Seward residents are quick to point out that their town is the historic start of the trail. In World War II, Seward became the largest U.S. military port north of Seattle, and there are still fortifications around Resurrection Bay where you can explore underground tunnels and bunkers.

Like much of the rest of Southcentral Alaska, Seward was hit hard by the Good Friday earthquake of 1964. Much of the town's old waterfront was on loose alluvial fill, which slid into the sea when the 3½-minute, 9.2-magnitude quake triggered a massive underwater slide on the steep underwater slopes of the bay. The small boat harbor, the docks, and most of the town's industry slid away with it. The tsunami generated by the slide then wiped out what little of the waterfront remained. When the town was rebuilt, most of the waterfront was made into a park, with plenty of tent sites and RV spaces. Walk along the shore today and you can still see a few twisted railroad ties and other remnants of the catastrophe.

LAY OF THE LAND

The Kenai Mountains snuggle up so closely to the sea on the east side of the Kenai Peninsula that they've left room for just one town, Seward. About 127 highway miles from Anchorage, Seward and its population of 3,000 sits at the end of the Seward Highway and at the head of 950-foot-deep Resurrection Bay. The scenery around Seward couldn't be more magnificent—snow-capped mountains and blue-white glaciers complement the shimmering, often white-cap-streaked waters

Alaska's (Male) "Betsy Ross"

A 13-year-old Native boy named Benny Benson was a seventh grader living in an orphanage just outside of Seward in 1927 when he answered a call from the Territorial Legislature for entries in a contest to design a flag for Alaska. Benson sewed the eight gold stars of the Big Dipper on a blue background and entered his design. It won and became the territorial flag, and later the state flag. You pass a small roadside monument to Benson when you drive into town, but better than that is what you'll find hanging on the wall of the young adult section of the **Seward Community Library** (corner of 5th Ave. and Adams St.; ☎ 907/224-4082)—one of the original flags sewn by young Benson himself. The blue background has faded to a light gray, but the gold stars have held their color through the decades. Benson won $1,000 for his design, which he used to move to Seattle to study diesel engine repair.

of the bay, while 3,022-foot Mount Marathon towers above the town and swallows it in its late afternoon shadow.

Seward is the gateway to **Kenai Fjords National Park,** 607,805 acres of protected forest, rock, sea, and ice. It's an area of deep fjords, hidden bays and inlets, rocky headlands and peninsulas, calving glaciers, coastal rainforest, and 5,000- and 6,000-foot mountain peaks. Dominating the park is the rarely visited Harding Icefield, a 35-mile-long remnant of the Ice Age nestled nearly a mile up in the Kenai Mountains. Three dozen named glaciers, and several nameless others, spill out of the ice field. Six reach all the way to the sea, and tour boats and kayakers set out from Seward to watch them calve icebergs into the water. Sea otters, harbor seals, sea lions, and whales feed in the fjords. Moose, minx, marten, wolverines, and black bears live in the patches and ribbons of forest growing between the cliffs, ice, and sea. The park is mostly accessed by boat. **Exit Glacier,** 13 miles north of town, is the only point in the park to which you can drive.

At the **Kenai Fjords National Park Information Center** (Seward Small Boat Harbor; ☎ 907/224-7500; www.nps.gov/kefj), you will find rangers to answer questions about the park and provide information on the all-important tour boats, and a small but handy bookstore. Call or drop by here for advice on public-use cabins for rent in the fjords, guidance on a sea-kayaking expedition there, or information on hikes and trail conditions. They're open Memorial Day through Labor Day daily 9am to 7pm. Hours in May and September will be shorter but had not been determined by press time. The center is closed October through April.

GETTING TO & AROUND SEWARD
Getting There
BY CAR
The best way to get to Seward is by car. Seward and Anchorage are connected by the 127-mile Seward Highway, which is about as scenic a highway as you'll find

anywhere. You can pick up a rental car in Anchorage from any of the national agencies. If you get to Seward without a car, you can rent one from **Seward Hertz Rent-A-Car** (☎ 800/654-3131 or 907/224-4378; www.rentacaralaska.com) starting at $75 per day. You'll probably find a better deal in Anchorage, where rental cars (at least in the shoulder seasons) go for as low as $49 per day.

BY RAIL

The **Alaska Railroad Corporation** (☎ 800/544-0552, 907/265-2494, or 907/265-2300; www.alaskarailroad.com) offers daily service between Anchorage and Seward from mid-May to mid-September (round trip $65 adults, $33 children), with a train leaving Anchorage for Seward in the morning and returning in the evening. The round-trip journey takes 8 hours, so savvy travelers should spend at least a night in Seward rather than rushing down and back in the same day. The railroad sells day-trip packages that include glacier tours, but they last 16 hours, and there's no reason to push yourself like that when you're on vacation.

BY BUS OR VAN

Faster and cheaper than the train is the **Seward Bus Line** (☎ 907/224-3608; www.sewardbuslines.net), which makes the daily 2½-hour run from Anchorage year-round, for $45 one-way or $85 round-trip, with a stop at the Anchorage airport for an extra $5. It arrives in Seward in the evening. **Homer Stage Line** (2607 Eagle St.; ☎ 907/235-2252 or 907/339-1847; www.homerstageline.com) runs a van to Seward that arrives before noon. It costs $50 one-way or $90 round-trip. If you're headed for Homer, too, you can make the complete Anchorage-Seward-Homer circuit for $140, starting at any of those points and returning to where you started from whenever you're ready.

Getting Around

If you're not driving, the best way to get around Seward is to rent a bike. The **Seward Bike Shop** (411 Port Ave., in a rail car near the depot at the harbor; ☎ 907/224-2448) has them for $23 per day, or $14 for a half-day. Seward is also compact enough to be walkable—you can walk from one end to the other in about 20 minutes. During the summer, a trolley runs twice a day from the harbor, site of the cruise-ship dock and the train depot, to downtown.

BY WATER TAXI

The most common way to get to camping areas, cabins, and kayaking waters around Resurrection Bay or in Kenai Fjords National Park is by water taxi. **Aquetec Water Taxi** (☎ 907/362-1291; www.sewardwatertaxi.com) is the best outfit and has reasonable rates—from under $100 to more than $200.

ACCOMMODATIONS, BOTH STANDARD & NOT

Seward has a broad variety of lodgings, from cheapo youth hostels, to over-priced hotels, to in-town campgrounds. The town also has a greater than usual number of residents cashing in on tourist season by renting out rooms, cabins, and apartments. Some of these places qualify as genuine bed-and-breakfasts, while others are simply cozy rooms that you can rent by the night. Whatever the case, they're almost always less expensive than a stay in most Seward hotels and thus constitute the best value in Seward accommodations. The easiest way to snag a short-term

Seward rental is through a local booking agency called **Alaska's Point of View Reservation Service** (☎ 888/227-2424 or 907/224-2323; www.go2seward.com or www.alaskasview.com), which has a database of more than 100 such places in and around town. "I represent about 90% of the places to stay around here," says Debra Hafemeister, the outspoken owner, who doesn't pull any punches when describing a place. "I honestly tell people about the positive and the negative comments I've heard."

I asked Deb to find me a place for two, in town, with a private bath, for under $100. She came up with two listings. I eliminated one from consideration after Deb said, "I've had people complain that it wasn't clean." Deb warned me that the other place was at the top of three flights of stairs, but that didn't phase me, so I checked it out. It turned out to be a budget traveler's delight—a simple, single room with a queen bed on the top floor of a plain-looking home with a good view of Resurrection Bay. Nothing fancy, but not bad at all for $95. A similar but larger two-room unit on the same floor rented for $145 for four people.

There's no charge for Deb's service, and if you use it to book a room, Deb will fix you up with a 10% discount on a glacier cruise with one of the three big tour boat operators. While the lodging Deb represents covers a broad range of prices, on average you can expect to pay about $130 for a place for two with a private

Seward's Military Resort

For active-duty and retired military personnel who are eligible for benefits, members of the National Guard and Reserves, and certain government-employed civilians (who know who they are), Seward has a World War II–era Army base that's been reassigned as a base for charter fishing, sightseeing, and other Alaskan forms of R&R. The **Seward Military Resort** (☎ 800/770-1858 or 907/224-2659; www.sewardresort.com; AE, DISC, MC, V; $–$$$$) has a variety of lodging options: squeaky clean motel-style rooms (which sleep four), a dozen town house units (with a bedroom for parents and a sleeping loft for kids, and full kitchens where you can save a bundle by cooking your own meals), and a half dozen yurts (barely larger than a four-person dome tent). There's also an old RV park, a log cabin that's been there longer than anyone can remember, and a pair of fish-cleaning houses that look like field hospitals. Rates vary by season and pay grade. For instance, E1s thru E5s pay $22 for the yurts (which have three cots and no electricity) and $163 for the town houses, while CW4s and CW5s are charged $26 and $210 for the same. The motel rooms go to the lowest pay grade personnel for $70, while top brass pays $116.

bath. To that you'll need to add a 10% tax, the same tax that you'll also pay for hotels in Seward.

Hotels & Inns

$$ One of Deb's more unique offerings is **Whistle Stop Lodging** (411 Port Ave.; ☎ 907/224-5050; http://whistlestop.sewardak.net; MC, V), a vintage 1940s Alaska Railroad troop carrier that's been transformed into two comfortable and spacious—if long and narrow—rooms. They go for $125, which is a decent price for Seward, but especially here at the small boat harbor, where right next door, at the Holiday Inn, rates *start* at $189. One side of the car looks out on the fishing fleet, and the other looks into a courtyard formed with three other retired railcars (one's now a bike shop, another houses a glacier trekking operation, and the old cooking car has been conveniently transformed into The Smoke Shack restaurant, p. ###, where you can get a hearty breakfast in the morning). The Whistle Stop's plush double beds are comfy and snug, and when the wind blows hard off Resurrection Bay, the whole place rocks soothingly on its shocks, like the trawlers tied up snuggly in their berths in the harbor outside the window.

$$–$$$$ Most of Seward's hotels are too expensive to cover in this guide (and not a very good value for what you get, to my mind). The one exception is the **Van Gilder Hotel** (301 Adams St.; ☎ 800/204-6835 or 907/224-3079; www.vangilderhotel.com; AE, DISC, MC, V). Built in 1916, it's a charmer and plenty affordable, with rooms ranging from $109 to $175, though if you book through Expedia or Travelocity, the rate will often drop to $98, even in high season (there are also AARP and AAA discounts). A compact, three-story building with no elevator, the Van Gilder has been thoughtfully restored to something like how it might have looked in its youth, with flocked wallpaper, hanging light fixtures, and plenty of other Edwardian-era trimmings. Like many old hotels, it's also got balky water pressure, especially in the morning when everyone's showering, and the rooms are smaller than today's hotel rooms, since the people back then were smaller too. But the big brass beds have pillow-top mattresses, soft sheets and comforters, and plenty of room for modern-size people. Some rooms have private baths—with either modern showers or claw-foot tubs—and some share a shower and old-fashioned water closet. The first floor has a sitting room and a communal kitchen, where you'll find coffee, bagels, and other guests to talk to in the morning. The second and third floors were the sites of murders (in rooms 212 and 312), and now harbor ghosts, according to local lore. (Ask at the front desk when they're not busy, and you may learn more than you wanted to know.)

Camping

The cheapest campgrounds in the area are the free tent sites near Exit Glacier at the **Exit Glacier Campground** (at Mile 8.5 of Herman Leirer Rd., aka Exit Glacier Rd.). Sites are far apart and almost completely private but lack amenities like picnic tables and fire grates. Snow lingers here into early June; later in the summer, the campground often fills by early evening. It's first-come, first-served.

A bit farther from town, you'll find more amenities (running water, flushing toilets, picnic tables, dumpsters, fire pits) at the U.S. Forest Service's **Primrose Campgrounds** (Mile 17, Seward Hwy.), scenically located on the edge of Kenai Lake. The fee is $10 per night, and it's first-come, first-served. No reservations are accepted.

There are campsites along the beach and among the spruce trees at **Miller's Landing** (☎ 866/541-5739 or 907/224-5739; www.millerslandingak.com), an old homestead just south of town on Lowell Point Road. Tent sites cost $23, and sleeping-bag cabins start at $45. As rustic as the place seems, it has Wi-Fi and public-access computers around the woodstove in the store.

DINING FOR ALL TASTES

$–$$$ Local barbecue joint **The Smoke Shack** ★★ (411 Port St.; ☎ 907/224-7427; Wed–Sun 7am–3pm; MC, V) isn't really a shack at all, but rather a retired World War II–era cooking car, once part of a troop transport train. Its straight-backed booths and tight quarters hint at what it must have been like to get shipped to Alaska to protect "America's back door" from Imperial Japan. But I doubt the troops were feasting on what you can get there today, such as juicy smoked hamburgers ($7.95–$11), or sticky slabs of baby back ribs, served with black beans, hobo fries, coleslaw, and Texas toast ($13 for a half order, $19 for a full order). This is an especially good place for breakfasts, which are huge and cost less than $10. (Try the $8.95 frittata, the house special, which comes with either Spanish chorizo or hollandaise sauce.) Sorry, there's no dinner.

$–$$$ **Yoly's Bistro** ★★★ (220 4th Ave.; ☎ 907/224-3295; summer Mon–Thurs 10am–9pm, Fri–Sun 10am–10pm, hours vary for rest of year; MC, V) towers above Seward's other restaurants in both its creative cuisine and its high-rise bar stools. Taking a seat at the bar here is not unlike climbing into the saddle of the stuffed moose by the harbor from which tourists have their pictures taken. The menu has

Choice Cabins

A stay in a ruined fort and a cabin at the doorstep of a glacier are only two of the options for adventurous, and affordable, lodgings in and around Resurrection Bay. Before booking, however, factor in the costs of transportation (or get ready for a challenging hike or paddle).

To reserve public use cabins at any Alaska state park, contact the **Department of Natural Resources Public Information Center** (☎ 907/269-8400 or 907/269-8411; www.alaskastateparks.org; MC, V). Also see p. 373 for more on public use cabins.

$ Bring flashlights if you're lucky enough to snag one of the two highly sought after cabins at **Caines Head State Recreation Area** and you can explore the pitch-black remains of World War II–era Fort McGilvray, a bomb-proof maze of corridors and rooms embedded in a promontory above Resurrection Bay. The cabins are nestled in a spruce and hemlock forest, and they rent for $65 a night during the summer high season, or $50 the rest of the year. You can't drive to Caines Head, but you can hire a water taxi to drop you off and pick you up for about $100, for two of you. Experienced sea kayakers can paddle there on their own, and backpackers can hike along a 4.5-mile tidal trail. Part of the trail slips beneath the waves at high tide, so time your trek to avoid that.

$ More public use cabins are available across the bay at **Thumbs Cove State Marine Park**, a popular spot with local boaters that's 7½ miles from Seward. Along with the two public use cabins (including one wheelchair accessible cabin), this lovely wilderness area offers hiking, salmon fishing, and protected waters for sea kayaking. The cabins cost the same as those at Caines Head, but the round-trip water taxi ride adds an additional $120 to the cost (seriously cut sea kayakers might get there under their own steam, but it can be a miserably choppy paddle).

$ Farther afield—and more spectacular still—are the public use cabins in **Kenai Fjords National Park.** As you lounge at **Holgate Cabin** ✯✯, which sits on a small bluff above a steep, cobble beach that's sometimes

an Alaskan-Asian thing going on, with gourmet health-food-store overtones. But what distinguishes the bistro more than anything are the sauces. There's a sauce for just about everything, apart from the burgers ($9–$14). The pesto penne ($14) comes in a savory basil pesto cream sauce, the mahogany duck ($22) is doused in a lovely Mandarin herb sauce, and the wasabi-peanut crusted halibut ($23) is sided by an addictive sweet wasabi aioli. Steaks, too, get the "wet" treatment and can be ordered with a blue cheese demi-glacé, a shiitake mushroom demi-glacé, or a toasted pecan–cilantro cream sauce ($19–$24). Even the elegant littered with glacial ice, you'll have the remarkable experience of watching Holgate Glacier calve into Aialik Bay without ever moving from the front porch. Instead of popcorn, you can gobble the berries you picked in the surrounding spruce forest while you watch the "show" in complete privacy (except for perhaps the occasional interference by bears that come by to forage for berries, too).

Kenai Fjords National Park has two other public use cabins, as well, but Holgate's got the best view—although the ear-splitting crack of calving icebergs might wake you in the night. They each go for $50 per night, but the round-trip water taxi ride adds at least $275 to the total cost. If you want one, make reservations before you arrive (through www.recreation. gov; ☎ 877/444-6777 or 518/885-3639); walk-in reservations are sometimes available at the **Kenai Fjords National Park Visitor Information Center** (p. 122).

$ The pair of privately owned cabins at **Kayakers Cove** (☎ 907/224-8662; www.kayakerscove.com; no credit cards; only open Memorial Day–Labor Day), back on Resurrection Bay, are a step up in comfort from the public use cabins and their bare plywood bunks. Each of these one-room cabins boasts a double bed plus a loft with fairly comfy sleeping pads. A wood-fired on-site sauna is another of the Cove's top niceties. For this uptick in amenities, there's no real uptick in price; expect to pay $60 per night with tax included (plus $5 per person for linens, so bring a sleeping bag if you can). Why are prices so reasonable? Kayakers Cove is essentially a wilderness hostel, so you'll have more company there than at a public use cabin. In the small main building, there's a kitchen and a common area, where vagabond sea kayakers play checkers and Monopoly. Upstairs is the communal sleeping loft ($20 per night for sleeping bag space). If you want more solitude and are rolling in dough, you can rent the entire place for $300 a night and send the backpackers, um, packing.

Note: Kayaker's Cove rents sea kayaks for $20 a day.

little desserts get a sauce. The Key lime cheesecake ($7) sits on the plate pointy end up, like the prow of a ship going down in a glassy sea of limey coulis.

$$$$ At the small boat harbor, you'll find two seafood restaurants with similar menus, prices, and postcard-perfect views of masts and booms with snowy mountains beyond. Which should you pick? Well, **Chinook's Waterfront Restaurant** ★ (1404 4th Ave.; ☎ 907/224-2207; www.chinookswaterfront.com; mid-Apr to mid-Oct only daily noon–10pm; AE, DISC, MC, V) is the newer of the two, thus boasting a sleeker look, in both the casual downstairs pub area filled with burnished steel

and blond woods and the quieter upstairs dining room with tall windows set into roasted-tomato red walls. However, its food can be hit or miss. On a good night you might get a memorable crab pot pie with a steamy bisque and a crispy puff pastry crust ($26), or a perfectly cooked piece of salmon stuffed with shrimp or crab ($24). On an off night, well . . . there's always the beer, which is brewed on the premises. If your need for a microbrew outweighs your need for a guarantee that your blackened halibut won't be as dry as a stack of napkins or your vegetables an overcooked mush, Chinook's is the clear choice. If Chinook's were on all the time, I'd give it three stars. Since it ain't, one star will have to do.

$$$$ Nearby, in the building with a lighthouse cupola, **Ray's Waterfront** ★ (1364 4th Ave.; ☎ 907/224-5606; mid-Apr to mid-Oct only daily 11am–10pm; AE, DISC, MC, V) is the darker and more dependable of the two. The service, however, isn't as reliable, and grouchy waiters can cast a pall across the dining room (sometimes it seems like the unhappy faces of the staff are being mirrored in the down-turned mouths of the giant halibut, rockfish, beluga whale, and the rest of the taxidermied marine menagerie adorning the cedar plank walls). Forget about that and focus on the food. You can count on the spicy cioppino ($24), the house special, to bring cheer to your table no matter what. Ditto for the salmon ($24) or the halibut ($27), which come in one of three ways: blackened with Cajun spices and served with raita, baked in Dijon, or broiled and topped with mango salsa. In fact, when the food arrives, even the creatures on the walls appear to feel better about things.

$$–$$$$ Along the 10-mile drive from Seward to Exit Glacier, you'll pass a log cabin restaurant advertising "Cheap food, lousy beer." Those claims aren't exactly true. First of all, **Exit Glacier Salmon Bake** ★★ (Mile 0.5 Exit Glacier Rd.; ☎ 907/224-2204; daily 5–10pm but closing hours vary, closed mid-Sept to May; MC, V) offers great beer—Alaskan brewed, on tap, and served in mason jars. Secondly, the "cheap food" is found only on the kids' menu—corn dogs, mac and cheese, and grilled cheese sandwiches for under $7. While broiled salmon priced at $20 and grilled halibut going for $22 isn't at all unreasonable by Alaskan standards, it's still not cheap. Ah, well—this place is nonetheless a gem. The atmosphere is classic Alaskana, with fishing tackle hanging from the peeled log beams, moose antlers tacked to the rough-cut plank walls, and a mismatched collection of furnishings that includes a cable spool acting as a round table. There's something warm and comforting about this place that extends beyond the heat lamps over the picnic tables on the enclosed porch.

WHY YOU'RE HERE: THE TOP SIGHTS & ATTRACTIONS

The **Seward Museum's** (336 3rd Ave.; ☎ 907/224-3902; $3 adults, 50¢ children; summer daily 10am–5pm, hours vary for rest of year) collection of Native baskets and ivory carvings, and its displays on World War II and the Iditarod are interesting enough, but I wouldn't go out of my way to see them. I would, however, go out of my way to see the museum's exhibit on the 1964 Good Friday earthquake. Seward got slammed by this largest earthquake in North American history. First, the quake sheered much of the waterfront loose from dry land, sending it sliding into the sea. Then, the slide generated a 40-foot tsunami, which crashed ashore and obliterated what the earthquake missed. Oil tanks and 40 rail cars filled with oil exploded into flames. The only bridge out of town became impassable, and fleeing residents were trapped in the burning city. It was a bad day indeed in Seward, and it's recalled at this little community museum in gripping detail, with photos and artifacts such as clocks with their hands frozen in time by the violent tremor.

I'm a sucker for a good aquarium, so it's not hard for me to get sucked right in to the **Alaska SeaLife Center** ★★★ (kids) (301 Railway Ave.; ☎ 800/224-2525 or 907/224-6300; www.alaskasealife.org; $15 adults, $12 children 7–12; Sept 16–Apr 14 daily 8am–7pm, Apr 15–Sept 15 daily 10am–5pm), a beautiful $56-million facility built largely with settlement money from the Exxon Valdez Oil Spill Restoration Fund. It's got diving sea birds, frolicking harbor seals, spindly king crabs, sea stars you can touch, a giant octopus (deceased, but still on display), and more shallow-water and deep-sea fishes than you can shake a kelp bulb at. Of course every aquarium worth its sea salt has one big headliner, and at the Alaska SeaLife Center, that would be Woody, the 2,300-pound Steller sea lion. Now, on a wildlife or a glacier tour you're likely to see all sorts of sea lions in the wild, so what's the big deal about a lone sea lion in captivity? Well, in the wild you'll most likely view the animals from afar and when they're hauled out on the rocks, where they're heavy and clumsy. At the SeaLife Center you get to see Woody up close and swimming underwater, where he moves with extreme grace, agility, and— sometimes—more than a little bit of aggression. Woody sometimes concludes his show with a series of balletlike moves and a charge at the glass wall of his tank, stopping just inches from the spectators. They laugh and applaud, but I swear, Woody wants to kill someone. The museum has all sorts of interactive exhibits too, including a scale large enough for an entire family to pile onto, so you see how you stack up against Woody, pound for pound.

Note: The SeaLife Center accepts volunteers to work with its marine mammals, birds, and other wildlife; call for info.

ACTIVE SEWARD
Hiking & Boating

One of the more unusual hikes around Resurrection Bay is along the 4.5-mile coastal trail to **Caines Head State Recreation Area** ★ (www.alaskastateparks. org), the site of an abandoned World War II–era strategic command center. **Fort McGilvray** was built on a 650-foot-high cliff to defend Seward from invasion. At the gunwales, where once two 6-foot guns stood, hikers get a superlative view of Resurrection Bay. Underneath are a spooky maze of underground tunnels and bunkers you can explore—carefully—with flashlights. One word on planning the hike: Because much of the trail slips beneath the waves at high tide, you can't hike out there just anytime. It's imperative that you head out at low tide and either hustle back before high tide; or make other arrangements. The best plan for hikers is to stay the night at the campground here or at one of the popular public use cabins (p. 373). Another option is to ditch the hike and make the excursion by boat. You can rent a kayak and paddle yourself, or you can work something out with a water taxi. **Aquetec Water Taxi** (☎ 907/362-1291) charges about $50 per person each way for two people, less with more passengers (for example, the cost for six would be $276). I like Aquetec more than other companies in town because its prices are the most straightforward; these rates include taxes and there are no hidden surcharges.

Scuba Diving

Scuba diving in Alaska may seem like a chilly proposition, but because of the warming effect of the Japanese current that swirls into the Gulf of Alaska, the ocean temperatures around the Kenai Peninsula and Prince William Sound are more comparable to those off the coast of California than the Arctic. For avid scuba divers, Resurrection Bay is a prime place to get face-to-mask with seals, sea lions, and other marine life. Anchorage-based **Dive Alaska** (1002 W. Northern Lights Blvd.; ☎ 907/770-1778; www.divealaska.net) offers 8-hour, two-tank dive tours out on the bay for $235 per person. The fee includes all the gear you need, including a dry suit (hey, the water temperature may be like California's—but that's still pretty darned cold), and a boat ride to the dive sites (which usually turn into impromptu wildlife spotting tours). But you don't need to be certified to explore beneath the surface of Kachemak Bay. For $175 per person, all equipment included, Dive Alaska will take you snorkeling instead. Snorkeling tours last about 4 hours, including 3 hours of travel, which can turn into impromptu wildlife watching tours. Snorkelers are more likely to encounter invertebrates—star fish, tube worms—than large marine mammals. Divers tend to see both.

ATTENTION, SHOPPERS!

Seward hasn't got much interesting shopping, but it does have a handful of places to find out-of-the-ordinary gifts and souvenirs. **The Ranting Raven** (238 4th Ave.; ☎ 907/224-2228; www.trailriver.com) boasts an interesting mix of items made in Alaska and elsewhere, such as jewelry incorporating Indian trade beads, clothing made in India, CDs, and saucers, mugs, and other wares that are both microwave and dishwasher safe. Along the walls of the coffeehouse **Resurrect Art** (320 3rd Ave.; ☎ 907/224-7176; www.resurrectart.com), are local (or at least Alaskan) pottery, postcards, paintings, and other artwork for sale, as well as a small selection of books of local interest. **Softly Silk** (416 4th Ave.; ☎ 907/244-6088; www.softly silk.com) specializes in, you guessed it, silks painted with oil or watercolors. Warmer wear is on offer too, including hats, gloves, and other things made of wool, both the common type from sheep and the exotic Alaskan stuff made from musk ox.

GET OUT OF TOWN
Kenai Fjords National Park

Look at the east side of the Kenai Peninsula on a map. It's ragged with fjords, long and narrow bays carved by glaciers. While the area's glaciers aren't what they used to be during the last ice age (when they were busy carving the fjords), they're still one of the most noteworthy features of the region—and one of the main reasons people go to Seward. Most of them are accessible only by sea, so I'll discuss the boat tours below. But first, here's info on the one glacier of the more than three dozen in the park that you can drive to:

EXIT GLACIER ✦✦
When you visit Exit Glacier, you won't see giant slabs of ice crashing into the sea, or spot whales and seals swimming among the icebergs, but you will get a sense

of how the land is reborn when ice retreats. And it will cost you just a tiny fraction of what a tour to one of the tidewater glaciers will. Exit Glacier descends for 3,000 feet from the Harding Icefield to the wildly braided Resurrection River, a popular fishing area that rushes the glacier's icy, cloudy runoff to the sea. There's a $5-per-vehicle day-use fee ($3 per bike) to get into the parking lot, where there's a ranger station (go in and check out the enormous relief map of the park). From there it's an easy half-mile walk to the glacier viewing area, which is far enough away from the glacier's face that you won't get crushed if a big piece of ice calves. Take the optional nature trail on the way back. It's an eye-opening, well-labeled trip through time and demonstrates the natural progression of plant life that moves in as a glacier retreats—the bright pink fireweed, green mosses, lichens, and the other "pioneer" species that are the first to appear when the ice recedes; then the young forest of cottonwoods, alders, and willows, which displace the pioneers; and finally the mature Sitka spruce and hemlock forest, which takes advantage of the groundwork laid by the earlier species. Two-hundred years ago, the edge of Exit Glacier stood where the edge of the mature forest stands now. All along the way are mounds of gravel—glacial moraines that mark where the edge of the glacier was at various points in time. **Directions to Exit Glacier:** Turn off at mile 3.7 of the Seward Highway onto Exit Glacier Road, and drive 9 miles to the end.

Exit Glacier is so named because early explorers found it offered a natural route off Harding Icefield back down to sea level. If you've got a day, and the stamina, you can climb up to the ice field along the **Harding Icefield Trail** ✪✪✪. Trekking the 3.9 miles up the valley wall alongside Exit Glacier is an unforgettable experience. Once you get to the top, a bright white land of ice stretches as far you can see, with the occasional nunatak, an Eskimo word for "lonely peak," punctuating the scene. It's a good 6- to 8-hour hike, round-trip, with a simple shelter near the top to hunker down in if the weather turns nasty.

Out on the Ice . . . Safely

With all of their deep, slippery-lipped crevasses, deceptively thin trapdoors of ice, and other hazards, glaciers are extremely dangerous places for the uninitiated to wander. Which is why the $125 that you pay to **Exit Glacier Guides** ✪✪ (in an old train car at the small boat harbor; ☎ 907/224-5569; www.exitglacierguides. com) may be the best investment you make while in Alaska. Exit Glacier Guides offer a number of hikes daily throughout the summer, but the one with the greatest variety combines a 1-hour hike up the Harding Icefield Trail, with a pass through an alpine valley and a scramble down a rocky scree. Participants then strap crampons on their feet, and spend an hour out on the blue ice of the glacier, peering into crevasses and listening to crystal clear ice streams deep within. The wisecracking guides (you may get Captain Crampon, The Silver Sherpa, or both) mix corny trail banter with sober bits of wisdom (how to make Devil's Club tea, what to do if you encounter a bear, and so on). **Warning:** You need to be reasonably fit to take on one of these challenging hikes.

SEA TOURS

And now onto seeing the glaciers of Kenai Fjords National Park by sea, which you'll do with one of three companies. Each price their tours competitively, so picking a tour operator is largely a matter of: 1) What time you want to go. 2) How long you want to be out (shorter cruises might be better if you've got small kids). 3) What you want to eat.

Note: Add Seward's 6% sales tax and $3.50 per-passenger harbor fee to all glacier, marine wildlife, and sea kayaking tours described in this section.

The rock-bottom lowest fare is the $119 ($59 kids 11 and under) charged by **Major Marine Tours** (☎ 800/764-7300 or 907/274-7300; www.majormarine.com) for an 8-hour tour. That's a good long tour for a good price, but it doesn't include lunch. You can either pack your own (and really save), or pay an extra $15 for the on-board, all-you-can-eat salmon and prime rib buffet. Pay the $15. Major Marine has the best food of the lot. The boat leaves at 11:45am and gets back 7:45pm.

Renown Tours (☎ 888/514-8687; www.renowntours.com) has a 6-hour tour leaving at 11:30am for $129 ($65 kids ages 3–11, toddlers and infants free), which includes a light lunch (smoked salmon, a bagel and cream cheese, fruit, and a cookie). Renown uses a triple-decker motor catamaran that looks top heavy but rides smoothly—it's the best for the rough seas, in fact.

Of the three big tour operators permitted to go to Kenai Fjords National Park, I prefer **Kenai Fjords Tours** ✦ (1304 4th Ave.; ☎ 888/478-3346 or 907/224-8068; www.kenaifjords.com) simply because of my peculiar inability to sit still for very long when at sea. I need to walk the decks, and Kenai Fjords Tours' vessels are the best for this. They've got lots of different decks and passageways, plus a great variety of places to sit inside and outside. The deck plan is such that you can make endless circuits, varying your route, with no need to backtrack—which is important to wanderers. It has 6-hour glacier tours for $129 ($65 kids 2–11). For just 10 bucks more, it also has 8½-hour tours ($139, or $70 kids) which include a stop at Fox Island along the way for a salmon bake. (Overnight packages are also available, starting at $349 adults, $179 kids, which combine glacier tours with a night at the company's Fox Island Lodge.) There's also a 9½-hour tour that goes

---

The Green Factor

A caveat about seasickness: Of all the tidewater glacier tours in Alaska you can go on, the ones that go to Kenai Fjords National Park are the ones most likely to make you seasick. To get from Resurrection Bay to the sheltered waters of the park, you have to enter the Gulf of Alaska for a spell, and there's about a 50/50 chance or so of hitting rough seas. Take Dramamine, Bonine, or another seasickness preventative prior to departing and spare yourself the indignity of heaving over the rail. By comparison, the waters of both Prince William Sound and Glacier Bay are well protected, and seasickness isn't an issue on those cruises. Seasickness is also hardly ever an issue on the wildlife tours that stay within the protected waters of Resurrection Bay.

Sled Dog Tours in the Summer

The wild, slobbery fun of running with a team of Alaskan sled dogs is a quintessentially "Alaskan" experience. Once used by the Alaska Natives to zip across the frozen landscape, dog sleds today are more commonly used for sport. And in the summer, to be honest, they're around for the tourists. Those who visit in the warmer weather, but want to get a taste of the over-the-snow speed of winter dog sledding, can choose **Godwin Glacier Dog Sled Tours** (☎ 888/989-8239 or 907/224-8239; www.alaskadogsled.com). It helicopters its clients across Resurrection Bay to a dog camp atop 10,000-year-old Godwin Glacier, home to their snowy summer dog camp. The entire trip takes about 2 hours, with a half-hour in a sled pulled by a team of Alaskan sled dogs bred to run. It's a costly if memorable splurge, at $430 for adults and $390 for children. Big discounts are sometimes available in the shoulder season, in late May and early June.

The other method for mushing in summer costs considerably less . . . but lacks snow. That being said, the tours of **Ididaride Sled Dog Tours** ✪ 🐾 (Mile 1.1 Old Exit Glacier Rd.; ☎ 800/478-3139 or 907/224-8608; www.ididaride.com) may well be the more in-depth experience. Tours are led by members of the Seavey family, who have been involved with the Iditarod race from the get-go. Dan Seavey helped found the race and is one of the original mushers; his son Mitch Seavey won the race in 2003; and the youngest generation of Seavey boys are now racing in the Iditarod or the Junior Iditarod. Over the course of the 1½-hour tour, guests visit the kennels, getting a chance to hold the puppies and handle the gear used in the race; watch a video with Iditarod wipe-out highlights (mushing is much more dangerous than you might have imagined); and take a 2-mile ride in a wagon hitched to a team of sled dogs in-training. The ride is a blast, but equally rewarding is the up-close look you get of the two sides of the unique athletic culture of the Iditarod: the elite world of the jockey-like mushers on one side, and the clamorous, closed community of the very un-petlike dogs on the other. Tours run throughout the day, but you should call ahead for reservations. They cost $59 for adults, and $29 for children (ages 2–11).

to a glacier deeper in the park than the other two tour operators go. It costs $159 for adults ($80 for kids), and includes breakfast and lunch. If Kenai Fjords Tours' vessels weren't as conducive to stretching your legs as they are, 9½ hours would be too long for me. Happily, that's not the case.

SEA KAYAKING TOURS

Visiting Kenai Fjords National Park aboard a tour boat with more than 100 other passengers is one thing. Floating there before a massive wall of ice in a sea kayak, among the cobalt blue icebergs and doe-eyed harbor seals is another experience entirely. Alone time with a glacier will cost you more than joining the crowd, but if there's room for a splurge in your budget, this would be a good place to let it loose. Only very experienced sea kayakers ought to consider going on their own; you can get tips on how to do so from the **Kenai Fjords National Park Visitor Information Center** (at the small boat harbor; ☎ 907/224-7500 or 907/224-2132 for recorded info; www.nps.gov/kefj). Otherwise, go with a guide.

Sunny Cove Kayaking (☎ 800/770-9119; www.sunnycove.com) carries kayakers to the park aboard a 40-foot cabin cruiser, stopping to sightsee and watch marine wildlife just as the big tour boats do, then turns you and a guide loose in kayaks to explore the glacier for 3 hours. The cost is $375 per person plus tax, and a minimum of four people are needed to book a charter. Short guided paddles closer to Seward—with no glaciers in sight—start at $59 per person.

MARINE WILDLIFE TOURS

Those who've gotten their fill of glaciers in other parts of Alaska should skip the pricey glacier tours out of Seward and concentrate on wildlife spotting around Resurrection Bay. On a wildlife tour, you're likely to take in seabirds, eagles, seals, sea lions, mountain goats, and possibly even bears. Your chances of spotting a whale aren't as good as they would be if you went on one of the glacier tours (which double as whale-watching tours), although there is a resident population of killer whales that comes and goes from Resurrection Bay, and humpback whales occasionally make appearances near the mouth of the long bay. Best of all, these wilderness-oriented tours are shorter and less expensive than the glacier tours, and they use smaller, more intimate boats. Each of the three glacier tour operators also does wildlife tours. **Major Marine** has the top deal: a 5-hour tour for $59 adults ($29 kids), which gets out to the mouth of the bay where you might actually spot whales. For an additional $15 for adults ($7 for kids), you can dine on salmon for lunch during the trip. **Kenai Fjords Tours** has the most options, including a 3-hour tour for $59 adults ($30 kids), and a 5-hour tour with a stop on Fox Island for the salmon bake for $79 adults ($40 kids).

SOLDOTNA/KENAI

For non-fishermen, there are no good reasons to spend vacation time in either Kenai or Soldotna, sprawling sister cities along the swift Kenai River. For sports fishermen, there are hundreds of thousands of reasons to visit—all of them swimming upstream to spawn (if they can avoid the summer frenzy of fishermen trying to pluck them from the water and plop them onto a hot grill, that is). The Kenai River is the most popular fishing river in Alaska, famous for its Mack Daddy–size king salmon. Kenai River kings, in fact, are the largest kings in the world. Land a 50-pound king in any other Alaskan river and the state Department of Fish and Game certifies it as trophy. On the Kenai River, where 50-pounders are more common than beat-up pickup trucks on an Alaskan highway, you've got to muscle in a 75-pounder before you're in the trophy class. Silver salmon and red salmon also fill the river, keeping the fishermen coming all summer long, and keeping hundreds of local fishing guides in business. Whether you're a seasoned angler or a green-behind-the-gills newbie, you'll have no trouble finding a guide happy to take you out on the river to reel in some big ones.

A BRIEF HISTORY

Kenai was founded in 1791 as a Russian fur-trading post at the mouth of the Kenai River, the site of an Athabascan Indian village. It was the second permanent Russian settlement in Alaska, after Kodiak. A few historic Russian-influenced buildings still stand on the site of the original settlement (the originals are long gone), along with a replica of the town's original Russian Orthodox Church school.

In the early–20th century, Kenai was a busy cannery town, and in the mid–20th century, when oil was discovered in Cook Inlet, it became an oil town, and has remained one ever since. Commercial fishing is also big here—the small boat harbor inside the wide river mouth is home to a considerable drift-net fleet. From the town's beach or bluffs you can watch parades of fishing boats coming and going. Occasionally, you'll spot some Cook Inlet beluga whales in the river, who chase salmon as fervently as any fisherman.

Soldotna, centerless and strung out along the highway, is a child of the Automobile Age. It was born in 1947, the year bulldozers started pushing across the Kenai Peninsula to build a road that would connect Anchorage with the towns on the Kenai Peninsula. In the aftermath of World War II, hundreds of veterans came to Alaska to take advantage of government programs giving them home-steading preferences. Many liked the looks of the new road's junction with the beautiful river and staked their claims there. While former soldiers clearly founded Soldotna, it's uncertain today whether the town's name came from the Russian word for "soldier" or the Native word for "creek." Quite possibly, it was a little of both.

LAY OF THE LAND

There are a bunch of smaller communities along the 80-mile Kenai River, but Soldotna and Kenai are the primary hubs. The river slices right through Soldotna, a rushing artery of wilderness enlivening an otherwise drab town of gas stations and fast food franchises. On the right side of the road, just after the bridge you cross when driving south, you'll come to the **Soldotna Visitor Information Center** (44790 Sterling Hwy.; ☎ 907/262-9814 or 907/262-1337; www.soldotna chamber.com; summer daily 9am–7pm, winter Mon–Fri 9am–5pm). Stop there to see the world's largest sport-caught king salmon (97 pounds, 4 ounces), and to get a close-up look at the Kenai River from the steel-boardwalk there that keeps visitors and fishermen from trampling the riverbank.

Kenai, built high on a bluff overlooking the broad mouth of the river, has its share of box stores and other unlovely development. But it's also got several miles of beach and a choice view of the wide mouth of the river and of the snow-capped volcanic peaks across Cook Inlet. Stop at the **Kenai Visitor and Cultural Center** (11471 Kenai Spur Hwy.; ☎ 907/283-1991; www.visitkenai.com; summer Mon–Fri 9am–7pm, Sat–Sun 10am–6pm; off season Mon–Fri 9am–5pm, Sat 11am–4pm) for free maps and information, to see exhibits documenting the Native, Russian, and American cultures that have made the area what it is today, and to marvel at the "King of Snags," a gargantuan knot of lost fishing lures, lines, rods, sticks, and branches recovered from the river. Also pick up the free brochure **Old Town Kenai Walking Tour,** which is a key to the old buildings at the top of the bluff where the original town site was. Highlights of the tour include a Russian Orthodox church built in 1894, and the offices of the Kenai Chamber of Commerce, which occupy "Moosemeat John's Cabin," built by a homesteader who hunted moose to feed his 13 children.

GETTING TO & AROUND KENAI

Because the drive from Anchorage to Soldotna and Kenai passes through such spectacular country, and because you'll be helpless in these two sprawling, public-transportation-free communities without a car, driving is the most sensible way to get to and around town. Soldotna is located about 150 miles from Anchorage along the Sterling Highway (about a 3-hr. drive, nonstop), which crosses the Kenai River at Soldotna before heading south to Homer. The Kenai Spur Highway branches off the Sterling Highway at Soldotna and leads to Kenai, 11 miles away.

The main airport for the Kenai Peninsula is at Kenai, a short 65-mile hop across the water from Anchorage. **ERA Aviation** (☎ 800/866-8394 or 907/266-8394; www.flyera.com) has frequent flights, starting at around $160 round-trip. Four rental car companies are at the airport, **Avis, Budget, Hertz,** and **Payless.**

Homer Stage Line (☎ 907/235-2252 or 907/339-1847; www.homerstageline.com) stops at Soldotna on its way to Homer. One-way fare from Anchorage is $50, and a round-trip fare costs $90.

ACCOMMODATIONS, BOTH STANDARD & NOT

Soldotna has a profusion of hotel and motel rooms indistinguishable from the standard fare you'll find along highways from Oakland, California, to Ocean City, Maryland. These places are fine for people from Anchorage or Fairbanks, down on the peninsula for a few days of fishing. But they certainly aren't ideal for travelers who want to get in touch with the real Alaska. In the Kenai-Soldotna area, you're better off staying at one of the many bed-and-breakfasts. Not only will you have a chance to get to know some bona fide Alaskans (and you'll never really get to know Alaska without getting to know real Alaskans), you'll also be in a good position to get the inside scoop on where the fish are biting, when they're biting, and what lures they're taking. There are several dozen local B&Bs, and all of the owners are fluent in fishing. Many are located right on the river and have boat launches, docks, or riverbank walkways that make getting to a good fishing spot as easy as walking into the backyard. Some have processing rooms where you can cut and gut your catch, as well as freezers where you can stash it. Most will also set you up with a local fishing guide, or at least tip you off on whom to avoid.

The best way to zero in on one of these truly authentic Alaskan accommodations is through the **Kenai Peninsula Bed & Breakfast Association** (☎ 866/436-2266 or 907/776-8883; www.kenaipeninsulabba.com), which has about 35 members. While the association purports to cover the entire Kenai Peninsula, most of its members are concentrated around Kenai and Soldotna. Not all B&Bs in Alaska necessarily have screens on their windows, or pay their local taxes, or keep their bathroom sinks hairball free. But all of the members of the Kenai Peninsula Bed & Breakfast Association do, and a peer review process and guest comment cards help to ensure that they continue to do so.

The thing to keep in mind if you call the association's hotline (the members take turns answering it) is that not all of the properties are in Kenai or Soldotna.

So check to make sure you're not booking someplace 2 hours away from where you want to be. "The Kenai Peninsula is a big place," says association member Diana Lofstedt, host of Harborside Cottages in Kenai (reviewed below). "You wouldn't believe how many people call and say, 'Oh, you mean Kenai Fjords National Park, which is outside of Seward, is not in Kenai?'"

Hotels & Bed & Breakfasts

$$-$$$ Some of the association's members put guests up in cottages or cabins, but most run traditional homestay-style B&Bs. A typical example is **Tanglewood Bed & Breakfast** (2528 Beaver Loop Rd.; ☎ 907/283-6771; www.tanglewoodbed andbreakfast.com; MC, V), a large country home with a front yard stocked with rusting cars and old commercial fishing paraphernalia (not at all unusual in rural Alaska, where storing junk in your yard is an emblem of practicality and self-reliance). The sprawling backyard runs right up to the edge of the Kenai River, where you can fish from the bank without another angler in sight. Across the river, and visible from most rooms in the house, is a broad and wild delta; grab a pair of binoculars and you might spot moose, caribou, and bald eagles there. The house is a three-level affair with an enormous upstairs suite boasting a queen-size canopy bed, a twin bed, a private bath, and a recliner from which you can watch TV, wildlife on the river delta, or both. It goes for $150. In the home's daylight basement (one side has windows, the other doesn't) there are four small, unadorned rooms that share two baths and have just enough space for the beds and your suitcases. They sleep either two or three people with various combinations of twins and queens, and they go for either $100 to $125. *Warning:* One room has no windows at all, a deficiency that the host, Delora Garcia, puts an almost convincing spin on when she says, "It's good if the summer light keeps you awake." Breakfast times are flexible, but Delora's menu isn't. "You tell me when you're eating. I'll tell you what you're having," she says. It's usually a large serving of hash browns and eggs, with bacon or sausage.

$$$-$$$$ Less typical of the Kenai Peninsula Bed & Breakfast Association members is **Harborside Cottages** ✿✿ (813 Riverview Dr.; ☎ 888/283-6162 or 907/283-6162; www.harborsidecottages.com; AE, DISC, MC, V), which is a B&B in the very loosest sense (you get a welcome basket with homemade bread and fruit when you check in, but after that you're on your own). I love this place anyway. Its five tidy, vinyl-clapboarded cabins are clustered among cottonwood, spruce, and birch trees atop a high, windy bluff at the mouth of the Kenai River. The cabins' little front decks are perfect perches from which to watch the comings and goings of fishing boats and, sometimes, beluga whales. Each has just enough room for two (some units have twins, some have two twins pushed together and covered with so many layers of padding that you'd never know you weren't on a genuine king-size bed). The location is quiet, romantic, close to the weathered Russian-style buildings of Old Town Kenai, and about a 5-minute walk to the beach, a dandy place for long strolls, driftwood fires, and agate hunting. The best rates are in May and September, when rooms are $135 a night. They go up to $150 in June and August, and peak at $170 in July, when the sockeye salmon peak, too (and sports fishermen overrun the town).

$–$$$$ Across the river mouth from Kenai, a decommissioned salmon cannery has been reborn as a vacation spot offering easy access to fishing and low-rate historic lodging. Accommodations at the **Kenai Landing** (2101 Bowpicker Lane; ☎ 907/335-2500; www.kenailanding.com; AE, DC, DISC, MC, V) range from tiny rooms in the former dormitories of the cannery workers, to one-room cottages where the resident ship captains slept, to a three-room cottage where ship officers and visiting dignitaries stayed. All are simply furnished, clean, and modern on the inside, with original corrugated metal roofing and siding on the outside. In addition, there are a bunch of two-room, riverfront suites in a set of buildings that weren't part of the cannery. During the peak season of July, the dorm rooms go for just $89 (they've got corner sinks in the rooms and shared baths down the hall), the captains' quarters (great for a couple) run $149 to $159, the cottages (good for a small family) are $209, and the suites run $165 to $185. In June and August the rates drop $20 to $30, and in May and September they drop by that much again (the place closes in the off season). A cavernous old warehouse has a few gift shops that you can rattle around in, and the hulking building where the canning line was located now houses a so-so restaurant with very high ceilings and lots of room between tables. But the real draw is the river. You can fish right from the cannery's dock, or you can arrange for a guide (p. 127) to pick you up there in a boat and take you out on the water. Long Cook Inlet beach is also nearby, where the non-fishing members of your party can beachcomb and make a driftwood fire while the fishermen catch dinner.

Camping

Tent sites are $11 a night at Soldotna's **Centennial Park Campground,** which runs along a bluff above the Kenai River. When heading southbound through town on the Sterling Highway, turn right on Kalifornsky Beach Road just after the bridge across the river and look for the campground sign on your right.

DINING FOR ALL TASTES

Fast food franchises dominate the dining scene in both Kenai and Soldotna, though there are a handful of more interesting eateries. I've listed them below.

$ For a quick bite at a popular local diner, stop at **Sal's Klondike Diner** (44619 Sterling Hwy., at corner of Lovers Lane; ☎ 907/262-2220; daily 24 hr.; AE, MC, V), which serves a typical menu of burgers, omelets, and chocolate malts, along with fried halibut sandwiches, sides of reindeer sausage, and locally made salmon sausage. Breakfast is served round the clock and the portions are huge. Most items cost less than $10, and certain breakfasts are priced at $5 for one and $9 for two (the fried egg with biscuits and gravy hits the spot). If you need help finding this place, when you're driving southbound on the Sterling Highway passing through Soldotna, just look for a space on the left with a portrait of a Klondike Girl and a miniature mining village on the roof—that'd be Sal's.

$–$$ The only Russian-style building in Old Town Kenai that's open to the public and isn't the Russian Orthodox church also happens to be the best place in town to eat, **Veronica's Cafe** ★ (604 Peterson Way, across from the Russian church; ☎ 907/283-2725; summer Mon–Wed 9am–9pm, Thurs–Sat 9am–9:30pm, Sun

11am–5pm; rest of year Mon–Wed and Sat 10am–4pm, Thurs and Fri 10am–9:30pm; MC, V). Built as a cabin in 1918 by a Russian Native family, it transformed from cabin to coffeehouse and was on the verge of going under when an anthropology instructor met a commercial fisherman in line there. They married, told each other they couldn't bear to see the place close, and bought it. The two talented chefs they found have free reign in the kitchen. Now, in addition to lattes and double espressos, you can get a chicken-cashew sandwich or a bowl of cabbage-and-kielbasa soup for less than $10, and dinner specials such as tamale pies, lasagna, and seared salmon with raspberry butter and saffron rice, usually for less than $15. With its sloping floors, exposed wood beams, mismatched place mats, live music, and general ramshackle state, Veronica's brings the town's present and past together, as well as its visitors and residents.

ACTIVE KENAI

For fishermen, there's no need to explain the appeal of battling with your own dinner at the end of a monofilament line that's taut as a harp string. For non-fishermen, there's no way for you to really know whether all the fuss will appeal to you until you try it. And the abundance of fish and guides in the Kenai and Soldotna area make it a fine place for beginning fishermen.

Newbies should go with a guide service. Standing on a bank trying to figure things out on your own will save you money, but cost you a bundle in frustration and time. Hiring an expert with a boat to give you a crash course in salmon fishing will be way more rewarding. After getting some training, you can spend as much time as you like honing your skills along the riverbank.

Guided charters average about $150 to $180 for a 6½-hour trip, and $250 to $275 for a full day. Check with the area visitor centers for assistance in weeding through the hundreds of guide services. Or try **The Sports Den** (☎ 907/262-7491;

When the Salmon Run

King salmon, aka Chinook—For this prized catch, you'll want to be on hand for one of two runs. The first one goes from mid-May to June (sometimes it's catch and release only). The second starts in early July and goes through the month. The first, in general, has more but smaller fish (though "small" on the Kenai River can still weigh 40 pounds). Most anglers fish for king from a boat—your chances of hooking one from shore are far slimmer.

Reds, aka the sockeye—The reds run from mid-July to early August, mixing in with the second king run. Reds are catchable from shore or from a boat. The most popular spots for reds are at the confluences of the Kenai River with the Russian River and the Moose River.

Silvers, aka coho—The silvers have two runs. The first starts in late July and goes into August. The second, and lighter run, occurs in September. Like the sockeye, silvers can be caught from shore as well as from a boat.

Warning: Hooking the Fisherman Instead of the Fish

Every summer about 100 people show up at Soldotna's emergency room with fishhooks stuck in their skin. Most of them are fishermen who snagged themselves, and the rest are bystanders. To avoid a Kenai River body piercing, do not stand behind a casting fisherman. And if you're fishing, dress defensively. The wide-brimmed hats and sunglasses everybody wears here aren't just for sun protection.

www.alaskasportsden.com), one well-established operator that offers salmon fishing day trips on the river for about $150.

Of course, you don't need a guide to fish if you have the know-how (though your odds of going home with salmon—especially king salmon—are better if you fish from a boat). Bring your rod and reel, get an Alaskan fishing license (and a king stamp if you're going for kings), and you're in business. Licenses and stamps are widely available at grocery stores and other retail outlets, or online at **www.admin.adfg.state.ak.us/license**. The cost for non-residents is $20 for a day, $35 for 3 days, $55 for 7 days, and $80 for 14 days.

There are more than two dozen public access points along the Kenai River. Many of them are so crowded with anglers, especially those along the lower part of the river, that fishermen stand shoulder to shoulder. Around Soldotna, steel boardwalks have been built to protect the riverbanks from the crowds. Get out of town, if you can, to find more elbow room.

For those who want true wilderness, the Kenai Airport is a jumping-off point for charter operators offering fishing trips across the water on the unpopulated, roadless side of Cook Inlet. Among them is **High Adventure Air** (☎ 907/262-5237; www.highadventureair.com). Day trips to fish on the west side of Cook Inlet range from $320 to $395 per person, depending on the location.

HOMER

Homer goes by a number of different monikers. Most apt, I think, is "Cosmic Hamlet by the Sea" as it's a town of artists, writers, fishermen, hippies, Russian Orthodox Church dissidents, Native seal hunters, moose slayers, drop-outs, drifters, seekers, cold water surfers, and all sorts of other free souls. It's the creative, experimental, diversity-honoring heart of Alaska. Other names include the "End of the Road," celebrating the fact that this is as far west as the continuous U.S. highway system goes before it runs out of pavement. Homer's also known as The Halibut Fishing Capital of the World, because it's the home port of Alaska's foremost commercial and sports halibut fishing fleets. T-shirts call it "a quaint little drinking town with a fishing problem," which sums up Homer's beach town, summer-party atmosphere pretty well.

But even if you don't drink or fish, Homer's got plenty going for it in its thriving local arts scene, its great restaurants, its long beaches and stunning scenery, and its proximity to a fabulous marine wilderness. Just across the water, at the foot of the Kenai Mountains, lies Kachemak Bay State Park, a roadless world filled with opportunities to hike, camp, and sea kayak.

A BRIEF HISTORY

Homer was founded in 1895 as a camp for gold prospectors, but coal turned out to be where the money was. Coal mining dominated Homer from the turn of the century until World War II, and there's still plenty of the black mineral in the ground. Walk along Bishop's Beach and you'll see long coal seams in the eroding cliffs. Fishing and tourism hold down the economy nowadays, though coal still makes an appearance, sometimes in the most unexpected places. Homer's got one of the few beaches in the world where you can collect both driftwood and coal to throw into a bonfire.

Homer has long appealed to mavericks. In the 1950s, "the barefooters," a communal group that eschewed footwear, even in the winter, made its home there. In the 1960s, hippies discovered Homer, and so did the reclusive Old Believers, an insular group of Russian-speaking fishermen and farmers who, after all these years, continue to object to reforms the Russian Orthodox Church implemented under Peter the Great. The Old Believers have taken root in a handful of rural villages they've established, and you'll see them all around town, the men and boys in their embroidered shirts and hand-woven belts, and the women in their ankle-length dresses. A lot of the hippies stuck around and now run businesses, farms, and fishing boats. Homer also has a substantial community of potters, sculptors, painters, woodworkers, and other artists, who give the town definite pizazz.

LAY OF THE LAND

Homer is a 238-mile drive south of Anchorage, at the bottom of the Kenai Peninsula and at the end of the Sterling Highway. It sits on the north shore of a beautiful, 40-mile-long fjord called Kachemak Bay. Protruding halfway across the bay is a 4½-mile bar of gravel, called the Homer Spit. The Spit is the focal point for vacationers. It's where the fishing harbor is, along with beach campgrounds, and all sorts of seasonal restaurants, shops, and charter boat outfits. The rest of the town is strung out along miles of Kachemak Bay shoreline and up nearby 1,200-foot bluffs. There's no downtown, which is a drawback. Homer's closest equivalent to a town square is driftwood-strewn Bishop's Beach, just south of The Spit. It's where people go to promenade, build bonfires, walk their dogs, surf, and show off their pickup trucks (locals drive up and down the beach at low tide).

The Homer Chamber of Commerce Visitor Information Center (201 Sterling Hwy.; ☎ 907/235-7740; www.homeralaska.org; Memorial Day–Labor Day Mon–Fri 9am–7pm, Sat–Sun 10am–6pm; rest of year Mon–Fri 9am–5pm) is one of the first buildings you come to as you drive into town and is a good source for visitor information.

Across Kachemak Bay, beneath the hanging glaciers creeping down the Kenai Mountains from the Harding Icefield, are the hiking trails and kayaking waters of **Kachemak Bay State Park.** There are two communities on that side of the bay to explore, as well, both inaccessible by road. **Halibut Cove** once had a thriving herring saltry (where the fish were packed in salt) and a population of 1,000. Now it has a population of 23, art galleries, and a good restaurant (called the Saltry).

Twelve blocks of boardwalks run along the waterfront, but it has no roads. **Seldovia** is a sleepy fishing village, with a few shops and an old Russian Orthodox church worth visiting.

GETTING TO & AROUND HOMER
By Car

Driving is the best way to get to Homer. From Anchorage, it's a 4½-hour drive down the scenic Seward and Sterling highways if you don't stop to see the sights. But there are plenty of sights, so give yourself a day for the journey. Once in Homer, it's also helpful to have a car. As nice a town as it is in other respects, it suffers from poor urban planning and isn't an easy place to get around by foot. And there's no public transportation. If you arrive in Homer without a car, you can rent one at the airport from **Hertz** (☎ 800/654-3131 or 907/235-0734; www. hertz.com).

By Shuttle

The cheapest way to get to Homer is via the **Homer Stage Line** (2607 Eagle St.; ☎ 907/235-2252 or 907/339-1847; www.homerstageline.com), which offers van trips from Anchorage to Homer for $60 one-way or $110 round-trip. If you're headed for Seward too, you can make the complete Anchorage-Homer-Seward circuit for $140, starting at any of those points and returning to where you started.

By Air

ERA Aviation (☎ 800/866-8394; www.flyera.com) flies between Homer and Anchorage several times a day in the summer. Round-trip fares start at around $224.

By Ferry

The **Alaska Marine Highway System** (☎ 800/642-0066; www.ferryalaska.com) connects Homer with Kodiak Island (9½ hr. away) and some of the Bush communities along the Alaska Peninsula and in the Aleutian Islands.

By Water Taxi

To get across Kachemak Bay to go hiking, camping, or kayaking, go with **Mako's Water Taxi** (☎ 907/235-9005; www.makoswatertaxi.com; $70 round-trip). Mako's also offers tours of the bay, starting at $40 per person for a 1-hour trip.

ACCOMMODATIONS, BOTH STANDARD & NOT

As one of Alaska's favorite seaside getaways, Homer has no shortage of places to stay. It's got more than 35 hotels, motels, and inns and more than 140 less standard lodging options, including bed-and-breakfasts, in-town campgrounds, hostels, and some apartments and rooms by the small boat harbor, which only the sports fishermen seem to know about.

I cover all the bases below, but because B&B stays, and to a lesser extent house rentals, are the most uniquely Alaskan way to go, I'll start with those. Homer has a shortage of labor, as do many cities in this relatively sparsely populated state. For the summer high season, therefore, it imports many of its hotel workers (a lot of them are college students), which means they'll be just as clueless as you about the area, should you need advice. Not so with the B&Bs. These are owned by real

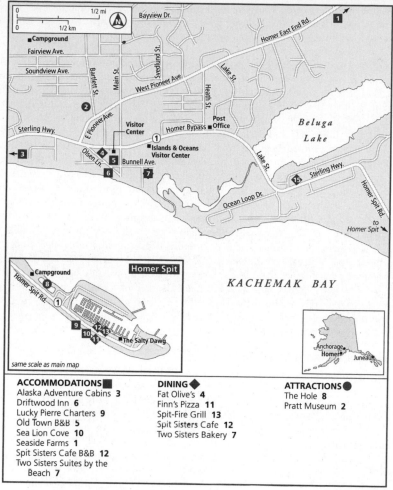

ACCOMMODATIONS ■
Alaska Adventure Cabins **3**
Driftwood Inn **6**
Lucky Pierre Charters **9**
Old Town B&B **5**
Sea Lion Cove **10**
Seaside Farms **1**
Spit Sisters Cafe B&B **12**
Two Sisters Suites by the
    Beach **7**

DINING ◆
Fat Olive's **4**
Finn's Pizza **11**
Spit-Fire Grill **13**
Spit Sisters Cafe **12**
Two Sisters Bakery **7**

ATTRACTIONS ●
The Hole **8**
Pratt Museum **2**

Alaskans, many with Alaskan roots going back several generations. "You actually meet people who live in Alaska when you stay in a B&B," says Don Cotogno, treasurer of the **Homer Bed & Breakfast Association** (☎ 877/296-1114 or 907/ 226-1114; www.homerbedbreakfast.com). "And they can tell you all about the area, what life is like here, where to eat, you name it."

If they're represented by Cotogno's organization, you can also be sure that they'll be fully inspected and up to snuff. In an effort to keep the state government out of their lives ("We don't want angry complaints going to state senators who then might write up silly laws governing B&Bs," says Cotogno), the Homer B&B Association initiated a rigorous process of peer review 3 years ago. They have a laundry list of what B&Bs must offer their clients and the standards of cleanliness and safety they must maintain to be represented by the Association.

Members are inspected yearly by their officers; in the past 2 years, they've kicked out two B&Bs who didn't comply. They also will move a client from one lodging to another if they're unhappy (a safety net you won't find with such direct-rental-from-owner sites as VRBO.com).

The Homer Bed & Breakfast Association currently has 40 members: 25 classic B&Bs (with an owner living on the premises and serving food in the am) and 15 other types of accommodations (B&Bs without breakfast or private vacation rentals). They're as diverse as the town they're in. B&B Junee's, for example, is run by a spry 70 year old, whose father was a gold miner and whose house is like a gold rush museum, it's so packed with mining memorabilia. Sometimes the other B&B owners send their guests over just to talk with Junee, as she's an admired storyteller and verbal historian in these parts. Another recommended B&B is run by the garrulous sisters who helm a popular local cafe (see Two Sisters Suites by the Beach, p. 133). Stay there and you're guaranteed to meet locals: Breakfast puts you right in the center of Homer's social swirl. While some of the Association's B&Bs go for as little as $95 per night double occupancy, most run between $110 and $130 per night—that's still lower than what you'll pay at most area hotels.

As I write this, Homer has a competing B&B organization called **Homer's Finest Bed & Breakfast Network** (☎ 800/764-3211 or 907/235-4983; www. homeraccommodations.com) but the two groups will probably be merged by the time this book comes out. The Homer Chamber of Commerce (www.homer alaska.org) also maintains lists of local B&Bs, but since they're not inspected, I'd recommend going with one of the other two organizations (or with the specific B&Bs I recommend below).

Hotels & Bed & Breakfasts

$ **Seaside Farms** (40904 Seaside Farm Rd.; ☎ 907/235-7850; www.xyz.net/~seaside; MC, V but rates are lower if you use cash) is by definition a hostel, but it's no ordinary hostel. It's also a working horse, cattle, and organic raspberry farm bordering Kachemak Bay. Inside its 1950s farmhouse, there are $20 bunks and $50 to $70 rooms, but forget about those and get one of the private cottages. They're tiny, homey, and set among the pastures, hayfields, wildflowers, birch grove, and shoreline of the farm. One, with a sleeping loft, a propane double burner, and raspberry bushes growing under its kitchen window, is snuggled up to a field where cows graze. Another, with a sagging porch and a fat-bellied little woodstove set upon beach rocks, sits on a bluff overlooking the bay. None have electricity or running water, but each has its own outhouse . . . and its own soul. Anybody with a drop of hippie in their blood will be spellbound. They go for $60 to $75, or you can do chores around the farm in exchange for your lodging. The owners also allow vacationers to camp on the premises for $10.

$$ The next place to consider was originally a Depression-era boarding house above a general store. The store is now the Bunnell Street Gallery and the living quarters above it have become **Old Town Bed & Breakfast** ★★ (106 W. Bunnell Ave.; ☎ 907/235-7558; www.oldtownbedandbreakfast.com; MC, V), which as you might guess from the name, is loaded with historic character. And except for a wildly listing stairway leading to the B&B, the old building is in beautiful shape. The early-20th-century feel of the upstairs is conveyed through the furnishings,

such as four-poster or brass beds, and original hardwood floors. One room has its own bath, and two share a bath. Choose either of the two corner rooms and you'll have a view of the snow-capped mountains across Kachemak Bay. Rooms range in price from $95 to $115 in summer (less the rest of the year). Breakfast and a 4pm tea is included in the price and prepared in the tiny Italian deli and catering business next door, whose owner, a young art school drop-out, proclaims: "I used to be a painting major. Now I'm a food artist."

$$$ There are ocean views upstairs, and sticky buns with steaming lattes downstairs at **Two Sisters Suites by the Beach** ★★★ (233 E. Bunnell Ave.; ☎ 907/235-2280; www.twosistersbakery.net; MC, V). The three $145 rooms (down to $95 from Sept 15–May 1) are located a block from Bishop's Beach, a half block from the wetlands of Beluga Sough, and right upstairs from Two Sisters Bakery. The nightly rate includes anything you want for breakfast in the artisan bakery and cafe, a casual place where none of the fishermen drinking coffee and reading the *Anchorage Daily News* will bat an eye if you show up in your jammies. But don't pick it just for the pastries. The rooms are lovely, too: artfully designed digs with bamboo laminate flooring, colorful paintings by local artists on the walls, overstuffed seating, plush queen-size beds, and creatively pleasant bathrooms (I especially like the thick, cotton towels and the beach stone accents in the showers). While each of the rooms is the same price, rooms no. 1 and no. 2 are the largest, and look out across Kachemak Bay at the jagged peaks and retreating glaciers of the Kenai mountains. All of them are well within the bakery's aroma zone.

$–$$$$ No lodging in Homer covers all the bases in price quite like **Driftwood Inn** (135 W. Bunnell Ave.; ☎ 800/478-8019 or 907/235-8019; www.thedriftwood inn.com; MC, V). The Driftwood's diversified strategy ranges from $43 RV sites to $275-per-night beach houses, all of them on the bluffs above Bishop's Beach. Unless you're driving your own lodging, you'll be best off staying in the inn's main building, a cluttered, time-worn place that tilts and sags behind its fresh vinyl siding the way casual, seaside getaways tilt and sag everywhere. The small and simple rooms come with various combinations of single-, double-, and queen-size beds, and private or shared baths. Some have built-in writing desks and fold-down bunks that give them the air of economy-class staterooms in old school ocean liners. Most range from $120 to $156, double occupancy, but a few go for as little as $72. Those would be what the Driftwood calls its "Ships Quarters," easily the tiniest rooms in Alaska. They are essentially 8-by-12-foot cedar closets with bunk room for three. Miraculously, a private bath has been squeezed into each of them. As cramped as they sound, they're oddly cozy, and perfect for an economy-minded, non-claustrophobic duo or trio, or older kids.

$$$$ When you see the decommissioned fishing vessel the *Double Eagle* for the first time, you get an idea of how the people who believe they discovered Noah's ark atop Mount Ararat in Turkey must have felt. This 75-foot Gulf Coast shrimper, which came to Alaska to help with the cleanup of the *Exxon Valdez* oil spill, now rests on a steeply sloping mountainside high above Kachemak Bay. It's one of four lofty and uncommon vacation rentals belonging to **Alaska Adventure Cabins** ★★ 🅺🅸🅳🆂 (2525 Sterling Hwy.; ☎ 907/223-6681; www.alaskaadventure cabins.com; MC, V), all suitable for big families. The kid appeal of the *Double*

The Homer Spit's Fisherman Hideaways

In addition to the obvious places to stay on the Spit—the campgrounds and RV parks, the $400-per-night luxury condos, the one big, fancy hotel—there are some hidden gems in the form of little-known rooms and short-term rental apartments perched above some of the area's businesses. These places cater mainly to sports fishermen who want to wake up close to their charter fishing boats, but anybody in-the-know can snag one. I'll list the most dependable ones here. Some of these places aren't available every summer, so keep your eyes peeled for for-rent signs in the ground-floor windows of businesses.

$$ On the absolutely-charming end of the spectrum is the teeny attic room above Spit Sisters Cafe (p. 135), which has a name that's bigger than it is, the **Spit Sisters Cafe B&B** ★★★ (Harbor View Boardwalk; ☎ 907/299-6868 or 907/299-6767; www.spitsisterscafe.com; MC, V). It's got a comfy double bed, a single bunk built into a dormer window, a kitchenette, an itty-bitty bathroom hiding behind a curtain, and a fun selection of books and DVDs filling the remaining nooks. Outside is a broad, private deck overlooking the perpetual action in the fishing harbor. Best of all—and what makes it a B&B—is that you get to have anything you want for breakfast downstairs in the cafe, which is the hippest place on The Spit for coffee, baked goods, biscuits and gravy, and free Wi-Fi. You'll pay $85 per night single occupancy, $100 double, and $120 for three people.

$$ On the really basic end of the spectrum are the three rooms with private baths above the offices of **Lucky Pierre Charters** (4025 Homer Spit Rd.; ☎ 800/478-8903 or 907/235-8903; www.luckypierrecharters.com; AE, DISC, MC, V). They are simple spaces where up to five people—usually Lucky Pierre clients—can sack out on a set of bunk beds, a queen-size bed, and a pull-out sofa. They go for $105 as a double, with $15 per extra person. Get the room on the end if you can—it has more windows.

$$–$$$ Nicer still are the two modern, sunny, studio apartments above the **Sea Lion Cove** (421 Homer Spit Rd., the 4th boardwalk on the right; ☎ 907/235-3400 in summer, 907/235-8687 in off season; www.sealiongallery.com/cove; AE, DISC, MC, V). They're small, but the long views of Kachemak Bay and its glaciated mountains more than make up for it. They share an outdoor deck above the beach, and both have a queen bed, a pull-out futon couch, and kitchenette. They go for $125 to $135 (or $95 in the off season).

Eagle is unparalleled. It's got three decks, a bedroom in the pilothouse, another bedroom in the hold, and a view more suited to aviators then mariners. It's also got three baths and a full kitchen. Elsewhere on the mountainside, there are two downright irresistible cabins, and a 1944 Pullman railcar which has been given a modern condo makeover on the inside. One of the cabins is a compact, three-story, treehouselike place folded into a snug canyon. The other is a luxurious A-frame, with a spiral staircase leading to a sleeping loft, moose and buffalo heads on the wall, and a glorious wide-angle view of the sea that takes in everything from the Homer Spit to St. Augustine Volcano smoldering away in the Gulf of Alaska. They range in price from $245 to $395, but go down a good $50 a night in winter.

Camping

The **City of Homer** (☎ 907/235-3170; http://publicworks.ci.homer.ak.us, click "Parks & Recreation"), runs campgrounds both on The Spit and up on the bluffs near the hospital. Tent sites go for $8 per night. The Spit can be windy and crowded, but that's where the action is. Pay for sites on The Spit at the log cabin across the road from the small fishing lagoon known as "The Hole." To get to the campgrounds near the bluff, the Karen Hornaday Campground, turn uphill on Bartlett off Pioneer Avenue, turn left on Fairview, then right on Campground Road. There's a self-pay box by the entrance.

DINING FOR ALL TASTES

Homer's got a wonderful variety of places to eat spread around town—too many to cover here. These are my favorites:

$ One good leisurely way to start your morning in Homer is with a cup of fair-trade coffee and a strawberry scone at **Two Sisters Bakery** ★★ (233 E. Bunnell Ave.; ☎ 907/235-2280; www.twosistersbakery.net; Mon–Fri 7am–6pm, Sat 7am–4pm, Sun 9am–4pm; MC, V). It's a homey place with a wraparound deck, a sandy yard filled with driftwood planters and Tonka Toy trucks, and a busy kitchen filled with people whose baking transcends boring old cakes and breads. All of the baked goods—from the enormous sticky buns to the light and steaming biscuits at the bottom of soupy bowls of biscuits and gravy (they're insanely good)—come out of a custom-built wood-fired brick oven, which makes an already warm and friendly spot near the Bishop's Beach all the cozier (and the breads all the crispier). One of the two sisters, filling a measuring cup with flour, describes the bakery's charm like this: "There's a lot of hand holding here. It's like you walked into mom's kitchen and she said, 'Oh, don't worry about that, I'll do it. You just sit down and take it easy. Here, try some of this.'" As an added bonus, there's a bed-and-breakfast upstairs (p. 134).

$ Two Sisters supplies sticky buns, quiche, muffins, bagels, and whatnot to an allied eatery on the Homer Spit called **Spit Sisters Cafe** ★★ (Homer Spit at Harbor View Boardwalk; ☎ 907/235-4921; www.spitsisterscafe.com; May–Sept only daily 5am–5pm; MC, V). It's a postage stamp of a restaurant, with limited seating that quickly fills up with fishermen and tourists, who stop in for hot panini sandwiches ($8) and the same insanely good biscuits-and-gravy you can get at Two Sisters Bakery ($7 for a full order). It's also got free Internet and Wi-Fi, and the unforgettable slogan "Hot Coffee, Fresh Pastries, Live Girls."

$-$$ Next door to Spit Sisters is another hole-in-the-wall whose tiny size belies its greatness, the **Spit-Fire Grill** (Homer Spit at Harbor View Boardwalk; ☎ 907/235-9379; summer only daily 10am–9pm; MC, V). Just eight seats along a wrap-around counter, plus a few outdoor tables, make up the place. Mike, the owner and head chef, once managed a natural foods store, which explains the hummus-and-greens sensibility he's brought to his restaurant. Lunches include the likes of a hefty grilled-chicken sandwich with pink lady apples for $8, or buffalo meat burgers in sizes ranging from a quarter-pound for $8 to a half-pounder for $12. Fresh fish comes in the back door every day, and ends up as the dinner special, usually priced around $14. "Just about all of the dinner specials were probably swimming around that morning," says Mike. All lunches and dinners include two sides—such as potato salad, beet salad, and organic watermelon. Fresh oysters raised across Kachemak Bay go for a reasonable $1.50 a pop.

$-$$$ Five customers make a crowd at tiny **Finn's Pizza** ★★★ (Homer Spit, Cannery Row Boardwalk; ☎ 907/235-2878; May–Labor Day only daily noon–10pm; MC, V), my favorite Homer pizza joint. Bjorn, the pony-tailed owner stationed in front of the wood-fired oven, loads his pies with more organic and wholesome ingredients than you might think a pizza could bear—and everything is piled on top of whole-wheat pastry dough molded into a light, crispy crust. A basic 12-inch pie goes for $9.25, while an 18-incher covered with Greek toppings is $23. When Bjorn used to work on The Spit cleaning and vacuum-packing fish, he lamented the dearth of places where a workingman could get a satisfying $5 lunch. He's fixed that. It's not on the menu, but if you ask for the Poor Man's Special, he'll serve you a slice and a half pint of beer. You can also get mixed organic greens (something you don't see just anywhere in Alaska) with vinaigrette for $4. And there's a fantastic view and some elbow room in the little solarium on the second floor.

$$-$$$$ What used to be the garage where the Kenai Peninsula Borough School District parked its buses is now one of Homer's most popular local eateries, **Fat Olive's** (276 Ohlson Lane, off Sterling Hwy. when you roll into town; ☎ 907/235-8488; summer daily 11am–10pm, rest of year daily 11am–9pm; MC, V). It's a minute, comfortable spot with a wood-burning oven, a marble wine bar, hints of the Mediterranean, and Neapolitan pizzas large enough to mount bus tires on (12–28 in. in diameter for $11–$36), with toppings that run the gamut from pepperoni to pineapple to basil pesto. The wood oven also produces hefty calzones ($12) and stromboli ($12), and hot sandwiches big enough for two ($11). Enormous salads ($14 for a seafood salad with fish and Dungeness crab) make for meals in themselves. Dinners include all of the above, as well as entrees such as an oven-smoked game hen ($18) and a roasted rack of lamb glazed with pesto and topped with feta cheese ($26). Finn's may have the healthiest pizzas, but Fat Olive's has the biggest.

WHY YOU'RE HERE: THE TOP SIGHTS & ATTRACTIONS

Homer has two first-rate museums that are must-sees, but your top priority should be finding a boat. Whether you paddle a sea kayak, catch a water taxi over across the bay, or charter a fishing boat, you owe it to yourself to somehow get out on the water; see "Active Homer" below for tips on doing so.

Raspberries: Tart, Sweet & All You Can Eat

After the second week of August or so through September, during raspberry season, you can wade into the brambles at **Seaside Farms** 🎈 (40904 Seaside Farm Rd.; ☎ 907/235-7850; www.xyz.net/~seaside) and pick as many ripe raspberries as you can. It's an organic, self-help operation, with 2 acres of raspberry bushes, and a charge of $2 per pound.

The Islands and Ocean Visitor Center ★★ (95 Sterling Hwy.; ☎ 907/235-6961; www.islandsandoceans.org; free admission; summer daily 9am–6pm, Labor Day–Sept 30 Tues–Sun 10am–5pm, Oct 1–Memorial Day Tues–Sun noon–5pm) takes a sweeping look at life along Alaska's 5,000 miles of Pacific coastline, from the bottom of the Inside Passage, clear out to the tip of the Aleutians, then all the way up to the Arctic. That long line matches that of the Alaska Maritime National Wildlife Refuge, 5 million federally protected acres of islands, headlands, islets, rocks, spires, and other wildlife habitats (the visitor center is, in fact, the headquarters for the refuge). In the museum, which sports a strong sense of theater, natural history goes hand-in-hand with 9,000 years of human history. An entire room is transformed into a seabird rookery, with sound and smell effects. A life-size trapper—"Mother was an Aleut, father was a Russian," he tells you—appears on a video screen in the door of a cabin, wanting to chat about the weather and fur prices. Special attention is given to the Aleutian Islands. The intimate relationship between the native Aleuts and nature is revealed in a rich collection of artifacts made with plant and animal materials (check out the surprisingly stylish seal intestines rain jacket with grass stitching). Native artifacts yield to displays on World War II in the Aleutians (the battle to dislodge the Japanese from Attu Island was the second bloodiest in the Pacific), and the Cold War military buildup and Atomic Age (three nuclear bombs were tested there).

An even richer array of artifacts and exhibits is housed in the **Pratt Museum** ★★★ (3779 Bartlett St.; ☎ 907/235-8635; www.prattmuseum.org; $6 adults, $3 children 3–18 years; summer daily 10am–6pm, rest of year Tues–Sun noon–5pm, closed Jan), which should be seen as soon as possible when you get to town. It will give you a thorough grounding in the region's natural and cultural history. And surprises lie in wait for you here at every turn. Look up and there's the front end of a Dall sheep, or the skeleton of a whale, or a kayak overhead. Look down and there's a drawer to peek into, containing samples of the coal, the shale, and the sandstone you'll see when you stroll Bishop's Beach; or the contents of a 2,000-year-old midden, a prehistoric garbage pile that reveals that the early people of Kachemak Bay ate things still served in Homer today (clams, halibut, salmon) and some things that aren't (beluga whales, murres, sea lions). Pick up the receiver of a marine radio and listen to Capt. Joseph Hazelwood notifying the Coast Guard that the *Exxon Valdez* is hard aground. Pull a bright orange survival suit from a bin, and see if you can get into it in 30 seconds, which is about how much time you'd get if your fishing trawler were to suddenly start going down.

Tip: Discount coupons for $1 off admission are often available at the info desk of the Islands and Oceans Visitors Center.

THE OTHER HOMER

A town with as many artists as Homer is bound to have **art workshops,** and Homer has them throughout the summer. Some last for weeks and others for just a few hours. For an alternative to the usual visitor activities, sign up for one of the shorter workshops and come away with, perhaps, a willow reed basket you wove yourself. Various galleries or artists run these workshops, and the quick way to find out who's offering what is to call **Homer Council on the Arts** (355 W. Pioneer Ave., Ste. 100; ☎ 907/235-4288; www.homerart.org), which keeps track of the schedule. Every summer brings a different set of courses. To give you an idea of what you might find, here are some examples of past 1- and 2-day courses: the basic techniques of screen printing ($50); beginning basketry, using wild grass, nettles, and willow ($35); beginning flamework, which covers the safety precautions, setup, prep-work, and torch techniques needed to make a pendant using borosilicate glass ($195); and one called "Exquisite Hors d'Oeuvres," described as "poetry with food" ($40—hey, in all-inclusive Homer, "food artists" are artists too).

If "Exquisite Hors d'Oeuvres" appeals to you, look into taking one of the **monthly cooking classes** led by Teri Robl, food columnist for the *Homer News.* Her specialty is cooking with, as she says "seafood caught from the cold, clean waters of Alaska: all species of salmon and crab, as well as halibut, cod and shrimp." Classes are intimate affairs, held in the kitchen of her home overlooking Kachemak Bay, and they cost about $125, depending on the ingredients. You pair what you've cooked together with wine from the local Bear Creek Winery to cap off the session. If you're more of an eater than a chef, you can try her food (for two weekends a month in the summer) at the wine and food pairing sessions held at the same winery ($35 for that meal). Call Robl or check her website for the schedule: ☎ 907/235-7191; www.acsalaska.net/~robl.

Every weekend in August an informal beach gathering called **Beach Sculpture Sunday** (Bishop's Beach, at the end of Beluga Place) offers an opportunity to

---

Fishing 101

You don't need a boat to go fishing in Homer. If you're after salmon, there are rivers to fish all over the Kenai Peninsula. On the Homer Spit, there's also **"The Hole,"** a small sea water lagoon where the Alaska Department of Fish and Games releases hatchery-raised king and coho salmon. Since the fish have no natural rivers to return to when spawning time comes around, they return to the lagoon where they were released. It's the easiest fishing in Alaska, and a great spot to teach the kids, or yourselves, the fundamentals. Buy a fishing license, rent a rod and reel, and get some basic instruction on what to do at an adjacent fishing shed. The kings begin arriving in late May, peak in mid June, and wrap things up in July. The coho begin arriving in early August and keep coming through mid-September.

work alongside local artists to create temporary public art using driftwood, seaweed, stones, jetsam, flotsam, and whatever else you can find on the sand. This is a particularly good event for kids, although when art supplies are abundant, free, and sometimes so large they take two people to carry, it's easy for anyone to lose themselves in the creative process. The time varies with the tide. Call the **Homer Chamber of Commerce** (☎ 907/235-7740) for the schedule, or just head down to Bishop's Beach when the tide is low.

ACTIVE HOMER

Ever get the yen to hook your own halibut dinner? Well, Homer—The Halibut Fishing Capital of the World—is the place to do it. You're virtually guaranteed to come back with fish, as the halibut grounds outside of Kachemak Bay are some of the most productive in the world, regularly yielding 200- and 300-pounders.

On a typical charter, you'll leave Homer around 6am and spend a couple of hours motoring out to the fishing grounds. Then for 6 hours or so you'll reel in what may be the biggest fish you've ever caught, weighing 50 pounds or more from around 200 feet; you can keep the two you like best, but you'll have to throw the others back. It all makes for a long, tiring, expensive (usually $200 per person, not including fishing license) but memorable day. Most boats carry 12 to 18 passengers and don't give discounts for kids, but there are some that carry just six passengers (known as "six packs" and even more pricey at $225–$250 per person). Half-day trips cost half as much and I think that's the way to go if you're taking kids, if you get seasick (the waters will be less rough closer in), or if a full day just sounds too darned long. The downside? The fishing isn't usually as good.

About 100 charter fishing boats operate out of the harbor in Homer. The **Homer Chamber of Commerce** (www.homeralaska.org) has links to most of them on its website. Shop around before picking a boat. Study the websites, call and talk to captains to try to get a feel for their personalities (you'll be on the boat together for a long time, and you don't want to get stuck with a Captain Bligh). For a short list of charter operators, contact the **Homer Charter Association** (☎ 907/235-2282; www.homercharterassociation.com), a group that formed to promote safety and good practices, as well as to protect the industry's political interests. One of the bigger operators in town is **Central Charters** (4241 Homer Spit Rd.; ☎ 800/478-7847 or 907/235-7847; www.centralcharters.com), which has an office on the Spit. It serves as a booking agent for all sorts of other activities as well.

Anyone who's fishing in Alaska and is over the age of 16 needs a state fishing license. Most of the charter operators will sell you one when you book a trip; see p. 386 in "Planning" for info.

ATTENTION, SHOPPERS!

Unlike the many gift stores throughout Alaska posing as art galleries, Homer's art galleries are the Real McCoy. And they're all over town. The most interesting times to visit them are on the first Fridays of the summer months, when—for **First Friday**—they stay open late, often host the artists, and have live music and free appetizers.

Bunnell Street Gallery ★ (106 W. Bunnell Ave.; ☎ 907/235-2662; www.bunnell streetgallery.org) has become the state's foremost center for innovative, contemporary art, which is not to say you won't find affordable and practical things

Kachemak Bay State Park & State Wilderness Park

Much of Homer's magic stems from its dazzling view of the jagged Kenai Mountains rising out of the sea on the opposite side of Kachemak Bay. Fortunately, you can do more than just gaze in awe at the dark blue-green forests, snow-capped peaks, ice-blue glaciers, and tantalizing little islands across the water. For about $70 round-trip, you can zip across the bay in a water taxi (there are no roads) to hike, kayak, and camp. Most of the bay's south side is within **Kachemak Bay State Park and State Wilderness Park** ★★★, 400,000 acres of twin wilderness area. The relatively low cost of the water taxi fare makes this the most affordable marine wilderness you can visit in Alaska (no pricey floatplanes or long hours in a water taxi are required).

Homer's water taxi operators have the place all figured out, and they're excellent sources for help planning a hiking or kayaking trip. Some even rent kayaks. The twin parks are close enough to Homer for you to do a day hike or kayak trip there, although they're also immense enough for you to spend weeks exploring. **Central Charters** (4241 Homer Spit Rd.; ☎ 800/478-7847 or 907/235-7847; www.centralcharters.com) works with all of Homer's various water taxis and will help you book a ride over and back, no matter how long you stay.

An 80-mile network of **hiking trails** winds through the parks, and generally hikers have two ways to go: high or low. Go low and the trails will lead you through the mossy forest to secluded beaches and hidden coves. Go high and you climb out of the trees to glaciers, snowfields, and alpine peaks. If you're not in great hiking shape, go low. The high trails climb

---

there—plates and mugs, silver jewelry sets with moonstones or jade, hand-printed postcards, even big cherrywood forks and spoons—are seamlessly folded in with the conceptual stuff. It was once a general store and community gathering place, where fisher folk and homesteaders went for hardware, dry goods, and the news of the day. Though practical items like oatmeal and overalls have been replaced with regularly changing art exhibitions (along the lines of an investigation into the nature of the spoon), the place is still a community gathering point. Concerts, plays, films, lectures by artists, and readings by writers are regular occurrences.

Other notable galleries include: the **Sea Lion Gallery** (Central Charters boardwalk, 4241 Homer Spit Rd.; ☎ 907/235-3400), which has works by artists from all over Alaska, as well as fine Alaska Native crafts; **Ptarmigan Arts** (471 E. Pioneer Ave.; ☎ 907/235-5345), a cooperative with work by a number of Homer artists; and the **Art Shop Gallery** (202 W. Pioneer Ave.; ☎ 907/235-7076; www.artshop gallery.com), which sells works by local artists and Alaska Natives in an octagonal, cedar-sided building that looks like an overgrown Russian blockhouse.

The most fertile shopping grounds are on The Spit, which has the greatest concentration of shops in one spot. They include **Lazy M Leather** (Homer Spit

from 1,200 to 2,400 feet, which will kick your butt big time if you've been letting your cardio slide. Whichever way you hike, keep your eyes peeled for wildlife along the trails. The parks crawl with moose, black bear, mountain goats, coyotes, and wolves.

Camping is allowed just about everywhere in the parks, and it's free. There are a few tent platforms, but most campers pitch their tents wherever they find a nice spot. There are also five public use cabins bookable through the **Alaska State Parks/Department of Natural Resources Public Information Center** (☎ 907/269-8400 or 907/269-8411; www.alaska stateparks.org; MC, V). They get snatched up a half year in advance, so plan ahead if you want one. See p. 373 for more on public use cabins.

The protected waters, hidden coves and beaches, forested islets, ample opportunities for alone time with large marine animals (seals, sea otters, porpoises, and whales), and the relatively easy access make Kachemak Bay State Park one of the top sea kayaking destinations in Alaska. Experienced sea kayakers can rent boats from one of the various guided kayaking tour operators or water taxis for about $45 a day for single seaters, and $65 for two-seaters. There are plenty of guided tour operators who come here, too. A solid one is **True North Kayak Adventures** (☎ 907/235-0708; www.truenorthkayak.com), which leads half-day paddles for $90, full-day paddles for $139, and overnight trips starting at $350 per person. Families get 10% discounts. For other operators, again, check with Central Charters (mentioned above).

Rd.; ☎ 907/235-4238), the most self-deprecating shop in town. The M is for Mary, but Mary is anything but lazy. She works all the time sewing exquisite, handmade leather goods, including handbags of all sizes, belts with removable brass buckles, and leather-bound photo albums. Just across the boardwalk from Lazy M is **Local Showcase** (Central Charters boardwalk, 4246 Homer Spit Rd.; ☎ 907/235-8415; www.stores.ebay.com/localshowcase), which boasts an intriguing selection of Alaskan crafts and keepsakes, such as the naturally shed antlers of caribou, elk, and deer fashioned into hair sticks or sliced to form big oval buttons. You'll also find Birchwood branches carved into mixing spoons or large ladles, walrus ivory jewelry, and rusting railroad spikes pried from the abandoned Wild Goose Railroad near Nome in order to serve as irresistible curios.

Farther out on the Spit, **Caroline's Handmade in Homer** (4460 Homer Spit Rd.; ☎ 907/235-2724) appeals to tourists and locals alike, with a mix of reasonably priced Alaskana and imports. Tourists go for things like the moose-antler letter openers, short strips of whale baleen etched with walruses and polar bears, caribou antlers transformed into cribbage boards, and odd little doll-like wall-hangings made from cottonwood and split reindeer hooves. Locals head to

Caroline's for the imported clothing, like Balinese sarongs, Indian cotton blouses, and wraparound pants. And there are all sorts of knickknacks for under $10—hemp hacky sacks, fossilized walrus vertebrae, and 25¢ slices of moose or caribou antler.

NIGHTLIFE IN HOMER

Homer's nightlife is concentrated in its dive bars, which are many and varied, but not so divey that tourists feel entirely out of place. In fact, Homer's most famous bar, **The Salty Dawg** ✹✹ (on the Homer Spit; ☎ 907/235-1678) is actually one of its foremost tourist attractions. Located on the harbor, amid all the fishing charters and trinket shops of the Homer Spit, the Dawg occupies an old log cabin that's slowly sinking into the sand. Sawdust and peanut shells cover the floor, and thousands of dollar bills—signed by the patrons who left them behind—cover the walls and ceiling.

On the most local end of the spectrum is **Kharacters** (197 E. Pioneer Ave.; ☎ 907/235-9932), a smoky, rough-and-tumble place with only the occasional tourist and plenty of commercial fishermen, just off their boats, rich with cash and falling over each other to buy the next round of shots. It's a great place to go for harrowing tales of fishing in Alaska. I went in for one quick beer and left several hours later with my eyes burning from second-hand smoke and my head spinning from tequila and stories of setting crab pots in the Bering Sea amid 50-foot swells, icy gales, and utter darkness.

Duggan's Waterfront Pub (120 W. Bunnell Ave.; ☎ 907/235-9949), near Bishop's Beach, is Homer's mecca for pool and darts. It's also one of the more dependable venues for live music, and it's got a great grill whipping up burgers and steaks until late in the evening.

In addition to dive bars, which you can find anywhere in Alaska, Homer's got theater, which is rare in the state. **Pier One Theatre** (☎ 907/235-7333; www.pier onetheatre.org) is a bona fide community theater that does actual musical, comedy, and dramatic productions—not corny shows aimed at tourists. Yes, it's an amateur affair, but there are a remarkable number of talented amateurs in this artsy, literate community and so the shows are on a par with the so-called "professional" theaters elsewhere in the state. There's usually something playing Thursday through Sunday evening, throughout the summer. Check the website or the *Homer News* for details.

KODIAK

The city of Kodiak, on Kodiak Island, is the most far-flung of the destinations in Southcentral Alaska. Once the capital of czarist Alaska, the island is now rich in Russian history, as well as Native history and culture. Alaska's largest commercial fishing fleet docks here and it dominates the economy and gives the place an unpretentious, non-touristy feel. Hunting and sports fishing draw many of the visitors who come to Kodiak, but the biggest reason to visit stands 10 feet tall, has 4-inch claws, and salmon breath. It's the Kodiak bear, the largest bear on the planet, and more than 3,000 of them call the island home.

A BRIEF HISTORY

For 8,000 years, Alaska's Alutiiq people had Kodiak Island to themselves, deferring only to the bears. The Alutiiqs lived in semi-subterranean homes called barabaras, and survived by polishing their hunting, fishing, whaling, farming, and berry-picking skills. The beginning of the end of that way of life came in 1763, when Russian explorers showed up. The Russians established a fort on the southeast side of the island, enslaved the Natives, and forced them to hunt for the furs so coveted in Moscow and Saint Petersburg. After an earthquake and tidal wave wiped out the original Russian settlement in 1792, a new one was established on the northwest side of the island, at the present site of Kodiak, which the Russians called Pavlovsk. Kodiak remained the capital of Russian America until 1804 when, after the region's population of fur-bearing animals had been depleted, it was moved to Sitka.

During World War II, Kodiak was home to a huge U.S. naval base and other fortifications. The old Navy yard is now the center of air operations for the Coast Guard in the North Pacific. Elsewhere on the island, you can crawl around the old bunkers, gun emplacements, and pill boxes built during the war at Fort Abercrombie.

Kodiak is no stranger to natural disasters. The Good Friday Earthquake and tsunami in 1964 wiped out much of the town and fishing fleet. In 1912, a sudden, volcanic eruption took place 100 miles away on the mainland, blackening the sky and covering the island beneath 2 feet of ash. Dig just beneath the surface of the ground here and you'll find the ash layer lying there. Dig further and you'll find earlier layers of ash layers, from prehistoric eruptions.

LAY OF THE LAND

At 3,588 square miles, Kodiak Island is the second largest island in the U.S., after the Big Island of Hawaii (some Kodiak residents claim that at an extreme low tide, Kodiak is even larger then the Big Island). It's the main island in the Kodiak Archipelago, which also includes Afognak, Shuyak, and some smaller islands. The archipelago is located on the eastern side of the Gulf of Alaska. Warm Japanese currents in the Gulf keep temperatures on Kodiak relatively mild, though the weather is often foggy, wet, and gray, and great storms batter the island. But sometimes, when the prevailing northerly winds shift slightly, the skies clear and Kodiak emerges from the gloom as an unspeakably beautiful island of dark spruce forests, emerald green grasses, and snow-capped mountains rising out of a glittering sea.

Two-thirds of Kodiak Island and its neighboring islands fall within **Kodiak National Wildlife Refuge.** These 1.9 million acres of deep glacial valleys, mountains, lakes, forests, and fjords are the uncontested terrain of the Kodiak bear. The refuge is inaccessible by road, so visitors and residents must use floatplanes to get in and out. In fact, all of Kodiak Island has just 82 miles of highway to explore. There are some remote beaches and other sites you need a car to get to. The best drive is out to Pasagshak, past domestic buffalo grazing in green fields, a missile launching facility, and—believe it or not—good surfing beaches. Few tourists get out this way, so you'll have the road and beaches more or less to yourselves if you decide to rent a car and explore Kodiak Island more deeply.

The **Kodiak Island Convention and Visitors Bureau** (☎ 907/486-5557; www.kodiak.org) is located in the ferry terminal building right downtown. Hours vary according to the ferry schedule.

GETTING TO & AROUND KODIAK

By Ferry

The most affordable way to get to Kodiak is aboard a ferry of the **Alaska Marine Highway Ferry System** (☎ 800/642-0066; www.ferryalaska.com), which run between Homer and Kodiak three or four times a week during the summer. The trip takes about 10 hours, and costs $74, one-way for adults, and half that for children. An extra $72 will rent you a stateroom for the night, but most riders simply bring a sleeping bag and sack out in one of the common areas (this ferry doesn't have the nice camping areas on deck like the ferries that ply the calmer waters of Southeast Alaska). If you're prone to seasickness, drop a Dramamine before you leave. The ferry travels through rough Gulf of Alaska waters for part of the trip, which definitely makes the ferry voyage a more memorable adventure than a plane ride. You never lose sight of land, and the Alaska Peninsula's jagged mountain scenery is marvelous.

By Air

If you don't have time for the trip to Homer and the ferry ride, you can make the 252 mile flight from Anchorage to Kodiak. A round-trip ticket aboard **Alaska Air** (☎ 800/252-7522; www.alaskaair.com) starts at about $252. **ERA Aviation** (☎ 800/866-8394 or 907/266-8394; www.flyera.com) also flies to Kodiak, using smaller, prop-driven aircraft. Its fares are competitive, but check online for Web specials. The airport is about 5 miles from town. A cab from the airport to town costs about $20. Of the local taxi agencies, I think **A&B Taxi** (☎ 907/486-4343) is the most reliable.

By Car

Car rentals with unlimited mileage cost about $67 a day, including tax. Both **Budget** (☎ 800/572-0700) and **Avis** (☎ 800/331-1212) have cars for rent at the airport.

ACCOMMODATIONS, BOTH STANDARD & NOT

Kodiak has an impressive variety of affordable accommodations, which can help you offset the cost of the airfare or ferry ticket you need to get there. Some of the best deals in town are at the bed-and-breakfasts, of which there are more than 30 on the island. Most are listed on the website of the **Kodiak Island Convention & Visitors Bureau** (100 Marine Way; www.kodiak.org).

A few miles out of town on Rezanof Drive, there are $10 tent sites amid the tall forest at **Fort Abercrombie State Historic Park.** It's run by the **Alaska Division of State Parks,** Kodiak District Office (☎ 907/486-6339; www.alaska stateparks.org, click on "Individual Parks").

There is a 5% borough tax on accommodations on Kodiak Island.

$ Typical of Kodiak's budget B&Bs is **Bev's Bed & Make Your Own Darn Breakfast** (1510 Mission Rd.; ☎ 907/486-0834; www.bevsbedandbreakfast.com;

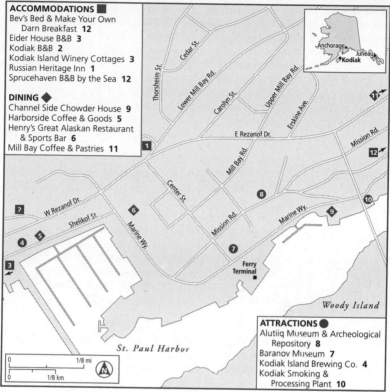

ACCOMMODATIONS ■
Bev's Bed & Make Your Own
  Darn Breakfast **12**
Eider House B&B **3**
Kodiak B&B **2**
Kodiak Island Winery Cottages **3**
Russian Heritage Inn **1**
Sprucehaven B&B by the Sea **12**

DINING ◆
Channel Side Chowder House **9**
Harborside Coffee & Goods **5**
Henry's Great Alaskan Restaurant
  & Sports Bar **6**
Mill Bay Coffee & Pastries **11**

ATTRACTIONS ●
Alutiiq Museum & Archeological
  Repository **8**
Baranov Museum **7**
Kodiak Island Brewing Co. **4**
Kodiak Smoking &
  Processing Plant **10**

Woody Island

St. Paul Harbor

MC, V), which takes up the entire ground floor of a commercial fishing family's home. The four rooms are named for animals you might find in the vicinity—bear, fish, deer, or wolf—and they have touristy bed spreads and sheet sets with drawings of those animals on them. Some will find them cute, others a bit tacky—but what do you want for a mere $70 to $80, double occupancy? At the lower end of the scale are two rooms that share a bath; you'll likely pay $80 for your own loo. As the name suggests, you're on you own for breakfast here . . . but not entirely. There's a big, bright community kitchen that Bev, the owner, stocks with eggs, cereal, and other basics so that you can cook for yourself. That means you'll save not just on lodging, but on food too (and do so in proximity to a hardworking Kodiak fishing family). Other bonuses here include laundry facilities; a fish freezer and vacuum packer to help you better preserve what you might catch; a covered porch with a grill and a meat smoker; and the unpretentious, accepting feel of a group home. And it's near town, too.

$ At **Sprucehaven B&B by the Sea** ★★★ (2145 Spruce Haven Lane; ☎ 907/486-5171; MC, V) a retired Kodiak physician and his wife put guests up in an efficiency apartment on the ground floor of their beautiful waterfront home. The hosts will be happy to give you utter privacy, but are even happier if you want to come upstairs to play pool or chat by the fireplace. They're an entertaining couple with a passion for history—especially Kodiak history. Their home is a few miles from town (so you'll need a car) in a quiet, wooded estate between a lake and a broad bay. Decor-wise, the apartment has both feet firmly planted in the 1970s, but with latter-day touches like satellite TV and Wi-Fi. It's as clean and orderly as a doctor's office, and has a library with all sorts of Alaska titles, a little Maupassant, and the entire Harvard Classics series. Breakfast is served upstairs at 7am sharp, or you can fix your own in the apartment whenever you like (the apartment's fridge is stocked with eggs, cheese, bread, and butter). The rate is $85 for doubles without breakfast, or $93 with breakfast, regardless of who prepares it.

$ Kodiak has six hotels or motels, including my budget fave, the **Russian Heritage Inn** (19 Yukon St.; ☎ 907/486-5657; www.russianheritageinn.com; AE, DISC, MC, V). Although it's a standard two-story, walk-up motel, it's a good choice given the competition. The Russian Heritage Inn is a way better deal than the over-inflated Best Western Kodiak down the street, and it's not at all dreary like its comparably priced neighbor, the Shelikoff Inn. Standard motel rooms at the Russian Heritage Inn start at $80, and spacious one-bedroom suites (with elbow room for families or fishing parties) with kitchenettes and vaulted ceilings go for $120. The heritage at the Russian Heritage Inn comes from the historic drinking well that's there, dug by the Russians sometime before 1867. Originally the well stood in an open field. Now it's in the parking lot of the motel.

$$ The most conveniently located B&B in Kodiak, and also one of the most pleasant, **Kodiak Bed & Breakfast** ★★★ 🧒(308 Cope St.; ☎ 907/486-5367; no credit cards) is set in a cute, diminutive two-story hillside home above St. Paul Harbor. The chipper hostess lives upstairs and serves breakfasts that typically involve fresh seafood and eggs. You get the entire downstairs for $115 per night, double occupancy. That's two small bedrooms, one with a double bed, and one with a pair of twins, as well as a cozy living room—perfect for a family group. It's got a private entrance and there's a lovely wooden terrace where you can sit during sunny days and survey the fishing fleet at berth.

$$ The much more rural accommodation **Eider House Bed & Breakfast** (782 Sergeant Creek Rd.; ☎ 907/487-4315; www.eiderhouse.com; MC, V) sits next to a rushing creek (a fave of bears hunting for salmon). Like the other Kodiak B&Bs I've reviewed, the entire downstairs of a private home here has been turned over to guests, meaning you can stretch out in the living room if you get tired of hanging in your room. The four handsome rooms have sumptuous beds, private baths, and subtle wildlife themes. They go for $120 a night for double occupancy. Guests also have use of the kitchen, though the hostess, a young mother, comes down each morning to prepare a continental breakfast and to socialize. Ask her to show you her video of a juvenile Kodiak bear trying to catch salmon from the opposite bank of the creek. It was torn between staying to fish and running away from the humans with the video camera at the B&B across the way.

$$–$$$ Surf, turf, and, of course, wine are the draws at the **Kodiak Island Winery Cottages** (Mile 36.4 Chiniak Hwy.; ☎ 907/486-4848; www.kodiakwinery. com; MC, V). Each of the three two-story cabins occupies a private niche carved

into the woods, but a short stroll away is a long, sandy beach, perfect for beach-combing and bonfires (two of the cabins actually sit both in the woods and right on the lake). All of the cabins have fully equipped kitchens, washer/dryers, La-Z-Boy recliners, plenty of sleeping options in attic bedrooms, and the party-ready feel of college-town rental houses. They go for $125 per night for multiple nights, or $135 for a single night. The location—besides its convenience for stocking up on wine and availing yourselves of the free tastings—is downright picturesque. Don't expect rolling vineyards, though. They make berry wine here, made from wild berries collected all over the island.

DINING FOR ALL TASTES

As the home port for a good part of the Bering Sea's storied crab fishing fleet, you might expect Alaskan king crab to be more affordable here than in other parts of Alaska. Sadly, a whole king crab at a Kodiak eatery commands the same $40-plus per plate that it does in other parts of the state. But there is good news about Kodiak's dining scene: It's jammed with otherwise affordable eateries dedicated to keeping their local customers fat and happy.

$ With its soft, warm lighting, slate floors, and cool jazz, **Harborside Coffee and Goods** (512 Marine Way; ☎ 907/486-5862; Mon–Sat 6am–8pm, Sun 7am–8pm; MC, V) could fit in nicely as a neighborhood cafe in downtown Portland or Boston, if it weren't for all the heavily bearded fishermen in weathered Carhartts and Xtratuf rubber boots. The fishing fleet out the window, bobbing at berth in St. Paul's Harbor, is another dead give-away that this is no urban coffee nook. The coffee is darned good, though, and the morning ambience can't be beat.

$–$$ For fish and chips made with fresh salmon or halibut (in either 8- or 10-ounce portions), head to **Channel Side Chowder House** (450 Marine Way; ☎ 907/486-4478; Mon–Fri 7am–7pm, Sat 8am–7:30pm, Sun 9am–4pm; MC, V). Or take a pass on the fryer oil and order a savory salmon wrap or a bowl of rich and chunky chowder. The ice cream parlor decor reflects the fact that Chowder House is also, actually, an ice cream parlor. On a sunny day, you can sit out on the deck beside a whale skull and watch the fishing boats go by.

$–$$ Kodiak isn't exactly a cultural hub, so you really don't expect a celebrated French chef to be running a humble little coffeehouse there, turning out artistic pastries and elegant breakfasts and lunches. But that's what's happening at **Mill Bay Coffee & Pastries** ★★ (3833 E. Rezanof Dr.; ☎ 907/486-4411; Mon–Sat 6:30am–7pm, Sun 8am–5pm; breakfast until 6:30am–11am, lunch 11am–2pm; MC, V). Joel Chenet (who was named best young chef in France in 1967) was cooking in the French embassy in New York City when he visited Alaska on vacation, fell in love with the place, and moved to Kodiak to start this way-off-the-beaten-path eatery with two partners. Unfortunately, Mill Bay doesn't serve dinner, though you can get soups, bagels, quiche, pastries, and really good coffee (roasted on-site) until early evening. Try to swing by for a meal. The changing breakfast and lunch menus feature lots of local seafood, eggs from free-range hens, loads of fresh veggies, and *tres chic* plate presentations. For breakfast, you might have the smoked salmon omelet ($9.95), as light and savory as an omelet can be.

For lunch, try the Kodiak Sea Burger ($11), which stars a plump patty made from salmon, crab, shrimp, and cream cheeses, proudly sitting atop a bed of wild greens, on a toasted brioche bun; a long wooden skewer pins a lemon wedge to the top and holds the whole thing together—the end result is as elegant as anything seen on the cover of *Gourmet* magazine.

$–$$$$ Henry's Great Alaskan Restaurant and Sports Bar (512 Marine Way; ☎ 907/486-8844; summer daily 11:25am–10:30pm, rest of year daily 11:25am–9:30pm; AE, MC, V) dishes up an extensive bar-and-grill menu, with dinners ranging from $9.50 for a chicken sandwich to $30 for the Double Seafood Combo (six prawns and 8 ounces of scallops), plus Kodiak Island Brewery beers on tap. It's a big, dark place, part of a strip mall near the waterfront that's usually packed with fishermen, off-duty Coast Guardsmen, and their respective clans. Try the outstanding bouillabaisse on Thursdays, or the enormous crawfish pie—it's bigger than your head—on Wednesdays.

WHY YOU'RE HERE: THE TOP SIGHTS & ATTRACTIONS

Back when Alaska was still part of Russian America, the Russians built a three-story log warehouse on the Kodiak waterfront to store the sea otter pelts awaiting shipment back to Mother Russia. Alexander Baranov, chief manager of the Russian-American Company, ran the show in Alaska, but as a reminder of who was ultimately in charge, he mounted a bust of Czar Alexander I atop the warehouse roof. The warehouse has survived to become the oldest Russian building in America, and it now houses the small but rich **Baranov Museum** (101 Marine Way; ☎ 907/486-5920; www.baranov.us; $3 adults, children 12 and under free; summer Mon–Sat 10am–4pm, Sun noon–4pm; rest of year Tues–Sat 10am–3pm). It's filled with items from that era, such as trade beads, flintlock pistols, and handcuffs, as well as Native artifacts, including a whole room devoted to intricately woven basketry. There are also oddball curios like a narwhal tusk, and furs and pelts you can run your fingers through (stroke a sea otter pelt and you'll get a good idea of why Russians coveted them so).

Long before the Russians ever showed their bearded faces around the Kodiak Archipelago, the Alutiiq people were there hunting, fishing, and hunkering down inside their semi-subterranean dwellings during the winter. Evidence of their 8,000 years of life before Russians came to the islands is on display at the **Alutiiq Museum & Archeological Repository** (215 Mission Rd.; ☎ 907/486-7004; www.alutiiqmuseum.com; $3 adults, children 12 and under free; June–Aug Mon–Fri 9am–5pm, Sat 10am–5pm; rest of year Tues–Fri 9am–5pm, Sat 10am–4:30pm). This small museum (and massive repository—it has more than 100,000 artifacts stashed away) seeks to preserve and share Alutiiq culture. Before inspecting the displays, watch the 20-minute video, "Stories From Stone: The Archaeology of Horseshoe Cove." Not only will you see how some of the artifacts on exhibit came to be there, you'll get a sense of how this Native-run museum has succeeded in bringing Native values to Western academic practice.

One of the densest accumulations of marine life you'll ever see is at the **Kodiak Fisheries Research Center** (301 Research Court; ☎ 907/481-1700; www.afsc.noaa.gov/kodiak/default.htm; free admission; Mon–Fri 8:30am–4pm). Across the bridge from Kodiak on Near Island, the center houses several governmental agencies involved with fisheries management and marine research. Its 10-foot cylindrical aquarium is stuffed with the most Alaskan marine life I've ever seen in one place, including red king crabs. I'd seen king crabs in freezers, on plates, and mounted to walls, but, until visiting the center, I'd never before seen them marching around like Japanese killer robots, ripping the legs off star fish, and dipping their claws inside to get at the meat. There's also an open tank filled with icy seawater and finger-friendly creatures like sea cucumbers and sea anemones that you can touch (be warned that anemone tentacles are surprisingly sticky).

THE OTHER KODIAK

The true "other" Kodiak is the Alutiiq Kodiak that existed for thousands of years before Western contact. It's a Kodiak that modern Alutiiqs and archaeologists learn about a little bit more each year as they continue to excavate ancient village sites. You can join them, either as a visitor or as a volunteer archaeologist, through the **Alutiiq Museum Community Archeology Program** (☎ 907/486-7004, ask for Patrick Saltonstall). The dig occurs each summer during the last week of July and the first 2 weeks of August. Up to 18 volunteers meticulously brush and sift through layers of dirt to unearth tools, hearths, fish bones, and who-knows-what. Believe it or not, you can simply call the museum for directions and then just show up to watch. If you want to volunteer, you should be prepared to dig for a least a full day, if not longer, and you should be totally self-sufficient. As a volunteer, you'll get instruction on how to dig and the tools you'll need to work with, but you're on your own for food, accommodations, transportation, and so forth. Most of the volunteers live on Kodiak, making this an unparalleled opportunity to meet and work with locals.

Tucked away in a warehouse beneath the bridge on Kodiak's nitty-gritty docks is the **Kodiak Smoking and Processing Plant** (420 Marine Way; ☎ 907/486-0450 or 907/486-4409), where sports fishermen and hunters have what they've caught or shot prepared to take home with them. A hard-working Laotian family runs the place, and they'll give you an informal tour (and possibly some smoked fish) if you drop by and they're not tied up with something else. There's no telling what will be going on when you visit. They might be smoking salmon, or vacuum sealing halibut, or wrapping deer meat, or turning moose into hamburger. When I dropped by, they were skinning a caribou suspended on meat hooks, and I thought it was the coolest thing I'd seen all day. My traveling companion, looking wan, said she could have done without seeing it at all.

You can go to every brewery in Alaska—and there are some good ones—but you won't find a better one than the **Kodiak Island Brewing Co.** (338 Shelikof Ave.; ☎ 907/486-2537; www.kodiakbrewery.com). You also won't find Kodiak beer anywhere but Kodiak. This brewery is a genuine craft brewery, small scale, independently owned, and proud to be making beer the traditional way. It produces just enough beer to sell on tap at local bars and restaurants, and from behind a small counter at the brewery itself. Drop by any day in the summer from noon to 7pm for a free sample and to mingle with the locals. There's usually a steady stream of folks bringing in growlers (pitchers) to refill. If the brewer isn't swamped, he may give you a quick free tour of the grain mill, fermenters, and other apparatus if you ask. It's a—er—pint-size operation so it won't take long

Getting Out to See the Bears

The brown bears on Kodiak Island have been isolated for so long that they've evolved into a separate sub-species, one with broader, thicker skulls and greater average weights and lengths than other brown bears. To stand in the presence of these enormous bruins is an uncommon thrill, and one that will disabuse you of any misconception you may have about being at the pinnacle of the food chain.

The experience doesn't come cheap, though.

Bear viewing takes place on the enormous swatch of Kodiak Island that falls into the Kodiak National Wildlife Refuge, which is inaccessible except by floatplane or boat. The easiest way to get in to see the bears is to go with one of several local floatplane operators that specialize in bear-viewing day trips. Half-day trips start at around $400 per person and typically involve about a 40-minute flight to a lake, where the plane lands. Then there's a guided hike to a salmon stream where bears congregate to feed. You might get 2 hours on the ground before flying off again. Be sure to bring binoculars and telephotos lenses, as guides will keep you at a safe distance (a Kodiak bear is not something you want to crowd).

During most of the year the bears stick to themselves, scattered throughout the wilderness. But when the salmon are running (July to mid-Aug), you can count on the bears to congregate along the stream banks to feed, making it the best time to visit. Earlier or later in the season, the

to—*ahem*—drink it all in. The brewery has a good variety of beers, and all of it is fresh, unfiltered, and made with certified organic base malt.

ATTENTION, SHOPPERS!

Every summer in August or September, Russian Orthodox pilgrims make their way to Kodiak to pay tribute to the island's homegrown saint, St. Herman, whose relics (that is, bones) are kept at the Holy Resurrection Russian Orthodox Church. One of their stops is usually **Monk's Rock** (202 E. Rezanoff; ☎ 907/486-0905), a coffee house and deli with a small gift shop and bookstore. It's run largely by the students and recent graduates of St. Innocents Academy, a Russian Orthodox boarding school with students from all over the Lower 48. Saint Herman items ($6–$20) are the big sellers here. You don't have to be a pilgrim to appreciate Saint Herman, with his long, snow-white hair and beard, his oddly kind but grim visage, and his wide-brimmed halo—a holy reminder of the legacy of Russian America. The shop stocks St. Herman icons, St. Herman books, St. Herman bookmarks, and St. Herman greeting cards. But lots of other saints make appearances in icon form here, too.

Native-made goods are the lure at the **gift shop in the Alutiiq Museum** (215 Mission Rd.; ☎ 907/486-7004; www.alutiiqmuseum.com), which has a small but bear-viewing operators typically fly across Shelikof Straight to spot brown bears (though not Kodiak bears) along the shore of the Alaskan Peninsula. They generally charge the same rates, regardless of where they fly.

For a longer stay in bear country, book a few days at one Kodiak's many backcountry wilderness lodges. Most cater primarily to hunters and fishermen, but some offer bear-viewing excursions as well. Check with the **Kodiak Island Convention and Visitors Bureau** (☎ 907/486-5557; www. kodiak.org) for a list of all the Kodiak wilderness lodges. The one outfit on the island that caters exclusively to those aiming to see and not shoot bears is **Kodiak Treks** ★★ (11754 S. Russian Creek Rd.; ☎ 907/487-2122), a low-impact, leave-no-trace, mom-and-pop operation run by a wildlife biologist and his wife. With Kodiak Treks, you have the option of setting off in search of bears on 2- to 6-day hiking expeditions, or to hunker down in a small, solar-powered lodge on an island deep in bear country. In order to take the camping option, you need to be able to carry a 40-pound pack and cover 5 to 10 miles a day. (In contrast, all you need to know about the lodge is that it has a steamy sauna house.) If you'd like to camp for a few nights and then spend the last night in the lodge, that's okay too. The $300 per person per day rate includes all food and equipment, but does not include the floatplane ride there and back, which is an additional $275 or so.

wonderful inventory of wares made by local artists from materials such as silver, bone, and walrus ivory. On the high and impractical end of the spectrum, you might find an Alutiiq headdress made from sea otter and caribou furs, which somehow stand straight up on end, for $200. In the more practical department, you might come upon a pair of baby dentalium (a tooth-shaped shell) earrings for $10 or a pair of iridescent abalone disk earrings for $38. T-shirts with Alutiiq phrases and translations are among the biggest sellers. Among the choices: *Mukuk'uungq'rtuten?*, which translates to, "Got milk?"; *Kapignangcuk,* meaning "Little nuisance"; and *Yugpakartuten,* or "You talk too much."

You'll need a car to get to the **Kodiak Island Winery** (Mile 36.4 Chiniak Hwy.; ☎ 907/486-4848; www.kodiakwinery.com) where you can pick up a bottle or two of a wine made with local raspberries, salmonberries, blueberries, or blackberries ($20 per bottle). The winery also makes a strawberry wine, but the strawberries are imported from Oregon, and, frankly, strawberries don't belong in wine. Stop by for free samples of each, and check out the small gift shop, which has nothing but Alaskan-made goods.

5 Southeast Alaska

The Alaskan Panhandle, where land & sea intertwine

SOUTHEAST ALASKA—OR SIMPLY SOUTHEAST, AS ALASKANS SAY—ALMOST isn't part of Alaska at all. Look at it on a map: It's firmly snuggled up against Canada, and it's just barely attached to the rest of state. The entire 540-mile-long region, with its multitude of islands, its sawtoothed mountains, and its millions of acres of coastal rainforest, is held to the greater part of The Great Land by a mere 11-mile-wide wisp of connective tissue. One well-aimed glacier or mighty earthquake could snip Southeast loose from the main body of the state entirely.

Yet that really wouldn't change much. Southeast is already a world unto itself, a land separate from and largely unlike the rest of Alaska. Sure, it's got Juneau, the state capital. But Juneau and all the other drizzly, mossy towns scattered across the region are more akin to Seattle than to Fairbanks or Nome. A trip to Southeast Alaska is a trip deep into the heart of the Pacific Northwest. It is a land of gray light, misty pine-forested mountains, and the glassy black-green waters of the Inside Passage. Though the rainfall is the highest in the state, the snowfall in Southeast towns is the lowest and the temperatures are milder overall, and though the summer days here aren't as long as they are in the Interior or the Far North, the winter days aren't as short. (See the "Land of Glaciers, Gore-Tex & Never-Ending Rain" box below for more on the weather here.)

One thing you need to realize about Southeast right up front is that you could easily spend your entire Alaskan vacation here and never see another part of the state. Southeast has that much to offer. It's got the tallest coastal mountains in North America, from which spring the greatest grouping of tidewater glaciers in the world. It has totem poles and clan houses, gold rush boomtowns and Russian colonial architecture, and gin-clear creeks and lonely bays. Practically every town has a fishing fleet, and practically every restaurant includes Alaskan salmon and halibut on the menu. There are vast congregations of migratory birds in the marshes, bald eagles in the cottonwood, whales in the fjords, hungry bears in the blackberry bushes and salmon streams, and tour operators eager to take you to see all of it.

Another thing you need to realize is that Southeast is a maritime region. You can't drive around it (you can't even drive to it without cutting through Canada). Nearly all of the towns and villages throughout the region are inaccessible by road. Locals travel most commonly by boat, hopping on the family fishing trawler or the state ferry to get from one place to the next. Not surprisingly, the cruise-ship

Land of Glaciers, Gore-Tex & Never-Ending Rain

Geologically, Southeast is part of an impact zone in which the great tectonic forces of the earth are shoving the Pacific plate beneath North America. The continent has crumpled under the pressure, shoving the Coast Mountains into the sky up to nearly 20,000 feet in places. The immense grinding of tectonic plates has also fractured the edge of the continent like a broken piece of china, creating the thousands of islands, large and small, that shelter Southeast's waters from nonstop storms on the Gulf of Alaska.

The gulf still gets the final say on the weather here, though. The Japanese current that swirls into that corner of the Pacific brings warm water that evaporates and blows toward shore. The moisture-laden air piles up against the barricade of the Coast Mountains, then lets loose—dumping up to 200 inches of rain per year on parts of the region. The driest and sunniest months are May and June, but even then you'd be wise to pack your Gore-Tex, because sunshine in Southeast Alaska simply means it will rain soon. The tumultuous Gulf of Alaska also keeps temperatures moderate in Southeast. Winter temperatures rarely get below zero (–18°C), while summer daytime temperatures tend to be in the 60s (upper teens Celsius). If it hits the 80s (upper 20s to lower 30s Celsius), it's a real heat wave.

The precipitation that falls in buckets in Southeast's lower elevations comes down as snow in the mountains, feeding vast ice fields that spill out where they can in the form of glaciers. At Glacier Bay, one of the top tourist attractions in Alaska, 16 glaciers reach the sea, while more hang in the alpine valleys. Whales feast and frolic in the bay among the icebergs, sea kayakers, tour boats, and cruise ships. In Juneau, you can actually drive a car right to Mendenhall Glacier—it reaches directly down into a suburban valley.

industry dominates tourism here, bringing a half million passengers into Southeast Alaska each summer. The port towns of Skagway, Juneau, Ketchikan, and Sitka bustle with tens of thousands of passengers who come ashore all at once, creating lively, sometimes frenzied, mass-tourism scenes. The biggest cruise ships do not dock in Haines, Petersburg, or Wrangell, where you can escape the shell-shock of summer tourism, and still spot plenty of glaciers, whales, and bears.

DON'T LEAVE SOUTHEAST ALASKA WITHOUT . . .

Witnessing the birth of icebergs. Glacier Bay National Park is the most popular place to watch icebergs calve from the face of a tidewater glacier into the sea, but there are lesser-known, equally awesome glaciers, just waiting to break off into icebergs, in the **Tracy Arm-Fords Terror Wilderness,** at LeConte Bay, to name just one other place. See p. 231.

Taking a hike. Stretch your legs and fill your lungs with the pure Southeast air while trekking through aromatic spruce and cedar forests, along ridgelines, across sub-alpine meadows, and along lonely beaches strewn with driftwood. There are opportunities to hike everywhere in this region, including a trailhead in downtown Juneau that leads to the top of the mountain rising above the town. See the **Perseverance Trail** on p. 224.

Spout spotting. Thousands of humpback whales spend the summer in the **Inside Passage,** cavorting and fattening up in the nutrient rich waters, before heading back to Hawaii or Mexico for the winter. Get out into the thick of them on a whale-watching tour, or spot them from shore or while riding a ferry.

Communing with the bruins. Southeast Alaska has two prime bear-viewing spots—**Pack Creek** and **Anan Creek**—where hungry black bears and brown bears gorge themselves on spawning salmon, ignoring the tourists . . . more or less. See p. 232 and 180.

Going native. Totem poles, clan houses, and Native dance demonstrations—all of these will give you a glimpse of the cultures of the Tlingit and Haida Indians, who have inhabited Southeast Alaska for centuries.

LAY OF THE LAND

On the Alaskan scale of things, Southeast is a compact little area, making up just 6% of the whole state. Still, it's big enough to contain New Hampshire, Massachusetts, Rhode Island, Connecticut, Delaware, and New Jersey. And it includes the 5.6-million-acre Tongass National Forest, the largest national forest in the country.

There are seven towns and several small villages scattered throughout Southeast Alaska. Life in the villages is largely devoted to hunting and fishing, and devoid of tourism. So I'll concentrate on the towns in this chapter, plus the hamlet of Gustavus adjacent to Glacier Bay National Park and Preserve.

KETCHIKAN   Ketchikan is known as Alaska's "First City" because it's the first major community you'll come to when sailing up the Inside Passage into Alaska. Once a rough-and-tumble logging and fishing town, it's now a fun if touristy stop for every big cruise ship plying the Inside Passage. It's known for its totem poles, its wooden streets, and its famous brothel—Dolly's House—now a museum. It's also the jumping-off point for trips to pristine and drizzly Misty Fiords National Monument. See p. 157.

WRANGELL   Wrangell is an ugly-duckling fishing community and one-time (until the mills closed in the 1990s) logging town, well off the beaten tourist path. It's not much of a destination in its own right, but it is the jumping-off point for Anan Creek, a top bear viewing spot. It's also the gateway for the Stikine River, which you can blast up in a jet boat for glacier viewing and a soak in hot springs.

Bird-watchers go cuckoo over the Stikine River Delta, where millions of migratory shorebirds stop in the spring on their flights north. See p. 172.

PETERSBURG Petersburg is another off-the-beaten-tourist-path town, only it's as picturesque as Wrangell is homely. Neat and tidy Norwegian-style shops, homes, and gardens reflect the Scandinavian roots of the town's settlers. As the home base for the world's largest halibut fleet, fishing is king here. Mom-and-pop tour operators offer whale-watching and trips to LeConte Glacier, a refreshing small-scale alternative to the larger tour operators in more touristy areas. See p. 181.

JUNEAU Of the three principal Alaskan cities, Juneau is by far the easiest to fall in love with. It's got none of Anchorage's Los Angeles–like sprawl, or Fairbanks' freezer-burned edges. Instead, it's like a miniature San Francisco, with colorful hillside neighborhoods, museums, yuppies, coffee houses, abandoned gold mines, politics (it's the state capital), a suburban glacier, and spectacular mountain trails that start at the edge of downtown. It's also the go-to place if you're heading to Glacier Bay National Park, the Tracy Arm-Fords Terror Wilderness, or the primeval forest of the Kootznoowoo Wilderness, the brown bear capital of the world. See p. 206.

SITKA Located on the western side of Baranof Island, Sitka is the only major Southeast Alaskan community fronting the Pacific Ocean. With sparkling waters on one side, emerald green mountains on the other, and dozens of forested islets dotting its protected sound, Sitka has one of Alaska's most beautiful settings. As the former headquarters for the fur trading operations of the Russian-American Company, Sitka also has more Russian colonial architecture than anywhere else in Alaska, including the house of a Russian bishop who became a saint. Tlingit history is even more deeply rooted here; you can chat with Native artisans in their workshops, wander through a rainforest filled with totem poles, and catch a performance by a Native dance troupe in the community's clan house. Getting out onto the water to see whales and other large marine mammals is another big Sitka attraction. See p. 189.

SKAGWAY No town in Alaska celebrates its boomtown beginnings more enthusiastically than Skagway, which sprung up overnight during the Klondike gold rush. Block after block of carefully preserved shops, saloons, hotels, and other buildings from the era stand along Skagway's boardwalk-lined streets, a National Park Service historic district. From Skagway you can follow in the footsteps of tens of thousands of gold-fevered stampeders on a 3- to 5-day hike up the Chilkoot Trail, or you can take a day trip into the scenic mountains in a vintage railcar of the White Pass & Yukon Railroad. Skagway's boom-or-bust origins replays throughout the summer, as tens of thousands of cruise-ship passengers course through the streets by day, then sail away in the evening. See p. 233.

HAINES With glacier-covered mountains all around and the graceful Victorian dwellings of a decommissioned U.S. Army post making up half the town, Haines is as picturesque as it could possibly be. No large cruise ships visit Haines, which half the town applauds and the other half wants to change. Meanwhile, Haines offers a quiet contrast to its nearest neighbor, bustling Skagway. For visitors, it's a jumping-off point for outdoor adventure, it's got an odd assortment of museums, and it's a hotbed for Tlingit art and culture. In the fall, it's also the home of the largest bald eagle gathering in the world. See p. 247.

GUSTAVUS   Gustavus isn't a town as much as a loose collection of homes and farms spread across the outwash plain created by the retreating glaciers of Glacier Bay National Park and Preserve. If you don't want to rush through Glacier Bay on a day trip, camp in the park, or stay at the park's touristy lodge at Bartlett Cove, Gustavus offers an appealing variety of country inns and bed-and-breakfasts. See p. 230.

GETTING TO & AROUND SOUTHEAST ALASKA
BY FERRY

The most common and best way to get around Southeast Alaska is via the ferries of the state's **Alaska Marine Highway System** (☎ 800/526-6781; www.akferry. org; see full discussion on p. 369). This ferry system serves all the major communities in Southeast Alaska, and you should use it as much as you can while you're here. You'll get an unmatched perspective of the land, the sea, and the locals. It's public transportation like no other.

There are frequent sailings between all the main Southeast Alaska towns during the summer season, which runs from May 1 until September 30, with less frequent sailings in the winter season. The shortest leg is the 1-hour run between Skagway and Haines, which costs $31 one-way. The longest run within the Southeast is between Juneau and Ketchikan, which costs $107 one-way, and takes between 18 hours and 1½ days, depending on the route.

You can also get *to* Southeast Alaska by ferry. Northbound ferries headed up the Inside Passage board in Bellingham, Washington, and in Prince Rupert, British Columbia. The trip from Bellingham to Juneau takes 2 to 3 days, depending on the route, and costs $326 one-way. The larger vessels have everything you'll need on board to make that extended trip pleasant: cafeterias, bars, reading rooms, movie theaters, showers, a video game arcade, gift shops, and even solariums with deck chairs. State rooms are available for overnight voyages, but most passengers simply bring sleeping bags and sack out on a deck chair in the solarium or find a spot on the observation deck or in the indoor lounges. Some people even pitch tents and duck tape them to the deck in designated areas. That's probably the best way to get an early morning peek at the whales, eagles, and other wildlife common to this area. Naturalists stationed aboard the ferries point out creatures and places of interest, answering questions and delivering impromptu, but in depth, lectures (another plus of this form of travel).

Twice a month from June through September, a ferry sails across the Gulf of Alaska between Juneau and Homer, where you can make connections for the more distant points of Kodiak, or Unalaska in the Aleutian Islands.

Reservations are strongly recommended if you want a stateroom, plan on traveling to Alaska from Bellingham or Prince Rupert, or plan on traveling across the Gulf of Alaska. You also need reservations if you're bringing a vehicle, since space for cars is tight.

Sailing times and fares change each season. Go online for the most up-to-date info if you intend to plan an itinerary around ship sailings.

BY AIR

Alaska Airlines (☎ 800/252-7522; www.alaskaair.com) flies daily from Anchorage and Seattle to five communities in Southeast Alaska: Juneau, Sitka, Petersburg, Wrangell, and Ketchikan. A one-way ticket from Anchorage to Juneau runs about $150 to $200, and a one-way ticket from Seattle to Juneau starts at about $240.

Two commuter airlines serve many of the region's smaller communities: **Wings of Alaska** (☎ 907/789-0790 or 907/983-2442; www.wingsofalaska.com) and **LAB Flying Service** (☎ 907/789-9160; www.labflying.com). They're competitively priced with Alaska Airlines.

BY CAR

There are only three communities that you can drive to in Southeast Alaska. One of them, Hyder, is so land-locked and disconnected from the rest of the region that it may as well be in Canada, whose border it sits on and whose currency it uses. That leaves Skagway and Haines for us to consider. These are the key gateways for motorists coming and going from Southeast Alaska aboard the state ferries. Still, to get anywhere else in the state from either town requires a trip through Canada and the proper proof of citizenship (see p. 365). Most tourists don't bother bringing cars aboard the ferry. It's too expensive, and you can get by very well without a car in Southeast anyway. Still, a rental car might be worth considering for a day or two in those destinations where you want to get out of town and explore on your own. See the individual towns throughout this chapter for info on recommended car rental companies.

BY OTHER MEANS

Just about every community in Southeast Alaska has a number of different floatplane pilots and water taxi services that carry passengers out to wilderness areas, for fishing, kayaking, stays in public use cabins, or whatnot. Floatplanes and water taxis are the only way to get to some of the more remote places in Southeast. Water taxis take longer, but they're always more affordable. The fares fluctuate with fuel costs. Visitor information centers are the best sources for tracking down the local operators; relevant info is listed under each of the towns discussed below.

KETCHIKAN

Built on salmon fishing, logging, gold mining, prostitution, steep hillsides, and a lot of pilings sunk into the mud, rainy old Ketchikan has grown up to become a charming and respectable town bustling with tourists in the summer. Known as the First City, because it's the first major Alaskan community you come to when sailing up the Inside Passage, Ketchikan is so far south that when the locals talk about going to the "Big City," they're usually referring to Seattle, not Anchorage. Ketchikan is famous for its totem poles (the largest collection in the world), its salmon fishing (some of the best in Alaska), its wilderness (nearby Misty Fiords National Monument), and its former boardwalk red light district, where today you can tour a historic brothel (Dolly's House), and its rain (it rains like mad here—14 ft. annually—but the weather shouldn't be an issue if you dress right and put yourself into a rainy-day mindset).

A BRIEF HISTORY

Ketchikan originated as a Tlingit summer fish camp, called Kitschk-Hin. Modern Tlingit joke that the name meant "place so rainy only a white man would build a town there," but the actual meaning is closer to "creek where eagles spread their thundering wings." Both the eagles and the Tlingit were drawn to Ketchikan by the salmon run in Ketchikan Creek, which passes right through town. The salmon still spawn there each summer, the eagles still hunt them, and the Native presence in this town of 8,000 is still strong.

Ketchikan's history is rooted in timber, fishing, and gold industries. As the first city in Alaska for northbound travelers along the Inside Passage, Ketchikan became a natural supply stop for the stampeders hurrying to the gold fields to the north, and prior to that it had its own minor gold rush. But it quickly became apparent to the newcomers that the real riches to be had in Ketchikan weren't golden but salmon-colored, and the fishing industry took off early on. The first salmon cannery opened in 1886, and by the 1930s there were more than a dozen canneries in town. For a while, Ketchikan was the uncontested "Salmon Capital of the World," but over-fishing knocked it off that pedestal as catches declined and canneries closed in the 1940s. Yet there were still plenty of trees around to cut down, and when the U.S. Forest Service opened Southeast Alaska to large-scale logging in the 1950s, Ketchikan became the center of it all. One of the largest pulp mills in the world opened here in 1954, literally liquefying forests until it closed in 1997, due to aging equipment and stiffer environmental regulations.

Today logging continues on a small scale, run by Native corporations. Commercial fishing has sprung back and is still a strong part of the economy. And tourism has taken on a major role. Cruise ships dock right along Water Street, in the heart of downtown, letting thousands of passengers loose each day in the summer. Though Ketchikan has cleaned up its gritty old self, and replaced its dark, dangerous waterfront dives with T-shirt emporiums and jewelry stores, it hasn't lost its charm.

LAY OF THE LAND

Ketchikan is on the southwest shore of Revillagigedo Island, named for the Spanish viceroy of Mexico from 1789 to 1794, and a tongue-twisting reminder that Spain was among the European nations staking claim to Alaska in the 18th century. Since the island's full name is such a mouthful, most people simply call it Revilla (rhymes with vanilla) Island. Neighboring Gravina Island is a 5-minute ferry ride across a long, narrow stretch of water called the Tongass Narrows. There's not much on Gravina Island other than the airport. Wedged into a wide spot in the Tongass Narrow, and right in front of Ketchikan's downtown, is little Pennock Island, which has several residences and vacation rentals set among the woods. You need a boat to get there. Downtown Ketchikan is compact and hilly, with crooked streets, streets built on pilings over the water, and lots of "stair streets," wooden staircases with official street status. The first few blocks around the cruise-ship wharf have been taken over by tourism, but the town gets real—and real fun to explore—as soon as the hills and stair streets begin.

Ketchikan

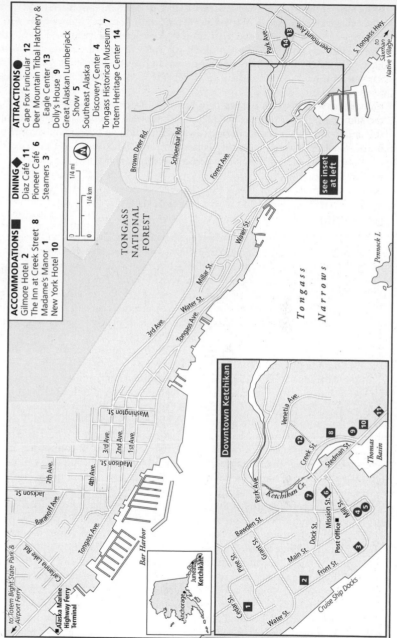

ACCOMMODATIONS ■
Gilmore Hotel **2**
The Inn at Creek Street **8**
Madame's Manor **1**
New York Hotel **10**

DINING ◆
Diaz Café **11**
Pioneer Café **6**
Steamers **3**

ATTRACTIONS ●
Cape Fox Funicular **12**
Deer Mountain Tribal Hatchery &
  Eagle Center **13**
Dolly's House **9**
Great Alaskan Lumberjack
  Show **5**
Southeast Alaska
  Discovery Center **4**
Tongass Historical Museum **7**
Totem Heritage Center **14**

1/4 mi
1/4 km

TONGASS
NATIONAL
FOREST

Brown Deer Rd.
Schoenbar Rd.
Forest Ave.
Park Ave.
Deermount Ave.
S. Tongass Hwy.
to
Saxman
Native Village

see inset
at left

Water St.
Millar St.
3rd Ave.
Water St.
Tongass Ave.
Washington St.
3rd Ave.
2nd Ave.
1st Ave.
Madison St.
4th Ave.
7th Ave.
Jackson St.
Baranof Ave.
Carlanna Lake Rd.
Tongass Ave.

to Totem Bight State Park &
Airport Ferry

Alaska Marine
Highway Ferry
Terminal

Bar Harbor

Tongass
Narrows

Pennock I.

Anchorage
Juneau
Ketchikan

Downtown Ketchikan

Venetia Ave.
Creek St.
Park Ave.
Ketchikan Cr.
Stedman St.
Thomas
Basin

Cedar St.
Pine St.
Grant St.
Bawden St.
Dock St.
Main St.
Mission St.
Mill St.
Front St.
Water St.
Post Office ■
Cruise Ship Docks

The only other community on the island is Saxman (population 425), a Native village 2½ miles south of town along the South Tongass Highway. Saxman's totem poles, wood carvers, and clan houses draw loads of visitors. The South Tongass Highway runs for 12 miles along the coast in one direction, the North Tongass Highway runs 18 miles north of town in the other direction—and that's as far out of town as you can drive in either direction. Most of Revilla Island is inaccessible by car.

The **Ketchikan Visitors Bureau,** 131 Front St., Ketchikan, AK 99901 (☎ 800/ 770-3300 or 907/225-6166; fax 907/225-4250; www.visit-ketchikan.com), stands right on the cruise-ship dock, offering town information and desks where tourism businesses sell their wares, including tickets for tours. The center is open daily in the summer from 8am to 5pm and when cruise ships are in town; it's open week-days only in winter.

GETTING TO & AROUND KETCHIKAN
Getting There

They say there are only three ways to get to Ketchikan: by air, by sea, and by birth. For obvious reasons, I'll cover just the first two. The **Alaska Marine Highway System** (☎ 800/642-0066; www.ferryalaska.com) links Ketchikan with the other Inside Passage communities by ferry, a fun way to travel. For tourists, the Juneau to Ketchikan route is most common and costs $104 for an adult (Juneau, of course, is just one of dozens of gateways). A stateroom costs an extra $70, but you're free to cram as many people as you can into it. Most passengers bring sleeping bags or blankets and sack out in the public areas. The ferry terminal is 2½ miles north of downtown, and a cab ride from there to downtown costs about $12. Try **Sourdough Cab** (☎ 907/225-5544).

Alaska Airlines (☎ 800/252-7522; www.alasakaair.com) connects Seattle and Ketchikan with nonstop service, and has flights between Ketchikan, Wrangell, Petersburg, Sitka, Juneau, and Anchorage. Various small flight services, using floatplanes or wheeled aircraft, connect Ketchikan with neighboring island com-munities, and run trips to Misty Fiords National Monument. The Ketchikan International Airport is on Gravina Island. There's no bridge connecting it to Revilla Island, an eighth of a mile away, so a small ferry runs people and cars back and forth all day, charging $5 for adults, $2 for kids ages 12 and under, and $6 for cars.

Taking a cab from the airport to downtown is a little complicated since the air-port is on an island separate from the rest of Ketchikan. To catch a cab, you have to schlep your bags to the airport ferry (about a 5-minute walk from the termi-nal), pay for the $5 ride across the water, then grab one of the taxis waiting on the other side. The fare to downtown is about $15, making the total cost $20 if you're solo, $25 if you're a couple, and so on in extra $5-ferry-ticket increments. There are two other options. One is to take the **Airporter Shuttle** (☎ 907/225-5429). It leaves directly from the airport terminal and charges $20 per person, which includes the ferry ride. It's a good deal if you're traveling solo, but not otherwise. Look for the driver holding a sign in the baggage claim area. The other option is to take the water taxi, which is both the fastest and the most stylish way to get from the airport to downtown Ketchikan. It costs $18 for the first person and $7 per additional person, so it's actually the cheapest way to go if you're on your own, and equal in price or just a wee bit more expensive if you're not. The catch is, it can't take you to the door of your hotel or B&B. It drops you off at the dock downtown, and then you're on your own again. But it gets you there in just 8 minutes, well ahead of the taxis and the Airporter Shuttle. Look for someone holding a sign for **Tongass Water Taxi** (☎ 907/225-8294) at the baggage claim area.

If you can get your luggage under the seat, you can take the bus to and from the airport ferry terminal or the ferry terminal of the Alaska Marine Highway System, as well. Buses come every half-hour and cost $1.00 to get downtown. Contact the **Ketchikan Gateway Borough bus** company (☎ 907/225-8726) for info.

Getting Around

If you're staying downtown, you don't need a rental car. It's easy enough to get around Ketchikan and to the outlying attractions without one. Ketchikan has a very workable public transportation system, with buses running to the two main out-of-town attractions—Saxman Native Village, and Totem Bight State Park—every half-hour. The fare is $1.00. There are also tour buses that take trips to the totem pole parks and other locations. Go to the visitor center (see above) to shop around for operators.

If you're staying out of town or you intend to explore the island more deeply than most visitors do, you can rent a car from any of the big national car rental chains at the airport.

ACCOMMODATIONS, BOTH STANDARD & NOT

Whatever flavor of lodging you prefer, you're likely to find it in Ketchikan (both in town and in the surrounding areas), whether you're looking for an affordable room in a historic hotel, a home-cooked meal in a Victorian bed-and-breakfast, or a chic Creek Street condo. If you're looking for a place in Southeast Alaska to hunker down with the family for a few days, you'll also find an abundance of choices among the apartment and vacation rentals here.

Note that Ketchikan has a 13% tax on all accommodations within the city limits, and a 6.5% tax on accommodations outside the city limits.

Vacation Rentals

Let's start with vacation rentals, which in this part of the state are usually the least expensive way to go (starting prices are $85, rather than $115 and up). Though there are dozens of them around Revilla Island, two local agencies have the lock on listings (both also represent local B&Bs). And you won't find much overlap in their stables—unlike the B&Bs, which advertise anywhere and everywhere, vacation rentals go with one or the other agency, so be sure to look at both before you make a choice. The older and smaller of the two, **Ketchikan Reservation Service** (☎ 800/987-5337 or 907/247-5337; www.ketchikan-lodging.com), is managed by Wanda Vandergriff, who divides her time between running her own B&B and directing business toward the 20 or so other properties she represents. In her stable she has the cheapest of the properties in the area (along with more cushy ones), perfectly fine lodgings that go for as little as $85 in summer, when booked for 2 or more nights. And though most agencies will negotiate with guests over rates, she's occasionally willing to do so not only in the off season but in the summer months as well. Give it a try! She's also a real mother hen when it comes to overseeing the properties she reps. "I inspect them before I say I'll handle 'em, making sure that everything is safe and clean," she reports. "And then I'll come by to visit with my hosts and take a look around, well, at least once a month, often more." In the 13 years KRS has been in business, she's stopped working with two B&Bs, but for the most part problems are rare and dealt with promptly. "If a guest is unhappy and I have to upgrade them, the B&B owner pays the difference," she reports.

As an example of what you might get with this service, I'll point you towards the **Thomas Street Vacation Rental**, two apartments set in a historic, cheerful yellow house built on a wooden plank street supported by pilings sunk into the water (the house rattles gently when garbage trucks roll by, but it's sturdy enough). A schoolteacher and her husband own and live in the house, and the two guest apartments boast the simple, indestructible orderliness of a grade school classroom. The nicer unit is the small upstairs apartment with a full kitchen, a tiny bedroom with a queen-size bed, and a narrow living room not much wider than the pull-out sofa. It doesn't feel cramped, though, thanks to the big window and a high ceiling with long skylights. It goes for $95. The downstairs unit, one of Vandergriff's few $85 options, is an efficiency apartment with less of a spacious feel and a weird entrance—you have to go through the owner's office to get to it. I'd recommend shelling out the extra $10 for the added privacy and space, if you can afford to. Both units come stocked with eggs, pastries, bread, and other basic breakfast fixings. Larger groups might go for the snug **Cottage at Herring Cove,** which features four bedrooms, and such homey touches as quilts on the beds, wooden rocking chairs for lounging, and a good-size, very usable kitchen. It starts at $125 per night in summer, though the price increases a bit if you cram it with people.

Mary Bolshakoff is in charge of the competition, **Alaska Travelers Accommodations** (☎ 800/928-3308 or 907/247-7117; www.alaskatravelers.com), and she does her best to hold her hosts and owners of her rental properties to the highest of standards. "I wouldn't list a property that wasn't immaculately clean," say Bolshakoff. "I also try to choose hosts who are warm and welcoming, people who are excited about their properties and love showing off the area to their guests." One of her most popular hosts is an expert in both fishing and jam and jelly making; stay with her, and she'll lead you to the best berry patches, and best places to drop your fishing line. She also runs classes on smoking salmon (for an extra charge).

Bolshakoff represents about 35 vacation rental homes and apartments, and a handful of B&Bs, with prices ranging from just $95 a night to more than $200. The majority are guest houses on the property of larger homes, giving her clients the best of both worlds: They have complete privacy, but there's a host right next door in case guests need advice or help.

One of Mary's best vacation rentals is called Grace Abounds, a renovated 1930s beach cabin and boathouse (it's owned by a Lutheran minister, if you were wondering about the name). It's the Alaskan equivalent of a Cape Cod summer home, a lovely, private place with red shingles, shiny brass gutters, exposed beams, dormers and bay windows, claw-foot tubs, and a private beach littered with driftwood and logs begging you to throw them into a bonfire. It goes for $180 double occupancy, with $25 per additional person, and it's got room for six. If that's too much house (and too much money), two of you can stay in the boathouse, which has been converted into a rustic one-bedroom efficiency, for $95 a night. There's a discount if you rent both buildings, and a 5-night minimum either way.

When booking through either service, keep in mind that some properties may have cleaning fees. In general, there's a 3-night minimum for rentals, but both agencies offer some 1-night rentals as well.

Hotels

$$ Though it's called the **New York Hotel** ★★ (207 Stedman St.; ☎ 907/225-0246; www.thenewyorkhotel.com; DISC, MC, V) this family run, historic charmer is "Olde" Ketchikan all the way. The decor is solidly retro, with dark wainscoting, tiled baths, and rooms furnished with burnished antiques that could be holdovers from when the hotel was built in 1925. (Don't worry, you'll also get modern TVs, dataports for free Internet access, a minifridge, and bathrooms with all the modern amenities.) Set in the old Creek Street red light district (you can guess what these hotel rooms were once probably used for!), it's smaller than other hotels in town, with narrow hallways and steep stairs, but it's quite comfortable and reasonably priced for the area, at $129 for a single night or $119 for multiple nights. The views are fetching too, as many of the rooms face the kaleidoscope of fishing boats docked in the Thomas Basin small boat harbor. So why does it only get two stars? Well, the hotel is hard to manage for those with mobility issues (in addition to the narrow hallways, there's no elevator) and the standard rooms are too cramped to fit a whole family. But these quibbles aside, it's one of the top choices in town.

$$–$$$ The **Gilmore Hotel** (326 Front St.; ☎ 800/275-9423 or 907/225-9423; www.gilmorehotel.com; AE, MC, V) is right in the middle of the action, which is both a selling point and a weakness. Located right across the street from the cruise-ship dock (with great views of the long wharf where all the luxury yachts line up), the Gilmore looks out on the busy shipping and floatplane activity in Tongass Narrows, or at least it does when a towering cruise ship isn't tied up outside blocking the view. The hotel is on Front Street, the city's main nightlife strip, and the traffic going into and out of the three nearby bars has been known to keep hotel guests up well past their bedtimes. Though the smallish front rooms are the nicest—with plush feathertop mattresses and silky comforters on the beds ($139 per night)—you may want to avoid them as their windows directly face the street party. Take away the fancy bedding and put a brick wall outside the window rather than a view, and what you're left with are the back rooms, which go for $115. They're dreary, but they're certainly quieter. Built in 1927, the three-story Gilmore has been remodeled a few times over the years, but has a mustier ambience than the New York Hotel (see above). On the plus side, the hotel offers free pick-ups from the airport and the ferry terminal, and room rates drop early and late in the season. In addition, the hotel restaurant, Annabelle's, is pretty good and has a long, old bar that's a great place to hang after a long day of sightseeing.

$$$–$$$$ The New York Hotel (reviewed above) also runs what it calls **The Inn at Creek Street** ★ (5 Creek St.; ☎ 907/225-0246; www.thenewyorkhotel.com; DISC, MC, V), which consists of three elegant apartments above the boardwalk shops of Creek Street, plus a nice single room with a Jacuzzi tub above an old dancehall and brothel. The room goes for $135 and the apartments for $179. The apartments make for especially romantic hideaway splurges. They have full kitchens, jet tubs, and spiral staircases leading to airy sleeping lofts with sumptuous beds. With their pull-out sofas, they can easily sleep four. From the balcony, depending on the time of year, you can watch spawning salmon below you in Ketchikan Creek, while seals slide in to feed on them. They're not doing it for your entertainment, of course, but it's a darned good show.

$$$–$$$$ Ketchikan has plenty of places calling themselves bed-and-breakfasts, but as of this printing, it had only one bona fide breakfast-serving bed and breakfast, **Madame's Manor** ★★★ (324 Cedar St.; ☎ 877/531-8159 or 907/247-2774; www.madamesmanor.com; no credit cards). Every other Ketchikan B&B gets by with a continental breakfast. Not Madame's Manor. Here, the pleasant and mildly eccentric proprietress sets her table with Limoges china and Waterford crystal, and serves her guests proper morning meals, which might include French toast with peaches and cream, followed by fresh-baked cobbler. The three rooms start at $149 in high season, and each has a kitchenette, private bath, canopied bed, and enough Victorian antiques for three simultaneous productions of *Arsenic and Old Lace*. The whole place truly excels at over-the-top Victorian extravaganza. Every wall, corner, nook, cranny, living ficus, and artificial rose bower is adorned, hung with chintz curtains, or laced with twinkling lights. Perched on a steep hillside in Ketchikan's historic Knob Hill neighborhood, two nearly vertical blocks above downtown, the house has a view from its parlor's crushed velvet fainting couch that alone can make you swoon. If this sounds like too much, there are two good-size, Victorian-era-free-zone apartments downstairs—a one-bedroom for $115 and a two-bedroom for $125—without a single doily or an antique vanity between them.

Camping

The U.S. Forest Service's **Signal Creek Campground** and **Last Chance Campground** (☎ 877/444-6777; www.recreation.gov) are both in a lovely patch of rainforest known as the Ward Lake Recreation Area, 8 miles from town on the North Tongass Highway. Both campgrounds are near fishing and hiking. Camping costs $10 per night.

Eighteen miles out North Tongass Highway, the Alaska Division of Parks' **Settler's Cove State Park** (☎ 907/247-8574) includes a sandy beach (a good place to watch whales, beachcomb, or even swim), a disabilities-accessible path to a spectacular waterfall, and a short coastal trail. Camping costs $10 a night.

DINING FOR ALL TASTES

$–$$ If reindeer sausage, clam chowder, or a big slice of pie sound good to you, head over post-haste to get a seat at the **Pioneer Café** (619 Mission St.; ☎ 907/225-3337; Sun–Thurs 6am–10pm, Fri–Sat 24 hr.; MC, V). This is the best diner in town, and it gets crowded. Locals often snag every vinyl upholstered booth and spin-top stool at the counter and settle in for good long sits. If you manage to grab a seat yourself, you'll find breakfast all day, with choices ranging from a healthy bowl of oatmeal for $3.95 to a satisfying double serving of 8-ounce pork chops with three any-style eggs for $15. Dinners range from hot turkey sandwiches to broiled halibut with mashed potatoes and gravy. The seafood here is frozen but less expensive than in other downtown restaurants.

$–$$ You might have better luck getting a table at **Diaz Café** (335 Stedman St.; ☎ 907/225-2257; Tues–Sat 11:30am–2pm and 4–8pm, Sun 11am–7pm; no credit cards). The menu has a broad selection of Chinese entrees and American diner fare, but Filipino food is the specialty here. Café Diaz doesn't look like much from the outside, but don't be fooled—the place is a venerable Ketchikan institution. It's been around since the 1950s, serving chicken adobo ($15) and *pancit bijon* (stir fried noodles; $14) to generations of Filipinos drawn to this corner of Alaska to work on the cannery slime lines. The cafe's screaming red and yellow interior reflects the preference for bold primary colors found in Manila. Once your eyes recover from the jolting color scheme, they'll pop out when they see how big the portions are—you'll get mountains of ginger beef, heaps of sweet and sour halibut, and enormous hamburgers. Go here to eat like a hungry cannery worker.

$$$–$$$$ If you decide to eat in the touristy heart of things, a good choice is **Steamers** (76 Front St.; ☎ 907/225-1600; summer daily 10am–10pm; AE, V), which is advantageously perched in a high, third-floor loft space directly across from the cruise-ship wharf. From there you can enjoy a nice view of Pennock Island across the water, unless a cruise ship is tied up. (Then you get an elevated and oddly intimate view of the side of a cruise ship.) Steamers specializes in seafood and steaks, with most dinners ranging from $18 to $30. Specialties include a dozen oysters ($16), raised in the nearby Tlingit village of Kake. They're broiled, then stuffed with a mixture of crab meat, spinach, and Parmesan cheese, and drizzled with a *beurre blanc* (white butter sauce) and baked until the cheese melts. All-you-can-eat Dungeness crab goes for $30 (the record is 12—the house definitely lost money on that customer). A half Dungeness crab, served with a claw reaching flamboyantly from a giant margarita glass, goes for $10. If you come for lunch, try the grilled oyster po'boy sandwich ($11), with fries.

WHY YOU'RE HERE: THE TOP SIGHTS & ATTRACTIONS

What's the top sight in Ketchikan? I can answer that in two words: totem poles. They're everywhere: Mounted to the front of buildings, planted along the road, preserved in a museum, and slowly weathering in the sun and rain at two totem pole parks.

The **Totem Heritage Center** ★★★ (601 Deermount St.; ☎ 907/225-5900; $5 adults, children 12 and under free; summer daily 8am–5pm, rest of year Mon–Fri 1–5pm) is a must visit, and so is a visit to at least one of the area's totem pole parks. But I recommend starting at the museum, so you'll better understand what you're seeing once you get to the parks. The exhibits here will give you a good grounding in the basics, like how to distinguish a Tlingit pole from Haida totems (the Tlingit stack one figure right on top of another, the Haida leave spaces), or how to distinguish an eagle figure, bear figure, and even a killer whale figure from each other.

Thirty-three poles carved in the 19th century are dramatically displayed inside the center, comprising the largest collection of totem poles in the United States. Traditionally, an important part of a totem pole's life cycle was rotting and returning to the earth. Prior to Western contact nobody would have thought about trying to preserve an old pole. But by the early–20th century, totem carving was rapidly dying, and Tlingit elders agreed that it made sense to save these poles so future generations or carvers would have references. And that's how this museum came to be.

The area's two totem pole parks are quite different from each other. One is free and designed for self-guided tours. The other is set up for guided tours, includes a Native dance performance and other cultural fanfare, and charges a fairly hefty fee for all the extras. I'll start with the freebie—**Totem Bight State Historical Park** ★★★ (Mile 9.9, North Tongass Hwy.; ☎ 907/247-8574; www.alaskastate parks.org; free admission; daily 24 hr.) allows visitors to spend some quiet time alone with totem poles in the woods, which is how I prefer to do it. The park is a product of a Depression-era Civilian Conservation Corps project that brought skilled elderly carvers together with young apprentices to salvage decaying poles (some of which eventually ended up in the museum) and to create reproductions. Altogether, there are 14 poles spread out along gravel pathways in the rainforest, covering a lovely spot along Tongass Narrows. In a clearing, you'll find a reproduction of a traditional Tlingit clan house—a cavernous, one-room, cedar building thoroughly adorned with Tlingit carvings. Back when the Tlingits had the world pretty much to themselves, 30 to 50 members of several closely related families would have lived in a house like this. Duck through the tiny doorway and check out the fire pit and the house posts inside (they're just like totem poles, only they hold the roof up). The house posts tell the story of Duktoothl, a legendary Tlingit figure partial to weasel-skin hats and ripping sea lions in half with his bare hands.

It doesn't take more than 30 minutes to walk through the entire park, but you could easily linger longer; the peaceful pebbly beach could be perfect for a picnic. If you don't have a car, the city bus runs by the park every half-hour in the summer. Rangers occasionally lead free summertime tours, but most of the time it's just you and the totems. Stop at the gift shop by the parking lot and pick up the self-guided tour brochure, which tells the stories behind each of the poles.

While Totem Bight is set up for individual exploration, the totem park at **Saxman Native Village** ★★ (Mile 2.5 S. Tongass Hwy.; ☎ 907/225 4421; www. capefoxtours.com; $3 for park, $35 adults for entire show, $18 children 12–17; hours vary, call in advance) is designed as a shore excursion for cruise-ship passengers, although independent travelers can tag along, too. If you like, you can wander the grounds and inspect the totem poles for a small fee. But you're better off buying a ticket, getting the guided tour, and enjoying the entire Saxman Native Village experience. I generally avoid the canned cultural programs of mass tourism destinations, but this one is fun, authentic, and has too much heart to hate. It starts with a crash course in the Tlingit language and a video of Saxman's history. Then the tour enters the Beaver Clan Tribal House, Saxman's community gathering spot and a more contemporary version of the clan house at Totem Bight. The tribal house is constructed from Western red cedar, and it's filled with that wood's wonderful aroma. After the fundamentals of life in a tribal house are covered, an old legend is acted out, and a dance troupe performs songs and dances unique to the local clans. Everybody gets to join in the last dance. Next comes an inspection of the totem poles. The park has 28 poles with a wide range of figures, including Abraham Lincoln. One particularly comical pole shows what happens when children put their hands in places they don't belong, like inside the mouths

Touring Ketchikan

Among the plethora of tours you can take in Ketchikan, my favorite kills two birds with one stone, or runs over them with one amphibious tour vehicle, anyway. It's the **Ketchikan Duck Tour** ★ (☎ 866/341-3852 or 907/225-9899; www.akduck.com), a cousin of similar tours now available in Boston, New York, and other major American cities. Like the others, it's good, hokey fun. The tour vehicle, a cross between a trolley car and a D-Day landing craft, does drive-bys of all the iconic sites in town, and then, as passengers gasp (well, the kids usually do), it rolls down a boat ramp and motors around the harbor for a while. The whole thing lasts 90 minutes, and costs $36 for adults and $22 for children 3 to 12 years old.

Budget travelers can save on the duck tour fare with a self-guided tour. Pick up a free copy of the Official Historic Ketchikan Walking Tour Map at the visitor center by the cruise-ship wharf.

of giant clams. The program culminates with a visit to the carving shed, where you can watch Tlingit artists coax wild-eyed totem characters out of fresh cedar logs, as their ancestors have done for centuries. The schedule fluctuates with the schedules of the cruise ships. Check at the visitor center for times.

Beyond Totem Poles

If the Totem Heritage Center totem poles whet your appetite for more ancient Native arts and crafts, visit the **Tongass Historical Museum** (629 Dock St.; ☎ 907/225-5600; $2 adults, children 12 and under free; summer daily 8am–5pm, rest of year Wed–Fri 1–5pm and Sat–Sun 1–4pm). Sharing the same building as the town's public library, the museum has a fine collection of Tlingit and Haida beadwork, moccasins, blankets, and baskets. Take a look at the museum's photographs of old, pre–cruise ship Ketchikan, from the days when all the streets were either made of wood or filled with mud.

Salmon's a big, big deal in this area, as you'll find out at the **Deer Mountain Tribal Hatchery and Eagle Center** ★ (1158 Salmon Rd.; ☎ 907/228-5530; www. kictribe.org/Hatchery/Hatchery.htm; $9 adults, children 12 and under free; daily 7:30am–4:30pm). Even those who can't tell the difference between a fingerling and a fry are sure to find this place interesting. The laboratory-like setting inside the hatchery is where Ketchikan Indian Corporation raises the 150,000 fish that it releases into the wild each year to supplement the area's natural salmon runs. If you're lucky, you'll get to see clinical fish technicians fertilizing salmon eggs by hand. If the eggs have already hatched when you visit, you might get to witness the feeding frenzy that ensues when you throw a handful of fish food into a big tank with several thousand baby salmon in it. As it happens, a creek running by the hatchery happens to be a wild salmon run, and in mid-summer you can stand beside it and see how salmon are made the natural way. The hatchery also doubles as a sanctuary for injured eagles. Their aviary is built right over a portion of the creek, and every now and then a bird swoops down from its perch and plucks a fish from the water. As this center is located right over the footbridge from the must-see Totem Heritage Center, you can easily combine the two.

The crooked boardwalk along Ketchikan Creek known as Creek Street has always been a top draw for visitors. Originally this was so because it was the town's red light district, which crawled with lusty fishermen and loggers looking for negotiable affection. Nowadays, the excitement surrounds the historic brothel tour. Of the 20 brothels that once lined the boardwalk, **Dolly's House** ★★★ (24 Creek St.; ☎ 907/225-6329; admission $5; daily 7am–5pm) is the only one still in business, though it's evolved from a bawdy house to a bawdy museum. Dolly Arthur, the madam, opened it in 1919, when prostitution was legal in Ketchikan, and she ran it openly until prostitution was prohibited in 1954, then ran it less openly. Dolly's House was so well known that when Dolly died in 1975, newspapers up and down the West Coast ran her obituary. Besides the red-light-district memorabilia, the house is filled with Dolly's belongings, which offer poignant glimpses into her personal life, including the rocky relationship with her one true love, a rakish longshoreman named Lefty. The 20-minute tour (you didn't think they'd let you wander around a brothel unescorted, did you?), led by a guide in a feather boa, is a bargain at $5. Kids are welcome, but I wouldn't bring one.

Walk all the way to the end of Creek Street and you'll come to the **Cape Fox Funicular** (800 Venetian Way; ☎ 907/225-8001; admission $2; daily 7am–midnight) a contraption that appears to be the unplanned offspring of a trolley car and an elevator. Hop aboard, press the up button, and ride 130 feet to the top of the steep wooded slope to the **Westcoast Cape Fox Lodge,** a pricey hotel with a panoramic view of the town and a lobby filled with Native art. It's worth the trip just so you can say you've ridden on a "funicular" (it's a real word—look it up).

Before wilderness adventurers head into the Tongass National Forest, they stop by the **Southeast Alaska Discovery Center** (50 Main St., a block from the cruise-ship dock; ☎ 907/228-6220; www.fs.fed.us/r10/tongass/districts/discovery center; admission $5; May–Oct daily 8am–5pm, Oct–May Thurs–Sun 10am–4pm) to pick up maps, books, permits, public use cabin descriptions, and trip-planning advice. This is the primary visitor center for the entire 17-million-acre forest, which covers three-fourths of Southeast Alaska. Even if you're not about to embark on a big backcountry hiking, kayaking, or camping adventure, you should still check this place out. It's got a swell natural history museum made up largely of dioramas offering ecological and historical vignettes about the Tongass National Forest, which range from Natives living in harmony with nature to loggers clear-cutting old growth forests.

If you hear the obnoxious buzz of chainsaws when you step out of the Discovery Center, it's not coming from the logging exhibit inside. It's coming from the logging exposition at the nearby **Great Alaskan Lumberjack Show** kids (☎ 888/320-9040 or 907/225-9050; www.lumberjackshows.com; $32 adults, $16 children 12 and under; hours vary). The energetic, noisy, expensive, hour-long show (scheduled three times a day according to the cruise-ship schedules) pits teams of lumberjacks from the U.S., Canada, and Australia against each other in a series of competitions, which include axe throwing, buck sawing, springboard chopping, and tree climbing. Logging in Southeast Alaska has wreaked havoc on the environment, and I'm certainly not shedding tears for the closing of Ketchikan's mills. Still, it's strangely encouraging to know that log rolling contests live on.

Misty Fiords' Molybdenum

When President Jimmy Carter proclaimed Misty Fiords a national monument in 1980, most of it was designated as protected wilderness. But Congress slipped in an exception—a 151,000-acre enclave with a particularly rich deposit of molybdenum, a rare metal used for nuclear isotopes and in alloy metals used for filaments, oil pipelines, and parts for aircraft or missiles. So far nobody has proposed mining there, but I'm sure that someday somebody will. It's an environmental battle waiting to happen.

THE OTHER KETCHIKAN

When the tourist season winds down in Ketchikan, the arts season cranks up with talks, plays, musical performances, and a once-a-month community get-together, talent show, dance, and cooking competition called **The Monthly Grind** (☎ 907/225-2211; www.ketchikanarts.org; tickets $5 adults, $1 children). Held in Saxman Tribalhouse, a modernized version of a traditional Tlingit clan house where the sweet smell of cedar hangs in the air, the Grind gives refunds to any ticket holder (tickets are available all over town) who brings a home-baked dessert. Desserts are judged, awards given, then all the entries are cut up into tiny pieces and consumed by the crowd. The Grind is held the third Saturday of the month, and it always sells out, leaving a few ticketless sad sacks outside while 320 revelers whoop it up inside.

In a lecture series entitled **Friday Night Insight** (Southeast Alaska Discovery Center, 50 Main St.; ☎ 907/228-6220; free admission; Fri 7–8pm) scientists, fishermen, birders, and others talk about their passions, usually with audio-visual aids. Past talks have featured an expert on Northwest Coast art, who, after 20 years of research, determined that a single carver working between 1770 and 1810 was responsible for many of the most significant totem poles and house posts in Native villages from Metlakatla to Klukwan; three law enforcement officers with the U.S. Forest Service who tackled the question, "Why does the Forest Service need law enforcement officers?"; and local artist Ray Troll, who creates quirky, aquatic images of the latest scientific discoveries. Troll entitled a presentation about his offbeat career, "Fish Worship: Is it Wrong?" The lectures are held most Fridays from September through April.

ATTENTION, SHOPPERS!

The rise of Ketchikan as a cruise-ship destination changed the downtown retail scene. Hardware stores, green grocers, barbershops, and general mom-and-pop establishments that once lined the waterfront were replaced by lame-o gift shops and foreign-owned jewelry stores. With so many sweatshop-made baubles and frightfully expensive gold chains being hawked, don't expect to find much of anything that you could afford or, more to the point, would want to buy. One saving grace is the **Tongass Trading Company** ★ (201 Dock St.; ☎ 907/225-5101), which has held its own on the waterfront since 1898. What started out as a well-stocked, 19th-century general store has evolved into a 21st-century, miniature

Wal-Mart, with historic roots, family owners, and better quality merchandise. You can get anything here—fishing line, pipe joints, hip waders, Gore-Tex, sleeping bags, spotting scopes, smoked salmon, the latest Patagonia organic cotton travel beanie, clean socks, a can of peanuts, whatever. Walk right past those tacky gift shops on the waterfront and buy all your cheesy Alaska souvenirs right here. There's a whole gift-shop-size section filled with more Alaska sweatshirts, postcards, key chains, golf balls, and plastic moose than you can shake a diamond willow walking stick (which they've also got) at. And the prices are as good as anywhere in town, if not better.

Venture beyond the waterfront and you'll find that Ketchikan also has all sorts of art galleries, filled with the work of local artists. When you're walking along Creek Street, pop into **Soho Coho Art Gallery** ★★★ (5 Creek St.; ☎ 800/888-4070 or 907/225-5954; www.trollart.com), which features the work of artist Ray Troll. Troll combines a quirky wit and an illustration style reminiscent of R. Crumb's with an obsessive interest in fish, fossils, science, evolution, and the landscape of Southeast Alaska. His work comes in many forms: books, posters, aprons, postcards, coffee mugs, and so on. It'll be hard not to leave sporting one of Troll's "Spawn Until You Die" hats or "Mad Cow, Happy Salmon" T-shirts.

For Native arts and crafts—a nice button blanket or a bent-wood box perhaps—head out to **Saxman and the Saxman Arts Co-op** (2706 S. Tongass; ☎ 907/225-4166). Local artists and artisans make pretty much everything here. Leave an imprint of your foot and they'll even make a pair of beaded leather moccasins for you.

NIGHTLIFE IN KETCHIKAN

If you're in Ketchikan in July, see if you can catch a production of **The Fish Pirate's Daughter** ★ (call the First City Players for a schedule; ☎ 907/225-4792). This long-running campy melodrama spoofs Prohibition, prostitution, and the once serious business of fish piracy, in which workaday independent fishermen took what they figured was rightfully theirs from the voracious floating fish traps that Ketchikan canneries set up (one of the first things Alaska did after it became a state was to ban these stock-depleting monstrosities). A damsel finds herself in distress, a hero arrives just in time, the audience quickly learns to cheer, hiss, and go ooh la la at the right moments, and a Creek Street madam with a heart of gold says things like, "Why don't you come up to see me sometime?" It's all been unfolding in Ketchikan since 1966. Advanced tickets, which are $40, include an all-you-can-eat crab feed. You can save a bundle by skipping the crab and just showing up at the door to buy a ticket for the show, which is $10. All tickets are half price for people 17 and under.

Ketchikan was once famous for its rough-and-tumble bars but with the demise of logging and the advent of the cruise-ship economy, the bar scene ain't what it used to be. Still, a few classic dives remain, where grizzled fishermen (the loggers are long gone) in greasy Carhartts and Xtratuf boots go to unwind. For a dose of unpolished, old-school Ketchikan, grab a can of beer and bar stool at the oddly intimate **Potlatch Bar** (along the boardwalk at Thomas Basin small boat harbor; ☎ 907/225-4855) where you can shoot pool, catch live local music most weekends, and find deckhand openings and diesel engine bearings advertised on the chalkboard by the door. Or try the dark and cavernous **First City Saloon** (830

Water St.; ☎ 907/225-1494), where you play darts or video games, and watch sports on big-screen TVs. There's usually a small cover charge on Friday and Saturday nights, when there's often a live band playing.

GET OUT OF TOWN

One way or another—whether by tour boat, kayak, or floatplane—you have to get out of Ketchikan for a visit to what might be the most untouched part of the planet you'll ever see, **Misty Fiords National Monument** ★★★. This 3,570-square-mile chunk of the Tongass National Forest has not a single road and scarcely any hiking trails. Most people get there by sea, and even the forest rangers patrol by kayak.

Misty Fiords rises from a shoreline laced with glacially carved waterways and up to 5,000-foot snow-capped peaks along the Canadian border. In between lies a varied landscape that includes glaciers, alpine meadows, coastal rainforest, and light-colored granite cliffs so reminiscent of Yosemite National Park that people call Misty Fiords "The Yosemite of the North."

The easiest and most inexpensive way to see Misty Fiords National Monument (the U.S. Forest Service uses the alternate spelling of "fjord," by the way) is on a tour boat. Two companies run tours, and both head for the same spot, Rudyard Bay, the heart of the monument. One company's boat tour lasts 6½ hours and passes the same terrain coming and going, while the other company's boat tour lasts 4½ hours and takes a different route out and back. The quicker tour is the way to go. It's run by **Allen Marine Tours** (☎ 877/686-8100 or 907/225-8100; www.allenmarinetours.com) and costs $149 ($99 for kids 12 and younger). Allen Marine's boats are newer and a little speedier than the competition's, but that's not why the tours are quicker. They're quicker because there's no passenger swap.

If you go with the competition, **Alaska Travel Adventures** (☎ 800/478-0052 in state, or 800/791-2673 out of state; www.bestofalaskatravel.com), some of the passengers you ride out to Rudyard Bay with will board a floatplane there for a flightseeing tour back to Ketchikan. They'll trade seats with floatplane passengers who flew out and are taking the boat tour back. Of course, if you really want to see Misty Fiords from top to bottom, you can join them in the air-sea excursion for $269 (or $229 for kids 12 and younger). If you do just the boat tour, the fare is $139 ($86 kids). That's a little cheaper than Allen Marine's, but you'll see the same terrain and have to listen to the tour guide's same spiel both coming and going. Allen Marine Tours covers more ground, in less time, and you don't have to listen to the same jokes twice.

Serious sea kayakers love Misty Fiords, but it's no place for the inexperienced to strike off on their own. Sudden storms can turn the black-mirror waters into nasty chop, and the crazy tides can turn by as much as 25 feet, inundating what might have seemed to be perfect campsites just hours before. Paddlers who need a guide should try **Southeast Sea Kayaks** (☎ 800/287-1607 or 907/225-1258; www.kayakketchikan.com; summer daily 8am–5pm, rest of year Mon–Fri 9am–3pm). I have to warn you, though, the 12-hour trip isn't cheap, at $399 for adults, and $369 for kids 8 to 12. It does include a lunch, paddling instruction, and about 6 hours of kayaking. A much more affordable option for kayaking is to go on one of the $99 day trips with **Southeast Exposure** (37 Potter Rd.;

☎ 907/225-8829; www.southeastexposure.com; daily 7am–7pm), which explores the shoreline of Revilla Island, but doesn't go to Misty Fiords.

The quickest way to see Misty Fiords is on a flightseeing trip, and several air taxis out of Ketchikan offer tours, which start at about $200 per person for a 2-hour trip. **Island Wings Air Service** (☎ 888/854-2444; www.islandwings.com; daily 7am–7pm) will take you there to see the sites aboard a floatplane, then land on a lake or calm bay and let you walk on the shore for half an hour. It costs $209 per person. For $325 per person, Island Wings adds 40 minutes and a glacier stop.

WRANGELL

Wrangell is a rough-hewn slice of real Alaska that's well off the beaten tourist path. Unlike its nearest neighbor, prim little Petersburg, there's nothing quaint about Wrangell. It's a simple, brawny community built on logging and fishing, and steeped in wood pulp and salmon guts. Why would anyone go out of their way to visit this ugly-duckling town? Because of the neighborhood. Wrangell is the jumping-off point for the stunningly beautiful Stikine River Delta, where you can paddle a canoe along braided waterways and come face to face with seals, sea lions, bald eagles, and some of the millions of migratory seabirds that pass through. To get deeper into the wild, you can hop aboard a jet boat and roar up the swift Stikine River to see glaciers and soak in a hot springs. And if it's bears you're looking for, Wrangell is a short hop from Anan Creek, one of the top bear-viewing spots in Alaska. There you can watch hungry black bears and brown bears fatten up for the winter as they feast on spawning salmon.

A BRIEF HISTORY

The Tlingits, the dominant Native group in Southeast Alaska, came into the world through a hole in the ice—that's according to Tlingit legend, anyway. A current theory holds that the Tlingit came to Southeast Alaska from the Canadian Interior, traveling down the Stikine River, one of the few corridors through the Coast Range. The glaciers along the Stikine River once engulfed the river. It's possible the river bored a path right beneath them, which means the Tlingit could have quite literally come to Alaska through a hole in the ice.

The one thing that's known for sure is the Tlingits have used the Stikine as a trade route for centuries, fiercely guarding its mouth from interlopers. Wrangell Island, situated near the mouth of the river, was the stronghold from which they kept an eye on things.

When Russian fur trappers came to Alaska, they found the Stikine River as useful for trade as the Tlingit did, and they guarded it just as carefully. The Russians planted the seed for the town of Wrangell in 1833 when they raised their flag over a stockade they built there. A powerful Tlingit ruler, Chief Shakes V, relocated his village from elsewhere on the island to an islet beside the fort, perhaps in accordance with the adage about keeping your friends close and your enemies closer. Today you can cross a small footbridge to the Chief Shakes Island, as it's called, and inspect a faithful reproduction of Chief Shakes' clan house, which is loaded with Tlingit art and artifacts.

After the Russians thoroughly decimated Southeast Alaska's populations of fur-bearing animals, they decided the British could have the place. In 1840 they leased a large part of Southeast Alaska, Wrangell Island included, to Britain's

Hudson Bay Company. The Brits moved into the Russian stockade, renamed it Fort Stikine, and raised the Union Jack. But with scarcely a sea otter left to club or a beaver left to skin, they saw no point in sticking around either, and they abandoned the fort in 1849. After the United States bought Alaska in 1867, American troops moved into the old stockade, renamed it Fort Wrangell, and raised the Stars and Stripes. At that point Wrangell became the only place in Alaska that has ever been under the control of four nations—Tlingit, Russian, British, and American—and under three flags.

The gold rush–era that came soon after the U.S. took over was good to Wrangell. The Stikine River was a natural route for the prospectors stampeding to the gold fields in the Yukon and beyond. Dance halls, gambling parlors, and bars blossomed like fast-food franchises and filling stations at a highway interchange. During the gold rush of 1898, famed lawman Wyatt Earp spent 10 days there on his way to the Klondike to hunt for gold. The town implored him to stay and be marshal, but he declined, leading residents to conclude that Wrangell was simply "too wild for Wyatt."

The fishing industry also blossomed under U.S. control, and so did logging, which was the dominant industry in town for most of the 20th century. For economic and environmental reasons, the logging industry collapsed in the 1990s. Most of the mills shut down, and the town's population began to decline. Today, just one mill remains, and it operates sporadically. Though Wrangell still hasn't gotten over the loss of its logging industry, the population has leveled out at about 2,100, and residents are friendly and eager to make a go of tourism.

LAY OF THE LAND

Wrangell sits on the northwest tip of Wrangell Island, 6 miles south of the Stikine River Delta. What passes as the business district sits on the waterfront, along Front Street, which runs between the small boat harbor and the ferry terminal, and passes the small cruise-ship dock along the way. Much of the rest of town lies along Church Street, a block uphill from Front Street. Only one road leads out of town, Zimovia Highway, which is 13 miles long and ends at the beginning of a 100-mile network of old logging roads. The **Wrangell Visitor Center** (296 Outer Dr.; ☎ 800/367-9745 or 907/874-3901; www.wrangell.com; May–Sept 30 Mon–Sat 10am–5pm, rest of year Tues–Sat 10am–5pm) is at the James and Elsie Nolan Center, right in the heart of town. For information about U.S. Forest Service recreation areas, hiking trails, and public use cabins on the island, contact the **Wrangell Ranger District** (525 Bennett St.; ☎ 907/874-2323; www.fs.fed.us/r10/tongass; Mon–Fri 8am–4:30pm).

GETTING TO & AROUND WRANGELL

By Ferry

The **Alaska Marine Highway System** (☎ 800/642-0066 or 907/874-3711; www.dot.state.ak.us/amhs) connects Wrangell with all the other cities of the Southeast, as well as Prince Rupert, British Columbia, and Bellingham, Washington. It's an 8- to 12-hour trip from Juneau ($84 adults, $42 children 6–11, children 5 and under free) or a 6-hour trip from Ketchikan ($36 adults, $16 children). One of the highlights of the ferry trip through the Inside Passage is the leg between Wrangell and Petersburg, which passes through the aptly named Wrangell Narrows.

That Curious Island by the Airport

The canneries in Wrangell once employed lots of Chinese laborers. If one of them died, then the body would be packed in salt brine for shipment home. As local lore has it, this was done on the little island adjacent to the Wrangell airport, which, consequently, is called Deadman's Island.

So shallow is this long, skinny waterway that ferries can run it only at hide tide. Large cruise ships can't squeeze through many of the tight passages, but a few small and midsize ships call on the port each summer.

The ferry terminal in Wrangell is right downtown. The ferry stopover is usually just half an hour, which isn't enough time to see much other than the Tlingit clan house on tiny Chief Shakes Island. Sometimes though, because of the tide, the ferry stays longer.

By Air

Alaska Airlines (☎ 800/252-7522; www.alaskaair.com) has daily summer service to Wrangell. The short flight from Ketchikan (about $200 round trip) takes 28 minutes, while the even shorter flight from Petersburg (about $200 round trip) takes 19 minutes, with the plane practically skimming along the treetops in both cases. The airport is 1½ miles from town. Cabs don't have meters in Wrangell. They just charge flat rates: $6 to transport one person between the airport and downtown, or $3 per head if you're traveling in a group. Try **Northern Lights Taxi** (☎ 907/874-4646).

By Boat

You need a boat more than you need a car in Wrangell. The compact town itself is quite walkable, but to see the surrounding natural wonders and wildlife, a watercraft is needed. If you're not going on a guided tour, and you're comfortable venturing into the wild on your own, you can rent a kayak or a canoe for about $65 per day. **Alaska Charters and Adventures** (No. 7 Front St.; ☎ 888/993-2750; www.alaskaupclose.com) and other outfitters do rentals. Most paddlers hire a water taxi to get out to the best paddling spots. **Sunrise Aviation** (☎ 800/874-2311 or 907/874-2319; www.sunriseflights.com) provides floatplane service.

By Car & Bike

If you want to get out and explore the one road out of town, **Practical Rent-A-Car** (at the airport; ☎ 907/874-3975), has a handful of vehicles for $47 to $55 per day. Reserve one ahead of time because they go fast. Bikes are available for $20 per day through **Rainwalker Expeditions** (☎ 907/874-2549; www.rainwalker expeditions.com), which also rents sea kayaks and canoes.

ACCOMMODATIONS, BOTH STANDARD & NOT

Accommodations in Wrangell have improved tremendously since naturalist John Muir came to town in 1879 and declared it "the most inhospitable place at first sight I have every seen." Muir went on: "There was nothing like a tavern or lodging

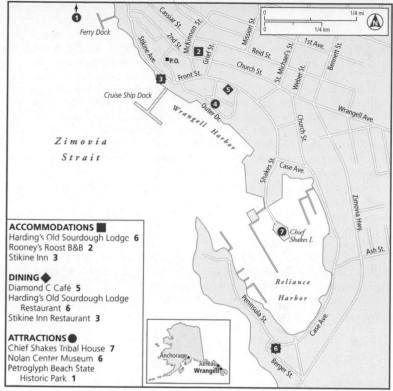

ACCOMMODATIONS
Harding's Old Sourdough Lodge 6
Rooney's Roost B&B 2
Stikine Inn 3

DINING ◆
Diamond C Café 5
Harding's Old Sourdough Lodge
Restaurant 6
Stikine Inn Restaurant 3

ATTRACTIONS ●
Chief Shakes Tribal House 7
Nolan Center Museum 6
Petroglyph Beach State
Historic Park 1

house in the village, nor could I find any place in the stumpy, rocky, boggy ground about it that looked dry enough to camp on until I could find a way into the wilderness to begin my studies." Muir would have nothing to complain about nowadays. Wrangell has campgrounds with dry and level tent sites, a hostel, a hotel, a fishing lodge, and a handful of cozy bed-and-breakfasts. On top of that, there are more than 20 public use cabins in the surrounding national forest. Most important, the local innkeepers are eager to please and the lodging prices are quite reasonable for Southeast Alaska.

Wrangell has a 7% sales tax and a 6% bed tax, bringing the cost of the rooms listed here up 13%.

Hotels

$ The most conveniently located B&B in town also happens to be the most affordable. It's called **Rooney's Roost Bed & Breakfast** (206 McKinnon St.; ☎ 907/874-2026; www.rooneysroost.com; MC, V) and it's run by the Rooney family, who have set aside six rooms for travelers in their grand, century-old home. Some rooms look down from giant dormer windows into the heart of downtown Wrangell, such as it is. Antiques fill the house and a rooster motif prevails among the artwork and knickknacks. The rooms themselves may be tiny, but they're homey and have beds covered with comforters and piled with overstuffed pillows. Three rooms share a bath and go for just $75. The others have private baths (one with the original claw-foot tub) and go for $95. The price of a room includes breakfast, which typically features seafood and wild berries, and the Rooneys readily shuttle guests to and from the ferry terminal or airport for free.

$–$$$$ You can get meals and a room bundled into a package that includes a fishing trip or other guided outings at **Harding's Old Sourdough Lodge** (1104 Peninsula; ☎ 800/874-3613 or 907/874-3613; www.akgetaway.com; AE, DISC, MC, V). A former Wrangell mayor owns the place and runs it in the fashion of a wilderness fishing lodge, which is what it's like, except that it's close to town (a mile from the ferry terminal) and you can get a room there without getting an entire package. Most of the rooms are small, woodsy, and simple, and all come with a continental breakfast. They range in price from $104 for a basic room with king-size bed and private bath to $179 for a suite with two queen-size beds, an in-room Jacuzzi, and a private bath with heated tile floor. The lodge itself is a handsome, red-cedar pole home, built along the water. You can warm up after a day in the wild in its sauna or steam room, then take a seat in the big, rustic dining room for a meal featuring homemade sourdough bread and fresh seafood. Dinners cost $19 to $24 when they don't come as part of a package, and they're served "family style," meaning you get what the mayor has made that night. If you're not a guest, you can make reservations and eat here anyway. It's actually one of the best dining spots in Wrangell.

$$–$$$ If you're more of a hotel person, the **Stikine Inn** (107 Front St.; ☎ 888/874-3388 or 907/874-3388; www.stikineinn.com; AE, MC, V) is the place to stay. It could not be more conveniently located, close to the ferry terminal and right on the water. The rooms are small and motel-like, but some of them have fantastic views across Zimovia Straight. The hotel even has its own private dock so you can come and go by kayak or canoe, Wrangell's answers to the rent-a-car. Rooms go for $103 to $143 during the summer high season, with big off-season discounts.

$–$$$$ The most fun and unusual place to stay in Wrangell is a cozy wooden houseboat called **Rain Haven** ✸ (☎ 907/874-2549; www.rainwalkerexpeditions. com; no credit cards). For something really different—where you can fish from what amounts to your front porch, and where the whole unit gently rocks you to sleep at night—this is the place. Rain Haven has a covered fore deck, an atrium, a thoughtfully assembled onboard library, an attractive galley stocked with staples, a hot shower, and bunks with feather bedding and room enough for three. You'll get the best deal early in the season, when the boat is docked in Shoemaker Harbor, about 5 miles from town (and right across the street from the hiking trail to Rainbow Falls, p. 181). It's a bargain then at $85 a night, which includes a lift into town and back, unless you prefer to bike or kayak. The price goes up in July, when the owners move the boat to a lovely cove in the wilderness, a short paddle from shore. At that point in the season, you can only reserve Rain Haven as part of 3- to 5-day packages, which include a ride to the cove, use of a canoe, and guided trips up the Stikine River and to LeConte Glacier. Packages start at $550.

A Cozy, Underutilized Cabin to Call Your Own

The 22 public use cabins in the U.S. Forest Service's Wrangell Ranger District are among the best deals—and apparently one of the best-kept secrets—in central Southeast Alaska. Renting for a mere $25 to $35 per night, they can sleep at least six people, and more often then not, they're vacant. The catch is that most are accessible only by floatplane or water taxi, which can add a few hundred dollars to the cost. The other catch is how rustic they are. As with all of the public use cabins in Alaska (see p. 373 for info), they're a step up from sleeping in a tent—but not a big step.

Many of the Wrangell Ranger District cabins are built along the water, spaced about a day's paddle apart. With some planning and luck with reservations, you can explore a big part of the region by kayak or canoe and stay at a different cabin every night.

One of the sweetest of these underutilized gems is the **Steamer Bay Cabin,** a modified A-frame on its own island, 27 miles west of Wrangell. In addition to the utter solitude, there's a lovely bay for leisurely walks, beachcombing, and watching the late summer sunsets. Several of the cabins are along the Stikine River, including the two Shakes Slough Cabins. After waking up in one of these cabins, you can paddle to Chief Shakes hot springs and sweat your cares away as the cold river rushes by.

For reservations, contact **ReserveUSA** (☎ 877/444-6777; www.reserve usa.com). For trip planning assistance, and a list of water taxi and float-plane operators, talk to the Wrangell Ranger District Office (525 Bennett St.; ☎ 907/874-2323; www.fs.fed.us/r10/tongass).

Camping

There are several attractive campgrounds in Wrangell. Five miles south of town, the **Shoemaker Bay Recreation Area** offers sites by the road overlooking the boat harbor, right across from the Rainbow Falls Trail. There are free tent sites and RV sites with electric hookups for $25 a night, $15 without electric; the camping fee includes use of the town pool and its showers. Contact the **Wrangell Recreation and Parks Department** (☎ 907/874-2444) for information. They also manage **City Park,** right at the edge of town on Zimovia Highway, where camping is permitted with a 1-night limit.

DINING FOR ALL TASTES

The dining scene is not fancy in Wrangell, but the seafood, served everywhere, is often same-day fresh. If you just need to fuel up, and don't mind simple, hearty diner fare, head to the **Diamond C Café** (215 Front St.; ☎ 907/874-3677; daily 6am–3pm; MC, V; $-$$). For something a tiny bit more memorable, try the following two joints.

$–$$$ Stikine Inn Restaurant (107 Front St.; ☎ 888/874-3388 or 907/874-
3388; daily 7am–8pm; AE, DISC, MC, V) is attached to the inn of the same name,
but gets as many locals as visitors, as this is where folks in the area come to cele-
brate their special occasions. Not that it's at all high end—it looks a bit like an
upgraded diner (you won't get white tablecloths, but flowers are often on the
tables). The fish is cooked up every which way but is always super fresh. Best of
all, you can tipple as you dine here: Most of the bars in town serve food, but this
is the only bona fide restaurant where you can get alcohol with your grilled hal-
ibut ($19), king salmon ($19), or shrimp fettuccine ($15).

$$$–$$$$ "Alaskan Style Dining" is what's advertised at **Harding's Old Sour-
dough Lodge Restaurant** ★★ (☎ 907/874-3613; hours vary according to guests'
schedules; AE, DISC, MC, V) which means, in the words of owner Bruce Harding,
"whatever I'm cooking, you're eating." Typically, he's cooking baked halibut or
salmon, or broiled shrimp, all fresh from local waters (all-inclusive meals are $19
per person, or $24 if you want turf with your surf). The portions are hungry-
man-size and always accompanied by fresh-baked sourdough bread. You're free to
pile as many fresh green things on your plate as you can at the serve-yourself salad
bar. But save room for the chocolate mousse.

WHY YOU'RE HERE: THE TOP SIGHTS & ATTRACTIONS

Wrangell's history is longer and more colorful than its simple, gritty face might
suggest, but after you visit the **Nolan Center Museum** ★★★ (296 Outer Dr.;
☎ 907/874-3770; admission $6; summer Mon–Sat 10am–5pm, rest of year Tues–
Sat 1–5pm) you'll see things in perspective. The museum, housed in the most
modern and impressive building in town, has a rich collection of historic photos
that are worth the stop alone. But put aside some time, too, for the galleries dedi-
cated to the Russian era, British era, and the American gold rush–era, as well as
the logging and fishing industries and Native culture. Among the Native artifacts
on display are century-old spruce root and cedar bark baskets, and some very old
carved house posts. Amazingly, the house posts still have some of their original
fish egg and mineral paints on them.

The house posts in the Nolan Center came from the clan house that Chief Shakes
V built when he relocated his village to be closer to the Russians. The original house
is long gone, but a reproduction called the **Chief Shakes Tribal House** ★★ stands
at the site of the original, on little Chief Shakes Island in the small boat harbor,
accessible by a footbridge. The house and totems were built by Natives using tra-
ditional tools as part of a Civilian Conservation Corps project in the 1930s.
Inside, the house is rich with historic artifacts and Pacific Northwest ambience.
Call the Wrangell Chamber of Commerce (☎ 907/874-3901) a week in advance
and they'll try to arrange a tour for you, for $3 per person. Even if you don't get
in, it's still worth a visit to check out the totems, have your picture taken beneath
the multi-faced figure over the door, and look for sea otters swimming in the har-
bor. You can also visit Chief Shakes' final resting place on Case Avenue. His grave
is set apart by a white picket fence and two killer whale totem poles.

Wrangell's most mysterious attraction is the collection of ancient rock carvings
at **Petroglyph Beach State Historic Park** ★★★ (half mile north of the ferry ter-
minal along Evergreen Rd.). Nobody knows the who, the when, or the why behind
the 50 or so spirals, faces, animals, and other images pecked into the rocks along

Fore Real

Surprising fact: Wrangell has the only regulation USGA-rated golf course in Southeast Alaska. **Muskeg Meadows Golf Course** (Ishiyama Dr.; ☎ 907/874-4653; www.wrangellalaskagolf.com) is a 9-hole course hacked out of the rainforest and laid out over the sawdust and wood chips produced by an old lumber mill. It actually makes for a course with remarkably good drainage. That being said, the course has some unique hazards. One of them resulted in the Raven Rule: If a ball is stolen by a raven, you may replace it with no penalty, provided you have a witness to the theft.

Given how unknown this course still is, the duffers hanging out in the pro shop and clubhouse here are pleasantly surprised when new people come by. Brace yourself for a friendly welcome.

the beach here. But it's fun to wander among them and formulate hypotheses. Scientists have estimated their age at between 3,000 and 10,000 years, and (to deepen the mystery) similar images have been found in Hawaii, Korea, Mexico, and France. Wait for low tide to go see them; at high tide they're submerged. A boardwalk has been built so visitors can get a view without trampling them. State and federal antiquities laws protect the petroglyphs from rubbings, which slowly damage them, but there are 10 reproductions on the site that you're free to rub away on.

ACTIVE WRANGELL

River Tours

The vast expanse of wild lands surrounding Wrangell offer scores of opportunities for fishing, sea kayaking, river rafting, wildlife watching, camping, and overnighting in public use cabins. The possibilities are too numerous to cover here, but any of the local outfitters or the U.S. Forest Service's Wrangell Ranger District (p. 173) can fill you in on your options. I'll cover Wrangell's two most popular out-of-town destinations here, Anan Creek and the Stikine River. Many of the local guides offer trips to another major attraction in the area, LeConte Glacier, but that's a trip that's best done from Petersburg (p. 181), which is closer to the glacier and where tours are more affordable.

The Stikine River ✯✯✯ is the fastest free-flowing navigable river in North America and it simply has to be experienced. This 400-mile-long river whips along at 6 to 8 mph, and slices right through the snow-capped, glacier studded Coast Mountains, linking rainy Southeast Alaska with the dry Canadian Interior. The river delta, which emerges just north of Wrangell, teems with wildlife.

Serious river rafters fly to Telegraph Creek, British Columbia, and launch weeklong rafting or kayaking trips down the river from there. You don't have to go all the way to Canada to experience the river, though. Tour operators in Wrangell take visitors part way up the river in jet boats just like those used on the shallow, reedy Everglades. A trip up the river to see wildlife and to watch the Chief Shakes Glacier calve icebergs into Chief Shakes Lake along the way will likely be a highlight of your trip to Alaska. If you include a stop at Chief Shakes Hot Springs for a steamy soak on the riverbank—the water's naturally 120°F (49°C), but you can decrease the temperature with buckets of icy river water—the trip will definitely be a highlight. Try **Breakaway Adventures** (☎ 888/385-2488 or 907/874-2488; www.breakawayadventures.com), which has reasonable rates and the newest boats, and is good about tailoring its tours to your interests (a soak at the hot springs if you like, more time wildlife viewing if not). A 7-hour up-the-river tour costs $150 (or $130 for kids 12 and younger). In March and April, when the hooligan are running and the birders are in town, it operates bird-watching tours to the **Stikine Flats**—a watery labyrinth of braided channels, marshes, and grasslands at the mouth of the river—for $80 ($60 for kids).

Rainwalker Expeditions Alaska Waters (☎ 800/347-4462 or 907/874-2378; www.alaskawaters.com), located in the lobby at the Stikine Inn (see above) is a good alternative, running 2½-hour tours of the river delta for $82. It also operates 5-hour jet boat tours ($179 adults, $150 children 12 and under) up the Stikine River, with stops at the hot springs for a soak and at the Chief Shakes Glacier. Rainwalker gives discounts to AARP and AAA members, so flash those cards.

It's not just tourists in river rafts hitting the waters around here come summer. In July and August, thousands of salmon literally queue up on Anan Bay, 35 miles southeast of Wrangell, for their annual spawning runs up Anan Creek. Lying in wait for them are dozens of hungry black bears and a handful of brown ones, tired of gorging themselves on berries and ready to feast on fish for awhile. Eager tourists crowd the viewing platforms at the **Anan Creek Wildlife Observatory** ✹✹✹, for the chance to see these powerful bears in the wild (but from a safe distance). During the peak season, from July 5 through August 25, the U.S. Forest Service limits the number of visitors to 60 per day through a permit system. You could secure a permit, hire a water taxi, and explore Anan Creek on your own. But unless you're a hard-core backcountry type who'd feel at home in bear country, this would be a good time to pay a little extra to go on a tour. Either way, contact the **U.S. Forest Service Office in Wrangell** (☎ 907/874-2323) for a list of guide services or water taxis.

Permits cost $10. If you go with a guide, you don't need to worry about getting them—the guide will take care of it for you. Otherwise you can go online and reserve permits for the season beginning in mid-February. Don't worry if you haven't thought that far ahead. A dozen permits for each day aren't made available until 3 days in advance, in order to accommodate late planners. With a little flexibility, you won't have any trouble getting some.

Hiking

In 1879, naturalist John Muir climbed what is known today as the **Mount Dewey Trail** ✹ and inadvertently scared the daylights out of the villagers below. Muir set a huge bonfire atop the hill when a storm blew in. The Tlingits in the village below couldn't see the fire, but they could see a mysterious orange glow emitting through the dark clouds, which grew brighter and brighter as the storm intensified. They had no idea what was going on, but it didn't look good. They were relieved and possibly a little miffed when they discovered it was only Muir trying to stay warm. Muir said the enormous fire was one of the most enjoyable of his life. Today, the half-mile trail up the 400-foot hill at the edge of town may not be the best place for a bonfire (at least without a license), but it offers a pleasant, quickie hike with a big payoff of a view. Walk to the end of 3rd Street for the trailhead.

For a longer hike (about 4 hr.) with a waterfall and a view, choose the **Rainbow Falls Trail**. It's a mile hike to the falls, and another 2.5 miles up to a ridge-top lookout. The upper parts of the trail are steep, but the view is worth the effort. The trailhead is 5 miles past the ferry terminal on Zimovia Highway. If you haven't got a bike or a rental car, a cab will carry you to the trailhead for $9. There's a pay phone across the street at Shoemaker Harbor, where you can call the cab from when you're ready to come back.

For info on the many other trails of Wrangell Island—trails where tourists rarely tread—inquire at **Wrangell Ranger District** (see p. 173).

ATTENTION, SHOPPERS!

In the world of minerals, Wrangell is famous for its raspberry-colored, geometrically perfect garnets. They come from an area at the mouth of the Stikine River called Garnet Ledge, which was once mined commercially but has been deeded to the children of Wrangell since the 1960s. Nowadays, only children are supposed to collect garnets there. Every spring a bunch of Wrangell families camp at the ledge to let their kids stock up on the precious gems, which are the birthstone of January. You can find them for sale around town, and when a cruise ship is in, kids hawk them down at the dock.

PETERSBURG

For an escape from the visiting masses clogging towns like Skagway and Ketchikan, for quality time among the humpbacks, for a look at the fastest-moving glacier on the continent, and to stroll along the plank streets of an utterly adorable Alaskan fishing town, go to Petersburg. Large cruise ships can't dock in Petersburg's shallow port, so visitors—delightfully—take a back seat to halibut, salmon, and pickled herring.

Known as "Alaska's Little Norway," Petersburg proudly wears its Scandinavian heritage on its arm. Residents adorn their tidy shops and homes with decorative Norwegian rosemaling (a distinctive floral pattern), they hold town meetings and play bingo in the Sons of Norway Hall, and they celebrate Norwegian Independence Day each year with a big bash. The phone book is filled with names like Havrilek, Hallingstad, and Severson, and the barbershop floor gets a regular covering of light blond hair.

A BRIEF HISTORY

Norwegian immigrant Peter Buschmann founded Petersburg in the 1890s, taking advantage of a ready supply of ice from nearby LeConte Glacier to start a fish packing plant and cannery. He also built a sawmill and a dock. Word spread that Buschmann would hire any Scandinavian who applied for a job, and soon the town was filled with tow-heads cutting timber, catching fish, and packing it into glacial ice for shipment to Seattle. Buschmann made some bad business deals and wound up committing suicide, but his town thrived. His cannery, now owned by a big Seattle seafood processor and called Petersburg Fisheries, has been in continuous operation since it opened. It shares the waterfront with two other canneries, two cold processing plants, and Alaska's largest halibut fishing fleet. Fishing boats come and go constantly throughout the summer.

Several tour boats come and go out of Petersburg as well, taking visitors on whale-watching expeditions or to LeConte Glacier. The glacier, 25 miles away from town, is one of the fastest-flowing on the continent, and it calves icebergs like mad.

LAY OF THE LAND

Petersburg sits on the northwest tip of mountainous, heavily forested Mitkof Island, about halfway between Juneau and Ketchikan. Mitkof Island is separated from its close neighbor, Kupreanof Island, by the 22-mile-long Wrangell Narrows, a crooked, shallow channel just 300 feet across at points. Petersburg is at the top of the Narrows, on Frederick Sound, a rich salmon and halibut fishery, and a popular feeding ground for humpback whales in the summer. On clear days you can get a spectacular view across the sound of the saw-toothed peaks and hanging glaciers of the Coast Range. A wicked-looking 9,077-foot peak called Devil's Thumb marks the Canadian border. The town has a permanent population of about 3,100, which swells in the summer when cannery workers and fishing crews come to town.

You'll find three small boat harbors here, which bustle with commercial fishermen throughout the summer. Much of the town is built on pilings over Hammer Slough, a creek mouth that floods at high tide and creates a postcard-quality reflecting pool beneath the waterfront. Sing Lee Alley, a wooden street built across the slough, is at the heart of town and what a picturesque heart it is, lined with freshly painted Scandinavian-style shops and homes. Nordic Drive is the main thoroughfare, running from the ferry terminal a mile through town, then changing into Sandy Beach Road, a few miles north of town. Nordic Drive becomes the unpaved Mitkof Highway to the south, and runs for 34 miles. Out of town, there are all sorts of opportunities for outdoor adventures since Petersburg is surrounded by the Tongass National Forest. For complete information on all of the camping, hiking, and kayaking options, contact the **Petersburg Ranger District** (12 N. Nordic Dr.; ☎ 907/772-3871; www.fs.fed.us/r10/tongass/districts/petersburg).

For info on Petersburg proper, stop by the **Visitor Information Center** (☎ 866/484-4700 or 907/772-4636; www.petersburg.org; Mon–Sat 9am–5pm, Sun noon–4pm) at 1st and Fram streets, near the boat harbor. It serves as a clearinghouse for tour companies and stocks lots of information on the area.

GETTING TO & AROUND PETERSBURG

Alaska Airlines (☎ 800/252-7522; www.alaskaair.com) has flights to and from Petersburg two times a day, with one northbound and one southbound jet. Round trip fares from Anchorage are about $350. Small charter companies also serve the community, doing flightseeing tours of LeConte Glacier and, carrying people to public use cabins in the surrounding Tongass National Forest. The airport is less than a mile from the heart of town.

Ferries run by the **Alaska Marine Highway System** (☎ 800/642-0066; www.ferryalaska.com) stop at Petersburg a few times a week. The fare is $66 from Juneau (8 hr. away), $45 from Sitka (9 hr.), or $34 from Wrangell (3 hr.). The

ACCOMMODATIONS ■
Scandia House **4**
The Tides Inn Motel **2**
Waterfront B&B **9**
Water's Edge B&B **1**

DINING ◆
Papa Bear's Pizza **8**
Rooney's Northern Lights
    Restaurant **7**

ATTRACTIONS ●
Clausen Memorial Museum **3**
Fishermen's Memorial Park **6**
Sons of Norway Hall **5**

ferry dock is about a mile from the center of town. Children ages 12 and under pay half the adult rate. It's a pleasant walk unless you've got lots of luggage, it's raining, or the ferry arrives very late at night (as it's prone to do) and you have no idea where you're headed. Many B&Bs pick up and drop off guests at the ferry terminal and airport, and you should take advantage of this if you can. **Metro Cab** (☎ 907/772-2700) charges about $5 for a ride from the airport or ferry port to the center of town.

You can walk the whole of Petersburg in about an hour. To explore the back-country, however, you'll need a bike, a car, or a boat. Both Tides Inn Motel and Scandia House (p. 184 and 185) rent cars. Their fleets are tiny though, so reserve one in advance. Rates at Tides Inn, an agent of Avis, run between $67 and $79 a day, plus 15% tax. Scandia House charges only $58 a day and allows customers to take its vehicles off the pavement—an important consideration. (Mitkof Island has more than 100 miles of unpaved roads, so an off-road vehicle comes in handy.) Scandia House also rents small boats, if you'd like to explore Kurpreanof Island or the Wrangell Narrows. An 18-footer with 40 horsepower engine rents for $125 per day, plus gas. If you stay a night or more at the hotel, you can rent the skiff for $115 per day; if you rent for 6 days, you get the seventh day free.

ACCOMMODATIONS, BOTH STANDARD & NOT

Lodging is a straightforward proposition in Petersburg. There are campgrounds, public use cabins, a hostel, two hotels, and about a dozen bed-and-breakfasts. For a complete list of B&Bs, check the website of the Chamber of Commerce (www.petersburg.org). Following are my favorites.

A 4% sales tax and a 6% bed tax apply to all accommodations described here, except the public use cabins.

Hotels & Bed & Breakfasts

$$ A convenient location and waterfront views are the main reasons to pick **Waterfront Bed & Breakfast** ★ (1004 S. Nordic Dr.; ☎ 866/772-9301 or 907/772-9300; www.waterfrontbedandbreakfast.com; MC, V). Waterfront is actually an understatement: This B&B sits on pilings out *over* the water. And it's practically next door to the Alaska Marine Highway System terminal, so if you come by ferry, you won't even need a cab. The five comfortable guest rooms—which range from $100 to $120—are appointed with heavy, mission-style oak furniture. Some rooms have a queen-size bed, some have double beds, and all the beds have puffy down comforters. When the weather's nice, guests sit out on the broad deck and watch the arrivals and departures of floatplanes, fishing boats, and the state ferry. The hostess prepares big, hearty Alaskan breakfasts (biscuits and gravy, pancakes, sausage-and-egg casseroles) that are included in the price of the room. If you like, she'll fix you dinner as well (though that costs more). It's an easy walk to the restaurants in town, or you can use the house kitchen to cook for yourselves. In foul weather, or whenever the spirit moves you, you can retreat to the communal hot tub.

$$ Outside of Petersburg proper (it's about 2 miles from the center, on the Frederick Sound) **Water's Edge Bed & Breakfast** ★★ (705 Sandy Beach Rd.; ☎ 800/868-4273 or 907/772-3736; www.petersburglodgingandtours.com; no credit cards) offers blessed privacy, quiet, and space. Along with your own comfortable room with either a king-size bed ($110, it can be split into two singles) or a queen-size bed ($100), rooms share a kitchenette and a spacious living room, with a big bay window where you can laze the afternoon away, watching eagles swoop over the secluded beach out front or whales spouting off in the sound. It's a perfect spot for groups, since the rate goes down if you rent both rooms for 3 or more nights: $185 a night with breakfast, $165 a night without. All rates include shuttle rides to and from the airport or ferry terminals and even the use of bicycles (now, that's generous). And your hosts—a marine biologist and retired teacher—are super-knowledgeable about the area. In fact, they run Kaleidoscope Tours and offer guests a 5% discount on their glacier and whale-watching trips. Reserve a room well in advance, as this place is very popular. Children under 12 aren't admitted, unless you rent both rooms.

$$ The **Tides Inn Motel** (301 N. 1st St.; ☎ 800/665-8433 or 907/772-4288; www.tidesinnalaska.com; AE, DISC, MC, V) also has the advantage of being on the water (noticing a trend here?). The harborside rooms give you a front-row seat on the best show in town—the comings and goings of the halibut fleet, with frequent guest appearances by sea lions and swooping bald eagles. It's also the least expensive option in the vicinity for those who don't want to go the B&B route (and as the

A Cabin with a View

The U.S. Forest Service has 20 rustic public use cabins in the Petersburg area. They're dirt cheap, but guests need a boat or a floatplane to get to most of them, which adds to the cost. There's one, however, that's accessible by foot—if you're up for a 3- to 4-hour uphill hike. **Raven's Roost Cabin** ★ is a lovely, custom-made alpine cabin on a ridgeline 1,745 feet above town. It's an idyllic place. From the deck you enjoy a mesmerizing view of Frederick Sound, the Wrangell Narrows, Kupreanof Island, and neighboring Canada. Guests spend their days hiking through the high mountain muskeg, or boggy terrain, returning to their rustic home away from home with piles of wildflowers and wild berries.

Though the cabin's affordable ($35 a night), it's minimally equipped: It has an oil heater, an outhouse, two single wooden bunks, and a sleeping loft (you bring the sleeping bags, camp stove, cooking utensils, toilet paper, and so on). The cabin is particularly popular with locals in the winter who hire helicopters to fly them to the ridge top, from where they ski down. The sleeping loft has a doorway, so people can get into the cabin even when the snow's really deep. (See p. 373 for public use cabin reservations.)

---

largest hotel in town, it's about as far from a B&B in ambience as you can get). The 45 recently refurbished, spic-n-span rooms go for between $100 and $110 for double occupancy. Even better, rooms with kitchenettes cost the exact same amount as those without (price variations are based on view, as most rooms are spacious, with a pair of queen-size beds). So if you want to cook—and that certainly will be a money saver—be sure to ask for a kitchenette. There are both smoking and nonsmoking rooms, a continental breakfast and coffee all day in the lobby, plus a courtesy shuttle to the airport or ferry dock.

$$–$$$$ The newest hotel in town, **Scandia House** ★★★ (110 Nordic Dr.; ☎ 800/772-5006 or 907/772-4281; www.scandiahousehotel.com; AE, DISC, MC, V) is also the oldest. Let me explain. Scandia was founded in 1910, but it burned down in 1995. It's since been entirely rebuilt, but with an eye to the town's signature Norwegian styling. That means the 33 rooms are simple and airy, but with lots of natural light; blond-wood trim; painted, curvaceous, floral accents called "rosemaling" here and there; and comfy chairs. Some even have Jacuzzis. You can choose from standard rooms with one or two queen-size beds, a room with a single king-size bed or a pair of twin beds, or a room with a kitchenette and two queens. Rates run from $110 to $140. If you want to splurge, there's a lovely, high-ceilinged suite with a view for $195. A courtesy shuttle takes guests to and from the airport or ferry terminal. Scandia House is a little farther from the water, but even more centrally located than Tides Inn.

Camping

The closest place to pitch a tent near Petersburg is the **Twin Creek RV Park** (☎ 907/772-3244), 7½ miles out the Mitkof Highway. It costs $15 to put a tent in one of the RV spaces, or $25 to put an RV there. The nearest natural campgrounds to Petersburg are the U.S. Forest Service's **Ohmer Creek Campgrounds** (☎ 877/444-6777; www.recreation.gov), 22 miles off the highway. The campgrounds feature a 1-mile trail, a floating bridge over a beaver pond, and summer trout and salmon fishing.

DINING FOR ALL TASTES

Petersburg is the 12th most productive fishing port in the United States, according to the National Marine Fisheries Service. What that means for you, the hungry traveler, is halibut for dinner that might have been caught that morning. It means Caesar salads topped with locally caught salmon smoked by the docks. It means jumbo prawns served within eyeshot of the boats that might have netted them. Dining in Petersburg isn't fancy, but it sure can be satisfying.

$–$$$ Just across from the ferry terminal is **Papa Bear's Pizza** (1105 S. Nordic Dr., across from the ferry terminal; ☎ 907/772-3727; summer daily 11am–9pm, rest of year daily 11am–8pm; MC, V), where, if you time it right, you can get a pizza to go and eat it on the ferry while Petersburg disappears over the stern. You can also get pizza by the slice ($3.50), calzones ($13), wraps ($7.95), ice cream ($2), and espresso ($1). And if you want to kill time and catch a beer buzz while waiting for a boat, there's a bar with pool tables upstairs. A large (16-in.) pizza with three toppings, big enough for three or more, costs $25.

$–$$$$ A seafood view—of sorts—is the lure at **Rooney's Northern Lights Restaurant** (203 Sing Lee Alley; ☎ 907/772-2900; daily 6am–9pm; DISC, MC, V), located across from the Sons of Norway Hall. Call ahead and reserve a table by the window, where you can watch sea lions dine in the harbor while you dine indoors. It's a casual place where Petersburg fishermen bring their families for inexpensive tacos and burritos, hamburgers and fries, spaghetti, cranberry pecan chicken, pastas, and—naturally—halibut and salmon dinners. It's open for breakfast, lunch, and dinner, with dinners ranging from $7 to $30, but averaging just about $12 to $17.

WHY YOU'RE HERE: THE TOP SIGHTS & ATTRACTIONS

After building his cannery, sawmill, and dock, Petersburg founder Peter Buschmann sunk a bunch of pilings into Hammer Slough and built a barnlike building on top of them. He painted the building white, slapped on rosemaling-adorned shutters, and named it the **Sons of Norway Hall** (23 Sing Lee Alley). It was finished in 1912, and it's been the social center of the town ever since. Norwegian dancers occasionally perform here in the summer, accompanied by a buffet that includes fish cakes, pickled herring, and Norwegian pastries. Check at the visitor center for dates. A replica of a Viking ship, which plays a big role in the Little Norway Festival, is usually parked out front. If nothing's happening at the Sons of Norway Hall while you're in town, at least take a snapshot of the building—it's the town icon.

Next, spend a little time in the **Fishermen's Memorial Park,** next door to the Sons of Norway Hall. This may be the only park you'll ever visit built on pilings over a tidal slough. There's also another photo-op here: A bronze statue of a Bojer Wikan, a lifelong Petersburg resident lost at sea. He represents all of the local

Petersburg's Super Seafood Sweepstakes

Between July 1 and August 15, you can take a shot at the $4,000-or-so purse in the annual Canned Salmon Classic. To win, correctly guess how many cans of salmon the local canneries will pack that season. Tickets are on sale at shops around town. Here's a tip to get you started: There were 6,345,790 cans packed in 2006.

mariners and serves as a reminder of the life-and-death stakes that accompany commercial fishing. (Cholesterol is *not* the only risk associated with beer battered halibut.)

To delve deeper into Petersburg history, walk 3 blocks inland to the **Clausen Memorial Museum** ★ (203 Fram St.; ☎ 907/772-3598; www.clausenmuseum. alaska.net; $3 adults, children 12 and under free; summer Mon–Sat 10am–5pm, call for off-season hours). It's a simple community museum that dwells lovingly on Petersburg's past, which means lots of Norwegian family photos and mementos, along with antique fishing gear and cannery equipment, tributes to loggers and logging, and Native artifacts—including a Tlingit canoe. One of the most interesting exhibits is the small model of the savage fish traps that canneries used throughout Southeast Alaska. These traps decimated fish populations and put fishermen out of work. Abolishing them for all time was one of the state legislature's first orders of business upon statehood. Be sure to take a look at the huge taxidermied salmon here—it's the largest one ever caught by commercial fishermen (127 pounds).

When you're ready for a stroll, head south of town along the water to nearby **Eagle Park,** which overlooks the Tongass Narrows. This is a lovely spot for tide pooling (at low tide anyway—free tide tables are widely available around town) and for spotting eagles, who are drawn by the bits of fish waste from a nearby cannery that wash ashore. If you don't spot them on the beach picking at halibut, look up in the treetops.

THE OTHER PETERSBURG

Petersburg's most anticipated event of the year is the 4-day **Little Norway Festival.** It's held the third full weekend in May, around Norwegian Independence Day, May 17. Residents dress up in Scandinavian costumes, parade through the streets with a Viking ship, play music, and dance in the streets. The festival culminates in a potluck Norwegian fish feed on the beach. This is the best time to see Petersburg at its proudest, hands down.

One great way to hang out with locals, no matter the time of year, is to go to the **Sons of Norway Hall** (see above) at 7pm on any Saturday and play bingo. It's good, wholesome, small-town fun and visitors are warmly welcomed (especially those who don't win).

ATTENTION, SHOPPERS!

You won't find any big box stores or a retail-sapping shopping mall in Petersburg. Happily, it instead boasts an old-fashioned downtown, with lots of colorful shops and galleries. Many of them are concentrated along Sing Lee Alley. The notables include an arts-and-crafts store called the **CubbyHole** (14 Sing Lee Alley; ☎ 907/772-2717) which is well stocked with the rosemaling patterns decorating everything in town, plus beads, yarn, and Norwegian souvenirs and gifts. Nearby, in a quaint old boarding house, where teachers and fishermen once lived, **Sing Lee Alley Books** (11 Sing Lee Alley; ☎ 907/772-4440) has a good selection of, among other things, Alaska titles, including a few by local authors.

GET OUT OF TOWN

Some of the best whale-watching waters in Alaska are just 30 miles from Petersburg, at the nutrient-rich point where the waters of Frederick Sound, Stephens Passage, and Chatham Straight merge. Literally hundreds of humpbacks gather to feed there in the summer and on the way out, you'll probably encounter sea lions, harbor seals, and other large marine mammals drawn to this fertile area.

Unlike the big commercial whale-watching tours that dominate other parts of Alaska, the handful of local operators here are strictly mom-and-pop operations using small boats that generally carry no more than six passengers. Not only are the boats less crowded, but you'll get more face time with the guide and a more eye-to-eye view of the whales. (Not to scare you, but I should point out that sometimes whale-watching from a small boat can lead to closer contact with the animals than anybody expects. Once, apparently by accident, a leaping whale landed on a boat, knocking people into the water. Nobody was hurt, but the whale must have been chagrined.) The downside is the cost—tours start at about $200 per passenger, with group discounts if there are more than three of you. That's more than you'll pay on the larger commercial tours elsewhere, so if price is your only consideration, then save your whale-watching for Sitka, Seward, or another port where these tours depart. If you do decide to do it here, know that tours generally last 6 to 10 hours and make for a sublime experience.

Whale-watching tours run from May into September. Don't wait until you get to Petersburg to book one though, or you might miss out, especially during the peak months of July and August. The best method of booking is through **Viking Travel** (☎ 800/327-2571 or 907/772-3818; www.alaskaferry.com) which keeps track of all four local tour operators and knows which boats have seats available on what days. There's no extra charge to go through Viking, and the company doesn't favor one operator over another. If you have a choice of boats, get one with a hydrophone, an underwater microphone that allows you to listen to the whales' songs. Viking Travel is also a clearinghouse for fishing charters, floatplane charters, kayaking trips, water taxis, and glacier tours.

You really need to stay at least 2 days in Petersburg, one so you can go whale-watching, and other so you can see LeConte Glacier. It's both the southernmost and the fastest-moving glacier in North America. (Incidental glacier trivia: LeConte Glacier is named for Joseph LeConte, a geologist and one of the founding members of the Sierra Club.) Fast moving translates into lots and lots of calving icebergs. The bay in front of the glacier, LeConte Bay, is filled with icebergs, and when the wind and tide are just so, they drift out into Frederick Sound and are sometimes visible from town. On very rare occasions, a big, blue iceberg will beach itself right in Petersburg. Tours generally start at about $150 and last 5 to 6 hours. Again, the best way to book a tour is through Viking Travel.

You can explore other sites along the roads north and south of town with a car or bike. Head north on Sandy Beach Road to **Outlook Park** ✪, an excellent place to scan Frederick Sound for humpback whales and rogue icebergs. For a better look, use the spotting scopes inside the timber-frame shelter (it was built by a local shipwright using Norwegian stave churches as a model). Keep going north until you come to **Sandy Beach Park,** known for its stone fish traps and petroglyphs. These are visible during low tides (when the tide pooling is good too), but they're not readily apparent even then. Ask a local to point them out, or catch one of the free ranger-led tours periodically put on by the U.S. Forest Service. Check with the **Petersburg Ranger District** (12 N. Nordic Dr.; ☎ 907/772-3871; www.fs. fed.us/r10/tongass/districts/petersburg).

SITKA

Sitka is more thoroughly steeped in Russian history than anywhere else in Alaska. It was, after all, the capital of Russian America, where Alexander Baranof—the Lord of Alaska—chased off the Tlingits and ran Russia's American fur trade empire. Atop Castle Hill, where Baranof lived in a hulking log mansion dubbed "Baranof's Castle," you can survey Sitka's spectacular surroundings—forested islets dotting Sitka Sound, snow-capped peaks rising up behind town, and a lop-sided shield volcano on the horizon, protecting Sitka from the full force of the Gulf of Alaska's storms. Wander around town and you can still see some of the buildings the Russians left behind. In fact, Sitka has more Russian-era buildings than anywhere else in Alaska, including the home of a saint, The Russian Bishop's House. Beneath the onion dome of the landmark St. Michael's Cathedral, you can inspect religious treasures and age-old icons. The influence of modern Russia can also be seen in the handmade Russian souvenirs filling Sitka's gift shops.

Of course, the Tlingits inhabited Sitka long before the Russians showed their bearded faces, and unlike the Russians, they're still around. Today you can visit a Tlingit community house to catch a performance by Native dancers. You can meet Native weavers, jewelry smiths, and carvers in their workshops. And you can walk through a forest filled with totem poles carved with images of whales, bears, beavers, ravens, a village watchman in his conical rain hat and shawl, and a sea monster known as Waasago. Cultural attractions aside, Sitka is also one of the best places in the Southeast for whale-watching, kayaking, and tide pooling.

A BRIEF HISTORY

Sitka is unlike the rest of Southeast Alaska in that it's the only community on the shore of the stormy North Pacific, rather than along the protected Inside Passage. The Tlingit acknowledged this geographical distinction when they named the large Native village that originally stood there Shee Atika—"people of the outside."

The People of the Outside weren't happy when Alexander Baranof, governor of the Russian-American Company, established a fort near their village in 1799. He left a few dozen bearded trappers and their women behind, then sailed back to Kodiak. In 1892, the Tlingit attacked the fort, killing nearly everyone inside and burning it to the ground. In 1894, Baranof returned, heavily armed, to even the score, and found the Tlingit had built their own fort. They held out for 6 days against the Russians. When they ran out of ammunition, they slipped away into the night, not to return for almost 2 decades.

In the meantime, the Russians took over the village and turned it into the town of Novoarkhangelsk, or New Archangel. The Russians had decimated the fur seal and sea otter populations in the Aleutians, and it was time to do the same here. For half a century the town thrived as the capital of Russian America and as a center for trade and ship building. Baranof threw lavish, vodka-soaked receptions for whatever ship captain came by. "They all drink an astonishing quantity, Baranof not excepted," wrote an American captain. "It is no small tax on the health of a person trying to do business with him."

When the fur trade collapsed entirely and Russia sold Alaska to the United States, New Archangel was the site of the transfer. The Russian flag came down, the U.S. flag went up, the Americans changed the name to Sitka—an approximation of Shee Atika—and within a week, two American saloons, an American restaurant, and a 10-pin alley opened up. Sitka remained the capital of Alaska under the U.S. until 1906, when the government seat moved to Juneau. Timber and fishing were the dominant industries through most of the 20th century, until logging collapsed in the 1990s. Now fishing and tourism are booming, with a major U.S. Coast Guard air station helping out the economy as well.

LAY OF THE LAND

Sitka is on the west shore of Baranof Island, a mountainous place roughly the size of Delaware. The island measures 100 miles across at its widest point and 30 miles at its narrowest. Several barrier islands protect Sitka from the brunt of the Pacific surf. Thirty-two-hundred-foot Mount Edgecumbe, shaped like a lopsided Mount Fuji, dominates the view to the west. Heavily forested mountains with towering granite peak up to 3,350 feet on the eastern edge of the city, while dozens of forested islets fill the waters of Sitka Sound to the south and southwest. There are only about 14 miles of paved road in and around town. Halibut Point Road runs north for 7 miles to the ferry terminal and dead ends soon after at a U.S. Forest Service campground. Sawmill Creek Road runs south of town past a variety of attractions, such as the Whale Park and the Theobroma Chocolate Factory. Most of the points of interest in town are located along Lincoln Street. The airport is located on little Japonski Island, connected to downtown Sitka by a short bridge. There is no deepwater dock, so cruise ships anchor in Sitka Sound and carry passengers ashore on little shuttle boats.

At Harrigan Centennial Hall (330 Harbor Dr.), next to the dock where cruise-ship passengers come ashore, there's a **visitor information desk** (☎ 907/747-3225; Mon–Fri 8am–10pm, Sat 8am–5pm, sometimes Sun), as well as a history museum and the auditorium space for a lively Russian dance troupe (p. 197). The town's professional visitor organization is the **Sitka Convention and Visitors Bureau,** at P.O. Box 1226, Sitka, AK 99835 (☎ 907/747-5940; fax 907/747-3739). They maintain a very useful website at **www.sitka.org.**

GETTING TO & AROUND SITKA

Alaska Airlines (☎ 800/252-7522; www.alaskaair.com) flies daily between Sitka directly to Ketchikan and Juneau, and flies from those two cities nonstop to Anchorage or Seattle. Ferry service is less frequent to Sitka, but it's more fun, and cheaper than flying. The ferry passes through some incredible passages, including Peril Straight, a tight squeeze where it appears you could almost grab a tree branch as you pass through. **Alaska Marine Highway System** (☎ 800/642-0066; www. ferryalaska.com) operates three types of ferries here: The old, slow ferries (9 hr. from Juneau), the new fast ferry Fairweather (4½ hr. from Juneau), and the small shuttle that sails between Sitka and the small communities of Petersburg, Wrangell, and Coffman Cove. The fare from Juneau to Sitka is about $40 on the older ferry, and $45 on the fast ferry. You might assume that the fast ferry is a better choice than the slower one, but not necessarily. You'll probably see more wildlife along the way on the slow boat—including whales, bear, and deer—making the trip a de facto wildlife tour (which means you might not need to spend money on an actual wildlife tour). There are often Park Rangers aboard the ferries lecturing on the nature you're seeing.

Once you've gotten to Baranof Island, **Sitka Cab** (☎ 907/747-5001) or **Hank's Taxi & Tour** (☎ 907/747-8443) will get you downtown from the ferry terminal for about $18 or downtown from the airport for about $10. The better bargain is to hop aboard the **Ferry Transit Bus** or the **Airport Shuttle** (☎ 907/747-8443), which wait at the ferry and the airport for passengers to arrive, then shuttle them to town for $6 one-way or $8 round-trip. No reservations are required. Just hop onboard and pay the driver.

You don't really need a car in Sitka. You can pretty much walk clear across town in 8 minutes or so, and you can bike to the end of the short road segments north and south of town. **Yellow Jersey Cycles** (329 Harbor Dr., across from Centennial Hall; ☎ 907/747-6317; www.yellowjerseycycles.com) rents bikes for $25 per day. But if you like, you can drive the short roads in a rent-a-car from **Avis** (☎ 800/230-4898 or 907/966-2404; www.avis.com) for $65 per day on average or from **North Star Rent-a-Car** (☎ 800/722-6927 or 907/966-2552; www.northstarrentacar.com) for $55 per day on average.

For water transport to kayaking locations, public use cabins, the hot springs, or wherever, **Ester G Tours & Sea Taxi** (☎ 907/747-6481 or 907/738-6481) is available, for $150 per hour.

ACCOMMODATIONS, BOTH STANDARD & NOT

The homestay-style B&B is the norm in Sitka, where you get a room in the hosts' home and sit at their dining room table for breakfast. But you can also go for the types of quirky digs that you might brag to your friends about once you get home, such as a floating cabin or an actual working lighthouse. And if all you want is a bed for the night, simple hotels are on offer, too. The best options follow below.

Hotels & Inns

$ Let's start with the **Sitka Hotel** ★ (118 Lincoln St.; ☎ 907/747-3288; www. sitkahotel.com; AE, MC, V), the oldest and most affordable of Sitka's three hotels, and frankly, the only one I would stay at. The others are too corporate, bland, and expensive. The rooms at the Sitka Hotel, on the other hand, are some of the most affordable hotel rooms in Alaska—and unless they were inside St. Michael's Cathedral itself, they couldn't be more centrally located. Yeah, they're motel-basic, but they're also white-glove clean, perfectly comfortable, and cost just $90 a night for a double with a private bath, and $70 a night for a double with a shared bath. The rooms in the back of the hotel, which was recently rebuilt from scratch after a fire, are larger and more modern than the rooms in the front of the house, but the front rooms have the sort of appealing high ceilings, decorative window mold-ings, and creaky floors you'd expect from a place built in 1939. Downstairs there's a nice diner posing as a Victorian restaurant, and a long, narrow, lively bar called the Pourhouse. (Note that if you want to get any sleep, you should ask for a room that's not right above the bar.)

$$–$$$ If you're willing to pay a little more and sacrifice the central location, you can get a place smack dab on the water at the **Cascade Inn** (2035 Halibut Point Rd.; ☎ 800/532-0908 or 907/747-6804; www.cascadeinnsitka.com; MC, V). It's 2½ miles from downtown, so you'll need a car or a bike to get around, but that may be a moot point when you get a load of the views: All of the rooms have pri-vate balconies right on the waterfront. Even the inn's cedar sauna has an ocean view, at least until the glass door steams up. The 10 units aren't big, but they're bright and clean. They come with one or two queen-size beds, and some have kitchenettes (but you'll pay a bit extra for those). Rates range from $115 to $140 in the high season, with big off-season discounts. The owners run Big Blue Charters, and you can book fishing-and-lodging packages through them. The unfortunate thing about the place is that it's attached to a gas station and conven-ience store, so while it's kind of like an oceanfront Maui condominium on one side, it's a little like a Kansas truck stop on the other. This also isn't the best choice for travelers with mobility issues, as there are stairs to climb.

$$–$$$$ In Sitka, most bed-and-breakfasts are much more amenity laden than any of the pricier hotels in town. Take, for example, the **Alaska Ocean View Bed & Breakfast** ★★ (1101 Edgecumbe Dr.; ☎ 907/747-8310; www.sitka-alaska-lodging.com; AE, DISC, MC, V). A handsome three-story home—and a short walk from downtown—it's just loaded with creature comforts. Each of the three guest rooms sports down comforters and pillows, oversize spa towels, cushy robes, fresh slippers, Bose Wave music systems, HEPA air filters, and other niceties. The par-lor boasts a library of Alaskana, filled with videos, maps, books, and magazines. In the yard, there's bocce ball, croquet, badminton, horseshoes, and a pond with a small waterfall. On the deck is a covered Jacuzzi, a perfect place to watch neigh-borhood eagles (oh yeah—there are neighborhood eagles!). And I haven't even mentioned the hosts, who walk the line perfectly between enthusiastic and dis-creet, making all their guests feel welcome but giving them a good amount of pri-vacy, too. For breakfast, you'll find locally roasted coffee, freshly baked goodies, sometimes blueberry pancakes or crab quiche, and a lot of support for people with dietary idiosyncrasies (Atkins people, you know who you are). Rooms range from $129 for the nice but small one, to $239 for the top-floor suite, which has a bal-cony with glass railings so that you can enjoy the ocean view from bed.

$$$ Ever wanted your own private island, where you can live out all of your hermit-in-a-lighthouse fantasies? If you've got a big group looking for an unusual getaway on a private island all to yourselves, then the **Rockwell Lighthouse** ★ kids (on an unnamed island in Sitka Sound; ☎ 907/747-3056; no credit cards) just might be for you . . . with some caveats. If your group is opposed to making its own beds, keep looking. The Rockwell Lighthouse is a few steps above rustic, and there's certainly no pampering there. The beds come with linens, but it's up to you to put the two together. If you find a spider in the shower, you should take it up

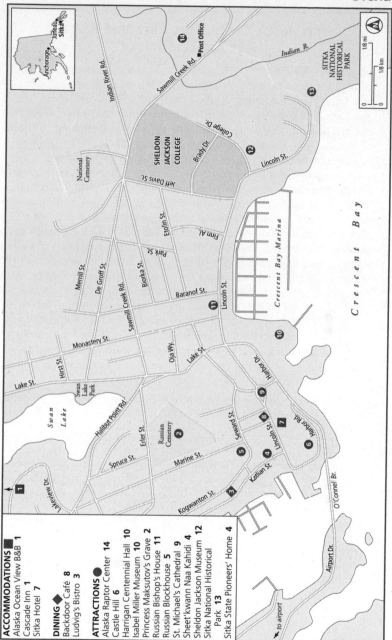

Sitka

ACCOMMODATIONS ■
Alaska Ocean View B&B **1**
Cascade Inn **1**
Sitka Hotel **7**

DINING ◆
Backdoor Café **8**
Ludvig's Bistro **3**

ATTRACTIONS ●
Alaska Raptor Center **14**
Castle Hill **6**
Harrigan Centennial Hall **10**
Isabel Miller Museum **10**
Princess Maksutov's Grave **2**
Russian Bishop's House **11**
Russian Blockhouse **5**
St. Michael's Cathedral **9**
Sheet'kwann Naa Kahidi **4**
Sheldon Jackson Museum **12**
Sitka National Historical
Park **13**
Sitka State Pioneers' Home **4**

193

Part Rustic Cabin, Part Anchored Barge: Meet the Floathouse

Floathouses, houses built on floating docks, are fairly common throughout watery Southeast Alaska. Entire logging camps were sometimes built on the water, with floatshops, floatsaloons, floatschools, and other float-buildings. In a peaceful wilderness bay 6 miles from Sitka, you can get off the grid and into the swing (and gentle sway—if you catch my drift) of floathouse living at **Camp Coogan Bay Hideaway** (☎ 907/747-6375; www. ssoceanadventures.com; MC, V; $$$$). It consists of several old barges lashed together and anchored at the edge of a heavily forested little island, deep in bear country. The main building is a rustic old floatcottage, a little grubby but charming nonetheless. It's got a kitchen, a living room, a sleeping loft, a bedroom, and a covered porch where you can sit in a rocker and look out over the dark, calm waters at the other islands and mountains all around. You could squeeze up to 12 people into the float-cottage, plus an extra two in a small float outbuilding. Camp Coogan is equipped with a floatouthouse, a floatoutdoorshower, and a float (wood-fired) sauna. For heat, there's a woodstove, for water there's a rain catchment system, and for light there are Coleman lanterns. This is an excellent choice for big fishing parties, huge families looking to get well away from it all but not from each other, and those seeking a remote but comfortable base for kayaking and canoe trips. The place can be yours for $180 a night, plus $30 for a water taxi ride out and back. You could also rent a kayak and paddle, but it's a long paddle.

with the spider, not the owner, who's the town's colorful veterinarian, and who has larger animals to worry about. The lighthouse sits on the shore of a ¾-acre wooded island, 1 mile from downtown, with delightful views of Sitka Sound and Mount Edgecumbe. It's got a kitchen, 1½ baths, and you can squeeze up to eight people into the beds on its three floors, though the bunk beds on the top floor are kid-size. It goes for $150 per night for two, $200 for four, and $35 per extra person after that. The price includes the use of a small motor boat for getting to and fro.

Camping

The primitive **National Park Service Dyea Campground** offers 22 well-separated sites near the water at the ghost town 9 miles from Skagway. You'll find pit toilets here, but no water. RVs over 27 feet are not allowed. The fee is $6. The **Pullen Creek RV Park** (☎ 800/936-3731 or 907/983-2768) is near the small-boat harbor, with coin-operated showers. RV sites with power, water, and dump station use are $30; car camping sites run $20; and tenting with no vehicle is $14.

DINING FOR ALL TASTES

The restaurant scene is surprisingly lackluster in Sitka, with a few exceptions. Here's where I would eat if I were you:

$ Tucked away behind the Old Harbor Books, the **Backdoor Café** ★ (104 Barracks St.; ☎ 907/747-8856; Mon–Sat 6:30am–5pm, Sun 9am–2pm; no credit cards) is one of those vibrant little coffee houses where people of the Pacific Northwest seek refuge on gloomy days and fortify themselves with free-trade organic coffee or peppermint tea. You can eat cheap and well here too, with wholesome sandwiches ($4.95) or hot bowls of homemade soup ($3.75) served with big hunks of bread. I'm also a fan of Backdoor's baked goods: fresh, fat, gooey cookies, chocolate peanut butter bars, date bars, and pies ($1–$2). Tourists occasionally stumble upon this place, but it's mostly filled with locals—environmentalists, fishermen, peaceniks, bookworms, and other coffee lovers.

$$ If there's a cruise ship anchored in Sitka Sound, look for a colorful tent with a sign reading **Crab Feast** ★★★ (located in the parking lot behind Brenner's Fine Clothing and Gifts, 124 Lincoln St.; no phone; hours vary; no credit cards). Plunk down $12 for a freshly steamed Dungeness crab, plus 50¢ for the melted butter, and feast away. This could be one of the most memorable meals you'll have in Alaska.

$$$–$$$$ At one point in the early–19th century, before either San Francisco or Seattle had emerged as ports of call, Sitka was the most cosmopolitan place on the West Coast of the Americas. Never mind that it was merely a scraggly collection of log shelters lining muddy streets, it was known as "The Paris of the Pacific." People from Hawaii, New England, Britain, and Mother Russia strode its boardwalks, mingled with its Natives, and downed its vodka. That tradition of cosmopolitanism in miniature continues at **Ludvig's Bistro** ★★★ (256 Katlian St.; ☎ 907/966-3663; Tues–Sat 2–10pm; MC, V; reservations strongly recommended), easily the top restaurant in Sitka. It's a tiny, lively, colorful place, done up in rustic Mediterranean colors. The kitchen puts French, Moroccan, Spanish, and Italian twists on Alaskan seafood and game. Specials might include an elk steak, rubbed in rosemary, paprika, and salt, then grilled and finished with sautéed wild mushrooms in blue cheese butter ($19). Among the regular entrees, try the Alaskan paella ($29), which is loaded with local smoked salmon, rockfish, scallops, prawns, grilled chicken, and cured chorizo. And definitely do dessert here. Perhaps the lavender baklava ($7.95), or maybe some chunks of dark Belgian chocolate ($7.95) served with a raspberry Rioja sauce. To try Ludvig's on the cheap, look for Ludvig's street cart behind the pharmacy on Lincoln Street. The spicy sausage and the clam chowder really stand out.

WHY YOU'RE HERE: THE TOP SIGHTS & ATTRACTIONS

It's one thing to see totem poles in the temperature-and-humidity-controlled environment of a museum, and quite another to see them standing tall in a dark, damp Pacific Northwest coastal rainforest. At the **Sitka National Historical Park** ★★★ (106 Metlakatla St.; ☎ 907/747-6281; www.nps.gov/sitk; admission $5 to visitor center; summer daily 8am–5pm, rest of year Mon–Sat 8am–5pm), you can see both. Two miles of pathways through the woods pass several Tlingit and Haida totem poles. (You can tell the difference because Haida poles leave blank spaces between figures, whereas Tlingit totems fill the entire pole with carvings. And, of course, you can also tell the difference because they're labeled.) This 107-acre national park is the oldest in Alaska, established in 1910 to commemorate the Battle of Sitka, the last major act of Tlingit resistance to Russian colonization. The woods are older but largely unchanged since the battle. Take some time to lay in the grass in the large meadow where the Tlingit built the fort for their last stand—there they endured 6 days of bombardment by Russian cannons, before finally slipping off into the night.

Park Service rangers lead tours in the park throughout the summer (call for the schedule), or you can wander through the park on your own for free. Pay the small admission for the visitor center and watch the short film about the battle. Be sure to look around the museum while you're waiting for the show to begin, as it's filled with Russian and Tlingit artifacts, including the war hammer wielded by Chief Katlian during the Battle of Sitka. Another highlight is the weathered ancient totem poles dramatically displayed in a special, high-ceilinged gallery. On-site are studios where modern Alaska Native wood carvers, weavers, and jewelry makers work; the visitor center doubles as a home to the Southeast Alaska Indian Cultural Center and you're welcome to chat with the artists there.

The Sitka National Historical Park has two off-site components: The **Russian Blockhouse** (206 Lincoln St.; ☎ 907/747-0110; $4 or $15 per family; summer daily 9am–5pm, call for off-season hours), a reproduction of the fortification that separated the Russian and Tlingit parts of New Archangel (under the theory that good fences, with big, heavily armed blockhouses attached, make good neighbors), and the former residence of a saint, the **Russian Bishop's House ★★★** (Lincoln and Monastery sts.; ☎ 907/747-4927; www.nps.gov/sitk/historyculture/russian-bishops-house.htm; free admission or $4 tour; summer daily 9am–5pm, off season by appointment only). The blockhouse, which you can view only from the outside, makes for a quick stop. But you can lose yourself inside the Russian Bishop's House for quite a while. The house was built in 1843, and it's the second oldest building in Alaska (the oldest, in Kodiak, was built in 1793). The original occupant, Bishop Innocent, oversaw the vast Russian Orthodox diocese that stretched across the top of the Pacific Rim all the way to Kamchatka, the Russian peninsula. Bishop Innocent was canonized in the 1970s, which means this boxy, square-log, two-story hulk of a house was actually the home of a saint. It was also the most refined building in the Russian colonies when it was built. Innocent himself considered it an "ecclesiastical palace." The first floor had church offices and a school for Native children. A chapel, the bishop's residence, and a public reception room were upstairs.

You can take a free self-guided tour of the downstairs, or for $4 you can go on a ranger-led tour of the whole house. The place was about to fall down when the Russian Orthodox Church sold it to the National Park Service in the 1970s. Since then it's been expertly restored to its old ecclesiastical, palatial self.

This is one of the few surviving structures in Alaska from the Russian American period, and it's the most impressive. One reason it's still around is because of the excellent workmanship of the Finnish shipwrights who built it. At different points throughout the building, the restorationists have revealed the notched joints the shipwrights fit together so snuggly, in lieu of nails. When the

Dance Revolution, Tinglit & Russian-Style

If you've ever wondered who created dance, it was Raven. Get the whole story by attending a performance of the **Naa Kahidi Dancers** ★★★ (Sheet'kwaan Naa Kahidi, 200 Katlian St.; ☎ 907/747-7290; www.sitkatours.com/dance.html; $7 adults, $5 children 12 and under). Don't be offended when the dancers, who range from gray-haired grandparents to babies on their mothers' backs, enter the stage with their backs to you. You're not being snubbed, you're being invited to examine the clan crests on their robes. They'll turn around and look at you when everyone's on stage. The performance is held in a modern version of a Tlingit community house, which fills with the sound of a beating drum box and the sweet smoke of burning cedar. Performances are scheduled around the arrival of cruise ships, and times are posted around town.

The New Archangel Dancers ★★★ (Harrigan Centennial Hall; ☎ 907/747-5516; www.newarchangeldancers.com; admission $8) offer half-hour shows throughout the summer, drawing from a deep repertoire of Russian, Byelorussian, Moldavian, and Ukrainian folk dances. The shows change all the time. Only the big Russian finale is the same in every performance. You may notice that the male Russian dancers don't look particularly manly. There's a reason for that. When the group formed in 1969, not a single man in Sitka would join it. So half the women put on trousers, and performed the men's parts themselves. It's been like that ever since, and now men aren't allowed to join. Shows are scheduled around the cruise-ship calendar, with as many as 17 shows a week during the peak season. Half the fun is in the costumes—vibrant floral prints, elegant Russian gowns, bright Ukrainian plaids and braids, and dark Moldavian outfits. Seeing women with fake beards dance is fun too.

Be sure to catch a performance by at least one of these Native troops, and do your best to see both. To me, they're equally worthwhile.

---

restorationists pulled up the old floorboards, they found cut stalks of devil's club, a common Southeast Alaska plant, tucked into the corners of the house. Tlingits believed the plant was a powerful charm; they believed it would protect the occupants from disease and from malicious people. The devil's club in the floorboards suggests that the Tlingit workmen who helped build the bishop's house wanted to protect the occupants, including the Native children who attended school there.

Saint Innocent was a proponent of translating the Bible into Native languages, which I suspect is a big reason why the Russian Orthodox Church is so strong in Alaska Native communities today. Compare Innocent's approach to that of the Rev. Sheldon Jackson, an American who came along later in the century, and who believed that turning Natives into good Presbyterians required squelching their indigenous culture. The effectiveness of that approach is evident in the dearth of Presbyterian churches in the Alaskan Bush these days. Say what you will about Jackson's cultural sensitivity, though, you can't deny that his voracious appetite for collecting Native artifacts has added to the world's knowledge about the cultures he worked so hard to alter. The wide-ranging personal collection he amassed while traveling around Alaska is the nucleus of the even larger collection of Native artifacts housed in Sitka at the **Sheldon Jackson Museum** ★★★ (104 College Dr.; ☎ 907/747-8981; www.museums.state.ak.us; $4 adults, children 18 and under free; summer daily 9am–5pm, rest of year Tues–Sat 10am–4pm). The museum's unusual, octagonal-shaped exhibit hall has some 1,700 pieces (out of 5,600 pieces in the whole collection) on display in concentric octagonal rings. It includes Eskimo masks and puppets, basketry, hunting implements, finely sewn and beautifully ornamented clothing, and totem poles. Throughout the summer, a rotating lineup of Native artisans sit in the exhibit hall and work on carvings, basketry, beadwork, and textiles not unlike the ancient artifacts on display. They're living proof that Jackson's legacy didn't work out quite the way he planned.

As you wander around Sitka, you can't help but wonder how it must have looked when it was in Russian hands. Pay a visit to the **Isabel Miller Museum** (330 Harbor Dr.; ☎ 907/747-6455; www.sitkahistory.org/museum.shtml; $4 recommended donation; summer daily 8am–5pm, rest of year Tues–Fri 8am–5pm, Sat 11am–5pm) and you'll find a marvelous visual aid that will pique your imagination. Among the hodgepodge of photographs, artifacts, and displays filling this little community museum is a scale model of New Archangel in 1867, the year the Russian flag came down, the U.S. flag went up, and the name of the settlement was changed to Sitka. The high school history teacher who made the model poured exhaustive research into it, and got down to a level of detail that includes fence posts, cows, and outhouses. It's a great blueprint for visualizing what the Russians did with the place during their 65 years.

It should be against the law to leave Sitka without walking to the top of **Castle Hill** ★. Beyond the commanding view of Sitka Sound, this is the spot where Russia officially handed Alaska over to the United States. If you had been here on that day, you might have heard the sound of weeping from an upstairs window in the mansion Alexander Baranof (the brilliant and fiercely alcoholic governor of the Russian-American Company—he used to greet ship's captains with a bucket of vodka and a ladle) built here. The tears would've been coming from Princess Maksutov, the wife of the last Russian governor, who wasn't, to put it mildly, in favor of the transfer. Before then, this unassuming wooded knob, wedged between the two busiest streets in town, was also the center of the Tlingit settlement here, and it was covered with Tlingit clan houses.

By the way, you can visit **Princess Maksutov's grave** at the Lutheran Cemetery, on Princess Way (near the Russian Blockhouse). If you make that trip, I know you're into cemeteries, so walk to the end of Observatory Street, which runs parallel to Princess Way, and spend some time in the old Russian Cemetery, too. This quiet and mysterious 2-block cemetery is filled with the remains of Russians who inhabited New Archangel and never left. Few tourists find it.

You don't need to go out of your way to find Sitka's most in-your-face historic site, **St. Michael's Cathedral** ★ (240 Lincoln St.; ☎ 907/747-8120; admission $2; open whenever cruise ships are in port) It sits right in the middle of town, splitting the main drag into a Y. It's a reproduction of the log church built on the site by Bishop Innocent, between 1844 and 1848. The original burned down in a 1966 fire that destroyed much of downtown. As firefighters tried to save the church, other Sitkans formed a human chain and pulled out much of its contents

Life in the Intertidal Zone

Sitka is tide pool central in Southeast Alaska. All you need is a low tide to get a close-up look at the sea stars, sand dollars, hermit crabs, mussels, anemones, barnacles, and other creatures that have adapted to life at the wet edge of the sea. Tide tables are available at Sitka National Historical Park (p. 195) or anywhere selling fishing supplies. Head to any of these spots on a low tide; the lower the better:

Totem Beach, at the Sitka National Historical Park. Don't just look down into the tide pools, scan the sky, too: This is a good place to look for bald eagles.

John Brown's Beach, on Japonski Island, across the bridge and a 5-mile round-trip walk from downtown. The headstone of this little beach's namesake sits in a one-grave cemetery along the path between the Coast Guard station and the water. Who John Brown was and why he has a cemetery all to himself is a local mystery.

Halibut Point State Recreation Area, located about 4 miles north of town on Halibut Point Road. In addition to tide pools, there's a fetching beach for strolling along, or—if the weather's really nice—taking a quick dip in the sea.

before the cathedral's familiar onion dome and spire collapsed in flames. They rescued crucifixes, chalices, vestments, chandeliers, the front doors, and almost everything else inside, including an altar cloth sewn by Princess Maksutov, and an icon of St. Michael, which was lost at sea en route to Sitka in 1813, then washed ashore, undamaged, 30 days later.

Sitka Wildlife

Bald eagles are as common in parts of Alaska as pigeons are in Venice or New York City. Still, it's hard to get a really good close-up look at them in the wild. For an eye-to-eagle-eye encounter, pay a visit to the **Alaska Raptor Center** ★★ 🧒 (100 Raptor Way; ☎ 907/747-8662 or 800/643-9425; www.alaskaraptor.org; $12 adults, $6 children 12 and under; May–Sept 8am–4pm), a nonprofit rehabilitation facility for injured eagles, owls, hawks, and other birds of prey. The main attraction is a 20,000-square-foot simulated rainforest, which serves as a flight training center where recuperating birds can test their wings. There's also an outdoor enclosure for the lifers—raptors with no chance of surviving in the wild. A nature trail runs through the wooded grounds, leading down to a river where salmon spawn, and where wild eagles, unaffiliated with the center, sometimes feed. The center is about a 20-minute walk from town. *Note:* You can volunteer to work side by side with staff here, doing everything from selling T-shirts to working with the birds.

Whale Park (Mile 3.8 Sawmill Creek Rd.), as you might guess from the name, is your spot to spot whales; you'll need a bike or a car to get to it from downtown. You'll find shelters with binoculars in them, whale interpretive signs, and—most unusual—a hydrophone that lets you listen along to the songs of the whales. If you don't make it to the park, tune into Whale Radio at 88.1 FM—it broadcasts the songs of the whales, live, 24 hours a day.

The cold, nutrient-rich waters around Sitka abound with humpback whales, sea lions, seals, sea otters, and other marine life. Therefore, you should make getting out onto the water—either in a kayak (p. 203) or aboard a tour boat—a priority. The **St. Lazaria Island National Wildlife Refuge** ★ is a popular attraction, though rough weather often prevents tour boats from going there. But when the sea is calm, boats can get up close to the island's soaring cliffs, where thousands of sea birds nest, including murres, tufted puffins, rhinoceros auklets, oystercatchers, cormorants, and the common seagull. Bald eagles frequent the island as well. Large marine mammals, including whales, are drawn by the multitudes of small schooling fish (good eats!) around the island.

About a dozen operators run wildlife tours out of Sitka, and a list of them all is available online at www.sitka.org/tours.html. The best deal is with **Allen Marine Tours** ★★ (☎ 888/747-8101 or 907/747-8100; www.allenmarinetours.com), which offers 2-hour and 3-hour tours, for $59 or $79 respectively. Go for the longer tour. The shorter one sticks around Sitka Sound, which isn't as exciting as some of the places the longer tour goes to. Allen Marine caters mainly to the cruise-ship industry, and its tour boats carry big groups. For $54 more, you and just five other passengers can take a more personalized 3-hour tour with **Ester G Sea Tours & Taxi** ★★★ (☎ 907/747-6481 or 907/738-6481). The captain, a former commercial fisherman and a state-certified high school biology teacher, is an amiable and deeply knowledgeable guide who customizes the trips to fit the interest of the passengers—a big advantage of going on a smaller boat. Schedule an evening tour when the sea is more likely to be glassy and the protracted Alaskan summer sunset bathes the sea lions, whales, and puffins in the most beautiful golden light. Three-hour tours cost $133 and 4-hour tours cost $155.

To get below the surface at the Sitka Sound—literally—take a ride aboard the 65-foot semi-submersible operated by **Sea Life Discovery Tours** ★★★ (kids) (☎ 877/966-2301 or 907/966-2301; www.sealifediscoverytours.com). A cross between a glass-bottom boat and a submarine, it's got window seats that sit beneath the waterline allowing passengers a peek at the near-shore marine life in the sound, such as crabs, moon jellies, anemones, sea slugs, fish, and lots of kelp. Divers equipped with cameras in their diving helmets send additional images back to the ship while naturalists narrate. The 2-hour tours cost $86. I give this tour a best-snacks award for serving kelp pickles and kelp marmalade while cruising through a—what else—kelp forest.

THE OTHER SITKA

Sitka is a vibrant, well-educated little community that keeps itself amused year-round with intellectually stimulating events and activities. That means discerning travelers have all sorts of opportunities to interact with the community at a more intimate level than most tourists ever do.

Like the vigilant little watchmen figures atop Haida totem poles, always on the lookout for threats to the village, members of the **Sitka Conservation Society** (201 Lincoln St., Room 4; ☎ 907/747-7509; www.sitkawild.org) keep an eye on the 17-million-acre Tongass National Forest, which comprises most of Southeast Alaska. The watchmen have mystical powers and a height advantage, but only this scrappy environmental group can file briefs. It regularly exercises this power in defense of the forest against the Canadian and U.S. timber industries, the state of Alaska, the U.S. Forest Service, and whoever else poses a threat to the largest remaining temperate rainforest in the world. In the summer, the Conservation Society also exercises its powers of public outreach. Operating under the premise that the more people experience the splendors of the wild Tongass, the more willing they'll be to help protect it, the society has a regular series of **free guided hikes** through the wilderness and reasonably priced 3- to 5-hour boat tours around the area's inlets, islets, fjords, and narrow straights ($25–$40). They draw about half locals and half visitors, making them a particularly fine option for those who want to get more of an insider's perspective on what they're seeing. Call or check the Internet for a schedule.

What started as a simple Sitka writers conference in 1984 evolved into something far more ambitious—and worthy of planning a vacation around. **The Sitka Symposium** (☎ 907/747-3794; www.islandinstitutealaska.org) brings together preeminent writers and thinkers from diverse backgrounds to tackle big social and cultural concerns. The typical lineup might include more than 40 novelists, journalists, astronomers, Zen Buddhists, Muslim peace activists, folklorists, poets, and biologists, with a strong mix of Native American and international voices. If you're in town during the week in June, or sometimes July, when the symposium is held, consider yourself lucky. The atmosphere in town is electric, and you might catch a reading by an author such as Barbara Kingsolver, Barry Lopez, or Terry Tempest Williams. The full week costs $365, but if you just want to drop in for a single reading or symposium, it'll just cost $10.

By day, when the cruise ships are in port, tourists swarm through **St. Michael's Cathedral** (240 Lincoln St.; ☎ 907/747-8120) to see its ornate interior and age-old religious icons. When St. Michael's isn't pulling duty as a tourist attraction, it's an actual work-a-day Russian Orthodox church. Few tourists come around for the services, but you'd be welcome if you did. As with all Russian Orthodox churches in Alaska, the congregation is largely Native, so attending a service is an excellent way to rub elbows with—and maybe get to know—some of them. Russian Orthodox religious services are highly ritualized, with lots of chanting, singing, and incense, and a prescribed call-and-response between the priest and the congregation. Most parishioners respond in English, but if they choose to do so, they can respond in their native tongue; you might hear people slipping into Tlingit, Yupik, or Aleut during the service. Everyone but the sickly is expected to stand throughout the ceremony, so be prepared to be on your feet for 45 minutes to 2 hours. Regular services are held Thursdays from 6pm to 6:45pm, Saturdays from 6pm to 7pm, and Sundays from 9:30am to 11:30am. Be sure to doff your cap if you're male, and to cover your head with a scarf if you're female. Don't worry if you don't have a scarf. If a woman walks into the cathedral bare-headed, a kindly parishioner will quickly offer her a loaner.

Alaskan old-timers are called "sourdoughs," and as it happens, one of the greatest gatherings of sourdoughs in Alaska can be found smack in the middle of Sitka. The 75 or so retired fishermen, loggers, longshoremen, pioneer housewives, and other residents of the **Sitka State Pioneers' Home** (120 Katlian St.; ☎ 907/747-3213; daily 8am–8pm) are full of colorful stories that stretch deeply into pre-statehood, territorial Alaska's past, and it's not hard to find someone there willing to bend your ear. The doors of the Pioneers' Home are wide open to unexpected visitors, and the home is so centrally located—right on the old Russian parade grounds along the waterfront—that it's quite easy for unexpected visitors to wander in. Hang out in the lobby long enough and you'll have no trouble rustling up a game of pinochle or Monopoly. Or you can simply sit with the fellas on the front steps looking out onto Sitka Sound, admire the flower beds, and listen for a while; do so, and you'll learn more about Alaska, its history, culture, and people, than you will from any guided tour. Trust me, this could be a highlight of your visit.

A final way to hang with Sitka's Native population is to join the modern ritual of **Sitka Tribal Bingo** (456 Katlian St.; ☎ 907/747-3207; $25 to play; Sat–Mon 5:30–11pm). Bingo is big here—in addition to raising money for tribal programs and services, it sometimes constitutes the most exciting nightlife in the area. Grab a stubby pencil, a bingo card, and a cup of bad coffee, and sit among the elders and others who gather here regularly.

ACTIVE SITKA
Hiking

Located at the foot of Baranof Island's heavily wooded mountains, Sitka is rich in hiking. A dozen U.S. Forest Service trails can be accessed right from town or a short drive from it. Many remote trails lace the island and are accessible by water taxi or floatplane. The Alaska Natural History Association trail guide, called **Sitka Trails** ($8, available at www.alaskanha.org) will give you details on dozens of them. Here are my picks of the bunch:

The most easily accessed trail on the island is the 2.2-mile **Sitka Cross Trail,** which starts right in town. This well-used trail runs along the edge of town, past peat bogs and through rainforest, then meets up with two other popular trails that take you deep into the mountains. The main trailhead is near the intersection of Charteris Street and Georgeson Loop, but there are lots of neighborhood access points along the way.

The Sitka Cross Trail first intersects with **Gavan Hill-Harbor Mountain Trail,** which climbs steeply for 3 miles to a spot with a bird's-eye view of Sitka from about 2,500 feet, then continues for 3 miles along a ridge to Harbor Mountain Road. The actual trailhead is at the top of the long staircase at the end of Baranof Street. It's an all-day trip up and back. The lazy-hiker's way to do it is to catch a cab to the Harbor Mountain Road end of the trail and walk down.

The Sitka Cross trail also connects to the **Indian River Trail,** which follows a salmon stream through the rainforest to a splendid 80-foot waterfall. The two trails meet about a third of the way up Indian River Trail. You can also drive to the Indian River Trail's trailhead, taking Sawmill Creek Road to Indian River Road, just east of town. It's a long hike—11 miles round-trip from the trailhead—but it isn't particularly steep.

Seven miles north of town, several easy, well-maintained trails loop along the shore and through the old growth coastal rain forest in the Starrigavan Recreation Area. They include the 1.5-mile **Mosquito Cove Trail,** which leads to a secluded gravel beach. The recreation area has lots of spawning salmon and wild berries in the summer, and, consequently, bears. So stay on your toes.

If you're feeling really ambitious, and really fit, climb 3,349-foot Mt. Verstovia behind town, or 3,201-foot Mt. Edgecumbe, the lopsided Mount Fuji that stands between Sitka and the open Pacific. The strenuous, 14-mile round-trip trail up **Mount Edgecumbe,** an extinct volcano, begins in the muskeg and rainforest, and ends amid heaps of volcanic ash at the edge of the crater. Just getting to the trail-head involves a boat ride to the Kruzof Island, where Edgecumbe's located (the water's too rough here for floatplanes). Water taxis charge about $125 each way (contact the Sitka Convention and Visitors Bureau for a list of operators). The view from the summit, overlooking the sparkling North Pacific on one side and the Southeast Alaska's vast mountainscape on the other, is simply astonishing. (On a clear day, that is.) It's an all-day hike up and back down, so it's best to stay the night on the island. Try to reserve the U.S. Forest Service's Fred Creek Cabin (see p. 373 for info on reserving public use cabins) at the base of the trail.

The view from **Mt. Verstovia** behind town is similarly stunning, but it's logistically easier to get at than Mt. Edgecumbe's. Most people don't go all the way to the summit, stopping instead at the mountain's big, broad shoulder, at about 2,500 feet. The trail starts out nicely enough, passing an old Russian charcoal pit, and it's only 2.5 miles up to the shoulder—but it's a hell of a climb. The trailhead begins about 2 miles out of Sitka on Sawmill Creek Road.

Much of Baranof Island, and Sitka's hiking trails, lies within the Tongass National Forest. Rangers with the National Forest Service lead free, local hikes. The times and trails vary. Check with the **Sitka Ranger District (☎ 907/747-6671 or 907/747-4225).**

Kayaking

Surrounded as it is by protected waterways and a multitude of inlets and passages, Sitka is a prime location for sea kayaking. Wildlife abounds, with sea otter, seal, sea lion, and eagle sightings practically guaranteed; there's also a good chance of spotting whales. **Sitka Sound Ocean Adventures (☎ 907/747-6375 or 907/738-6375; www.ssoceanadventures.com),** located in an old blue school bus parked at the main harbor, rents kayaks and leads tours. Single-person kayaks start at $35 for 4 hours. Guided tours start at $63 per person for two to three people for a couple hours on the water.

ATTENTION, SHOPPERS!

Not surprisingly, Sitka is awash with Russian goods. So if you've had a secret yen to own Fabergé eggs, some St. Petersburg amber jewelry, an antique samovar, a set of Lomonosov porcelain or Khokloma dishware, Russian Orthodox icons, or faux fur Soviet military caps embossed with a hammer and sickle—well, you've come to the right place, Comrade.

Sitka's original Russian import store, **The Russian-American Company** (407 Lincoln St.; ☎ 907/747-6228) borrows its name from Alaska's original Russian fur exporter. When it opened in 1986, the lid on trade with the Soviet Union was screwed on tight, and the store's owners competed with buyers from Gumps and Saks Fifth Avenue for the meager supply of lacquer miniatures and other prized goods trickling through the Iron Curtain. Today its shelves are dense with arts and crafts from all over Mother Russia, including enough matryoshka (Russian nesting dolls) to repopulate Chernobyl. It's got so much stuff that that it needs two locations. I was impressed by the range of matryoshka themes, which go from the folkloric (stories like "The Giant Turnip" and "The Frog Princes"), to the pop cultural (unlicensed Simpsons, Flintstones, and Disney characters), to the political (Putin concealing a succession of leaders leading back to Stalin; American presidents from Bush to "Cannady"). You'll find some unique stocking stuffers here.

For locally made Native arts and crafts, stop by Sheet'ka Kwaan Naa Kahidi, the latter-day Tlingit clan house where the New Kahidi Dancers perform, and see what's on the small shelves at the **Made In Alaska Gift Shop** (200 Katlain St.; ☎ 907/747-7290). On first glance, this little gift shop appears to be meagerly stocked, but there are some real gems there—from the rawhide drums to the Fireweed Honey. All of it is made by Natives on Baranof Island. I got my sister, a genius in the kitchen, a ring-bound, desktop-published cookbook called *Tlingit Recipes of Today and Long Ago* ($15), which explains how to prepare dishes such as seal flipper (start by burning off the hair), fiddlehead ferns (prepare with a little bit of sugar or seal oil), and porcupine liver (slice thinly, roll in flour, and fry in bacon grease). Some dishes are quite simple (octopus head: skin head, boil water, add head to water, serve as finger food), and some are more complex (venison demi-glacé takes a pound of deer bones and more than 8 hr. to prepare).

You'll find handcrafted soaps and salves with the Wintersong label on them all over Alaska, but in Sitka you can buy them in the town where they're made. Located on the ground floor of a beautiful old Queen Anne Victorian home, the **Wintersong Soap Company** (419 Lincoln St., next to the Russian Bishop's House; ☎ 888/819-8949; www.wintersongsoap.com) store is about the size of a large bathroom, heavily scented by frou-frou bath products. I wish I could tell you that you'll save money by buying these soaps here, but there's no real discounting (there is, however, a bigger selection here than in many other stores).

Of all places to shop Sitka, the place Sitkans get most excited about is a thrift store that's closed more often than not, called **The White Elephant** (323 Seward St.; ☎ 907/747-3430). When news breaks that a "White E" opening has been scheduled, giddy anticipation spreads through the community. Bargain hunters gather outside the door a half-hour before it's unlocked. By selling things like jeans for $2 and hardback novels for $1, the store raises more than $50,000 a year for local charities. Almost everything's under $5. If you need a pair of shorts or forgot to pack a sweater, and you happen to be in town at the right time (ask any local), this is the place to shop.

Years ago Ed Iwamoto, a fisheries biologist with a passion for chocolate, was reading up on his favorite cacao-based comfort food when he came across the Latin name for the cacao tree, Theobroma cacao. Theobroma, he discovered, means "food of the gods," and that, he thought, would be a cool name for a chocolate company. When he finally hung up his transect study grids to become a chocolatier, he named his business **Theobroma Chocolate Company** (Sawmill Creek Rd.; ☎ 888/985-2345 or 907/966-2345; www.theobromachocolate.com).

Iwamoto dislikes sweet chocolate, gooey chocolate, and coconut, so you won't find any of that at his factory and store, located about 7 miles from town. But he loves nuts, caramels, toffees, and those rich buttery chocolate truffles, so you'll find plenty of those. Go on Tuesday or Thursday morning and you can watch the chocolate being made. Keep your fingers crossed that the antique wrapping machine breaks down, as it's prone to do, because the mis-wraps are sold at a deep discount.

NIGHTLIFE IN SITKA

Sitka doesn't have much nightlife outside of the fishermen's bars. But so what? Those are classic, salt-of-the-sea dives. Among them is the Pioneer Bar (212 Katlian St.; ☎ 907/747-3456), aka the P-Bar. It's got occasional live music, pool, crusty fishermen, loads of local color, and an extensive photo gallery of fishing boats. **The Pourhouse** (118 Lincoln St.; ☎ 907/747-3288) on the ground floor of the Sitka Hotel is another favorite with the fisher folk.

And I should mention that for 1 month each year, Sitka nightlife gets tremendously cultured. In fact, musicians from around the world gather in Sitka each June for Alaska's foremost chamber music festival, the **Sitka Summer Music Festival** ★ (☎ 907/747-6774; www.sitkamusicfestival.org). The 3-week event features formal performances in Harrigan Centennial Hall, where musicians play with a marvelous view of Sitka Sound behind them. Tickets cost about $15 and tend to sell out. Free, informal brown-bag concerts are also held around town.

GET OUT OF TOWN

Southeast Alaska has plenty of hot springs, but most of them are so remote and expensive, they're out of reach for most budget travelers. **Goddard Hot Springs** ★, located 17 miles south of Sitka, is an exception—well, sort of. There's no charge to use the springs—you just show up, wait for a bathhouse to open up, then slip into the steamy water and enjoy the view of boats at anchor offshore and Mount Edgecumbe in the distance. (It's owned by the city of Sitka and maintained by volunteers.) But there's no road to the springs, and no cheap way to get there unless you're a strong paddler. Experienced sea kayakers can get to the springs from Sitka with a full day's paddle, then camp anywhere in the surrounding Tongass National Forest. Otherwise, it's about a $600 round-trip sea-taxi trip. (Check with the Sitka Convention and Visitors Bureau for a list of water taxis.) If you're paying that kind of money, the only sensible thing to do is to combine a trip to the hot springs with a stay at one of the nearby public use cabins managed by the U.S. Forest Service. The Kanga Bay Cabin and Sevenfathom Bay Cabin are within 8 miles of the springs to the north and south respectively (for info on public use cabins, see p. 373).

Locals cherish this place and put it to good use, so you may have to wait your turn for a soak. The two cedar bathhouses each come with its own naturally heated cedar hot tub. If the wait for a bathhouse is too long, there's an undeveloped spring with a muddy bottom you can console yourself in, but it's not as hot or as nice as the tubs.

JUNEAU

With a population of about 31,000, Juneau is the third largest city in Alaska (after Anchorage and Fairbanks), and hands down the most appealing of the three. Unlike sprawling, unlovely Anchorage and squat, frostbitten Fairbanks, Juneau is a looker and with a great personality to boot. It's a drizzly cosmopolitan town with crooked streets twisting through a historic district filled with coffee houses, movie theaters, restaurants, and gold rush–era bars that are still as shadowy as ever. Colorful Victorian homes cover downtown hillsides, some of them so steep that the wooden staircases and boardwalks that reach them have been given official city street status. The population is a mix of shuffling old men in quilted flannel shirts, government office workers, drunks from the villages on long-term benders, yuppies, pierced and tattooed 20-somethings in black-hooded sweatshirts, and overeducated fishermen and artists who left their emergency room practices or tenured chairs to net salmon or carve whales. As the state capital, where Alaska's Republican-dominated legislature meets from January to May, Juneau is also a town of politicians, lobbyists, and power brokers—at least part of the time. The city has a political season in the winter and spring, a tourist season from spring to early fall, and a short off season in the fall when residents breathe a sigh of relief and take off on vacation themselves.

A BRIEF HISTORY

Juneau was both the first Alaskan town established after the U.S. take-over in 1867, and the first of many Alaskan boomtowns to arise during a gold rush. Two unlikely prospectors, Joe Juneau and Richard Harris, are commonly cited as the town's founding fathers, but a local Tlingit leader, Chief Kowee, deserves at least as much credit. The Tlingits knew about the gold-laced rock in the mountains behind the Tlingit fish camps where Juneau would arise all along. They just had no use for it. Then, in 1880, a mining engineer working out of Sitka, George Pilz, offered 100 Hudson blankets to any Tlingit clan who could lead him to gold. Chief Kowee paddled to Sitka and showed Pilz an impressive chunk of gold ore. Pilz dispatched Juneau and Harris to investigate. But instead of looking for gold, the pair traded their provisions for the Native hooch, got rip-roaring drunk, and returned to Sitka empty-handed.

Kowee followed, explained the situation to Pilz, and escorted Juneau and Harris back to his fish camp. This time, he practically dragged the two up a gulch and into the Silverbow Basin, where gold-laced rock and chunks of gold glistened all around. Juneau and Harris were flabbergasted. Harris wrote in his journal: "We knew it was gold, but so much, and not in particles; streaks running through the rock and little lumps as large as peas or beans . . . I took the gold pan, pick, and shovel and panned $1.20 to $1.30 to the pan."

Juneau and Harris quickly staked out 160 acres by the water for a town, which Harris, as the only one who could write, generously lent his name to. But the first wave of miners to arrive soon changed the name of the fledgling town from Harrisburgh to Rockwell, and later to Pilzburg. Juneau, unhappy that nothing had been named after him, used his first summer's earnings to buy enough votes from his fellow miners to rename the town in his honor. And that name has stuck. For Kowee's part in sparking Alaska's first gold rush, the people of the newly minted town of Juneau made him an officer of the peace—the "Indian police-man," they called him—and gave him a $10 a month salary.

In the late 1800s, as Juneau morphed from a home of Tlingit fish camps into a boomtown filled with rowdy saloons, trading posts, brothels, canneries, sawmills, and so forth, Sitka—the territorial capital at the time—was waning. In 1906 Alaska's capital was relocated to Juneau. Gold mining in Juneau ended in World War II, when the U.S. government declared it was non-essential to the war effort. There's still plenty of low-grade gold ore in the mountains, but it's not valu-able enough to tempt modern mining companies. Government is the main game in town today. Nearly 45% of employed adults work for the state or federal gov-ernment, with the number climbing even higher from January to May, during the legislative session.

LAY OF THE LAND

Juneau is nestled between a deep, ice-carved passageway called the Gastineau Channel, and the waterfall-streaked granite cliffs of the Coast Range. Two com-manding mountains shoot up right behind downtown, 3,576-foot Mount Roberts (which has a tram up to an observation deck you should see) and 3,819-foot Mount Juneau (which has a grueling trail to the top). The summits of the mountains are often covered with clouds, as it rains in Juneau 222 days of the year, on average. Behind the green mountains lies the Juneau Icefield, which stretches for 85 miles from north to south, and 45 miles from east to west. The ice field feeds 35 glaciers, including one of Juneau's biggest attractions: Mendenhall Glacier, 12 miles north of downtown.

Downtown Juneau is compact and walkable, with lots of hills to keep residents fit. Much of the waterfront was built on tailings, the rocky debris from old gold mines that were dumped into the channel to create more buildable land. Across the channel from downtown and over a bridge is Douglas Island, now a suburb of Juneau (it used to be its big rival). The island has bed-and-breakfasts, some beautiful rocky beaches, and the Eaglecrest Ski Area. Juneau stretches north of downtown into the Mendenhall Valley, where there are suburbs housing most of the city's 31,000 people. That's where the airport is too, as well as Mendenhall Glacier. There are no roads to Juneau, although construction of a road to Skagway is slowly progressing—much to the dismay of residents who fear the corrupting influence highway traffic will have on the place. As it is now, the main road sys-tem runs just 45 miles from one end to the other, making the ratio of highway to hiking trails in Juneau 45:130.

You can pick up a free Juneau map, the ferry schedule, brochures of every sort, and input from a volunteer visitor greeter at one of the three visitors centers in town. One is at the airport, next to the baggage claim. Another is in a kiosk on the ferry docks. The mother of them both is located in **Centennial Hall** (101 Eagan Dr.; ☎ 907/586-2201; www.traveljuneau.com; summer Mon–Fri 8:30am–5pm, Sat–Sun 9am–5pm; rest of year Mon–Fri 9am–4pm).

GETTING TO & AROUND JUNEAU

It's a 2-hour flight from Seattle and a 90-minute flight from Anchorage to Juneau International Airport with **Alaska Airlines** (☎ 800/252-7522; www.alaskaair.com).

There are also flights to and from Juneau to most of the main communities in the Southeast, and other parts of Alaska. Fares are about $220 round trip from Anchorage to Juneau. Smaller carriers, such as **Wings of Alaska** (☎ 907/789-0790 or 907/983-2442; www.wingsofalaska.com), fly from Juneau to the places Alaska Airlines can't access, like Skagway and Haines, where the runways are too short for jets. *A word of warning:* All too often, all flights in and out of Juneau are cancelled or diverted—locals call it "overheading"—because of fog. The airlines will put you on the first flight in or out, but they won't cover hotel costs. Travel insurance (p. 376) is your only source for protection.

A cab ride to downtown costs about $20. Call **Capital Cab** (☎ 907/586-2772 or 907/789-2772). The city bus, **Capital Transit** (☎ 907/789-6901), runs regularly from the airport to downtown. It costs $1.50 in exact change, and your bags must fit under the seat.

The ferries of the **Alaska Marine Highway System** (☎ 907/789-7453 or for a recorded schedule 907/465-3940; www.akferry.com) connect Juneau with all of the major communities in the Southeast, and, in the summer, make monthly runs across the Gulf of Alaska to Prince William Sound and points beyond. The ferry terminal is at Auke Bay, 14 miles from downtown. A cab ride costs about $30. If you're getting off the ferry and trying to get downtown, you can usually find other passengers who'll share the fare with you. The city bus, aggravatingly, stops just 1½ miles short of the ferry terminal. The cab ride from there is about $7. If you're taking the bus, call the cab before you board and have it meet you at DeHarts Marina, which is as close as the bus gets to the ferry.

If you're in Juneau for just a day or two, you won't need a car (shuttles leave regularly for the biggest attraction outside of downtown, Mendenhall Glacier). If you're staying longer than a couple of days and want to get out to see things like the Shrine of St. Therese or to explore Douglas Island, you can rent a car via any of the major national rental car agencies at the airport. Or, if you're a gearhead, you might consider biking. Once you get out of downtown, the terrain is generally flat. Bike rentals are available at **Driftwood Lodge** (435 Willoughby Ave.; ☎ 800/544-2239 or 907/586-2280; www.driftwoodalaska.com), for $15 per half-day, $30 per full day.

ACCOMMODATIONS, BOTH STANDARD & NOT

Downtown is where you want to be. It's where the action and most of the city's attractions are, and it's got a broad inventory of hotels, inns, and bed-and-breakfasts to choose from. Your second choice, which is best if you need more peace and quiet, is to stay across the Gastineau Channel on Douglas Island. It's a short hop from downtown, but it feels miles away.

Note that you need to add a 12% tax to all accommodations in Juneau.

The Juneau Convention and Visitors Bureau website (www.traveljuneau.com) has a list of virtually all of the accommodations in Juneau, but there's no criteria for listing other than membership in the visitors bureau. To narrow things down and weed out, say, the B&Bs with stacks of lumber in the yard and hair in the sinks, check out the listings at **Alaska Travelers Accommodations** (☎ 800/928-3308 or 907/247-7117; www.alaskatravelers.com). The Ketchikan-based company typically lists about a dozen properties in Juneau. Most of them are bed-and-breakfasts, with rooms ranging from $125 to $279. The company is owned by

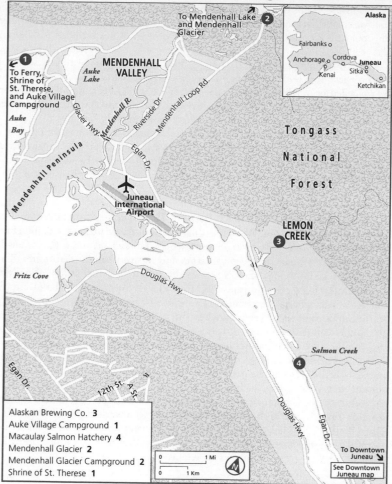

To Mendenhall Lake and Mendenhall Glacier **2**

Alaska

Fairbanks
Anchorage Cordova **Juneau**
Kenai Sitka
Ketchikan

To Ferry, Shrine of St. Therese, and Auke Village Campground **1**

MENDENHALL VALLEY

Auke Lake

Auke Bay

Mendenhall Peninsula

Glacier Hwy *Mendenhall R.* Riverside Dr. Mendenhall Loop Rd.

Egan Dr.

Juneau International Airport

Tongass National Forest

LEMON CREEK **3**

Fritz Cove

Douglas Hwy.

Salmon Creek

4

Egan Dr.

12th St. A St.

Douglas Hwy.

Egan Dr.

To Downtown Juneau

See Downtown Juneau map

Alaskan Brewing Co. **3**
Auke Village Campground **1**
Macaulay Salmon Hatchery **4**
Mendenhall Glacier **2**
Mendenhall Glacier Campground **2**
Shrine of St. Therese **1**

0 ———— 1 Mi
0 ———— 1 Km

Mary Bolshakoff, who has met all of the owners and inspects each of the properties she recommends on a yearly basis. "The B&Bs I recommend are owned by people who are warm and friendly and enjoy meeting people," she says. "That and cleanliness are the most important things to me."

In addition to B&Bs, Mary also has some vacation rentals, and even—in the off season—a few private apartments. The best listings are:

♦ The Indian Cove B&B, which sits right at the high tide line on Auke Bay, near the ferry terminal (you'll fall asleep at night to the sound of the water lapping against the pilings). A hot tub makes this a romantic choice, but it's also recommended for families, thanks to the spacious two-bedroom suite on-site, including a kitchenette (great if you've got picky eaters in tow). The decor is streamlined, with neutral rugs and furniture enlivened by splashes of color—a bit of burgundy here, some navy there. The two bedroom is $165 per night for four, but can sleep up to six ($10 per night for each additional guest). The one-bedroom here is $140 per night. Rates include breakfast and daily maid service.

◆ A simple but colorfully decorated one-bedroom apartment attached to a newer home with a two-car garage on Douglas Island, a short bus ride over the bridge to downtown. It goes for $125 a night for double occupancy, $140 for triple. Visit in winter and host Caroline will show you her favorite cross-country ski trails. Children ages 10 and up only can stay.

◆ Five small apartments, each with private entrances in a robin's-egg blue, 1914 home in what was one of Juneau's first B&Bs. Decor would be best described as quaint—lace curtains, patchwork quilts, and flowery wallpaper. These comfy rooms start at just $95 per night; those with full kitchens go for $155.

Bed & Breakfasts & Hotels

$ **The Alaskan Hotel** ★★ (167 S. Franklin; ☎ 800/327-9347 or 907/586-1000; www.thealaskanhotel.com; AE, V) is one of those classic old Alaska hotels that either charms people or repels them. Alaskan Hotel lovers like the timeworn rooms with their ancient steam radiators and mirrored antique armoires. They cherish the creaky floors, the off-plumb door frames, the labyrinth of hallways with their floral red carpeting and their flocked wallcovering above dark wainscoting. And heck, when it comes to the bay windows from which prostitutes used to solicit business off the street back when the hotel was a brothel, they're in ecstasy (it's fun to wonder what twisted stories the bay windows would tell . . . if bay windows could talk). I think everyone can agree that the hotel's central location in the downtown historic district is a major plus, and those who defend the hotel aren't particularly bothered by the noise from the nearby bars, including the best one in Juneau, the Alaskan Bar, which is on the premises. Alaskan Hotel naysayers, on the other hand, dislike all of these things. They would have sided with the Juneau's Fire Marshal and Litter Control Board, who wanted to tear the building down in 1977, before a couple of hippie carpenters bought it and brought it up to code. Love it or hate it, you can't deny that the Alaskan Hotel is one of the best deals in town, if not the state, with rooms priced between $60 and $80, with either shared or private baths.

$$–$$$$ When the Baranof Hotel, now the **Westmark Baranof** (127 North Franklin St.; ☎ 800/544-0970 or 907/586-2660; www.westmarkhotels.com; AE, DISC, MC, V), was built in 1939, she was the grand hotel in Territorial Alaska. Now she's a dimly lit reminder of a grand hotel, filled with standard burgundy-and-cherrywood chain hotel decor, sub-standard size rooms, and a steady procession of business travelers and airline crews. The $179 summer rack rate is simply too high for what you get. But don't write off the Baranof just yet. Westmark doesn't advertise it, but the second floor has 16 rooms that go for $119. They've got unlovely rooftop views and haven't been remodeled in years, but at that price they're worth a look. While the Baranof reminds me of a long-forgotten former debutante self-deluded enough to think that she's still a grand dame, she still has a few charms. There's her rich collection of mid-20th-century Alaskan oil paintings in her updated Art Deco lobby. Some of her rooms still have the original beaded

Downtown Juneau

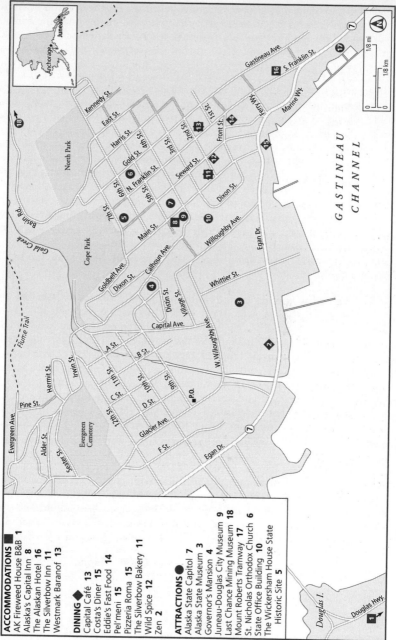

ACCOMMODATIONS ■
Ak Fireweed House B&B **1**
Alaska's Capital Inn **8**
The Alaskan Hotel **16**
The Silverbow Inn **11**
Westmark Baranof **13**

DINING ◆
Capital Café **13**
Costa's Diner **15**
Eddie's Fast Food **14**
Pel'meni **15**
Pizzeria Roma **15**
The Silverbow Bakery **11**
Wild Spice **12**
Zen **2**

ATTRACTIONS ●
Alaska State Capitol **7**
Alaska State Museum **3**
Governor's Mansion **4**
Juneau-Douglas City Museum **9**
Last Chance Mining Museum **18**
Mount Roberts Tramway **17**
St. Nicholas Orthodox Church **6**
State Office Building **10**
The Wickersham House State
Historic Site **5**

door casings and other original architectural flourishes. And then there's her proximity to power, just 2 blocks from the state capitol. No matter what, the Baranof will always have her lobbyists and legislators, who sit at the white-clothed tables in her elegant Gold Room restaurant, conferring over Scotch and king crab legs.

$$$–$$$$ Occupying a downtown three-story building built in 1914, **The Silverbow Inn ★★★** (120 2nd St.; ☎ 800/586-4146 or 907/586-4146; www. silverbowinn.com; AE, DISC, MC, V) has a quirky, casual, comfortable feeling about it. Family photos in the hallway and waterproof frog radios with suction cup feet in the showers give the place a homey feel. "It's more like a pension than anything—the Europeans get it," says the owner. "It's a small, family-run motel, but we're not a bed-and-breakfast." Still, guests can amble downstairs in the morning and find freshly ground hot coffee, granola, and hotel pans filled with eggs and French toast, plus hot bagels and other goodies from the adjacent Silverbow Bakery (p. 214). In the evenings, there are wine and cheese tastings. Besides the bakery downstairs, there's a cavernous back room where locals sip coffee and use the free Wi-Fi by day, and where movies are shown and beer is served at night. Rooms are priced from $156 to $188, with the less expensive rooms being smaller and the top-priced room being huge, with views of Mount Jumbo, and a whirlpool tub.

$$$$ Just a few minutes from downtown, the **AK Fireweed House Bed and Breakfast ★★** (8350 N. Douglas Hwy.; ☎ 800/586-3885 or 907/586-3885; www. fireweedhouse.com; AE, DISC, MC, V) feels far more remote, located as it is on the edge of a wetland and amidst a forest of spruce, pine, and hemlock frequented by deer and bears. The main building--a somewhat mossy family home with just one guest room--doesn't look particularly promising from the outside. That's because the owners have poured all of their nesting energy into the interior, the way Alaskans tend to do. The guest room is light, airy, and inviting, with a vaulted ceiling and walls of honey-colored Western cedar. It's got a luxurious king bed with a pillow-top mattress, an elegant tiled bathroom with a Jacuzzi tub and shower tower, amenities such as Dish TV, and a solarium with wicker chairs and a spotting scope, which you can use to study the blue ice of hanging glaciers in the mountains above Juneau. It goes for $189, and comes with breakfast at the family table (a random sample: poached pear with cream cheese, plus smoked salmon and wild rice quiche). For groups of four or more, there's an outbuilding with a second-floor studio apartment that includes a small wood-burning stove starting at $239, and there's a luxurious two-bedroom, double-walled cedar cabin for $329. Pay by cash or check and Fireweed House will give you a 5% discount.

$$$–$$$$ Lobbyists and power brokers favor **Alaska's Capital Inn ★★★** (113 W. 5th St.; ☎ 888/588-6507 or 907/586-6507; www.alaskacapitalinn.com; AE, DISC, MC, V) for its elegantly restored rooms. Built in 1906 by a successful prospector for his child bride, the current owners have spiffed up the old home and restored its original Arts and Crafts–style grandeur with a historic preservationist's scrupulous attention to minute detail. Beyond the Arts and Crafts–style furnishings are Persian rugs, Alaskan artwork, claw-foot tubs, and feather-top beds. An air of gentility and almost decadent comfort prevails. Rates range from $149 for the former maid's quarters beneath the kitchen (two twins, and a private entrance

A Shrine to Lay Your Head

Old-fashioned Catholic-style spiritual renewal—think meditative walks around a Medieval labyrinth, plus quiet contemplation inside a chapel dedicated to a virgin saint—is the lure that attracts guests to the **Shrine of St. Therese** 🧒 (21425 Glacier Hwy., 22 miles north of Juneau; ☎ 907/789-9815; www.shrineofsainttherese.org; no credit cards; $–$$$$). The Diocese of Juneau, which owns this seaside shrine (see p. 221 for info on simply visiting the shrine), has four cabins there for guests seeking spiritual refuge (**Be warned:** if your idea of getting closer to God involves alcohol, loud voices, and bonfires, neither you nor the Diocese will be happy with your stay). The cabins vary drastically in price and comfort. An ascetic monk would feel right at home in the **Hermitage Cabin,** which was, in fact, originally occupied by a reclusive priest. Nestled among the conifers and alders with a view of the Inside Passage, it has two twin beds, a table and chairs, a woodstove—and that's it. It goes for just $35 a night, double occupancy; for that price, don't expect running water (there's a public restroom nearby). A step up on the austerity scale is the **Post Office Cabin,** a log cabin originally used as a rural post office. It's got a kitchenette, a bathroom, and a postage-stamp-size bedroom. Put in some additional cots and it can accommodate a family of six; it rents for $100. Big groups on retreat go for the **Jubilee Cabin,** which is modern and roomy, costing $230 a night for its four bedrooms and two baths. Work it right, and 13 could spend the night here. The swankiest cabin of the bunch is the **Little Flower Cabin** ⭐⭐⭐, which might as well have been plucked from the pages of *Sunset Magazine*—the sunset views are that good. It's got a wraparound octagonal deck, a panoramic ocean view, stained glass windows, marble countertops, a gas fireplace, and two bedrooms with comfy queen-size beds. Double occupancy units start at $170. (If you're booking rooms as a family, the Diocese will let you have it for the double-occupancy rate.)

that opens onto a backyard urban garden), to $275 for the Governor's Suite, a huge attic room from where you can sit in a bubbling, double-seater Jacuzzi and spy on rivals on the upper floors of the state capitol—a block away—out a large dormer window. The hosts have discreet private quarters on-site, and they've done a savvy job of creating a space where their politico guests can meet and mingle. The inn's signature breakfast, which is included with the room, features Dungeness-crab eggs Benedict, hickory smoked ham, home fries with herbs, and rhubarb muffins. Children under 11 are not admitted.

Camping

$ The rock-bottom cheapest place to stay in Juneau is in a tent. And the U.S. Forest Service **Juneau Ranger District** (☎ 907/586-8800; make reservations by calling ☎ 877/444-6777, or online at www.recreation.gov) makes that prospect pretty pleasant with the two lovely campgrounds it operates. At the **Mendenhall Glacier Campground** ★ (take Mendenhall Loop Rd. to Montanan Creek Rd. to Skaters Cabin Rd.) you can unzip your tent flap and ponder the glacier across the lake before you even crawl out of your sleeping bag. This beautiful campground, one of the nicest in the state, has 68 well separated tent sites. It's also got a half-mile wheelchair-accessible nature trail, and clean restrooms with hot showers and flush toilets. Sites are $10 per night. At the **Auke Village Campground** (1½ miles west of the ferry terminal) you can wake up at the edge of a forest, looking out upon a rocky beach and the little islands in Auke Bay. The campground was once the site of a Tlingit Native village. There are just 11 sites here, for $8 per night.

DINING FOR ALL TASTES

Juneau resembles a miniature San Francisco or a little Seattle in a lot of ways, but not when it comes to fine dining. You might expect that a city so rich in art, culture, and out-of-towners would have a restaurant scene that foodies would get all worked up about. Sadly, it's not so. Juneau's high-end restaurants are solidly ho-hum. But not to worry, because the city shines where it really counts in Pauline Frommer's Alaska—at the budget-end of the spectrum. For those who thrive on cheaper eats, Juneau has plenty to get excited about.

$ Huge breakfasts bring the crowds to **Costa's Diner** ★★★ (Merchants Wharf, 2 Marine Way; no phone; Mon and Wed–Fri 7am–2pm, Sat–Sun 8am–2pm but hours vary; no credit cards). But dining here is an experience, to put it mildly. There's no menu, and little tolerance for needless questions. To avoid asking any needless questions yourself, take a look at the instruction sheet by the "cash register," (it's a copper pot), before ordering. You either pick one of the specials written on the board above the grill, or you design your own breakfast and jot it down on a sticky note. Then—and this part is critical—make sure the cooks see your sticky note. Otherwise, you'll be in for a long, fruitless wait. The basics you have to work with are eggs, vegetables, potatoes, cheeses, French toast, and some excellent coffee. Most breakfasts fall between $5 and $10.

$ Fat deli sandwiches ($6.15–$8.50), darned exciting salads (no, really—both the Mediterranean and the Caesar are a meal-and-a-half; $4.35–$9.50, including a bagel), a rotating roster of soups ($4.50 cup, $5.70 bowl, includes bagel), and breakfasts of oatmeal, egg-and-cheese bagels, and bread pudding are all on offer at **The Silverbow Bakery** kids (120 2nd St.; ☎ 907/586-4146; summer daily 6am–8pm; AE, DISC, MC, V) which also has the distinction of being the oldest bakery in Juneau. It still uses the same sourdough starter it's used since 1897 and that's a good thing. Get one of the 16 varieties of boiled-not-baked New York–style bagels there, with a smear of cream cheese/goat cheese, or cream cheese and salmon. Don't be discouraged if the handful of tables by the counter are occupied—there's a cavernous back room with lots of additional seating, and usually a bunch of young people taking advantage of the free Wi-Fi. It's like a speakeasy for laptop people back there.

$–$$ Everyday hash browns and fried eggs or memorable seared crab cakes with poached eggs and hollandaise—the **Capital Café** (lobby of Baranof Hotel, 619 Mission St.; ☎ 907/586-2660; daily 6:30am–2pm; AE, DISC, MC, V) can deliver it

Where the Stewards, Boatswains & Engineers in First Class Dine

One of my favorite places to eat in Juneau is a simple hole-in-the-wall called **Eddie's Fast Food** ★★★ (225 Front St., Miners' Mercantile building; ☎ 907/523-8026; daily 10am–7pm; no credit cards). When the cruise ships are in—all summer long, in other words—you can find their ships' Indonesian and Filipino crews here, dining on the comfort foods of home. By its own account, Eddie's serves "Oriental & American Food," which includes a toasted vegetarian sandwich and a bunch of different burgers (including a salmon burger) for less than $10, as well as Chinese dishes cooked to order for less than $12. Indonesian and Filipino fare is the real specialty, though. Once I had a memorable Filipino combination special: the *talilong* with *kalabasa,* which turned out to be deep-fried mullet and squash, with a scoop of rice ($8). The squash was cut into bite-size chunks and then bathed in a buttery broth. The cod was fried whole, spine, tail, fins, eyes, and all. It was crispy as a french fry on the outside, moist and steamy on the inside. It was one of the best meals I had in Juneau, and it cost just $8.95.

all. With its beige walls, dim lighting, and 1930s ambience, it's a little dreary, but the menu is heartening. For breakfast ($8.25–$15), try omelets with salmon and asparagus. For lunch choose from sandwiches, wraps, seafood, and burgers ($9–$30), which are made with free-range, antibiotic-and-hormone-free beef, aged 21 days. The seafood includes macadamia-nut-crusted halibut for $15, and a pound of king crab legs for $30—the best price in town.

$–$$$ Pizzeria Roma (Merchants Wharf, 2 Marine Way; ☎ 907/463-5020; daily 11am–10pm; AE, DISC, MC, V) serves good pizza on a thin, crispy crust in a small, warmly lit, often packed-to-the-gills space. It may be much lighter than the pizza you're used to. The veggie pie ($8.25), for instance, relieves cheese of its muscle-bound role and relies on light-footed pesto instead. Assisting the pesto are spinach, red pepper, sun dried tomatoes, onions, and Greek olives; cheese only makes a cameo appearance with some crumbles of feta and a light sprinkling of mozzarella. Pizzeria Roma also serves focaccia sandwiches ($7.95), calzones ($8.95), and big mixed-green salads ($6.75), as well as draft beer and wine by the glass, and of course traditional pizzas coated with melted cheese. With its well-deserved reputation, its limited seating, and its proximity to the cruise-ship docks, Roma is typically packed at dinner. Service might be slow and harried, so don't go unless you have some time to spare.

$$–$$$ You get to put together your own meal and watch as it's cooked at **Wild Spice** (140 Seward St.; ☎ 907/523-0344; www.thewildspice.com; Mon–Thurs 11am–6pm, Fri–Sat 11am–10pm, Sun 11am–6pm; AE, DISC, MC, V), which offers Mongolian barbecue by day, and Mongolian barbecue with a full dinner menu at night. The

---

Late-Night Dirt-Cheap Downtown Dumplings

Pel'meni (Merchants Wharf, 2 Marine Way; no phone; daily 11am–late; no credit cards; $) serves one thing: Russian dumplings. Simple, delicious dumplings. All you have to decide is whether to get dumplings filled with meat or dumplings filled with potatoes. Both varieties are scooped from steaming pots, drizzled with a peppery hot sauce, topped with cilantro and curry powder, and served with a side of sour cream. This is precisely the kind of food people crave after stumbling out of Juneau's downtown bars at 2:30am, which is why Pel'meni's stays open until 3am on weekends. Forget about eating there amid the unfriendly jumble of little tables and glaring fluorescent lighting. Step outside along the waterfront where you can enjoy your hot dumplings in the fresh air, while studying the floatplanes and cruise ships.

---

entrees read something like a world-beat music playlist: Peruvian Blue Corn Crusted Halibut ($18), Jamaican Blue Mountain Chicken ($16), Hawaiian Hoisin Glazed Salmon ($19), and Brazilian Santos Bouillabaisse ($19). Dinners are cheaper in the Mongolian barbecue part of the world. For $11, you can stuff a bowl with as much raw squid, catfish, beef, pork, chicken, vegetables, and noodles as it will hold, then hand it to a cook who splays it all out on a sizzling flat-top grill before cooking it right in front of you.

$$–$$$$ The lobby restaurant at the Goldbelt Hotel, **Zen** (51 Eagan Dr.; ☎ 907/586-5075; daily 6am–10pm; AE, MC, V), strives for Ring-of-Fire chic. With its polished black river stone, protruding bamboo stalks, and flowy ceiling fabric, Zen tries desperately to bring a little minimalist West Coast cool to Juneau. In its mind, it's doing the Asian-fusion thing, so it serves fried rice alongside a modest portion of salmon ($22), and slathers New York strips in oyster sauce ($25). In reality, though, Zen is a simple Chinese restaurant putting on airs. It's like a small-town kid just back from L.A. with a funny new haircut, an eyebrow ring, and a pair of ultra hip trousers that sag in the butt. Humor its pretension, ignore the high-end entrees, and go for the Szechuan string beans ($12), the beef broccoli ($14), and kung pao shrimp ($15). The Chinese dishes are solid—and they're the most affordable, to boot.

WHY YOU'RE HERE: THE TOP SIGHTS & ATTRACTIONS
Downtown
From the observation deck at 1,800 feet, at the top of the **Mount Roberts Tramway** ★★★ 🧒 (490 S. Franklin St.; ☎ 888/820-2628 or 907/463-3412; www.goldbelttours.com; $24 adults, $13 children 6–12, children 5 and under free; daily 9am–9pm) downtown Juneau looks like it does in a Google Earth map—the town is so far, far below, that the enormous cruise ships at dock look no more imposing than bathtub toys. This vantage point makes the tramway the one unmissable

attraction in downtown Juneau—the long views up and down the Gastineau Channel should make you straighten your spine, fill your lungs with fresh air, and generally feel alive. Go up and drink in the view, and after the exhilaration eases up, have a look around the small mountain complex: It includes a restaurant and bar, a gift shop, a nature center, and a theater showing a 20-minute film on Tlingit culture.

The complex also includes the **Juneau Raptor Center** (kids) (☎ 907/586-8393; www.juneauraptorcenter.org; free admission; daily 10am–6pm), which treats and rehabilitates injured wild birds and has a small visitor center, where there's usually a tethered eagle or two to see.

Hiking trails at the top of the Tramway lead deeper into the mountains, through the spruce and hemlock forest. Look for the live trees with Native carvings on them ("culturally modified trees," as the Goldbelt Native Corporation, which owns the land and runs the tram, calls them). Most visitors take the 6-minute tram ride to the top, but there's a cost-saving trick if you're up for some exercise: Simply hike up and back for free (see "Mount Roberts Trail" on p. 225). Or hike up and spend $5 at the mountain complex (on a nice cold beer maybe?). Save the receipt and you can ride the tram back down at no charge.

I can't say that others visiting the **Alaska State Museum** ★★★ (395 Whittier St.; ☎ 907/465-2901; www.museums.state.ak.us; $5 adults, children 19 and under free; summer daily 8:30am–5:30pm, rest of year Tues–Sat 10am–4pm) will feel this way, but I was taken by the surprisingly personal dimension in the artifacts on display there. The heavy wool broadcloth cape worn by William Henry Seward, the secretary of state who brokered the purchase of Alaska from Russia, looked as crisp and new as if Seward had laid it there while running down the hall to the restroom. The caribou-skin diapers stuffed with disposable moss got me thinking about the practical considerations of Native life I'd never considered before. While I've always been impressed by the resourcefulness and craftsmanship Alaskan Natives put into their garments, I was really struck by their fashion sense at the Alaska State Museum—the exquisite beadwork on the his-and-hers Athabascan moose-hide suits; the neatly tailored swan's-down Eskimo baby parka; the fine, decorative tassels adorning the waterproof gut-skin parkas made by Aleuts from sea lion, seal, and bear intestines. I was also surprised by the collection of gold rush–era curios made by Natives to sell to the stampeders—proof that the demand for Native-made souvenirs goes way back.

What the Alaska State Museum does for the history of the state, the **Juneau-Douglas City Museum** ★★ (114 W. 4th St.; ☎ 907/586-3572; www.juneau.org/parksrec/museum; admission $4; Mon–Fri 9am–5pm, Sat–Sun 10am–5pm) does for the city, almost as well. This small but richly curated museum has exhibits that exceed what you'd expect in a place of its size. I was fascinated by the 9-foot-long Tlingit basket-style fish trap that was found protruding from a creek bank near Mendenhall Glacier. Carbon dating shows that the trap—fashioned from split hemlock sticks and spruce hoops, all lashed together with split spruce root—was made sometime between 1300 and 1500. It survived the centuries because it was buried suddenly in oxygen-free glacial silt. A timeline beside the fish trap sets the world scene 500 to 700 years ago: Joan of Arc lived and died, Leonardo da Vinci was born and living, playing cards and flush toilets were invented, the Leaning

Tower of Pisa was built, and cocoa was all the rage among upper class Aztecs (who usurped it from the Mayans).

Each Tuesday, Wednesday, and Thursday in the summer, the museum sends a costumed guide out to lead historic downtown walking tours. Tours start at 3pm, last 1 hour, and cost $10 for adults, $7 for children 18 and under (the price includes museum admission; call in advance to reserve). You can also pick up a free brochure for a self-guided downtown walking tour at the museum's little but well-stocked gift shop.

The Juneau-Douglas City Museum also has its share of artifacts from Juneau's gold-crazed youth, but to dig even deeper into Juneau's heyday of hard-rock mining there, go to the **Last Chance Mining Museum** (1001 Basin Rd., at the end of the road; ☎ 907/586-5338; admission $4; daily 9:30am–12:30pm and 3:30–6:30pm). It's packed with rusting mining equipment and displays dedicated to hard-rock mining, which is fitting since it occupies the old buildings of the Alaska-Juneau Mine, once one of the most productive hard-rock gold mines in Alaska. A multi-tiered glass map shows the intricate network of tunnels that miners blasted deep into the earth here. The train cars and engines that carried miners into the mountain are slowly rusting away outside. The museum's a mile out of town, on forested Gold Creek, a nice long walk or a short drive from downtown. Check out the view of the Mount Juneau Waterfall on the way.

Walking Tour: Downtown Juneau

> **Start:** St. Nicholas Orthodox Church.
>
> **Finish:** Evergreen Cemetery on the long tour.
>
> **Best times:** Whenever it's not raining . . . or at least, not raining *too* hard. Head uphill on Franklin Street, turn right on 5th Street, and start your tour at:

❶ St. Nicholas Orthodox Church

Built in 1893, this is the only surviving example of the small, octagonal, onion-domed Russian Orthodox churches that were once found all over Alaska. St. Nicholas's founding involved a miracle. The story goes like this: A young Tlingit man awoke from a dream in which an elderly white man with a long white beard told him to go to Sitka to be baptized as a Russian Orthodox Christian. The young man did and then became gravely ill. The bearded man continued to appear in his dreams, urging that all Tlingits convert to Russian Orthodoxy. After the young man died, the dream spread among other Tlingits, including an influential chief named Ishkanalykh. The chief went straight to the Russian Bishop of Alaska, and pledged to labor to build a church in Juneau. When Ishkanalykh saw an icon of St. Nicholas, he recognized the face as the white man in his dreams. And so the church was dedicated to the saint with the long, white beard. As long as there's no service in progress, you can drop $2 in the donation box and go inside to look at 18th- and 19th-century icons, vestments, and relics. The church is still active (p. 227), and its congregation is still largely Tlingit.

Continue the uphill trudge on Franklin until you come to 7th Street, go left and find:

❷ The Wickersham House State Historic Site

This is where pioneer judge and statesman James Wickersham, a towering figure in Alaska history, retired. Wickersham arrived in Alaska in 1900 and presided over a wild, 300,000-square-mile judicial district with no roads, no public facilities, and a firm tradition of frontier justice. He traveled through the land aboard steamboats in the summer and dog sleds in the winter, settling claim-jumping disputes, holding murder trials, straightening out corruption in Nome, and collecting license fees from saloons and mercantile exchanges, the court's only source of revenue. In 1908 he became Alaska's delegate to Congress, where he won the right of home rule for Alaska, and advocated for its admission as a territory and later a state. He overcame strong opposition to federal funding to build the Alaska Railroad, and he helped establish both the University of Alaska and Denali National Park. He's also credited as the first white man to attempt to climb Denali. The house was closed to visitors in 2006 for restoration work, and it wasn't known at press time when it would reopen. If it's open when you visit, go inside and check out Wickersham's personal effects, including his collections of carved Native ivory, basketry, and other mementos from his travels. The house is located on Chicken Ridge, which got its name because early miners hunted ptarmigan (the state bird) there. Chicken Ridge might have been called Ptarmigan Ridge, but the miners had a hard time with the word ptarmigan, and preferred the name "miners chicken."

Continue on 7th Street to Seward Street, turn left and head downhill to the corner of 4th Street, where you'll find:

❸ The Alaska State Capitol

The State Capitol was built by the federal government in 1931 as the Federal and Territorial Building, which became Alaska's upon statehood in 1958. It's stately enough from the front, with a handsome facade of Alaskan marble and Indiana limestone, but the brick-faced concrete of the building's sides and rear is that of an oversize, out-of-date public school. The governor's office is here, as well as the chambers for the state legislature, which meets for 120 days from January to May. Feel free to go in and poke around. Inside, the territorial-era ambience has been restored to many parts of the building. Throughout the building there are historic photographs and public art on display, including a map of Alaska cut from a section of the Trans-Alaska Pipeline. During the summer, free tours are offered every half-hour from Monday through Saturday, 9am to 4:30pm. Or you can pick up a brochure in the lobby and take a self-guided tour.

Across Main Street from the capitol building, and kitty-corner from the courthouse, you'll see two totem poles standing in front of the:

❹ Juneau-Douglas City Museum

This is a rich little museum devoted to local history (p. 217). Stop in and grab a copy of the Historic Downtown Juneau Guide, which covers more historic buildings than I'm getting into here. (Downtown has 60 buildings from 1904 or earlier.) The museum was built in 1951 as a library, the first in the state. Out front are two totem poles. One, carved in 1967, is called Harnessing the Atom. At the top is an eagle, which stands for the United States. Below it is a Russian priest, standing for the USSR. Below them is Man on Top of the Sun, who represents the Tlingit legend of the origin of the universe and the harnessing of energy. At the bottom, supporting the others, is Raven, the creator of all things in Tlingit culture. The other pole is the Four Story Totem Pole. I won't go into the stories, but they involve a frog, a man, Raven, a monster frog, Bear Chief, a fish trap, a black bear, a shaman holding a land otter, a black oystercatcher rattle, an octopus, a halibut, and a halibut hook baited with a supernatural mouse.

Across the street from the museum, at the curve where 4th Street turns into Calhoun Street, you'll find:

⑤ The State Office Building

Known locally as The SOB (I kid you not), the State Office Building was built along the side of a cliff. To see the dramatic views that come with that setting, head to the 4th Street entrance, which will take you right to the 8th floor, where there's an atrium overlooking the Gastineau Channel. Keep your eyes peeled for the historic photos taken from the archives of the Alaska State Library (which is in the building, too). You'll also find the Old Witch Totem, a well-weathered totem pole that tells the Tlingit story of Gunakadeit, a sea monster with human origins (it's the second most popular legend for totem pole art after ravens, and is considered a good-luck sea monster). The SOB elevators are the local shortcut for getting from the hilly part of downtown at the top of the cliff to the flatlands at the bottom. Originally the flatlands were part of Gastineau Channel, but mine tailings were dumped there for years, increasing Juneau's buildable land twofold.

Exit the SOB where you entered and walk 2 blocks north on Calhoun Street to:

⑥ The Governor's Mansion

Except for the totem pole out front, this Greek Revival–style mansion could be a stately home in New England. Built in 1912, the mansion is currently home of Sarah Palin, the perky former mayor of Wasilla, who soundly defeated the unpopular incumbent, a member of her own Republican Party, in 2006. There are no public tours, but you're free to stand on the sidewalk and look all you want. The totem pole, by the way, tells the story of how the stars, sunlight, tides, land animals, marine mammals, and mosquitoes were made (Hint: A giant was involved).

Continue along Calhoun for a few blocks until you reach:

⑦ Gold Creek

Chief Kowee led the shiftless prospectors Joe Juneau and Richard Harris to the mouth of this creek, where they left their canoe and hiked up the gulch to the creek's headwaters, an area known to the Tlingit as Bear's Nest and now called the Silverbow Basin. There the two white men found the large pieces of quartz "all spangled with gold" just as Kowee reported, and with that, the gold rush that led to the founding of Juneau was on.

Cross the bridge over Gold Creek, stay on the street that started out as Calhoun but which, you may notice, changes names a few times. At the fork you'll come to, bear right on Martin Street, and pay your respects to Juneau's early inhabitants at:

⑧ The Evergreen Cemetery

Chief Kowee, Joe Juneau, and Richard Harris (see "A Brief History" above for info on exactly who these guys are) all ended up here. Harris's body was shipped from Oregon, where he died in 1907, broke, nearly blind, and in a sanitarium. Juneau's body was shipped back from Dawson City, where, after unsuccessfully searching for gold in Klondike, he ended up running a restaurant. When Chief Kowee died in 1892, he lay in state for 2 days in his police uniform. Then his people removed the uniform, painted his face with a red and black Tlingit design, and cremated him at the entrance of the cemetery. Look for the bronze plaque marking the spot.

Beyond Downtown

In many ways Juneau's suburban Mendenhall Valley is just like any suburban area anywhere—except for the glacier plowing through it. While the **Mendenhall Glacier** ★★★ isn't one of the bigger or more active Alaskan glaciers, it's certainly the most accessible. It's known as the drive-up glacier, and it's well worth the 12-mile trip from downtown to see (you can drive, or hop one of the shuttles that leave throughout the day from the cruise-ship docks; these cost $6). Think of it as a starter glacier, and check it out before feasting your eyes on the more spectacular glaciers in Glacier Bay National Park, Tracy Arm-Ford's Terror Wilderness, or other parts.

The Mendenhall Glacier flows 13 miles from the Juneau Icefield tucked into to the mountains down to Mendenhall Lake, 54 feet above sea level. Like almost all of Alaska's glaciers, it is in retreat. Ice still flows down it, but its forward edge is moving steadily backward. As recently as the 1930s, the glacier covered the smooth, striated rocks where the **Mendenhall Glacier Visitor Center** (8645 Old Dairy Rd.; ☎ 907/789-0097; www.fs.fed.us/r10/tongass/districts/mendenhall; $3 adults, children 12 and under free; summer only 8am–7:30pm) is now, 1 mile from the glacier's front edge. There's no charge to see the glacier itself, but there's a small admission to the visitor center. Pay the admission and you'll get a crash course in glaciology through film and various exhibits, including a cool scale model of the Juneau Icefield that shows how the Mendenhall Glacier fits into the bigger picture. After getting up to (glacial) speed, go outside and stroll the paved, half-mile Trail of Time to see first-hand the succession of life that returns as a glacier retreats, starting with moss and lichens, followed by fireweed, then cottonwood trees, and finally a spruce and hemlock forest. If you want to get to the face of the glacier, where the refrigerated air creates its own micro wind patterns, a fairly steep 3.5-mile trail will take you there. Pick up a map of all the nearby trails in the visitor center, and you can make a day of hiking in the area.

Less of an adrenaline rush, but still a rush of sorts for spiritually minded travelers, the **Shrine of Saint Therese** (Mile 22 Juneau Veteran's Memorial Hwy.; ☎ 907/780-6112; www.shrineofsainttherese.org; free admission; daily 8:30am–10pm) is another draw just a short drive from Juneau. A seaside, beach-rock chapel, it's dedicated to Saint Therese of Lisieux, Catholicism's patron saint of Alaska. Known as The Little Flower, Saint Therese was a Carmelite nun who died at age 24, in 1897. The Little Flower's chapel sits on its own wooded little island, attached to shore by a causeway. After looking around inside, walk around the island to see the 14 stations of the cross, which have carvings of oddly large-headed characters, as if everyone at Calvary, including Jesus, were a dwarf. On shore, take a spin through a reproduction of a spiraling Medieval labyrinth laid out in the sand, then find the columbarium, where plants from the Bible grow.

Mother of All (Juneau Area) Glaciers

The Juneau Icefield, a massive remnant of the ice sheet that once covered most of North America in the Ice Age, is firmly seated in the Coast Mountains 4,500 feet above Juneau, and just out of town. Thirty-five big glaciers and dozens of smaller ones flow from the 1,500-square-mile sheet of ice. She's one big mama, and a sight well worth seeing. The only practical way to get up to her is to fly, and there are helicopters and planes that specialize in Juneau Icefield trips. Personally, I prefer the copter rides. The planes cover a broader area, but the choppers actually land on the ice and let you out to run around—and doesn't that sound like more fun than just looking at the ice from the air? Both types of tours are very popular, and flights often book up 2 to 3 days in advance. Which leaves you with this question: Do you wait to see what the weather will be like (since a cloudy day can diminish the view or ground flights altogether), or do you take a chance and secure a seat? I think the latter course of action is smarter: Book in advance and take your chances with the weather (it may be less of a risk than taking a chance with the limited number of flights).

One of the oldest and most well-respected of the ice field tour operators is **Era Helicopters** (☎ 800/843-1947 or 907/586-2030; www.flight seeingtours.com). Its 1-hour flights, with a 15-minute landing on the Juneau Icefield's Norris Glacier, go for $229, which is standard. A 2-hour flight adds a stop at a sled dog camp, where you hop aboard a dog sled and go mushing across the ice. It's an experience of a lifetime, but at a pricey $445.

Afterwards, pop into the little serve-yourself gift shop and pick up a St. Therese icon, key chain, or votive candle. Catholics make pilgrimages to the shrine, but you don't have to be Catholic to visit. Many simply come for the sheer peacefulness of the place. There are cabins for rent, too (p. 213).

Just beyond the Shrine at the end of the road there's a lovely tidal estuary called Eagle Beach State Park. Bring a picnic; you might just see eagles swooping down and snatching salmon out of Eagle River during your own meal. Walk north along the beach to the rocky outcropping to look for fossils, and keep an eye peeled for whales in the distance.

Just as wild salmon instinctively return to their home streams to spawn and die, hatchery salmon return to the hatcheries from which they came. So when you take the tour of Juneau's **Macaulay Salmon Hatchery** (2697 Channel Dr.; ☎ 877/463-2486 or 907/463-4810; www.dipac.net; $3.25 adults, $1.75 children 12 and under; summer Mon–Fri 10am–6pm, Sat–Sun 10am–5pm; off season appointment only), you'll watch the miracle of life—salmon hatchery style—unfold. Each summer millions of coho, pink, and chum salmon return to the big, red-roofed building on the edge of Gastineau Channel where their mothers' eggs and their fathers' milt were mixed in 5-gallon buckets to create them. To complete the cycle, they must dodge the crowds of salmon-loving seals gathered in the waters outside the hatchery and scale a 450-foot fish ladder. At the top of the ladder, they enter into a sorting mechanism and then fall into the hands of hatchery technicians with filet knives, who slit them open to get at their eggs and milt. And then their job is done. The best time to go is from mid-June to October, when the salmon are running. Earlier in the season, all you'll see are the juveniles before they're released. Other local marine species are on display in a big, naturalistic aquarium. It's inhabited by some peculiar creatures, such as the Pacific spiny lumpsucker, a prickly bubble of a fish with an adhesive pelvic disk for clinging to rocks. Then there's the alarmingly odd-looking fish called the decorated warbonnet, with its googly eyes and fright wig.

If you'd like to join the crowd of predators attempting to intercept a few home-coming coho, there's a bait-and-tackle shop outside, where you can get a license and a pole, and try your hand at salmon fishing from the pier. The hatchery is a short drive, bike ride, or bus trip north of downtown. Give yourself about 45 minutes to tour it.

THE OTHER JUNEAU

Small city Juneau is ripe with opportunities for you to break off the beaten tourist path, rub elbows with the locals, and see what makes Alaskans tick.

You'll get to see a broader cross-section of Juneau at any of the local festivals held throughout the year. Juneau has a busy festival calendar. No matter what month you're there, you stand a good chance of arriving close to one annual festival or another. All of them are geared toward the local populace, more than the tourist, which makes them all the more appealing for discerning travelers. If you're in town in April, for example, you might catch the weeklong **Alaska Folkfest** (www.akfolkfest.org). It really consists of two parallel festivals: One is the official festival, in which back-to-back, 15-minute performances are held throughout the day at Centennial Hall. The other is the unofficial after-festival at the Alaskan Hotel (p. 210), where musicians book all the rooms, leave their doors open, and stage impromptu jam sessions. Folk aficionados wander the halls with six-packs of beer, popping into this room and that, finding a different micro-variety of folk music in each.

For 3 days in early June, during even numbered years, Tlingit, Haida, and Tsimshian Natives gather for a cultural celebration called, simply, **Celebration** (☎ 907/463-4844; www.sealaska.com). It's 3 days of dancing, parades, sports, and juried art shows. The winning entries from the art show are kept on display year-round in the lobby of the **Sealaska Heritage Institute** (1 Sealaska Plaza; ☎ 907/463-4844; www.sealaskaheritage.org).

During the last weekend in June, Juneau holds **Gold Rush Days** (☎ 907/780-6075), which features 2 days of intense mining and logging competitions. Logging events include ax throwing, stock power sawing, speed climbing, tree topping, log rolling, vertical chopping, and horizontal chopping. The mining competitions include spike driving, jack leg drilling, team drilling, hand mucking, 12B overshot mucking, and, thank goodness, gold panning.

If you're in Juneau late in the season, you'll be there at the start of the weekly fall lecture series, **Evening at Egan** (Egan Hall, University of Alaska Southeast;

www.uas.alaska.edu; free admission; Thurs at 7pm). The lectures, which run from September to December, delve into a wide range of topics, which almost always have an Alaskan connection. Past lectures have featured:

♦ A cultural anthropologist on what Natives have learned about polar bears over thousands of years, and what he learned about them while living near the Arctic Circle.
♦ An Iraq war veteran on conscientious objector status and the year he spent in prison for desertion.
♦ A renowned whale researcher on why whales sing.
♦ An Alaskan Native on her childhood in a Tlingit village, her moves to Seattle and San Francisco, and her return home.

During Juneau's booming gold rush years, it had five breweries (my kind of town!). Now it has just one, the **Alaskan Brewing Company** (5429 Shaun Dr.; ☎ 907/780-5866; www.alaskanbeer.com; daily 11am–5pm), which brews and bottles enough beer to ship all over Alaska and the Pacific Northwest. If you're passionate about beer, go on the free brewery tour. After taking a quick spin through the plant to see how Alaskan Brewing Co.'s half dozen beers are made, you'll get to taste each of them. The brewery's lineup includes Alaskan Amber, a revival of an alt-style brew made at one of the city's original breweries. It's the same rich, malty, long-on-the-palate beer that Juneau's gold miners slaked their thirst on.

If you play lacrosse, you can join the local players for a rousing session of drop-in box lacrosse, Monday and Wednesday from 6pm to 8pm at the **Treadwell Ice Arena** (105 Savikko Rd.; ☎ 907/586-0410; www.juneau.org/parksrec/icerink) on Douglas Island. Box lacrosse is an indoor version of lacrosse played on a covered or defrosted hockey rink. You pay $3 to play, and sticks are provided, but you'll have to try and borrow gloves and a helmet.

ACTIVE JUNEAU
Hiking
Wedged between 3,000-foot mountains and the sea, Juneau has an exhaustive variety of hiking trails, some of which begin right downtown. The city's most popular hike is the **Perseverance Trail** ★★, which begins at the end of Basin Road, a 1.5-mile walk from downtown. The trail itself is an easy, 3-mile round-trip on an old wagon road that takes you back into the Silverbow Basin, where the gold that sparked the gold rush was first discovered. Along the way you'll encounter plenty of mining ruins and rusting equipment and you can step up to the edge of the Glory Hole, a broad 1,000-foot-deep pit miners dug into the earth. Ebner Falls is another highlight. The trail begins near the Last Chance Mining Museum (p. 218), which makes for an agreeable stop while you're in the neighborhood.

The more challenging **Granite Creek Trail** begins 2 miles along the Perseverance Trail and climbs 3.5 miles and 1,200 feet to a glorious basin, past waterfalls and alpine lakes. There are loads of wildflowers and wild berries along the way in the summer. This is a good route to take if you want to get away from the light traffic of joggers, mountain bikers, and babies in knobby-tired strollers along Perseverance Trail. *Warning:* There's avalanche danger along all three of these trails through the winter and into the spring.

There are a few ways to approach the **Mount Roberts Trail ★★★**, a 4.5-mile climb from the edge of downtown to a 3,819-foot summit. The obvious way is to start at the trailhead, which begins at the top of a wooden staircase at the end of 6th Street, in a hillside neighborhood of old, colorful homes. Another way is to cheat, and take the Mount Roberts Tramway (p. 216) up to the little visitor complex at 1,760 feet and pick up the trail there. Or you can hike up to the top and take the tram back down (buy something at the tram complex for $5 and you can ride down without buying a ticket). For a shorter hike, but one that's still a good climb, hike only as far as the tram complex, which is at the tree line. The view from the summit is really something. It rivals that of the top of Mount Juneau, only the trail isn't as dangerous.

The best family hike around is across the bridge from downtown Juneau on Douglas Island. The hour-long walk on the **Treadwell Mine Historic Trail** loops through a forest that has grown up through the ruins of an old mining complex dating to 1882. The mine's tunnel system, which ran beneath Gastineau Channel, partially collapsed and flooded with seawater in 1917, closing the mine. More than 300 miners were underground as water began to fill the tunnels. All were safely accounted for but one (it's not clear if the missing man drowned or skipped town for personal reasons, happy to be presumed dead). The trail is an easy walk, but don't stray into the woods—they're honeycombed with mining shafts and holes. To find the trail, cross the bridge to Douglas Island and turn left, drive down 3rd Street to the fork and bear left on Savikko Street, and continue to Savikko Park (aka Sandy Beach Park). The trail starts at the far end of the park. A brochure detailing the history of the mine and providing a key to the numbered posts along the trail is available at the visitor center.

The Mendenhall Glacier (p. 221) has several trails, ranging from a short nature walk to a pair of steep 3.5-mile trails up either side of the glacier. You can pick up a brochure at the Mendenhall Glacier Visitor Center with maps of them all.

To find out about all the hikes in the area, get a copy of the U.S. Forest Service map called Juneau Area Trail Guides, a detailed map widely available where free visitor material is found. Or check with the **Juneau Parks and Recreation Department** (155 South Seward St.; ☎ 907/586-5226; www.juneau.org/parks rec), which leads guided hikes Wednesday and Saturday mornings throughout the summer.

Rock Climbing

Although Juneau is surrounded by mountains, their loose shale makeup doesn't make for good rock climbing. The city has a vibrant rock climbing scene nonetheless thanks to its climbing gym, the **Rock Dump Indoor Climbing Gym** (1310 Eastaugh Way; ☎ 907/586-4982; Mon–Fri 4pm–10pm, Sat–Sun noon–8pm) This is no hard-knuckled clubhouse where tawny rock hounds make beginners feel completely intimidated. Rather, it's a community-focused place that draws people of all climbing abilities (including those with no climbing abilities at all). You have to be at least 14 to climb alone or to belay another climber, but otherwise there's no age restriction. It's not unusual to see 4-year-olds scaling the walls like spiders (nor, I'm afraid, is it unusual to see 4-year-olds who wet their pants, throw gravel, cry, and refuse to climb). Done up in muted blues, reds, and yellows, the roomy gym has 30-foot walls, a bouldering area, a free-standing tower, a chimney, and a bunch of other fun climbing features.

Yoga

To yoke body and mind with breath among the local yogis, check out **Rainforest Yoga** (174 S. Franklin St., Ste. 202; ☎ 907/789-6392; www.rainforestyoga.org; hours vary), a quiet yoga studio on the second floor of an old building in bustling tourist heart of town. Drop by or check the website for the schedule, which changes periodically.

ATTENTION, SHOPPERS!

Downtown Juneau has loads of shopping. In the historic district, by the cruise-ship docks, you'll find a plethora of gift shops, T-shirt dealers, ice cream and tof-fee places, and touristy art galleries. Push farther into downtown and the crowds of tourists quickly thin as the level streets give way to hilly streets. Here are my favorites from both areas:

To pick up a little freshly smoked salmon or halibut in Juneau, stop by the **Taku Store** (550 South Franklin, across from Mount Roberts Tram station; ☎ 800/582-5122), which is right in the touristy heart of things, across from the Mount Roberts Tramway. Help yourself to some free samples, while watching workers behind glass filleting, smoking, and packing the fish.

The hand-written note taped inside the window of the **Alaska General Store** ★★★ (224 Front St.; ☎ 907/463-4616) reveals a lot about this tiny shop's inventory and how it's acquired. It says, "We buy old Native art, old jewelry, antiques & funky junk." This is the place to go to look for bona fide Alaskan curios, such as old Chilkat blankets, antique hide-web snowshoes, 49-star Alaskan state flags, and the little totem poles carved from bone that tourists used to buy in Alaska in the 1920s. The shelves and display cases are loaded with inexpensive curios for less than $10: small Japanese fishing floats, walrus ivory shards, Indian trade beads, old poker chips, and Alaska license plates. Still, funky junk isn't nec-essarily what the majority of tourists in town are looking for. So the store stocks a bunch of tasteful modern souvenirs too—Alaska-made soaps, candles, and black T-shirts bearing bright red Kwakwaka'waka and Tshimshian symbols. In the back of the store, there's a small woman's clothing boutique, with jeans and tops by LTB and Free People. See what's hanging on the 40%-off rack.

"We only stock things that are associated with the Alaska State Museum," says a volunteer at the downtown location of the **Friends of the Alaska State Museum Store** ★★ (124 Seward St.; ☎ 977/523-8431; www.foasm.org). "The museum has a great display of Northwest Coast art, so we have Northwest Coast art. The museum has a big section on Russian-America, so we have Russian crafts. The museum has a collection of Native ivory carvings, so we have Native ivory carv-ings." Get the idea? Most of the stock is handmade in Alaska, and some of it would take a museum's acquisition budget to acquire. There are carved Native dance masks costing thousands of dollars. There are Native carved wood halibut hooks with bone barbs from $250, and tightly woven beach grass baskets the size of a lime for $125 and up. There are also precious knick-knacks for less than $50—such as a little ivory whale carving with baleen eyes for $40. In two back rooms of the store, smaller versions of the museum's rotating art exhibits can be seen. I asked the Friends of the Alaska State Museum volunteer if a traveler on a really tight budget might save himself the price of admission to the museum by just visiting the store. "The store exists to supplement the museum's budget," he said, frowning. "So that would defeat the purpose."

The old rectory beside the **St. Nicholas Russian Orthodox Church** (325 5th St.; ☎ 907/586-1023; www.stnicholasjuneau.org) (p. 218) is now a small, one-room gift shop, which has a small but unusual collection of mostly Russian-made gifts. There are Russian nesting dolls and nesting eggs of various sizes ($12–$50); Russian Orthodox books; Russian Orthodox music; and lots and lots of Russian Orthodox iconography, done the way Russian Orthodox believers like their icons—painted on simple wooden canvasses. This is also a good place to stock up for Christmas; tree ornaments on sale include little Russian angels, little Russian Orthodox churches, and even a little Santa Claus, the jolly old namesake of the church himself.

NIGHTLIFE IN JUNEAU

South Franklin Street in Juneau's old red light district has nearly a dozen bars, most deeply historic and total dives. The most touristy, and least authentic, is the **Red Dog Saloon** (278 Franklin St.; ☎ 907/463-3658), which has swinging saloon doors, walls covered with old-timey Alaskana, and loads of lubricated cruise-ship passengers. It's worth stopping there for a quick beer just to deepen the appreciation for the town's real bars. The best of the lot is **The Alaskan** (167 S. Franklin; ☎ 907/586-1000), in the basement of The Alaskan Hotel. With its antique chandeliers, flocked red velvet wall papering, massive mirrored oak bar, and dark nooks and crannies, the place looks every bit like the brothel bar it used to be. There's live music (and sometimes dancing) throughout the week, and usually no cover.

Bar hopping is popular in Juneau, but it's not the only thing to do there. If you're around early or late in the tourist season, you get a chance to catch a production by the **Perseverance Theatre Company** (914 3rd St., Douglas Island; ☎ 907/364-2421; www.perseverancetheatre.org). The company, which draws too many seasoned, out-of-state theater people to Juneau to qualify as pure community theater, tends to favor Shakespeare, rock musicals, and regional Alaskan plays, including an all-Native production of *Macbeth,* set in Tlingit culture. Ticket prices are kept low, around $25 usually, and admission to some shows is on a sliding scale.

GLACIER BAY NATIONAL PARK

The profusion of glaciers and wildlife at **Glacier Bay National Park** ★★★ (☎ 907/697-2230; www.nps.gov/glba) has made the icy marine wilderness 60 miles northwest of Juneau *the* most popular visitor attraction in Southeast Alaska. It's not a cheap trip—and there are other spectacular tidewater glaciers you can see more affordably—but for many visitors, skipping Glacier Bay would be unthinkable. It's Southeast's marquee attraction, and the whole point of visiting Alaska in a nutshell. And yes, you too should see it . . . unless you opt for the lesser-known but far more affordable alternative glaciers near Juneau in the Tracy-Arm-Ford's Terror Wilderness. I'll come back to them in a bit. First, let me give you an idea of what to expect at Glacier Bay:

Glacier Bay National Park and Preserve takes in a 65-mile-long, Y-shaped bay, and its surrounding horseshoe of mountains, at the top of the Inside Passage. Sixteen tidewater glaciers creep to the bay from ice fields in the snowy St. Elias and Fairweather mountains. Nowhere on earth is there a larger cluster of glaciers reaching the sea. With the same thunderous booms of artillery fire, office-building-size slabs of ice sometimes crack off from the leading edges of a dozen of these glaciers and crash into the water, kicking up waves big enough to surf. Littered with icebergs, the water of the bay sometimes crackles like Rice Krispies as long-frozen air bubbles break open and send thousands of tiny, ancient breaths back into the atmosphere. The bay is rich with marine life, including humpback whales, which feed on teeming schools of tiny fish, and killer whales, which pursue doe-eyed harbor seals, that sometimes rush to tour boats for cover. High up on the barren cliffs, mountain goats leap among the crags, while black bears, brown bears, and even the unusual blue bear (a rare variety of black bear) pad around in the forested areas along the shore. On sun-warmed rocks in the bay, cantankerous groups of sea lions sun themselves and complain loudly about each other, like members of some dysfunctional social club.

One of the most remarkable things about Glacier Bay is how new it is. Just 200 years ago, the whole bay was filled by a single immense glacier, 100 miles long and 4,000 feet thick in places. When British explorer George Vancouver sailed by in 1794, Glacier Bay did not exist. One hundred years later the ice had retreated 48 miles, and today it's pulled back 65 miles. It's the fastest glacial retreat ever recorded. It's also a living laboratory where scientists study the re-colonization of plant life that returns when glaciers retract. As you venture into Glacier Bay, you can see for yourself all the steps between the colorful lichens grabbing a foothold at the head of the bay and well-established old growth spruce forest at the mouth of the bay.

GETTING TO & AROUND GLACIER BAY

The only development in the park is near the mouth of the bay, at Bartlett Cove, the hub for transportation and commercial activities. There's a lodge there, campgrounds, kayak rentals and tours, and a dock for the ferry and tour boat. About 10 miles away from Bartlett Cove, outside the park's boundary, is the pastoral settlement of Gustavus, which has several bed-and-breakfasts and an airport.

You can get to Glacier Bay by plane or by ferry. The ferry is a bit cheaper but it takes longer and rules out making a day trip to Glacier Bay, which is fine because you really should take your time there and soak in the place. And in any case, traveling by boat is one of the highlights of traveling in Southeast Alaska. You're likely to see whales and other wildlife while en route, so a ferry ride can also double as a wildlife watching tour.

The ferry is operated by the same company that runs the lodge that does the day tour of the park, **Glacier Bay Lodging and Tours** (☎ 888/229-8687; www.visit glacierbay.com), a joint venture between the local Native corporation and the National Park Service's concessionaire. The ferry is a 72-foot high speed catamaran called *Glacier Bay Express II,* and it makes runs between Juneau and Bartlett Cove only on Wednesdays, Fridays, and Sundays. The round-trip fare is $140 (or $80 for children ages 2–12), and the trip takes about 3 hours. Go early in the season and you might luck out and get a two-for-one special. The *Glacier Bay Express II*

is also the same boat used for the daily tours of Glacier Bay (something for which you have to buy a separate ticket). It doesn't become a ferry until 4:30pm, when it leaves Bartlett Cove for Juneau. It makes the return trip at 8pm, arriving at 11pm—so if you're an early-to-bed type, be prepared to stay up late.

If you've only got a day to see Glacier Bay—and I hope you've got more time to spare than that—you'll have to fly in and out. **Alaska Airlines** (☎ 800/252-7522; www.alaskaair.com) has afternoon flights between Gustavus from Juneau each day in the summer, for about $174 round-trip. Smaller carriers such as **Wings of Alaska** (☎ 907/789-0790 or 907/983-2442; www.wingsofalaska.com) charge about the same, and have flights throughout the day. Shuttles meet the planes and charge $12 a pop for the ride to Bartlett Cove. Most of the accommodations in Gustavus will pick you up for free, if you're checking in.

Once you've gotten to Glacier Bay, you've got a few options for getting around. There are private charter boats that run out of Gustavus, but they're super pricey. The best deal, and the most popular way to see the bay, is to go on the 8-hour **Glacier Bay Tour** offered by Glacier Bay Lodging and Tours. The *Glacier Bay Express II* carries 149 passengers, along with a National Park Service naturalist who narrates the trip and answers questions. It costs $160 (or $80 for kids 2–12).

The most adventuresome way to see Glacier Bay is from a sea kayak. If you're an experienced kayaker, you can rent boats from **Glacier Bay Sea Kayaks** (☎ 907/697-2257; www.glacierbayseakayaks.com) for $40 a day and spend several days camping and exploring the bay on your own. It's possible to set off in a kayak directly from Bartlett Cove, but since the nearest glaciers are 50 miles away, most paddlers hitch a ride aboard the *Glacier Bay Express II*, which charges $100 for a drop-off or a pick-up. If you're new to sea kayaking, take a guided tour. Glacier Bay Sea Kayaks also offers full-day tours for $140 and half-day tours (which don't go near the ice) for $90. Longer guided tours are led by **Alaska Discovery** (☎ 800/586-1911 or 907/780-6226; www.akdiscovery.com) which offers 5 days of camping, sea kayaking, and hiking for $1990 per person.

Note that you should add 7% to the cost of lodging and tours at Glacier Bay.

ACCOMMODATIONS, BOTH STANDARD & NOT

If you're not on a multi-day kayaking trip around Glacier Bay, camping as you go, there are two areas where you can spend the night: at Bartlett Cove or in nearby Gustavus.

Bartlett Cove

$ How's this for affordable: The wooded **Bartlett Cove Campground** ★ (no phone) has no charges attached to it for stays (nor does it require reservations). Just show up (it's a short walk from the dock), check in at the visitor information station by the dock, and go put up your tent. When you register, a ranger will brief you about the campground rules, which mainly deal with cooking and storing food in places that won't draw bears. Borrow a wheelbarrow there to lug your gear in and to tote the free firewood available at the campground to your fire pit. Showers and meals are available in the Glacier Bay Lodge (see below).

$$$–$$$$ Extraordinarily convenient and well located, the **Glacier Bay Lodge** (☎ 888/229-8687; www.visitglacierbay.com; AE, DISC, MC, V), is right next door to the dock. If you take the ferry to Bartlett Cove you can walk right from the boat to your room when you arrive, then walk from your room to the tour boat or the kayaking concessionaire the next morning. The rooms are standard-issue motel fare, but the location more than makes up for it. Set among the spruce trees at the edge of the cove, the lodge has a grand stone fireplace in the lobby and huge windows with a phenomenal view across the bay of 15,320-foot Mount Fairweather. Rooms with that Mount Fairweather view are the most expensive, going for $170. Save some money and go for one of the $150 forest-view rooms. You'll get plenty of scenery when you get out on the water, and if you dine in the lodge restaurant.

Gustavus

A stay at one of the B&Bs, lodges, or other accommodations in Gustavus will be a less convenient but more personal experience than a stay at Glacier Bay Lodge. Whether it costs more or less will depend on where you land. The complete list of lodging is available through the **Gustavus Visitors Association** (☎ 907/697-2454; www.gustavusak.com). Just about all of the places offer free shuttle runs from the airport or dock at Bartlett Cove.

$–$$$ One of the best deals in Gustavus is a studio apartment available for $100 a night above an artists cooperative called Smokehouse Gallery. The studio, which overlooks a meadow sometimes filled with wildflowers, is one of the two apartments that make up **Aimee's Guest House** (Shooting Star Lane; ☎ 907/697-2330; www.glacierbayalaska.net; no credit cards). Both are bright, spacious, and handsomely appointed. A two-bedroom apartment, which has an enclosed deck overlooking the salmon stream running through the meadow, goes for $150 double occupancy. It's got a semi-enclosed deck with a day bed and a hammock on it, nice places to sleep for kids or anyone else who can slumber in the bright dusk of a Gustavus summer night.

$$$–$$$$ Another good choice in Gustavus is **Blue Heron Bed and Breakfast at Glacier Bay** (off Dock Rd.; ☎ 907/697-2337; www.blueheronbnb.net; no credit cards), where you can get one of two rooms for $145 or one of two single-room cabins for $185, double occupancy. Located near the Gustavus waterfront, the 10-acre homestead occupied by Blue Heron B&B is filled with wildflower meadows, wetlands, and an enormous organic garden, fertilized with seaweed raked from the beach of a nearby island. The rooms and cabins all have sweeping views of the surroundings, and they all come equipped with binoculars so you can spy on the animals outside. The congenial hosts—who'll loan you bikes to explore Gustavus—live in a octagonally shaped cedar home, which has a sun room on its south side where guests gather for big breakfasts of pancakes, waffles, potatoes, eggs, and fruit salad. The rooms, which have private baths, are in a separate building, above a workshop. They're best for couples. Larger parties should go for one of the cabins, which have two queen-size beds, and either a roll-away twin or a bunk bed (best for kids, but long enough to fit grown-ups). The cabins also have small kitchens, where you can save money by cooking your own meals.

TRACY ARM-FORDS TERROR WILDERNESS

As an alternative to visiting Glacier Bay, consider a cost-saving trip to **Tracy Arm-Fords Terror Wilderness** ★★; its glaciers rival Glacier Bay's in awesomeness, if not number. Closer to Juneau and considerably less expensive to get to than Glacier Bay, Tracy Arm has just two tidewater glaciers there to see, as opposed to the 16 in Glacier Bay. On the other hand, it's not nearly as well-known (although word is spreading), so the waters aren't nearly as crowded with sightseers.

Located about 40 miles southeast of Juneau, the Tracy Arm-Fords Terror Wilderness features two long, narrow fjords, Tracy Arm and Endicott Arm, which cut deeply into the Coast Mountains. Tour operators out of Juneau run daily sightseeing trips up Tracy Arm, which twists and turns for more than 30 miles, passing beneath 4,000-foot peaks and along sheer rock palisades streaked with waterfalls. Humpback whales and orcas travel into the 1,000-foot-deep arm to feed, sea lions live there year-round, mountain goats dot the mountainsides, bald eagles nest in spots along the way, and kittiwakes (cute little seabirds that look like a baby seagulls) make common appearances. At the head of the fjord are a pair of glaciers, Sawyer Glacier and South Sawyer Glacier, which are known for calving exceptionally large icebergs into the sea. Sometimes, giant icebergs calve unseen underwater, then come shooting to the surface unexpectedly, like giant, frozen submarines suddenly bursting from the blue-green waters milky with glacial silt.

The family-owned **Adventure Bound Alaska** (215 Ferry Way; ☎ 800/228-3875 or 907/463-2509; www.adventureboundalaska.com) does 8-hour tours of Tracy Arm aboard a 56-foot monohull vessel with lots of deck room. It charges $130 for adults and $90 for children 4 to 18 (the rate includes tax). If you can't get a seat on Adventure Bound's boat, call the **Juneau Tour Center** (☎ 800/820-2628 or 907/586-8687), which runs an almost identical tour, using a similar boat leased from Adventure Bound, but charging $5 more per passenger.

ADMIRALTY ISLAND

Twenty miles and a half-hour floatplane ride from Alaska's capital city is the brown bear capital of the world, Admiralty Island. This 1-million-acre island, the second largest in Southeast Alaska after Kodiak Island (and third largest in the U.S.), has an estimated 1,600 brown bears on it—the highest concentration of brown bears anywhere, and more than there are in the entire Lower 48. The Tlingit name for the island is Kootznoowoo, "fortress of the bears." It's a rugged land covered with lakes, old growth rainforest, and mountains with peaks up to 4,650 feet. Almost all of the island is protected within the Tongass National Forest's Admiralty National Monument and the Kootznoowoo Wilderness. There's only one human settlement, the Native village of Angoon. The village has about 500 people, meaning Admiralty Island's bear population outnumbers its human population by more than 3 to 1. The island also has large populations of boreal toads, Sitka black-tailed deer, and bald eagles.

Most visitors to Admiralty Island come on day trips from Juneau to see bears at the mouth of Pack Creek, a salmon stream where the bruins come to feast on the fish in the summer. Officially known as the Stan Price State Wildlife Sanctuary, the site has a bear viewing platform and a tower where visitors can get a good look at the animals without getting in their way (and from which visitors are not allowed to stray). The U.S. Forest Service tries to minimize the impact of tourists on the bears with a permit system that, between June 1 and September 10, limits the number of visitors to 24 per day—that means this is one outing you definitely want to plan ahead for. The best time to go is during the peak salmon spawning season (July 5–Aug 25). During peak season, the permits cost $50 for adults, and $25 for children 16 and under or for adults 62 and older. Permit prices drop in off season, but so do the odds of seeing bears.

The simplest way to visit Pack Creek is on a guided tour, where you don't need to worry about the permit (the tour operator takes care of it for you). The Forest Service sets aside half of the two dozen daily permits for tour companies. Only one tour company per day gets permits, so your choice of companies might be limited by the days you can go. Check the Forest Service website for the list of tour operators.

Expect to pay about $600 per person for a full-day trip to Pack Creek. **Alaska Discovery** (☎ 800/586-1911; www.akdiscovery.com) offers a full-day trip to Admiralty Island which includes the flight, a sea kayaking trip, gear, lunch, and bear viewing at Pack Creek, for $590.

If you're the hardy outdoors type and want to see Pack Creek on your own, get yourself one of the 12 daily permits the Forest Service issues to individuals. Backpackers can turn a visit to Pack Creek into an extended sea kayaking or canoeing trip around or across the island. Seymour Canal, on the east side of the island, is a popular destination for sea kayakers. It has two areas—Swan Cove and Windfall Harbor—where bears congregate and permits aren't needed to see them. The Cross-Admiralty Canoe Route crosses the island and connects Seymour Canal with Angoon. This 32-mile route consists of a series of lakes and portages, along with four U.S. Forest Service public use cabins. There are also three-sided shelters and other places to camp along the way. Boardwalks built by the Civilian Conservation Corps in the 1930s run between some of the lakes, and in one stretch there's a hand tram that you can roll your canoe along on so you don't have to carry it on your head. Contact the **Forest Service Information Center** (☎ 907/ 586-8800; www.fs.fed.us/r10/tongass) for trip planning assistance.

SKAGWAY

The biggest attraction in Skagway today is simply Skagway itself. Spared from the destructive forces of fire and urban renewal that wiped out so much of the rest of the Old West, the town's 6-block historic district is filled with original gold rush–era buildings with false fronts and boardwalks. The White Pass & Yukon Route Railroad still runs here, and you can climb aboard one of its vintage railcars for a ride into the beautiful, treacherous mountains the stampeders faced. Or if you've got 3 to 5 days for a backpacking expedition, you can walk in the footsteps of those gold-crazed fellows over the Chilkoot Trail, which is still lined in places with rusting rotting artifacts they cast off along they way.

That being said, Skagway is as touristy as it gets in Alaska. It's a major cruise-ship stop, and on busy summer days, 20,000 passengers course through the streets, keeping the cash registers singing in the T-shirt emporiums and jewelry shops that now inhabit the town's old mercantile exchanges and dentist offices. The town's year-round population is less than 900. Yet that number nearly triples in the summer when part-time residents show up to make their summer money driving historic tour buses and waiting tables.

A BRIEF HISTORY

If life were fair—or at least if it had been fair to Captain William Moore—Skagway would be called Mooresville.

Moore was a retired Canadian steamboat captain who staked a 160-acre homestead in a narrow, windy valley at the top of the Inside Passage in 1887. His homestead had a good anchorage on one side, and one of the few trails from Southeast Alaska through the mountains into Canada on the other. Moore predicted that someday somebody would find gold in the Yukon, and then his little homestead would blossom into a thriving port town. It would be called Mooresville, and its founding father would become very rich.

It didn't quite work out that way.

Someone did discover gold in the Yukon, in 1896, along a tributary of the Klondike River. The *Seattle Post Intelligencer* broke the news in the Lower 48 with the screaming headline "Gold! Gold! Gold!" and the Klondike gold rush was on. Fortune seekers came stampeding into Moore's valley, just as Moore had predicted. The problem was, they didn't stop coming. First there were hundreds, then thousands, then tens of thousands. They had no respect for Moore's claim to the land, nor the toll he attempted to collect for those using the White Pass Trail through the mountains. They didn't even call the place Mooresville, opting

Skagway's Favorite Scoundrel: Soapy Smith

During the heyday of the Klondike gold rush, Skagway was peopled by dreamers and get-rich-quick schemers yes, but also by the conmen, thieves, and other crooks who came to prey on them. At the top of the heap was a smooth-talking Texan named Soapy Smith, who led a notorious gang. Soapy and his pals used everything from fixed poker games, to rigged sweepstakes, to fake telegraph offices, in order to separate hapless stampeders from their money. Dubbed by newspapers as "the king of the frontier conmen," Smith had a long payroll, which included the police, politicians, and even the local barber. Any customer who revealed to the barber that he was carrying a lot of cash or gold left the barbershop with a nick on his ear, literally earmarked for Smith's men to prey upon.

Smith drank heavily, had a ferocious temper, and was—of course—a shameless criminal. But he had some endearing qualities too. He was generous to charities, he helped build churches, and he paid for the burial of indigent prostitutes. But public opinion in Skagway turned against Smith when his men snatched a bag of gold from a Klondike miner and ran off with it. A vigilante committee demanded that Smith return the gold, but Smith refused, insisting that the miner had lost it fair and square in a rigged game of three-card monte. When the committee held another meeting, on July 7, 1898, to discuss what to do, Smith tried to storm it with a shotgun. A gunfight broke out, and Smith and one of the vigilantes were both killed. The legend of Soapy Smith, however, is alive and well in Skagway today, and you'll hear stories about him—some may even be true—everywhere you go.

instead to use the area's Tlingit name, "Shgagwie," or "Skaguay" in their best approximation (the post office, which preferred "Skagway," had the final say).

By the fall of 1897, Skagway had grown "from a concourse of tents to a fair-size town, with well-laid-out streets and numerous framed buildings, stores, saloons, gambling houses, dance houses and a population of 20,000," according to Canada's Northwest mounted police, who were keeping close tabs on the rising human tide on Canada's doorstep. Canada didn't want thousands of ill-prepared gold seekers starving when winter came, so it required everyone entering the country to bring a year's worth of supplies with them. This slowed the stampede, as the gold-seekers had to trek back and forth across the border, hauling their ton of goods one trip at a time. This was a boon to business in Skagway and helped the town flourish.

When the stampeders finally reached the gold fields, they found almost all of the land had already been claimed before they had even left the Lower 48. There was nothing left for them. Many returned home in disgust. Others followed new gold rushes to places like Fairbanks or Nome, or went to work building the White Pass & Yukon Route Railroad connecting Dawson City to Skagway. Skagway might have faded away altogether if not for that railroad. The railroad even gave Skagway strategic importance in World War II, when it was the port for supplies arriving to build the Alcan Highway connecting Alaska with the Lower 48 through Canada.

As for Captain Moore, he settled a lawsuit with the newly incorporated town of Skagway and made a small fortune despite everything. His home is now a small museum that you can visit. See p. 243.

LAY OF THE LAND

Skagway is located in a narrow valley at the top of the Inside Passage. It's one of only two coastal communities in Southeast Alaska connected to the rest of North America by road (Haines is the other), so it's a key stop in the state ferry system, and a bustling place for all sorts of traffic in the summertime. The waterfront is taken up by a small boat harbor and several large cruise-ship docks. A small airstrip runs along one edge of town. Skagway's streets are laid out in simple grid, 15 blocks long and 4 blocks wide. Broadway is the main drag, and its first 6 blocks are so chock full of historic buildings that the National Park Service has made it part of the Klondike Gold Rush National Historical Park. While the town is flat and easy to walk, the tall ridges on either side offer aerobically challenging sub-alpine terrain to hike, and there are a couple of glaciers not far up the valley that you can get to by train.

The **Skagway Convention and Visitors Bureau Center** (245 Broadway; ☎ 907/983-2854, fax 907/983-3854; www.skagway.com), occupies the historic Arctic Brotherhood Hall, the building with the driftwood façade; it's open in summer daily from 8am to 6pm and winter Monday through Friday from 8am to 5pm. The website contains links to lodgings and activities, or you can request the same information on paper (order at ☎ 888/762-1898).

GETTING TO & AROUND SKAGWAY

By Sea

Most visitors get to Skagway by sea, either aboard cruise ships or aboard the ferries of the **Alaska Marine Highway System** (☎ 800/642-0066 or 907/983-2941; www.ferryalaska.com). The ferries connect Skagway with Juneau, Haines, and other points throughout Southeast Alaska. The fast ferry to Juneau takes 2½ hours, while the standard ferry gets there in a more leisurely 7 hours (and it's a nicer boat). Round-trip fare is $96 for adults, $48 for children. There's a boat from Juneau almost every day in the summer. **Chilkat Cruises** (☎ 888/766-2103 or 907/766-2100; www.chilkatcruises.com) makes several trips daily between Haines and Skagway, charging $30 one-way and $53 for adults round-trip. The boat stops to look at marine life and a waterfall during the 45-minute ride.

By Air

Jets can't land in the narrow valley Skagway sits in, so to get there by air, you need to go with one of three air taxi operators: **Wings of Alaska** (☎ 907/789-0790 or 907/983-2442; www.wingsofalaska.com), **LAB Flying Service** (☎ 907/789-9160; www.labflying.com), and local favorite **Skagway Air Service** (☎ 907/789-2054; www.skagwayair.com). They all charge about $200 round-trip from Juneau. Wings of Alaska offers discounts for online bookings.

By Shuttle or Car

Skagway is compact and easily walkable, with the airport and the ferry docks right in town. If you're not much of a walker, or you've got too much luggage to lug around, you can get a ride with **Dyea Dave's Shuttle & Tours** (☎ 907/983-3512), which has a bus waiting for passengers at the ferry docks and which will come get you at the airport if you call. The rides are free, under an arrangement Dave's made with the local hotels. The one local taxi service was out of business as of press time.

A rental car is a good option in Skagway—not for getting around town, but for getting out of it. The South Klondike Highway is one of the most spectacular drives in Alaska. It loosely follows the route gold-crazed stampeders took through White Pass into Canada, 14 miles from Skagway. In total the highway stretches 99 miles, from Skagway to the Alaska Highway, then another 13 miles to Whitehorse, capital of Yukon Territory. The short drive to the pass and back is worth the trip, even if you don't have a passport to get over the border (for information about crossing the border, see p. 370). The White Pass & Yukon Route Railroad makes the same trip, more or less, but it charges $199 per person round-trip. In comparison, you can rent a car for about $60 and cram as many people as you like into it. The desk for **Avis** (3rd Ave. and Spring St.; ☎ 800/230-4898 or 907/983-2247; www.avis.com) is in the lobby of the Westmark Inn. **Sourdough Car & Bicycle Rentals** (350 6th St.; ☎ 907/983-2523) has cars starting at $60 a day, and fat-seated cruiser bikes for $10 a day.

ACCOMMODATIONS & DINING

Skagway has loads of big, crowded, gold rush–themed eateries along Broadway. They're easy enough to find. The real scores are the cozy, dirt-cheap little hideaway spots, the places the locals actually patronize, and those are the ones I'll concentrate on here. One is a simple diner with big storefront windows that flood it with light called the **Sweet Tooth Café** (Broadway by corner of 3rd Ave.; ☎ 907/983-2405; daily 6am–2pm; MC, V; **$**). American comfort food is the draw here, and they whip up solid hash browns and eggs, sandwiches and chips, burgers, shakes, and sundaes all for under $10.

Skagway gets thousands of tourists each day in the summer, but most of them arrive aboard cruise ships and don't need lodging ashore. Consequently, the town has far fewer places to stay than you might expect at such a popular tourist destination. There's a big, lackluster hotel, but you're far better off staying at one of the historic or at least family-run B&Bs in town, which are far more in touch with the spirit of the place (and competitively priced, to boot).

Skagway has an 8% city bed tax, and a 4% sales tax, which apply to all of the accommodations listed here except the public use cabins.

Hotels & Bed & Breakfasts

$–$$ The cheapskate's choice in Skagway is **Sergeant Preston's Lodge** (370 6th Ave.; ☎ 866/983-2521 or 907/983-3500; http://sgtprestons.eskagway.com; AE, DISC, MC, V). I found myself drawn to its neat, tidy grounds: The U.S., Canadian, and Alaskan flags fly side by side out front, and simple gray buildings with green roofs are arranged in a horseshoe around a miniature parade field of a lawn. It's

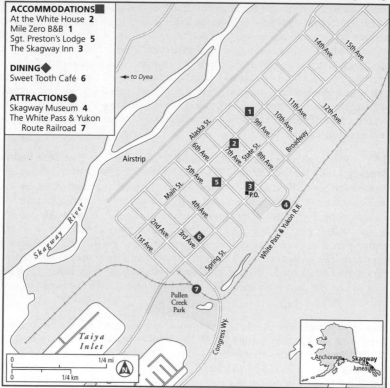

ACCOMMODATIONS ■
At the White House **2**
Mile Zero B&B **1**
Sgt. Preston's Lodge **5**
The Skagway Inn **3**

DINING ◆
Sweet Tooth Café **6**

ATTRACTIONS ●
Skagway Museum **4**
The White Pass & Yukon
    Route Railroad **7**

← to Dyea

14th Ave.
15th Ave.
11th Ave.
12th Ave.
10th Ave.
9th Ave.
Broadway
Alaska St.
6th Ave.
7th Ave.
State St.
8th Ave.
Airstrip
5th Ave.
Main St.
4th Ave.
P.O.
White Pass & Yukon R.R.
Skagway River
2nd Ave.
3rd Ave.
1st Ave.
Spring St.
Pullen
Creek
Park
Congress Wy.
Taiya
Inlet

0   1/4 mi
0   1/4 km

Anchorage Skagway
Juneau

all a little like you've happened upon an outpost of the Royal Canadian Mounties. Actually, the place was influenced by a radio show from the 1930s and 1940s called "Sergeant Preston of the Yukon," about the crime-fighting adventures of a Mountie and his loyal sled dog. The rooms aren't fancy, but they're affordable, they all have private baths, and they're just a block from Broadway, the main drag. The smallest rooms—which are just large enough to turn around in—go for $90, double occupancy. They step up in size and price to $105 and then $115. In addition there are a few one-bedroom apartments (where you can save money by cooking your own meals) for $150. Historical footnote: Although Mounties were never stationed here, the oldest building on-site was a barracks for U.S. Army officers during World War II.

$$–$$$$ Occupying a comfortably settled old building that—like so many places in Alaska—started out as a brothel, **The Skagway Inn** ★★ (655 Broadway; ☎ 888/752-4929 or 907/983-2289; www.skagwayinn.com; AE, DISC, MC, V) is filled with period furnishings, lacy curtains, and luxuriously fat mattresses with puffy comforters that give guests a sense of Victorian languor. Each of the 10 rooms is different, and each has a name—Hattie, Dottie, Birdie, and so on—that's somehow supposed to evoke the spirit of the women who plied their trade there. Rooms with shared baths go for $119, and those with half baths go for $149. The rooms with full baths go for $189, and come with a pair of robes on hangers that seem to be waiting expectantly to see which of you will wear the silky one and which will wear the cotton. Downstairs, a big breakfast (included with the room) is served at Olivia's, a hideaway restaurant with a tapas menu at night. Outside, the yard has a big, raised-bed produce garden, with gravel paths to stroll and a cozy nook where you can sit on sunny days and muse on how perfectly respectable the neighborhood, once Skagway's rollicking red light district, has become. Internet specials sometimes knock $20 off the price of a room, so check online before calling.

$$$ Or how about a newly built, hotel-B&B hybrid? The **Mile Zero Bed and Breakfast** (901 Main St.; ☎ 907/983-3045; www.mile-zero.com; MC, V) has some elements of both. What makes it hotel-like are the modern, roomy, business-class ambience rooms, with sound-proofed walls and private entrances. In true hotel fashion, some even have TVs mounted high in the corner. What makes it a B&B is that, well, it sort of is one. There are just seven rooms, a homey common area, and owners who live on-site and set out fresh fruit and muffins in the kitchen for breakfast. The rooms, which all have two queens and sleep up to four, have private baths and go for $135 double occupancy during the high season. The Mile Zero sits on the corner of a quiet, nicely kept neighborhood a few blocks from the historic district.

$$–$$$ If Mile Zero is too schizophrenic for your tastes, then turn to a B&B with some solid history behind it: **At the White House** ★★★ (475 8th Ave.; ☎ 907/983-9000; www.atthewhitehouse.com; MC, V). This lovely old place was built as a home in 1902 by a successful Skagway gambler and saloon owner. The miniature Doric columns over a pair of porticoes out front are vaguely reminiscent of the actual White House (hence the name), and the original woodwork in the elegant entryway and dining room (where continental breakfasts are served) give guests a sense of turn-of-the-20th-century showiness. The rooms, which are all upstairs along either side of a long hallway, were all built recently after a fire destroyed the top part of the inn. They're got plush beds with handmade quilts, ceiling fans, and screened windows (for the odd hot day). They vary in size and range in price from $125 to $150 for double occupancy during the high season, with substantial off-season winter discounts.

$$$–$$$$ To spend the night away from the hustle and bustle of summertime Skagway (or if you're a backpacker coming or going along the Chilkoot Trail), give a thought to the **Chilkoot Trail Outpost** ★ (Mile 8.5 Dyea Rd.; ☎ 907/983-3799; www.chilkoottrailoutpost.com; MC, V). Located along the scenic road to Dyea, near the start of the route to the Klondike that most stampeders preferred, Chilkoot Trail Outpost has cabins that are rustic on the outside but surprisingly modern, lovely, and well-finished inside. Small touches like log porch swings and prominent ridgepoles carved with Tlingit animal designs supporting their roofs are a big part of the appeal. Most rooms have either an open floor plan with two queen beds, or one bedroom with a queen or pair of twins and a living room with a futon couch that folds out into a double bed. They go for $165, double occupancy. If you've got a sleeping bag and don't mind sleeping in a bunk bed with no

A Glacier Cabin or a Little Red Caboose, for $35 a Night

As I've said before in this chapter, the public use cabins of the U.S. Forest Service represent the best lodging values in the state—if you come prepared. Visitors must bring their own bedding, cooking supplies, and other essentials (see p. 373 for more on these cabins). And interestingly, sometimes these cabins aren't even, well, cabins. In the Skagway area, intrepid travelers can bunk in a retired White Pass & Yukon Route Railroad caboose, called the **Denver Caboose.** It sleeps up to six (with four single bunks and one double) and is located nearby but not on the railroad tracks (thankfully) at the head of the trail to the Denver Glacier, which is about 3 miles away. It's a bit of a tight squeeze inside, but, with its oil stove for cooking and warmth (you bring the fuel), it's cozy enough. And the views of the mountains and the Skagway River are world-class. Another option in the vicinity is **Laughton Glacier Cabin,** which lets you sleep near the lip of an actual glacier. The cabins sit along a trail that leads to the spot where the glacier meets Skagway River, about a mile away (it's about 15 miles from Skagway). It's teeny tiny (13 ft. by 14 ft.), but if you're part of a friendly group, you can sleep up to six here (in two single-person plywood bunks and a pair of two-person bunks).

Both cabins use oil stoves for heat, have outhouses, and depend on nearby streams for water. The only means of transportation to either of them is via the **White Pass & Yukon Route Railroad** (☎ 800/343-7373; www.wpyr.com), which offers daily flag-stop service in the summer. Round-trip fare is $30 to the Denver Glacier trailhead, and $60 to the Laughton Glacier trailhead. (If you're not staying in the cabins, you can spend about 4 hours hiking to the glaciers and back before the train comes by again to pick you up.)

linens, there are hikers' duplexes, which have private baths, for $135. In the evening, guests gather around the fire pit, near a little waterfall, and make s'mores with ingredients supplied by the hosts. A buffet breakfast is served in the log dining hall, which is like a little cafe, and you're free to use the screened-in cookhouse to prepare other meals if you like.

Camping

A primitive **National Park Service Dyea Campground** has 22 well-separated sites near the water at the ghost town 9 miles from Skagway. The campground has pit toilets and no water. RVs over 27 feet are not allowed. The fee is $6. The **Pullen Creek RV Park** (☎ 800/936-3731 or 907/983-2768) is near the small-boat harbor, with coin-operated showers. RV sites with power, water, and dump station use are $30; car camping sites are $20; tenting with no vehicle is $14.

WHY YOU'RE HERE: THE TOP SIGHTS & ATTRACTIONS

The Klondike gold rush gets all the attention, but Skagway's history has far more layers than that, and you'll get a good sample by visiting the **Skagway Museum** ★ (7th and Spring sts.; ☎ 907/983-2420; $2 adults, children 12 and under free; Mon–Fri 9am–5pm, Sat 10am–5pm, Sun 10am–4pm). The collection spans the ages with artifacts including: a long, dark woolly mammoth tusk; a Tlingit war canoe; a gold rush–era slot machine and roulette wheel; an amazing patchwork feather quilt, made by missionary women from duck skins and lined with peppercorns to discourage moths; Victorian-era women's lace blouses and cinch-waist wool jackets (man, they cinched their waists in tight!); and World War II–era canteens, helmets,

---

A Train Ride into the Mountains and Back in Time

Keep your fingers crossed for good weather when you're in Skagway so you can properly enjoy a ride in one of the vintage railcars of the **White Pass & Yukon Route Railroad** ★★★ (☎ 800/343-7373; www.wpyr.com). The historic, narrow gauge train climbs high into the mountains, across high trestles and bridges, through tunnels, along steep cliffs, past waterfalls, glaciers, and historic sites such as Dead Horse Gulch, where you can still see the bleached bones of pack animals worked to death by the gold-crazed stampeders.

Under clear skies, a ride aboard the White Pass & Yukon Route Railroad will be a highlight of your visit to Skagway. (In foul weather, it will be an expensive trip into the clouds.) Seats usually book up in advance though, so take a chance and make reservations as early as you can. If the mountains are socked in on the day of your trip, you can change your reservation with no charge. If you cancel, there's a 10% penalty.

There are various trip options. The quickest and cheapest—and the only one you can do if you haven't got a passport—is the trip up to 2,685-foot White Pass, where the Alaska-Canada border is. The 3-hour, 40-mile round-trip costs $95 (all fares are half price for children ages 3–12). It leaves daily.

With your passport, you can easily go on one of the two trips into Canada. The most popular is the trip to Lake Bennett, 20 miles past the border (Fri, Sat, and Sun departures only). There's a 2-hour layover at the lake for a walking tour of the area and a look at the artifacts on display in a 1903 train station. Lake Bennett is at the end of the Chilkoot Trail, and backpackers who hike up the trail usually hop the train here and ride back down to Skagway. If you're a serious train buff, do the Lake Bennett trip on Friday, when a vintage steam engine is used, rather than the modern diesel engine used the rest of the time. The Friday fare is $180. If you could care less what kind of engine is used, go on the weekend, when the fare is $150. On Wednesday, there's a shorter trip into Canada, which turns around at Fraser, 6 miles over the border. Travelers heading for Whitehorse hop off in Fraser and take the bus from there. Round-trip from Skagway to Fraser is $125.

and bayonets. You'll also find hands-on exhibits like whale baleen to feel, stereo-scopes with historic scenes to peer at, and wildlife skeletons to handle. The museum shares space with Skagway's city hall, in a handsome old school that was the first stone building in town.

Tours

In a town so fully focused on separating tourists from their money, it's a pleasant surprise to learn that one of the most worthwhile things you can do in Skagway costs absolutely nothing. I'm referring to the **free historic walking tours** led by National Park Service rangers around Skagway's historic downtown. The Park Service has restored 17 buildings downtown (and is slowly adding more) as part of the Klondike Gold Rush National Historical Park. The free tours around this area, which last 45 minutes, leave from the park's Visitor Center at the corner of 2nd and Broadway. They're limited to 30 people, and they fill up fast. So stop by the Visitor Center and get your tickets early in the day.

Don't feel like walking? The **Skagway Streetcar Company** ✦ (270 2nd Ave.; ☎ 907/983-2908; www.skagwaystreetcar.com) hires witty and theatrical drivers for its faux-classic tour buses, puts them in period costumes, and sends them off to lead humorous and historical tours of town. The tours are loosely based on the tour given to President Warren G. Harding when he passed through in 1923. Of all the commercial tours in Skagway, this one is by far the best (and most fun). Reservations are a good idea. They cost $42 per adult, and $21 for those 12 and under. Tours take 2 hours and leave roughly every 2 hours from 8:30am to 3:30pm.

There is, of course, far too much history in Skagway's 6-block historic district to squeeze into a 45-minute tour. If the ranger-led walk leaves you thirsting for more, I've got your back. With another 45 minutes and the guidebook you hold in your hands, you've got everything you need to embark upon a . . .

Walking Tour: Historic Skagway

Start: Park Visitor Center, 2nd Avenue and Broadway.

Finish: In the vicinity of Broadway and 7th, in the town's former red light district.

Time: 45 minutes if you breeze by the museums, longer if you linger.

Best Times: Whenever it's not raining.

❶ White Pass and Yukon Railroad Depot & Administration Building

Take a close look at the depot building. Pretty plain, huh? It actually has no architectural ornamentation, because it was built in the frenzy of the gold boom, using recycled lumber, old packing crates, and whatever other materials the carpenters could get their hands on. The administration building right beside it has more of the standard ornamentation because it was built a little later and under less frenzied circumstances. Both buildings are now used by the National Park Service as the Klondike Gold Rush National Historical Park Visitor Center.

Quickly stroll the small, free museum here for a crash course on the Klondike gold rush. A relief map provides a scale model of the mountains and two routes through them that the stampeders had to choose from. Canadian Mounties didn't try to stop the onslaught of Americans entering their country along these trails, but they did require the travelers to bring a ton of supplies so they wouldn't starve in the winter. It took multiple trips for a stampeder to haul an overload of supplies across the border on his back. One exhibit illustrates what a ton of supplies looked like; you'll understand how a stampeder—going back and forth, carrying one crate at time—might have hiked 1,000 miles to complete the 33-mile Chilkoot Trail.

Cross Broadway on 2nd Avenue and head for the second building on the left, which is:

② Soapy Smith's Parlor

This simple shedlike structure is where Soapy Smith, Skagway's favorite conman, ran one of his creative scams: the telegraph to nowhere. Stampeders fresh off the boat, who didn't realize that Skagway had no telegraph service, would pay Soapy's morse-code operator to wire messages home. Home would soon reply "Family emergency, send money." Thus one victim would be twice fleeced.

Across the street, on the corner of 2nd and Broadway, is:

③ The Red Onion Saloon & Brothel

When the White Pass & Yukon Route Railroad was built, the tracks were laid right down the middle of Broadway. The owners of businesses along Main Street, the town's original commercial strip, suddenly wanted to be on Broadway, too. So they slipped log rollers under their buildings and hauled them over a block to where the action was. Somehow, when a popular saloon and brothel called the Red Onion was moved, it wound up with its back end facing Broadway. Instead of spinning the whole thing around, the movers sawed off the front and back of the building and swapped them. Look down when you enter the Red Onion and you can still see the cut line in the floor. Business is still going strong at the **Red Onion Saloon** (p. 246) where corseted waitresses with heaving breasts serve burgers and tall beers to mobs of tourists. For $5 you can go on the **15-minute brothel tour** (scheduled throughout the day) ✪✪ and see the layers of water-stained, peeling wallpaper that once decorated the cubicles of the working girls. Check out the small collection of turn-of-the-20th-century sex toys that were found hidden beneath the floorboards.

Two doors north on Broadway (away from the water) is a building covered with driftwood, known as:

④ Arctic Brotherhood Hall

More than 8,000 pieces of driftwood adorn the unusual facade of this building, an exquisite example of architecture in the Victorian Rustic style. The building, built in 1899, was originally the clubhouse of the Arctic Brotherhood, a secretive fraternal order dedicated largely to drinking. Look closely at the driftwood and you'll see the organization's initials, as well as its symbol, a gold pan and nuggets. The City of Skagway Visitor Information Center has taken up residence in the building hall these days. If you ask to see the meeting hall, they might let you peek in back at the grand room where the Arctic Brothers did whatever it was the mysterious, alcohol-based fraternal orders did in those days.

Cross Broadway at 3rd Avenue, and drop by:

⑤ The Mascot Saloon

During the gold rush, saloons in Skagway were like visitor information centers. They're where you went to find out what was going on, what trail conditions were like, and where you might get a good price on 100 pounds of beans. Skagway had some 80 saloons in its heyday, and the Mascot was one. Most of the buildings along Broadway have false fronts, but the Mascot, with its simple gable roof, is an oddball. It's one of the gold rush buildings that was restored by the National Park Service. Without the benefit of photos, park service historians recreated the interior of the Mascot as best they could, guided by old newspaper accounts, oral history, and wallpaper remnants. After they finished, a photo of the saloon turned up, and—to the restorationists' delight—the re-created Mascot Saloon matched the original pretty closely, from the wallpapering to the taxidermied blond raccoon (the Mascot's mascot) standing atop the cigar counter.

One block away, on the southwest corner of Broadway and 4th Avenue, is:

⑥ The Pack Train Building

This is kinda the tallest historic building in Skagway. Look at the building from the rear and you'll see what I mean by "kind of." The third floor is actually an elaborate false front, a common architectural pretension that gives a building a stronger presence on the street than it really deserves. The Pack Train Building's real upstairs—the second floor—originally had hotel rooms on it. On the ground floor there was a saloon called The Trail, which was run by the mayor and his partner. The message built into the facade on the 4th Avenue side of the building—"U-AU-TO-NO-THE-TRAIL"—is a standing, phonetic advertisement for a long-gone saloon.

Go up Broadway to 5th Avenue, turn right and go to a little shack known as:

⑦ The Goldberg Cigar Store

This nicely restored little hut represents the type of simple, unambitious shacks that started replacing the canvas tents that first went up in Skagway. Nobody knew then that Skagway would get a railroad, and that, therefore, the town would last. So the architecture was very simple. A cigar seller named Goldberg owned this one, running his business in the front and living in the back.

Right behind the Goldberg Cigar Store you'll find:

⑧ The Ice House

The building's thick, heavily insulated walls and the tracks on its ceiling tipped off historic preservationists that this barnlike structure was once used to store ice, an important commodity in a town with 80 saloons. It's a restoration work in progress.

Next door to the Ice House is:

⑨ The Moore Cabin

This is the simple cabin where Captain William Moore, whose homestead was overrun by the gold hungry stampeders, lived. For more on Moore, go to p. 233.

Next door to the Moore Cabin is:

⑩ The James Bernard Moore House

Moore's son, Ben, lived here. It's furnished in a combination of Native, frontier, and Victorian styles, and if it's open you can go inside for a look around.

Head up Broadway to the corner of 7th Avenue. You're now in the old:

⑪ Red Light District

In the beginning, all of Skagway was a red light district. But as the town grew up and matured, it realized that to be a proper town it needed a properly defined red light district. So this became the neighborhood where Houses of Negotiable Affection, as they were sometimes called, were concentrated. It's not the least bit seedy anymore. The two former brothels that are still there now have new, respectable identities. One is the Historic Skagway Inn, at the corner of Broadway and 7th Avenue, and reviewed earlier. The other, a red Victorian house with a white picket fence at the corner of 7th and 8th avenues, is a private residence (look from the sidewalk, but don't go knocking).

ACTIVE SKAGWAY

Yes, it takes 3 to 5 days to backpack in the footsteps of the Native traders and gold-crazed stampeders who once made the **Chilkoot Trail** ★★★ almost as crowded as a NY subway at rush hour. But it's worth it. Literally tens of thousands of stampeders trudged it back and forth, while hauling the year's worth of supplies the Canadian Mounties required them to have so they didn't starve in Canada. And long before the gold seekers took to the Chilkoot Trail, Tlingit Indians used it as a trade route to do business with the Athabascans of the Interior. The Tlingit carried fish, seal oil, and seaweeds up the trail, and brought back caribou hides, moose meat, and plants not found near the sea. Today the trail is sort of an outdoor museum, where snowy winters and the National Park Service have helped to preserve all sorts of possessions the overburdened stampeders cast off along the way, including cans, boots, boats, even a pot-bellied stove.

The 33-mile trail begins at Dyea (p. 246), a 15-minute drive from Skagway. It ends at Lake Bennett, in British Columbia, where the stampeders built or bought boats to complete the long trip to the Yukon gold fields. The trail starts out muddy and thick with mosquitoes, then climbs into alpine terrain with spectacular views. The most difficult section is near the top, a steep final climb dubbed The Golden Stairs, where prospectors hacked a staircase into the ice (it's a scramble among the boulders in the summer). Most backpackers hike up the trail (which is actually easier on your knees than hiking down it), then hop the White Pass & Yukon Route Railroad (p. 239) for a ride back to Skagway ($90 one-way).

You need to do a lot of planning before tackling the Chilkoot Trail. You also need a permit and, since you're crossing an international border, your passport (as of early 2008; check with the State Department for final dates). The trail is jointly managed by the National Parks Service and its Canadian equivalent, Parks Canada, which limit the number of users to 50 per day. Permits cost $50. Make reservations through the **National Park Service Trail Center** (in Skagway at 2nd St. and Broadway; ☎ 907/983-9234; www.nps.gov/klgo), or through Parks Canada Reservations (☎ 800/661-0486; www.wpry.com).

A trek through Skagway's historic gold rush cemetery and on to a pretty waterfall is the choice for those in search of a less challenging hike. It too is full of gold rush sights. Dominating the cemetery is a monument to Frank Reid, the local hero who died in a shootout with infamous conman Soapy Smith. A humble wooden marker 3 feet outside the cemetery marks Smith's grave, who also died in the shootout. A short forest trail behind the cemetery leads to the Lower Reid

Falls. To get to the cemetery, head up Main Street until it crosses 23rd Avenue, then follow the gravel road over the train tracks to the graveyard. It's a 2-hour walk from downtown to the cemetery and back, or a short drive.

ATTENTION, SHOPPERS!

Skagway's entire 6-block historic district is loaded with shopping. Purveyors of mass-tourism junk dominate the scene, but there are a few gems in the mix.

Skagway has nearly 30 jewelry stores catering to cruise-ship passengers, who apparently buy a lot of jewelry. Most of these shops are identical to the ones you'll find at cruise-ship ports in Hawaii and the Caribbean. There are, however, a few locally owned jewelers that are worth a stop, most notably a tiny shop in an old candy store called **Taiya River Jewelry** (252 Broadway; ☎ 800/943-2637 or 907/983-2637). It hasn't got $89,000 South African diamond chokers on display, like its foreign owned competitors might, but it does have pendants made with real gold nuggets found by placer miners in the Yukon. A tiny one costs about $40, while one with a seriously chunky nugget costs about $200. Also on sale are forget-me-not charms, with "Made in Skagway" etched on the back.

Skaguay News Depot & Books ✦ (264 Broadway; ☎ 907/983-3354) takes its history so seriously, it spells Skagway the old-fashioned way. Its selection of Alaskan history titles is small but solid, with an emphasis on the gold rush. You won't find any daily newspapers on sale, but for $2 you can pick up a reprint of the front page of the edition of the *Skaguay News* detailing the shooting of Soapy Smith.

Foodie shopping alert! **Dejon Delights** ✦✦✦ (5th and Broadway; ☎ 907/983-2083) is a must-visit. It produces some of the best smoked seafood I, for one, have found in Alaska. If that sounds like hyperbole, sample the smoke eye cured in a mixture of brine and Alaskan-made stout or taste the lox cured with brine and dark rum for proof. Even the tried and true smoked Alaskan salmon and halibut are first rate. Smoked fish runs from $7 to $9.95 per pound, and it comes from 15 miles away, in Haines.

Ignore the yarn, fabrics, and "needle-arts" at **The Rushin' Tailor's Quilt Alaska** (371 3rd St.; ☎ 800/981-5432; www.changingthreads.com) and head for the shelves filled with Russian nesting dolls. These are the real deal, made and hand-painted in Russia. You'll find them all over Southeast Alaska, but because of the large selection, this is the best place in Skagway to pick them up. A little Eskimo holding a fish, inside of a bigger Eskimo holding a fish, inside of an even bigger Eskimo holding a fish, costs $16. You can keep adding Eskimos with fish all the way up to $80.

Thailand has no historic connection to Alaska, but I love Skagway's Thai import store, **Maya's Curios** (5th Ave. between Broadway and Spring St.; ☎ 907/983-3970), anyway. The owner, a Thai import herself, has filled the tiny space with a rich variety of textiles, carved wood, and handicrafts—all reasonably priced. Thai silk scarves go for $15 to $25. A lovely candleholder carved from mango wood goes for $4.25. A waist-high mango wood vase carved like a honey dipper will be about $70. The shack the store occupies was one of the first permanent structures built in Skagway, when it was in the transition phase between muddy tent camp and enduring community.

NIGHTLIFE IN SKAGWAY

Though **The Red Onion Saloon** (corner of Broadway and 2nd Ave.; ☎ 907/983-3181; www.redonion1898.com) is packed to the gills with cruise-ship passengers by day, the crowd thins out at night, when the ships depart. It's still got bartenders in white cotton shirts and suspenders, and barmaids with cinched corsets, but it turns into a locals bar after dusk. The Tuesday open-mic night sometimes draws some real talent. A DJ throws down the beats on Thursdays, and traveling blue grass, rock, and country bands sometimes jam on other nights of the week.

Skagway lore has it that the homegrown stage show called **"Days of 98"** (6th and Broadway; ☎ 907/983-2545; matinees $14, evening $16, half price for

---

The Ghost Town that Rivaled Skagway

Nine miles north of Skagway is **Dyea** ★★★, a ghost of a ghost town, which has done as good a job at vanishing as Skagway has done at sticking around. If you have a thing for American history, or for places that seem to just shout out "Carpe Diem!" by reminding us of the impermanence of civilization (and the fleeting nature of life itself), Dyea is well worth a visit. Once upon a time, it was a thriving community of 10,000 on the plains of the Taiya River, crowded with outfitting stores, restaurants, hotels, saloons, tent cabins, and everything else a gold rush boomtown needed. It competed with Skagway for dominance, and it had the upper hand awhile. Its harbor wasn't as good as Skagway's, but it sat at the head of the Chilkoot Trail, the preferred route to the Klondike. Then Skagway got the railroad, and overnight the Chilkoot Trail and Dyea became obsolete. By 1903 its population had dwindled to three, and dairy cows roamed where stampeders once congregated. A forest has grown up where the town and the cows once were, and now there are just a few faint traces of the boomtown left. Wharf pilings come out at low tide. You can see some rusting junk and find the rotting timbers of a boat in the brush, if you know where to look. The most obvious evidence of Dyea's existence is a single, weathered false front, which has been propped up and preserved. It was part of a real estate office, of all things. When you find it, look closely in the forest around you and you'll see a row of evenly spaced and aged trees that were planted more than a century ago along the edge of a long-gone street.

On the road to the town site is a graveyard known as Slide Cemetery. Forty-nine or more people who were killed along the Chilkoot Trail in an 1898 avalanche are buried here. Some were found frozen in running positions.

The Dyea town site is part of the Klondike Gold Rush National Historical Park, and park rangers lead free walking tours each day during the summer. Tours are held at 2pm, with additional tours at 10am on Friday, Saturday, and Sunday. If you don't have a car, you can ride out to Dyea on a rental bike (p. 236), or you can arrange a lift with Dyea Dave's Shuttle & Tours (☎ 907/983-3512; p. 236).

children 15 and under) has been in production since the 1930s, when it was first performed as a fundraiser for the local hockey team. The rise and fall of the town's esteemed conman kingpin, Soapy Smith, is recounted with cancan girls, ragtime piano, actors from around the country, and all the conventions of melodrama. It's mildly bawdy, but no worse than what kids see on TV all the time. Performances are scheduled throughout the day, and times change with the cruise-ship schedules. Matinees are cheapest, but evening performances include a round of mock gambling, using Soapy Dollars and a vintage Skagway roulette wheel. The venue, which is the meeting hall of the local Fraternal Order of Eagles, was built using walls salvaged from the old Mondimen Hotel, where Soapy used to live.

GET OUT OF TOWN

Some visitors break up their stay in Skagway with a day trip to Juneau aboard a 65-foot motor catamaran run by **Alaska Fjordlines** (☎ 800/320-0146 or 907/766-3395; www.alaskafjordlines.com). As they say, it's not so much the destination as the journey, and you'll certainly get an abundance of wildlife viewing along the way, including a stop at a Steller sea lion rookery, a bus tour of Juneau's highlights, with a 1-hour stop at Mendenhall Glacier, and 3 hours of free time downtown. The total outing is about 12 hours and costs $149 for adults and $119 for children 3 to 12.

Skagway's even closer to Haines, and **Chilkat Cruises** (142 Beach Rd.; ☎ 888/766-2103 or 907/766-2100; www.chilkatcruises.com) makes the 45-minute-or-so trip back and forth all day long. You can leave Skagway anytime before noon and have plenty of time to sightsee before the last boat back at 5pm. A round-trip ticket is $53 for adults, and $27 for children 12 and under.

HAINES

Every town in Southeast Alaska is blessed with beautiful surroundings, but Haines's really stands out. The jagged mountain peaks around Haines are taller, snowier, and more numerous than those around other communities in the region. And because Haines is one of the sunniest towns in the Panhandle—it gets half as much rain as Juneau and a third as much as Ketchikan—the odds are good that you'll actually get to *see* the spectacular natural surroundings.

It's hard to lay eyes on the landscape here without also feeling drawn to explore it, and you'll have many opportunities to do so. Hiking trails start right from town, including one that climbs to a dizzying 3,650-foot peak. In the winter, snowboarders and skiers ride in helicopters to impossibly steep peaks and shoot back to earth so quickly that they're practically free falling.

The sunny weather and thermal springs beneath Haines's Chilkat River mean a late freeze, and consequently, a late salmon run. Bald eagles from all over the Pacific Northwest are well aware of this fact, and they gather just outside of Haines in the fall for an end-of-season-salmon-feed blowout. It's the largest gathering of bald eagles in the world. Quite a few eagles hang around all summer long. A good way to see them is from aboard a rubber raft, floating down the lazy Chilkat River. Eagles perched in the cottonwoods along the banks stare back as you drift by.

Large cruise ships do not go to Haines, which has helped this community of 1,715 preserve its tranquil, slightly oddball character. Lately Haines has been gaining a reputation as the quintessential small American town, thanks (or no thanks, some locals would say) to the attention it keeps getting from national magazines. *Outside* magazine has singled Haines out twice, once naming it a "dreamtown," and another time calling it one of the most desirable "Towns to Live In If You Don't Have to Make a Living." The town's obituary writer, Heather Lende, has deepened that idyllic image in her popular book, *If You Lived Here, I'd Know Your Name: News from Small-Town Alaska*. While it's true that everybody knows everybody and nobody locks their doors in Haines, it's not unlike most of the rest of Southeast Alaska in that respect. The big difference? It's sunnier.

A BRIEF HISTORY

Haines originated as a summer fishing camp for the Tlingit village of Klukwan, 20 miles up the Chilkat River. The camp was called Die Shu, meaning "end of the trail," as it sat at the end of the ancient trade route through the Chilkat Pass that linked the coast with the Interior. Klukwan is still there, Westernized and ramshackle, but ensuring that Haines remains grounded in its Tlingit past, and supplying it with totemic art, Native crafts, and dancers who perform at the Old Tribal House.

Missionaries arrived in Die Shu in 1879 and started a school and a mission. They named their settlement after the secretary of the Presbyterian Women's Executive Society of Home Missions, Francina Haines, who had raised the money for the endeavor. With the Klondike gold rush, the ancient Tlingit trade route became a freight trail, and Haines grew into a mining supply town. The Haines Highway, one of just two roads linking Southeast Alaska to the rest of the world, traces much of the original trail through the mountains.

The gold rush heated up a border dispute between the U.S. and Canada, which led the U.S. to build a military base in Haines. If Haines is in Canada, the reasoning went, why's there a U.S. Army fort here? Until World War II, Fort Seward was the only permanent U.S. military base in Alaska. During the war it was a training camp and recreation area. The bars and brothels in town were all many of the troops needed on their break from the war. After the war the fort was decommissioned, and its buildings turned into private homes and businesses, including some of Haines's most appealing lodging. Today you'll find a quiet town that has cleaned up its act, and that survives largely on fishing and tourism.

LAY OF THE LAND

Haines sits on the east side of narrow, heavily wooded Chilkat Peninsula, on the edge of Portage Cove, at the tip top of Inside Passage. The glacier-filled St. Elias Mountains and the misty Coastal Mountains converge all around. The St. Elias range creates a rain shadow that spares Haines from the Gulf of Alaska's storminess.

The town has two distinct parts, divided by the Haines Highway. To the north is the little downtown and the small boat harbor. To the south is the old Army post, Fort Seward, where stately officers' homes (some of them open to travelers) are built around a large parade ground.

Haines is one of only two coastal communities in Southeast Alaska connected to the rest of North America by road, which makes it a key stop for the state ferry. Skagway is the other community with a road. Haines is 15 miles away from Skagway by boat, or 359 miles away by car.

Drop by the **Haines Convention and Visitors Bureau** (122 2nd Ave.; ☎ 907/766-2234; www.haines.ak.us), located near the small boat harbor, to collect brochures and get oriented. It's open summer Monday through Friday from 8am to 7pm, Saturday and Sunday from 9am to 6pm; in winter, hours are Monday through Friday from 8am to 5pm.

GETTING TO & AROUND HAINES

By car, it's a 760-mile drive to Haines from Anchorage and a 644-mile drive from Fairbanks, with two Canadian-American border crossings (see p. 370 for information on border crossings). The last leg of the drive to Haines is the 155-mile Haines Highway, which connects Haines with the Alaska Highway. It's a spectacular drive that descends from Chilkat Pass at 3,510 feet to sea level, running along the Chilkat River for a while.

Most tourists get to Haines aboard the ferries of the **Alaska Marine Highway System** (☎ 800/642-0066 or 907/766-2111; www.ferryalaska.com). The cruise up the Lynn Canal is one of the highlights of the beautiful Inside Passage. It takes about 4½ hours to get to Haines from Juneau aboard the slow ferry, and about 2¼ hours aboard the faster boats. The fare is $37 for adults, and $19 for children. The state ferries also connect Haines and Skagway, but they don't run nearly as often as the boats of **Chilkat Cruises** (142 Beach Rd.; ☎ 888/766-2103 or 907/766-2100; www.chilkatcruises.com) which make several trips back and forth each day in the summer, charging $25 one-way and $45 round-trip.

The state ferry dock is a few miles from town. There's no public transportation, and the one cab company that was in business when I was last there was charging a scandalous $20 for the short trip into town. Most hotels and B&Bs, and all of the car rental places, will pick you up at the ferry terminal. So skip the cab and make arrangements with one of them. Don't rent a car to get around town—it's easy enough to walk everywhere. Rent one only if you want to explore the surrounding attractions, such as the Chilkat Bald Eagle Preserve, on your own rather than in a tour group. You'll miss the narratives that way, but you'll save money and you'll have more freedom. **Eagle's Nest Car Rental** (☎ 800/354-6009 or 907/766-2891) has the best rates on rental cars, at $45 per day (plus 9.5% tax). The **Captain's Choice Motel** (☎ 800/478-2345 or 907/766-3111), and **Hotel Hälsingland** (☎ 800/542-6363 or 907/766-2009) also rent vehicles.

Two air taxis fly between Juneau and Haines, charging about $200 for a round-trip flight. **Wings of Alaska** (☎ 907/789-0790; www.wingsofalaska.com) offers a discount if you book online. **LAB Flying Service** (☎ 907/789-9160; www.labflying.com) is the other.

ACCOMMODATIONS, BOTH STANDARD & NOT

On the whole, accommodations are less expensive in Haines than in other parts of Southeast Alaska, with steep off-season discounts (though that's the norm everywhere). And as in other, larger cities, you'll find everything from homestay B&Bs to short term apartments to standard hotels where you can lay your head.

I've picked what I consider to be the two best value choices downtown, which are closer to most of the restaurants and museums, and four alternatives at Fort Seward, which are both more picturesque and closer to the ferry dock to Skagway.

You'll need to add a 5.5% sales tax and 4% bed tax to rates I've listed below.

Take a Day Trip to Skagway

If you plan to visit both Haines and Skagway, consider staying in Haines—the cheaper and quieter town—and making Skagway a day trip (a day in Skagway is enough for most people).

From Haines, it's a 45-minute hop to Skagway with **Chilkat Cruises** (142 Beach Rd.; ☎ 888/766-2103 or 907/766-2100; www.chilkatcruises. com). You can leave Haines anytime before noon and have plenty of time to sightsee in Skagway before the last boat back departs at 5pm. A round-trip ticket is $53 for adults and $27 for children 12 and under. Chilkat Cruises also has package deals with the White Pass Railroad (p. 239) that will save you a few bucks on its spectacular train ride into the mountains.

Downtown

$$ Among Haines's handful of local motels, **Captain's Choice Motel** kids (108 2nd St.; ☎ 800/478-2345 or 907/766-3111; www.capchoice.com; AE, MC, V) is my first choice. It's got a central location and a pleasant seaside vibe. The nautically themed rooms have ship's lanterns, lots of honey colored pine, and blue carpeting that climbs the wall like wainscoting. If it's available, get room no. 26. It's an end unit with a private deck, and it's got the best view in the hotel. If you can't snag 26, simply ask for a room with a view; they're the same price as those without ($117 for double occupancy). This is also a good place for families, thanks to oversize digs that go for just $132 (sleeping four).

$–$$ After Skagway's infamous conman Soapy Smith died in a shootout, his gang of thugs and bad men scattered. One of them, Tim Vogel, landed in Haines, where he established himself as a respectable businessman and built himself a home. Although Vogel was, in the vernacular of the day, a bit of a dandy (a fastidious dresser who strutted around town twirling his golden-headed cane like Charlie Chaplin), the simple farmhouse-style home he built has nothing more ostentatious about it than the weather vane on the roof. Vogel's house is now **The Summer Inn Bed and Breakfast** (117 2nd Ave.; ☎ 907/766-2970; www. summerinnbnb.com; MC, V). The five guest rooms boast wood flooring, throw rugs, minimal furnishings, and a tranquil country vibe. You can have one for $90 to $105. They share three baths, including one with the original claw-foot tub that Vogel drew his baths in. The young innkeeper, who lives in a back apartment on the inn's grounds, serves sourdough pancakes each morning for breakfast.

Fort Seward

$ Like all military bases, the housing at Fort Seward was stratified by rank. The block with the two-story duplexes where the non-commissioned officers and their families lived was dubbed Soap Suds Alley, because it's where the non-coms' wives did the base laundry. The current owner of one of those duplexes has knocked out dividing walls and turned the place into a simple, affordable, homestay-style B&B called **Chilkat Eagle Bed and Breakfast** (69 Soap Suds Alley; ☎ 907/766-2763;

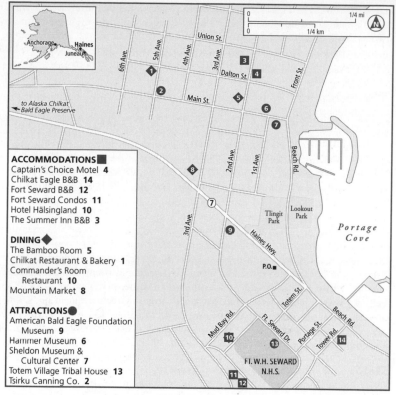

ACCOMMODATIONS ■
Captain's Choice Motel **4**
Chilkat Eagle B&B **14**
Fort Seward B&B **12**
Fort Seward Condos **11**
Hotel Hälsingland **10**
The Summer Inn B&B **3**

DINING ◆
The Bamboo Room **5**
Chilkat Restaurant & Bakery **1**
Commander's Room
    Restaurant **10**
Mountain Market **8**

ATTRACTIONS ●
American Bald Eagle Foundation
    Museum **9**
Hammer Museum **6**
Sheldon Museum &
    Cultural Center **7**
Totem Village Tribal House **13**
Tsirku Canning Co. **2**

www.eagle-bb.com; AE, DISC, MC, V). The three plainly decorated rooms, which are upstairs and share two baths, go for a double occupancy rate of just $80. Hang out there for a while and you'll get an earful about small-town social dynamics. The congenial host is a retired fisherman and former chairman of the town planning commission. He knows Haines inside and out and will talk about the place eloquently and with a conspiratorial gleam in his eye. He's also a good cook who's flexible about breakfast hours and about ferry or airport pickup times. He'll be there to pick you up at the ferry dock even if your boat doesn't arrive until at 2am—which, unfortunately, happens sometimes.

$ You can move up the ranks onto stately Officers Row and have more privacy too at the **Hotel Hälsingland** (Fort Seward parade grounds; ☎ 800/542-6363 or 907/766-2000; AE, DISC, MC, V). The hotel comprises three sprawling buildings— the commanding officer's quarters, the captain's quarters, and the bachelor officer's quarters—which have been spliced together and subdivided so no two rooms are quite the same. Some have decorative fireplaces and sweeping views of Lynn Canal and the Chilkat Mountains. Some are a bit dark and forlorn. Ask to take a look at what's available before you check in. Rates run from $69 for rooms with shared baths, to $89 for rooms with private baths (featuring either a shower or claw-foot tub). The Hälsingland has been a hotel since just after World War II, and it's changed little since then. It's a little ragged around the edges, but new owners are gradually fixing it up, and I actually enjoy its musty, 1940s-in-amber quality. The hotel has a swell restaurant and bar, which have also changed little with time. If young Humphrey Bogart were to sit down next to you at the bar, you in your early-21st-century attire would seem more out of place. The hotel shuttles guests to and from the ferry or airport for free.

$–$$$ Traditionally, U.S. Army forts have the same layout wherever they are. The first house along Officers Row is always set aside for the post commander, the preeminent soldier on the base. At Fort Seward, that house is now the preeminent bed-and-breakfast in Haines, **Fort Seward Bed and Breakfast** ★★★ (1 Fort Seward Dr.; ☎ 800/615-6676 or 907/766-2856; www.fortsewardbnb.com; DISC, MC, V). This is one of those wonderful homestay B&Bs where you get the benefit of sharing a home with a nice family (and this is a truly warm, gracious, and welcoming bunch) without feeling like you're invading the nice family's space, or vice versa. The family resides on the third floor, leaving the first two floors entirely to the guests, except at breakfast when someone comes down to cook things like whole-wheat sourdough pancakes. At other times, guests are allowed to use the kitchen, too (a valuable perk). The seven high-ceilinged rooms have a lot of personality with comfy beds and pretty cabinets in some; prices range from $85 to $135 for double occupancy. Some rooms are huge, with two queen beds, kitchenettes, decorative fireplaces, and private baths with claw-foot tubs. If you've got a large group, get two of the big rooms and open the door between them to make one enormous suite.

$$–$$$ You don't have to move to Haines to get your own apartment there. If you're staying for at least 2 nights, you can get a fully furnished one- or two-bedroom unit in the former lieutenants' family quarters on Officers Row. This is a good option if you want space and privacy, and you want to save money by cooking some of your own meals. **Fort Seward Condos** (in House 2 and House 5; ☎ 907/766-2708; www.fortsewardcondos.com; no credit cards) rents apartments for $113 to $131 (stay 1 week and get a night free). They're all in a pair of three-story duplexes with wraparound front porches and views across the parade grounds to Lynn Canal and the saw-toothed Chilkat Mountains beyond. The apartments are clean and well-kept, but they're definitely dated. The furnishings appear to be straight out of the swinging 1960s. If you're into retro, however, you'll love 'em.

DINING FOR ALL TASTES

Haines has a lot of eateries for a town of 1,715, thanks largely to the fact that food is the first thing many automobile drivers and passengers think of after the long drive down the Haines Highway or following a voyage aboard the state ferry. The restaurants tend to be less touristy and more locally oriented than in other Southeast Alaskan cities.

$ At **Mountain Market** (151 3rd Ave.; ☎ 907/766-3340; daily 7am–6pm; MC, V) locals come in the a.m. for darn good coffee and fresh baked muffins, as well as scones, bagels, wraps, smoothies, smoked salmon spread, and something called "Died and Gone to Heaven," which is a fresh roll filled with pesto, tomatoes, brie, and fresh basil ($7). This is one of the town's two morning meeting spots (Chilkat is the other one). Here, the crowd is a mix of bearded, grizzled year-rounders and fresh-faced, young "adventure people," as the seasonal workers employed by the guided tour operations are called. Mountain Market is an actual natural foods market, so it's a good place to stop for picnic fixings, too.

$–$$$ The regulars at **Chilkat Restaurant and Bakery** ★★ (corner of 5th Ave. and Dalton; ☎ 907/766-3653; May–Oct only Tues and Thurs 7am–3:30pm, Wed, Fri, and Sat 7am–8pm; MC, V) tend to be clean-cut and well scrubbed, as if they've just come from church, which they probably did. The Covenant of Life Center church originally owned this restaurant and hired only from its flock. Sagging membership and a diminished employment base led the church to sell. The original clientele still frequents the place, and the new owners have added Thai food to the straight-up country-kitchen fare. Go at breakfast or lunch and get hot cakes ($3.25), biscuits and gravy ($5.95), or a hot roast beef sandwich ($8.95 for a massive "half" sandwich). Better yet, go for lunch on Tuesday or Friday, or for dinner on Friday and Saturday, when the Thai menu is on. The curries ($11), beef asparagus ($11), and other tasty Thai dishes have a wonderful home-cooked quality, as if somebody brought their mother from across the Pacific to run the kitchen—which, in fact, they did.

$$–$$$ The enormous baskets of halibut fish and chips ($18) are the big draw at **The Bamboo Room** (11 2nd Ave.; ☎ 907/766-2800; www.bamboopioneer.net; summer daily 6am–10pm, rest of year daily 6am–9pm; AE, DISC, MC, V), a vinyl-boothed diner fastened at the hip to the dark, spacious Pioneer Bar. These co-joined establishments share a cheerful old building sheathed in corrugated red siding. In the early–19th century, the building functioned as a hotel with a genuine French restaurant, then it went through a phase as a speakeasy and (like so many places in Alaska) a brothel. The family that bought it in the 1950s, and put it back on the straight-and-narrow course, still owns it. Though big baskets of fish and chips get all the raves, healthier choices are on offer, such as pastas and grilled salmon ($13–$18). If you'd prefer to dine in the bar, you may.

$$$–$$$$ The restaurant at the Hotel Hälsingland, **Commander's Room Restaurant** ★★★ (13 Fort Seward Dr., at the Hotel Hälsingland; ☎ 907/766-2000; www.hotelhalsingland.com; summer only daily 5:30–9pm; AE, DISC, MC, V) is one that time forgot. Tall double doorways, high ceilings, white-clothed tables—it has the perfectly simple charm of a place that's changed little since the post-war 1940s, when it opened. Entrees on the changing menu are honest and elegant: pan-roasted duck breast with sautéed cabbage, bacon apple, and chanterelle ragout ($22); braised lamb shank with mustard spaetzle, pancetta, and cremini mushrooms ($23); prawns and grits, with braised greens ($19). Take a look at the vegetable garden out back where the chef starts work by picking the produce he'll work with that evening. With the 1940s so well preserved all around, it could easily be a Victory Garden.

WHY YOU'RE HERE: THE TOP SIGHTS & ATTRACTIONS
Bald Eagles & Other Wildlife

Topping your list of things to do in Haines should be a visit to the **Alaska Chilkat Bald Eagle Preserve** ★★★ (contact **Alaska State Parks** for info at ☎ 907/766-2292; www.alaskastateparks.org—click on "Individual Parks"), where the largest concentration of bald eagles in the world can be found. More than 3,000 eagles perch in the preserve's leafless cottonwood trees along a 5-mile stretch of the Chilkat River during the fall, with numbers peaking around Thanksgiving. In the summer you can still find dozens of the enormous birds there, and if you watch long enough, one might swoop down from a tree and snatch a fish out of the water with its talons. Bring binoculars, as a bird in a tree, even one with a 6-foot wingspan, still looks kind of small to the naked eye. The main viewing areas are from the pull-outs and pathways along the Haines Highway, between mileposts 18 and 24. The eagles know that this stretch of river has a late-season salmon run, and they fly in from hundreds of miles away to take advantage of it, some from as far as the state of Washington. If you don't have a car to get out to the preserve on your own, go with **Alaska Nature Tours** (☎ 907/766-2876; www.alaskanature tours.net), which runs eagle-watching tours in the fall, starting at $60 per person. Through the rest of the summer the company also runs more general wildlife watching tours, which are well worth the $60 for adults or $50 for children (12 and under) for the 2-hour outings, and which may include bear viewing.

Museums

With four museums and 1,715 residents, Haines has the highest per capita museum rate of any small town I've ever seen. You don't need to see all of them, but they are small enough for you to squeeze in a visit a day without feeling like you're stretching it. The common denominator shared by them all is the quirky obsessions of their founders.

A couple of commercial fishermen, feeling nostalgic for the days when Haines had nine salmon canneries rather than the one that remains, started a small museum devoted to canning's heyday, the **Tsirku Canning Co.** (5th and Main St.; ☎ 907/366-3474; www.cannerytour.com; $12 adults, children 12 and under free; mid-May to mid-Sept only, tour hours vary). Go in and stand beside a vintage

---

Rafting Down the Chilkat

If staying in one spot to watch the eagles seems too stationary for you, there's another way to go. The Chilkat River runs right through the bald eagle preserve, and you can float down it in an inflatable raft with **Chilkat Guides** (on Sawmill Rd., Mile 1 Haines Hwy.; ☎ 888/282-7789 or 907/766-2491; www.raftalaska.com). Besides the eagles perched on stumps and in the cottonwood trees that you'll see along the way, you may spot moose and bears too. The 3½-hour trips costs $79 for adults or $62 for children (7–12). This is no rip-roaring white water trip, but rather a mellow float down a gentle, shallow river. If the raft grounds itself on a gravel bar, as sometimes happens, everybody gets out to haul it off.

1920s canning line as it clacks and whirs to life, cuts and bends sheets of metal into cans, stuffs fake salmon into them, seals and labels them, and then—voila!—spits out canned fake salmon. The demo has the same appeal as the book *The Way Things Work,* but with moving parts you could actually lose a finger to if you weren't kept at a safe distance by a fence. Tour times vary, so call for a schedule. The whole experience lasts an hour, including the 10-minute video.

Steve Sheldon, one of the early settlers in Haines, wore a lot of hats. He was a shopkeeper, grocer, surveyor, laundryman, postmaster, U.S. Commissioner, and a Prohibition-era deputy U.S. Marshall. In addition to all that, he was a rabid collector of everything from presidential election buttons to Native basketry. When he died, his collection of Native artifacts became the stem cells from which the town's most traditional museum sprung. The **Sheldon Museum and Cultural Center ★★** (11 Main St.; ☎ 907/766-2366; www.sheldonmuseum.org; $3 adults, children 12 and under free; Mon–Fri 10am–5pm, Sat–Sun 1–4pm) is one of those simple community museums that doesn't look like much on the surface but sucks you in deeply. That's always been my experience, anyway. Go upstairs first to see the exhibits on Tlingit art and culture. You'll see bentwood boxes (made from single pieces of wood, soaked for months, and then bent into shape), grass baskets, a reassembled section of an old Tlingit clan house, and the cheap flintlock rifles that early traders exchanged with Natives for furs (the price of a rifle equaled the number of furs you could hang from the muzzle; as time went on the muzzles grew longer and longer). The artifacts downstairs concentrate on later arrivals to the land: The bright, idealistic young Presbyterian missionary couple who left behind Bibles and a surgical kit filled with sharp, shiny instruments; the Chinese cannery workers, who left behind rice bowls, tea sets, and opium pipes; the miners who heeded the call of the triangle dinner bell that hung outside the Porcupine Mine's cook shack.

Walk into the **American Bald Eagle Foundation Museum** (113 Haines Hwy.; ☎ 907/766-3094; www.baldeagles.org; $3 adults, $1 children 8–12; Mon–Fri 9am–6pm, Sun 1–4pm) and you'll feel like you've walked into a life-size wildlife diorama. The museum is a celebration of taxidermy, where you'll find yourself eyeball-to-glass-eyeball with more than 180 stuffed wolves, bears, moose, sheep, wolverines, bald eagles, and all the other major animal species found in the nearby Chilkat Bald Eagle Preserve. The museum is a nonprofit operation dedicated to protecting bald eagle habitats, and it's run by a guy in a wheelchair who was paralyzed in a construction accident while building the place. Despite the accident, his enthusiasm for bald eagles remains undiminished, and talking to him (he's usually there) is as interesting as seeing his lifeless, lovingly posed creatures.

The most unlikely of the Haines museums is the **Hammer Museum ★★★** (108 Main St., across from the bank; ☎ 907/766-2374; $3 adults, children 12 and under free; Mon–Fri 10am–5pm, Sat noon–4pm), which is devoted exclusively to the simple hammer. At first, I thought hammers sounded like a pretty dumb idea for a museum, but as it turns out, hammers are fascinating. You'll see cooper's hammers, cobbler's hammers, bookbinder's hammers, hammers used to post bills, hammers used to stamp furs, hammers with names like "bung starter" and "bung pick," magnetic hammers, triple-clawed hammers, an 800-year-old Tlingit war hammer used to smash in heads, little wooden drink hammers from the Roaring

Tlingit Storytelling

Before Southeast Alaska got electric lights, DVDs, and Nintendo, Tlingits entertained themselves on long, cold, gloomy evenings by gathering around the fires in clan houses and telling age-old stories. Some of those stories are re-told regularly in Haines by Native theater and dance groups called the **Chilkat Dancers** ★★★ (☎ 907/766-2540). Wearing elaborate costumes that include traditional, hand-carved wooden masks, the troupe acts out four ancient Tlingit legends: Raven Goes Berry Picking, Tide Woman, the Cannibal Giant, and The Mystery of Frog Woman. The quirky characters, the enchanting stories, the mesmerizing music and lighting, and the evocative setting—at the **Totem Village Tribal House**, a reproduction of a traditional clan house on the Fort Seward Parade Field—all help create a delightfully memorable hour of very old-school Alaskan entertainment. Performances are held weekdays at 4pm. Tickets are $15 for adults, and $7 for children 12 and under.

20s used to knock on the table to show applause, and more. There are 1,400 hammers in all, each with a story. Really this museum is about what happens when a hobby turns into an obsession, and how an obsessive collector got his collection to help pay for its own storage.

ACTIVE HAINES

Haines is rich with hiking opportunities. For a comprehensive guide to the trails, stop by the Haines visitor center and get a free copy of *Haines is for Hikers*. The easiest, most family-friendly hike here is the 2-mile **Battery Point Trail**. It passes through a forest and emerges at a Lynn Canal beach, which is sometimes lined with wild irises, and where you might see a whale. The trail begins at the end of Beach Road, south of the Chilkat Cruises ferry dock.

The toughest hike around is also one of the easiest to get to. The 7-mile round-trip **Mount Ripinsky Trail** ★ starts right in town, at the end of Young Street. It climbs to a 3,650-foot summit with an astounding view of surrounding mountains, ice fields, and the inland sea. Bring food and plenty of water, and don't go unless you're in great shape and have a day to spare. And expect sore legs the next morning.

ATTENTION, SHOPPERS!

Haines has some fun little shops specializing in local goods, but you have to hunt for them—they're pretty spread out around town. They're worth tracking down, though. The prices for Native arts and crafts in Haines tend to be markedly better than in nearby Skagway, and the shopkeepers like to chat, which makes shopping in Haines fun even if you hate to shop.

When you're at Fort Seward, drop by the old Army hospital at the south end of the parade grounds, which is now a nonprofit gallery and cultural center called **Alaska Indian Arts** ★ (13 Fort Seward Dr.; ☎ 907/766-2160; www.alaskaindian arts.com). You'll find a variety of locally made Native arts and crafts there spanning a broad range of prices. Wander around and find the workshops where carvers and craftsmen create totem poles, dance masks, rattles, paddles, and other things. If you don't get a chance to see the Chilkat dancers, you can at least look at their elaborate animal costumes, which are displayed here when not in use.

After returning home from a visit to Alaska, there's nothing I'd rather pull from my suitcase than some hefty packages of smoked salmon and smoked halibut. Some of the best smoked seafood I found in the state came from **Dejon Delights** ★★★ (37 Portage St., Fort Seward; ☎ 800/539-3608 or 907/766-2508), located in the old quarter masters building at Fort Seward. Tuck a few pounds of sockeye salmon cured with brine and Haines Brewing Company stout in the back of your suitcase, toss in a packet of lox cured with brine and dark rum, then forget all about it until you get home. The fish can go unrefrigerated for 10 days before the quality starts to suffer, Dejon Delights says, but I ate some that sat forgotten in my bag for far longer than that, and it still tasted great. Prices range from about $7 to $9.95 a pound.

For less perishable mementos, shop at **Uniquely Alaskan Arts** (210 Willard St.; ☎ 907/766-3225). It stocks a wonderful variety of made-in-Haines items ranging from a $4,500 Native bear totem pole, to $350 Native animal masks (with real human hair), to carved walrus tooth necklaces starting at $30, to silver jewelry for even less. A local teenager on a hunting trip with her dad shot a black-and-white photo of a group of bears they surprised. The picture won a blue ribbon at the state fair, and for $3 you can get a greeting card with the image held to the front by photo-corners.

In the 1991 Walt Disney film *White Fang,* a young gold prospector and a wolf-dog hybrid become friends and face unsavory characters who steal gold and stage dog fights. The film was shot outside of Haines, and after it wrapped, the Western street-front set that Disney built was moved to the community fairgrounds. Some of the false fronts now have actual buildings attached. The spaces are leased by small businesses, such as a wood turner, an oils and aromatics shop, a massage therapist, and an art gallery. After exploring the shops on both sides of the street, pop into the **Haines Brewing Company** (108 White Fang Way; ☎ 907/766-3823) for some free samples of beer and possibly a quick tour. I recommend picking up a $9 growler of the signature brew, Spruce Tip Ale, which is made with actual spruce tips.

Alaska's Interior

Land of the midnight sun & the northern lights

WHEN I TRAVEL THROUGH THE ALASKAN INTERIOR—THE VAST HEARTLAND of the state—I feel like I've slipped out of the ordinary, three-dimensional, physical world I know and entered into a curious, pleasant, and potentially dangerous land of magical realism. The landscape is so immense, the light so unusual, and the weather swings so extremely, that the lines separating the real from the fantastical start to melt and bend in my mind.

The Interior is the only place in Alaska where blue skies, puffy clouds, and temperatures in the 80s (upper 20s to lower 30s Celsius) are the norm in the summer, while winter temperatures drop (and stay) so far below zero that you can throw a cup of boiling water into the air and watch it freeze before it hits the ground. It's a region where the locals have grown so accustomed to the mesmerizing blue, green, yellow, and red curtains of the northern lights that they won't bother looking up unless the colors are really, *really* bright. It's a land where gold miners and eroding streams unearth Ice Age animal remains so regularly that you can buy shards of woolly mammoth tusk by the handful in local gift shops.

Since the Arctic Circle transects the Interior, that also makes this the true beginning of the land of the midnight sun. At the height of summer the daylight never ends, and in the depths of winter it never comes. The long spells of light and dark throw the brain's pineal gland, which helps to regulate cycles of wakefulness and sleep, into overdrive. A giddy, sleepless energy fills you in the summer; as the sun does its 360-degree loop in the sky, shining on you from every angle, you end up packing more into a day of vacation time than you knew you could. In the winter, melancholy prevails, drinking intensifies, and people sleep 10 or 12 hours a day. If you're headed to the Interior in the winter, March is the sanest time to go. There's still plenty of snow around for winter sports, but enough daylight has returned for you to see what you're doing and not want to sleep all day.

The inhabitants of the Interior are a proud, practical, slightly cracked bunch who never question the logic of the bizarre land in which the live. They just organize their lives around it, playing midnight baseball and throwing festivals that run late into the bright nights of summer or lacing up their insulated Arctic bunny boots and wearing lots of layers in the frigid winter. Their emblem is duct tape, a fix-it-all that can mend a broken fishing rod as well as it can repair a torn parka. They have a passion for travel. Whoever can get away in the winter, it seems, does—at least for a week or two. And they enjoy talking to other travelers. You'll find them to be generally kind, curious, and perhaps even protective toward any less-hardy creatures who somehow found their way into their strange, menacing, and beautiful world.

DON'T LEAVE INTERIOR ALASKA WITHOUT . . .

Boiling yourself like a tea bag. Soak in the 104°F (40°C) thermal springs at **Chena Hot Springs,** either under the midnight sun or beneath the northern lights in the winter, depending on when you visit. See p. 290.

Taking in the indoor wonders at the Museum of the North. The natural and cultural wonders on display at Fairbanks' **Museum of the North,** part of the University of Alaska, feature the enigmatic Native carving called the Okvik Madonna and a mummified Ice Age steppe bison, which was killed by lions and preserved for 36,000 years in the permafrost. See p. 277.

Ice, ice baby. Watch the world's top ice carvers compete in the **World Ice Art Championships** in March, or take a look at the winners at the **Ice Museum** in downtown Fairbanks in the summer. See p. 363 and 276.

Getting around the Interior the old-fashioned way. Take a lazy canoe ride or a touristy paddle-boat trip down a peaceful river in the summer or enjoy a sled dog ride in winter.

Exploring the hinterlands. Drive deep into gold mining country on the **Steese Highway,** or—if you're really adventuresome—drive up to the Arctic Circle or beyond on the **Dalton Highway.** See p. 291 and 297.

Enjoying the greatest light show on earth. Bundle up in the winter and feast your eyes on the enchanting and mysterious cosmic light show of the **aurora borealis,** aka the northern lights. See p. 278.

LAY OF THE LAND

The scale of the Interior is dizzying. To the south, the region is defined by the Alaska Range, the highest mountains on the continent. The highest of them all, stupendous 20,320-foot McKinley, is actually taller than Everest when measured from base to summit. To the north, the Interior boasts the otherworldly Brooks Range, barren and Mars-like in the short summer, and caked from top to bottom with snow in the long winter. Tens of thousands of caribou call these alien Arctic mountains home, and if you're in the right place at the right time, you'll witness a migrating herd running across the tundra in perfect sync, like a flock of birds or a school of fish.

Spread out between the two great mountain ranges are 175,000 square miles of rolling hills and river valleys—a landscape so large it could swallow Ohio, Indiana, Pennsylvania, and New York. Denali National Park and Preserve alone is so big it could hold New Hampshire and a couple of Hawaiian Islands to boot (it's so huge, it's gotten its own chapter in this guidebook). In the middle of all of this is Fairbanks, the only community in the entire Interior large enough to call a city. From there the grand Alaska Range, so awe inspiring up close, lines the southern horizon like a low jagged row of baby teeth. Expansive stretches of tundra and forests of birch, aspen, and spruce cover fill the Interior. The opportunities to get out into the wild to hike, camp, canoe, encounter wildlife, snowshoe, cross-country ski, and dog sled abound.

FAIRBANKS   Famously described as "a touristy cross between Kansas and Siberia," Fairbanks is the crossroads of and the gateway to Interior Alaska. Just about everyone coming or going from the Interior passes through, but the city is worth at least a day or two in its own right. You'll want to take some time to visit the Museum of the North and the Large Animal Research Station at the University of Alaska Fairbanks. See p. 261.

THE RICHARDSON HIGHWAY   In the early days, trails radiated from Fairbanks like spokes on a wheel. The more popular routes evolved from dog sled trails into gravel roads or paved highways. The Richardson Highway was the first asphalt between Fairbanks and the outside world. It links Fairbanks with the port town of Valdez, 366 miles away, and it runs parallel to the Trans-Alaska Pipeline, which also ends at Valdez. Twelve miles south of Fairbanks is the town of **North Pole,** where Christmas decorations are kept up year-round. See p. 289.

THE PARKS HIGHWAY   The George Parks Highway, originally known as the Anchorage-Fairbanks Highway, runs for 362 miles between Anchorage and Fairbanks, cutting through the Alaska Range and passing Denali National Park and Preserve. It traverses some of the most spectacular scenery in Alaska, as well as some long, dull stretches. Fifty-eight miles out of Fairbanks, the highway crosses the Nenana River at the little town of **Nenana,** terminus for tugs and barges that carry freight to Native villages inaccessible by road. Ten miles from Fairbanks, the highway passes **Ester,** an old mining camp that's now notable for its all-you-can-eat great crab feed and after-dinner vaudeville show at the Malamute Saloon. See p. 269.

THE STEESE HIGHWAY   The 161-mile Steese Highway runs through one of the most scenic parts of the Interior, through the richest gold mining district in Alaska, and past natural features like Eagle Summit, where you can get an unobstructed view of the midnight sun on summer solstice. It passes through the mining town of **Central,** where gold dust is still legal tender, and ends on the banks of the **Yukon River,** at the tiny town of **Circle.** See p. 291.

CHENA HOT SPRINGS ROAD   Chena Hot Springs Road begins 5 miles out of Fairbanks off the Steese Highway. It runs through the Chena River Recreation Area, where you can hike among granite tors that jut out of the ground like so many Easter Island statues. At the end of the 56-mile road is Chena Hot Springs, a private hot springs resort that's open year-round. See p. 284.

THE ELLIOTT HIGHWAY   The Elliott Highway begins 11 miles north of Fairbanks and runs 152 miles to the little town of **Manley,** a remnant of pioneer Alaska where you can stay at a 1906 road house and soak in a hot springs inside a greenhouse. The highway rises and falls over ridges and hills, with views that stretch for hundreds of miles in all directions. See p. 296.

THE DALTON HIGHWAY The 414-mile, mostly unpaved Dalton Highway is the only road in Alaska to the Arctic. It's also known as the Haul Road because it was built for trucks to carry supplies to the oil fields on the Arctic Ocean at Prudhoe Bay. Not a road for the faint of heart, the Dalton crosses the Yukon River, the Brooks Range, and the Arctic Slope before dead-ending 9 miles short of the Arctic Ocean. There are few services along the way, but lots of trucks barreling down the road at demon speeds. See p. 297.

GETTING TO & AROUND INNER ALASKA

Fairbanks is the hub of Interior Alaska, the place from which most forays into the wild are staged (see p. 263 for the scoop on getting to and from Fairbanks). All destinations discussed in this chapter are accessible by automobile, which is the most practical way to get around. If you're not headed off into the Bush by canoe, dog sled, snowmobile, or bush plane, then you really ought to have an automobile—preferably a 4×4—to get around.

FAIRBANKS

Fairbanks is called the "Golden Heart" city because it sprang up in the wilderness smack in the center of Alaska during an early-20th-century gold rush. It has since grown into a low-rise, ruggedly individualistic city of 31,000—making it the second largest city in the state. As the gateway to the Interior, it's the supply center for dozens of Native villages spread out in the Bush, as well as for the oil drilling operations at Prudhoe Bay in the Arctic. Natives from all corners of Alaska gather in Fairbanks in the summer for the World Eskimo Indian Olympics.

Fairbanks offers plenty to keep visitors well occupied for a few days. The city is the site of the main campus of the University of Alaska, home of a fantastic museum of cultural and natural history, a research farm where you can meet reindeer and musk ox, and some of the most forward-edge research into global climate change. Firmly grounded in its pioneer past, Fairbanks has even preserved some of the original log cabins of its frontier-town baby years at the historically themed Pioneer Park, which is part tourist trap, granted, but also part town commons. In addition, you don't even need to leave town to get into the Great Outdoors. In the summer, you can paddle a canoe through town down the Chena River, or catch a ride on a paddle-wheel-driven riverboat. In the winter, you can bundle up tightly against the 40-below weather and marvel at the aurora borealis, try your hand at dog mushing, and watch artists create larger-than-life ice sculptures from crystal-clear blocks of ice cut from frozen lakes.

A BRIEF HISTORY

When E. T. Barnette, the founder of Fairbanks, got booted off the riverboat *Lavelle Young* and left on the banks of the Chena River, deep in the heart of the Alaskan Interior, he had absolutely no intention of starting a town there. Yet that's how Fairbanks got its start.

Barnette had actually intended to start a town 200 miles farther east, at a spot along the Tanana River near the Canadian border where there were plans to put a railroad crossing. Barnette imagined starting a trading post at the crossing and making a fortune off the gold seekers, trappers, and other adventurers coming and going by river and rail. He gathered several tons of merchandise—beans, whiskey, that sort of thing—and employed the captain of the *Lavelle Young* to transport it upriver. Nobody had ever gone that far up the Tanana in a riverboat before, and the captain was doubtful that it could be done. He agreed to try on the condition that, should the river prove to be un-navigable, Barnette would unload his cargo on the nearest riverbank. It was one thing to carefully crawl up an uncharted river with a fully loaded stern-wheeler, and quite another to run down it with the swift current, when the danger that a low-riding vessel would run aground was magnified.

The *Lavelle Young* set off on the journey, but had to turn back after encountering a waterfall on the Tanana River, which proved impossible to get around (even via the slough known as the Chena River). A frustrated and disappointed Barnette, along with his tearful wife and four men traveling with them, had no choice but to unload their stuff on the banks of the Chena River, in the middle of nowhere.

As a stranded Barnette stood along the Chena River wondering what his next move was, an Italian prospector named Felix Pedro stepped out of the forest and introduced himself. He had been panning for gold in the nearby hills, and came down to investigate when he saw the black smoke from the stacks of the riverboat. Pedro told Barnette that there were more prospectors in the hills, which convinced Barnette to start a temporary trading post on the spot until he could figure out a way to get his stuff farther upriver. The following summer, in a creek 12 miles north of Barnette's camp, Pedro found the gold for which he was looking. When word got out, gold seekers poured into the area. The first of many gold rushes into Interior Alaska was on, and Barnette hunkered down and played founding father to the boomtown that sprung up around him.

Initially he named his town Chena City, but he later switched it to Fairbanks in a deal he made with the federal district judge—the judge was a big fan of a senator from Indiana named Charles Fairbanks. In return, the judge, who presided over 300,000 square miles of raw Alaskan wilderness, agreed to relocate the district court from Eagle, near the Canadian border, to Barnette's boomtown.

Barnette became Fairbanks' first mayor, and for a while he was its leading citizen. But 10 years after he'd arrived, an ugly banking scandal made his life in Fairbanks very uncomfortable, and he and his wife loaded up a dog sled and slipped away in the middle of the night, never to return. While the little frontier town grew to become the second largest city in Alaska, with a population of 82,000 when you count the city and its surrounding areas, it's never lost touch with its frontier roots.

LAY OF THE LAND

Located about 160 miles below the Arctic Circle, Fairbanks is laid out along the banks of the Chena River, which ambles lazily through town in the summer, and freezes solid in the winter. It used to overflow its banks and wreak havoc in the spring until the Army Corps of Engineers built a huge flood control project upriver. The **downtown** area is concentrated on the east side of town, on the south bank of the Chena. Its riverfront plaza, called **Golden Heart Park,** makes a good starting point for a visit. Pop into the sod-roofed log cabin there that houses the **Visitor Information Center** (550 1st Ave.; ☎ 800/327-5774 or 907/456-5774 for a recorded message; www.explorefairbanks.com; daily 8am–8pm), where you can get oriented, grab a free city map, pick through brochures for every

Adventure Advice

For the lowdown on everything to do with the outdoors—hiking, camping, canoeing, not getting eaten by bears—in state parks, national forests, wildlife refuges, and other outdoor recreational sites throughout the Interior and the state, head to the **Alaska Public Lands Information Center** (3rd Ave. and Cushman St.; ☎ 907/456-0527; www.nps.gov/aplic; daily 9am–6pm). It's in the basement of Fairbanks old Art Deco post office. Even if you aren't venturing into the wild, stop in to check out the free natural history museum, which ain't dull at all. It features a lot of stuffed wildlife, Native handicrafts, and looping videos on the area, as well as the Alaska Natural History Association Bookstore.

conceivable visitor activity and service, and get free Internet. A footbridge leads across the river to the **Church of the Immaculate Conception,** which has an unusual combination of Roman Catholic and gold rush decors, and a parking lot next door where you can park for free while you explore downtown.

Fairbanks is crisscrossed with commercial strips. **Airport Way** is one of the main east-west thoroughfares, running from downtown to the airport, which is on the west end of town. Along the way it passes **Pioneer Park,** a funky frontier theme park and community gathering place.

The campus of the **University of Alaska,** which has some attractions like the **Museum of the North** and the **Large Animal Research Station,** is on the northwest side of town. The main entrance is at the corner of University Avenue and College Road. The commercial area serving campus is thinly spread along **College Road,** with a small concentration of businesses—a pizza shop, used bookstore, and coffee house—at the corner of **University Avenue.**

GETTING TO & AROUND FAIRBANKS
Getting There

The cheapskates' way to get between Fairbanks, Denali National Park and Preserve, and/or Anchorage is aboard one of the vans or minicoaches run by **Alaska/Yukon Trails** (☎ 800/770-7275 or 907/479-2277; www.alaskashuttle.com). A one-way ticket costs $65 to Denali and $91 to Anchorage, with daily service during the summer. Children ages 3 to 10 pay half price, and 2 and under are free, but parents are expected to provide a car seat for the ride. For those coming or going though Canada, the company makes runs to Dawson City three times a week during the summer, for $162 one-way.

Several small airline carriers at Fairbanks International Airport offer service between Fairbanks and the communities of the Bush. Many of them fly to Anchorage, too, but it's usually cheaper to get there on Alaska Airlines or Frontier. **Alaska Airlines** (☎ 800/252-7522; www.alaskaair.com) has direct flights from the Lower 48 to Fairbanks International Airport year-round and they offer connecting flights to Anchorage. **Frontier Airlines** (☎ 800/432-1359; www.frontier airlines.com) connects Fairbanks and Anchorage, as well, charging on average

$250 for that round-trip. **Delta Airlines** (☎ 800/221-1212 or 907/474-9244; www.delta.com) and **Northwest Airlines** (☎ 800/225-2525; www.nwa.com) also offer direct flights between Fairbanks and the Lower 48 in the summer.

A taxi ride from the airport to downtown costs about $20. Call **Yellow Cab** (☎ 907/455-5555). Or better yet, take the **Fairbanks Shuttle** (☎ 800/770-2267), which charges just $7 from the airport or the train station to any Fairbanks hotel or bed-and-breakfast (so it's cheaper than a cab if there are two of you, about the same as a cab if there are three, and just not cost efficient if there are four or more of you).

It's a lot cheaper to fly from Anchorage to Fairbanks, but the train is a lovely and leisurely alternative. You'll be able to take in the landscape, and there's guided commentary along the way. If you do decide to train it, the **Alaska Railroad's Denali Star** (☎ 800/321-6518 or 907/265-2494; www.akrr.com) runs from Anchorage to Fairbanks, with stops at Denali National Park along the way. During the high season (May 19–Sept 19), the adult one-way fare is $47 to Denali, and $189 to Anchorage; in low season, those rates are often significantly discounted.

Getting Around

BY SHUTTLE & BUS

If you're not renting a car, the shuttle is the smartest way (for small parties) to get around Fairbanks. Its regular rates are $5 one-way and $8 round-trip for anywhere in the city but the airport or train station. The wait time is generally about 15 minutes. The trade-off is you might have to share the ride with the other passengers the shuttle picks up or drops off along the way.

In a pinch, you can get around town via the Fairbanks North Star Borough's **MACS Transit bus system** (☎ 907/459-1011; www.co.fairbanks.ak.us, click Departments, then Transportation). Buses run from downtown, out to the University of Alaska, and to points in between. The waits between buses are usually long, however, and they don't run on Sundays. The adult fare is $1.50, or $3 to ride all day. Even with the savings, it's probably worth your while to rent a car instead (why waste your precious vacation time waiting for the bus?).

BY CAR

Several national car rental franchises are at the airport, and one's as good as another if you plan to stay on the blacktop (you'll find these cars average $50 a day for an economy class vehicle). But some of the Interior's most alluring roads are topped with gravel, and most rental car firms will prohibit you from taking their vehicles off the pavement. There are two exceptions:

- ◆ **National Car Rental** (at the airport and at 49960 Dale Rd.; ☎ 800/227-7368 or 907/451-7368) allows its 4×4 diesel pickup trucks onto unimproved roads. They rent for $125 a day or $750 per week.
- ◆ **GoNorth Alaska Adventure Travel Center** (3500 Davis Rd.; ☎ 866/236-7272 or 907/479-7272; www.gonorthalaska.com) goes one better. It rents 4×4 pickup trucks with campers on the back, which frees vacationers to go wherever they like and sleep wherever they park. During the peak season, the budget model camper rents for $87 with a 100-mile-per-day limit, or $141 a day with no mileage limit. SUVs rent for the same amount, but fancier campers go for a bit more (up to $154 with 100 miles, or $219 with unlimited miles).

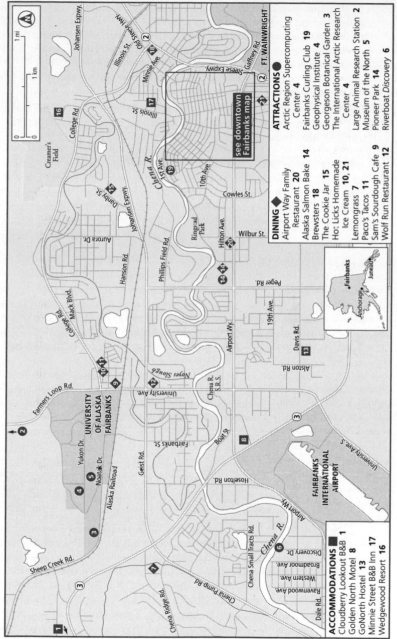

ATTRACTIONS ◆

Arctic Region Supercomputing Center **4**
Fairbanks Curling Club **19**
Geophysical Institute **4**
Georgeson Botanical Garden **3**
The International Arctic Research Center **4**
Large Animal Research Station **2**
Museum of the North **5**
Pioneer Park **14**
Riverboat Discovery **6**

DINING ◆

Airport Way Family Restaurant **20**
Alaska Salmon Bake **14**
Brewsters **18**
The Cookie Jar **15**
Hot Licks Homemade Ice Cream **10, 21**
Lemongrass **7**
Paco's Tacos **11**
Sam's Sourdough Cafe **9**
Wolf Run Restaurant **12**

ACCOMMODATIONS ■

Cloudberry Lookout B&B **1**
Golden North Motel **8**
GoNorth Hostel **13**
Minnie Street B&B Inn **17**
Wedgewood Resort **16**

A 7-day minimum on rentals is the norm, though sometimes walk-ins or late bookers can get vehicles for shorter durations, if there are holes in the schedule to fill. Insurance is required and costs $18 to $24 a day, unless you have proof of your own coverage. Find out what documents you need before leaving home. GoNorth (which, by the way, also runs a tent camp hostel—with a tepee!—that I recommend on p. 271) is near the airport, but doesn't do airport pickups. That means you'll have to find your own way there.

Fairbanks has a 10% vehicle rental tax, and a 3% motor home tax (which applies to GoNorth campers). In addition, all vehicles rented at the airport incur a 10% airport concession tax.

ACCOMMODATIONS, BOTH STANDARD & NOT

The variety of accommodations in Fairbanks and its environs ranges as far and wide as the seemingly limitless Alaskan Interior itself. There are some two dozen hotels, dozens of bed-and-breakfasts in the city and deep in the hinterlands, four hostels, a smattering of vacation rentals and public use cabins, and campgrounds galore, including a wooded car camp on the banks of the Chena River, right in the heart of the city.

Fairbanks has an 8% city bed tax.

Bed & Breakfasts

Almost all of the 40-some bed-and-breakfasts in Fairbanks belong to the **Fairbanks Convention and Visitors Bureau** (550 1st Ave.; ☎ 800/327-5774 or 907/456-5774; www.explorefairbanks.com), which has a website that gives a good overview of the field. The site's major failing is that the only criterion for inclusion is membership in the visitor's bureau. I wish I could tell you about a bed-and-breakfast association in Fairbanks that sends inspectors to objectively scrutinize new members and ensure that existing members maintain high levels of cleanliness and friendliness. But Fairbanks has no such beast. The closest thing to one is the **Fairbanks Area Bed and Breakfast Association** (no phone; www.pti alaska.net/~fabb), which declares that "our members' facilities have been inspected and meet the required quality standards set forth in our by-laws." The only trouble with that declaration is that by "inspected," they mean "self-inspected." In other words, each B&B gives itself the once over and reports the results to the association. Don't worry, I'm here to help: I can personally vouch for the B&B's reviewed below.

$–$$ Sean McGuire was always the shortest kid in his class, and—for some reason—he always dreamed of building towers. When he grew up, he built a home in the woods outside of Fairbanks, and the tower he put on it is a doozy. His unusual place, which rises well above the canopy of dwarf black spruce trees surrounding it, doubles as **Cloudberry Lookout Bed & Breakfast** ★★★ kids (351 Cloudberry Lane; ☎ 907/479-7334; www.mosquitonet.com/~cloudberry; MC, V), and it's a marvel of cozy nooks, skylights, and soaring spaces. The highlight is the spiral staircase, built around a 60-foot white spruce center pole, which corkscrews up to a cupola/belvedere with a walk-around deck and a commanding view. Cloudberry has six appealing bedrooms, each filled with pretty antique furniture, four with spectacular bathrooms of their own. They're priced between $75 and $125.

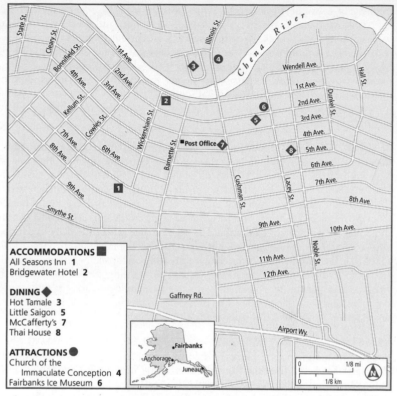

ACCOMMODATIONS ■
All Seasons Inn 1
Bridgewater Hotel 2

DINING ◆
Hot Tamale 3
Little Saigon 5
McCafferty's 7
Thai House 8

ATTRACTIONS ●
Church of the
   Immaculate Conception 4
Fairbanks Ice Museum 6

The two cheapest rooms, the Gallery Room and the Owl Room, are smaller than the rest, with lower ceilings, and they share a bathroom. If you were wondering how they got their names, that's because the "Gallery" has lots of pictures on the walls and the Owl room has lots of pictures on the walls . . . but only of owls. For breakfast, guests descend the spiral staircase to the cozy kitchen and have French toast while swapping stories with Sean and the other guests. There's a 3-acre thermokarst lake (which means it sits above the permafrost) on the property with a swimming dock for any who care to brave the bracing cold waters.

$$$ Imagine spending the night backstage at a community theater, with all sorts of costumes and props to play with, and you'll have some idea what it's like to stay at the **Aurora Express Bed and Breakfast ✸✸** (1540 Chena Ridge Rd., about 20 min. out of town; ☎ 800/221-0073 or 907/474-0949; www.aurora-express. com; closed mid–Sept to mid–May; MC, V). Now imagine this community theater is housed in seven retired train cars, hauled up to a hillside overlooking Fairbanks, and presided over by a hostess inclined to dress up as "Margarita the Mexican Girl" and blast mariachi music when serving *huevos rancheros* for breakfast, and you'll have an even better idea of what it's like to stay there. Each of the seven rooms at Aurora, which range from $135 to $150 per night, has a name and a theme. The Can-Can Room, for instance, sports a wire corset lampshade, a bed-side table with mannequin legs in fishnet stockings, and leopard-skin panty valances over the windows. The Immaculate Conception Room has stained glass, altar chairs, a bathroom that looks like a confessional, and a statue of the Virgin Mary looming over the bed. The dining car is loaded with goodies like rattles, drums, native dance robes, floozy dresses, and a moose suit. Two suites, sleeping up to four people, go for between $150 and $225 a night. Sorry, though young 'uns would enjoy playing with all the bric-a-brac, only those over the age of 8 are welcome here.

$$–$$$$ On a quiet residential street within easy walking distance of Fairbanks' downtown core is a natural cedar home that's been transformed into the **All Seasons Inn** (763 7th Ave.; ☎ 888/451-6649 or 907/451-6649; www.allseasons inn.com; DISC, MC, V). It's a homey, country-inn-like bed-and-breakfast, with a tiny and tidy yard, cozy common areas, lots of rugs and runners, and a hostess from Atlanta who has brought a measure of Southern hospitality—and a charming Southern accent—to Fairbanks. The eight rooms are a little frilly but simple and comfortable. During the summer high season, they range in price from $100 for the smallest unit to $175 for the largest, and you'll usually get the best rates by booking directly with the owner (rather than trying for an Internet deal). Breakfasts are generously portioned and likely to include quiches, egg puffs, apple pancakes, and fruit-filled crepes. The proximity to downtown and the grace of the hostesses are what make this place really shine, though.

$$–$$$$ Farther away from the downtown core, but not too far to walk if you don't mind hoofing it for 5 blocks, is a larger, somewhat more upscale option, the **Minnie Street Bed & Breakfast Inn** ★ (345 Minnie St.; ☎ 888/456-1849 or 907/ 456-1802; www.minniestreetbandb.com; DISC, MC, V). Located on a busy street, the four buildings that make up the inn are built around a garden courtyard, which serves as a calming counter weight to the street traffic. The inn's got a dozen bright Martha Stewart–esque rooms, along with a three-bedroom, two-bath house that sleeps up to six. The house, which comes with a fully stocked refrigerator, rents for $179 during the summer high season. The rooms range in price from $125 (for the smallest, with twin beds) to $189 (roomier digs with queen beds), and while you can't raid the fridge for those rates, you will get a full breakfast each morning at the long dining room table. Interestingly, the Minnie Street seems to be trying to appeal to the demanding and/or unusually large traveler: Beds are triple-sheeted, with hypo-allergenic down duvets and a choice of pillows, and many of the beds are extra long. For an extra $85 per hour per person, you and your partner can hop out of the steam shower and lay side-by-side while a pair of massage therapists set hot rocks on your back—one of the unusual-for-a-bed-and-breakfast spa packages offered here. There are 10% to 20% discounts for multiple-night stays if you book before May 31, as well as discounts on local tourist activities, such as the River Boat Discovery. Look on the website before calling, as there are often serious rate reductions posted there (often in winter but sometimes even during the high season, since this is a discount happy place).

Hotels

$ Six miles west of Fairbanks on the Parks Highway is the turnoff to the **Ester Gold Camp** ✸✸ (Mile 35, Parks Hwy.; ☎ 800/676-6925 or 907/479-2500; www.akvisit.com; AE, DISC, MC, V), an old mining camp that's been turned into a tourist attraction. Most visitors go there for the all-you-can-eat Dungeness crab feed (p. 274) and the vaudeville show at the Malamute Saloon (p. 288). Less known is that Ester offers cheap, historic accommodations. Upstairs above the old mess hall, where the crab feed occurs, there are several simple, 1930s-era rooms where the gold mine's middle management used to sleep. For $70 a night double occupancy, you'll snag a double bed with a shared bath. There's also a campground with tent sites for $10. While Ester is a full-blown visitor attraction, the eleven buildings of the mining camp are well-preserved and little changed, so you really get a nice sense of how the place was when its business was mining ore, not tourists.

$ A long-time Alaskan family owns and operates **Golden North Motel** (4888 Old Airport Rd.; ☎ 907/479-6201; www.goldennorthmotel.com; AE, DISC, MC, V), and they get much of their business from other Alaskans, including quite a few Native families making their annual trips into the big city in the summer. These locals know that this two-story converted apartment building, right in Fairbanks proper, offers some of the best deals in the area. Its 60 comfortable if somewhat worn rooms are well-maintained though small; larger rooms are actually two small rooms put together and boast a pair of queen beds with a separate (if windowless) TV room for $99 a night. Those with a single queen tend to go for $85. Niceties such as DVD/VCR players in the rooms, free coffee and pastries in the lobby, and a complimentary business center for guest use add to the appeal. But be sure to bring earplugs if you stay here, as you'll be right in the airport flight path and across from the freeway off-ramp and snowmobile lot.

$$–$$$$ When the population of Fairbanks boomed in the 1970s with the construction of the Trans-Alaska Pipeline, all sorts of new apartment complexes shot up. Some of them have been converted into hotels, which is why the larger units at **Wedgewood Resort** (221 Wedgewood Dr.; ☎ 907/452-1442; www.fountainheadhotel.com/wedgewood/wedgewood.htm; AE, DISC, MC, V) are genuinely huge, with one or two bedrooms, living rooms, dining rooms, balconies, full kitchens, and big bathrooms. The furnishings have, mercifully, been updated since the swinging '70s, but it's still easy to imagine the place filled with gangs of burly construction workers sporting feathered hair, handlebar mustaches, and cans of beer, and carrying on from their Barcaloungers as they watch the NFL. Today these apartments go for $174 to $225 in the summer, and they're especially suited for groups who want to hunker down in Fairbanks for a while. Consisting of eight buildings arranged on 23 acres, Wedgewood Resort is right next to Creamer's Field bird sanctuary (p. 284), a great spot for rambling walks through the wetlands.

In addition to the full-blown apartments, Wedgewood also has some more affordable standard hotel rooms in a building it calls the Bear Lodge, which is open in the summer only. Sometimes people complain because they were expecting a place called the Bear Lodge to be a little rustic, which it isn't (it looks like your run-of-the-mill hotel). But if you know what to expect—and you book a

---

The Low Vacancy Game

Many of the major hotels in Fairbanks, such as the Wedgewood, do big business with package tour operators taking cruise-ship passengers on land trips to the Interior and Far North. These hotels go through weekly boom-and-bust cycles during the summer, with certain nights regularly booked solid while other nights are completely dead. Interestingly, the hotels are on different schedules, so when one place has no vacancies, another might have nothing but vacancies. Your challenge is to pinpoint the hotels hurting for business on the night you're in town, and see how low you can get the front desk to make the price go. Simply get on the phone and ask. You'll find Web links and phone numbers for all of the hotels at the **Fairbanks Convention and Visitor's Bureau information line** (☎ 907/456-4636; www.explorefairbanks.com).

---

room on the weekends when visitors on package tours aren't filling the place—the Bear Lodge can be a good deal, going for as low as $125. Look under "special rates" on the website for the best deals. A shuttle, included in the room rate, ferries guests to and from the airport and to various tourist sights (another reason this place can be counted as a value).

$$$ A central, downtown location, within walking distance of most everything in Fairbanks, is the **Bridgewater Hotel's** ★★ (723 1st Ave.; ☎ 907/452-6661 or 800/528-4916; www.fountainheadhotels.com; AE, DC, DISC, MC, V) most obvious attraction. It's just 1 block from the downtown Marriott, but it's usually $50 less expensive. What's less obvious, until you stay there, is the remarkable care bestowed on each guest by the unusually gracious and friendly staff. They set out punch and cookies in the lobby, man a breakfast buffet, and generally do their utmost to keep guests comfortable. As for the physical property, it's an older, five-story building overlooking the Chena River, which somehow has the feel of a small European hotel. (Let's say it has an air of casual refinement.) Rooms are on the smaller side, as in Europe, and don't have full baths, only cramped showers. As for the rates: They're officially priced at $149 in the summer, but they can go as low as $99, especially on weekends, when the package travelers aren't packed in. The buffet breakfast I mentioned is available each morning in the basement restaurant.

$ Half an hour out of Fairbanks on the Steese Highway, rooms at the **Historic Chatanika Gold Camp** ★ (Mile 27.9, 5550 Steese Hwy.; ☎ 907/389-2414; www.fegoldcamp.com; DISC, MC, V) offer a time warp experience that's far from fancy but darn authentic. The camp is where the miners working the gold dredge that plowed through the lowlands digging up riches from the 1920s to the 1950s once resided, and it hasn't changed much at all over the years. At its peak, the camp housed 200 miners, most of whom slept in a hulking bunkhouse with metal siding. Today you can get one of their tiny, unadorned rooms for $60 a night. They all share baths and have the same sloping, well-worn wood floors that creak under foot. Newer, roomier digs are available in a pair of four-plex cabins for $76, but they lack the historic flavor of the bunkhouse, and they too share baths. You'll find relics from the mining days all around the property, including in the kitchen of the saloon, where the world's largest coal-fired cook stove (or so I'm told) turns out burgers, steaks, halibut, and other fare (it's the best food along the Steese Hwy.; prices range from $11 for a Caesar salad to $25 for prime rib). The dark and friendly saloon, a gathering spot for locals, offers up cold, cheap beer. Chatanika Gold Camp is a swell, low-cost base for hiking trips in the summer, and for cross-country skiing and viewing the northern lights in the winter.

Camping & Hostels

$ At the **Chena River State Recreation Site** (221 University Ave.; ☎ 907/451-2695; www.chenawayside.com; MC, V) you can enjoy the beauty of an Interior Alaskan forest, with all of the conveniences (and traffic noise, I'm afraid) of the city, thanks to its central location. In all, it's got 57 car camping sites and a few walk-in tent sites scattered among the wooded banks of the Chena River, not far from the University of Alaska campus. A car spot goes for $17, and a tent site for walk-ins goes for $10.

$ For a more unusual urban camping experience, stay at **GoNorth Hostel** (3500 Davis Rd.; ☎ 866/326-9292 or 907/479-7272; www.gonorthalaska.com; AE, DISC, MC, V), which has a tepee, tent cabins, and a shady grove where you can pitch a tent of your own. Tent cabins are the surprisingly comfy missing link between the old-fashioned canvas tents and solid-wall cabins. GoNorth's four tent cabins have raised plank flooring, small porches, and five single beds with crisp, clean sheets, which go for $24 per person per night. As this is a hostel, you might end up sharing the tent cabin with other hostellers. For privacy, rent the tepee, which you get all to yourself for $18 per person. It's much brighter and roomier inside than you might expect, and set up on a raised platform to keep you off the chilly ground. A stay in the tent grove costs $6 per site, plus $6 per person. The hostel has a nice screened pavilion with a kitchen and picnic tables, and shared baths with pay showers.

DINING FOR ALL TASTES

Since it's still something of a frontier town, Fairbanks doesn't have a lot of use for fine dining. The restaurant scene is dominated by places like **Sam's Sourdough Cafe** (3072 Cameron St., near the University of Alaska at Fairbanks just off University Ave.; ☎ 907/479-0523; daily 6am–10pm; MC, V), a bustling place with faded Norman Rockwells on the walls and big Alaskans squeezed into little booths; the **Airport Way Family Restaurant** (1704 Airport Way; ☎ 907/457-5182; daily 24 hr; AE, DISC, MC, V), which is most notable for staying open 24 hours a day; and **The Bakery Restaurant** (69 College Rd.; ☎ 907/456-8600; Mon–Sat 6am–9pm, Sun 6am–4pm; MC, V), a greasy spoon occupying an old Jack in the Box, which dishes up the best sourdough pancakes in town.

I list a couple of slightly more upscale joints below, but generally this is a town where you'll do better ordering the meatloaf than the seafood (which will likely be frozen). Heck, here you can even try musk ox meatloaf. Now that's something to put on a postcard. Most eateries are open late in the summer, and casual attire prevails.

$ Little Saigon (527 2nd Ave., across from the Marriott; ☎ 907/978-1793; daily 11am–7pm; no credit cards) is a simple shack where the proprietors grill meat on a backyard barbecue, and diners sit around a few plastic tables outdoors beneath shade umbrellas. Still, the spring rolls are cool and crunchy and the steaming bowls of *pho* (Vietnamese noodles in a clear beef broth with some veggies and usually beef) will satisfy. You certainly can't beat the price: It's a snap to order a full meal here for under $10. That being said, the language barrier makes pointing at what you want on the menu the surest way to order.

$ If you're driving in the campus area and want a quick roadside taco, pull into the gravel parking lot of **Paco's Tacos** (1335 Hayes Ave., next to Radio Shack; ☎ 907/451-8226; Mon–Sat 11:30am–7pm; no credit cards). An unpretentious *taqueria* with mariachi tunes blasting from outdoor speakers, it offers a good selection of comforting Mexican grub for $8 or less. There's some outdoor seating, but nothing's so messy or complicated that you couldn't eat it while driving. If there's nobody at the order window when you show up, that rock-filled can on the counter is for rapping on the glass to summon help.

$ Muffins, soups, bagels, smoothies, and the best coffee in town are the star attractions at a little downtown coffeehouse called **McCafferty's** (408 Cushman St; ☎ 907/456-6853; Mon–Thurs 7am–6pm, Fri 7–11am, Sat 10am–11pm, Sun 10am–4pm; MC, V). The other reason to go here? Entertainment, in the form of free Wi-Fi and an Etch-a-Sketch on every table. You'd be hard-pressed to spend more than $12 here.

$–$$ Sit-down Mexican (and you're going to need to sit down if you finish one of their big pitchers of margaritas), is on tap across the river at **Hot Tamale** (112 N. Turner, downtown; ☎ 907/457-8350; daily 10am–9pm; AE, DISC, MC, V). The inside is a dark warren of booths, alcoves, passageways, and dead ends. Looking for a table here is sort of like exploring the tunnels of a hard-rock mine that someone has decorated with Mexican pottery, terra-cotta tiles, and fake cacti. All day Friday, there's an all-you-can-eat buffet—with brisket, *carnitas,* halibut, *rellenos,* fajitas, and so on—for $12. On Saturday until 4pm there's a scaled-down version for $8.95. Otherwise entrees run from $11 to $14.

$–$$ **The Cookie Jar** ✦ 🄺🄸🄳🅂 (1006 Cadillac Ct.; ☎ 907/479-8319; www.cookie jarfairbanks.com; Mon 6:30am–8:30pm, Tues–Sat 6:30am–9pm, Sun 8am–7pm; AE, DISC, MC, V) is the kind of solid, affordable, family-style place where people go after church. It offers a slew of unpretentious, reasonably priced choices, from halibut burgers ($8.95) and hoagies ($7.95) to steaks ($18) and bubbly lasagnas smothered in sauce ($13). With the exception of that one steak dish, lunches and dinners never cost more than $15 and are usually much less.

$–$$$ When it comes to Thai food, Fairbanks is divided. One faction insists that **Lemongrass** ✦ (388 Old Chena Pump Rd.; ☎ 907/456-2200; Mon–Sat 11am–4pm and 5–10pm; MC, V) serves the best Thai food in the Interior, while another

Cold Cones, Hot Licks

As cold as Fairbanks gets in the winter, summers can be downright hot, with temperatures in the 90s (30s Celsius) for days on end. It's perfect ice cream weather, in other words, and **Hot Licks Homemade Ice Cream** ★ (3453 College Rd. and 1521 South Cushman; ☎ 907/479-7813; www.hot licks.net; Cushman location Apr–Sept daily 3pm–10pm, College Road location daily noon–11pm; AE, DISC, MC, V; $) is the place to go to make the most of it. Both locations do nonstop business all through the summer, serving cones, sundaes, shakes, banana splits, fountain drinks, and—in recognition of the close ties between the 49th and 50th states—Hawaiian shave ice. The homemade ice cream (my favorite's the blueberry) makes use of local ingredients such as wild berries.

faction swears by **Thai House** ★ (26 5th Ave.; ☎ 907/452-6123; daily 11am–4pm, 5–9:30pm; MC, V). I like them both equally, so I'm afraid the best I can do here is be "fair and balanced"—I'll report, you decide. Here's how the two restaurants are similar: The two are comparably priced, with dinners ranging from $9–$15. Both are run by gracious Thai families, who wear their native costumes while serving. They also both go heavy on the halibut in their seafood dishes, and both use fresh Alaskan produce during the summer. If location and organic food are important to you, however, that's where the restaurants differ: Lemongrass makes a big deal about using organic produce as much as possible, while Thai house is silent on the matter. But Thai House is located downtown, which makes it easier to find. (Its big, boxy dining room with high ceilings also gives it a more formal look than its competitor.) In contrast, Lemongrass is in an out-of-the-way strip mall on the airport side of town. That puts it squarely in the path of the University of Alaska crowd, who arguably give it more of a party vibe.

$–$$$ In another strip mall on the north side of town, a popular family-style restaurant with a good bar called **Brewsters** (kids) (345 Old Steese Hwy., ☎ 907/374-9663; daily 11am–11pm; MC, V) presents a wide-ranging menu that includes burgers and sandwiches for under $10, steaks and ribs in the $16 to $24 range, and a child's menu with a half dozen items under $6 (kids who get the comfortingly sweet penne with marinara sauce often find themselves defending it against grabby adult fingers), plus big $5 milk shakes. The dining room is spacious and done up to look like a 19th-century saloon, with dark wainscoting and Tiffany-style lamps. The original Brewsters is on the other side of town (3575 Airport Way; ☎ 907/456-2538), but the Steese Highway location is the nicer of the two.

$$$–$$$$ The owners of a lovely old Fairbanks home with a big stone fireplace gave it up when the expressway went in next door, and now the **Wolf Run Restaurant** ★★ (3360 Wolf Run Rd., at the corner of University Ave. and Johansen Expwy.; ☎ 907/458-0636; Sun–Thurs 11am–9pm, Fri–Sat 11am–10pm; AE, DISC, MC, V) occupies the premises. It's a funny, homey little spot, with a wild yard in

A Salmon Bake or a Crab Feed

The Alaskan salmon bake is the 49th state's equivalent of the Hawaiian luau—a touristy, all-you-can-eat affair usually followed by a show. That's mainly the case at Fairbanks's **Alaska Salmon Bake** (Pioneer Park, Airport Way and Peger Road; ☎ 800/354-7274 or 907/452-7274; www.akvisit. com/salmon.html; summer only daily 5–9pm; MC, V; $$$$); unfortunately, the show is separate. At the salmon bake you can stuff yourself to the brim with king salmon (which is glazed with brown sugar, butter, and lemon juice, then grilled right in front of you), halibut, and Alaskan cod (which is lightly battered and deep fried), as well as prime rib, and a buffet with salads and plenty of side dishes. Tickets are $31 or $15 for kids ages 3 to 12. For kids who don't need the all-you-can-eat option, there's a $6 hot dog, salad bar, and dessert option. The salmon feed runs from 5pm to 9pm. Time it right and you can wander over to the 8:15pm performance of The Golden Heart Revue (p. 288) after you eat.

At the **Ester Gold Camp Dining Hall Buffet Dinner** ✸ (Mile 35, Parks Hwy.; ☎ 800/354-7274 or 907/452-7274; summer only daily 5–9pm; MC, V), an early-20th-century mining camp 8 miles south of Fairbanks, there's a similar all-you-can-eat seafood extravaganza where Dungeness crab from the icy Alaskan waters of Yakutat takes top billing from the salmon. You'll dine in the camp's old mess hall, so get ready to be friendly, as you'll be sitting on long benches at shared tables (that's part of the fun . . . really). How much you pay depends on whether or not you go for the crab. With it, the buffet is $31 for adults, and $15 for kids under 12. Without it, the tab's just $22 for adults and $10 for kids; and heaven knows there's enough to stuff you to the gills without the crab, such as halibut, pork tenderloin, reindeer stew, seafood chowder, country fried chicken, corn on the cob, steamed veggies, and hot biscuits. Most guests wander over to the Malamute Saloon after eating to catch the show, Service with a Smile, described on p. 288.

front and small woods out back. Diners have just a few tables to choose from, but there are well-worn leather winged-back chairs at some. The food is hearty, excellent, and not terribly expensive. Dinners, priced at $16 to $25, center around such continental classics as Cornish game hens ($22) and four-cheese ravioli Florentine in a pesto cream sauce ($16). Sometimes the classics get Alaskan twists, such as the fresh halibut awash in a succulent white wine, shallots, and sour cream ($22). The mountainous salads ($5.25 and big enough for a meal) are given a special zing with caramelized walnuts and Mandarin oranges. For dessert, try the delightful cherry amaretto pie ($5.50).

$$$–$$$$ At the center of **The Turtle Club** (Mile 10, Old Steese Hwy., Fox; ☎ 907/457-3883; Mon–Sat 6–10pm, Sun 5–9pm; AE, DISC, MC, V; reservations recommended), a steakhouse 10 miles north of Fairbanks in the little bedroom community of Fox, is a big, horseshoe-shaped bar where a party-ready crowd of locals often gathers. You can have your meal in the bar or in the dining room, but be warned: If you choose the bar, you'll probably be inducted into the "turtle club," which will put you at the center of the merry-making for that evening (don't worry, there's no hazing, just a silly oath to swear and a membership card to receive). If you like those kinds of frat party antics, and you enjoy the kind of food that truckers eat when they're celebrating (tender prime rib, as thick as the rough hewn planking on the walls, is the house specialty), you'll love The Turtle Club. (If it's all too testosterone-laden for your tastes, choose the Wolf Run instead.) Along with slabs of meat, the menu features a slew of seafood dishes like Australian lobster, Alaskan king crab legs, halibut chunks, and enormous prawns, lightly battered and the size of small zucchinis. Dinners range from $19 to $31, but because they're so massive, a couple can share one plate and still have enough left over to save for lunch the next day.

WHY YOU'RE HERE: THE TOP SIGHTS & ATTRACTIONS

Most visitors to Fairbanks stop there on their way to somewhere else, usually Denali National Park and Preserve or the Arctic. But Alaska's Golden Heart city has enough homegrown attractions to easily fill a day or two. Some of these attractions were created explicitly for tourists, others are organic parts of the community that tourists happen to enjoy, and some are a little of both.

Pioneer Park ★★ (kids) (Airport Way and Peger Rd.; ☎ 907/459-1087; www.co. fairbanks.ak.us; free admission; Memorial Day–Sat after Labor Day daily 11am–9pm) is one of Fairbanks' attractions that falls into both camps. For locals, it's the town commons, with picnic pavilions, a playground, riverfront fishing, and meeting space for community groups and square dancers. For you and me, it's a 44-acre frontier theme park. Don't expect a Knott's Berry Farm or Disneyland, though. Pioneer Park is a *low-keyed* theme park. The rides are limited to a historic merry-go-round, a train that circles the park on a small-gauge track, and a dog cart pulled by sled dogs. Many of Fairbanks' original log cabins have been relocated from downtown here to serve as gift shops and concession stands. Also plopped down in the middle of it all is the restored railroad car that President Warren G. Harding rode in when he came to Alaska to drive the golden spike into the track and dedicate the new railroad. They even brought in one of the original riverboats that plied the Yukon in the 1930s and 1940s, the 227-foot stern-wheeler *Nenana*. It's filled with dioramas illustrating its glory days. And Pioneer Park has not just one museum, but three—one dedicated to Native Alaskans, one for the pioneers, and one for aviation. Rounding out its shameless tourist trap side, Pioneer Park is the home of the Alaska Salmon Bake (p. 274) and a vaudeville show called the Golden Heart Revue (p. 288). Admission to the park is free, but there are charges to get into some of the attractions. Depending on how deeply you get sucked in, you could either breeze through the park in under an hour or spend a half day there.

Riverboats were the Interior's original form of mass transit, and a marvelous way to see the land, to boot. The Binkley family, which has been in the riverboating business since the Klondike gold rush, still runs a stern-wheeler out of

Fairbanks. These days, instead of transporting gold miners, fur trappers, and farmers, it carries tourists on 3½-hour excursions. A ride aboard the 156-foot *Riverboat Discovery* ★ (1975 Discovery Dr.; ☎ 866/479-6673 or 907/479-6673; www.riverboatdiscovery.com; $45 adults, $30 children 3–12; tours mid-May to mid-Sept daily, 8:45am and 2pm) is one of the major attractions for visitors to Fairbanks on package tours, for all the good and bad that implies. The *Discovery* chugs from one point of interest to another along the clear Chena and the silty Tanana rivers. At one point, a bush pilot demonstrates a take-off and landing on a riverbank airstrip. At another, sled dogs and their musher come out to the bank to greet you. Finally, you disembark for a tour of an Athabascan village replica. It's fun, but touristy and a little pricey.

The Binkleys also run another big local tourist attraction, the **El Dorado Gold Mine** (off Elliott Hwy., 9 miles north of town; ☎ 907/479-6673; www.eldorado goldmine.com; $35 adults, $23 children 3–12; tours mid-May to mid-Sept Sat 3pm, Sun–Fri 9:45am and 3pm). Like the riverboat tour, it's elaborately staged—I'm talking a train ride through a tunnel in the permafrost, a meet and greet with Alaskans who spend a good part of their summers panning for gold in icy streams, and the chance to pan for gold yourself in a sluice box loaded with pay dirt. That being said, it is painlessly educational and good for kids.

If you can live without the train ride, there's a competing gold mining attraction outside of town that won't cost nearly as much to see, and which reveals more about the destructive nature of mining. **Gold Dredge Number 8** ★ (Mile 9, 1755 Old Steese Hwy.; ☎ 907/457-6058; www.golddredgeno8.com; $21 1-hr. tour or $10 for children 10 and under; tours daily 9:30am–3:30pm) is a five-deck-tall floating dredge that collected millions of dollars in gold while wreaking havoc on the landscape from 1938 until 1959. In that time, the dredge crawled 3½ miles across the land, digging up creek beds with huge scoops on its bow, sifting out the gold inside its beastly belly, and then spitting out the tailings from its stern. You can take a 1-hour tour of the monstrous contraption and the stark camp where the miners lived for $21 (or $10 for kids 12 and under). For $6 more ($3 for kids) you can try your hand at panning for gold in sluice boxes where you're guaranteed to find color, and for an additional $16 (or $7.50 for kids) you can pan for gold *and* have all-you-can-eat beef stew in the mess hall. The shed there is filled with the fossilized bones of woolly mammoths and other Ice Age animals, which were unearthed by the miners and are now stacked up like firewood.

If it's 85°F (29°C) and sunny while you're in town, and you're having a hard time envisioning the city when it's 20 below, you can get a little taste of winter in an old downtown movie palace that's been transformed into the **Fairbanks Ice Museum** ★★ (kids) (500 2nd Ave.; ☎ 907/451-8222; www.icemuseum.com; general admission $6; May 15–Sept 30 only daily 10am–8pm). The museum displays some of the huge sculptures from the previous winter's outdoor ice carving competition, the World Ice Art Championships (p. 363). As part of the experience, you'll watch a live sculptor at work creating new carvings and take in the multimedia presentation on ice sculpting that begins on the hour. The sculptures are in freezers that you walk in and out of, including one with a long ice slide running from the top row of the theater to the bottom. (You can actually zip down it.) In another freezer, you can get a taste of what 20 below feels like. Admission is $12 for adults, $11 for seniors, and $6 for kids ages 6 to 12 (5 and under free) with a multimedia presentation.

University of Alaska Fairbanks

Why am I sending you back to school? Well, the **University of Alaska Fairbanks** has far more reasons for out-of-towners to visit campus than your average big state university does. Its biggest attraction is the **Museum of the North** ★★★ (907 Yukon Dr., University of Alaska campus; ☎ 907-474-7505; www.uaf.edu/museum; $10 adults, $9 seniors, $4 children 7–16; daily 9am–7pm), which dazzles before you even get in the door—it occupies a spectacular "concept building" that's all swoops, curves, and silvery skin. Designed by a disciple of Frank Gehry, the building is supposed to evoke glaciers, alpine ridges, the northern lights, and the spring ice breakup on the Yukon River. I never would have figured that out without help, but once I read it, I could kinda see it. When you go in, plunk down the extra $4 for the self-guided audio tour—it's well worth it.

The main attraction is the ground floor Gallery of Alaska, which offers an overview of the last 11,000 years of human history, and the past few million years of natural history preceding that. The gallery has an extensive collection of Alaska Native, Russian, gold rush–era, and other artifacts that tell Alaska's story of cultural change. Among the whiz-bang natural history highlights are:

♦ Mammoth tusks, mastodon molars (which you can run your fingers across), and a 36,000-year-old mummified steppe bison named Blue Babe (look closely and you'll see the wounds left by the lions who killed it).
♦ Alaska's largest public display of gold: Millions of dollars of coins, nuggets, spoons, jewelry, and other golden objects are squeezed into a display case the size of half a phone booth.
♦ Looping videos on the northern lights, Native dance, and Arctic whale hunting.

If you get lucky, or if you call ahead and find out the hours, you can see Native athletes in the lobby demonstrating traditional games of skill.

Upstairs, in the Rose Berry Alaska Art Gallery, thousands of years of Alaskan art is on display. Contemporary multimedia pieces, paintings, and photography are presented alongside ancient Native artifacts, such as carved ivory harpoon weights, and a pair of good shaman/bad shaman masks made from whale bone. An enormous painting of Mount McKinley by Sydney Laurence (p. 46) is juxtaposed against the tiny Okvik Madonna, carved into a piece of walrus tusk. Where McKinley is immense and awe-inspiring, the Madonna is tiny and mysterious. She's more than 2,000 years old, and worn smooth by the ancient fingers of her owners. In her arms, she holds some sort of creature—it's not clear if it's a child, a sea otter, or what—and on her lips she has a curious smile not unlike the Mona Lisa's.

Natural history is on-the-hoof, if you will, at the University of Alaska's **Large Animal Research Station** ★★ (along Yankovich Rd. on the campus; ☎ 907-474-7207; www.uaf.edu/lars; admission prices vary by tour; Memorial Day–Labor Day daily 9:30am–5pm). Scientists curious about the unique adaptations of Arctic animals maintain herds of musk ox, reindeer, and caribou to study here. Happily, the scientists also let visitors enjoy a close-up look at these beasts—animals so well suited to the punishing cold that they take ice ages in stride. Half-hour tours ($6)

Greatest Light Show on Earth

You've heard, no doubt, about the aurora borealis (aka the northern lights), the dancing, glowing, multi-colored curtains of celestial light that wash over the skies in these parts, come winter. While every so often the aurora will make an appearance in the northern reaches of the Lower 48, they're as common as moose in the Alaskan Interior, which falls squarely beneath the auroral belt, the magnetically charged region around the north pole where the aurora most frequently occur. In the Interior, they're visible more often than not in the winter. Low to moderately intense auroral displays that would wow most people elicit yawns and shrugs from the locals. But when the aurora really go off, even the most jaded sourdoughs will bundle up in warm parkas and run outside to lay in the snow and stare at the heavens, mouths agape.

Alaska Natives had various explanations for this phenomenon. One Eskimo tale explained the northern lights as spirits playing ball in the sky with a walrus skull. According to another Native legend, the lights are given off by flaming torches guiding the newly dead into the afterlife. Scientists have come up with a less imaginative explanation, which involves fast-moving streams of protons and electrons that get molecules high in the earth's atmosphere so excited that they glow like neon signs.

The best time to view the aurora is any time between December and March, when the nights are long and the skies are dark. They're plainly visible within Fairbanks, but they're more intense if you get away from the city lights and view them in total darkness. Ask a local for suggestions on good viewing spots. During the long days of summer, when darkness never really comes, the aurora can't be seen.

For an aurora forecast, done by scientists at the **Geophysical Institute at the University of Alaska Fairbanks,** call ☎ 907/474-7558 or visit www.gedds.alaska.edu/auroraforecast.

---

are offered throughout the day, and hour-long tours ($10 adults, $9 seniors, $6 students) start at 1:30pm and 3:30pm. Both tours literally cover the same ground, a short path leading past the farmlike fields where the animals live. On the longer tour, you can spend more time chatting with the naturalist, but the short tour is enough for most people.

Not only hearty critters survive in this extreme region, as you'll discover at the **Georgeson Botanical Garden** 🧒 (117 W. Tanana Dr.; ☎ 907/474-1744; admission $2; May 31–Sept 2 only daily 8am–8pm), where you'll stroll among gigantic Alaskan vegetables, dahlias the size of dinner plates, and thousands of other plants thriving beneath the midnight sun. The garden is an intriguing combination of serious Arctic botany and sheer whimsy. There are all sorts of smaller gardens within the larger garden, including a children's garden with a tree house, a goldfish pond, a stream with flow meters and a flume you can manipulate, a stepping stone maze that tells the Athabascan story of how Raven made the world, and another maze that spirals back in time to the age of dinosaurs.

Whatever you're on campus to see, make a few minutes to stop at the **Alaska Range Overlook** ★ (Yukon Dr. near the top of the ridge), the best vantage point in all of Fairbanks for views of the Alaska Range. Several major peaks are visible from there on a clear day, including Denali. In the winter, this is the classic vantage point for watching the sun make its brief, low arc across the southern sky. Pick up a free **campus map** at the Museum of the North, to figure out what's where and for details on taking the handy campus shuttle.

THE OTHER FAIRBANKS

How can you, the Fairbanks visitor, dig beneath the cheery low-rise exterior of the Golden Heart city and gain insight into the big, freezer-burned hearts of its colorful residents? Easily. Opportunities abound to get off the beaten tourist path, and mingle with and get to know the locals. In general, they're a welcoming, curious, chatty bunch, streaked with eccentricity. In addition to seeing the standard sights, I encourage you to pursue at last one or two of the activities that follow.

Just by going to Fairbanks, you are greatly increasing your odds of meeting real Alaskans who will be happy to talk to you about the things real Alaskans like to talk about. To hedge your bets even further, sign up with the **Golden Heart Greeter Program** (☎ 907/456-5774; goldenheartgreeter@explorefairbanks.com), which will ensure you a sit-down with an amiable local eager to shoot the breeze. There are greeter programs like this in places all over the world, but this is the only one in Alaska. The volunteer greeters aren't visitor industry professionals, but rather friendly Fairbanks folks with so much enthusiasm for the place they call home that they're gung-ho to meet with perfect strangers to help them make sense of it (either that, or they're really lonely, but you can't knock 'em for that). Some are retirees, some are working stiffs, and some have special interests, such as gold mining, fur trapping, fishing for Arctic char, or moose hunting. The Fairbanks Convention and Visitors Bureau, which runs the program, tries to match the interests of visitors and volunteers. But more than anything, the visitors' bureau finds, everybody involved just wants to talk about the great land of Alaska in general.

In the movies, scientists don't work in soulless cubicles or colorless laboratories. Their workspaces are visually rich environments, where researchers toil behind sleek, silvery skinned walls, fiddling with the controls in rooms filled with blinking electronics, or disappearing into virtual reality rooms where the data comes to life. It's not like that in the real world . . . usually. But at the University of Alaska Fairbanks, well, science is pretty dramatic, so much so that the public is invited to tour these cutting edge labs throughout the summer. All tours are on Wednesdays; you have the choice of doing one or all three. The first begins at 1pm sharp in the basement of the Butrovich building, when visitors are ushered into the **Arctic Region Supercomputing Center** (☎ 907/450-8600). The guides aren't lying when they call the computers here "super computers"—they're among the fastest in the world. And whether they're standing before the lab's giant, stereoscopic wraparound screens, plotting graphs with x, y, *and* z axis, or spinning planet earth around like a top to speed up time, the guides make science look mighty cinematic.

The second tour begins at 2:30pm and covers the **Geophysical Institute** (☎ 907/474-7558), inside the neighboring cube-shaped building (The Elvey Building). The range of research conducted there stretches literally from the center of the earth to the center of the sun, taking in earthquakes, volcanoes, sedimentation, plate tectonics, the earth's atmosphere, the aurora borealis, and all sorts of other areas of geophysical interest. Scientists at the institute gather a lot of data from polar orbiting satellites, which downlink directly to the giant dish you'll spot on the roof as you enter. A highlight tour is a visit to the satellite control room, which is filled with banks of electronics with colored lights—again, just like in the movies. Another highlight is a visit to the institute's Alaska Earthquake Information Center, which monitors tremors with seismographs set up around the state. If you're lucky, you might get to see an earthquake in, say, the Aleutian Islands, graphically recorded in real time by a needle moving on a rolling drum.

The final tour of the day begins next door at 4pm in the lobby of **The International Arctic Research Center** (☎ 907/474-7558), an architectural beauty of a building, with swooping lines and silvery skin, and the flags of many nations displayed in the entryway. This is the world headquarters for research into global warming and climate change. A veritable United Nations of scientists gather here to do work in a variety of fields on a variety of different pieces of the climate change puzzle. The actual offices and cubicles where the toil takes place aren't particularly glamorous, but the building sure is cool. The tour is filled mostly with a PowerPoint presentation on the very latest about what scientists know about the rapidly changing subject of global warming. The tour also passes through an earthquake-proof library where much of the work of renowned Japanese wildlife photographer Michio Hoshino, who was eaten by a bear, is kept.

Tours are offered from June through August. If you're in town in the winter and need a science fix, check out the **Science for Alaska lecture series** (☎ 907/474-7558; www.scienceforalaska.com). Each Tuesday night, a scientist from the university's Geophysical Institute gives a presentation on the latest in Arctic or other high-latitude or Alaskan research. The talks are geared for a general audience, including kids. Past lectures have discussed things like:

- Why northern sky aurora and southern sky aurora sometimes mirror each other and sometimes don't.
- The science and the nonsense surrounding safety in bear country (with gruesome slides).
- Why scientists got so worked up over the single dinosaur footprint discovered in Denali National Park in 2005.
- The warming global climate, the thawing permafrost, and the outlook for seals on thinning ice (not good, I'm sorry to say).

Call for the location. I have no doubt you'll count these lectures among the highlights of your visit to Alaska.

Have you ever watched curling on TV and thought, "What's so hard about that?" Fairbanks might just be the place to find out, since curling is as popular as bowling here. The ancient Scottish team sport, in which one team member slides a polished granite stone along the ice toward a target while the others use brooms to sweep the ice like mad to influence the stone's course, has been played in Fairbanks since the city was founded. (It was brought to town by Scotsmen who joined the gold rush to the Interior.) The **Fairbanks Curling Club** (1962 2nd Ave.; ☎ 907/452-2875; www.curlfairbanks.org) has 200 members and the distinction of being "the oldest organized sports group in Alaska." The club used to play on the frozen Chena River during the winter, but now they've got their own curling arena, which has a spectator gallery heated to 68°F (20°C). If you're in Fairbanks from early October through April, you can drop by on any weeknight and watch the leagues compete for free.

If you call ahead of time, you might be able to line up a volunteer to teach you basic stone sliding and ice brushing techniques. There's no charge, no set time, and no guarantee that you'll get a lesson, but curlers are a pretty enthusiastic bunch, so odds are good that someone will step forward to coach you. Club members range in age from children, who play on teams with names like The Ice Chips and The Little Rockers, to octogenarians who have passed through the ranks of competitive curling and now just curl socially.

On a good day, the signal from radio station KJNP, "the gospel station at the top of the nation," carries clear across the Bering Straight to Russia. The rest of the time, it reaches radios deep in the Alaskan Bush, carrying the Good News as told by the Calvary Northern Lights Mission. The broadcasting facilities of **KJNP** (along Mission Rd.; ☎ 907/488-2216) are located just outside of Fairbanks in the oddball little town of North Pole (the call letters stand for King Jesus North Pole), where Christmas decorations are left up year-round (p. 289). The studios of the radio station and its sister TV station (which broadcasts locally) are located in a super-size log cabin billed as "the largest sod-roofed log cabin in the world." Some of the all-volunteer staff that runs KJNP live around it in smaller cabins scattered about a 48-acre wooded compound known locally as **Jesus Town.** Drop by any time between 9am and 5pm and you can take a free, informal tour of the studios. It doesn't matter if your interest in Christian broadcasting is spiritual or purely anthropological, if you just want to see the giant log cabin, or if you're simply intrigued by a place known as Jesus Town—you'll be welcomed. On the tour, you'll see the newsroom, offices, studios—and if you're lucky—a True Believer with a microphone, a Bible, and a 50k-watt signal reaching out to the world across the invisible airwaves.

Festivals & Events

Fairbanks is mad for festivals, celebrations, dog-sled races, and any other excuse it can think of for people to get together. The city's community calendar is kept full all year long, sub-zero weather or not. For the most current happenings, check with the **Fairbanks Convention and Visitor's Bureau information line** (☎ 907/ 456-4636; www.explorefairbanks.com). What's nice about these events is that they're not contrived for tourists. They're genuine local gatherings put on by a town that loves to shine up its classic cars, hitch up its dog teams, and dress up like saloon girls and take to the streets.

The **Tanana Valley State Fair** (☎ 907/452-3750; www.tananavalleyfair.org), which brags that it's Alaska's oldest fair, happens in early August. You'll find everything there that you'll find in a county fair in the Lower 48—carnival rides, livestock, 4-H exhibits, rodeo, washed-up pop bands from the '80s and beyond—plus you can gawk at Alaska's giant summer vegetables.

World Eskimo Indian Olympics

It's well worth it to plan a visit here in mid-July, simply to catch the **World Eskimo Indian Olympics** (www.weio.com), where Native athletes from around the state compete in games like the stick pull, the ear pull, and the two-foot high kick. While this event is popular with visitors, I'm putting it in the Other Fairbanks section because it is, more than anything, a Native get-together. The annual 4-day event emulates the gatherings Alaska Natives have had for centuries, where families or villages celebrate good hunts, exchange news, and demonstrate their physical abilities. Most of the age-old athletic games have some clear parallel to real-life survival skills. In the Indian stick pull, contestants try to yank a greased stick away from each other, which requires a powerful grip not unlike the one needed to grab slippery fish from a fish wheel. In the ear pull, contestants loop twine around each other's ears and pull hard until one of them can't take it anymore, a game requiring a high threshold for pain, a desirable attribute for people living in such an unforgiving climate. The premier events are the one-foot high kick and two-foot high kick. High kick competitors stand beneath a target suspended from a string, jump straight up and kick the target with one or both feet, then land without losing their balance. Top competitors can reach the bottom of a basketball net. On the flat Arctic tundra, a messenger with a good vertical leap could deliver urgent news to a village before he got there. One kick might mean, "Whale caught, everybody come help," while two might mean, "Caribou spotted, everybody come help." Then there's the blanket toss—a crowd favorite— a trampoline-like event where contestants are judged on height, balance, grace, and airborne maneuvers. Alaska Natives disagree about the origins of the blanket toss. Some say it developed in Native whaling communities as a way to get a look over the horizon. Others say it started just for the sheer fun of it.

You can attend the World Eskimo Indian Olympics during the day, when the preliminary competitions are held, but it's better to go at night for the finals. The preliminaries are free, but there's a small admission fee at 6pm. In the evening you can also catch a traditional dance, the Native baby contest, the Miss WEIO contest, and the handmade parky (that's what Alaskans call parkas) contest. Arts and crafts vendors are there day and night, as well as vendors selling Native foods. If you get a chance, try the Eskimo ice cream, made with whipped berries, seal oil, and snow.

Note: The World Eskimo Indian Olympics have traditionally been held in Fairbanks, but in 2006, after years of debate, the organizers decided to hold the 2007 games in Anchorage. The games are scheduled to return to Fairbanks in 2008, though. Check the WEIO website for updates.

Fairbanks calls itself the "Sled Dog Racing Capital of the World" (a title claimed by more than one Alaskan community), and, as such, there are races held all winter long. If you're visiting in the winter, you should definitely try to catch one. One of the biggies is held in mid-February, the **Yukon Quest International Sled Dog Race** ★ (☎ 907/452-7954; www.yukonquest.com). The start and finish of the 1,000-mile race, which follows early gold rush and mail trails along the Yukon River, alternates between Fairbanks and Whitehorse, Canada (Fairbanks gets the start in even-numbered years). The Iditarod is more famous, but the Yukon Quest is more grueling, according to mushers who've done both. In March you might catch the **North American Open Sled Dog Championship** (☎ 907/457-MUSH; www.sleddog.org). It's held over two weekends and is known as "Alaska's oldest running sled dog race." Unlike the Yukon Quest, which is a marathon, the North American Open Sled Dog Championship is a sprint—right through the frozen streets of downtown Fairbanks. There's no limit on how many dogs a musher can use, and dog teams with two dozen yelping animals aren't uncommon.

ACTIVE FAIRBANKS

The residents of the Interior are an active, outdoorsy bunch, in both summer and winter. For locals and visitors alike, getting out into the immense landscape to play—whether it's hiking, canoeing, golfing under the midnight sun, or cross-country skiing under the northern lights—is a huge part of the allure of the Alaskan heartland.

Canoeing

Unlike the wild white water rivers rollercoasting through more mountainous parts of the state, the rivers of the Interior are generally slow and lazy. This is canoe country. Strap on a life vest, pack a week of provisions or a simple picnic, and take advantage of it.

When it's not frozen solid, the lower part of the **Chena River** runs gently right through the heart of Fairbanks. So spend a few hours leisurely exploring this urban stretch of the river, stopping at one of the restaurants along the way, like the Pumphouse, then meeting the driver from your canoe rental outfit at a designated end point for a ride back to where you started. The upper part of the river gets a wee bit more challenging, with some class I rapids. It runs through beautiful wild land, with good opportunities to see wildlife such as moose, beavers, and muskrats. A trip down the Chena's full 100 miles takes 3 days, with camping along the way.

For water that's a bit more tricky, head out the Steese Highway into the backcountry north of Fairbanks and canoe down the **Chatanika River.** It has lots of class I rapids and opportunities for trips that could last from a day to a week. The upper part of the Chatanika, which cuts through some of Alaska's richest gold mining country, is swift and shallow, and riddled with sweepers, snags, and log jams. You don't need to be an expert to paddle it, but you don't want to be entirely green either. The lower stretches are slow enough to give you a chance to eyeball a lot of critters along the way, including black bears, brown bears, caribou, and Dall sheep. There are also campgrounds and a few public use cabins along the banks. For information about the cabins, or about camping along either the

Chena or the Chatanika rivers, inquire at **Alaska Public Lands Information Center** (see p. 263). Another excellent statewide resource for river runners is Karen Jettmar's *The Alaska River Guide: Canoeing, Kayaking & Rafting in the Last Frontier* (Alaska Northwest Books, $19).

Several outfitters in Fairbanks rent canoes but **7 Bridges Boats & Bikes** (4312 Birch Lane; ☎ 907/479-0751; www.7gablesinn.com), is possibly the most conveniently located, and its prices are fair at $35 a day or $100 a week, with discounts if you rent three or more canoes at a time. A van ride for you and your canoe to or from the river costs $3 per mile. The company also rents bikes, for $25 a day for non-guests, and $10 for guests. If you like, they'll set things up so you can paddle down the Chena River in town, then bike back to where you started. **Alaska Outdoor Rentals & Guides** (☎ 907/457-BIKE; www.akbike.com) right in Pioneer Park (p. 275) is another good pick; it will rent you a canoe for $33 and pick you and the boat up downstream for $17.

For a guided canoe or rafting trip, check with **Canoe Alaska** (☎ 907/883-2628; www.canoealaska.net), one of the oldest river running operations in the state. Trips start at $80 a day (or $50 for children 12 and under), and can be customized to your liking. Two-day paddling classes cost $190. Experienced paddlers can rent canoes for $35 a day.

Hiking

IN TOWN

Fairbanks doesn't have phenomenal mountain trails within its city limits, like Anchorage and Juneau. You have to get out on the gravel roads and into the countryside for prime hiking in these parts. That being said, the 2-mile nature walk through boreal forest and seasonal wetlands at **Creamer's Field** ★ within the city limits, is lovely. In fact, it's something like an All-Star Revue of Interior Habitats. It passes through seasonal streams and ponds, through woodlands and floodplains, across tussock meadow and muskeg. And while you're admiring all of these different habitats, be sure to look up: This 1,800-acre former dairy farm is a refuge for migratory waterfowl. Thousands of birds, including Canada geese, a variety of ducks, and songbirds from as far away as South America, stop there in the spring and fall on their way to and from the vast wetlands of the Arctic. Sandhill cranes stay all summer long, and don't be surprised if a moose makes an appearance. A local betting pool forms around the arrival of the first Canada goose at Creamer's Field, one of the harbingers of spring. The **Friends of Creamer's Field** (☎ 907/452-5162) lead **free guided tours** that leave from the parking lot Monday through Friday at 10am, with a second walk on Wednesday evenings at 7pm, from June until September. It takes 1 to 2 hours. Check out the old Creamer's farmhouse, which is on the National Register of Historic Places (it has a visitor center explaining why).

OUT OF TOWN

The hiking trails along the Steese Highway, the Elliott Highway, and Chena Hot Springs Road will get you deep, deep into the wilds of Interior Alaska. For a comprehensive list of Interior Alaska trails, trail conditions, and trip-planning assistance, check in with the **Alaska Public Lands Information Center** (see p. 263). I'll highlight some outstanding hikes along the Steese (p. 291) and Elliott (p. 296) highways in the driving tours sections that follow.

The best hiking along Chena Hot Springs Road is within the **Chena River Recreation Area.** Of those, **Angel Rocks Trail** ★★★ (mile 48.9) is the most popular hike in the Interior, a 3.5-mile round-trip loop that begins at a peaceful riverside picnic area and climbs through the boreal forest up to 1,750 feet and the tors known as Angel Rocks. It's got some steep sections, and takes 1 to 2 hours to complete.

About a half-hour up the Angel Rocks Trail, you'll come to the trailhead for the **Chena Hot Springs Trail** ★, which leads along a ridge 8.3 miles to Chena Hot Springs Resort. It's a delightful hike with beautiful views of valleys on either side, granite tors along the way, and very little foot traffic. (The sweetest way to do this all-day hike is to start at the hot springs, hike to Angel Rocks, then take a long, well-deserved hot soak when you get back.)

A tougher and even more awe-inspiring hike along Chena Hot Springs Road, the **Granite Tors Trail** ★★★ (mile 39) climbs to 3,300 feet and boasts a breathtaking collection of tors, some of them towering 100 feet above the alpine tundra. Give yourselves at least 6 hours for this 15-mile loop trail. If you're up for a 3-day backpacking expedition, the **Chena Dome Trail** (one trailhead at mile 49, the other at mile 50) makes a broad 30-mile loop that climbs along ridgelines and drops into valleys, peaks at 4,421 feet, and passes granite tors and the wreckage of a military airplane that crashed in the 1950s. You can take shorter, scenic day hikes up and back from either of the Chena Dome trailheads.

Hiking trips in the Chena River Recreation Area can be combined with stays at the six public use cabins there managed by the **Alaska Division of Parks** (3700 Airport Way, corner of University Ave.; ☎ 907/451-2705). Only one can be reached by automobile, the **North Fork Cabin** (Chena Hot Springs Rd., mile 47.7), a simple, classic Alaskan log cabin with firewood stacked on the porch and room enough to sleep eight. You have to hike to the others, and the shortest hike is 3.5 miles.

Golf

The **North Star Golf Club** (330 Golf Club Dr., off old Steese Hwy. past Chena Hot Springs Rd.; ☎ 907/457-4653; www.northstargolf.com), claims to be the northernmost course in North America. It may also be one of the few in the world to be open 24 hours a day in the summer (ah, the perks of that midnight sun; even when it's technically set, there's enough light to swing by). Its 18 holes are laid out over permafrost, which creates an ever-changing pattern of dips, swales, and mounds. Don't fret if a raven or a fox steals your ball. The local rule allows you to replace it in such cases without penalty. You can play 9 holes for just $20 and 18 for $36; golf cart rental is $15 and club rental is $20.

The **Fairbanks Golf and Country Club** (1735 Farmers Loop Rd.; ☎ 907/479-6555) has 9 holes, and hazards that include moose and marmots. Lately it's been having a nasty problem with bald spots on the greens caused by snow mold. Games cost $20 and cart rental is $12, depending on the length of the game. You can rent clubs for $15.

Skiing

During winter only (obviously), the Fairbanks area offers first rate cross-country skiing trails and some perfectly respectable downhill runs, as well. Cross-country trails are both near the campus of the **University of Alaska Fairbanks** and at the

Birch Hill Recreation Area at Fort Wainwright. Both areas are lit, so you can ski even on the darkest winter day. Birch Hill also has beginner and intermediate runs for downhill skiers, with chair lifts. For more serious downhill schussing, head to **Mt Aurora/Skiland** (20 miles outside Fairbanks, along the Steese Hwy.; ☎ 907/456-7669 or 907/389-2314; www.skiland.org; lift tickets $32 adults, $10 seniors, $22 children 7–11, children 6 and under free; hours vary), which has a 1,100-foot drop and more than 20 runs, for intermediate and advanced skiers. It's about 20 miles out of Fairbanks on the Steese Highway, and it bills itself as "The home of the farthest north chairlift in North America."

Chairlifts aren't to be taken for granted in the Interior. **Moose Mountain** (Moose Mountain Rd.; ☎ 907/479-8132; www.shredthemoose.com; $35 adults, $30 seniors and students, $20 children 7–12, children 6 and under free; Fri–Sun but hours vary) has two peaks and 42 runs for all ski levels. It doesn't, however, have chair lifts. Instead, you have to take off your skis and board a bus for a ride up to the peaks.

Yoga

Ask anyone in Fairbanks how people deal with the long, super-cold, sunless winters, and they'll tell you the same thing—you have to stay active. Snowshoeing, dog sledding, and cross-country skiing are among the more celebrated outdoor activities. Yoga, surprisingly, is quite popular too. And it's practiced year-round. If nothing says "vacation" to you quite like "adho mukha svanasana" (downward-facing dog), join the local yogis at **Interior Yoga** (Regency Court Mall, off College Rd. across from Jiffy Lube; no phone; www.interioryoga.com) in their pursuit of balance and bliss. Drop-in classes are held throughout the week and cost $12. Better yet, if you're around Saturday morning, join the **University of Alaska Fairbanks Yoga Club** (University Park Gym, on University Ave. just past the railroad tracks; call Maya at ☎ 907/388-1080). The club meets between 9:30am and 11am, and everyone—from loose-limbed devotees to stiff-as-a-board newbies—is welcome. A $5 donation is suggested.

ATTENTION, SHOPPERS!

The best places to shop in Fairbanks are, unfortunately, scattered all over town. Some of them are real finds, though.

Before Chris McCandless, the hapless and ill-prepared idealist who was the subject of the Jon Krakauer book *Into the Wild*, starved to death in a school bus near Denali National Park, he stopped at **Big Ray's** ★ (507 2nd St; ☎ 907/452-3458) in downtown Fairbanks and bought a rifle. He shot a moose with it, but he didn't know how to cure the meat and it spoiled. Big Ray's no longer sells firearms and it can't be expected to help you with common sense, but it does have just about everything else that someone preparing to venture into the Alaskan wild might need, from sleeping bags rated for 30 below zero, to bug-proof net clothing, to big bags of beef jerky. Even if you're not in the market for gear, browsing at Big Ray's is fun and full of surprises. Who would have expected, for instance, that among all the insulated camouflage clothing, the 100%-wool field pants, flannel shirts with quilted lining, and the oil-cloth ball caps, you'd find a bright blue Conoco-Phillips jumpsuit, just like the oil workers of Prudhoe Bay wear?

Another top-notch outdoor store is **Beaver Sports** (3480 College Rd.; ☎ 907/479-2494; www.beaversports.com) near the university. It stocks a larger selection of outdoor sports supplies than Big Ray's, and has a large selection of camping gear and accessories—from bungee cords to bear repellant.

You can pick up Alaskan souvenirs that are both useful and unusual at the **Great Alaskan Bowl Company** (4630 Old Airport Rd.; ☎ 907/474-9663). Its specialty is birchwood bowls of all sorts, sold in the same factory where they were turned on a century-old lathe. On sale are soup bowls, cereal bowls, laser-engraved bowls with Alaskan wildlife or sportsman themes, nested salad sets, and big, knotty bowls not good for liquids but perfect for popcorn or fruit. After they're lathed and kiln dried, and even sometimes etched with a laser, all bowls are coated with a mix of soybean oil, carotene, vitamin E, and lemon.

When old T-shirts, wool sweaters, and long johns outlive their usefulness in Fairbanks, they end up in the donation bin of The Fairbanks Community Behavioral Health Center, the starting point for their new lives as rag rugs, rag runners, rag place mats, and rag drink coasters. The center has a vocational program, which works to improve the job prospects of people struggling with depression, fetal alcohol syndrome, schizophrenia, and other such problems. The program is organized around turning rags into things to sell at the two locations of the nonprofit **Alaska Rag Company** (603 Lacey St., corner of 6th and Lacey; ☎ 907/451-4401; also at Pioneer Park, Cabin no. 4; www.alaskaragco.com). At either of them you can pick up a drink coaster for $6, a placemat for $14, a table runner for $30 to $40, and a rug for $32 on up into the hundreds. All of it is made largely from Fairbanks' cast-off insulating layers. If you happen to have packed some beloved jeans or worn-out T-shirts that you really shouldn't be wearing anymore, but which are too dear to part with, the Rag Company will gladly turn them into a tightly-woven, one-of-a-kind something-or-other that you can use for years to come.

Once a year, the musk ox at the University of Alaska Fairbanks' Large Animal Research station get combed to collect their soft, wool-like qiviut, which is sent to Native weavers in the Bush, and then returned in the form of articles of clothing for sale in the **Large Animal Research Station Gift Shop** (along Yankovich Rd.; ☎ 907/474-7207; www.uaf.edu/lars). Qiviut is warmer than wool, softer than cashmere, and not surprisingly, more expensive than either of them. If a qiviut night stole for $375 is beyond your budget, you might find a simple headband with a snowflake pattern for $155. And if that's too much, you can pick up a 1-ounce skein of pure qiviut for $60 and make something yourself. It really is remarkable stuff. You can also buy a 1-ounce bag of raw qiviut for $25, or (like I did recently) a tiny sample bag of it for $1—a little musk ox memento. Proceeds go toward the maintenance of the animals.

As unlikely as it seems, the Alaskan Interior was ice-free during the last ice age, though massive ice sheets and glaciers surrounded it on all sides. All sorts of creatures found refuge there, cut off from the rest of the world by the frozen walls of their immense fortress. The fossilized remains of many of them are encased in the permafrost today. They're unearthed all the time by erosion, mining operations, and fossil hunters. At **The Craft Market** ★★★ (401 5th Ave.; ☎ 907/452-5495), a cluttered Fairbanks shop in an old home on the edge of downtown, these fossils are sold by the pound. There are boxes filled with fossilized bone, tusk, teeth, antler, and other hardened bits and pieces of creatures that once roamed the Interior or swam in the Arctic Ocean or Bering Sea. Most are just shards or fragments, sorted by animal, but you might find a box filled with whole fossilized walrus jaws or good-size segments of woolly mammoth tusk (the state fossil). Alaskan crafts-people are the main buyers, but some tourists shop here, too—after all, fossils make for unique souvenirs. The store's packed with more common craft supplies too, such as glass beads and dyed feathers, as well as Alaska T-shirts, shot glasses, and other souvenirs that aren't quite as exotic as a Pleistocene-era animal part.

NIGHTLIFE IN FAIRBANKS

Put on by the same company that runs the Alaska Salmon Bake (p. 274) at Pioneer Park, **The Golden Heart Revue** ★★ (At the Palace Theater; ☎ 800/354-7274 or 907/452-7274; www.akvisit.com/palace.html) is a polished, corny, sometimes bawdy exploration of the central question surrounding Fairbanks' existence: Why? In the course of explaining how a city sprang up in a swampy valley bedeviled by gigantic mosquitoes in the summer, and 40-below temperatures in the winter, the cast hits on topics such as self-expression through outhouse design, prostitution in frontier-era Fairbanks' log-cabin red light district, sled dog names, Hawaiian vacations, and fashion statements that include parkas with extended-wear duct tape elbow patches. Tickets are $18 or $9 for children 12 and under, and showtime is at 8:15pm, with a 6:30 pm show sometimes added, during summer only.

Eight miles south of Fairbanks, at the Ester Gold Camp, the competing summer vaudeville show is a wee bit more high-falutin' (but just barely), built around the gold rush–era poetry of Robert Service, "The Bard of the North." **Service With a Smile** ★★ (Mile 35, Parks Hwy.; ☎ 907/479-2500) is performed in the Malamute Saloon, which has the swinging doors and sawdust floor of a frontier watering hole, just like the fictional Malamute Saloon that Service wrote about in "The Shooting of Dan McGrew." Unlike the theater where the Golden Heart Revue is performed, you can actually order a beer while watching the show (heck, it's the best way to get into the spirit of the production). Take a gander at the old, battle-scarred bar. It's from the saloon in Dawson City that Robert Service modeled his Malamute Saloon on. That's what the bartender told me anyway, and she swore she wasn't making it up. Tickets are $18 or $9 for children 12 and under. Most people combine the show with the crab feed described on p. 274. There are also cheap, historic rooms available on-site (p. 269).

For mellower summer evening entertainment, and to get a good picture of just how phenomenal the northern lights (which can only be seen in the winter) really are, take in the **PhotoSymphony** ★ (☎ 907/479-8097; www.photosymphony.com) in Ester. Okay, it's a slide show, but man, what a slide show—a large-screen presentation of panoramic photographs of the aurora borealis taken by photographer LeRoy Zimmerman, and set to music. Tickets are $10, or $6 for children 12 and under.

Downtown Fairbanks has no shortage of dive bars that open early, close late, and cater to a population of people with serious drinking problems. They're concentrated along 2nd Avenue in downtown. My favorite is **The Mecca Bar** (549 2nd Ave; ☎ 907/456-6320), a long dark cave of a bar with the same decor it had when it opened in 1946, including smoke-stained mirrors on the ceiling. Every so often a band will play.

More lively, less divey watering holes are outside of downtown. In the campus area, check out the compact basement bar called **The Marlin** (3412 College Rd.;

☎ 907/479-4646). Okay, it's a dive, too, but it's a university dive bar and so is different from a downtown dive bar. Go there Thursday through Saturday evenings to check out whatever band has squeezed itself onto the tiny stage. There's usually no cover charge, unless the band has driven in from out of town and needs to pay for gas. Because the place is so small, it gets crowded quickly when there's music. Whenever you go, it will have Pabst Blue Ribbon on tap, in mason jars, for $3. And there's always lots of dark, intimate, basement dive ambience, free of charge.

Fairbanks' most celebrated bar is the **Howling Dog Saloon** ★★★ (2160 Old Steese Hwy.; ☎ 907/456-4695; www.howlingdogsaloon.com; closed in winter) which is actually 10 miles north of Fairbanks in the bedroom community of Fox. The Howling Dog has a long bar with a diverse crowd, where diesel mechanics knock down pints alongside aurora scientists. The floor's littered with peanut shells, and the ceiling's covered with ball caps, bras, and dollar bills autographed by whoever wants to stick a dollar on the ceiling. There's a big dance floor and a little stage. Check out the old worn-out carpeting on the stage—it's the red carpet that was rolled out at Fairbanks International Airport in 1984 when President Ronald Reagan met very briefly with Pope John Paul II, before both reboarded their planes and went their respective ways.

Three miles south of town is the somewhat more upscale dance club and theater called **The Blue Loon** ★★ (Mile 353.3, 2999 Park Hwy.; ☎ 907/457-LOON; www.theblueloon.com). While it looks like a tractor barn from the outside, the interior is cool and stylish, with lots of dark wood, rope lighting, and a vaulted ceiling that's ribbed and looks like the inside of a giant overturned canoe. Along with a concert and dance space (which may get performances from such well known, if now second-tier, acts as the Indigo Girls and Hot Tuna), the Loon has a movie theater with balcony seating, which gets second-run films and a stage for live performances, including go-go dancers in cages. The crowd's a mix of military personnel and students from the University of Alaska, with a smattering of tourists in summer.

GET OUT OF TOWN
North Pole

The community of North Pole is a hard-luck little town 15 miles south of Fairbanks that's been confusing children about geography since the 1940s. Postwar homesteaders named the budding community after the place where Santa Claus lives in a gambit to lure toy factories there. They got an oil refinery instead, but the name stuck, and North Pole has been working the Christmas angle ever since. The streets have names like Kris Kringle Drive and are lined with street lights shaped like candy canes. The businesses leave Christmas decorations up year-round and have names like Santa's Suds Laundromat. It all may seem a little treacly, especially in the hot summers when green and red tinsel glitters under the midnight sun, but therein lies the appeal, at least for those drawn to displays of American garishness. The main attraction is the **Santa Claus House** 👦 (101 St. Nicholas Dr.; ☎ 800/588-4078 or 907/488-2200, press 5 for a message from Santa; www.santaclaushouse.com; free admission; summer only daily 8am–8pm). When you're driving down the Richardson Highway, you can't miss it. It's the enormous barnlike complex beside the Santaland RV Park and beneath the 42-foot giant Santa checking his list. There are toys and Christmas ornaments galore for sale inside, and somebody in a Santa suit is available for photos most of the time. Say hi to the forlorn reindeer outside in the pen and consider a stop at **Jesus Town,** too (p. 281).

One of the best things North Pole has to offer is its postmark, which you can get without getting out of your car. In about 10 minutes you can pull off the Richardson Highway, drop post cards in the drive-by mailbox at the **North Pole Post Office** (325 S. Santa Claus Lane), then get back on the highway and be on your (ho, ho, ho) merry way. (The post office, incidentally, gets nearly a half million pieces of mail a year addressed to "Santa Claus, North Pole.")

Chena Hot Springs Resort

Fairbanks residents and tourists alike love **Chena Hot Springs Resort** ✹✹✹ (Mile 56.5, Chena Hot Springs Rd.; ☎ 800/478-4681 or 907/451-8104; www.chenahot springs.com; $10 adults, $7 children 6–17, children 5 and under free; daily 7am–midnight). So do I. It's about a 2½-hour round-trip drive from Fairbanks, so you can get there and back in a day. But be nice to yourself and stay the night, so you can really lose yourself in the peaceful, unpretentious ambience of the place. For centuries, Alaska Natives knew about the springs and probably used them for medicinal purposes. Some prospectors found out about the place in 1905, and before long they'd developed it into a resort where trappers and other prospectors could soothe their aching backs and arthritic hands, and forget their frontier worries for a spell. The resort still has a rustic atmosphere, and even a few of the original cabins. It is by no means a resort in the sense of a "luxury resort." In fact, it's actually a little ratty around the edges, like an old summer camp. But if you relish a good, long, steamy soak in fresh, untreated mineral water bubbling straight from the fiery bowels of the earth, you'll have found your slice of sub-Arctic heaven.

The water here seeps from the ground at about 165°F (74°C), and sits in a cooling pond before it's pumped into the various soaking areas. The main one is a gorgeous 160-foot-long, boulder-lined lake, with water temperatures between 100° and 104°F (38°–40°C). A cold-water fountain in the middle of the lake shoots from a boulder, which you can haul yourself out on like a sea lion if you need to cool off. There are also hot tubs, and for kids (who aren't allowed in the rock lake), there's an indoor swimming pool—heated but not too hot.

Soaking is the big attraction at Chena Hot Springs, but the resort offers plenty of other activities, too. Cross-country skiing, snowshoeing, ice skating, and snowmobile rides are big winter draws. In the summer, there are sled dog rides (the dogs pull carts since there's no snow), horseback riding, and guided fishing trips. There are also flightseeing tours ($390 per person) across the Arctic Circle to the Native village of Beaver, where visitors spend an hour poking around and sampling Native food.

Chena Hot Springs is as jammed with visitors in winter as it is in summer—the springs are especially popular with young Japanese couples, who believe that children conceived under the northern lights will be lucky. Since it's so far north and so far away from any city lights, the views of the aurora borealis can be stupendous here, and you'll have lots of good vantage points: You can simply watch the lights as you float on your back in the thermal lake, or ride a Sno-Cat to the top of a hill with a 360-degree view of the sky and a warm-up lodge, or rent one of the resort's Arctic snow suits, so that you can lay comfortably in the snow, losing yourself in the natural light show.

In keeping with its frontier roots, this resort is admirably self-sufficient. It generates its own electricity at a geothermal plant, and it raises much of the produce served in its restaurant in an organic summer garden and in a year-round, hydroponic greenhouse heated by a system of hot-water pipes.

Need more reasons to come here? One is the resort's **Aurora Ice Museum** ($15 for adults and $7.50 for children 6–17), where you can check out ice sculptures like a life-size jousting ice knight, a giant ice chess set, and a two-story ice turret that you can climb to the top of via a spiral ice staircase. Sit on an ice stool at the ice bar, and order a vodka martini served in—what else?—a martini glass carved from ice (which you can keep until it melts). It's open year-round.

The most affordable lodging options at the resort, for those who don't mind roughing it (and are willing to carry their own bedding), is a simple yurt with three cots, which goes for $65 as a double, or $85 as a triple. There's a nearby outhouse, and showers in the bathhouse where you wash off before getting into the hot springs. The resort also has camping sites along a creek that go for $20 a night. (There's an 8% bed tax on everything at the resort but the tent sites.) Since these options are too rustic for many, there are motel-like rooms at the Moose Lodge—a big, faceless room with 2 queens and a full bath goes for $200, or a smaller room with two double beds and a three-quarter bath costs $165.

INTERIOR DRIVING TOUR #1: THE STEESE HIGHWAY ✸✸✸

The old chestnut that it's "not the destination but the journey that counts," really applies to the Steese Highway. This 162-mile highway runs out of pavement halfway along, gets rougher and narrower as it goes, and dead ends on the Yukon River at a misnamed little town that, apart from the river and the mosquitoes, has nothing going for it. Along the way, though, you'll pass through Alaska's richest gold mining country, chock full of mining relics, heaps of old mine tailings, well-staked claims, and the largest working gold mine on earth. At a few creek-side spots, you can try your hand at panning for gold without the risk of getting shot for claim jumping. At Eagle Summit, you can climb to a peak so tall that around solstice you can see the midnight sun rolling along the horizon, even though you're south of the Arctic Circle. And if that's not enough adventure for you, there are opportunities galore for overnight hiking, camping, river paddling, and even touring a rocket launching facility.

More than anything, though, a drive along the Steese Highway is a trip deep into the entrancing sub-Arctic landscape of Interior Alaska. The undulating hills roll off in all directions, covered with wildflowers from mid-May through July, and glowing with fall color in late August and early September. The hills crawl with wildlife—moose, wolves, hoary marmots, peregrine falcons, ptarmigan, you name it. Late in the summer, a herd of 50,000 migrating caribou cut through the area. Go expecting nothing but stay open to anything, and a trip down the Steese Highway will be a delight.

I've put together a highway log covering the Steese Highway highlights. Mile zero is in Fairbanks, where the Steese Highway begins as a four-lane expressway. To get anywhere north of Fairbanks by car, you have to start out on the Steese

---

Pipeline Problems: Age, Eco-Terrorists & Yahoos

In the Trans-Alaska Pipeline's 20-some years of use, a few saboteurs have succeeded in temporarily shutting it down. The reasons people attack the pipeline are various. Sometimes they're fossil-fuel-hating environmental "monkey wrenchers," known in these parts as "eco-terrorists." Sometimes they're just drunk and want to shoot at something. The pipeline is supposed to be bullet-proof, but in one case an inebriated local guy shot a hole into a weld, causing a 250,000 gallon spill that destroyed 2 acres of tundra, and earning himself a 10-year prison sentence. Lately the problems have had to do with upkeep, as the pipeline is showing its age. In the summer of 2006, a spill on the North Slope led to a government ordered inspection that found 16 of the 22 miles of the feeder pipes at Prudhoe Bay were so badly corroded they needed to be replaced.

Highway. Both the Elliott Highway and Chena Hot Springs Road, the two other main routes above the city, split off from the Steese after the first few miles. The Steese is open year-round, but if you're driving it in the winter, call the **Department of Transportation** (☎ 907/451-5204) for a recorded message on road conditions. Keep in mind that a lot of the road is unpaved, and that only certain rental car companies (p. 264) have vehicles they allow off the pavement. Also, bring bug protection—the mosquitoes here are thick as hail.

Mile 8.4—Stop here at the **Trans-Alaska Pipeline Viewpoint** (☎ 907/457-3344) to get a look at the 799-mile-long conduit carrying crude oil from the Arctic Ocean at Prudhoe Bay to the Pacific Ocean at Valdez. Since it began operating in 1975, more than 15 billion gallons of crude oil have been pumped through it and loaded onto tankers for transport to West Coast refineries. The pipeline is operated by the Alyeska Pipeline Service Company, a consortium of Big Oil firms, and believe it or not, this is such a popular sight, they now run a little gift shop and visitor center at the viewpoint.

Mile 9.5—If you're headed for the environmental disaster and big visitor attraction called **Gold Dredge Number 8,** discussed on p. 276, the turnoff is here.

Mile 13.6—Those oversize satellite dishes you'll see here are part of the **NOAA/NESDIS Command and Data Acquisition Station,** a facility that tracks and controls polar satellites. You can't get in, but you can stop at the front gate and study the information kiosk if you like.

Mile 16.6—Pull over here to see **Felix Creek.** In 1902, Felix Pedro, an Italian prospector, found the first gold in the Tanana Valley right along this creek, thereby setting off a stampede of other prospectors, which in turn led to the founding of Fairbanks. If you've got a pan, you can try your hand at panning in the creek here, just like the old Alaskan sourdoughs did. The **Felix Pedro Monument** is here, too.

Mile 20—You'll pass Twin Creek Road here, which leads to the largest gold mine in Alaska, the **Fort Knox Gold Mine,** a gaping pit in the earth where cyanide is used to leach gold from rock. There are no tours or public access of any sort, I'm sorry to say. I'm simply pointing it out so you know it's there. It's been in business since 1996.

Mile 20.9—This road climbs to 2,233 feet, so pull over and have a look around at the **Cleary Summit scenic viewpoint.** You can see the White Mountains and the sweeping Chatanika Valley to the north, and, on a good day, Denali to the south. Below are where old mining operations once took place, and where current ones are underway. This is a good vantage point for watching the midnight sun in late June.

Mile 27.9—You'll find food, lodging, and a saloon here, at **The Historic Chatanika Gold Camp** (p. 270).

Mile 29.5—Here is Neal Brown Road, the turnoff for the University of Alaska at Fairbanks' **Poker Flat Research Range,** the only university-owned scientific rocket launching facility in the world. (If you're very, very, very lucky, you may see a launch as you drive by).

Mile 39—One of the most attractive campgrounds in the Interior is the state's **Upper Chatanika River Campground** ($10 tent sites). This is a popular spot for grayling fishing and for launching all-day kayaking or canoeing trips to the Lower Chatankia River State Recreational Area, at mile 11 of the Elliott Highway (covered next). The Chatanika River is a class II, moderately difficult paddle. There's a scenic rocky beach, wild roses blooming everywhere in June, and—like every moist part of Interior Alaska during the summer—thick swarms of oversize mosquitoes.

Mile 57—As you've been driving, you may have noticed a rusty pipe cutting across hillsides. That would be part of the 90-mile system of pipe, tunnel, and ditch called the **Davidson Ditch,** which once carried water from the Chatankia River to gold mining operations. It was built between 1924 and 1929, and was considered an engineering marvel in its day. Steam shovels from another engineering marvel, the Panama Canal, helped with the construction. Davidson Ditch is mostly ditch, but about 6 miles of it were pipe. The pipe (which happens to be almost the same diameter of the Trans-Alaska Pipeline) was used to siphon water through the low points. For a few years in its later life, the Ditch was used to generate electricity, but a 1967 flood, which knocked out a 1,000-foot section of pipe, brought its usefulness to an end. Stop here at **U.S. Creek** and take a close-up look at some of the rusting remains.

Mile 57.3—If you didn't find any gold back at Felix Creek, you'll get another chance at the **White Mountains National Recreational Area Nome Creek Valley.** Turn off here and drive 7 miles to the beginning for a 4-mile stretch of the Nome Creek set aside by the Bureau of Land Management for recreational gold panning.

Hiking the High Country

The **Pinnell Mountain National Recreation Trail,** which runs for 27 miles entirely above the tree line, is regarded as one of the best short backpacking routes in the state. The views are eye popping, summer wildflowers are everywhere, and wildlife spotting opportunities are abundant. Migrating caribou pass through the area in droves from mid- to late summer. On the downside, the weather can go from good to horrendous in nothing flat. The two emergency shelters along the way (at mile 10.7 and mile 17.7) are especially welcome sights when things get nasty. Of course, you don't have to do the full grueling trip. You can start from either end and make a short day hike out and back—views are great from the get-go. The trail stretches between 3,624-foot Eagle Summit (mile 107) and 2,982-foot Twelvemile Summit (mile 85). Eagle Summit is the better starting point if you're going the distance because it's more of a downhill walk from there.

Before setting off on any backcountry hike in the Interior, check in with the **Alaska Public Lands Information Center** (see p. 263) for trail conditions and trip planning assistance.

All you need is a pan and some patience. You can get more information at the **Public Lands Information Center in Fairbanks** (p. 263) or at the **BLM website** (www.ak.blm.gov).

Mile 85.6—Here at **Twelvemile Summit** there's an easy 2-mile hike that climbs to an overlook with a spectacular view of the surrounding countryside. Unusual rock formations and lots of caribou abound in the area. From late July to mid-September, you can usually spot bands of migrating caribou if you sit and wait for a bit. The summit is located along the divide between two watersheds: To the west, all waterways lead to the Tanana River; to the east they lead to the Yukon River. Hikers will also find the trailhead here for the **Pinnell Mountain National Recreation Trail** (above).

Mile 107—Even though **Eagle Summit** is 50 miles south of the Arctic Circle, the line of latitude is lofty enough to give you a peak over the horizon at the midnight sun anyway. Because of that little geographic peculiarity, there's always a big crowd from Fairbanks gathered atop Eagle Summit on the solstice, celebrating the longest day of the year like a Super Bowl win. This is the tallest (3,624 ft.) peak along the Steese Highway, and the views are marvelous. The hike to the top is less than a mile, and not particularly tough, and it's worth a visit even if it's not solstice-time. On a good day you can see the Alaska Mountains, 100 miles to the south. The wildflowers in the area are the best on the whole drive, and help to offset the piles of rubble and eroded scars on the land left from all the small-scale gold mining operations in the area.

Mile 116.5—The Steese Highway crosses **Mammoth Creek** here, where a woolly mammoth tusk and the fossilized remains of other ancient creatures have turned up. You can see some of the fossils just up ahead, at the museum in Central (see below).

Mile 127.5—The rugged little town of **Central,** population 113, has a grocery store, a couple of diners, a laundry, a motel, a museum, and a saloon with a scale that patrons can shake gold dust out onto to settle their tabs. The market price of gold is posted at the bar, so there's no confusion. Check out the **Circle District Historical Museum** (☎ 907/520-1893; $1 adults, 50¢ children 12 and under; in summer only daily noon—5pm), a big log building with an impressive display of 20 different types of gold, which members of the community have donated or put here on loan. Also on view are exhibits on early mining techniques and freight hauling by sled dog, an old miner's cabin, and the first Alaskan printing press ever hauled north of Juneau, as well as a photo gallery of wildflowers (which can come in handy if you've been trying to figure out what you've been looking at all day). And did I mention all the rock? There's a gallery of minerals, and some of the fossils found in Mammoth Creek. If you've driven this far, you should definitely stop at the museum for a look around.

Mile 127.8—Just out of town is the turnoff to what used to be the biggest draw along the Steese Highway, **Circle Hot Springs.** Unfortunately, the springs were closed at press time due to a big fire, and there was no word on the future of the place. The hot springs were originally a gathering place for Athabascan Indians. The whites caught on to the springs, as the story goes, when a miner out hunting in the winter wounded a moose, which escaped by swimming across a stream. That was odd, since the stream should have been frozen. The miner returned in the spring, and the hot springs were developed not long after into a frontier resort, where other miners came to soak away their aches and pains. Call the Fairbanks Visitor's Bureau (p. 281) to check on the status of the springs.

Mile 162—The Steese Highway narrows and worsens until it finally stops at the misnamed wilderness town of **Circle,** population 73. The miners who founded the town in 1896 gave it the name Circle because they thought they were on the Arctic Circle. Turned out they were off by 50 miles, but the name stuck (whoops!). It's nearly a ghost town today, though it was a gold rush boomtown once, with two theaters, eight dance halls, and 28 saloons. It once called itself "the largest log cabin city in the world," but the Yukon River has swept away much of the original town. Now, there's one gas station and a grocery store, the **H.C. Company Store** (☎ 907/773-1222). When the Yukon River floods, so does the H.C.—the flood dates and high-water marks are marked on the piling inside. The grocery store is one of the two things to see in Circle: The other is the **Pioneer Cemetery,** which has a lot of graves from the 1800s scattered among the trees. Walk upriver along a gravel road paralleling the bank of the Yukon until you come to a path through a thicket, then follow the path until you find headstones. Circle also has a free campground by the river, and mosquitoes so big, thick, and aggressive, they sound like rain when they hit the outside of your tent

INTERIOR DRIVING TOUR #2:
THE ELLIOTT HIGHWAY

The Elliott Highway is like the Steese Highway in that it takes you deep into mining country, it's rich with views of Interior Alaska's wild, rolling countryside, and it's only partially paved. Unlike the Steese Highway, the Elliott Highway has a big reward at the end: **Manley Hot Springs,** where you can sit in a greenhouse and soak in steaming hot mineral water. There aren't as many points of interest along the way, however, so instead of including a highway log like I did for the Steese Highway, I'll just describe the highlights here.

The Elliott Highway begins 10 miles north of Fairbanks, at the bedroom community of Fox, and ends 152 miles away at the little town of Manley. It parallels the Trans-Alaska Pipeline for several miles, rising and falling all along the way with the rolling hills and ridgelines it crosses. After the first 73 miles, the pavement ends, and the highway continues as a largely rough, pot-holed road with narrow shoulders, steep grades, frost heaves, and blind curves (beware of moose in the road). Where the pavement ends is also where the Dalton Highway, the only road to the Arctic, begins. The Elliott gets plenty of truck traffic up to this point, with steady streams of big rigs coming and going from the oil fields at Prudhoe Bay.

If you plan to drive the Elliott Highway, make sure you've got the right vehicle. Only a handful of Fairbanks car rental firms allow their vehicles to go off the pavement (p. 264).

At milepost 71, you'll come to the turnoff for Livengood. On a map Livengood has more of a presence than it does on the actual landscape. There's nothing there but a sparse collection of rural homes. Don't bother with it. If you want to go exploring off the beaten track, turn off at milepost 110 and drive 11 miles south to **Minto,** an Athabascan village of about 200 people on the banks of the Tolovana River. There's a small arts and crafts center here, where, if it's open or if you can find someone to open it for you, you can buy birch-bark basketry and other beautiful Minto-made Native handiworks at great prices.

Make an excuse to get out of the car, as there are top-notch hiking trails at **White Mountains Recreation Area** at milepost 28; or you can trek 8 miles to **Hutliana Hot Springs** at milepost 129 (see p. 297 for details).

At the end of the road, you'll come to the rustic little community of **Manley ★**, on a slough of the Tanana River. Manley has about 100 people and at least as many sled dogs. It also boasts a gas station, a grocery store, a post office, two public campgrounds, and lodging at **The Manley Roadhouse** (100 Front St.; ☎ 907/672-3161). Built in 1906, the Roadhouse is the oldest lodging in Interior Alaska. Downstairs there's an informal sitting room with all sorts of Alaskana on display, as well as a restaurant and a bar with an extensive selection of spirits. The simple, country-style rooms start at $65 a night, double occupancy. The hot springs here consist of three concrete soaking tubs in a greenhouse filled with grapes and hibiscus. Each tub is kept at a different temperature and—for $5 per person, per hour—you get all three tubs and the entire greenhouse to yourselves. Call ☎ 907/672-3231 to book a slot.

Hikes Off the Elliott Highway

Trails in the **White Mountains Recreation Area** (Mile 28, Elliott Hwy.) are the way to go if you really want to get away from it all. The recreation area has more than 200 miles of trails and nine public use cabins. The area is busiest in the winter, when dog mushers, snowshoers, cross-country skiers, and snowmobilers take to them. Most are too muddy in the summer for hiking, but there are a few exceptions. The scenic **White Mountains Summit Trail** keeps dry by following the ridgeline to the top of Wickersham Dome, which has nifty views of the White Mountains' jagged peaks in the distance. Wild berries grow along the trail in the summer. A half-day challenge for those who follow its first few miles, it can also be done as a multi-day backpacking trip by those who follow its 18-mile length of trail to Beaver Creek. The Bureau of Land Management has a public use cabin there, the **Borealis-LeFevre Cabin,** where you can bed down for the night if you make reservations (see p. 373 for reserving public use cabins).

This area also offers up an unremarkable 8-mile trek through the woods with a swell pay-off: the **Hutliana Hot Springs** (trail begins a quarter of a mile east of the one-lane bridge at mile 129). The springs at the end of this trail fill a 3-foot-deep pool built from rocks and maintained by hot springs enthusiasts. There are absolutely no services or amenities here of any kind—it's a total soak in the wild. If you're rugged enough to make it this far, you may as well make a night of it. Bring food, camping gear, and plenty of water so you don't get dehydrated.

Check in with the **Alaska Public Lands Information Center** (see p. 263) for trail conditions and trip planning assistance.

INTERIOR DRIVING TOUR #3:
THE DALTON HIGHWAY ★★★

The Dalton Highway will take you as far as you can go on the U.S. Highway system, to the very top of the continent. It's the only road in Alaska that leads to the Arctic, and it's one of the planet's all-time spectacular road trips traversing vast stretches of tundra, crossing through black spruce forests dwarfed by the permafrost, dropping to near sea level where it crosses the broad Yukon River, and crossing the Arctic Circle. It also climbs to 4,800 feet into the otherworldly Brooks Mountains, before it descends onto the vast North Slope and the Arctic plain, where it skirts the edge of Arctic National Wildlife Refuge.

As you can tell, I'm a fan. That being said, it's also a challenging, hazardous, punishing drive, and not one to undertake casually.

Most of the Dalton Highway is unpaved. Each summer, the state lays a little more asphalt (and backs up traffic), but only about 25% of the road has been improved so far. The rest is fraught with soft shoulders, sheer drop-offs, steep grades, blind curves, sharp rocks, and long stretches of potholes and wash board.

It's also imperative to bring along food and water and go with a full tank of gas. Services are few and far between. There are just two truck stops along the way.

A BIT OF BACKGROUND ON THE DALTON   The Highway branches off the Elliott Highway, 84 miles north of Fairbanks, and runs 414 miles to the well-secured gates of the oil fields at Prudhoe Bay, 9 miles short of the Arctic Ocean. It was built in 1974 to haul building materials and supplies to the construction camps working on the Trans-Alaska Pipeline. Nowadays, thousands of 18-wheelers scream up and down annually, hauling freight to Prudhoe Bay. Truckers own the road. The maximum speed limit is 50 mph, but they blast down the highway at 70 mph, kicking up gravel showers and dust storms in their wake. Pull over when you see them coming and give them room, but do so carefully so you don't roll off an embankment and end up upside down on the tundra.

Crazy things happen along the Dalton Highway. Truckers tell stories of rut-crazed bull moose staring down tractor trailers. When I was there last, wolves stalking people at rest stops were a problem. Around mile 115, a wolf chased a young schoolteacher and nipped her in the buttocks before she locked herself in an outhouse. On the very same day, at mile 75, a wolf leapt onto the road and ran after a bicyclist (who was on a long-haul ride from Tierra del Fuego to the Arctic). An approaching trucker saw the wolf closing in on its frantically pedaling prey and swerved to run down the animal, then just kept driving.

PREPLANNING YOUR TRIP   Most visitors go no farther than the Arctic Circle, which can be done in a long day trip from Fairbanks. If you go all the way to Deadhorse, give yourself at least 4 days (it's about a 1,000-mile round-trip from Fairbanks). Stay in Wiseman (discussed later) along the way. Then make reservations to go on a tour of Prudhoe Bay and book a room in Deadhorse, both discussed in the section on p. 303.

Check in with the **Alaska Public Lands Information Center** (p. 263) in Fairbanks before attempting to tackle the Dalton. If you're driving your own car, bring two spare tires. Most rental car agencies in Fairbanks don't allow their vehicles to travel the Dalton Highway, but two do. (See p. 264.) If you don't feel up for driving yourself, tours are available through **Northern Alaska Tour Company** (☎ 800/474-1986 or 907/474-8600; www.northernalaska.com) which does 3-day trips to Prudhoe Bay for $789 per person. On the tour you'll fly over the Brooks Range in a small plane, land at Coldfoot where you'll spend the night, and drive back down in a van, with another night in the historic gold mining village of Wiseman.

Following is a highway log that offers a brief sketch of the Dalton Highway.

Mile 0—The Dalton Highway begins 84 miles north of Fairbanks, at milepost 73 of the Elliott Highway.

Mile 53—This is where you get your first view of the broad and mighty **Yukon River,** with the Fort Hamlin Hills rolling off in the distance behind it. The Yukon is the longest river in both Alaska and in the Yukon Territory of Canada, where it originates. It stretches 1,980 miles from its Canadian headwaters to the Yukon

Dalton Highway Driving Times from Fairbanks

Under perfect driving conditions, and without stops, the journey from Fairbanks will generally take:

3 hours to Yukon River
4½ hours to Arctic Circle
6 hours to Coldfoot
8 hours to Atigun Pass
13 hours to Deadhorse

Factor in extra time for road work, nasty weather, sightseeing, and rest stops.

River Delta in Western Alaska on the Bering Sea. Athabascan Indians used to travel the Yukon in birch bark canoes. Later, wood-burning paddle-wheel riverboats carried gold seekers and supplies up and down the river. During the Klondike gold rush, it was a main thoroughfare. Stern-wheelers continued traveling the Yukon River to the Yukon Territory until the Klondike Highway opened in the 1950s. Nowadays, people in the roadless villages on the banks of the Yukon travel the river in motorboats during the summer, and on snowmobiles or dog sleds during the winter, when it becomes a frozen expressway.

Mile 56—The Dalton Highway is the only road in Alaska to cross the Yukon River, and it does so here using the **Yukon River Bridge.** Pull off before the bridge and take some pictures. The 2,290-foot bridge, which arches gracefully over the river, is covered with wooden planking, which expands and contracts as the temperatures change without causing any structural problems. Across the river at the **Yukon River Camp** (☎ 907/474-3557; hours vary; MC, V) you'll find the first of two truck stops along the Dalton. It's got gasoline, $89 motel rooms, and a great diner where road crews and truckers mingle at communal tables with package tourists and independent travelers. The gas is expensive and the hotel rooms are horrid (*Tip:* Stay in Wiseman, p. 302, instead), but the diner is fantastic. Breakfast is served all day ($7.95–$12), lunch features enormous hamburgers, salmon burgers, and veggie burgers ($8.25–$9.75), and dinners include horseradish encrusted halibut and salmon fettuccine ($22).

Mile 60—Just down the road, there's another dining option tucked back in the Bush and not visible from the road. It's the **Hot Spot Café** (☎ 907/451-7543; hours vary; no credit cards; $–$$); go if you want a really hefty hamburger, and other diner fare.

Mile 86—If you're in no particular hurry, take the 1-mile side trip here to the very scenic **86-Mile Overlook,** though I'll warn you—the road is narrow and rocky, with no turning back until you get to the top. Once you get there, you'll be rewarded with sweeping views. To the northeast are an impressive collection of granite tors. To the southeast, you'll see the rolling Fort Hamlin Hills. To the east, you stare into the massive and marshy Yukon Flats National Wildlife Refuge, a waterfowl nesting area that's larger than Vermont and Connecticut combined.

Mile 90—If you're trying to make good time, skip the 86-Mile Overlook and stop at the pullout on the crest hill here. There's a long view of the Dalton Highway vanishing into the north, with the Trans-Alaska Pipeline zigzagging alongside it— a photo-op if there ever was one.

Mile 98—Ancient hunters used to camp at the 40-foot pinnacle here called **Finger Rock,** where they could spot herds of bison and woolly mammoth for miles around. Early Alaskan bush pilots said the rock pointed toward Fairbanks, and they used it as an aid in navigation. Today, truckers stop for the outhouse, and tourists stop for that and because it's one of those riveting features on the landscape that you can't possibly pass without exploring. Besides the rock itself, which is a granite tor, there's a half-mile trail across the alpine tundra. Stretch your legs on the trail and study the low, sturdy Arctic alpine plants, such as low-bush cranberries and leathery-leafed Labrador tea. Athabascans and Eskimos use Labrador tea for its cathartic and medicinal effects, as well as to season strong-tasting meat, such as brown bear.

Mile 115—Congratulate yourself—you've made it to the **Arctic Circle.** This is the line of north latitude at which the sun stays completely above the horizon for 1 full day on summer solstice, and below it for 1 full day on winter solstice. One-third of Alaska lies above the Arctic Circle. There's an undeveloped campground, outhouses, and a sign you can have your picture taken in front of that says "Arctic Circle, Dalton Highway, Alaska, Latitude 66 degrees, 33 seconds." I can think of no better place to stop and visualize how the seasons change as the earth, tilted on its axis, orbits the sun. This is as far as most visitors go up the Dalton.

Mile 132—Keep your eyes peeled for the pull-out, where you can stop for your first view of the daunting Brooks Range. For an even better look, park there and climb to the top of the 1,500-foot hill called **Gobblers Knob.** The facility you can see along the pipeline is Pump Station No. 5, one of many pump stations that keep the oil flowing south. Despite the name, though, this particular pump station doesn't do any pumping. It's actually a pressure relief station that slows the gravity-fed flow of oil as it descends from the Brooks Range. You can also see Prospect Creek up ahead, the next point of interest.

Mile 150—Archaeologists have found charcoal, stone scrapers, and other evidence that indicate that the area around here was used by ancient hunters for thousands of years. Read about them at an interpretive display at the **Grayling Lake Wayside.** There's a turnout to the east that accesses shallow Grayling Lake, where you might find moose in the water munching on aquatic plants.

Mile 156—After you cross the bridge over the **South Fork of the Koyukuk River** here, the landscape begins to change. You're now traveling through the foothills of the Brooks Range. This is active gold mining territory, and many of the side roads you'll see lead to private mining claims. It's not a good place to go exploring.

Mile 175—At about the halfway point on the Dalton Highway, you'll come to **Coldfoot,** an unlovely little truck stop on the Middle Fork of the Koyukuk River. This is the last place for northbound travelers to get anything—food, gas, tire repairs, whatever—before Deadhorse. Coldfoot dates back to around 1899, when it was a center for prospectors and was called Slate Creek. In the summer of 1900, a wave of stampeders arrived with plans to stay the winter, but then got cold feet and beat it before the snow came. That's how the story goes, anyway. In 1981 the legendary Iditarod musher Dick Mackey began selling hamburgers to truckers here from an old school bus. The truckers later helped Mackey build a permanent truck stop, **Coldfoot Services Truckstop** (☎ 907/474-3500; daily 24 hr.; MC, V; $). It is the best place hereabouts to get a cheap, hot meal and to catch up on the news of the road. Everyone sits at oilcloth-covered common tables with long wooden benches. Check out the gallery of truck wrecks on the wall and the center post of the building, which is carved with the names of truckers who helped build the place.

Most of the buildings in Coldfoot are modular ATCO units, salvaged from pipeline construction camps. A notable exception is the big, handsomely designed log building housing the **Arctic Interagency Visitor Center** (☎ 866/AK-PARKS or 907/274-8440; www.alaskanha.org; late May to early Sept daily 10am–10pm), which is jointly run by the National Park Service and other government agencies. Inside you can get the low-down on road conditions and camping, borrow bear-proof containers, buy hunting or fishing licenses, study natural history exhibits, and browse at a bookstore run by the Alaska Natural History Association.

Mile 188—Just after the bridge over the Middle Fork of the Koyukuk River, there's a turnoff on your left to **Wiseman,** a gold mining village of log cabins and about 29 residents in clearings among the spruce forest on the banks of the Koyukuk River. It's 3 miles from the Dalton Highway. Wiseman exists in an Arctic time warp. Many of the cabins date to the early days of the village, a 1908 boomtown founded when gold was discovered on nearby Nolan Creek. If you just drive into Wiseman and out again, you won't see much. Spending the night at one of the lodgings there (see the "Where to Stay" box, below) is the best way to get in touch with the surprising, frontier character of the place.

Mile 203—Watch for **Sukapak Mountain** coming into view to the north. It's a bald, 4,459-foot granite rock that glows like gold in the summer afternoon sun. "Sukapak" means "marten deadfall" in the Iñupiat Eskimo language. When the Iñupiat look at the mountain from the north, they see a resemblance to a care-fully balanced log, like the kind used to trap marten. The short mounds between the highway and the mountain you might notice are called palsas, which are formed when ice heaves the vegetative matt upward.

Mile 211—The highway crosses **Disaster Creek** here, which used to be as far as the public could travel up the Dalton Highway. It took a big battle in the state legislature to do away with the gate that blocked the road to private vehicles here. The forces of open-access prevailed in 1994.

Mile 235—Alaska is divided into boroughs, rather than counties. At this point, you'll enter the North Slope Borough, the world's largest municipality, in land area anyway. It covers a good portion of the Alaskan Arctic, and has about 8,000 year-round residents. As the road begins climbing into the Brooks Range, the landscape changes considerably, with the boreal forest thinning out until—at one

Where to Stay along the Dalton Highway

The hotels at both Yukon Crossing and at Coldfoot are depressing places made from pre-fabricated, modular ATCO units salvaged from old pipeline construction camps. It's nice to know that they're there in a pinch, but you'll do a lot better staying in Wiseman.

$ At the **Wiseman Gold Rush B&B** ★ (Mile 1886; ☎ 907/678-3213; no credit cards) you can sleep in either a brand-new spruce wood cabin or in a tent cabin (wood frame and floor, canvas walls and ceiling), like the kind Alaska's pioneers often used. Both are set on the edge of a grassy field and go for about $75 double occupancy. Neither has electricity, but both have Coleman lanterns and woodstoves, which adds to the old-timey ambience (I think). Outside, there's a fire pit made from a section of the Trans-Alaska Pipeline, and plenty of dogs, who may either howl at you or greet you with soggy tennis balls or severed caribou hooves in their mouths. The tent cabin is surprisingly comfortable, with two soft double beds that you sink into deeply. The spruce cabin is small and cozy but tall, sporting a high loft equipped with a log-framed bed. It shares its bath with the tent cabin next door—"It's got the only flush toilet this side of Wiseman," the owner, Lourna Loundsbury, will tell you proudly. Lourna and her barrel-chested husband, Jim "Clutch" Loundsbury, live nearby in their own one-room cabin. Lourna calls the place a "B&B or Not" because she will cook sausage and eggs for you in the morning, but only if you're really inter-ested. Ask Clutch to show you his mining museum, kept in a separate one-room cabin.

$$$ Berni and Uta Hicker, who run **The Arctic Getaway** ★★★ (Igloo No. 8; ☎ 907/678-4456; www.arcticgetaway.com; no credit cards), are Arctic transplants from Munich and consummate do-it-yourselfers. They home-school their children, hunt their own meat, trap animals for fur, grow their own vegetables, tend to their sled dogs, and generate their own power with windmills and banks of solar panels. They also generate cash flow by running a year-round bed-and-breakfast. Guests can stay in one of two adjoining cabins, connected at the shared bath. The one-room cabin goes for $90, while the two-story, two-room cabin goes for $150. Both are rustic, but comfortable and warm, with kitchenettes and oil stoves. Uta serves sourdough pancakes for breakfast in the dining room of the family's home, which is Wiseman's old log dance hall, built in 1910. Berni's mar-mot, wolf, bear, and lynx hides hang from the rafters, and photos of min-ers standing stiffly with Native women, taken when the dining room was still used for dancing, hang on the walls. If you want to spend winter in the Arctic, this is the place to do it. The northern lights are directly over-head, and Berni and Uta will ensure that you don't starve or freeze to death (two very real risks in the Arctic).

last tree along the road marked with a sign that says **"Farthest North Spruce Tree on the Alaskan Pipeline. Do Not Cut"**—it gives up entirely. The Farthest North Spruce, which was about 273 years old, was killed by a vandal in 2004. But you can still see its weathering remains.

Mile 245—The Dalton climbs steeply to **Atigun Pass** at 4,739 feet, the highest highway pass in Alaska. Pull over at the turnout, shut off your engine, stretch your legs, listen to the wind, think about how deep you are in the wilderness, and try not to freak out.

Mile 284—Of all the amazing and beautiful things I saw when I last drove the Dalton Highway, perhaps the most surprising was the beautiful young college student alone on the North Slope, in the middle of nowhere, jogging. Actually, she wasn't in the middle of nowhere. The University of Alaska Fairbanks Institute of Arctic Biology has a field station here, where it does research on global warming. The Toolik Field Station on **Toolik Lake** isn't open to the public, but you can find places along the shore of the lake where, if you are so inspired, you can take a freezing cold Arctic dip. I did, and it's freaking cold.

Mile 302—Watch for Dall sheep around here on the steep, rocky sides of Slope Mountain. Watch for grizzly bears, too, in May and early June, when they come to hunt on the sunny slopes

Mile 326—Keep an eye out here for peregrine falcons, gyrfalcons, rough-legged hawks, and other raptors, which hunt along the cliffs beside the Sagavanirktok River.

Mile 344—Look for falcons and hawks nesting in the bluffs above the Sagavanirktok River here.

Mile 354—Stop here at the **Last Chance State Wayside** and consider the changing geography. This is where the diminishing lowlands of the Brooks Range and the North Slope begin to give way to the flat expanse of the Coastal Plain. The Coastal Plain has the unusual distinction of being both desert and wetlands. It's desert because it gets so little precipitation, about 5 inches per year. It's wetlands because permafrost seals the ground, keeping the water that does collect on the surface from draining. Protein-rich sedges and an enormous population of insects thrive on the surface in the summer, drawing birds from as far away as Asia, Africa, and Tierra del Fuego. Caribou descend upon the plains in vast numbers in late June and July, and you may see them from the highway—or even crossing the highway—then.

Mile 414—The Dalton Highway ends for the public on the windswept tundra at **Deadhorse,** 8 miles short of the Arctic Ocean. Deadhorse is an unsightly little company town that exists solely to serve the oil drilling operation at **Prudhoe Bay.** Tourism there is an afterthought, at best. Yet each summer a handful of curious travelers (mostly cruise-ship passengers on pricey land tours, but always a few intrepid travelers who drive up the Dalton Hwy.) come for a bit of high-latitude industrial sightseeing.

Where to Dine & Stay in Deadhorse

The two Deadhorse hotels that take tourists (there are two other hotels just for workers) are as spartan as unlovely little Deadhorse itself. Both hotels are made up of ATCO units, the prefabricated modular dwelling structures of choice in the Arctic. There is very little difference between the two hotels except in their prices, their meals, and their bathroom arrangements. Apart from the Deadhorse's general store, where you can buy snacks, the hotels are the only places in town to find food.

At the **Prudhoe Bay Hotel** ✯ (☎ 907/659-2449; AE, MC, V; $$$$) all the rooms share baths, and all the room rates include three all-you-can-eat meals. The food is basic cafeteria chow, but it's good for what it is, and it's consumed in great quantities by the truckers and oil field support personnel who frequent the hotel to engage in Deadhorse's number one leisure time activity—eating. (There's really nothing else for them to do.) A no-frills double-occupancy room with two twin beds, a small closet, and a shared community bath goes for $180 a night for two. A double-occupancy room with a queen-size bed, a bath shared with just one other room, a small closet, plus a TV and a phone, goes for $200.

In contrast, all the rooms at the **Arctic Caribou Inn** (☎ 877/659-2368 or 907/659-2368; www.arcticcaribouinn.com; AE, MC, V; $$$$) have private baths and a pair of twin beds, for $235. Since the beds are built for one, this hotel really isn't a good choice except for a couple (unless you're not getting along). Like the Prudhoe Bay Hotel, the Arctic Caribou Inn has a cafeteria, with similar food and all-you-can-eat buffets at each meal. But meals cost extra: $12 for breakfast, $15 for the buffet, and $18 for dinner. All in all, the Prudhoe Bay Hotel is a far better deal.

There are two reasons to visit Prudhoe Bay. One is to see the largest domestic source of oil in the United States. More than 13 billion barrels of crude have been pumped from the frozen ground at Prudhoe Bay since oil production in the Alaskan Arctic began in 1977. Prudhoe crude is pumped through the Trans-Alaska Pipeline to the port town Valdez, 900 miles to the south, where it's loaded aboard oil tankers and shipped to West Coast refineries.

Prudhoe has to be one of the strangest workplaces in the world. The scene is otherworldly. The heathery tundra, which workers are forbidden to set foot upon, is dotted with gravel pads supporting oil wells, processing facilities, and support structures for as far as the eye can see. The year-round population is about five, but at any given time there will be thousands of workers there. Their schedules go something like this: Work, eat, sleep, start over. They do this for 2 to 6 weeks at a time, then fly back to wherever they're from—Fairbanks, Anchorage, Dallas—for a 2- to 4-week break. Work at Prudhoe continues round the clock, year-round, right through winter's blinding snow storms, sub-zero temperatures, and long months of utter darkness. Winter is especially busy, since it's the only time of year when the ground is hard enough to support the heavy equipment used for new construction.

The second reason to visit Prudhoe Bay is to see the Arctic Ocean. Thanks to the Dalton Highway, you can get to Prudhoe Bay more cheaply than Alaska's other gateway to the Arctic Ocean, Barrow, which you have to fly to. The beach may be littered with ice, but bring a bathing suit and towel anyway. If you've made it to the Arctic Ocean, you've got to at least dip your toes in the chilly water. If you really want to brag, take the full plunge and become a member of the Polar Bear Club.

You can't drive around Prudhoe Bay on your own. You have to sign up for one of the four daily tours, which are offered in the summer only. They last about 1½ hours, and they cost $37, unless you're a child 12 or under, in which case they're $17. Most of the tour is spent in a van, which drives past oil wells and processing facilities toward the beach as the driver gives you a broad overview of Prudhoe's history and production volumes. You can't get out of the van until you reach the shore, when you're free to walk around and swim. Make reservations through the **Arctic Caribou Inn** (see the box, above) at least 24 hours in advance so that security has time to size you up. Otherwise, you won't get through the gates.

7 Denali National Park & Preserve

Easy-access wilderness with wildlife galore & the continent's highest peak

THERE ARE THREE BIG REASONS TO GO TO DENALI NATIONAL PARK AND Preserve: to see Alaskan wildlife in a bona fide Alaskan wilderness, to marvel at the tallest mountain in North America . . . and because you can.

Although this 6-million-acre park is larger than New Hampshire, it's just one of the gang when compared to the other enormous swaths of national park land in Alaska—nearly 55 million acres in all. Mind blowing scenery and loads of wildlife are the norm in these places. What really sets Denali apart (besides The High One, Mount McKinley) is its accessibility. You can get deep into the park, among the moose, caribou, and bears, without spending a small fortune on a bush pilot to get you there. And you don't need the survival skills of a mountain man to get out alive. Denali is set up for tourists, with ranger-led hikes, shuttles for backpackers, tour buses for the sedentary masses, and visitor centers where you can buy bug spray and Caesar salads. Everyone can do Denali. You don't need to know how to kill a moose and restring your snowshoes with its entrails to have a good time there (and hunting is prohibited, in any case). Denali is a tourist-friendly wilderness.

Maybe even *too* tourist friendly. These days a half-million visitors per year flock to the park, most of them squeezed into June, July, and August. The front part of the park seems more like a carnival than a wilderness, and the commercial strip just outside the park is so wholly devoted to mass tourism the locals call it Glitter Gulch. But don't let the long shadow of mass tourism discourage you. There's plenty of room to get away from it all and experience wilderness that would have made Thoreau's eyes pop out. The National Park Service does a good job at managing the multitudes and preventing them from trampling the tundra and scaring off the wildlife. One way it does this is by restricting the use of the single road into the park. You can only drive the first 14 miles on your own. To go farther, hop one of the regular shuttle buses that carry visitors as deep into the heart of the park as they care to ride. You can get off anywhere along the way and wander in the wilderness all day long, then flag down an outgoing shuttle when you're ready to return. Better yet, get a free backcountry permit and disappear into the park for up to 30 days. Bicyclists are free to pedal the road, but bikes can't be taken off road.

Whether you're afoot, in the saddle of a mountain bike, or bumping along the road in a bus, you're going to see wildlife at Denali. The park is an intact sub-arctic ecosystem, and home to 39 types of mammals, 168 bird species, 14 fish species, and one species of amphibian (the little wood frog). On any given summer day you might spot caribou loping along a ridge top, Dall sheep leaping from one cliff-side crag to another, moose munching on the shrubbery, bald eagles riding the thermals, and maybe even a grizzly bear or a black wolf rambling across the tundra.

Your odds of seeing the park's namesake, the 20,320-foot mountain Denali (McKinley), aren't as good, despite the fact that it's a star attraction. The summit is obscured more often than not by a blanket of clouds it pulls up around itself. The sad truth is you're more likely to see Denali from Anchorage or Fairbanks, where it's often visible protruding from the clouds, than you are to see it from the park itself.

If the mountain does make an appearance while you're in the park, count yourself lucky and prepare to be flabbergasted. It's so big it makes neighboring peaks like 17,400-foot Mount Foraker look like shrimps. By some measures, Denali is actually *the* tallest mountain on earth. Yeah, Mount Everest tops out at 29,035 feet above sea level, but it cheats, starting high up on the Himalayan plateau. From base to summit, Everest rises just 12,000 feet. Denali, with its base about 2,000 feet above sea level, rises some 18,000 feet.

A BRIEF HISTORY

Geologists have determined that Denali's towering peaks, and the rest of the Alaskan range, are the result of the smashing together of two tectonic plates—an ongoing process that slowly continues to push the mountains up even higher. The Athabascan Indians had other explanations for Denali. In one legend, Totson the Raven chief sent an enormous wave to destroy Yako, his enemy. Yako saved himself by turning the wave to stone, and the frozen wall of water is the mountain range we're left with today.

Archaeological records indicate that the first humans in the area came on hunting trips 12,000 years ago. A later people, the Athabascan Indians, settled in summer camps around some of Denali's rivers and lakes, where the fishing was good. The salmon runs around Denali have never been great, so Native settlement was always rather thin.

In the modern era, Charles Sheldon, a blue-blooded Easterner and buddy of Theodore Roosevelt, fell in love with the Denali area after spending the winter of 1907–1908 there in a cabin on the Toklat River. Sheldon spent the next 9 years pulling strings and lobbying Congress to protect the land. His persistence paid off in 1917 when President Woodrow Wilson signed a bill creating Mount McKinley National Park. Alaskans were never wild about the name Mount McKinley, preferring to call the mountain by one of its Athabascan names, Denali. In 1980 the park was renamed Denali. The mountain, however, is still officially known as Mount McKinley, and a lot of people, myself included, use the names interchangeably. The park and preserve has been expanded three times since it was founded, and now covers 9,492 square miles. It is a complete sub-arctic ecosystem.

LAY OF THE LAND

The eastern edge of Denali National Park butts up against the Parks Highway, the main route between Anchorage and Fairbanks. The park has just one entrance, which is located 237 miles north of Anchorage and 125 miles south of Fairbanks. Ninety-one-mile **Denali Park Road,** the park's only road, scales mountains, runs along cliffs (some with hair-raising drop-offs), rolls across hills, crosses rivers, traverses boreal forest and sub-arctic tundra, pit stops at Wonder Lake, and dead-ends at **Kantishna,** smack dab in the middle of the park. On the map, Kantishna looks like it's in the park, but it's actually outside the park boundaries. It's a very rural, private enclave surrounded by park on all sides, the hole at the center of a 6-million-acre, national park donut.

Tucked among the trees at the entrance to the park, in the area known as Front Country, are the park's administrative offices and most of the visitor facilities. These include the railroad depot, an airfield, a post office, a general store, a cafeteria, some campgrounds, and the kennels for the rangers' sled dogs (the rangers patrol the park by dog sled in the winter).

The most important resource for setting up a trip is the concessionaire: **Doyon/ARAMARK Joint Venture,** 241 W. Ship Creek Ave., Anchorage, AK 99501 (☎ 800/622-7275 or 907/272-7275; fax 907/258-3668; www.reservedenali.com). The concession is operated by a joint venture of ARAMARK, which manages affairs at many parks around the country, and the Doyon Native Corporation of Interior Alaska. They handle the reservations system for the campgrounds and shuttle buses, as well as several hotels, bus tours, a rafting operation, and a dinner theater. The best place to make in-person contact with the concessionaire is at the reservation and ticketing desks in the **Wilderness Access Center,** on Denali Park Road, half a mile from the park entrance. The access center is open from mid-May to mid-September daily from 5am to 8pm; it's closed October through April. Since there's no park entrance station, this center is also a good stop for the park map, a copy of the *Alpenglow* park newspaper, and other handouts. A small store offers a limited selection of conveniences and camping supplies, including hiking boots.

The **National Park Service** can be reached at P.O. Box 9, Denali National Park, AK 99755 (☎ 907/683-2294; www.nps.gov/dena). Or make contact in person at the spectacular **Denali Visitor Center,** near the railroad depot at mile 1.5 of the park road on the right side. It is open summer daily 9am to 6pm.

COMMUNITIES OUTSIDE THE PARK

Most visitors to Denali stay outside of the park in one of the little communities along a 40-mile north-south stretch of the Parks Highway. The main choices are **Healy, Carlo Creek, McKinley Village,** and **Nenana Canyon,** aka **Glitter Gulch.** Some Denali visitors also stay in **Cantwell,** at the junction of the Parks Highway and the unpaved Denali Highway. But its distance from the park entrance—27 miles—is too much of a drawback, so I don't recommend it. (I'll discuss which of the other park communities you may wish to lodge in below, in the section on Accommodations.)

The back door to Denali National Park is **Talkeetna,** a funky community of dirt streets, boardwalks, and log cabins that swarms with mountain climbers who come to scale McKinley and its neighboring peaks each spring. It's located so far south of the park entrance—138 miles away—and it's so fun and interesting in its own right, that I've given it its own subsection in this chapter (p. 328).

GETTING TO & AROUND DENALI

GETTING TO DENALI

The entrance to Denali National Park is about a 6-hour drive on the Parks Highway from Anchorage, and a 3-hour drive from Fairbanks. The rock-bottom cheapest way to get there is aboard one of the vans or mini-coaches of

Alaska/Yukon Trails (☎ 800/770-7275 or 907/479-2277; www.alaskashuttle. com), which is the way locals without cars and penny-pinching backpackers travel. The drawbacks? It stops frequently to pick up and drop off passengers along the way, and there aren't on-board bathrooms. But it's *cheap*. A one-way ticket to the park costs $46 from Fairbanks and $65 from Anchorage. If you're traveling between Fairbanks and Anchorage, you can stop at the park for an indefinite amount of time, then continue your journey for $91.

A pricier if cushier way to go is via the Alaska Railroad's **Denali Star** (☎ 800/ 544-0552; www.akrr.com) which offers daily service to Denali in the summer from Fairbanks and Anchorage (mid-May to mid-Sept). Because the train averages less than 40 miles per hour, it actually takes longer to get to Denali by rail than on the highway—8 hours rather than 6 hours from Anchorage, and nearly 4 hours rather than 3 from Fairbanks. So why take the extra time? One reason is the sight-seeing opportunities: Local high school students work on the train as tour guides, telling stories, discussing points of interest along the way, and making sure you don't miss any wildlife. The Denali depot is located at the park entrance, right across from the main visitor center. One-way fares during the peak season, from June 1 through early September, are $135 from Anchorage (or $68 for children ages 2–11) and $59 from Fairbanks ($30 for children).

Glitter Gulch and McKinley Village hotels will usually pick up guests at the train station at no extra charge (and sometimes at the Alaska/Yukon Trails bus stop, as well). In addition, all run shuttles to and from the park, so you can cut costs by skipping the rental car if you're staying in these areas. That's not doable in such outlying communities as Healy or Carlo Creek, where you'll be stranded without a car, so pick one up before you get to Denali. You can expect to pay between $50 and $90 per day for a car rental out of Anchorage (p. 32), or about $50 for a car out of Fairbanks (p. 264). Cars are a non-issue if you're lodging at Kantishna, the private enclave inside the park, or camping in the backcountry, as Denali Park Road is closed to private automobiles.

GETTING AROUND INSIDE THE PARK

You can drive the first 14 miles of the Denali Park Road ($20 per car for a 7-day pass) as far as the Savage River Bridge. Beyond that point, the Park Service uses a

---

Booking Tent Sites & Bus Rides in the Park

The park service sets aside some walk-in campsites and seats on the shuttle and tour buses for reservation no more than 2 days in advance. The rest can be booked up as early as December 1 if you go online (www. reservedenali.com) or starting February 15 by phone (☎ 800/622-7275 or 907/272-7275). Buses, tours, and campgrounds sometimes book up solid, so make your reservations as soon as you know your schedule. The week around the Fourth of July is the busiest time of year, so book way, way in advance then to ensure you don't get skunked (or avoid the park altogether then and sidestep the crowds).

mass transit system to minimize the impact of visitors on the wilderness. To go beyond the checkpoint at the mile 14 mark, you can travel on foot, by bike, or aboard a shuttle bus or a tour bus (p. 322). At the front end of the park, a free shuttle runs in a loop every 15 minutes in the summer, stopping at the various visitor centers, the railroad depot, and the campgrounds.

ACCOMMODATIONS, BOTH STANDARD & NOT
WHERE TO STAY INSIDE THE PARK

To really get to know Denali, camp there. Pitch a tent, warm your toes by a camp fire, and let the peace of the tundra and spruce forest wash over you. Even if you don't usually "rough it" in this way, you'll be glad you tried it—Denali really rewards those who place themselves in the middle of its extraordinary land. The park has six campgrounds spread out along Denali Park Road. They vary in size, remoteness, and price. Except for the two backpacker campgrounds, you can and should reserve a spot before you arrive, either online at **www.reservedenali.com** or by calling ☎ **800/622-7275.** Tent sites at the backpacker campgrounds are made available no more than 2 days in advance, and you have to show up in person at the Wilderness Access Center near the entrance to the park to get reservations (get there before the door opens at 7am so you'll be at the front of the line). Reservations for 35% of the spots at the other campgrounds are also handled like this. The rest can be reserved as far in advance as February 15 by phone or December 1 online. Occasionally, some of the campgrounds fill up (especially around the Fourth of July, which is peak season), so you'd be wise to make a reservation as soon as you know when you'll need a spot. You can camp at Denali for a total of 14 days per year; if you go over the limit and aren't done camping yet, there are private campgrounds available outside the park, up and down the Parks Highway.

Here's a rundown of your in-park options:

Riley Creek Campground, at the park entrance, is the largest and most easily accessible but the least "wilderness like" of the campgrounds. It's got 150 sites for tents and recreational vehicles spread out along gravel loops in a forest of birch and spruce. Right next door is the park's general store, showers, and laundry. Stay at this one for the convenience of being near the park entrance, or if you need a place to cool your heels while waiting for reservations at a campground deeper in the park because you didn't plan ahead (it's the least likely of the in-park campgrounds to fill up). Riley Creek is open year-round. Cost: $20 per night if you drive in, $12 if you walk in.

A far more desirable spot is **Savage River Campground** ★★ at mile 13, about as far as you can drive into the park on your own. Tucked away in a thin spruce forest on the tundra beside an icy river clouded with glacial silt, it's an enchanting spot. With numerous tent and RV sites, flush toilets, and potable water, it can handle groups of up to 20. Best of all, you can set off on some of the best hikes in the park from here. Cost: $20 per night.

While Savage River is ordinarily as far as you can drive into the park on your own, you can go farther if you have a permit to camp at **Teklanika Campground** ★ at mile 29. It offers 53 sites for tents and RVs set among a low boreal forest. There's a 3-night minimum, and once you drive in you can't drive out until your 3 days are

Denali National Park

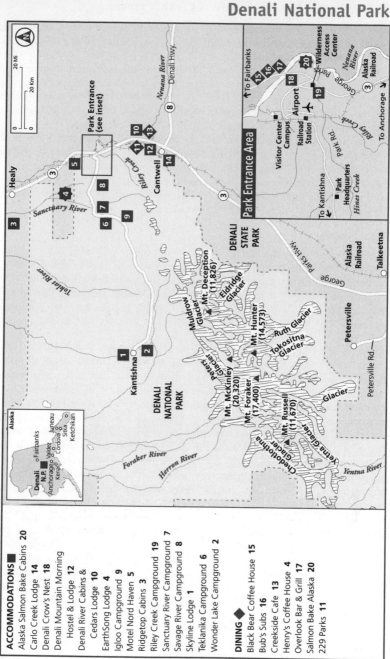

Park Entrance Area

ACCOMMODATIONS ■
Alaska Salmon Bake Cabins **20**
Carlo Creek Lodge **14**
Denali Crow's Nest **18**
Denali Mountain Morning
  Hostel & Lodge **12**
Denali River Cabins &
  Cedars Lodge **10**
EarthSong Lodge **4**
Igloo Campground **9**
Motel Nord Haven **5**
Ridgetop Cabins **3**
Riley Creek Campground **19**
Sanctuary River Campground **7**
Savage River Campground **8**
Skyline Lodge **1**
Teklanika Campground **6**
Wonder Lake Campground **2**

DINING ◆
Black Bear Coffee House **15**
Bub's Subs **16**
Creekside Cafe **13**
Henry's Coffee House **4**
Overlook Bar & Grill **17**
Salmon Bake Alaska **20**
229 Parks **11**

up. (The rule cuts down on traffic.) It's as nice as the Savage River Campground, but because of the limited access, I give it just one star instead of two. Cost: $16 per night with a 3-night minimum.

To get away from the cars, pack rations into the bear-proof container the rangers loaned you at the visitor center (they insist) and backpack to either **Sanctuary River Campground** at mile 23 or **Igloo Campground** at mile 34. These are both "primitive" campgrounds, with pit toilets and no potable water. Reservations are handled on a walk-in basis. Cost: $9 per night.

Near the end of the road, at mile 85, is **Wonder Lake Campground** ✸✸✸, the most spectacular campground of the bunch. It's got 25 tent sites near the edge of the postcard-perfect Wonder Lake, the sometimes placid pond at the foot of Denali's north face. Under the right conditions, the lake produces a perfect mirror image of the mountain. It takes 6 hours on the park shuttle to get there, but sites are still in high demand. Cost: $16 per night.

Kantishsna

Kantishna, the privately owned enclave in the center of Denali National Park, has some wonderful but phenomenally expensive wilderness lodges. They're the sorts of places where the First Lady might slip away for a week, and where even the outhouses have million-dollar views of Mount McKinley, just 20 miles away. Don't rule Kantishna out entirely, though. It does have one affordable splurge:

$$$$ Called, appropriately enough, the **Skyline Lodge** ✸✸✸ (☎ 907/683-1223; www.katair.com/skyline.html; DISC, MC, V), Kantisha's one affordable option is perched at the top of a lofty hillside above a river valley and beneath the reinforced radio antenna for Kantishna Air Taxi. A solar-powered, backcountry summer lodge, it doubles as the headquarters for the air taxi, so guests share meals and common areas with the company's bush pilots. There are just three small guest rooms, but each offers comfortable sleeping lofts and smashing mountain views right from their double beds. The downside: rooms share a bath that's in the main building, a short walk away—after all, this is the wilderness. Skyline books up fast, so reserve your room as far ahead as possible—like the summer beforehand (I'm not kidding). They go for $185 a night, double occupancy, with an additional $30 for meals. Don't skip the grub, as the food is excellent: You'll get fresh baked breads and muffins in the morning, a make-your-own sandwich station for lunch, and a home-cooked meal with crisp greens plucked from the lodge's greenhouse for dinner (on my last visit, they were serving marinated short ribs with rosemary potatoes and roasted asparagus). Expect something fresh from the oven for dessert, like extra-gooey chocolate chip cookies. The sunny sitting room with a high ceiling and long mountain views invites lounging, but leave yourself time to borrow a mountain bike and pedal to Wonder Lake for a hike in the park. In the evening, you can play Ping-Pong with the bush pilots, or stoke up the wood-fired sauna and have a good sweat. The park shuttle (see above) can take you here, or you can fly in with Kantishna Air (guests usually get a discount on the flight), which can double as a flightseeing tour.

WHERE TO STAY OUTSIDE THE PARK
Nenana Canyon, aka Glitter Gulch

The vast majority of Denali goers flock to the mile-long touristy commercial strip just north of the park entrance, an area officially called Nenana Canyon, but better known as "Glitter Gulch." This is Denali's epicenter of mass tourism, where you'll find the biggest hotels (many corporate chain establishments), most of the area's souvenir shops and restaurants, and one busload of visitors on package tours after another. Glitter Gulch starts just a mile north of the park entrance, a short bike ride away. If you haven't got a car, the proximity to the entrance is the main draw, as you'll be close to food, services, and the park entrance. Otherwise, there are better choices up and down the Parks Highway.

There's a 7% tax on all the accommodations listed here.

$–$$$ Sadly, there is just one budget option among all the premium priced rooms in Glitter Gulch: the employee housing at the big salmon bake. If you can snag one of the **Alaska Salmon Bake Cabins** (along the Georges Park Hwy. at mile 238.5; ☎ 907/683-2733; www.denaliparksalmonbake.com; AE, DISC, MC, V) you'll be staying on a wooded hillside on the edge of the commercial hustle and bustle, among the cooks, waitstaff, and dish washers from the Salmon Bake. This option has three things going for it: It's cheap, it's in Glitter Gulch, and it's quiet. Because some of the restaurant employees shifts start at 4:30am and others start at 9pm, a 24-hour "no noise" policy is strictly enforced. The most basic accommodations are the tent cabins, which share a bath. From the outside, they look more like storage sheds with tarps thrown over them than tents (the tarps cover foam insulation), but on the inside they've got painted plywood walls, a pair of double beds, and a rustic coziness that you can feel good about for $74 per night double occupancy. A step up in comfort are the standard cabins, which have a pair of double beds, private baths, TVs, and refrigerators. They go $140 double occupancy. Backpackers keep these places pretty solidly booked, so make reservations as far in advance as possible.

$$$$ I don't think a big splurge in Glitter Gulch makes sense. But a smaller splurge might, especially if you head up the wall of the canyon to the secluded **Denali Crow's Nest** (Crow's Nest Rd. off the Georges Park Hwy. at mile 238.5; ☎ 888/917-8130 or 907/683-2723; www.denalicrowsnest.com; MC, V). Set into a steep hillside of Sugar Loaf Mountain, high above the commercial ruckus down below, the lodgings here consist of 39 cozy log cabins. Yes, the cabins are small (you'll get bigger rooms in the 100 and 200 level), and without TVs or phones, but they've all got glorious views of the mountains, so why would you want to stare at a tiny screen or yak on the phone, anyways? The front desk is open 24 hours, and it will arrange to shuttle you to and from the park entrance or the train depot for no extra charge. After a long day of play, you can soak outdoors under the late-night sun in a hot tub; nearby are two of the area's best restaurants. During peak season, from early June until early September, cabins go for $189 double occupancy (children 11 and under stay for free). If you cram 'em with extra adults, you'll pay $199 for three and $209 for four. In the short shoulder season—Memorial Day through the first week of June—the double occupancy

Finding a Denali Area Bed & Breakfast

There are several bed-and-breakfasts in the area from Healy to Carlo Creek. As in the rest of Alaska, the term B&B is used loosely here. Some places serve hot breakfasts, some serve continental breakfasts, and some serve no breakfast at all. I wish I could tell you about some selective B&B association that sorted out the good from the bad, but no such thing exists. The best I can offer is the **Greater Healy/Denali Chamber of Commerce** (☎ 907/683-4636; www.denalichamber.com) which has a fairly complete list of all the lodgings in the area. Yet it doesn't vet the properties, so its usefulness is limited. You'll find about 30 different properties listed there, including most of the places I reviewed here (which are the pick of the litter).

rate is $139. The hotel shutters from mid-September through Memorial Day. One warning: Because the cabins are connected by stairs, this is not the best choice for people with mobility impairments.

McKinley Village

Six miles south of the park entrance, there's a junior version of Glitter Gulch called McKinley Village. It's not so much a real community as a collection of three hotel and lodge complexes, spread out among the spruce trees on the banks of the Nenana River. It's a mellower alternative to Nenana Canyon, however, just a short drive up the highway to the park entrance.

$$$–$$$$ If a cozy little cabin sounds good, but the $189 rate for a cabin at Denali's Crow's Nest doesn't, head down the highway to **Denali River Cabins and Cedars Lodge** (Mile 231 Parks Hwy.; ☎ 800/230-7275; www.denaliriver cabins.com; AE, DISC, MC, V). There you can get a lovely little cedar cabin along the Nenana River for $149 double occupancy in high season (in late May and early Sept, shave $30 off that rate; the rest of the year, it's closed). Like a high-end summer camp, the 54 cabins here are clustered closely together, and set along a raised boardwalk that's there to protect the river bank. Most come with two comfy queen-size beds, and all have TVs and tiny baths. They've also got Dutch doors that you can leave open to better hear the river or meet your neighbors. There's a good on-site restaurant, and the lodge has a free shuttle to and from the park entrance. Best of all, there's a huge Finnish sauna right on the river, and close enough to the cabins for you to dash to in a towel. Roomier but pricier motel rooms with cedar walls and ceilings go for $189, but the cabins are the real draw.

Carlo Creek

More laid-back still is Carlo Creek, 13 miles south of the park entrance. Slow down as you approach mile 224 of the Parks Highway and don't blink, or you'll miss this small collection of restaurants and affordable accommodations.

$-$$ The first place in Carlo Creek to consider has to be the most appealing hostel I've ever seen, **Denali Mountain Morning Hostel & Lodge** ✪✪✪ (Mile 224 Denali Park Hwy.; ☎ 907/683-7503; www.hostelalaska.com; AE, DISC, MC, V). Along with dorm rooms ($25 per person), it's got an oddball assortment of attractive and private little cabins, which range in size from a two-person number that looks like an oversize outhouse, to a two-story place with a nearly vertical staircase. The cabins (which are clean and with truly comfortable beds—no planks and thin mattresses here), cost between $75 and $125 a night, double occupancy, with a $10 charge for additional people. None of the cabins have their own baths, but there are plenty of outhouses and communal facilities strategically placed around the property. Costing less than the cabins but more than the hostel beds are dome tents, which are set up on raised platforms to keep you off the damp ground and away from creepy-crawly things. Tents go for $25 for one or $40 for two, and come equipped with two cots (add $5 more per sleeping bag, if you don't bring your own). The hostel is spread out in the low woods along rip-roaring Carlo Creek, which has been known to flood in the spring and knock cabins off their foundations. The architectural centerpiece of the place is The Octagon, a handsome eight-sided lodge where you can play Pictionary by the woodstove, sink into an overstuffed sofa with a book, whip up a meal (in the clean, usable community kitchen—another big money saver!), and socialize with your fellow hostellers, usually a highly international bunch. Cheap shuttle rides to and from the park, backpacking gear rentals, a small natural foods store, a fire pit along the creek, and of course the steady stream of eager, young world travelers, are among the key attractions.

$-$$$ The tone of **Carlo Creek Lodge** (Mile 224 Parks Hwy.; ☎ 907/683-2576; www.carlocreek.com; MC, V) is set at the office, a spruce log building covered with horns, antlers, snowshoes, old woodstoves, saw blades, and other miscellaneous surplus items, along with hanging baskets of flowers. The nine spruce log cabins are just as picturesque and exactly what comes to mind when you think Quaint Alaskan Cabin in the Woods. From the moose antler doorknobs, to the burled spruce roof poles, to the tiny windows that conserve heat in the winter and keep the places dark enough to sleep in during the bright summers, these cabins are the real deal. One even has a sod roof. The least expensive go for $85 and share a spruce log bathhouse, while the $130 cabins come with private baths. Sheltered tent sites on the lodge's 32-acre wooded property have granite slab picnic tables, like something out of the Flintstones. They go for $12 per tent plus $4 per person.

Healy

You'll find the largest assortment of Denali-area lodgings in rural Healy, which begins 11 miles north of the park entrance. With about 1,000 residents living along the gravel roads spread out across its forest and tundra, it's the largest Denali-area community, as well as the only one offering year-round visitor services (gas stations, motels, and the like). During the summer, flightseeing operations operate from Healy's air strip. Healy has a coal mine, too, along with a coal-burning power plant that generates electricity for Fairbanks. But the community is so spread out, you'd never know it was there.

$$–$$$$　　Bears, moose, and all sorts of other wildlife wander along the wooded ridge top above Healy Valley where **Ridgetop Cabins** ★★☆ (Mile 253.3 Parks Hwy.; ☎ 907/683-2448 or 866/680-2448; www.alaskaone.com/ridgetop; MC, V) is located. Built on the 80-acre homestead of a long-time Alaskan couple who are as congenial as they could possibly be, the cabins are light and airy, thoroughly modern, and filled with blond wood furnishings and cabinetry. Although they're just a pine cone's throw from one another, they all have a feeling of utter privacy. Prices range from $120 for a small single-room unit to $165 for a big, two-bedroom model with full kitchen. The owners lay out a continental breakfast in their kitchen each morning, and you're free to raid the big blueberry patches any time. Just make a lot of noise so you don't catch any bears by surprise. To get there, you have to drive up a narrow, mile-long, rocky, rutted road. Go slowly so you arrive with all the car parts you started with.

$$$–$$$$　　The **Motel Nord Haven** 🧒 (Mile 249.5 Parks Hwy.; ☎ 800/683-4501 or 907/683-4500; www.motelnordhaven.com; AE, DISC, MC, V) is a peaceful, tidy, two-story motel surrounded by a low taiga forest and nothing else. This one's particularly good for groups or families because there's one price for these spacious rooms no matter how many people bed down for the night. They'll even supply cribs and rollaway beds at no extra charge. Nightly rates range from $140 to $168 (for a kitchenette room) during the summer high season; $90 to $111 in shoulder seasons (May 1–June 2 and Aug 27–Sept 30); and $75 to $90 the rest of the year. Though the rooms are pretty plain, they're spruced up a tad by Alaskan art on the walls, and cheery flowered coverlets. I also like the fact that the rate includes a complimentary breakfast of fruit, muffins, and hard-boiled eggs and use of the house library (pick up a tome on Denali to read yourself to sleep by).

$$$–$$$$　　**EarthSong Lodge** ★★☆ 🧒 (on Stampede Rd., 4 miles from Parks Hwy.; ☎ 907/683-2863; www.earthsonglodge.com; MC, V) is an even more secluded gem where you can sit on the front porch of your own rustic cabin and gaze across wide open alpine tundra, with nothing to break the silence except the howls of happy sled dogs at feeding time. The lodge is on a 4-mile-long panhandle of private land surrounded on three sides by Denali National Park and Preserve, and it feels like it could be a wilderness outpost at the edge of the known world. It would be a comfortable outpost, though, one where you can hang out in the lodge playing board games or singing songs around an old piano, and where you can get breakfast sandwiches and Thai food at a delightful little cafe (see Henry's Coffee House, p. 318). The dozen spruce log cabins, connected by boardwalks and built on short stilts so they don't thaw the underlying permafrost, range from $145 to $185 in summer, and $85 to $125 the rest of the year. The basic models are one-room affairs, and the most deluxe cabin has two bedrooms. All have handmade quilts, small private baths, and historic photos from the University of Alaska archives. None have TVs or telephones, which makes it that much easier for you to concentrate on the quiet of the surrounding wilderness. The owner is a former backcountry ranger and a one-time unofficial Iditarod contestant (he ran the race, he just never bothered to enter). If you ask, he'll give you a free tour of his sled dog kennels. In the winter, he will even take you on dog sled expedition, but at about $620 per person per a day, it's a major splurge.

DINING FOR ALL TASTES

As a general rule, Denali's restaurants disappoint. Most are seasonal operations that charge too much and herd as many tourists through as they possibly can in 115 days, with no thought about cultivating repeat customers. Like tourist-trap restaurants everywhere, they simply don't care enough to offer quality. Happily, Denali does have a few exceptions, which I list below.

GLITTER GULCH

$–$$ Ask the locals about good places to eat and inevitably they'll recommend **Bub's Subs** (at Denali Dr. and Parks Hwy., along the boardwalk; ☎ 907/683-BUBS; mid-May to mid-Sept only daily 11am–9pm; MC, V). For simple, fast meals, I'll second their endorsement. You'll find all kinds of sandwiches here: hot hoagies, stuffed with meatballs ($12), Philly cheese steaks ($13), or Italian sausages on freshly baked buns ($9.50). There are even healthy options such as a pita sandwich overflowing with hummus ($9.75) or a chicken Caesar salad ($12). Seating's limited, so you're better off scoping out a spot by the river (try Riley Creek, at the first left after the post office at the entrance to Denali Park) and having a picnic.

$ More seating can be found a few doors down at **Black Bear Coffee House** (boardwalk at Denali; ☎ 907/683-1656; mid-May to mid-Sept only daily 11am–9pm; MC, V), a coffee house and bakery that doubles as a soup-and-sandwich shop and bar (it serves beer and wine along with lattes and cappuccinos). This is where the off-duty bush pilots, river guides, and young East European hotel workers hang out, sipping chai teas and nibbling on turkey-herb sandwiches. Prices are reasonable, at $2.50 for most baked goods, $7.95 for all sandwiches, $5 for a bowl of soup, and $3.50 for a cup.

$–$$$$ The big hotels in Glitter Gulch don't have good restaurants—they tend to be large, pricey, mediocre affairs, geared toward the package tour masses. Though it deals with the same volume of customers, **Salmon Bake Alaska** (Mile 238.5 Parks Hwy.; ☎ 907/683-2733; mid-May to mid-Sept only daily 7am–midnight, bar open until 4am; AE, DISC, MC, V) is more authentically Alaskan than any of those hotel restaurants. "The Bake," as locals call it, is a family-style place in a ramshackle building with multiple dining areas, wildly sloping floors, and a big, busy upstairs bar. Alaskan king salmon (baked, grilled, or blackened, $19) and halibut (grilled or blackened, $21) are the big things here. But you can fill up and save money with a blackened halibut sandwich or an enormous king salmon quesadilla (both go for $12).

$$–$$$$ The food's good but the views are even better at **Overlook Bar and Grill** (Mile 238.5 Parks Hwy.; ☎ 907/683-2641; mid-May to mid-Sept only daily 11am–11pm; MC, V), which is perched on a mountainside high above the commercial clamor of Glitter Gulch. Try to get a table on the big sun deck, but don't sweat it if you don't—enormous windows give just about every seat in the house a view of the peaks of the Alaska Range. Inside, the Overlook is split neatly down the middle, divided between a dining room and a bar. The bar has plenty of tables and more windows, as well as a bountiful selection of booze, including all of the premium liquors (some mixed into glacier-themed cocktails) and a whopping 76 varieties of beer, heavy on Alaskan brews. Given that there's so much potential for heavy drinking to be had here, it's a good thing the food portions are massive enough to soak up all the alcohol. The grilled salmon ($22) and halibut ($25) are the most popular, if pricey, menu choices. The better deal—and the house specialty—are the various types of burgers ($9.95–$11), which come on onion buns with french fries, jojos (potatoes coated in egg and seasonings then fried), or a baked potato. The veggie burger made with black beans, brown rice, onion, tomato, and green chiles ($9.95) is especially good.

CARLO CREEK

$$–$$$ Right next to gurgling Carlo Creek itself is the **Creekside Café** ★ (Mile 224 Parks Hwy.; ☎ 907/683-2277; mid-May to mid-Sept only daily 6am–10pm; DISC, MC, V), a simple A-frame restaurant with plank flooring, country-inn decor, and entrees that are affordable (most dinner entrees cost no more than $18) and thoughtfully prepared. The annually changing menu has included grilled salmon with a spicy plum glaze ($17) or a rib-eye steak with roasted peppers and artichoke relish ($23). The atmosphere and the service is casual and comfortable, and the portions are generous. For breakfast, the signature dish here is a massive chunk of moist meatloaf topped with eggs ($9.95) but I also highly recommend the skillet entrees, like the bed of fried potatoes topped with two eggs, reindeer sausage, mushrooms, onions, olives, and a heap of other toppings ($8.95).

$$–$$$$ **229 Parks** ★★★ (Mile 229.7 Parks Hwy.; ☎ 907/683-2567; www.229parks.com; summer Tues–Sun 5–10pm, rest of year Fri–Sat 9am–10pm, Sun 9am–1pm; MC, V; reservations recommended) is a shape shifter. In the winter, it's a community gathering place, with knitting circles, movie nights, sled dog hitching posts in the gravel parking lot, and a simple menu of soups, sandwiches, and extraordinary baked goods (the pastry chef got her training in France and is a certified member of the European Pastry Union). In the summer, 229 Parks turns into one of Alaska's most exciting fine-dining establishments. Super fresh, locally grown produce is a big reason why. What's in season, and the whims of the kitchen, dictate what's on the ever-changing menu. Green beans were in season when I was last there, and they made crisp, steamy plate companions for the rosemary-skewered Alaskan halibut, the herb and feta phyllo bundles ($30), and the prosciutto-wrapped rack of elk rubbed with a juniper marinade ($32). On the lighter and more affordable side of the menu, you might find locally grown red peppers, scallions, carrots, daikon radish, mint, cilantro, and baby mizuna stuffed into vegan spring rolls ($9).

HEALY

$–$$ Healy's offers convenient-but-nothing-special roadside diners along the Parks Highway. Skip 'em and go instead to **Henry's Coffee House** (on Stampede Rd., 4 miles from Parks Hwy.; ☎ 907/683-2863; www.earthsonglodge.com; summer only daily 7–9am and 6–9pm; MC, V), an offbeat, out-of-the-way eatery stuck out on the alpine tundra and named after a beloved sled dog. This is the tiny, rustic in-house restaurant for the EarthSong Lodge (p. 316), and it's open for breakfast and dinner. If you show up for breakfast, try the bagels stuffed with sausage, egg, and cheese ($5) or one of the great hulking cinnamon rolls ($2.50). But if you're going to go to the trouble of finding this place, come for dinner so you can hang out in the upstairs dining room surrounded by sled dog art and route maps, and see the 8pm slide show on dog sledding (it's actually quite entertaining). The dinner menu boasts homemade soups, sandwiches, and salads (less than $10), pasta specials (less than $15), and the house specialty, spaghetti and meatballs ($14).

WHY YOU'RE HERE: THE TOP SIGHTS & ATTRACTIONS

Before you can strike out into the Denali wilderness to ramble through the pristine landscapes and search for critters, you must first satisfy the demands of the gatekeepers at the park entrance. That's where the tickets for the shuttle and tour buses, as well as the permits needed for backcountry hiking and camping, are sold. With practically a half-million tourists flocking through Denali these days in the course of a single summer, the front of the park can be something of a mad house. Making reservations for the campgrounds and buses before you leave home can minimize the amount of time you spend in the park's maw of mass tourism. If you don't have reservations, or if you're gunning for backcountry hiking permits, get up early and hustle over to the **Wilderness Access Center,** or the **WAC** (near the park entrance), before it opens at 7am so that you can stake out a spot at the front of the line. You'll cut way down on the hassle of the process this way, and you'll have your pick of available camping sites or shuttle bus slots.

For backcountry hiking permits, which can be reserved no more than a day in advance, go to the **Backcountry Information Center,** or the **BIC,** housed in a trailer in the WAC parking lot. The 6-million-acre wilderness is divvied up into 43 backcountry units, and a limited number of permits are issued for each unit. The most popular units are around the base of McKinley, and they get snatched up quickly. Don't fret if you can't hike at the very foot of The High One. There are plenty of equally spectacular but less coveted parcels of the wilderness to explore. The rangers at the BIC are expert trip planners and they'll be happy to help you hash out an itinerary. The whole process may take an hour or more, not including the half-hour safety video you'll have to watch and a 5- to 10-minute safety briefing a ranger will give you.

Permits are not required for day hikes; you just hop off the shuttle bus anywhere along the road and hike until you're ready to get back on the bus again.

Entrance & Reservation Fees

The park's entrance fee, good for a week, is $10 per person or $20 per family (up to eight of you). You pay it when you pay for camping, shuttle bus seats, or the bus tours. In addition, there's a $4 reservation fee, which is tacked on to whatever campground, tour bus, or shuttle bus reservations you make. You don't need to pay the entrance fee if you hold an "America the Beautiful pass," (see p. 375), which allows the bearer unlimited visits to National Parks and Federal Recreation areas around the U.S. for 1 year.

First to the Top

It's the biggest. That's why climbers risk their lives on Mount McKinley. You can see the mountain from Anchorage, more than 100 miles away. On a flight across Alaska, McKinley stands out grandly over waves of other mountains. It's more than a mile taller than the tallest peak in the other 49 states. It's a great white triangle, always covered in snow, tall but also massive and strong.

The first group to try to climb Mount McKinley came in 1903, led by Judge James Wickersham, who also helped explore Washington's Olympic Peninsula before it became a national park. His group made it less than halfway up, but on the trip they found gold in the Kantishna Hills, setting off a small gold rush that led to the first permanent human settlement in the park area. Wickersham later became the Alaska Territory's nonvoting delegate to Congress and introduced the bill that created the national park, but the government was never able to get back land in the Kantishna area from the gold miners. Today that land is the site of wilderness lodges, right in the middle of the park.

On September 27, 1906, renowned world-explorer Dr. Frederick Cook announced to the world by telegraph that he had reached the summit of Mount McKinley after a lightning-fast climb, covering more than 85 miles and 19,000 vertical feet in 13 days with one other man, a blacksmith, at his side. On his return to New York, Cook was lionized as a conquering explorer and published a popular book of his summit diary and photographs.

In 1909, Cook again made history, announcing that he had beat Robert Peary to the North Pole. Both returned to civilization from their competing treks at about the same time. Again, Cook was the toast of the town. His story began to fall apart, however, when his Eskimo companions mentioned that he'd never been out of sight of land. After being paid by Peary to come forward, Cook's McKinley companion also recanted. A year later, Cook's famous summit photograph was re-created—on a peak 19 miles away and 15,000 feet lower than the real summit.

In 1910, disgusted with Cook, four prospectors from Fairbanks took a more Alaskan approach to the task. Without fanfare or special supplies—they carried doughnuts and hot chocolate on their incredible final ascent—they marched up the mountain carrying a large wooden flagpole they could plant

Check the bulletin boards at the WAC or talk to a ranger there to find out about areas of the park that may be temporarily closed due to wildlife activity.

Once you've jumped through the appropriate hoops, you'll probably have some time to kill before your scheduled bus. If so, head to the auditorium at the WAC, where a short but helpful film on the history of the park plays throughout the day.

Another thing you should make time for is a visit to the **sled dog kennels.** During the winter, park rangers use dog sleds to patrol the park, and during the on top to prove they'd made it. But on arriving at the summit, they realized that they'd climbed the slightly shorter north peak. Weather closed in, so they set up the pole there and descended without attempting the south peak. Then, when they got back to Fairbanks, no one could see the pole, and they were accused of trying to pull off another hoax.

In 1913, Episcopal archdeacon Hudson Stuck organized the first successful climb to reach the real summit—and reported he saw the pole on the other peak. Harry Karstens led the climb (he would become the park's first superintendent in 1917), and the first person to stand at the summit was an Alaska Native, Walter Harper.

Although McKinley remains one of the world's most difficult climbs, about 10,000 people have made it to the top since Hudson Stuck's party. Since 1980 the number of climbers has boomed. Garbage and human waste disposal are a major problem. One recent June day, 115 climbers made it to the summit. In 1970, only 124 made the attempt all year; now more than 1,200 try to climb the peak each year, with about half making it to the summit. The cold, fast-changing weather is what usually stops people. From late April into early July, climbers fly from the town of Talkeetna to a base camp at an elevation of 7,200 feet on the Kahiltna Glacier. From there, it takes an average of about 18 days to get to the top, through temperatures as cold as −40°F (−40°C).

Climbers lose fingers, toes, and other parts to frostbite, or suffer other, more severe injuries. More than 90 climbers have died on the mountain, not counting plane crashes. During the season, the park service stations rescue rangers and an emergency medical clinic at the 14,200-foot level of the mountain, and keeps a high-altitude helicopter ready to go after climbers in trouble. In 2002, under pressure from Congress, the park service started charging all climbers a $150-a-head fee, defraying a portion of the rescue costs. The park and the military spend about half a million dollars a year rescuing climbers, and sometimes much more. The cost in lives is high as well. Volunteer rangers and rescuers die as well as climbers. Plane crashes, falls, cold, and altitude all take a toll. Monuments to those who never returned are in the cemetery near the airstrip in Talkeetna.

—*Charles Wohlforth*

summer they introduce visitors to the dogs, let them pet the puppies, and give demonstrations. The schedule is posted at the WAC (there are one morning and two afternoon demos), and a free shuttle bus leaves from there and goes to the kennels.

To get a grand geographic overview of Denali, spend some time in the **Denali Visitor Center** (p. 329). I'm a sucker for a good map, and the giant relief map of the park they've got there will give you a fine overview of how all of the park's

Along Denali Park Road

Ninety-one-mile **Denali Park Road,** the only roadway in the 6-million-acre park, scales mountains, runs along cliffs, rolls across hills, crosses rivers, traverses boreal forest and sub-arctic tundra, pit stops at Wonder Lake, and dead-ends in the private in-holding of Kantishna. Here are some highlights of the trip to give you an idea of what you're in for:

Mile 9   This is the first point in the park where you can see mighty Mount McKinley on a clear day. You don't get a lot of views of the mountain when you're driving up the Parks Highway to the park, thanks to all the other mountains that get in the way. And you can't see it from the park entrance. So when you finally do see it—weather permitting—it's a thrill. If the clouds have obscured the mountain, look for moose. They're especially plentiful in this area, especially in September and October, the fall rutting season. Never mess with a moose, and that goes double when they're looking for love (or at least procreation). In addition, most bulls have one thing on their minds—cows—and they'll skewer and trample anything that looks like it might be an obstacle.

Mile 14   This is the end of the line for private vehicles, a policy enforced by the park services check point. If you're in a rent-a-car, park by the bridge and go for a little hike up the dry tundra to **Primrose Ridge.**

Mile 29   If you're on the bus, it will probably stop here at the overlook above the wildly braided **Teklanika River,** which is fed by melting glaciers, and which consists of a series of shifting concourses that snake back and forth across the gravel bottom of the valley floor, sweeping across an area more than a mile wide in places.

mountains, glaciers, rivers, valleys, ridges, and whatnot fit together. A ranger with a laser pointer is stationed there to answer questions. The visitor center also has a fine natural history museum chock-full of stuffed grizzly, Dall sheep, birds, and other creatures that—with any luck—you'll soon see alive and well in the wilderness.

To delve deeper into the park's wildlife biology, geology, and ecology, spend some time at the **Margaret Murie Science & Learning Center,** which has all sorts of exhibits, as well as animal skulls that you can handle and fur samples you can run your fingers through. The Murie center becomes the main visitor center from mid-September until mid-May.

TOURS & TRANSPORTATION

Those planning to power around sections of the park on their own two feet—perhaps a day hike or simply a short stroll into the wilderness—should catch one of the park's **green shuttles.** Traveling varying distances along the entire length of

Miles 38 to 43 Watch for grizzly bears roaming across the tundra here. The bears in this area are so thick that the area is closed to visitors (so you can't get off the bus here), as the partially eaten sign at **Sable Pass,** at mile 39, explains. Grizzlies are primarily vegetarians, subsisting on roots, berries, and other plants they find on the tundra. Only occasionally do they supplement their high fiber diet with protein—old or injured caribou, moose calves, carrion, and the odd arctic ground squirrel.

Mile 46 This is **Polychrome Pass,** a 5-mile-wide mountain gap where bright, multi-colored layers of rock have been exposed on either side by a long-gone glacier. You're at 3,700 feet here, with a broad view of the Tolkat River in the valley below. Keep an eye peeled for wolves around the pass, and look for caribou in the valley it overlooks.

Mile 58 Here, the road reaches its highest point—3,980 feet—at **Highway Pass,** so turn on your camera and get ready to capture some dramatic views.

Mile 63 The **Fish Creek Turnaround** here is where the 8-hour bus trip usually turns back.

Mile 66 Stop at the newly built **Eielson Visitor Center** to stretch your legs, feast your eyes on the mountain, if it's visible, and maybe buy a postcard. (The newly constructed visitor center is scheduled to open in summer 2008.)

Mile 86 **Wonder Lake** is 4 miles long and 280 feet deep. It's home to loons, grebes, and mergansers. The mountain is about 27 miles away from the lake, and it looms very large here.

Denali Park Road, they allow passengers to hop off anywhere along the way (except in areas closed because of wildlife activity) and pick up passengers who flag them down. The only catch is that if they're full, you may have to wait for the next to come along before hopping aboard. These trips are informal. Some drivers like to narrate, while others don't say much. They all usually stop, or at least slow down, when there's wildlife to see.

Camper buses are for more ambitious folks who are planning to overnight in the wilderness. On these buses, seats have been removed in the back to make room for bicycles and backpacks. Reservations are required for camper buses and are only given to those with reservations at one of the campgrounds in the park or a backcountry hiking permit (discussed later).

Depending on how far into the park you go, shuttle or bus prices will range from $23 to $29 for adults. Fare for kids 15 to 17 ranges from $11 to $15; those 14 and younger ride free. The most popular routes are the 6½-hour round-trip to the Toklat River and the 8-hour round-trip to Fish Creek. The full 11-hour

The Denizens of Denali

The Serengeti of the North, as Denali's called, is a protected, fully intact ecosystem so chock full of animals that you're virtually assured of sightings. The creatures visitors most want to see are known as the Big Five. They are:

Moose, which tend to live in forested areas close to lakes, marshes, and other bodies of water. In addition to grasses, leaves, and coniferous needles, they like to eat underwater vegetation. They're surprisingly good swimmers, so keep your eyes peeled for a demonstration when you come to ponds or lakes.

Caribou, which belong to a group of about 1,800 animals known as The Denali Herd. The herd's range falls almost exclusively within the boundaries of the park.

Dall sheep, which tend to be spotted in the high mountains in the eastern and western parts of the park. They feed on the park's ridges and steep slopes, and retreat to the rocks and crags to avoid predators. From afar, they appear as white dots on the mountainside.

Grizzly bears, which eat a wide variety of foods, including grasses, roots, berries, fish, whatever carrion they happen upon, and whatever moose or caribou calves they can catch. They're most commonly seen near their food sources, such as blueberry patches or salmon streams.

Wolves, which are divided among about 14 packs in the park, made up of about 92 animals. They range far and wide, traveling as much as 30 miles in a day, and trotting across the tundra—and sometimes right down the Park Road—at about 5 mph (they can run as fast as 45 mph when they want to run something down).

Wildlife activity at Denali varies with the season. Summer is the busiest time of year. It's when the animals raise their young and are always on the

round-trip to Wonder Lake is simply too long for most kids . . . and most adults, for that matter. If you show up late in the day, a good alternative to the longer routes is the 5-hour round-trip to Polychrome Pass.

Interpretive Bus Tours

Guided bus tours are more expensive and they don't allow passengers to jump on and off at will, but they're the way to go for people who want a wilderness experience that doesn't require getting their boots dirty. Unlike the park's shuttle buses, which are run by the Park Service, these tours are privately run, in a joint venture between the Doyon Native corporation and the big national park concessionaire ARAMARK, which owns many of the hotel rooms in Glitter Gulch. In addition, Doyon runs a tour to the high-priced wilderness lodge it operates in the center of the park.

move looking for food, as they fatten up as much as possible for the coming winter. The animals have various strategies for dealing with the winter. Some, like grizzly bears and arctic ground squirrels, hibernate. Others, like mice and voles, retreat to their burrows and tunnels and live off their stockpiles of nuts and seeds. Moose, Dall sheep, and caribou spend their winters on the go, searching for food and trying to avoid wolves, which spend their winters on the go looking for moose, Dall sheep, and caribou to eat. Eighty percent of Denali's birds, including golden eagles and trumpeter swans, simply fly away to warmer climes. Those that remain, such as spruce grouse and great horned owls, are experts at finding food in the snowy landscape while conserving their energy.

Altogether, there are 39 species of mammals in the park, ranging in size from 1,400-pound bull moose to tiny shrews and voles no heavier than a Ping-Pong ball. A whopping 167 species of birds flutter through the skies here. Most of them are migratory, showing up just in spring or summer. But 18 hardy species live there year-round. Denali has 10 species of fish, even though most of its streams and lakes are too clouded with glacial silt to make for a great fish habitat (the fishing's terrible, although it is allowed in most of the park). Interestingly, there's not a single species of reptile in the park, and there's just one amphibian—the tiny wood frog, which stops breathing and freezes solid in the winter, then thaws out and hops back to life in the spring.

See the "Alaska on the Wild Side" appendix, p. 389, for more info on common wildlife in Denali and throughout Alaska.

These are four choices (*note:* the prices do not include the $10 park entry fee):

- **Denali Natural History Tour** 🧒: This is a quickie 4-hour dip into the park, focusing on its natural and cultural history. You'll only get to mile 17 of Denali Park Road, and won't have as much of a chance to see wildlife as you would on a longer tour. The tour makes several stops, starting with a stop at the Wilderness Access Center to watch a movie about the park's history. At the turnaround point, an Alaskan Native greets passengers and gives an informal talk on the Native way of seeing the world. Tours cost $52 or $26 for kids 14 or younger, and they include a snack and a hot drink.
- **Tundra Wilderness Tour** ★★: The opportunities to see wildlife are far better on this tour, which lasts 6 to 8 hours and goes about 60 miles into the park. Costs are $84 for adults, $32 for kids 14 and younger, which includes a box lunch. Though the tour is offered both in the morning and afternoon,

you'll have a better shot at seeing McKinley's peak on the morning tour. When it's cloudy and McKinley is hidden behind the clouds, the tour wraps up after 6 hours. When Denali's out, the tour goes deeper into the park, and lasts up to 8 hours. A truncated version of this tour, called the **Teklanika Tundra Wilderness Tour,** is offered for a few days early and late in the season, when snow keeps the buses from going more than 30 miles into the park. It costs $56 for adults or $18 for kids.

◆ **Kantishna Experience:** This is a marathon 12-hour, 190-mile round-trip ride all the way to the end of the park road (at Kantishna) and back. If you've got the stamina to be on a bus that long, you'll get to see more of the park, more wildlife, and get a closer look at Mount McKinley (weather permitting) than on the other tours. There are bathrooms stops along the way, as there are on all of the tours, and in Kantishna, you'll visit the historic cabin of one of the pioneers who settled here during the gold rush of the early 1900s. The bus driver narrates the tour until it reaches Wonder Lake, where a park service ranger hops aboard to lead the Kantishna portion of the trip. This one costs $139 for adults or $129 for kids.

◆ **Kantishna Wilderness Trails:** This tour is very similar to the Kantishna Experience, except its ultimate destination is Kantishna Roadhouse, one of the private wilderness lodges in the middle of the park. You'll get a hot lunch in the lodge's dining room, then you can attend either a dog mushing demonstration (which involves a motley but enthusiastic team of past-their-prime sled dogs, rescued from shelters) or a gold panning demonstration (in which you can try your hand at panning for gold in a chilly stream). This tour is geared mainly to guests of the Kantishna Roadhouse, who, since they don't have to spend 12 hours on the bus, aren't nearly as grumpy at the end of the day as those who do the road in one fell swoop. It costs $139.

To make reservations for the Denali Natural History Tour, the Tundra Wilderness Tour, or the Kantishna Experience, go online at www.reservedenali. com or call ☎ 800/622-7275. To go on the Kantishna Wilderness Trails tour, call ☎ 800/230-7275 or book online through www.denaliwildlifetour.com.

Flightseeing Tours

Unless you're part of that rare breed of death-defying, world-class mountain climber drawn to Alaska to stand on McKinley's 21,000-foot summit with crampons on your feet and very thin air in your lungs, the only chance you'll have to really get to know The High One up close and personal is on a flightseeing tour. From one of the many small aircraft that buzz around the mountain like gnats around a refrigerator, you'll get an unparalleled sense of its massive scale. A variety of different flightseeing operators offer a number of different trips, including tours that circle the mountain, tours that buzz the summit, and tours that land on one of McKinley's glaciers so that you can actually set foot on the face of the mountain. Flights originate from airstrips near the park's entrance and from Talkeetna, and they're all competitively priced from company to company, though you'll save money by flying out of Talkeetna. Although the town is a long way from the park entrance, it's actually closer to the mountain than Glitter Gulch or neighboring communities.

There are plenty of flightseeing operators to choose from, and they're all pretty competitively priced, but the one I like best is **Talkeetna Aero Services** (☎ 888/733-2899, in Talkeetna 907/733-2899, at Denali Park 907/683-2899). It appeals to me because you can catch flights out of either Talkeetna or Healy, and because they've got planes with pressurized cabins that can circle the very tip-top of the mountain—which at 20,000 feet is out of reach for aircraft with unpressurized cabins. Flights start at $175 per passenger for a tour of Ruth Glacier out of Talkeetna, and $245 for a tour with a landing on Ruth Glacier. A tour in a pressurized plane—which climbs above 20,000 feet to give you a closer look at Denali's summit than most people will ever get—costs $265 out of Talkeetna and $295 out of Healy. Whichever tour you take or company you go with, one of you should try to snag the co-pilot's seat (don't worry, you don't need to know how to fly). Ask the pilot, who will assess the weight and balance of the plane, then give you a thumbs up or thumbs down.

ACTIVE DENALI

MOUNTAIN BIKING

If you have the time and don't mind inhaling the dust kicked up when buses pass, mountain biking is a great way to see Denali Park Road on your own terms. On a mountain bike, you can break away from the crowds and pedal right past the checkpoint where private automobiles are turned back. The only thing you can't do is take the bike off the road (read up on all the rules at the visitor center).

This is truly a park set up for cyclists: The camper shuttle has room for bikes, so you can mix up time in the saddle with time in the bus. And you'll find bike racks at all the campgrounds, so you can park while you hike or camp.

To rent a bike, call the **Denali Outdoor Center** 🛈 (Mile 240 Parks Hwy.; ☎ 888/303-1925 or 907/683-1925; www.denalioutdoorcenter.com). Mountain bikes rent for $40 for 1 full day, or $35 per day for multiple days. Reserve ahead of time, as they do sell out occasionally.

RIVER RAFTING

Blasting down the silty, ice-cold Nenana River in an inflatable raft is a wild and woolly way to round off a visit to Denali National Park. The Nenana runs between the park border and the Parks Highway, right through Glitter Gulch. The upper portion is slow and smooth and good for folks looking for a mellow, not-too-terrifying float along the edge of the wilderness. The lower portion speeds up markedly and squeezes between the rock walls of Nenana Canyon. It's loaded with class III and class IV rapids, which leave big, goofy grins on even the most jaded adrenaline junkies. The scenery all along the way is spellbinding. A gaggle of competing rafting outfits keeps prices in the reasonable range. The oldest and most experienced of the bunch is the **Denali Outdoor Center** (Mile 240 Parks Hwy.; ☎ 888/303-1925 or 907/683-1925; www.denalioutdoorcenter.com). It offers whitewater trips for $73 (or $53 for children 10–13) and trips down the mellow stretch for the same adult price (or $37 for children). Both trips last about 3½ hours all together, including 2 hours on the water, and time spent driving to and from the river and suiting up. The best deal is the combo trip, which hits both the slow-moving and the rollicking stretches of river, lasts 4 hours, and costs $98 (or $73 for children). If you've got enough people to fill an eight-person raft, you'll get a 10% discount. Discount coupons are often found in the freebie local visitor publications, widely available throughout the area, so take a look before booking a trip (reservations are strongly recommended, because trips can book up fast).

NIGHTLIFE IN DENALI

Nightlife around Denali is concentrated in the bars (and at two touristy dinner theaters). Of all of them, the **Salmon Bake Alaska** (p. 317) has the liveliest after-hours scene. It's the main hangout for Denali's young seasonal workers, and keeps 'em coming back with shuffleboard, video games, and the occasional live band.

The dinner theaters are geared for visitors on package tours, and tend to be corny in the extreme. Don't come expecting Broadway-quality performances and you might get a chuckle or two out of the proceedings. **Cabin Nite Dinner Theater** (Mile 238.0 Parks Hwy.; ☎ 800/276-7234 or 907/683-8200), at the McKinley Chalet Resort, is a rowdy, lively musical revue in which the actors and the waitstaff are one and the same. The plot involves a gold rush–era woman who runs a roadhouse in Kantishna, and the dinner involves large platters of food served at long, family-style tables. It costs $57 (half price for kids 2–12). This is the better show for kids.

At **The Music of Denali** (Mile 238.5 Denali Parks Hwy.; ☎ 800/426-0500 or 907/683-2282), at the Denali Princess Lodge, you're served dinner first and then watch the performance. My advice: Skip the mediocre dinner and just catch the show, which concerns the first party of mountain climbers to reach McKinley's south summit, in 1913. It costs $50 for dinner and a show, or half price for kids 2 to 12. If you skip the dinner, you have to buy tickets at the door, for $21.

TALKEETNA: BACK DOOR TO DENALI

Unless you're a world-class mountain climber, Talkeetna makes a lousy base for expeditions into Denali National Park. Although the tiny, rustic town is just 60 miles from Mount McKinley, it's 138 miles from the park entrance—too much of a drive for easy access. Still, Talkeetna is worth a visit on your way to or from the park. Why? For one thing, when Mount McKinley decides to emerge from the clouds, the views from Talkeetna are phenomenal. The town is just far enough away from the mountain that you can often see The High One from there, poking through the same clouds that obscure the view from within the park itself.

Another good reason to visit Talkeetna is because it's such a funky town, a real step back in time to Alaska's pioneer past. Yeah, it crawls with international alpinists in the spring and with everyday tourists on package tours through the summer, but all that attention has done remarkably little to change the place. The same dirt streets, narrow boardwalks, log cabins, and clapboard houses that have been there since the town was founded as a supply center for trappers and gold prospectors around 1900 are still in use today. Talkeetna's unvarnished, unaffected character is the perfect antidote to the over-commercialized madness of Glitter Gulch, just outside the park entrance.

Yet another reason to visit Talkeetna, at least early in the season, is to rub elbows with the mountain climbers. They come from all over the world to scale, or attempt to scale, McKinley and other peaks in the Alaska Range during the spring, when the mountains are still frozen solid and the avalanche danger is low. The town buzzes with a giddy, swaggering, globally flavored energy when the climbers are in town, psyching themselves up for high-stakes expeditions that could end in glory, disappointment, or death.

GETTING TO & AROUND TALKEETNA

Driving is the most practical way to get to Talkeetna, which is located roughly half way between Anchorage and the entrance to Denali National Park. Get off the Park Highway near mile 99 onto Talkeetna Spur Road and go 14 miles to its end. Once you get to Talkeetna, you can park your car and walk all over the tiny town, which sits at the confluence of the Susitna, Chulitna, and Talkeetna rivers.

The **Talkeetna/Denali Visitor Center** (☎ 800/660-2688, summer 907/733-2688, off season 907/733-2641; www.talkeetnadenali.com) is located at the junction of the Parks Highway and Talkeetna Spur Road—which makes it a convenient stop even for those bypassing Talkeetna altogether. Unlike most visitor centers in Alaska, which are associated with the local chamber of commerce or the state visitors bureau, this one is owned by a local flightseeing service (Talkeetna Aero Services). It's an excellent source for maps, brochures, trip-planning assistance, and outhouses, but don't expect impartiality when it comes to flightseeing.

The **Alaska Railroad Star** (☎ 800/544-0552; www.akrr.com) stops twice daily in Talkeetna during the summer on its way to and from Denali National Park. The fare between Anchorage and Talkeetna during the summer high season is $82, or $41 for kids ages 2 to 11. From Talkeetna to Denali National Park, the fare is $63 for adults or $32 for kids.

ACCOMMODATIONS, BOTH STANDARD & NOT

Talkeetna has lots of bargain-rate accommodations, starting with the $13 tent sites at the large, wooded RV park on the riverbank, **Talkeetna RV** (☎ 907/733-2604). If you haven't lined up a place to stay before you get to town, stop at the **Talkeetna/Denali Visitor Center** mentioned earlier and let them know. They'll call around and find all the places in your price range with vacancies. What follows is the cream of the budget crop.

$ At first glance, **House of Seven Trees** (Main St.; ☎ 907/733-7733; no credit cards) appears to be a B&B, located as it is inside a stately old clapboard home with a white picket fence out front. In fact, it's actually an unusually homey hostel, where the common area is like grandma's living room and the four small but comfy upstairs guest rooms all have dormer windows and quilted beds. They share a bath, have either a queen or two twin beds, and go for $75 or $85. In the backyard off the alley is an even cheaper option, the bunkhouse, where you can sleep for just $25 (or $20 if you brought a sleeping bag and don't need sheets). Wherever you lay your head, you get use of the house's full kitchen, where you can cook whatever you like (a grocery store is just down the street).

$ The **Fairview Inn** (101 Main St.; ☎ 907/733-2423; AE, DISC, MC, V) hasn't changed much since it opened in 1921. The downstairs is still a popular little bar (p. 331) with oak flooring and a giant buffalo head on the wall, and the upstairs still has spartan rooms that rent by the night. The five rooms share two baths, and they're all just big enough for their beds and beat-up old dressers. They go for $85 double occupancy, and have different configurations of twin and queen beds. This certainly isn't a good place to stay if you intend to turn in early. The lively bar downstairs is simply too noisy. Stay here only if you can sleep through anything, or if you intend to party downstairs into the wee hours yourself.

$–$$ The rooms are cheap, the atmosphere is historic, and the breakfasts can't be beat at the **Talkeetna Roadhouse** ★★★ kids (13550 East Main St.; ☎ 907/733-1351; www.talkeetnaroadhouse.com; MC, V). Built with logs in 1917 as a freight distribution warehouse, then expanded over the years, the Roadhouse has bunks in a co-ed room ($20 per night), and small private rooms ($65 or $85). There are just five private rooms, plus the bunk room and one private cabin, so you definitely want to make reservations here. The two downstairs rooms, which are the least expensive, have low ceilings and the vague feeling of a stateroom on an old riverboat. For $20 more, the three upstairs rooms are a bit roomier and have a log-cabin vibe. If you have a family, go for the cabin, which rents for $105 as a double, plus $10 per extra person. It's got a full-size bed, a twin, and a sleeping loft, as well as a kitchenette. For the Roadhouse's low prices, you can't expect maid service or a private bath (not even in the cabin). But you can count on the delightful aroma of cinnamon rolls, muffins, and French roast coffee wafting through the building in the morning. The Roadhouse's bakery is one of the best in Alaska, and the enormous egg and pancake breakfasts served there will stick to your ribs for a while.

DINING FOR ALL TASTES

There are a few high-end places in town where you could easily drop $100 on a meal for two, but cheap eats are the way to go in Talkeetna. The bargain places dish up generous servings, have memorable dishes or decor, and genuinely aim to please.

$–$$ It's not hard to tell that the **West Rib Café & Pub** (behind Nagley's General Store on Main St.; ☎ 907/733-DELI; www.westribpub.info; summer daily 11:30am–midnight, pub until 2am; fall and spring daily 11:30am–10pm, pub until midnight; winter Thurs–Sun only, hours vary; AE, DC, DISC, MC, V) is a climbers' hangout. Those little finger holds that rock climbers use to train are mounted to the walls and ceiling, which are also covered with graffiti and climbing gear left behind by climbers who've summited successfully. Among the beers on tap is an exceptionally potent one (9.2% alcohol) called, appropriately enough, Ice Axe Ale, which is brewed exclusively for the West Rib Café & Pub by the Glacier Brewhouse in Anchorage. In fact, the West Rib started out as a climbers bar with a little barbecue outside where people could cook their own food. The barbecue evolved into a screened-in cookhouse, and professionals now do the cooking. Alaskan pub-style fare is the name of the game here, from chili made with black beans, to kidney beans and ground caribou, to crab sandwiches, to musk ox burgers. Most dinners cost less than $10, except the filet of halibut or salmon, which goes for just $13.

$–$$ Fiddlehead ferns are a rare delicacy that you're most likely to find unfurling in a dark northern forest during their 1-week spring sprouting season or adorning a plate of blackened scallops at a white tablecloth restaurant in Kona. So when you come to the simple roadside stand attached to a burled-spruce pavilion called **Dancing Bear Salmon Bake** ✪✪ (corner of Main St. and Talkeetna Spur Rd.; ☎ 907/430-1318; summer only daily 8am–11pm; no credit cards) and find that you can get a bowl of fiddlehead ferns, sautéed in garlic butter, for just $5, you have to try it. They're harvested when they make their brief annual appearance in the Ostrich fern grottoes along the river here, then frozen so they can be used all summer. Shaped as the name suggests (like the head of a violin), the food has a delicate flavor that's comparable to asparagus with a nutty bite. For $6.75, you can get a bread bowl of king salmon chowder as well. Or go for the grilled king salmon entree ($14), with home fries, cold corn, and a tomato and onion salad. All the salmon served here is wild king salmon, a rare delicacy—"Not that farm raised crap," the waiter says with sneer.

WHY YOU'RE HERE: THE TOP SIGHTS & ATTRACTIONS

Since it's strategically located at the confluence of three rivers, Talkeetna is a hot spot for fishing and riverboating.

Several companies cater to anglers, who come for the summer salmon and trout runs. One long-time fishing outfit is **Mahay's Riverboat Service** (☎ 907/733-2229 for fishing, 907/733-2223 for sightseeing; www.mahaysriverboat.com), which whisks fishermen upriver in jet boats that fly along at 35 mph, drawing just 8 inches of water. Five-hour fishing charters cost $155 per person and 8-hour trips cost $205. For those who want the thrill of the jet boat but could do without the fishing, there's a 2-hour jet boat sightseeing tour for $55 (or $28 for kids 12 and younger). It includes a stop along shore for a quarter-mile hike through a forest, with visits to a replica of a Native shelter and a restored trapper's cabin (which includes a chair upholstered in bear fur).

A mellower way to get out on the water is by raft. River rafting around Talkeetna is not like rafting in the wild, woolly white water of Nenana River near the entrance to Denali National Park. Instead, the trips are scenic floats on swift but placid class I water. While there's no guarantee that you'll see any wildlife, you stand a good chance of spotting eagles, moose, beavers, maybe foxes, and possibly a bear or two, as well as spawning salmon. Several companies offer these trips, but the most fun (I think) is **Denali View Raft Adventures'** 🧒 (☎ 907/733-2778; www.denaliviewraft.com) "Flag Stop Rail 'n Raft" tour, in which you ride the Hurricane Turn train of the Alaska Railroad 11 miles out of town then float back to Talkeetna in an inflatable rubber raft. The whole trip takes about 4½ hours and costs $155, or $105 for kids 12 and younger, including lunch. The company also offers a 2-hour float for $65 ($45 kids), and a 3-hour trip for $95 ($65 kids), but there's no choo-choo involved. Regardless of how you get out on the water, bring layers of clothing; even on the sunniest Alaskan day, the breeze on a glacially fed river can chill you to the bone.

NIGHTLIFE IN TALKEETNA

The West Rib (see above) is one of Talkeetna's two watering holes, where grizzled locals, jaunty climbers, and everyday travelers meet and mingle. The other is the **Fairview Inn** (101 Main St.; ☎ 907/733-2423; summer Sun–Thurs noon–2am, Fri–Sat noon–3:30am; rest of year roughly daily 4pm–2am; AE, DISC, MC, V), a small, dark drinking establishment that oozes old-timey Alaskan ambience. The same giant buffalo head that greeted President Warren G. Harding when he swung through Talkeetna (there's a photo of him at the inn to prove it) greets you when you walk in. A grizzly bear hide (complete with head) is tacked to the ceiling, and various other animal parts adorn the walls. On Deadman's Wall, there's a photo gallery of climbers who did not make it off the mountain alive—a somber counterpoint to the spirited crowd that fills the joint on summer Fridays, Saturdays, and Sundays, when there's live music and hardly ever a cover charge. Wednesdays are reserved for jazz players, and Mondays are open-mic nights.

THE BUSH IS OFTEN DEFINED AS THE PART OF ALASKA THAT IS INACCESSIBLE by road—most of the state, in other words. By that definition, many of the isolated communities discussed elsewhere in this guidebook fall squarely within the Bush. For one reason or another, though, they also fall more logically into other chapters. This chapter is concerned with those far-flung Bush communities that simply don't fit anywhere else—the deep, deep, *deep* Bush. Geographically, "the Bush" of this chapter stretches from the Aleutian Islands in the south, up the coastline of the Bering Sea, and along the shores of the Arctic Ocean. That's a mind-bogglingly vast area, yet this chapter is short because there simply aren't a lot of destinations to cover there. In fact, there are just three: Dutch Harbor/Unalaska, Nome, and Barrow.

Sure, there are a few hundred Native villages in the Bush where the locals hunt, fish, and gather wild foods, in much the same way their ancestors did (firearms and fossil fuels being the biggest difference). But tourism doesn't fit into the fabric of life there, and if tourists did somehow show up, there wouldn't be anything for them to do anyway. A handful of Bush communities, such as Bethel and Dillingham, have wilderness lodges catering to millionaire hunters and sports fishermen. But since they're outrageously expensive, and since this guidebook's focus is on value travel, we're going to ignore them. There are also millions of acres of national parks, preserves, and monuments that stretch out across the Bush. Each summer a few extremely hardy backpackers venture into these wildernesses. But to get in and out alive, you need serious backcountry survival skills and pockets deep enough to hire a private Bush pilot. For the vast majority of travelers, these places are just too dangerous and expensive to visit.

That leaves us with our three rough-hewn outposts of civilization, each with its own Bush character. There's Dutch Harbor/Unalaska, the bustling fishing port in the stormy, treeless Aleutian Islands. There's Nome, the wacky little gold rush–era boomtown clinging to life on the edge of the Bering Sea. And there's Barrow, the Eskimo-dominated Arctic beach town at the tip top of the continent. All are worlds apart, yet all share some Bush qualities in common. The weather is dependably lousy (if not life threatening). The food tends to be expensive and greasy. The architecture is shabby and anything but quaint. The lodging tends to be bare boned and basic. And the cost of travel can be prohibitive. So why the heck would you want to visit one of these far-flung, hard-bitten places? Quite honestly, you might not. However, if you really want to get to know Alaska—I mean the *real* Alaska—well then, you just might.

DON'T LEAVE BUSH ALASKA WITHOUT . . .

Dipping your toes in the Arctic Ocean. In Barrow you can play footsie with the Arctic sea ice in the summer. Or you can become an immediate lifetime member of the Polar Bear Club by taking the full plunge (your head has got to be all the way under, or it doesn't count). See p. 356.

Looking for polar bears. The polar sea ice is thinning and polar bears are rapidly headed toward endangered species status, but in the winter they still come ashore at Point Barrow, and sometimes even wander into the town of Barrow itself. See p. 357.

Panning for gold. There's still gold in them thar' grains of sand on the beach at Nome, and it's finders keepers. After filling your poke with color, get out of town and explore the derelict railway cars of the Last Train to Nowhere and the abandoned gold dredges all slowly rusting away on the tundra. See p. 347 and 349.

Remembering "The Forgotten War" in Alaska. During World War II, the Japanese spent 2 days bombing U.S. fortifications on the windswept volcanic slopes above Dutch Harbor, and you can easily spend a half-day exploring the old bunkers, tunnels, and zigzagging trenches that remain. See p. 336.

Pick up Native handiworks at bargain prices. The Bush is the best place to find deals on Native arts and crafts, because the Bush is where these things come from. See the "Shopping" sections throughout this chapter for info.

LAY OF THE LAND

This chapter takes in two regions, Southwest Alaska and the Far North. The Far North includes Barrow in the Arctic and Nome in the sub-Arctic. Unalaska/Dutch Harbor, the hub of the Aleutian Islands, falls into the Southwest region. Kodiak Island is considered part of Southwest Alaska, as well, but because it's so readily accessible from Southcentral Alaska, that's the chapter I put it in (see p. 142).

SOUTHWEST ALASKA

UNALASKA & DUTCH HARBOR　Located on the second largest of the Aleutian Islands, the town of Unalaska was the headquarters of the Russian-American Company's sea otter fur trade in the 1700s, and the site of a little-known battle between the U.S. and Japan in World War II. Across a short bridge, on neighboring Amaknak Island, is the port of Dutch Harbor, one of the world's most productive seafood processing ports. Most visitors to Unalaska are drawn by the legendary halibut fishing or by the opportunities to see rare sea birds such as the gray whiskered auklet. See p. 335.

THE FAR NORTH

NOME　Nome is a weather-beaten little beach town sitting between the Bering Sea and the vast tundra and mountain wilderness of the Seward Peninsula. It was born at the tail end of the 19th century amid one of the biggest gold rushes in history. Mining for gold and other minerals is still at the heart of its economy, and prospectors still find gold dust in the dark sands along the beach the town sits on.

Nome is also the finish line for the famed Iditarod sled dog race. Its official, if tongue in cheek, motto is "There's no place like Nome." See p. 342.

BARROW Located on the shore of the Arctic Ocean, 330 miles north of the Arctic Circle, Barrow is the northernmost community in the United States. It's largely populated by Iñupiat Eskimos who have adapted many of their ancient hunter-gatherer ways to the modern world. Visitors go to see Native whaling culture, polar bears, the northern lights, and the midnight sun (though not all at once). They also head here for the bragging rights of having stood at the northernmost point in North America (Point Barrow). See p. 351.

GETTING TO & AROUND THE BUSH

Alaska Airlines (☎ 800/252-7522; www.alaskaair.com) flies out of Anchorage and Fairbanks to Nome and Barrow. It also has the exclusive right to sell tickets to Unalaska aboard a smaller carrier. You'll typically pay about $320 round trip to get from Anchorage to Nome, and about $400 round trip from Anchorage to Barrow. You can also get to Unalaska via the **Alaska Marine Highway System** (☎ 800/642-0066; www.ferryalaska.com). It's a 3-day voyage from Homer, but cheaper than flying.

You won't need a rental car in Unalaska or Barrow, which are quite walkable. But you should definitely get a rental car in Nome. The city itself is compact, but you'll want a car to get out onto the tundra and into the mountains. You can drive to Prudhoe Bay on the Dalton Highway, one of the most spectacular—and gnarly—drives in America (p. 297). But nobody will think badly of you if you choose to take a tour out of Fairbanks instead. Tours typically drive one leg of the trip and fly the other. I give the pricing for all of these options below, on a destination by destination basis.

UNALASKA & DUTCH HARBOR

The tiny wind-scoured community of Unalaska is set amid the remote, storm-battered, spectacularly beautiful Aleutian Islands, an area so meteorologically turbulent it's known as the "Cradle of Storms." Home of Dutch Harbor and the storied Bering Sea crab fleet, Unalaska is a tough, scrappy commercial fishing town, as well as a halibut fisherman's paradise, a birder's dream, and a place not too many tourists ever see. Go there to hike through the treeless, emerald-green slopes of the Aleutians. Go there to kayak in the waters at the very edge of the North Pacific, where kayaks were popularized. Go there to try and hook one of the largest halibut on the planet, or to spy on a rare whiskered auklet as it dives for herring. Or go there simply to spend a little time in an outpost of civilization that's way, *way* off the beaten path.

A BRIEF HISTORY

Unalaska is and always has been the center of the Aleutian community in Alaska. The Aleut people have lived there for thousands of years, fishing and hunting for seals and sea lions from their kayaks, gathering berries on the windswept volcanic slopes, and escaping from the bitter cold in their underground, sod-roofed houses. Archaeologists have found remnants of such dwellings around Unalaska that date back 6,000 to 8,000 years.

Tight Schedules & the Aleutians Don't Mix

Do not plan a trip to Unalaska if you don't have some leeway in your itinerary. Foul weather in the Aleutians typically delays flights for a day or two in the summer, and far longer in the winter. This is one destination where **travel insurance** (p. 376), which probably won't cost more than a single night in a hotel room and which will cover your expenses if things go amuck, is a no-brainer.

When Russian explorers arrived in 1759, they found a dozen Aleut villages and more than a 1,000 people on the island of Unalaska and its close neighbor, Amaknak, a stone's throw away (the population today is around 4,000). Russian trappers showed up soon afterward and made Unalaska the headquarters of the Russian-American Co.'s sea otter trade. They also made slaves out of the Aleuts, kicking off a long history of abuse of the Aleuts by outsiders. Reminders of the Russian era in Unalaska include the onion-domed Church of the Holy Ascension, which has one of the most complete collections of Russian art and icons in the Americas inside, and a little graveyard filled with Russian crosses outside.

The U.S. Army heavily fortified Dutch Harbor in 1939, and when the U.S. entered World War II, it deployed thousands of troops to the Aleutians to protect "America's back door," as Alaska was called. The Japanese attacked in 1942, bombing Dutch Harbor for 2 days. At the Aleutian WWII National Historic Center, you can hike around the former Army fort that defended Dutch Harbor. It's filled with bunkers, tunnels, and other reminders of what historians have dubbed "The Forgotten War" in Alaska. The Aleuts didn't fare much better with Japanese and American armies in the Aleutians than they did with Russian fur traders. Some Aleuts were captured by the Japanese and stuck in harsh prison camps in Imperial Japan, and the rest were evacuated by the U.S. to squalid wartime refugee camps in Southeast Alaska. Today, though, through the village-owned Ounalashka Corporation, the Aleuts own most of Unalaska and its surrounding areas. You can hike and camp on their land, but you first must buy a permit for a small fee (see p. 340 for info).

LAY OF THE LAND

People refer to Unalaska and Dutch Harbor interchangeably, although Unalaska (pronounced Oon-ah-*lah*-ska) is the town and Dutch Harbor is the port within the town. Unalaska sits on Unalaska Island, about 800 miles southwest of Anchorage, at the beginning of the 1,000-mile-long Aleutian Archipelago. Dutch Harbor and the airport occupy neighboring Amaknak Island, which is across a short bridge from Unalaska (it's got a real name but everybody just calls it "The Bridge to the Other Side"). Amaknak Island is much smaller than Unalaska Island, and it's dominated by Makushin Volcano, which rises above the fishing fleet. The Aleutian Islands form the divide between the Gulf of Alaska and the Bering Sea, marking the spot where the warm Japanese current meets the cold air and waters from the Arctic, generating legendarily wicked weather. (Expect rain,

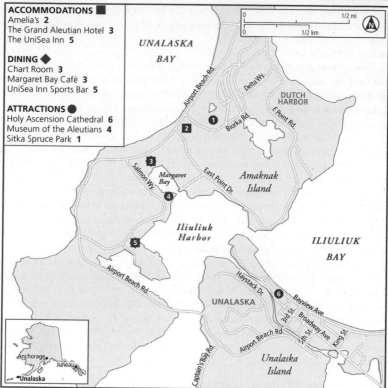

ACCOMMODATIONS
Amelia's **2**
The Grand Aleutian Hotel **3**
The UniSea Inn **5**

DINING ◆
Chart Room **3**
Margaret Bay Café **3**
UniSea Inn Sports Bar **5**

ATTRACTIONS ●
Holy Ascension Cathedral **6**
Museum of the Aleutians **4**
Sitka Spruce Park **1**

fog, and lots of wind.) On the plus side, the maritime climate means temperatures here are more moderate than in other parts of Alaska. In the summer, they range from about 45° to 65°F (7°–18°C). Winter temperatures are in the 20s and 30s (minus single digits to single digits Celsius). Every now and then, especially in the early summer and in the fall, the skies clear, the winds die, and the emerald green volcanic peaks of the Aleutians emerge in their eye-popping glory.

You'll find a good amount of info on the area in this chapter, but if you need more, go to the **Unalaska/Port of Dutch Harbor Convention and Visitors Bureau** (corner of 5th and Broadway; ☎ 877/581-2612 or 907/581-2612; www.unalaska. info; daily 8am–5pm).

GETTING TO & AROUND UNALASKA

Alaska Airlines (☎ 800/252-7522; www.alaskaair.com) stopped flying its own jets to Unalaska because of weather delays and the town's short runway (which is just 4 feet longer than the FAA's minimum requirement—that, combined with the area's severe winds, had jet pilots referring to the airport as the Super Bowl of Alaska airfields). Nowadays, Alaska Airlines leases the 30-passenger turbo prop aircraft of **Peninsula Airways** (☎ 800/446-4228; www.penair.com), which are better suited to the job. You can book a flight to several small communities along the Aleutian chain directly through PenAir, but to buy a ticket for the 3-hour flight to Unalaska, you have to go through Alaska Airlines. Round-trip airfare from Anchorage starts at around $900. (The airlines, by the way, refer to Unalaska as Dutch Harbor.)

If you have 3 days for a sea voyage, you can cut down on the cost of a trip to Unalaska by about $100 if you do one leg of the trip by boat. The **Alaska Marine Highway System** (☎ 800/642-0066; www.ferryalaska.com) ferry arrives at Dutch Harbor twice a month in the summer. It's an 82-hour voyage from Homer, with short stops on Kodiak and at seven Native villages along the way. Unfortunately, the ferry docks at Dutch Harbor for only half a day before heading back—not enough time to justify the trip. So unless you're content to wait 2 weeks for the boat to return (which is way too long), you've got to fly back. Still, using the ferry for one leg of the trip is a blast if you've got the time. Both the scenery and the Native villagers you'll see along the way will make deep impressions on you. That said, the voyage is a real open-sea adventure, so seasickness can be a problem. The passenger fare is $351 one-way, if you camp out on deck or sack out in the common areas (as many do) or $170 for kids ages 6 to 11 (5 and under are free). For a two-berth cabin with shared baths, add another $361.

You can get by without a car in Unalaska, because it is easily walkable in good weather and it has a thriving taxi business. (The cabs are used mainly by the many transient fishermen and cannery workers heading to and from town.) For a ride to the Grand Aleutian Hotel, **Blue Checker Taxi** (☎ 907/581-2186) charges $5 from the airport and about $9 from the ferry terminal. To explore the island more thoroughly, though, you need a car. **North Port Rentals** (☎ 907/581-3880; www. northportrentals.net) rents cars and trucks, starting at $60 a day (plus a 10% state and 3% city tax).

ACCOMMODATIONS, BOTH STANDARD & NOT

When it comes to lodging in Unalaska, you've just two choices: upscale or budget. There are, in fact, just two places to choose from. Both are owned by UniSea, the town's big multinational seafood processor. Add Unalaska's 8% tax on accommodations to the prices given here.

$ Your budget hotel option is a two-story place by the harbor called **The UniSea Inn** (185 Gilman Rd.; ☎ 866/581-3844 or 907/581-1325, register at the Grand Aleutian; DISC, MC, V). Rooms are clean and simple, and they go for $99 double occupancy. Ask for one with a harbor view; it costs the same as one without a view. There's a sports bar on-site, where hard-bitten Bering Sea fishermen like to watch hockey or shoot pool, and where local bands periodically play Top 40 and country covers. If the fierce Aleutian winds knock your coiffeur out of whack, Rosalinda's unisex hair salon is right off the lobby.

$$$$ The other choice is **The Grand Aleutian Hotel** ✫ (498 Salmon Way; ☎ 866/ 581-3844 or 907/581-3844; www.unisea.com/grand_aleutian_hotel.htm; DISC, MC, V), which is big, luxurious, and a total oddity. It's an attractive, sprawling, 112-room hotel, as nice as the nicest hotels in Anchorage, incongruously stuck out on one of the stormiest, remotest places on the planet. It's a bizarre delight to step out of a dark, wicked Aleutian gale into the Grand's handsome, warmly lit three-story lobby, where you can warm up beside an enormous stone fireplace and then repair to the piano bar for a snifter of brandy (you may want to hang out in the lobby, even if you choose the cheaper digs at the Inn). The rooms are spacious, come with either one king or a pair of queens, and go for $164 double occupancy, except the suites, which go for a walloping $269. All have broad views of the sea and surrounding mountains, and are loaded with amenities. Artwork from local and regional artists ground the hotel thoroughly in Alaska.

DINING FOR ALL TASTES

Steaks, burgers, Mexican, and seafood are the dietary staples in Unalaska, where the dining scene is as straightforward and unpretentious as the town itself.

$–$$ Restaurants come and go here, but there's always a fair selection of places serving big, hearty, reasonably priced meals. The best place in town for a fat burger and fries ($8.40) and a thick, frosty milkshake ($5.75) is a basic, brightly lit diner called **Amelia's** (On Airport Rd., in the heart of town; ☎ 907/581-2800; daily 5am–10pm; AE, DISC, MC, V). It's also a good bet for a fisherman's size breakfast.

$–$$ To mingle with off-duty fishermen, catch some ESPN on TV, and down a pizza (from $22 for a pie) or some late-night appetizers (try the wings, $11), head for the **UniSea Inn Sports Bar** ★ (185 Gilman Rd., at the UniSea Inn; ☎ 907/ 581-7246; Mon–Thurs 11:30–2am, Fri–Sat 11:30–3am, Sun noon–10pm; AE, DISC, MC, V). After you eat, you might play a round of darts, shoot some pool, or buy a fisherman a shot and listen to hair-raising accounts of king crab fishing on the freezing Bering Sea in the dark depths of winter.

$–$$ Slightly spiffier (mostly because of the lovely views of the harbor) is the Grand Aleutian Hotel's casual dining option, the **Margaret Bay Café** (498 Salmon Way; ☎ 907/581-3844, ext. 7122; daily 7am–3pm; DISC, MC, V). Basic staples like grilled cheese sandwiches ($7.25) and fish and chips ($14) are on offer here and are fine. The Café is only open for breakfast and lunch, though.

$$$–$$$$ The only place in town to really splash out is at the Grand Aleutian's other restaurant, the **Chart Room** ★ (498 Salmon Way; ☎ 866/581-3844 or 907/ 581-3844; daily 6–11pm; DISC, MC, V), which has steaks, seafood, pasta, and a pretty swell second-floor waterfront view. While the food isn't of the quality you'd get in a fine dining establishment in say, Anchorage, it's the best this town's got. Head there on Sunday for the brunch buffet ($25), or catch the Wednesday night seafood buffet—a good deal, for Alaska, at $32, as it includes halibut, salmon, and king crab (a single serving of king crab costs more than $30 in most restaurants, so the Chart Room's seafood feast can be counted as a steal). It's open for Sunday brunch and for dinner only.

WHY YOU'RE HERE: THE TOP SIGHTS & ATTRACTIONS

The Russian-American Company, which was busy decimating fur-bearing marine mammals in the Aleutians long before commercial fishing caught on, was required under the terms of its charter with the czar to support Russian Orthodox missionaries in America (even as it enslaved the Aleuts). So it built the **Holy**

Ascension Cathedral ($5 suggested donation; hours vary) in 1825, using California redwood. The church, which sits on a grassy slope overlooking Iliuliuk Bay, is the oldest Russian Orthodox Church in America. Imagine the boxy structure at the heart of the church without the smaller wings on the front and sides, as that's how the building looked originally. The additions, which give the church a cross-shaped floor plan, were added in 1894. With its three-story bell tower, twin onion domes, and small graveyard filled with Russian crosses, the church is irresistible to photographers. If you can get inside it, you'll find one of the richest collections of Russian artifacts, icons, and artwork in the Americas. To arrange a tour, contact the Unalaska **Convention and Visitors Bureau** (☎ 907/581-2612). The church is still active. To attend a service, show up Sunday at 10am, cover your head with a scarf if you're a woman, and doff your cap if you're not, and be prepared to stand for about 1 and a half hours.

Another living remnant of the Russian area, the **Sitka Spruce Park** in Dutch Harbor is home to six spruce trees that the Russians transplanted from the mainland in 1805. They're still thriving. The Aleutians are naturally treeless, so the park really stands out. The trees are the only ones in the United States designated as National Historic Landmarks.

Traditionally, the Aleuts were too busy eking out their hardscrabble existences on their treeless, storm-wracked island homes to put the kind of energy into art that other Alaska Natives did, such as the Tlingit with their enormous totem poles or the Athabascans with their flashy beadwork and embroidery. The arts and crafts of the Aleuts tend to be small, plain, and totally practical. They're most famous for their beach grass baskets, which are simply but gorgeously patterned, and so tightly woven that some can even hold water. The **Museum of the Aleutians** ✦✦ (314 Salmon Way; ☎ 907/581-5150; www.aleutians.org; admission $5; Tues–Sat 9am–5pm, Sun 11am–5pm) has a fine exhibit of old Aleut basketry for you to examine, along with all sorts of hunting and fishing implements, a waterproof kayaker's parka made from sea lion intestines and esophagus, and a bunch of other artifacts that shed a little light on Aleut resourcefulness.

Artifacts from the Russian and World War II eras round out the collection. One of the overall highlights is an original 18th-century pencil drawing of a young Aleut woman, *Woman of Unalaska,* by John Weber, the illustrator who sailed to Alaska with Captain James Cook, in order to document the expedition. The woman's facial tattoos, piercings, carefully styled hair, and tasseled garment show that while the Aleuts may not have had a lot of time for aesthetics, they didn't neglect them entirely. The woman's gentle eyes and shy smile also suggest that, while life might have been hard for the Aleuts, it didn't break their spirit.

You'll see remnants of World War II all over the Unalaska and Amaknak islands, from the pillbox beside the school playground, to the sunken ship in the harbor, to the old submarine dock where fishing boats are now overhauled. Overlooking the Dutch Harbor is 1,589-foot **Mount Ballyhoo,** which is covered with the remains of the old Quonset huts, bunkers, pillboxes, tunnels, gun mounts, and zigzagging trenches that made it impossible for an attacking aircraft to strafe the whole trench at once. Take a few hours to hike around the mountainside and explore the ruins, which are now part of the **Aleutian World War II National Historic Area** (☎ 907/581-9944; www.nps.gov/aleu; $4 permit; Thurs–Sun 1–6pm). Before visiting, you'll first have to go to the **Visitors Bureau** (p. 337), located in a World War II–era building at the airport, and buy the $4 permit needed to set foot on the land.

ACTIVE UNALASKA
HIKING

The Aleutians boast some of the most unique and pleasant hiking options in all of Alaska. Because there are no trees on the islands, the views from the trails are always unobstructed. Wind keeps the bugs away, and there are no bears to worry about. Along the way, you'll spot wildflowers, wild berries, and birds (including bald eagles) galore in the summer, and occasionally red foxes and wild horses. Much of the island is covered with springy grasses and heather, which turn bright green when it's warm, and which you can stretch out in to feast on all those ripe wild blackberries you'll gather during your trek.

Many of the trails on the island were established thousands of years ago by Aleut hunter-gatherers. In addition to hiking **Mount Ballyhoo** (see above), I'd recommend a walk up to the 421-foot **Bunker Hill,** with its old WWII gun emplacement, and 2,136-foot **Pyramid Peak,** which has a spectacular view in good weather.

Before setting out, you can pick up a brochure describing all the island hikes at the offices of the **Ounalashka Corp.** (400 Salmon Way, in Dutch Harbor; ☎ 907/581-1276; Mon–Fri 8am–5pm), which owns most of the island. When you drop by for the brochure, you can also buy the $6 permit needed to hike on Ounalashka land (it's $10 per family group).

FISHING

Most visitors to Unalaska Island come either to see birds or to catch fish. Sports fishermen tend to ignore the island's rich salmon runs and go straight for the trophy fish, which in this case are the humongous halibut. A 459-pound world record halibut was caught here in 1996 (go to Unalaska City Hall to see the full-scale model). Currently there are just two sports fishing operators in town. The first is run by Dave Magone, who will run you out to the flatfish grounds for a day of angling aboard his 32-foot **fishing vessel** *Lucille* (☎ 907/581-5949; www.unalaskahalibutfishing.com). Charters cost $180 per person and last 8 hours. The other charter operator is **Aleutian Island Outfitters** (☎ 907/581-4557 or 907/359-4557; www.aleutianislandoutfitters.com) which charges $200 per person a day for 6-hour day trips (you may be able to bargain them down on the prices for kids). Why does Aleutian charge more than the competition for a shorter trip? Because its boat, the 32-foot *Suzanne Marie,* gets to and from the fishing grounds faster than the *Lucille.* Otherwise, the time you spend with halibut hooks in the water is the same.

BIRDING

Birders know all about Unalaska and the 100-plus species of birds that nest and fly around the islands. Unlike other locales, where you trudge through trees to spot your life-list addition, birding here is a water-sport: The rarest birds of Unalaska are best seen from a boat. Unfortunately, you can count the bird-watching boats in this area on one finger. The sole operator, **Aleutian Island Outfitters** (see fishing above), will take you 10 miles offshore to the feeding grounds where various species of albatross and other pelagic birds congregate. Or it will take you along the coast to watch a tiny gray seabird known as the whiskered auklet dive for herring, sardines, and other little fish. The 6-hour tour is just as pricey as the Aleutian fishing expedition (at $200 per person) and since Aleutian has no competitors, you can be darn sure you won't get a discount. That said, Unalaska is one of the few places on the planet where you can see a whiskered auklet, and for some that makes the price worth it.

KAYAKING

Though the ocean surrounding Unalaska Island is rough, there are plenty of sheltered harbors, bays, and coves to explore by kayak. Rent a single-person kayak from **Aleutian Adventure Sports** (☎ 888/581-4489 or 907/581-4489; www.aleutian adventure.com) for $69 per day or a tandem for $89. Take a tour if you don't feel confident paddling alone. Tours range from $55 per person for 3 hours to $75 for 5 hours, and that includes instruction, if you like.

THE OTHER UNALASKA

Like other parts of the Alaskan Bush, Unalaska is so far off the beaten path that it has no beaten path of its own for you to steer clear of once you're there. Just to be in Unalaska is to see a side of Alaska few tourists ever do. If you really want to dig even deeper though, you can. Literally. Join the **Museum of the Aleutians** (314 Salmon Way; ☎ 907/581-5150; www.aleutians.org) on one of its summer archaeological digs at an ancient Aleut village site, and you'll get to help brush and sift through centuries of dirt in search of Alaska's earliest history. Evidence from these digs has emerged suggesting that the Aleutian Islands may have been the first place in North America inhabited by humans. Some have theorized (controversially) that people first came to the Americas from Asia by boat, island hoping along the Aleutians to the mainland. The more widely accepted theory is that the first people came over the Bering Land Bridge. You don't need to pick a side in the debate to participate in the dig. All you need are a few hours to get dirty. Or stick around for a few weeks if you're really into it—who knows, you might be the one who unearths something momentous, like the miniature pumice masks or the pair of 3,000-year-old labrets (the studs worn through pierced lips) found in past summers. There are no minimum or maximum time commitments, and no charge. You are, however, totally responsible for yourself, including getting to and from the dig site and bringing food and water.

NOME

Unlike most Bush communities, which have Native village roots, Nome sprung up as a gold rush boomtown. It was founded by the largely American stampeders who flocked to the Seward Peninsula at the tail end of the 19th century in search of riches and adventure (people still find gold dust on the beach here, and all you need is a pan to sift the sand with to join them in the hunt). This weather-beaten little town has held fast to the shore of the Bering Sea for more than a century despite a series of catastrophic storms, fires, and epidemics that would have wiped a less tenacious community off the map. For visitors, Nome itself has precious little in the way of attractions. So it's important to rent a car so you can get out onto the tundra to see Native fish camps, abandoned gold dredges, the hot springs, the nearby ghost town, and the rusting remains of the Last Train to Nowhere. Don't be surprised if you see a herd of reindeer or musk ox along the way.

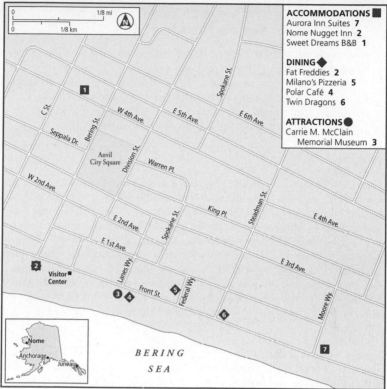

ACCOMMODATIONS ■
Aurora Inn Suites 7
Nome Nugget Inn 2
Sweet Dreams B&B 1

DINING ◆
Fat Freddies 2
Milano's Pizzeria 5
Polar Café 4
Twin Dragons 6

ATTRACTIONS ●
Carrie M. McClain
    Memorial Museum 3

A BRIEF HISTORY

Nome got its start as a wild, lawless, gold rush boomtown. In 1898, three prospectors, known as the Three Lucky Swedes (even though one was Norwegian), discovered gold in a creek near Nome. Word soon reached the stampeders in Canada, who had chased the Klondike gold rush only to get skunked when they reached the Yukon and found every claim already staked. Thousands of them came straight to Nome. By the summer of 1899 Nome was a tent city with 10,000 inhabitants.

It was an ailing prospector, left behind on the beach that summer as his comrades fanned out across the peninsula in search of gold, who discovered that the Nome beach itself was laced with gold. Once news got out about the easy riches on the strand, Nome's population swelled to 20,000. For a while it was the largest city in Alaska (today it is home to just 3,500 people, counting those who live within the city limits). Although by now the dark sands of Nome have been pretty thoroughly sifted, gold still turns up, and prospectors still camp there all summer and hunt for it, many finding enough to cover their expenses and break even (the ultimate budget vacationers!). Whatever gold turns up on the beach belongs to whoever finds it, and all you need to look for it is a pan and a little time.

Nome's Irreverent Side

Nome's goofball sense of humor is so well established that even the official city motto is a pun, "There's no place like Nome." Nomeites' irreverent nature is probably best exemplified by their tradition of propping discarded Christmas trees in a cluster on the frozen Bering Sea and telling visitors it's the Nome National Forest. Those who walk through the "forest" will find little wooden gnomes tucked here and there—the gnomes of Nome.

The rest of the world doesn't give Nome much thought until March, when it becomes the finish line of the Iditarod Trail Sled Dog Race. The Iditarod is rooted in a 1925 diphtheria epidemic among the Eskimos of Nome. An epic dog sled run was launched to deliver the serum needed to halt the epidemic. Twenty dog mushers and more than 100 dogs rushed the medicine 674 miles from Nenana near Fairbanks to Nome in 5 days. The humanitarian relay effort is commemorated in today's Iditarod, a grueling 1,151-mile dog sled race that begins in Anchorage and ends in Nome. Dog mushing fans and media people from around the world descend on Nome for the finish of the race, and special events are held all month long. See p. 75 in Anchorage for more info on the race.

LAY OF THE LAND

Nome sits on the southern shore of the Seward Peninsula, which juts out into the Bering Sea toward Russia like a big fat thumb. The peninsula is an upland remnant of the Bering Land Bridge, which connected Asia with North America when sea levels were lower, and which many anthropologists believe was the route by which human beings populated the Americas.

The 3,500 residents of Nome live and work in a ramshackle collection of weathered homes and businesses built on small stilts that keep them from melting the underlying permafrost. The town is laid out in a grid along the Bering Sea, with Front Street following the seawall, 1st Avenue a block away and parallel, and so on. Nome is 539 miles from Anchorage by air, and 160 miles from Russia. You can't drive there—unless you drive a dog sled—but once you've arrived, you'll find nearly 300 miles of gravel roads in the area worth exploring. Three main roads radiate from town, and I describe them on p. 349.

Nome is 102 miles south of the Arctic Circle. On the shortest day of the year, the sun is up for just 3 hours and 54 minutes. Visit on the longest day and you can work on your tan for 21 hours and 39 minutes (probably a dumb idea, on second thought).

The **Nome Convention and Visitors Bureau** (301 Front St.; ☎ 907/443-6624; www.nomealaska.org) has free maps and information on all the tour operators, accommodations, and whatnot not covered here. In the off season, the office is open daily from 9am to 6pm and it's open 9am to 9pm in the summer. If you're going to explore the road system around Nome—and you really should—stop in at the visitor bureau or at the **Alaska Department of Fish and Game** (corner of

Front and Stedman sts.; ☎ 907/443-5796) to pinpoint the best places to spot reindeer, musk ox, bears, and other wildlife before you go.

GETTING TO & AROUND NOME

Flying is the only practical way to get to Nome. Round-trip airfare on **Alaska Airlines** (☎ 800/252-7522; www.alaskaair.com) from Anchorage starts at around $420. Direct flights take about 90 minutes, but some flights stop in Kotzebue as well. Many visitors to Nome go on package tours, which save you a lot of money but prevent you from getting to know Nome and the surrounding tundra wilderness one-on-one. Since exploring the tundra is one of the great reasons to go to Nome, you'll get a lot more out of a trip here as an independent traveler. Still, **Alaska Airlines Vacations** (☎ 800/468-2248) charges $558 for an overnight stay at the Nome Nugget Inn, and $474 for a day trip with an 8-hour tour.

The airport is about 2 miles from downtown, and taxi fare from there to town is $5 per person. Call **Checker Cab** (☎ 907/443-5211 or 907/443-5136), or **Louie's Cab** (☎ 907/443-3600). But if it's a nice day and you're not overburdened with luggage, you can walk from the airport to town—it can be a pleasant stroll.

You can easily get anywhere in Nome on foot, but getting out onto the tundra takes a vehicle. Gravel roads make trucks or SUVs the vehicle of choice, and **Stampede Ventures** (at the Aurora Inn; ☎ 800/354-4606 or 907/443-3838) rents them for $95 per day. **Alaska Cab Garage** (4th Ave. and Steadman St.; ☎ 907/443-2939) rents cars with two-wheel drive for $85 a day, and four-wheel-drive vehicles for $100 a day.

ACCOMMODATIONS, BOTH STANDARD & NOT

If you're up for **camping,** you can pitch a tent on the beach that Nome is built along and camp for free. Public restrooms are available, and campers can head to the town's recreation center to shower. Nome's B&Bs tend to be cheaper than Nome hotels, and they offer the additional advantage of hosts who can help you get to know the community better than anyone working at a hotel ever would. Go to the visitor center's website (www.nomealaska.org) for a complete list of B&Bs and other accommodations. Local taxes add an 8% tax to the cost of rooms.

$–$$ My choice among Nome's bed-and-breakfasts is **Sweet Dreams B&B** ✮✮ (406 W. 4th St.; ☎ 907/443-2919; MC, V), which is run by a former Nome mayor and his wife. Their plain, two-story home, set on stilts, looks like any other modern Nome house from the outside. When you're on the inside, however, where the walls are covered with ancient, weathered wood, you'd swear the house is one of Nome's original, gold rush–era buildings. The place might also pass as a museum, filled as it is from floor to ceiling with Alaskan artwork and Native arts and crafts. Downstairs is a single-occupancy room with a private but detached bath ($85); the two double-occupancy rooms upstairs, which share a bath, go for $120. All rates include breakfast, which the mayor's wife cooks when she has time, and which the mayor cooks when she doesn't. The real draw here is the good humor and keen insight into local affairs offered by the hosts—the ex-mayor just happens to be one of the foremost authorities on Nome history.

Nome's Overflow Accommodations

During the Iditarod, when thousands of people flock to town and take up every single room, dozens of Nomeites open their homes as temporary bed-and-breakfasts. The **Overflow Housing Program,** as it's called, is run by the **Visitor and Convention Bureau** (☎ 907/443-6624; www.nomealaska.org) and involves about 50 homes. Participants run the gamut from friendly folks who will become your best friends in the Alaskan Bush to indifferent hosts who will take your money, show you your bed, and leave it at that. Some serve breakfast, some don't, and prices vary, but range from around $75 to $100 per person. Unfortunately, overflow housing becomes an option *only* after every single year-round B&B and hotel room is booked up. That always happens in March during the week of the Iditarod, and occasionally when a convention comes to town (yeah, they have conventions in Nome). Check with the visitor bureau for the list of housing options available during your stay.

$$ Of the hotels in town, the one with the kitschiest sense of fun is the **Nome Nugget Inn** (315 W. Front St.; ☎ 877-443-2323 or 907/443-2323; AE, DISC, MC, V). The Paul Bunyan–size gold pan nailed to the front, the weathered fishing hut with a parka-clad Native and husky perched on the roof above the entrance, and the inauthentic but enthusiastic gold rush Victorian decor in the lobby and lounge make the place festive and photogenic. The rooms, unfortunately, aren't as fun. They're small and basic, and go for $100 for those with a queen-size bed or $120 for those with a pair of twins, for double or single occupancy. The daily rate drops by $10 if you stay for 7 days.

$$–$$$$ The newest, largest (68 rooms), and cushiest hotel in town is **Aurora Inn Suites** (302 E. Front St.; ☎ 800/354-4606 or 907/443-3838; www.aurora innome.com; AE, DISC, MC, V). It's got a country-inn theme going, complete with a sauna to warm up in after walking on the cold beach out front. If you ask, you can get a room with a view of the Bering Sea right outside the window. In terms of accommodations, they come in all configurations, from rooms with two queen beds, to kitchenette units, to swank 1-bedroom suites with full kitchens, bay windows, and sleeper sofas. They range from $130 to $220 for double occupancy, depending on size and amenities.

DINING FOR ALL TASTES

Eating out in Nome means pizza, Japanese, or Chinese, and good ole' fashion' diner grub—sometimes all under one roof. You won't find any innovative upscale eateries tempting you to spend more than you planned. The travelers' rule of thumb about economizing on food costs by eating where the locals eat is easy to follow here, since every eatery in town is a local's joint.

$–$$$ For breakfast beside the Bering Sea, go to the **Polar Café** (205 E. Front St.; ☎ 907/443-5191; daily 6am–9pm; AE, DC, DISC, MC, V), which is tucked off an alley along Front Street and boasts a broad and lovely oceanfront view. In many respects—its all-day breakfast menu, its blistering love affair with the deep fat fryer, its knots of locals chewing the fat over coffee while studiously ignoring you—the Polar Café is just like any American diner anywhere. Except here you can sink your knife and fork into a big fat omelet ($9.25–$13) or a crispy country-fried steak ($14) while gazing across a sometimes frozen sea toward Siberia.

$$–$$$ For Nome's version of Asian fusion cuisine, try **Twin Dragons** ✰✰ (100 Front St.; ☎ 907/443-5552; Mon–Sat 11am–11pm, Sun 11am–5pm; MC, V), where your party might share a California roll ($9.95) as an appetizer, then split a small cheese pizza ($12), and finally order up some Mongolian beef ($11) as a chaser of sorts. For the Bush, the food is pretty darn tasty.

$$–$$$ **Milano's Pizzeria** (503 Front St., in the Old Federal Building; ☎ 907/443-2924; Mon–Sat 11am–11pm, Sun 12:30–11pm; MC, V) is another of Nome's inadvertent Asian fusion practitioners. I'd say skip the pizza and spaghetti and go for the halibut tempura ($18) and a sushi roll or two ($8.95–$13). It's not that the Italian food's bad, it's just that the Japanese food is so much better.

$–$$$$ Another greasy spoon with a view, **Fat Freddies** (315 W. Front St.; ☎ 907/443-5899; daily 11am–11pm; DISC, MC, V) is a busy local hang-out attached to the Nome Nugget Inn, right next to the Iditarod finish line. You can eat cheap and well here off the burger menu, where a basic burger is just $4, a veggie burger or a surprisingly tasty black bean burger costs $5, a salmon burger is $5.50, and a halibut burger goes for $6.50. For the bigger spenders, Fat Freddies has entrees like its big, fat pork chop plate for $16, or a seafood special, usually grilled halibut, for the market price, usually in the low $20s. Sometimes the seafood special is locally caught Alaskan king crab, typically for less than $24. That's an excellent price for king crab, so jump on it if you get the chance.

WHY YOU'RE HERE: THE TOP SIGHTS & ATTRACTIONS

People have been searching for gold in the dark sands of Nome for more than a century. Even though the beach has been thoroughly sifted and re-sifted by now, the gold still turns up. In the summer, you'll see prospectors camping on the beach, using hand-fed rocker boxes and small portable dredges to sift through the sand. They're not getting rich, but some of them make enough to cover their expenses for the season. Don't go to the beach and pretend that you can rise above gold fever. Give in. Go to any gift store in town, buy a plastic gold pan there, and try your luck in the sand "looking for color," as they say. Panning is allowed on the 2-mile stretch of beach between town and the Fort Davis Roadhouse. Even if you don't find gold, you might pick up some pretty beach glass or some interesting shells from the Bering Sea. And who knows? You might get lucky. In 1984 a visitor who was just beachcombing, not even looking for gold (or so he said), overturned a rock and discovered a 3½-inch gold nugget worth a fortune.

As you walk down the beach, you'll see the old **Swanberg Dredge,** one of 44 abandoned gold dredges on the Seward Peninsula. The dredges look like monstrous, derelict houseboats, floating in ponds they dug for themselves as they crawled across the tundra scraping up bucket after bucket of ground, shaking out tiny flecks of gold dust, and spitting out the ground up earth behind them. This one was in use from 1925 to 1949, and it's on the National Register of Historic Places. A boardwalk has been built over the marsh, so you can walk out to get a close-up view of the dredge, but, unfortunately, you can't go aboard.

When Carrie McLain was 8 years old, her father caught gold fever and followed the gold rush to Nome, bringing the whole family with him. She grew up and became the town's historian. Now, in the basement of the Nome library, you'll find the town's memory bank named in her honor, the **Carrie M. McClain Memorial Museum** ★ (200 E. Front St.; ☎ 907/443-6630; free admission; summer daily noon–8pm, rest of year Tues–Sat noon–6pm). Go in and thumb through some of the thousands of gold rush–era photos of early Nome, check out the exhibits on Eskimo culture and the Bering Land Bridge, and say hi to Fritz, a taxidermied Siberian husky. Fritz was one of the lead dogs in the 1925 Nome serum run that stopped a diphtheria outbreak and became the inspiration for the Iditarod.

ATTENTION, SHOPPERS!

As the hub for Natives flying out of the Bush to Anchorage and Fairbanks, Nome is probably the top place in Alaska to shop for carved ivory and other Iñupiaq Eskimo arts and crafts. And you won't have any problems finding these goods, as there are plenty of gift shops along Front Street dealing in carved bone and ivory, fur slippers and mittens, dolls, beadwork, jewelry, and all sorts of other Native handicrafts. Shop around to your heart's desire, though you may ultimately end up at the **Arctic Trading Post** ★★ (110 W. Front St.; ☎ 907/443-3879; www.nomechamber.org/arctictrading.html), which has one of the most extensive selections of Native goods in the area (if not the state), along with gold jewelry and other arts and crafts.

Also try **Chukotka-Alaska** ★ (514 Lomen Ave.; ☎ 907/443-4128), which boasts a mix of Native goods and Russian imports, such as Lomonosov porcelain, lacquerware, samovars, amber jewelry, nesting dolls, and warm, furry hats, as well as books on the Arctic, the Bering Strait, and Native culture.

Another key buy here: Iditarod tees. You don't have to be in town for the race to outfit yourselves in these collectibles. **Fat Freddies** (315 W. Front St.; ☎ 907/443-5899), the restaurant at the Nome Nugget Inn, has them on sale all year round, in both long- and short-sleeve styles.

NIGHTLIFE IN NOME

Nightlife in Nome—indeed, much of *life* in Nome—is concentrated in a dozen or so saloons (as Nome still calls its bars). Most of them are along Front Street, and some are pretty rough-and-tumble places with restive, early-morning drinking crowds. The one you shouldn't miss (and that you should feel relatively safe in) is **The Board of Trade** ★★★ (212 Front St., next to the Nugget Inn; ☎ 907/443-2611). Though most of historic Nome has been destroyed by fire or storm, the Board of Trade has survived since 1900, making it the oldest watering hole in

Booze & the Bush

Many of the Native communities in the Bush are either "dry," meaning alcohol is prohibited, or "damp," meaning the sale of alcohol is prohibited but you can legally possess a certain amount. Nome is "wet," meaning there are no restrictions on alcohol. As such, the drinking problems that have been controlled in the dry and damp communities run amuck in the saloons and streets of Nome. Just a little heads up.

these parts. Sit at its hand-carved bar, fix your hair in its gilded mirrors, and take in the cross-section of life in the Far North: Iñupiat whale hunters, crusty old Sourdoughs, prospectors who camp on the beach all summer sifting the sands for gold, and only the occasional tourist. The quietest, most unintimidating place in town is the **Anchor Tavern** (114 Front St.; ☎ 907/443-2105), where you can belly up to the bar and meet interesting locals or just quietly take in the grand view of the Bering Sea outside.

GET OUT OF TOWN

It takes just half a day to get to know Nome backward and forward. Once you've got the town down, the surrounding tundra and mountains will naturally beckon. The nearly 300 miles of gravel roads that radiate from town provide access to the countryside, which is dotted with Native fishing and berry-picking camps, historic ruins, wildflowers and wildlife, knockout scenery, a hot springs, and solitude a plenty.

Here's a run-down of the three roads you can take:

Nome-Council Road ✪✪✪

With its abandoned gold dredges and slowly decaying ghost town (and train), the Nome-Council Road, has more points of interest worth stopping for than either of the other two roads profiled in this chapter. Running east of town for 73 miles, the Nome-Council Road's first 30 miles run along the shoreline and pass Native summer fish camps, where long strips of bright orange salmon hang in the sun on driftwood drying racks during spawning season. After the road turns inland, it crosses a bridge and then comes to **The Last Train to Nowhere.**

Just past the train are the weathered remains of **Solomon,** once a gold mining boomtown with seven saloons and 1,000 residents. After the gold rush, a catastrophic storm and then a flu epidemic reduced Solomon to a ghost town. Feel free to wander around the well-weathered ruins, but take care not to end up with a rusty nail in your foot. After mile 40, the road passes two abandoned **gold dredges,** which you can explore, then it begins climbing until it reaches **Skookum Pass,** at about 1,500 feet. Stop there and take in the view. After 73 miles the road ends, more or less, at the **Niukluk River.** Across the river is the little community of **Council,** which is inhabited only in the summer. The locals drive right through the river, but think twice before you risk getting your rental car stuck in the cold water. Council has no shops or services, but if you're drawn to explore anyway, leave your car at the end of the road and ford the river. It's only about 3 feet deep.

Nome-Taylor Road ★★

No matter which road you take out of Nome, you'll stand a good chance of spotting something big and four-legged out on the tundra, such as moose, reindeer, and possibly bears. Explore the 85-mile Nome-Taylor Road, aka the Kougarok Road, and odds are good that you'll spot wild musk ox as the road climbs into the Kigluaik Mountains. Along the way, stop at mile 40 to have a look at the beautiful **Salmon Lake** (which has an inviting free shoreline campground). The Pilgrim River flows into the lake at one end, and in August you can see sockeye salmon spawn there.

Four miles after the lake is a turnoff for the **Pilgrim Hot Springs** ★, where you can take a relaxing soak in a weathered wooden hot tub filled with mineral water that bubbles up through the permafrost at 175°F (79°C) (don't worry—it's cooled down in the tub to a manageable 125°F/52°C or so with water from the Pilgrim River). The springs were initially developed by miners, who built a roadhouse, a saloon, and a dance hall there. The Catholic church later acquired the springs, building a mission and an orphanage there for children whose parents died in a 1918 flu epidemic. The church still owns the land, and if you can get in touch with the caretaker, you can arrange a visit. Call ☎ 907/443-5583, or inquire at the visitor center. Farther along Nome-Taylor Road, between about mile 60 and the end of the line at mile 86, you'll pass through musk ox country. This is one of the few places in Alaska where you'll see wild herds of shaggy musk ox, which look like little bison but are actually more closely related to goats.

Nome-Teller Road ★

The 73-mile-long Nome-Teller Road is the westernmost road in North America. It runs between little Nome and the even smaller Iñupiat village of **Teller,** which has a population of 250. Stop just outside of Nome to examine the **Alaska Gold Company Dredge,** which was busy tearing up the tundra in search of gold until the mid-1990s. After passing the dredge, the road climbs steeply through the rolling tundra, offering spectacular views along the way. You might spot musk ox in the distance or reindeer. The village of Teller communally owns a huge herd, which grazes out on the tundra.

The Railroad That Never Was

One of the stranger things you'll see on the Alaskan tundra are several abandoned turn-of-the-20th-century train cars from an elevated railway in New York City. They are what's left of a railroad that was supposed to run between the gold rush boomtowns of Solomon and Council City. The railroad idea was abandoned in 1907 when the gold rush waned. The tracks were never completed, and the train cars never got farther than the point where they were left to rust. They've been dubbed The Last Train to Nowhere.

Nome with Help

All you need is a rental car to explore the roads outside of Nome, but if you'd prefer to leave the driving to someone else and have a local who really knows the land show you around, take a guided tour. There are several outfits in town you can go with, including **Nome Discovery Tours** (☎ 907/443-2814; www.nomechamber.org/discoverytours.html). The knowledgeable and witty owner and guide is a long-time Nome resident and a one-time professional actor. His all-day tours include wildlife viewing, a stop to inspect an old gold mining dredge, a picnic lunch, and a visit to the tiny Native village of Teller, where an Iñupiaq Eskimo carver and his wife invite you in for coffee and show you home videos of their summer fish camp. Tours last from 5½ hours to 8 hours and range in price from $60 to $150. The visitor center has a complete list of other operators, too.

BARROW

Barrow is the northernmost community in the United States, which is exactly why people go there. In the summer, you can dip your toes—or your entire body if you're crazy enough—into the Arctic Ocean. In the winter, you can get as far beneath the northern lights as you possibly can, and see polar bears, whose numbers may be dwindling but who still frequent the area and even wander into town on occasion. Year-round, you can get acquainted with the Iñupiat Eskimos, who have carried their ancient traditions and ways of life into the modern world, and who made a killing drilling for oil. And you can go to Barrow to stand on Point Barrow, the very tip-top of the continent. But ultimately, you should visit because when you get home from Alaska everyone will ask, "Did you go to Barrow?"

A BRIEF HISTORY

Two-thirds of Barrow's 4,500 residents are Iñupiat Eskimo, which makes the community the largest Eskimo village in the world. Barrow is also both the largest community on Alaska's North Slope and the seat of the North Slope Borough, which is essentially a Minnesota-size county. The Iñupiat have been living in and around Barrow for thousands of years, occupying semi-permanent communities along the coast, which they moved among as the hunting seasons changed. The Iñupiat name for Barrow is "Ukpiagvik," which means "place to hunt snowy owls." In addition to snowy owls, the Iñupiat's survival depended on catching goose, ducks, fish, caribou, polar bears, walrus, seals, and—most challenging of all—whales. The hunting of bowhead whales, which pass close to shore off nearby Point Barrow in the spring and fall, is still at the heart of Iñupiat culture. While most whaling has been outlawed in U.S. waters, Native whalers such as the Iñupiat are allowed to hunt whales, with strict quotas. Wander around town among the satellite dishes, Ski-Doo snowmobiles, and other conveniences of the modern world, and you'll see the overturned *umiaqs,* the 20- to 30-foot seal-skin boats that Native whalers still use to pursue their quarry in the spring, when the sea ice is still close to shore (in the fall, when the ice is further out, they switch to aluminum boats). If you're in town in June after the spring hunt, you might get the chance to sample muktuk (whale blubber) and participate in a blanket toss (in which a group holds a blanket and tosses a jumper high into the air) at a Nalukataq celebration, which successful whaling captains throw. When a Nalukataq happens, everyone's invited.

LAY OF THE LAND

Barrow is located at 71 degrees north latitude. It is 330 miles above the Arctic Circle and 725 miles north of Anchorage. It sits along the shore of the Arctic Ocean, and with its weathered wooden buildings and unpaved streets of gray sand, it is every bit a beach town—albeit a very odd beach town. The sun does not set there between May and August, and it does not rise between November and January. The temperature ranges from an average of 40°F (4°C) in the summer, to around 15 degrees below zero (–26°C) in the winter. The ocean freezes in the winter. Outside of town, the surrounding tundra, which goes on as far as you can see, freezes too. In the summer it thaws on the surface, creating thousands upon thousands of little lakes dotting the North Slope. The frozen ground beneath the surface, the permafrost, keeps them from draining. Millions of birds, and hundreds of birders, travel thousands of miles to revel in this huge seasonal wetland. Despite the region's swamplike nature, it gets so little rain or snow that it's classified as a desert. So, in addition to being a very odd beach town, Barrow is also a very odd desert town.

Ten miles north of the town of Barrow is Point Barrow, the literal tip of North America. It's a long, narrow gravel spit marking the divide between two of the various seas of the Arctic Ocean, the Chukchi Sea to the west and the Beaufort Sea to the east. Native whalers dump the remains of their catch at the end of the point, which helps to keep the polar bears away from town. It's not a foolproof strategy, and the bears, which can be extremely dangerous, sometimes amble through Barrow's streets. Watchmen chase them off with firecrackers and rubber bullets.

The town itself has two distinct sections: Barrow proper, which is the older part of town, and Bowersville, which is the newer part. They both stretch along the beach, separated from each other by a lagoon. When the lagoon freezes in the winter, locals play golf on it, and sometimes polo, using cars instead of horses.

Out on Point Barrow is the world's largest Arctic research site, the **Barrow Arctic Science Consortium** and other science facilities. Everyone in town refers to the place as **NARL,** using the acronym for the place's old name, the Naval Arctic Research Laboratory, even though the Navy's no longer involved. Hundreds of scientists come to Barrow each year because of NARL. On the north side of campus is the **UIC Science Center** (☎ 907/852-3050), where you can see exhibits on some of the science being done there, including research into global warming, as well as an exhibit on Arctic anthropology.

The City of Barrow's **Visitor Center** (Momegana and Ahkovak sts., near the airport and Wiley Post & Will Rogers Monument), operates in the summer daily from 10am to 4:30pm (hours vary in off season). To obtain advance information, contact the **City of Barrow** (Office of the Mayor, P.O. Box 629, Barrow, AK 99723; ☎ 907/852-5211, ext. 221; www.cityofbarrow.org).

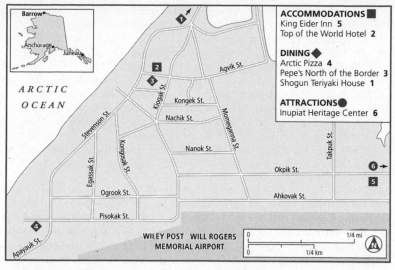

Barrow

ACCOMMODATIONS ■
King Eider Inn **5**
Top of the World Hotel **2**

DINING ◆
Arctic Pizza **4**
Pepe's North of the Border **3**
Shogun Teriyaki House **1**

ATTRACTIONS ●
Inupiat Heritage Center **6**

GETTING TO & AROUND BARROW

Short of chartering a private plane, the only way to Barrow is via **Alaska Airlines** (☎ 800/252-7522; www.alaskaair.com), which has a few flights a day from Anchorage, with a stop along the way in Fairbanks. Round-trip fares usually run around $600 from Anchorage, or $500 from Fairbanks. Most visitors to Barrow get there on package tours. For most of Alaska, I say leave the package tours to the lazy and less intrepid and take your brave selves there on your own. But for Barrow, package tours make good sense. They take in just about everything there is to do in Barrow, and they can save you a heap of dough over traveling independently. **Alaska Airlines Vacations** (☎ 800/468-2248; www.alaskaair.com/vacations), working with the Native-owned **Tundra Tours,** charges $569 for an overnight stay, and $469 for a 1-day, fly-in-and-fly-out tour.

Barrow is spread out, but city buses run every 20 minutes between all major points of interest in town. If you need a cab, try **Barrow Taxi** (☎ 907/852-2222), **Arcticab** (☎ 907/852-2227), **Alaska Taxi** (☎ 907/852-3000), or **City Cab** (☎ 907/852-5050). Cabs charge a flat $5 to get anywhere in town, $10 for a ride beyond town, plus $1 per additional passenger. Rates are set by the city and no tips are expected. To get out to Point Barrow, it's safest to go with a tour. You don't really need a rental car in Barrow, but **UICC Barrow Car Rental** (☎ 907/852-2700), charges $110 a day with proof of insurance, and $130 without.

ACCOMMODATIONS, BOTH STANDARD & NOT

There's not a lot to choose from when it comes to lodging in Barrow and it's all pricey. (Though unusual as it may be, there is no sales tax or bed tax in Barrow. Enjoy it while you can.) Here are your best bets:

$$$$ If you were thinking that while you're in Barrow you might inaugurate yourself into the Polar Bear Club with a bracing dip in the icy Arctic Ocean, you'll only have to run 50 yards back to your hotel to warm up if you stay at the **Top of the World Hotel** (1200 Agviq St.; ☎ 800/478-8520 or 907/852-3900; AE, DISC, MC, V). It's both the most centrally located hotel in town (right next to a good Mexican restaurant) and the only one on the dark, windy shores of the Arctic. A stuffed polar bear, a stuffed polar bear head, and often a small crowd of Iñupiat Eskimos watching TV and smoking cigarettes can be found in the lobby. The building is a few decades old but the rooms have been recently refurbished. They're clean and spacious, but otherwise just standard hotel rooms, except for the views of the Arctic Ocean available on the beach side of the building. The native corporation that owns Tundra Tours also owns the Top of the World Hotel, and if you come to Barrow as part of a package tour, this is where you'll stay. Standard summer room rates hover at $190 for double occupancy.

$$$$ The nicest place in town is just a snowball's throw from the Alaska Airlines terminal, the **King Eider Inn** (1752 Ahkovak St.; ☎ 888/303-4337 or 907/852-4700; www.kingeider.net; AE, MC, V). It has a spic-n-span, spankin'-new feel about it, which is partly due to the ban on shoes—you have to leave them at the door. It's also one of precious few nonsmoking places in a town that's a hotbed of smokers. Rustic pine furnishings and Native artwork form the decor throughout the building (though the teddy bears on the beds are a creepy touch I could live without). You'll enjoy kicking back on the leather sofa or rocking chair by the fireplace in the homey lobby, where you can help yourself to a cup of hot coffee at any time of day. Most rooms go for $180 double occupancy in the summer, with winter discounts. Rooms with kitchenettes cost $10 more. And you'll usually pay less by calling direct, rather than booking online.

DINING FOR ALL TASTES

Restaurants in Barrow tend to stay open very late, offer free delivery, and keep their TVs on at all times. Asian food dominates the dining scene, although the most famous place in town (the owner appeared on Johnny Carson's *Tonight Show*) is a Mexican place.

$-$$$ That famed place, "blessed" by Carson himself, is **Pepe's North of the Border** ★ (1204 Agviq St.; ☎ 907/852-8200; Mon–Sat 6–10pm, Sun 7–10pm; MC, V). Eat here and you can say you ate at the world's northernmost Mexican restaurant. You can also say you ate at the biggest restaurant in Barrow, for whatever that's worth. If you go on a package tour, this is where you'll stop for lunch. In addition to a wide selection of Americanized Mexican fare (guacamole salad, $9.75; enchilada plate, $18), the menu features cheeseburgers ($9.75), fried chicken ($20 for three pieces with vegetables and a baked potato), and grilled halibut ($26). The Mexican murals and mission-style decor suggest that you're south of the border. Only the parkas on the coat rack hint that you're north of most of Siberia.

$$–$$$ Do tacos and burritos seem somehow out of place at 71 degrees north latitude? Well, how about some teriyaki chicken, chow mein, or kim chee then? Japanese, Chinese, and Korean chow is the name of the game at **Shogun Teriyaki House** (1906 Pakpuk St.; ☎ 907/852-2275; daily 11am–midnight; MC, V). This

Booze & Barrow

Barrow, like a lot of communities in the Alaskan Bush with serious drinking problems, is a damp town, meaning it's BYOB. Alcohol is not sold there, but it's not banned entirely, as it is in dry towns. You are allowed, for personal use, to bring 1 gallon of beer, or 1 liter of distilled spirits, or 2 liters of wine. You can get a permit to bring more by contacting the **Office of the Mayor** (☎ 907/852-5211), or you can just wait to tie one on until you get back to Anchorage or Fairbanks. Bring in more without a permit and you can be charged with bootlegging.

place is as plain as a high school cafeteria, and the owners are grumpy and can barely speak English, but the $12 Chinese lunch buffet is one of the better deals in town.

$$–$$$$　By Barrow standards, the most elegant place to eat in town is the upstairs dining room at **Arctic Pizza** ★ (125 Upper Apayauq St.; ☎ 907/852-4222; daily 11:30am–11:30pm; MC, V). It's a quiet, newly remodeled space, with soft music playing, tablecloths, and neatly folded cloth napkins, and a sweeping second-floor view across 16 ancient Eskimo dwelling mounds toward the Arctic Ocean. Kids aren't allowed upstairs, but there's no such prohibition in the more pizza parlor–like downstairs dining room. Besides the pizza ($14 for a small pepperoni, $20 for a large), there's Mexican fare (burrito with beans and rice on the side, $16), pasta (chicken fettuccine, $16), and other good-size entrees.

WHY YOU'RE HERE: THE TOP SIGHTS & ATTRACTIONS

One of the main reasons people go to Barrow is simply to **stand on the top edge of the continent** and face the Arctic Ocean. Once you've gotten that out of your system, stretch your legs on the dark, windswept beach that the town is built along. Then you can say you walked along the top edge of the continent, too. Walk back along the gravel road that parallels the beach and you'll see the skin boats that Iñupiat use to hunt whales. Stop for a photo of yourselves beneath Barrow's famous whale-bone arch framing the Chukchi Sea. It's made from a pair of enormous bowhead whale ribs. Dress warmly. The beach is cold, often foggy, and sometimes littered with a jumble of ice, even in June. Occasionally, erosion reveals ancient whale bones or mammoth tusks, so keep your eyes peeled.

After you've chilled yourselves to the bone on the Arctic seashore, go indoors to warm up at Barrow's other visitor lure, the **Iñupiat Heritage Center** ★ (kids) (5421 N. Star St.; ☎ 907/852-4594; $5 adults, $2 teens, $1 children; Mon–Fri 8:30am–5pm). It's both a tourist attraction and local gathering place, modeled on the traditional Iñupiat community house known as a *qargi*. Besides the dancers, drummers, and storytellers there to entertain and enlighten you, there are workshops you can visit where Native boatwrights build skin boats, drum makers make skin drums, and craftspeople carve walrus ivory, etch bowhead whale baleen, and produce other arts and crafts. Pop into the Heritage Center's museum and look at the exhibit featuring the remains of Pleistocene-era creatures like mammoths and lions that wandered into the Arctic when the Bering Land Bridge was above water. Check out the frightening exhibit on how the planet's changing climate is changing life in the Arctic today.

By 1854 commercial whaling ships and fur traders were calling on Barrow, bringing firearms and alcohol to trade with the Natives, along with measles, small pox, influenza, and syphilis. A field base built by whalers in 1893 at what's now the Bowersville part of town, the **Cape Smythe Whaling and Trading Station** (☎ 907/852-3456; Mon–Sat 11am–11pm), is the oldest wood-frame building in the Arctic. It's still in use as a restaurant.

Predating the whaling station by 5 centuries or so are the remains of sod-roofed underground houses where the ancestors of modern Iñupiat Eskimos lived. The 16 dwelling mounds of the **Birnirk Archaeological Site** (about 2 miles north of Barrow airfield) are built in rows that parallel the shoreline.

THE OTHER BARROW

A surefire way to get a glimpse of the real Barrow, the part not so readily evident to tourists on quick jaunts through town, is to party with the locals. And that doesn't mean alcohol and drugs, it means mushing, mukluk, and muktuk (I'll explain about the last two below). Check at the **Iñupiat Heritage Center** (see above) to find out what's happening while you're in town.

If you're in town in January or February and lucky you might catch the midwinter festival of **Kivgiq,** the Messenger Feast. It's 3 days of song, dance, bartering, and eating that draws Eskimos from across the North Slope, Canada, Russia, and Greenland. You have to be lucky to catch it because it's not held in Barrow every year.

Your chances of catching a week-long spring snow festival called **Piuraagiaqta** are much better, since it's held every April. It features snowmobile and mukluk races (foot races in Eskimo boots), igloo building, dog mushing, goose calling, and golf on the frozen Arctic Ocean, among other Barrow-style events.

If the spring whale hunt is successful, the community divvies up the catch at a **Nalukataq,** a blanket toss celebration. June is usually Nalukataq month, and there may be more than one, depending on how many whaling crews caught whales. Everyone in the community, including tourists, is welcome to attend, and there's no charge. A feast is held, featuring traditional dishes like caribou, duck, goose, and of course, whale. This is your best opportunity to try muktuk, or whale blubber, a tough and chewy Eskimo treat. Eat it boiled, pickled, or raw. Or you can try muktuk sushi—just mix up a little dish of mustard and soy sauce and dip

---

The Coolest Club Ever

If you've got the nerve, you can take a dip in the Arctic Ocean and automatically become a member of the **Polar Bear Club** ★★★. Bring your surf shorts and some witnesses (so they can celebrate with you when you emerge, or call for help if you don't), and make sure you submerge your entire body, including your head— otherwise, your efforts won't count.

Polar Bear Tours

Barrow is the only place in the United States where you can go on a commercial tour to see polar bears. Whenever the pack ice in the Arctic Ocean comes near shore—historically from October through June—so do the polar bears. The best place to see them is at the tip of Point Barrow, where the town dumps the butchered remains from the whales it catches in spring and fall. Because polar bears are so dangerous, and because you can't drive out to the gut dump without a serious four-wheel-drive vehicle anyway, it's smartest to go on a tour. **Arctic Tours** (☎ 907/852-4512 or 907/852-1462) uses Humvees to take visitors out to the point, for $60 per person, with a two person minimum (children 12 and under go free). If you want to shop around for a better price, inquire at the Top of the World Hotel or the King Eider Inn for other operators. That being said, Arctic Tours has the best reputation for these tours; others seem to come and go each season. If you come to Barrow on a package tour when the bears are around, there's no need to book one of these extra tours: The guides will take you out to the point to look for them.

Global climate change and the shrinking Arctic ice packs mean you can't count on the old visit-from-October-through-June rule of thumb anymore. The new rule is that the earlier or the later you go in the season the better. And the sooner you get around to it the better. The loss of ice means that polar bears have to swim farther than ever before to get to their food sources, and scientists have documented several polar bear drownings in recent years—something they'd never seen before. Documented cases of polar bear cannibalism are also on the rise. This all has some scientists worried that polar bears may become extinct within the next century. See p. 382 for more info on climate change issues in Alaska.

the muktuk into it, like with other sushi. Nalukataqs always feature blanket tosses, and you may have an opportunity to get tossed yourselves. Just be warned that sprains and fractures are an accepted risk. The whaling captains pick the date of Nalukataq, and if they don't catch whales, they don't celebrate (although somewhere Greenpeace does). Any local will be able to tell you if one is happening while you're there.

Modern Iñupiat Eskimo culture isn't just muktuk and blanket tosses. Softball plays a big role too, so if you really want to see Barrow being its modern self, take in a **softball game.** Barrow is fanatical about the sport. It has nearly two dozen teams, it has produced several high school state champs, and it happily shelled out $1 million to build a new softball field. The game is played a little differently in Barrow, though. Grass doesn't grow on the North Slope, so the field is made of gravel. The winds are fierce, sometimes the fog is so thick the outfielders can barely see the batters, and 0°F (−18°C) weather isn't considered a good reason to cancel a game—occasionally a polar bear even wanders onto the field and disrupts play. When it gets too cold, spectators simply watch the game from their cars, honking for good plays.

ATTENTION, SHOPPERS!

Barrow is a sensible place to shop for Iñupiaq crafts, since they're made in town and have little or no markup. You won't find much difference in pricing from store to store, but you'll pay much less for crafts of the same standards that you'll find in Anchorage, Fairbanks, and most other parts of the state. To pick up an ivory carving, a baleen basket, or perhaps a fashionable seal skin bag, wait until the end of the presentation at the Iñupiat Heritage Center. The craftspeople who work at the center sell their excellent wares after the performance. If you want to shop around a little, head to the **AC Value Center** (4725 Ahkovak St.; ☎ 907/852-6711; www.alaskacommercial.com), which the Iñupiat simply call the Stuaqpak, or "Big Store." It's mainly a grocery store, but it's also got locally made arts and crafts, plus furs, parkas, and mukluks.

9 The Essentials of Planning

ALASKA GETS SOME 1.6 MILLION VISITORS A YEAR, AND THE VAST MAJORITY of them—more than a million—come by cruise ship. Once they buy their tickets, the only decisions they have left are what shore excursions to take and how many trips to the buffet line to make. The independent traveler has a lot more homework to do. And this is the chapter that will help you get it done. Here you'll find the essential information you'll need for planning a trip to the Great Land, such as when to go, what to pack, and which wildlife might kill you if you don't give it plenty of room.

The state's official visitor agency is the **Alaska Travel Industry Association** (☎ 907/929-2842; www.travelalaska.com). It sends out general printed information, which you can also find online, but it refers specific questions to the visitor bureaus in each town. For information about camping, hiking, and other outdoor recreation opportunities on state and federally owned land—which makes up 85% of the state—check with the **Alaska Public Lands Information Center** (www.nps.gov/aplic) which has branches in Anchorage (☎ 907/271-2737), Fairbanks (☎ 907/456-0527), Ketchikan (☎ 907/228-6234), and Tok (☎ 907/883-5667). They are operated collectively by the various land agencies involved, such as the U.S. Forest Service and the National Park Service, and they are invaluable sources of information.

WHEN TO VISIT

Winter in Alaska takes up most of the year, summer is brief and brilliant, and the fall and spring slip by so quickly hardly anyone notices them. The bulk of the state's million and a half annual visitors arrive between mid-May and mid-September, in order to take advantage of the brief Alaska summer. It makes sense in this case to join the crowd. The summer high season—June, July, and August—is when the days are at their longest, the temperatures are at their warmest, and every seasonal visitor attraction, activity, and lodging is open for business (with the exception of Denali, where things aren't fully up and running until mid-June). The rhythm of tourism is different in the cruise ship port towns of Southeast Alaska. There, the season kicks straight into high gear starting May 1, with the arrival of the first ship, and it runs at full tilt until the last ship sails away in October.

There are some good reasons to break away from the crowds and travel during the shoulder seasons, though. Saving money is the biggest one. In early May, and from late September through October, many lodgings and tour operators offer discounts of 10% to 25%. The weather is still mild in the shoulder seasons, the mosquitoes are at a minimum (they peak with the tourists, from late June through July), and you may encounter a more laid-back vibe at some of the more popular visitor attractions, which you'll have more or less to yourselves. Also, the first visitors of the season often get especially warm receptions.

A Canary in a Coal Mine: Alaska & Climate Change

Climate change is affecting Alaska faster and more severely than anywhere else on the globe (see "The Warming Climate" box below for info). But even the most committed environmentalists in Alaska have a hard time reducing their carbon footprint (the amount of carbon dioxide each of us causes to be emitted to the atmosphere), which increases global warming. Getting to and around Alaska uses a lot of fuel. A single passenger flying from Seattle to Anchorage and back is responsible for about 1,700 pounds of CO_2. Cruise ships emit twice as much carbon dioxide per passenger-mile as airliners. Driving to Alaska emits even more than taking a ship, partly because you have to go three times as far to cover the same distance.

Other than walking, rowing, or riding on horseback to Alaska, the only solution is to offset your carbon emissions by doing good somewhere else. To make that easy, a market has developed in carbon offsetting that allows buyers to fund a piece of a larger project that will cut emissions. The idea is that the offsets you buy account for what you emit during your trip. This concept is still in its infancy, however, and there's work left to make it fully credible. Critics have pointed out that whether the offsets really reduce carbon emissions depends on the quality of the projects they fund and if those projects actually take place. Until the market matures, it's buyer beware. Make sure you're buying something real by reading up and checking that the seller is audited. U.S. companies selling carbon offsets include **Carbonfund.org** (www.carbonfund.org) and **TerraPass** (www.terrapass.org), and, in the U.K., **Climate Care** (www.climatecare.org). Best of all, reduce your own impact as much as possible—that's more important than offsetting.

Many other environmental issues affect Alaska—the tour operator you choose to work with makes a difference. Eco-tourism has had a significant role over the years in helping conservation. One of Alaska's best eco-tourism operators, **Alaska Discovery** (p. 374), started leading groups because its founders wanted to develop a constituency to save beautiful places by taking people there. The **Alaska Wilderness Recreation and Tourism Association** (www.awrta.org) is a large and effective coalition of eco-tourism operators who communicate an environmental message to clients and use their political muscle to support conservation causes. The association's website makes it easy to find homegrown eco-tourism operators in Alaska.

Information sources nationally include: **Responsible Travel** (www.responsibletravel.com), a source of sustainable travel ideas; the **International Ecotourism Society** (www.ecotourism.org), offering eco-friendly travel tips, statistics, and touring companies and associations; and **Ecotravel.com,** an online magazine and eco-directory that lets you search for touring companies. In the U.K., **Tourism Concern** (www.tourismconcern.org.uk) works to reduce social and environmental problems connected to tourism.

—*Charles Wohlforth*

Discounts are even greater in the winter, especially on accommodations. Luxury hotels are often priced like budget motels when the mercury starts to drop. I'm talking rates slashed by 50% or more. And for snow lovers, winter in Alaska can be paradise. Much of the wildlife may be hibernating and many tourist attractions and tours won't be operating, but the northern lights are out, winter sports are on, and the local culture that goes on hiatus during the summer cranks into gear. Alaskans embrace the darkness and cold and keep themselves busy with concerts, theater, downhill and cross country skiing, snowshoeing, ice climbing, sled dog and snowmobile racing, and winter carnivals. The prime time for a winter visit is between February 1 and mid-March, when the darkness is beginning to abate and there's still plenty of snow on the ground.

In broad terms, June is the driest summer month here, July is the warmest, and August is the rainiest (though it's warmer than June). Weather-wise, you never know what you're going to get, though. In the summer it might be sunny the whole time you're in Alaska, or it might be rainy the whole time, or you might get some of both. Between the shoulder season months of May and September, May tends to be drier. However, the farther north you go in May, the greater your chances of running into mud, snow, and cold. My best advice is to hope for good weather and come prepared for bad. The chart that follows, "Alaska's Climate, by Months & Regions," will give you a statistical idea of what to expect.

Alaska's Visit-worthy Events

Alaskans love festivals, fairs, winters sports competitions, and any other excuse for a big, outdoor community get-together. Cold weather doesn't stop them. In fact, winter is the main season for this sort of thing. Here's a sampler of some of the bigger community events in the state. Dates shift from one year to the next, so check for exact dates before making plans around any of the events that follow.

JANUARY

The Anchorage Folk Festival (☎ 907/566-2334; www.anchoragefolkfestival.org): Catch Celtic, bluegrass, jazz, klezmer, and other performances, along with storytellers, dancers, and singers from around Alaska and beyond. There are enough performances and workshops to fill the first 2 weeks of the month.

FEBRUARY

Yukon Quest International Sled Dog Race (☎ 907/452-7945; www.yukonquest.org): The Iditarod may be longer, but this 1,000-mile race along historic gold rush and mail delivery routes between Fairbanks and Whitehorse, Canada, is more grueling. The race changes direction each year, starting in Fairbanks in even-numbered years, and ending there in odd-numbered years. It's held in early February.

Winterfest at Alyeska Resort (☎ 907/754-1111; www.alyeskaresort.com): Girdwood fills a 3-day weekend in early February with snowboard competitions, mountain bike slalom, games for kids, wine tasting, and a "polar bear" plunge (that is, an icy winter swim).

The Anchorage Fur Rendezvous Winter Festival (☎ 907/274-1177; www.furrondy.net): A huge, month-long, city-wide celebration that includes fireworks, craft shows, dog sled rides, snowshoe softball, and dozens of other events. The end of the Rondy runs into the beginning of the Iditarod.

Alaska's Climate, by Months & Regions

	Jan	Feb	Mar	Apr	May	June	July	Aug	Sept	Oct	Nov	Dec
Anchorage: Southcentral Alaska												
Average high**	21/-6	26/-3	33/1	44/7	55/13	62/17	65/18	63/17	55/13	40/4	28/-2	22/-6
Average low**	8/-13	11/-12	17/-8	29/-2	39/4	47/8	51/11	49/9	41/5	28/-2	16/-9	10/-12
Hours of light*	6:53	9:41	12:22	15:20	18:00	19:22	18:00	15:15	12:19	9:29	6:46	5:27
Sunny days†	12	10	13	12	11	10	9	9	9	10	10	10
Rainy or snowy days	8	8	8	6	7	8	11	13	14	12	10	11
Precipitation‡	0.8	0.8	0.6	0.6	0.7	1.0	1.9	2.7	2.6	1.9	1.1	1.1
Barrow: Arctic Alaska												
Average high**	8/-13	-12/-24	-8/-22	6/-14	25/-4	39/4	46/8	43/6	34/1	20/-7	5/-15	-6/-21
Average low**	-20/-29	-24/-31	-21/-29	-8/-22	15/-9	30/-1	34/1	34/1	27/-3	10/-12	-6/-21	-17/-27
Hours of light*	0:00	8:05	12:33	17:43	24:00	24:00	24:00	17:34	12:30	7:46	0:00	0:00
Sunny days†	7	18	21	18	8	9	11	5	4	6	8	4
Rainy or snowy days	4	4	4	4	4	5	9	11	11	11	6	5
Precipitation‡	0.2	0.2	0.1	0.2	0.2	0.3	0.9	1.0	0.6	0.5	0.2	0.2
Cold Bay: Aleutian Archipelago												
Average high**	33/1	32/0	35/2	38/3	45/7	50/10	55/13	56/13	52/11	44/7	39/4	35/2
Average low**	24/-4	23/-5	25/-4	29/-2	35/2	41/5	46/8	47/8	43/6	35/2	30/-1	27/-3
Hours of light*	8:05	10:10	12:17	14:36	16:32	17:25	16:33	14:34	12:17	10:04	8:01	7:08
Sunny days†	8	6	8	4	3	3	3	2	4	6	6	7
Rainy or snowy days	19	17	18	16	17	16	17	20	21	23	22	21
Precipitation‡	2.8	2.5	2.3	2.0	2.5	2.3	2.4	3.7	4.3	4.2	4.2	3.3
Fairbanks: Interior Alaska												
Average high**	-2/-18	8/-13	24/-4	42/6	60/16	71/22	73/23	66/19	55/13	32/0	11/-12	1/-17
Average low**	-19/-28	-15/-26	-2/-19	20/-7	38/3	52/11	52/11	47/8	36/2	17/-8	-5/-21	-16/-27
Hours of light*	5:46	9:14	12:22	15:54	19:22	21:48	19:26	15:52	12:24	9:04	5:39	3:43
Sunny days†	15	14	17	14	16	13	12	10	10	9	12	12
Rainy or snowy days	8	7	6	5	7	11	12	12	10	11	11	9
Precipitation‡	0.6	0.4	0.4	0.2	0.6	1.4	1.8	1.8	1.1	0.8	0.7	0.8
Juneau: Southeast Alaska												
Average high**	29/-2	34/1	39/4	48/9	55/13	62/17	64/18	63/17	56/13	47/8	37/3	32/0
Average low**	18/-8	23/-5	27/-3	32/0	39/4	45/7	48/9	48/9	43/6	37/3	28/-2	23/-5
Hours of light*	7:31	9:55	12:18	14:55	17:11	18:17	17:13	14:54	12:20	9:49	7:27	6:22
Sunny days†	8	7	7	8	8	8	8	9	6	4	6	5
Rainy or snowy days	18	17	18	17	17	15	17	17	20	24	20	21
Precipitation‡	4.3	3.9	3.5	2.9	3.5	3.1	4.2	5.3	7.2	7.8	5.4	5.1
Valdez: Prince William Sound												
Average high**	27/-3	30/-1	37/3	45/7	53/12	60/16	63/17	61/16	54/12	43/6	33/1	29/-2
Average low**	18/-8	19/-7	24/-4	31/-1	39/4	45/7	48/9	46/8	41/5	33/1	23/-5	19/-7
Hours of light*	6:54	9:41	12:22	15:19	17:58	19:20	17:57	15:14	12:20	9:30	6:48	5:29
Sunny days†	9	9	11	11	9	8	8	10	8	8	10	7
Rainy or snowy days	17	14	16	14	17	15	17	17	20	20	16	18
Precipitation‡	5.7	5.5	4.7	3.2	3.2	2.8	3.6	6.5	9.3	7.9	5.7	7.6

*Hours of light is sunrise to sunset on the 21st day of each month.

**All temperatures are given in degrees Fahrenheit first, with degrees Celsius after the slash.

†Sunny days include the average observed clear and partly cloudy days per month.

‡Precipitation is the average water equivalent of rain or snow.

MARCH

The Iditarod Trail Sled Dog Race
(☎ 907/376-5155; www.iditarod.com):
"The Last Great Race on Earth," as it's called,
runs for 1,150 miles from Wasilla outside of
Anchorage to Nome in early March. The cer-
emonial start is held in Anchorage a day
before the "Re-start." Nome goes nuts, with
awards banquets, dart tournaments, arts
and crafts shows, a reindeer potluck, golf
on the Bering Sea, movies, slide shows, lots
of drinking, and more.

World Ice Art Championships (☎ 907/
451-8250; www.icealaska.com): The
world's top ice sculptors spend the first 2
weeks of March in Fairbanks turning enormous blocks of ice into works of art, some
as tall as two-story buildings. During the
last 2 weeks of March, the sculptures are
lit and put on public display.

The Nenana Ice Classic (☎ 907/832-
5446; www.nenanaakiceclassic.com):
Correctly guess the moment the frozen
Tanana River at Nenana begins to break up
and you win a bunch of money, or more
likely, split a bunch of money with the
other correct guessers. The tradition dates
back to 1917, and in recent years the purse
has exceeded $300,000 (while the number
of correct guessers has exceeded 40).
Tickets are sold from February 1 through
April 5 at locations throughout the state,
all of them listed on the website.

APRIL

The Alaska Folk Festival (☎ 907/463-
3316; www.akfolkfest.org): A free, laid-
back, week-long celebration of music that
draws musicians from all over Alaska and
beyond to bring cheer to dreary wintry
Juneau, usually in early April.

Kodiak WhaleFest (☎ 907/486-4782;
www.kodiak.org): In mid-month, Kodiak
marks the annual migration of gray whales
with 10 days of music, workshops, and other
events. The whales, traveling from the sunny
waters of Baja California to the cold Bering
Sea, pass so close to shore that you don't
need a boat to get a good look at them.

**Alyeska Resort Spring Carnival and
Slush Cup** (☎ 907/754-1111; www.
alyeskaresort.com): Girdwood bids its ski
season goodbye with events such as a
mountain bike slalom race (the rule
prohibiting studded tires encourages wipe-
outs), and a competition in which costumed skiers and snowboarders attempt
(and usually fail) to hydroplane across a
100-foot-long ice-filled pond. Call for the
schedule.

MAY

Copper River Delta Shorebird Festival
(☎ 907/424-7260; www.cordova
chamber.com): Five million northbound
migrating shorebirds stop for a spell to
rest their wings and fill their bellies on
the Copper River Delta outside of Cordova.
Hundreds of bird-watchers come to see
the epic early May breather, and Cordova
throws a 3-day bash filled with workshops
and outdoor events.

Kachemak Bay Shorebird Festival
(☎ 907/235-7740; www.homeralaska.
org/shorebird.htm): Cordova's not the
only destination for birders in May. So is
Homer, where shorebirds and wetlands are
at the center of a 5-day celebration featuring guided bird-watching hikes and
boat tours, workshops, art shows, music,
a wooden boat festival, a film festival,
and other events. Again, the birds usually
alight early in the month.

Little Norway Festival (☎ 907/772-
3646; www.petersburg.org): Founded in
the late–19th century by Norwegian fishermen (who packed their catch in ice from a
nearby glacier), Petersburg does Norwegian
Independence Day right, with pageantry,
dancing, a Fish-O-Rama Seafood Feast,
and, naturally, a parade with a Viking ship
in it. The festival lasts 3 days, over the
third full weekend in May.

Kodiak Crab Festival (☎ 907/486-
5557; www.kodiak.org/crabfest.html): At
this festival, Kodiak honors the crustacean
that keeps its storied king crab fishing fleet
in business. Survival suit races, carnival

rides, a seafood cook-off, a wacky golf tournament in which spray paint and chainsaws are sometimes employed, demonstrations by the U.S. Coast Guard, and a blessing of the fleet are some of the highlights of the 5-day event, held in late May.

JUNE

Sitka Summer Music Festival (☎ 907/277-4852; www.sitkamusicfestival.org): Chamber musicians from around the world come to Sitka for a music series that fills most of June.

Midnight Sun Baseball Game (☎ 907/451-0095; www.goldpanners.com): Right around summer solstice, Fairbanks' semiprofessional sluggers, the Alaska Goldpanners, play a late-night game in the bright summer twilight.

The Midnight Sun Festival (☎ 907/443-6624): Nome may be south of the Arctic Circle, but it's close enough to get 22 hours of direct sunlight on summer solstice, more than enough time for a weekend festival that includes a parade, a softball tournament, an anything-goes raft race, and a "polar bear swim," sea ice permitting.

JULY

Most cities in Alaska go all-out with Fourth of July **Independence Day** celebrations, despite the fact that the skies never get dark enough for fireworks displays. The small towns really get creative. Check with local visitor information centers for details. Ketchikan, Skagway, Juneau, and Seldovia go especially nuts.

Mount Marathon Race (www.sewardak.org): Seward bursts at the seams with out-of-towners on the Fourth, who come for a grueling foot race from the middle of town to the top of a 3,022-foot peak looming above it, and back down again. There's lots of falling, sliding, and leaving-behind-of-skin involved.

Southeast Alaska State Fair (☎ 907/766-2476; www.seafair.org): For 4 days in late July, Haines hosts this cross between a country fair and a music festival, with livestock, logging demonstrations, a parade, and lots of bands kicking out the jams.

AUGUST

The Tanana Valley State Fair (☎ 907/452-3750; www.tananavalleyfair.org): Arts and crafts displays, rodeo shows, carnival rides, and livestock round out the offerings at this early August fair, Alaska's oldest.

The Alaska State Fair (☎ 907/745-4827; www.alaskastatefair.org): Alaska's single largest event, with carnival rides, livestock, monster trucks, bands you used to love in the '80s, and a giant vegetable competition. It's held for 12 consecutive days, ending on Labor Day.

SEPTEMBER

Kodiak State Fair and Rodeo (☎ 907/486-4782; www.kodiak.org): An old-timey country fair, with pie eating, seed spitting, and bubble-gum blowing contests, paired with calf roping, bronco riding, and barrel racing. It's held Labor Day weekend.

OCTOBER

Alaska Day Festival (☎ 907/747-8806): Sitka, the former capital of both Russian America and U.S. Territorial Alaska, throws a bash marking the day (Oct 18, 1867) that Russia handed Alaska over to the U.S.

NOVEMBER

Sitka WhaleFest (☎ 907/747-7964; www.sitkawhalefest.org): Sitkans celebrate cetaceans with whale-watching tours, concerts, an art show, and a 3-day symposium in which whale experts from around the world discuss the latest research. It's usually held over one weekend early in the month.

The Alaska Bald Eagle Festival (☎ 907/766-3094; www.baldeaglefestival.org): This festival in Haines in mid-November celebrates the world's largest gathering of bald eagles, who come to town for the late-season salmon run in the late-freezing Chilkat River.

ENTRY REQUIREMENTS

Be sure to check with the U.S. embassy or consulate for the very latest in entry requirements, as these continue to shift since the September 11, 2001, terrorist attacks. Full information can be found at the **U.S. State Department**'s website, www.travel.state.gov.

VISAS

As of this writing, citizens of western and central Europe, Australia, New Zealand, and Singapore need only a valid passport and a round-trip air ticket or cruise ticket to enter the U.S. Canadian citizens can also enter without a visa; you simply need to show proof of residence.

Citizens of all other countries will need to obtain a tourist visa from the U.S. consulate; depending on your country of origin, there may or may not be a charge attached (and you may or may not have to apply in person). To get the visa, along with a passport valid for at least 6 months from the end of your scheduled U.S. visit, you'll need to complete an application and submit a 1½-inch square photo. It's usually possible to obtain a visa within 24 hours, except during holiday periods or the summer rush.

For information about U.S. visas, go to **http://travel.state.gov** and click on "Visas."

PASSPORTS

To enter the United States, international visitors must have a valid passport that expires at least 6 months later than the scheduled end of your visit.

For Residents of Australia: You can pick up an application from your local post office or any branch of Passports Australia, but you must schedule an interview at the passport office to present your application materials. Call the **Australian Passport Information Service** at ☎ **131-232,** or visit the government website at www.passports.gov.au.

For Residents of Canada: Passport applications are available at travel agencies throughout Canada or from the central **Passport Office,** Department of Foreign Affairs and International Trade, Ottawa, ON K1A 0G3 (☎ **800/567-6868;** www.ppt.gc.ca). *Note:* Canadian children who travel must have their own passports. However, if you hold a valid Canadian passport, issued before December 11, 2001, that bears the name of your child, the passport remains valid for you and your child until it expires.

For Residents of Ireland: You can apply for a 10-year passport at the **Passport Office,** Setanta Centre, Molesworth Street, Dublin 2 (☎ **01/671-1633;** www.irl gov.ie/iveagh). Those under age 18 and over 65 must apply for a 123€ 1-year passport. You can also apply at 1A South Mall, Cork (☎ **021/272-525**), or at most main post offices.

For Residents of New Zealand: You can pick up a passport application at any New Zealand Passports Office or download it from their website. Contact the **Passports Office** at ☎ **0800/225-050** in New Zealand or 04/474-8100, or log onto www.passports.govt.nz.

For Residents of the United Kingdom: To pick up an application for a standard 10-year passport (5-yr. passport for children under 16), visit your nearest passport office, major post office, or travel agency; or contact the **United Kingdom Passport Service** at ☎ 0870/521-0410. You can also search its website at **www. ukpa.gov.uk**.

MEDICAL REQUIREMENTS

No inoculations or vaccinations are required to enter the United States, unless you're arriving from an area that is suffering from an epidemic (cholera or yellow fever, in particular). A valid, signed prescription is required for those travelers in need of **syringe-administered medications** or medical treatment that involves **narcotics.** It is extremely important to obtain the correct documentation in these cases, as your medications could be confiscated; and if you are found to be carrying an illegal substance, you could be subject to significant penalties. Those who are **HIV-positive** may also require a special waiver in order to enter the country (as you will be asked on your visa application whether you're a carrier of any communicable diseases). The best thing to do is contact **AIDSinfo** (☎ 800/448-0440 or 301/519-6616; www.aidsinfo.nih.gov) for up-to-date information.

CUSTOMS REGULATIONS FOR INTERNATIONAL VISITORS

Strict regulations govern what can and can't be brought into the United States—and what you can take back home with you.

WHAT YOU CAN BRING INTO THE UNITED STATES

Every visitor more than 21 years of age may bring in, free of duty, the following: (1) 1 liter of wine or hard liquor; (2) 200 cigarettes, 100 cigars (but not from Cuba), or 3 pounds of smoking tobacco; and (3) $100 worth of gifts. These exemptions are offered to travelers who spend at least 72 hours in the United States and who have not claimed them within the preceding 6 months. It is altogether forbidden to bring into the country foodstuffs (particularly fruit, cooked meats, and canned goods) and plants (vegetables, seeds, tropical plants, and the like). Foreign tourists may carry in or out up to $10,000 in U.S. or foreign currency with no formalities; larger sums must be declared to U.S. Customs on entering or leaving, which includes filing form CM 4790. For details regarding U.S. Customs and Border Protection, consult your nearest U.S. embassy or consulate, or **U.S. Customs** (☎ 202/927-1770; www.customs.ustreas.gov).

WHAT YOU CAN TAKE HOME FROM THE UNITED STATES

For a clear summary of **Canadian** rules, write for the booklet *I Declare,* issued by the **Canada Border Services Agency** (☎ 800/461-9999 in Canada, or 204/983-3500; **www.cbsa-asfc.gc.ca**).

For information, **U.K. citizens** can contact **HM Customs & Excise** at ☎ 0845/010-9000 (from outside the U.K., 020/8929-0152), or visit their website at **www.hmce.gov.uk**.

Exporting Wildlife Products

Alaska Natives put the bone, fur, and other byproducts of the animals they hunt to a variety of uses, including arts and crafts, which have become an important source of income for many Natives. Native hunters are allowed to take many animals that are otherwise protected, such as whales and walruses. Alaska Native art and crafts made with parts of protected marine mammals or from bear, bobcat, wolf, lynx, or river otter, are therefore legal, but permits are required to take them out of the country. The easiest way to deal with this is to have the shop where you made the purchase take care of the paperwork for you, then mail you the item. Otherwise, contact the **U.S. Fish and Wildlife Service** (☎ 907/271-6198) in Anchorage regarding a permit for wildlife products that don't involve marine mammals. Permits take a few days to process. For protected marine mammal products, contact the Washington, D.C., office of the **Fish and Wildlife Service** (☎ 800/358-2104; http://international.fws.gov), and be prepared to wait. It can take a month to get one of these permits.

A helpful brochure for **Australians,** available from Australian consulates or Customs offices, is *Know Before You Go.* For more information, call the **Australian Customs Service** at ☎ **1300/363-263**, or log onto **www.customs.gov.au**.

Most questions regarding **New Zealand** rules are answered in a free pamphlet available at New Zealand consulates and Customs offices: *New Zealand Customs Guide for Travelers, Notice no. 4.* For more information, contact **New Zealand Customs,** The Customhouse, 17–21 Whitmore St., Box 2218, Wellington (☎ **04/473-6099** or 0800/428-786; **www.customs.govt.nz**).

GETTING TO & AROUND ALASKA

BY AIR

GETTING THERE   You can fly in and out of Alaska through Fairbanks or one of the several communities in Southeast Alaska between Juneau and Ketchikan. But you're most likely to arrive and depart through Anchorage, the main air hub of the state. Several major airline carriers land at **Ted Stevens Anchorage International Airport,** which is named after Alaska's long-time sitting senator. Most flights—and the cheapest flights—originate in Seattle. Overseas flights sometimes originate in Asia. The dominant carrier in the state is **Alaska Airlines** (☎ 800/252-7522; www.alaskaair.com), which has more daily flights than all the other major carriers combined—up to 20 a day in the summer.

The flight line-up changes all the time, but as of this writing, these were the other major airlines serving Alaska: **Air Canada** (☎ 888/247-2262; www.aircanada.com); **China Airlines** (☎ 800/227-5188; www.china-airlines.com); **Condor Airlines** (☎ 800/524-6975; www4.condor.com); **Continental** (☎ 800/525-0280; www.continental.com); **Delta** (☎ 800/221-1212; www.delta.com); **Frontier Airlines**

(☎ 800/432-1359; www.frontierairlines.com); **Northwest** (☎ 800/225-2525; www.nwa.com); **Sun Country Airlines** (☎ 800/359-6786; www.suncountry.com); **United** (☎ 800/241-6522; www.united.com), and **US Airways** (☎ 800/428-4322; www.usairways.com).

GETTING AROUND   To fly to a roadless village, or to fly between most towns without returning to a hub, you will take a small, prop-driven plane with an Alaska bush pilot at the controls. Small air taxis also charter to fishing sites, lodges, remote cabins, or anywhere else you want to go—even a sand bar in the middle of a river. An authentic Alaskan adventure can be had by taking a Bush mail plane round-trip to a village and back. The ticket price is generally less than that of a flightseeing trip, and you'll have at least a brief chance to look around a Native village, although don't expect to find any visitor facilities without making arrangements in advance. Kodiak, Homer, Nome, Kotzebue, and Barrow are places from which you can do this with a little research. To find a bush pilot, inquire at local visitor centers, or ask around at local airfields.

Getting the Best Airfare to Alaska

Know a good deal when you see one. Airfares to Alaska rise and fall all the time. One key to getting a good airfare is recognizing a good airfare. Anchorage travel consultant Scott McMurren monitors the lowest fares from many cities and posts them online at **www.alaskatravelgram.com/airfares**. You'll also be able to make broad and impartial searches through such "aggregator" websites as **Sidestep.com**, **Kayak.com**, **FareCompare.com**, or **Mobissimo.com**, which search airline sites directly, adding no service charges and often finding fares that the larger travel sites miss.

Try booking through a consolidator. Persons traveling to Alaska from another country may wish to use a consolidator or "bucket shop" to snag a ticket. These companies buy tickets in bulk, passing along the savings to their customers. If you reside in Europe, the best way to find one that services your area is to go to the website **www.cheapflights.co.uk**, which serves as a clearinghouse for bucket shops both large and small. Many will also advertise in the Sunday papers. Be careful, though: Some charge outrageous extra fees, so read the fine print before you purchase your ticket. Bucket shops aren't useful for those flying within the U.S., as they are not generally able to undercut standard pricing on domestic travel.

Go at the drop of a hat. Alaska Airlines, and some other airlines, have last-minute web specials that can save those willing to fly on very short notice a bundle. Discounts of up to $100 are possible on the Seattle to Anchorage flight. Sign up for the My Alaska Air online newsletter at the Alaska Airlines website, **www.alaskaair.com**.

Book at the right time. Sounds odd, but you can often save money by booking your seat at 3am. That's because unpaid-for reservations are flushed out of the system at midnight, and as airfares are based on supply and demand, prices often sink when the system becomes aware of an increase in supply. Also consider booking on a Wednesday, traditionally the day when most airfare sales are announced.

Be sure to monitor such sites as Frommers.com and SmarterTravel.com, which highlight fare sales.

BY SEA

It's worth repeating that a majority of the 1.6 million annual visitors to Alaska travel via cruise ship. Chapter 2, "Cruising Alaska's Coast," goes into detail about cruising in Alaska.

But the large cruise ships aren't the only way to see watery Alaska. A less structured, less commercial, yet still affordable way to traverse the spectacular routes the cruise ships ply is via the ferries of the **Alaska Marine Highway System** (☎ 800/ 642-0066; www.ferryalaska.com). This is the way the residents of maritime Alaska—especially in the southeast part of the state where most towns have no roads to the outside world—get around (so you have the added bonus of meeting locals as you travel). By ferry you can ride all the way from Bellingham, Washington, up the famed Inside Passage to the towns of Haines or Skagway, where there are highway links to the rest of the state (through Canada). There are stops or connections to all the major Southeast communities along the way. In the summer, a ferry sails across the Gulf of Alaska twice a month, connecting Southeast with the central parts of the state. Also in the summer, a ferry runs every 2 weeks from Homer out to Unalaska in the Aleutian Islands, with stops in several remote Native communities along the way (see the chapters on Southcentral Alaska and Bush Alaska for specifics). Travelers can bring bicycles, kayaks, pets, and automobiles with them, for an extra charge.

Do you sacrifice comfort aboard these ferries? Not necessarily. While the ferries aren't at all luxurious, they're perfectly comfortable. Those that make longer runs are equipped with bright cafeterias (and the food's pretty good) and darkened bars. Some even have small movie theaters. The ferries assigned to shorter runs have snack bars, and often a U.S. Forest Service naturalist aboard, who points out marine life and natural features along the way. And while many passengers on overnight voyages simply pitch tents in designated areas on deck or sack out in common areas, it is possible to rent a private stateroom (albeit for an additional fee). Most have two single bunks; some have bunks for four but you pay one rate for them, regardless of how many passengers share the room. To snag a stateroom you'll need to make reservations at least several days in advance (more for such popular periods as the Fourth of July holiday). You'll also need reservations to bring aboard automobiles.

You'll find specific prices on ferry routes and pricing in the chapters (particularly the Southeast Chapter) that cover destinations served by ferries. Unless mentioned otherwise, fares quoted are one way.

BY RAIL

You can't take a train to Alaska, but you can catch a train to one of two Alaska Marine Highway System ports of call and hop the ferry there. From the West Coast, **Amtrak** (☎ 800/872-7245; www.amtrak.com) heads to Bellingham, Washington, with the ferry terminal a short walk from the train station. If you're coming from the east, it's easier to travel aboard Canada's **Via Rail** (☎ 888/VIA-RAIL; www.viarail.ca). Its transcontinental route starts in Toronto and winds up in Prince Rupert, British Columbia, which is another ferry stop in the Alaska Marine Highway System.

BY CAR

GETTING THERE   Don't drive to Alaska from the Lower 48 unless you've got lots and lots of time. No matter where in the U.S. you hit the road headed for Alaska, it will be a long haul. (Just consider that the distance from Seattle to Anchorage—2,250 miles—is nearly as long as the drive from New York to Los Angeles—about 2,800 miles.) If you plan on driving straight up from Seattle without stopping, you'll need to give yourself 4 to 5 days to get to Anchorage. To really enjoy the trip, you should give yourself a full 7 days, so you have time to rest and explore a little along the way (the 1,400-mile Alaska Highway that runs through Canada from Washington to Alaska has some spectacular stretches).

You can avoid the Alaska Highway by putting your car on the ferry in Bellingham and shipping it up the Inside Passage, but it will cost you an arm and a leg—$772 for an economy car, and more for larger vehicles. For that money, you could rent a car in Alaska for 2 weeks, which is to the most sensible option unless you're staying for an extended period.

As of press time, U.S. Customs & Border Protection planned to implement a requirement that all travelers entering the U.S. by land from a foreign country carry a passport beginning January 31, 2008. Check for the most up-to-date entry requirements on the U.S. Customs & Border Protection website, **www.cbp.gov**, or call the field offices in Tok (☎ 907/774-2252) or Haines (☎ 907/767-5511). To drive into Canada, you need to show Canada Customs (☎ 907/767-5540) proof of citizenship (a passport or birth certificate will do) and a government-issued photo ID. U.S Aliens should bring their Alien Registration Card, and naturalized citizens should bring their naturalization paperwork.

GETTING AROUND   Driving is the best way to see the Interior and the Southcentral parts of the state and most towns and cities in those regions have at least one rental car agency. But if your destination is Southeast Alaska, which is mostly detached from the state's road system, leave your car at home and rent bikes in the towns you want to explore.

An indispensable text for drivers in Alaska is **The Milepost** (p. 384), which documents every highway in Alaska mile by mile, with every roadside diner and anticipated construction delay along the way. For up-to-date reports on road conditions, check with the **Alaska Department of Transportation** (☎ 511; http://511.alaska.gov).

BY RV

Touring Alaska in an RV makes a good deal of sense. The home on wheels offers spontaneity by freeing you from hotel reservations, and it gets you out of town and into the countryside, closer to the natural Alaska most visitors come for. At the same time, an RV is more comfortable than a tent in cool, unpredictable weather conditions.

Many retirees drive to Alaska in their motor homes, park the RV by a salmon stream, and spend the summer fishing. Sounds nice, but for most of the rest of us, with limited time, it makes more sense to rent an RV after flying to Alaska. Unless you have a large family, an RV rental saves little over traveling with a rental car, staying in hotels, and eating in restaurants (RVs rent for around $1,500 a week, plus gas and possibly mileage charges), so you make this choice to gain sightseeing

Beware of Moose

Moose are one of the biggest (they literally weigh in at 1,400 pounds) driving hazards in Alaska. They're found just about everywhere the highways go, and they seem especially fond of blind curves on those highways. Always be on moose alert when you're driving, and watch your speed.

advantages, not avoid costs. **Alaska Motorhome Rentals** (☎ 800/254-9929; www.bestofalaskatravel.com) rents RVs one-way from Skagway to Anchorage with a $695 drop-off fee, plus the cost of the rental, mileage, and gas.

The same company, under a different name—**Alaska Highway Cruises** (☎ 800/323-5757; www.bestofalaskatravel.com)—offers the unique option of traveling one-way on a Holland America cruise ship then picking up an RV for a land tour. You can choose a package that ends up back at Seattle by road or by air. The tours follow set itineraries with reservations along the way—the service is designed for first time Alaska travelers and RV drivers who don't want to worry about the details—so some spontaneity is sacrificed. You get the security and simplicity of a package without being marched around in a group or cooped up in hotels. A cruise of a week followed by a week-long tour costs around $2,800 per person, double occupancy; a 3-week cruise to Alaska and drive back (or reverse) is around $4,100 per person. There are various discounts, including for third and fourth passengers.

SAVING MONEY ON ACCOMMODATIONS

Getting the best price on accommodations is an art and takes effort, even in Alaska. But if you take the following steps, you may be able to game the system effectively.

1. **Go in the off season.** Okay, that one's obvious and not always doable, but I include it here because it truly is the best way to pay less on accommodations.
2. **Pay cash.** Many hotels will knock 10% or so off your nightly rate if you avoid credit cards. Always ask.
3. **Surf the Web.** Such sites as Sidestep.com, Hotels.com, and Quikbook.com can be very helpful for zeroing in on "distressed merchandise": hotel rooms that have gone unsold and are therefore available at a discount. In the opaque website category, Priceline (www.priceline.com) and Hotwire (www.hotwire.com) are even better for hotels than for airfares; through both, you're allowed to pick the neighborhood and quality-level of your hotel before paying.
4. **Consider vacation and condo rentals instead of hotels.** You'll save money on food (since you'll have the option of cooking) and you'll often pay less or just as much for five times the space. These types of accommodations are particularly well suited to families and large groups, as the more people who bunk down in the house, the less you'll be paying per person. Because I think this is such a terrific way to enjoy Alaska, I've included information about local rental companies in nearly every area I cover in this book.
5. **Bargain.** Never haggled? It's easier than you think and can lead to big savings, if you do it intelligently. By that I mean don't try it if it's Iditarod time—in fact, if the prices seem to be high across the boards, it's a good sign

that something's going on and all of your bargaining won't get you a bargain. And just as important, do your research first. If you're going to a major area, you'll get an idea what the more established hotels are charging at such sites as Expedia.com or Travelocity. For smaller properties or less well-known areas, you'll have to rely on the prices in this book to judge the going rate. Once you have the correct price range under your belt, call the hotel directly and ask to speak with a manager (only they have the authority to play "let's make a deal"). Be nice, be friendly, be downright charming, but don't beat around the bush. Tell them that you'd sure like to give your business to hotel X, but you can't pay more than such and such a price. Stand firm and see what happens. If you're traveling with a group of people or staying for longer than 5 nights, use those facts as well when making your case. You could end up with a group discount or a "long stay" rate.

6. **Consider house swapping.** Simply pony up for a membership in a home swap organization (about $75 a year), and you'll get a list of people you can contact about staying in their homes. Because you'll exchange a number of e-mails before your visit, you'll be able to set the ground rules for how your home is to be treated and get to feel comfortable with your "swapee." It's this personal exchange that keeps the activity safe; those who engage in it rarely have problems. And it has some hidden perks. Families can pack more lightly than usual when they exchange with other families, as they know they'll be going to a place crammed with toys, cribs, high chairs, and more. And because it's common for the owner to send over friends to check up on the "swapee," this method of travel is a near-guaranteed way to meet people in the area you'll be visiting—a highlight of any trip.

Dozens of organizations promote home exchanges nowadays, but the following two seem to have the best coverage for Alaska: **The Home Exchange** (www.homeexchange.com) had several listings in Alaska at the time of writing. **Intervac** (www.intervac.com) had five listings in Alaska at the time of writing.

CAMPING

Campgrounds are almost everywhere in Alaska, many in extraordinarily beautiful natural places. Public campgrounds outnumber commercial ones. They're usually located where they are because there's something special about the place: a great view or beach, an exceptional fishing stream or trailhead. Only some take credit cards and rarely will you find running water or flush toilets; most are seasonal, with hand pumps for water. (When it's time to wash up, stay at a commercial campground.) Alaska's public campgrounds fill up only in certain times and places (the Kenai River and Denali National Park campgrounds are among the exceptions), so campers have flexibility to stop when and where they like.

I've mentioned some great campgrounds throughout the book, but there are many more than I had space to cover. A free map that lists all the public campgrounds along Alaska's highways is available from the **Alaska Public Lands Information Centers** (www.nps.gov/aplic). If you are planning to camp the whole way, get a copy of *Traveler's Guide to Alaskan Camping,* by Mike and Terri Church (Rolling Homes Press; $22), which contains detailed reviews of virtually every public and commercial campground in the state.

PUBLIC USE CABINS

Alaska's extensive collection of public use cabins offers some of the best deals on accommodations you'll find in the state. But public use cabins aren't for everyone. The cabins are bare-boned affairs. They generally include just a heating stove, bunks or sleeping platforms, a table and chairs, and an outhouse. You bring the food, cooking utensils, cook stove, water or water purification supplies, toilet paper, and bedding. And just getting to many of these cabins can be a challenge. Most require a hike, at the minimum, and many require a bush plane or a boat ride to get to—which adds significantly to the cost.

Five state and federal agencies have more than 200 cabins available throughout Alaska (the number fluctuates as new cabins are added, and old cabins burn down or are taken out of service). They range from $20 to $50 per night.

- The **U.S. Forest Service** (☎ 877/444-6777 or online at www.recreation.gov; AE, DISC, MC, V) has far and away the largest number of cabins to choose from, with more than 40 cabins scattered around Prince William Sound in Southcentral Alaska and more than 150 cabins distributed throughout the Tongass National Forest in Southeast Alaska. Reserve well in advance.
- **Alaska State Parks/Department of Natural Resources Public Information Center** (☎ 907/269-8400 or 907/269-8411; www.alaskastateparks.org; MC, V) has 53 cabins as far north as Fairbanks and as far south as Ketchikan.
- **The National Park Service** (☎ 907/271-2742; www.nps.gov/aplic/cabins/nps_cabins.html; MC, V) has 20 cabins in the Yukon-Charley Rivers National Park, the Kenai Fjords National Park, and the Wrangell-St. Elias National Park.
- The **U.S. Fish and Wildlife Service** (☎ 907/487-2600; http://alaska.fws.gov; DISC, MC, V) has 21 cabins in the Kenai National Wildlife Refuge and the Kodiak National Wildlife Refuge.
- The **Bureau of Land Management** (☎ 907/474-2250; www.blm.gov/ak/ak930/cabins2.html; MC, V) is the smallest renter, with just 12 cabins, mostly in the White Mountains Recreation Area north of Fairbanks.

If you'd like more information on staying in one of the state's public use cabins, contact the **Alaska Public Lands Information Center in Anchorage** (☎ 907/271-2737; www.nps.gov/aplic/center), which is an excellent clearinghouse for information.

OUTDOOR ADVENTURES/TOURS

ESCORTED PACKAGE TRIPS

Hundreds of thousands of visitors come to Alaska each year on escorted tours, leaving virtually all their travel arrangements in the hands of a single company that takes the responsibility for ushering them through the state for a single, lump sum fee. The perk of this sort of travel is that an escorted package tour provides security. You'll know in advance how much everything will cost, you don't have to worry about making hotel and ground-transportation reservations, you're guaranteed to see the highlights of each town you visit, and you'll have someone telling you what you're looking at. For those traveling at a higher price point than this book covers, escorted tours can be cost effective (as group tours can rent spaces at the large chain hotels for less than an individual traveler could). If you sometimes feel like you're a member of a herd on an escorted tour, you'll also meet new people, a big advantage if you're traveling on your own. Many passengers on these trips are retired, over age 65.

If you're short on time, escorted package tours make the most of it, as they often travel at an exhausting pace. Passengers get up early and cover a lot of ground, with sights and activities scheduled solidly through the day. However, stops only last long enough to get a taste of what the sight is about, not to dig in and learn about a place you're especially interested in. On an escorted trip, you'll meet few if any Alaska residents, since most tour companies hire college students from "Outside" (a term Alaskans use to refer to any place other than Alaska) to fill summer jobs. You'll stay in only the largest hotels and eat in the largest, tourist-oriented restaurants—no small, quaint places loaded with local character. For visiting wilderness, such as Denali National Park, the quick and superficial approach can, in my opinion, spoil the whole point of going to a destination that's about an experience, not just seeing a particular object or place. Here are the top operators for this type of tour:

Holland America Line Tours (☎ 800/544-2206; www.graylineofalaska.com or www.hollandamerica.com) is the giant of Alaska tourism and thousands of visitors do business with no one else when they come. Most clients arrive in the state on one of the company's ships (see chapter 2), but even within Alaska, chances are good that a tour you sign up for will put you on a Gray Line coach and exclusively in Westmark hotels, both owned by Holland America. Schedules are generally tightly planned and daily departures are early. The company goes more places than any other, with a catalog that covers just about anything in the state that could possibly be done with a group. Prices depend on a variety of factors, but in general a weeklong tour runs $1,400 per person.

Many feel that **Princess Cruises and Tours** (☎ 800/426-0550; www.princesslodges.com) surpasses Holland America with the consistently outstanding quality of its smaller list of offerings. The five Princess hotels are all among Alaska's plushest and Princess operates its own coaches and has superb railcars on the Alaska Railroad route to Denali. Most people on the tours come to Alaska on a cruise ship, but tours are for sale separately, too.

OUTFITTERS & OUTDOOR PACKAGE TRIPS

Besides the outfitters and tour guides listed below, I've noted other operators in the destination chapters covering the towns where they are based. Browse through those chapters before deciding on a trip, as a trip with a home-town guide service can be wonderful. There are many other larger operators, too; increasingly, international adventure travel companies bring groups to Alaska, renting equipment or even hiring guides here. Although those trips may be excellent, I've listed mostly homegrown operators who know their territory intimately.

An eco-tourism pioneer, **Alaska Discovery** ★ (☎ 800/586-1911; www.akdiscovery.com), was bought out by the famous Mountain Travel Sobek expedition company, but still keeps local staff in Juneau and offers some of the best guided sea-kayaking trips in Southeast Alaska. Glacier Bay and Admiralty Island outings cater to both beginners and the truly rugged. Their inn-to-inn trips are essentially outdoor-oriented package tours, taking groups to the best spots for day activities like kayaking, rafting, or watching wildlife. Extended river trips float through the

Arctic and on the Tatshenshini and Alsek rivers. Sample prices: A 3-day kayak expedition near Juneau is $1,090, while 10 days in the Arctic is around $4,400.

Equinox Wilderness Expeditions (☎ 604/222-1219; www.equinoxexpeditions. com) is owned by Karen Jettmar, author of *The Alaska River Guide,* the standard guidebook on floating Alaska's rivers. She leads challenging rafting, sea-kayaking, and hiking trips and base-camp wildlife viewing each summer in some of the wildest and most exotic places around the state. Her groups are tiny, with five to eight members, and she offers co-ed, family, and women's trips. A 9-day sea-kayaking trip cost $2,895 in 2007.

The guys who founded **Nova** ★ (☎ 800/746-5753 or 907/745-5753; www. novalaska.com) started commercial rafting on Alaska's rivers in 1975, but as the industry developed, they expanded only slowly, keeping their base in a tiny village on the Matanuska River, northeast of Anchorage, and primarily employing Alaskan guides. Their catalog covers longer expeditions on some of the state's wildest rivers, but also includes more affordable itineraries of 2 or 3 days. Two days on the Matanuska costs $295. Nova offers trips from Copper Center and Hope, as well.

Choose **Sport Fishing Alaska** (☎ 888/552-8674 or 907/344-8674; www.alaska tripplanners.com) to plan a fishing vacation. The owners, former guides and float, charter, and air-taxi operators Larry and Sheary Suiter, know where the fish will be week to week. After receiving a $95 advance fee, they plan a fishing vacation tailored to your budget that puts you right where fishing is hot at the time when you can travel.

For birders, there are two companies I recommend: First is **High Lonesome BirdTours** (☎ 800/743-2668 or 520/458-9446; www.hilonesome.com) which, though based in Arizona, is expert in Alaska and prides itself on relaxed trips for small groups. All-inclusive tours visit Kenai, Denali, Nome, Gambell, Barrow, Unalaska/Dutch Harbor, Adak, and the Pribilof Islands. And the second is Texas-based **Victor Emanuel Nature Tours** (☎ 800/328-8368; www.ventbird.com), which counts well-known authors among its leaders.

ALASKA SPECIALIST TRAVEL AGENCIES

Alaska Bound (☎ 888/ALASKA-7 or 231/439-3000; www.alaskabound.com), a Michigan-based agency, is the only one I know of in the Lower 48 that specializes in Alaska with a staff of former Alaskans. It started as a cruise planner, but now

---

The America the Beautiful Pass

In 2007, the National Parks Pass—which allows the bearer unlimited access to all the parks in the National Parks system for one year—got a name change (to the "America the Beautiful Pass") and a price hike. At $80, it's no longer the value it once was, so figure out how many days this year you'll be spending in the National Parks before purchasing one (it may not pay off). The pass covers everyone traveling together in one vehicle. Almost free, lifetime passes (you'll have to pay a processing fee) are available to senior citizens and persons with disabilities. Go to **www.nps.org** for more information on those.

plans many independent trips, too, charging a per person fee which depends on the length of the trip ($100 per person would not be exceptional).

Started in 1995 and steadily growing, **Alaska Tour & Travel** (☎ 800/208-0200; www.alaskatravel.com) now claims to be the largest custom vacation company in Alaska. The same folks operate the Park Connection shuttle between Denali and Kenai Fjords national parks, and that central part of the state is what they know best and cover deeply. The website is remarkable, including a search tool that brings up pre-set itineraries based on criteria you specify, and a live availability-and-rate calendar for a range of Denali hotels.

Alaska.org is a deep and well-built website that allows users to shop and customize tour packages or design their own vacations in the Southcentral-to-Fairbanks region with as much or as little structure and guidance as they choose, and without surcharge. When you've seen enough, call the toll-free number for questions and booking. Or don't. Uniquely for this kind of site, you can use it just to get information and call the listed operators yourself.

TRAVEL INSURANCE—DO YOU NEED IT?

When purchasing a big-ticket travel item—a guided tour or a cruise—it's essential to buy travel insurance. Many unforeseen circumstances can interrupt or cause you to cancel a trip, and with these types of trips, those events can lead to a large financial loss. But do you need such a policy for your trip to Alaska? Not necessarily. If you're purchasing the insurance to cover unforeseen medical expenses, lost luggage, or a cancelled flight, you may already be covered by your regular insurance if you're an American citizen. And hotel stays should never be insured, as hotels will usually allow you to cancel 24 hours in advance with no penalty (the only exception being if you book through a website such as Priceline that requires payment upfront for your stay).

So what might you want to insure? If you've booked a **vacation rental** and have had to put down a large deposit, that should be insured. If your homeowners insurance does not cover lost luggage, you may want to insure any **valuables you may be carrying with you** (as the airline will only pay up to $2,800 for lost luggage domestically, less for foreign travel). If you're an **international visitor** coming to Alaska, you should probably invest in insurance that will **cover medical expenses.** Unlike most European nations, the United States does not have any form of socialized health care, meaning that hospitals and doctor visits can be extremely expensive. In non-emergency situations, both doctors and hospitals have the right to refuse care without advance payment or proof of coverage. (*Note:* We're not utter barbarians; if you're in a life-or-death situation, you won't be denied health care. But as with non-emergency care, the uninsured pay dearly for any services rendered—you'll just get the bill a bit later.) American citizens usually find that their regular insurance will cover them in Alaska, making additional health insurance unnecessary (the exception being certain HMOs, so check first). Finally, if you're traveling to and from one of the more remote areas of the Alaskan Bush, places where banks of fog often ground planes (sometimes for days), insurance to cover additional costs is a necessity (see p. 336 for such info on Unalaska/Dutch Harbor).

If you do decide to buy insurance, you can easily assess the different policies by visiting the website **InsureMyTrip.com**, which compares the policies of all

Made in Alaska

A broad variety of goods manufactured in Alaska bear a sticker authenticating that fact. The state's Made In Alaska program has two different stickers. Alaska Native handicrafts get a sticker with a silver hand and the words "Authentic Native Handicraft from Alaska," while other Alaska-made products come with a polar bear and cub symbol and the words "Made in Alaska."

---

of the major companies. Or contact one of the following reputable companies directly:

- **Access America** (☎ 866/807-3982; www.accessamerica.com)
- **Travel Guard International** (☎ 800/807-3982; www.travelguard.com)
- **CSA Travel Protection** (☎ 800/873-9844; www.csatravelprotection.com)

MONEY MATTERS

Banks and ATMs are everywhere but in the smallest villages throughout Alaska. ATM machines and debit cards work just like they work elsewhere, and they've largely supplanted the need for travelers checks. Most ATMs impose surcharges of at least $1.50 if you're not a member of the affiliated bank.

All of the car rental companies and many hotels here require credit cards, while many of the smaller restaurants and places of lodging do not accept them or charge higher rates for those who use them (this is true of lodgings more than restaurants). I've listed credit card information for every hotel and restaurant mentioned in this book, but if you're going to businesses not mentioned in the book, be sure to call ahead to find out if your plastic will be accepted.

American currency, naturally, is the standard in Alaska. However, you may find that people in communities close to the Canadian border are willing to accept Canadian currency. Foreign currency can be exchanged at banks all over the state, though you'll generally get better exchange rates by simply using an ATM card.

HEALTH & SAFETY

AVALANCHE It's foolish to go into the snowy backcountry without a locator beacon, probes, and shovels. If you don't feel secure in how to use this equipment, go with a guide. It's near impossible to dig yourself out of an avalanche with your bare hands, and each winter lives are lost to avalanches.

BEARS & MOOSE There are two bear safety rules of thumb: Don't tempt them and don't surprise them. The first rule gets at tidiness with food and garbage when camping and backpacking. Never keep food, anything pungent, or even clothing with food smells on it inside your tent. Food should be stored in air-tight containers, and garbage placed in bear-proof garbage bins or air-tight containers outside your tent. Bear proof canisters are widely available for loan at ranger stations throughout the state. The second rule gets at the fact that you should make your presence known when hiking in bear country. Talk, sing, or wear bells when hiking. "Here, bear, bear, bear" is a common refrain among hikers. Avoid thick brush, take wide detours around dead animals (bears will defend their food), and never, ever get between a mother bear and her cub. If you come upon a bear, give it plenty of room, and slowly back off. Don't run or you might trigger a charge. If a bear does attack, lie flat on your stomach or curl up into a ball, protect your head, and play dead. Generally the attacking bear will back off after mauling you a bit. If the attack continues, change tactics and fight for your life. Bear deterrent sprays such as **Counter Assault** (☎ 800/695-3394; www.counterassault.com) are widely available.

A moose attack can be as deadly a bear attack. Give moose plenty of room, especially if they're with their young. Crowding moose may trigger an attack (they pummel their victims with their powerful forelegs).

BOATING SAFETY   Always wear a life-jacket when boating in Alaska. Because of the frigid water temperatures, even strong swimmers are often unable to swim if their boats capsize or they fall in the water. The shock of the cold water causes people to sink much faster, making boating accidents much more lethal in Alaska than they are in places with milder climates (you have only 15 min. to a half an hour before the cold water immobilizes you completely). Once you're out of the water but wet from the fall, it's just as important to get warm and dry, as hypothermia (or extreme lowering of core body temperature) can be deadly. Always use float bags (basically rubberized bags) to carry dry clothes in case of an accident. See more on hypothermia below.

CRIME   Alaska ranks high in the nation for total crime, and has especially high reports of rape. But take the same precautions to avoid crime in Alaska that you would take anywhere else, and you'll do okay. You'll be pretty safe in areas where tourists commonly frequent in the daylight hours, but a little less safe at night when leaving a bar or walking in deserted areas. Car break-ins are sometimes a problem at remote trailhead parking lots. Don't take a chance by leaving valuables in an unattended vehicle.

DANGEROUS PLANTS   In addition to poison oak and poison ivy, there are two shrubs to avoid contact with. **Pushki,** aka cow parsnip, is a large-leafed plant with white flowers and a celery-like stalk. It grows up to shoulder height by the end of the summer, and if you get the sap on your skin it will intensify the burning power of the sun and cause rashes. Wash it off quickly. **Devil's club** grows on steep slopes and has woody stalks with long, mean spines, which can stick you right through your clothing. All you have to do is look at it to know it's to be avoided. As for **wild berries,** they grow like mad along Alaskan trails in the summer. Some are edible, while others are poisonous. If you can't identify a berry with 100% confidence, don't eat it.

GETTING LOST/WILDERNESS COMMUNICATIONS   It's not difficult to get lost while hiking, canoeing, rafting, or kayaking; it happens to even experienced folks. But experienced outdoors enthusiasts always travel in twos, leave a written travel plan with a person who can call rescuers if you're late (for extended trips, not day trips), or at the very least leave a note in their car showing where they're bound. Since cellphones tend not to work in wilderness areas, really gung-ho travelers invest in Personal Locator Beacons with built-in GPS. The beacon is a small device that, when activated, transmits a distress signal and your exact location to an orbiting satellite. Authorities receive the message and find out who you are from a database. After verifying you are really missing, they can then go to the exact spot where the beacon is broadcasting. ACR Electronics' Aquafix or Terrafix PLB (for marine or land use, respectively) cost from $550 to $700 at stores such as West Marine or REI. If you don't want to shell out that much money, or if you want a device that also allows you to stay in touch in the wilderness, it is possible to rent an Iridium satellite phone that will work outdoors anywhere on earth. The drawback of this approach is that it is less useful in an emergency than a beacon: You need to know where you are and whom to call, and you have to be able to get the phone to work. With the Canadian outfit **RoadPost** (☎ 888/290-1616 or 905/272-5665; www.roadpost.com), prices start at $79 for the first week, $7 for each additional day, plus around $2 a minute for calls, plus the $35 delivery fee. They send you the phone by DHL express. But again, these electronic devices are only recommended for hard core adventurers on extended trips.

HYPOTHERMIA Hypothermia, the potentially fatal lowering of the body's core temperature, can occur in any season. People have gotten hypothermia on sunny, warm late winter days, and on cool summer days when temperatures were in the 50s (low teens Celsius). It's caused by cold and aggravated by exhaustion, wind, and wetness. To protect yourself, wear wool or a wool-like synthetic material that keeps its warmth when wet. Also, wear layers you can strip off to avoid chilling perspiration.

INSECT BITES Alaska doesn't have poisonous spiders or snakes, but it does have a bumper crop of mosquitoes in the summer. As of this writing, the West Nile virus has not been found in Alaska, so mosquitoes aren't dangerous. Just annoying. Mosquito repellant is a must in many parts of the state in the summer, and head nets and mosquito-proof clothing are widely used by wilderness trekkers.

WATER No matter how clean it looks, purify river or lake water before drinking. *Giardia lamblia,* that microscopic parasite so common in the rest of the United States, is common in Alaska too. Handheld filters sold in sporting-goods stores for around $75 will take care of the problem. So will iodine tablets or the good old-fashioned boil-before-drinking trick.

TIPS ON PACKING

Be prepared for anything. Bring wind and rain protection for foul weather. If you've got some good long underwear, such as Capilene from Patagonia, definitely bring it (it absorbs moisture when you sweat, and it looks cool enough that you can wear it in lieu of a cotton shirt on warm days). Bring a fleece jacket, a sweater, or some other light, warm middle layer. Also bring a breathable, waterproof shell.

If you go out on the water, on a whale-watching tour or fishing charter perhaps, you'll be glad if you brought a socking cap to keep your noggin warm. Bring

An Alaska Glossary

If Alaska feels like a different country from the rest of the United States, one reason may be the odd local usage that makes English slightly different here—different enough, in fact, that the Associated Press publishes a separate style-book dictionary just for Alaska. Here are some Alaskan words you may run into:

breakup   When God set up the seasons in Alaska, he forgot one: spring. While the rest of the United States enjoys new flowers and baseball, Alaskans are looking at melting snowbanks and mud. Then, in May, summer miraculously arrives. Breakup officially occurs when the ice goes out in the Interior's rivers, but it stands for the time period of winter's demise and summer's initiation.

bunny boots   If you see people wearing huge bulbous white rubber boots in Alaska's winter, it's not necessarily because they have enormous feet. Those are bunny boots, superinsulated footwear originally designed for Arctic air force operations—and they're the warmest things in the world.

cheechako   A newcomer or greenhorn. Not used much anymore because almost everyone is one.

dry or damp   Many towns and villages have invoked a state law that allows them to outlaw alcohol completely (to go dry) or to outlaw sale but not possession (to go damp).

Lower 48   The contiguous United States.

Native   When capitalized, the word refers to Alaska's indigenous people. "American Indian" isn't used much in Alaska, "Alaska Native" being the preferred term.

shorts for sunny weather. Pack a bathing suit in case your lodging has a hot tub or Jacuzzi, or if you get the urge to join the Polar Bear Club by plunging into the Arctic Ocean. And take a backpack to stash your layers in when you're not wearing them.

SPECIALIZED TRAVEL RESOURCES
FOR TRAVELERS WITH DISABILITIES

Getting off the beaten path in Alaska can be a real challenge for people with mobility issues. In the Alaskan Bush, for example, accommodations for people with disabilities are virtually nonexistent. It's a different story at the popular tourist destinations such as Denali or Anchorage. There wheelchair access is the norm, as it is at just about every hotel, many campgrounds, some B&Bs, and a few public use cabins.

Native corporation In 1971, Congress settled land claims with Alaska's Natives by turning over land and money; corporations were set up, with the Natives then alive as shareholders, to receive the property. Most of the corporations still thrive.

oosik The huge penile bone of a walrus. Knowing this word could save you from being the butt of any of a number of practical jokes people like to play on cheechakos.

Outside Anywhere that isn't Alaska. This is a widely used term in print and is capitalized, like any other proper noun.

PFD No, not personal flotation device; it stands for Permanent Fund Dividend. When Alaska's oil riches started flowing in the late 1970s, the voters set up a savings account called the Permanent Fund. Half the interest is paid annually to every man, woman, and child in the state. With nearly $40 billion in investments, the fund now yields from $900 to $2,000 in dividends to each Alaskan annually.

pioneer A white settler of Alaska who has been here longer than most other people can remember—25 or 30 years usually does it.

Southeast Most people don't bother to say "Southeast Alaska." The region may be to the northwest of everyone else in the country, but it's southeast of most Alaskans, and that's all they care about.

village A small Alaska Native settlement in the Bush, usually tightly bound by family and cultural tradition. The word *village* is roughly analogous to *tribe* elsewhere in the U.S.

—*Charles Wohlforth*

Among the various advocates in Alaska for people with disabilities is the Anchorage-based nonprofit **Challenge Alaska** (3350 Commercial Dr., Ste. 208; ☎ 907/344-7399; www.challengealaska.org). Contact them for more detailed information about outdoor recreation in Alaska, such as white-water rafting and skiing trips for people with disabilities. The group also runs the **International Sports, Recreation and Education Center** (☎ 907/783-2925), an adaptive ski school for people with disabilities at Alyeska Resort in Girdwood. In the summer, the center organizes kayaking trips, as well.

Alaska Welcomes You! (☎ 800/349-6301 or 907/349-6301; www.accessible alaska.com) is a local-to-Alaska travel agency expert that specializes in accessible tours and cruises. They also offer trip planning assistance to independent travelers with disabilities.

The Warming Climate

In the past 2 decades, winters have warmed and shortened and summers have gotten hotter. Individual years are sometimes closer to the long-term norm, but the trend is for warming. Years of bizarrely warm weather have become common and records have been broken so often they are hardly noted. In Anchorage, where I live, that has meant ski seasons ruined by rainy weather, massive insect kills of trees, and extraordinary forest fire danger, among many other changes. My friends and I, who grew up in Anchorage, never heard thunder until our teens; now it's commonplace, even early in the summer. Starting in the summer of 2004, the ocean warmed so much we were able to swim in it in places. That's never been possible before in my 44-year life. Alaska didn't even smell like Alaska that summer. Something about how the sun heated the ground and the plants created an odor I remember from travels in the Lower 48, not here.

In Arctic Alaska, the changes are much more pronounced: Sea ice is withdrawing from shore, catastrophic erosion washing away bluffs and villages, permafrost softening and giving way, winters warming and shortening, and ecosystems becoming disrupted as plant and animal life is stressed by the new conditions. A team of 300 scientists from all the Arctic nations, including the United States, completed a 4-year Arctic Climate Impact Assessment in 2004 and 2005. The report documented the changes and said they were largely driven by human carbon dioxide emissions. It predicted more changes, most of them negative. For example, if the sea ice continues to melt at the current rate, this century will see the end of

FOR SENIORS

Those over 65 are eligible for senior discounts at many Alaska attractions, and many accommodations have discounts for members of **AARP** (☎ 888/687-2277; www.aarp.org), which is open to anyone over 50. Be sure to inquire about the discounts before booking. Most Alaskan towns have senior centers, including Anchorage, which has the **Anchorage Senior Center** (☎ 907/258-7823), a good source for statewide information and advice. The nationwide **Elderhostel** (☎ 877/454-5768 or from overseas 978/323-4141; www.elderhostel.org) program offers weeklong educational vacations in Alaska for seniors. Check the website for specifics. Seniors traveling via the **Alaska Marine Highway System** (☎ 800/642-0066; www.ferryalaska.com) ferries can get discounts of up to 50%, depending on the route and season.

FOR STUDENTS

Bring your student ID and you'll get into most museums for a reduced price. If you're looking for summer work in Alaska, the **Alaska Department of Labor** (www.jobs.state.ak.us) has a database with job openings and online applications.

the ecosystem that lives upon it, including the likely extinction of the polar bear.

Carbon dioxide warms the earth by trapping the heat of the sun in the atmosphere, a phenomenon understood since the late 1800s. Climate records reconstructed from ancient ice show the amount of carbon dioxide in the atmosphere has closely matched average temperature and climate conditions for more than 400,000 years. Due to human burning of fossil fuels, the carbon dioxide level in the atmosphere now is higher than at any time in that period. And now Arctic temperatures are rising at a rate that appears unprecedented in thousands of years.

Does this mean adjusting your plans as a visitor? Yes and no. Tourists in recent years have enjoyed sunny weather, but also suffered through forest fire smoke and rainy skiing. But how the changes will play out in any particular year cannot be predicted, just as you cannot set your vacation dates based on a TV weather forecast. On the other hand, we may all need to adjust our plans. The amount of carbon dioxide each of us is responsible for emitting relates directly to the nonrenewable energy we use. You can help save Alaska by carpooling or turning off an extra light.

The Whale and the Supercomputer; On the Northern Front of Climate Change (North Point Press, $14) tells the story of how Alaska's Iñupiat and scientists are experiencing and learning about the changing climate. You can read more about it at www.wohlforth.net.

—*Charles Wohlforth*

For the most part, Alaska hostels are not affiliated with groups such as Hostelling International (☎ 301/495-1240) that offer member discounts. For a comprehensive listing of Alaska hostels, go to **www.hostels.com**.

FOR GAY & LESBIAN TRAVELERS

Alaska is a deeply conservative state, but it's a form of conservatism fiercely rooted in individual liberty and privacy. There's a real live-and-let-live ethos there. That said, Alaska isn't all that much different from the U.S. as a whole in regard to gays and lesbians, with generally higher quotients of queer friendliness in the most urban areas. For more specifics, call the **Gay and Lesbian Community Center of Anchorage** (☎ 907/929-4528). Another Anchorage-based resource is **Identity Inc.** (www.indentityinc.org), which does referrals and puts out a newsletter called *Northview*. It also sponsors activities in summer and winter, and it operates a gay and lesbian helpline (☎ 888/901-9876 or 907/258-4777).

Some Alaska bed-and-breakfasts and tours cater to gay and lesbian travelers. **Olivia Cruises and Resorts** (☎ 800/631-6277; www.olivia.com), for instance, organizes a lesbian cruise ship trip to Alaska each summer.

FOR FAMILIES

As a family destination, Alaska is a mixed bag. Foremost among the drawbacks is the expense of traveling here with kids in tow. Airfares are high, meals are costly, and many lodgings tack on extra fees when more than two share a room, even if the extra guests are kids. A prime way to offset costs, and enhance your Alaska adventure, is by camping (for information on all public campgrounds in the state, contact the **Alaska Public Lands Information Center; ☎** 907/271-2737; www. nps.gov.aplic/camping.htm). The kids will love being out in the wilderness, and you'll stay within your budget. To keep things (and yourselves) fresh, simply check into a hotel every few days for hot showers and cable TV fixes.

Other considerations? When it comes to wildlife viewing, young children probably won't have the patience for it. They may be disappointed that the animals are so far away, and they may not have the visual skills to spot distant animals in the landscape. Also, keep in mind that the distances you have to cover in Alaska are often immense, so bring activities with you that'll keep the kids amused and, if you're driving, plan on stopping at regular intervals to let everyone run around and decompress. Turn to p. 11 to see the kid-friendly itinerary I recommend.

STAYING WIRED

In all of the state's larger communities and many smaller ones, Internet is widely available in coffee shops and Internet cafes. Many accommodations also make Wi-Fi available to their guests, often for free. Websites such as **www.cybercaptive. com** and **www.cybercafes.com** list Internet cafe locations around the world, including some in Alaska.

Most towns reachable by road or ferry have cellphone service. The largest cellphone service provider is called **ACS,** which has contracts to provide service to customers of many other cellphone service providers without a presence in Alaska. ACS has calling area maps posted on its website, www.acsalaska.com. *Just be warned:* Once you get away from populated areas, don't expect to get any bars on your cellphone—service can be spotty in much of the state.

RECOMMENDED READING

A bit of background reading, beyond this guide, will immeasurably improve your enjoyment of Alaska. Here are a few tomes that I recommend.

For road tripping: The book you're most likely to see on the floor or passenger seat of a car in Alaska is *The Milepost* (☎ 888/440-6070; www.themilepost. com). It's an infinitely practical, mile-by-mile log of every roadside sightseeing attraction, campground, restaurant, gas station, and public restroom, along the highways of Alaska, British Columbia, the Northwest Territories, and the Yukon. It's loaded with mileage charts, maps, and color photos.

For history: *Alaska: Saga of a Bold Land* by Walter R. Borneman. A detailed narrative history of Alaska from the arrival of the first Russian to the battle over the Arctic National Wildlife Refuge.

Alaska's History: The People, Land, and Events of the North Country by Harry Ritter. A concise narrative history, starting with the hunters who followed game from Siberia into Alaska across the now-vanished Bering land bridge, and leading up to the modern era.

Travels in Alaska by John Muir. Naturalist Muir's classic account of exploring Southeast Alaska in the late–19th century.

For perspective on Alaska Native culture: *Two Old Women: An Alaska Legend of Betrayal, Courage, and Survival* by Velma Wallis. A retelling of a classic, uplifting Athabascan (an early Native group) legend set in the boreal forest and involving the most unlikely of heroines.

Native Peoples of Alaska: A Traveler's Guide to Land, Art, and Culture by Jan Halliday. A very readable general survey with an emphasis on cultural tourism.

The Native People of Alaska by Steve Langdon. A solid overview of Alaska Native cultures that was originally intended for first-time visitors to the state and has somehow become a required text in many introductory Alaska cultural studies courses.

For a great read: *Coming into the Country* by John McPhee. A sweeping look at the Great Land broken into thirds—urban Alaska, Bush Alaska, and total wilderness Alaska—and covering the lore and techniques of placer mining, the habits and legends of grizzly bears, the viewpoint of a young Athabascan chief, and the fortitude of the settlers, among other topics.

For wildlife: *Alaska Wildlife Viewing Guide* by Michelle Sydeman and Annabel Lund. A concise, illustrated guide to the critters of Alaska and how to view them without scaring them off or getting attacked.

ABCs of Alaska

Area Codes Alaska has just one area code, **907.** You don't need to use it for local calls within a city or town. You must use the prefix "1" and the area code before you make a toll call within the state.

Business Hours In general and at a minimum, **stores** are open Monday through Friday from 10am to 6pm, and on Saturday afternoons. Many have longer hours, especially during the summer. In the cities and larger towns, **grocery stores** stay open until late at night and carry a wide variety of goods besides food. **Banks** may close at 5pm, may have limited Saturday hours, and will be closed on Sunday. **Bars** are allowed by state law to stay open until 5am, unless local law says otherwise. And many local laws dictate that 2am is late enough. Note that many visitor attractions in Alaska operate during the summer season only and close for the winter; I've indicated summer-only places throughout the book.

Drinking Laws The drinking age in Alaska is 21. Most restaurants serve beer and wine, and some serve liquor as well. Packaged beer, wine, and liquor are sold in licensed stores, but not in grocery stores. More than 100 rural communities are "dry," meaning they prohibit the possession or importation of alcohol. Other communities are "damp," meaning alcohol can be consumed but not sold there. Almost all of these communities are Native villages in the Bush, where alcohol abuse has caused serious problems.

Electricity The United States uses 110–120 volts AC (60 cycles), compared to the 220–240 volts AC (50 cycles) that is standard in Europe, Australia, and New Zealand. If your small appliances use 220–240 volts, be sure to buy an adaptor and voltage converter before you leave home, as these are very difficult to find anywhere in the United States, and especially in Alaska.

Embassies & Consulates All embassies are located in the nation's capital, Washington, D.C. Some consulates are located in major U.S. cities, and most nations have a mission to the United Nations in New York City. If your country isn't listed below, call for directory information in Washington, D.C. (☎ 202/555-1212) or log onto www.embassy.org/embassies.

The embassy of Australia is at 1601 Massachusetts Ave. NW, Washington, D.C. 20036 (☎ 202/797-3000; www.austemb.org). There are consulates in New York, Honolulu, Houston, Los Angeles, and San Francisco.

The embassy of Canada is at 501 Pennsylvania Ave. NW, Washington, D.C. 20001 (☎ 202/682-1740; www.canadianembassy.org). Other Canadian consulates are in Buffalo (New York), Detroit, Los Angeles, New York, and Seattle.

The embassy of Ireland is at 2234 Massachusetts Ave. NW, Washington, D.C. 20008 (☎ 202/462-3939; www.irelandemb.org). Irish consulates are in Boston, Chicago, New York, San Francisco, and other cities. See the website for a complete listing.

The embassy of New Zealand is at 37 Observatory Circle NW, Washington, D.C. 20008 (☎ 202/328-4800; www.nzembassy.org). New Zealand consulates are in Los Angeles, Salt Lake City, San Francisco, and Seattle.

The embassy of the United Kingdom is at 3100 Massachusetts Ave. NW, Washington, D.C. 20008 (☎ 202/588-7800; www.britainusa.com). Other British consulates are in Atlanta, Boston, Chicago, Cleveland, Houston, Los Angeles, New York, San Francisco, and Seattle.

Emergencies Call ☎ 911 for the police, to report a fire, or to get an ambulance. If you have a medical emergency that does not require an ambulance, you should be able to walk into the nearest hospital emergency room (see "Hospitals," below). On rural highways, there may be gaps in 911 service, but dialing 0 will generally get you an operator who can connect to 911.

Fishing Licenses Non-resident fishing licenses are widely available at grocery stores and other retail outlets, or online at www.admin.adfg.state.ak.us/license. The cost is $20 for a day, $35 for 3 days, $55 for 7 days, $80 for 14 days, or $145 for a year (at which point you might as well become a resident).

Holidays Banks, government offices, post offices, and some businesses close on the usual national holidays, as well as on Seward's Day (the last Mon in Mar) and on Alaska Day (Oct 18, or the nearest Fri or Mon if the 18th falls on a weekend). The national holidays are: New Year's Day, January 1; Martin Luther King Jr. Day, the third Monday in January; Presidents' Day/Washington's Birthday, the third Monday in February; Memorial Day, the last Monday in May; Independence Day, July 4; Labor Day, the first Monday in September; Columbus Day, the second Monday in October; Veterans' Day/Armistice Day, November 11; Thanksgiving, the fourth Thursday in November; and Christmas, December 25.

Hospitals All of Alaska's larger cities have modern, full-service hospitals. Just about every smaller town has some kind of clinic, usually staffed with physician assistants rather than medical doctors.

Mail Mail in the United States must have a five-digit postal code (or zip code) after the two-letter abbreviation of the state to which the mail is addressed. You can receive mail addressed to you at "General Delivery" at the post office. To find post office locations in Alaska, go to www.usps.com/locator.

Newspapers & Magazines The *Anchorage Daily News* (www.adn.com) is Alaska's largest newspaper, and it's widely available throughout the state, with the exception of Southeast Alaska, where it's sometimes hard to find. *Alaska Magazine* is a good general-interest magazine, available pretty much throughout the state. The weekly *Anchorage Free Press* is another good general-interest publication that is widely available throughout the state.

Smoking In Anchorage, smoking is prohibited in all public places, including restaurants and bars. In the rest of the state, smoking in restaurants or bars that serve food is restricted to designated areas.

Taxes Alaska does not have a state sales tax nor a state income tax (it finances its operations with oil revenues). Most local governments do, however, impose sales taxes, accommodations taxes, and taxes on rental cars. These are noted throughout the book in the appropriate sections.

Telephone Check for surcharges on **hotel phones** before using them. These charges are common and ridiculously expensive. **Public telephones** are cheaper and cost 25¢ for local calls. Prepaid calling cards are available in many convenience stores and are generally the most affordable way to call long distance. For **long-distance calls** within Alaska or the U.S., dial 1, then the three-digit area code, then the seven-digit number. The area codes 800, 866, 877, 888 are toll-free from anywhere. For **international calls** to places other than Canada, dial 011, then the country code, city code, and telephone number. For **collect, operator-assisted,** or **person-to-person calls,** dial 0, the area code, then the phone number. An operator will come on the line to assist. For local **directory assistance,** dial 411. For long-distance information, dial 1, the area code of the place you're calling, and 555-1212.

Time Alaska is so huge, it spans five time zones. However, in the 1980s the middle time zone was stretched to the east and west so that almost all of the state falls within a single time zone, known as Alaska Time. It's an hour earlier than Pacific Time and 9 hours behind Greenwich Mean Time. The tip of the Aleutian Islands and St. Lawrence Island in the Bering Sea are on Hawaii-Aleutian Standard Time, which is an hour earlier then the rest of the state, and 10 hours behind Greenwich Mean Time. Daylight saving time moves the clock an hour ahead across all of Alaska between the second Sunday in March and the first Sunday in November.

Summer days in Alaska are *long*. For instance, on the longest day of the year in Anchorage, the sun rises at 4:30am and sets at 11:42pm. Above the Arctic Circle on the longest day of the year, the sun does not set at all. During the winter, the days are short. In Barrow, daylight is non-existent for the 64 days that the sun remains below the horizon. Anchorage gets 6 hours of daylight on the shortest day of the year. From there, daylight returns rapidly, by up to 5 minutes a day.

Tipping Tips are customary here and should be factored into your budget. Waiters should receive 15% to 20% of the cost of the meal (depending on the quality of the service), bellhops get $1 per bag, chambermaids get $1 to $2 per day for straightening your room, and cab drivers should get 15% of the fare. Tip fishing, kayaking, and other outdoor guides $10 to $20 per person.

Appendix: Alaska on the Wild Side

ALASKA TEEMS WITH MAJESTIC WILDLIFE, LARGE AND SMALL, FEATHERED, finned, and furred. Seeing these critters is probably a main reason you chose to come to Alaska, and happily, it's not too difficult to do. You can spot wildlife aplenty simply by driving around or getting out on the water. Incidental spottings are typical, and sometimes quite surprising. I've seen whales while driving along coastal highways, and bears while riding aboard the state ferry (they were on the shore, of course).

BLACK BEAR   The most common bear in Alaska—not to mention North America—is the black bear. They're found throughout most of the state, especially in Southeast and Southcentral Alaska, and along Prince William Sound. In fact, they're so ubiquitous, they can make pests of themselves. They're drawn to garbage dumps and fish drying racks, and occasionally even break into houses in Anchorage, Juneau, and Fairbanks. Since they subsist on insects, fish, berries, and other vegetation, they're usually not considered dangerous to humans, but it's wise to keep your distance. Grizzly or brown bears (see below) can be quite dangerous, so it's important to know how to tell them apart (and it won't be by color: "black bears" are often brown, blonde, or an unusual bluish shade). You can tell a black bear from a brown bear by the black bear's smaller size, more pointed head, and the absence of the brown bear's back hump. Want a peek at one? During salmon spawning season, you stand a good chance of seeing them feasting on fish along river banks and salmon streams; in late summer, they forage for blueberries.

Brown Bear

Black Bear

BROWN BEAR   Remember the movie *The Edge* in which Anthony Hopkins and Alec Baldwin are tracked by a ferocious bear? That ursine was a brown bear, and while most don't go out of their way to hunt humans, they can be dangerous and they certainly are massive. After a summer of calorie-loading, fully grown males will weigh between 500 and 900 pounds, with the occasional 1,400-pounder waddling off to the den for a long winter's nap. Brown bears and grizzly bears were once classified as separate species, but taxonomists had second thoughts about that and now say they're one and the same. Nonetheless, brown bears frequenting inland areas are still called grizzlies, and they tend to be smaller than the salmon-fed brown bears along the coast, which are simply called brown bears. Then there are the brown bears on Kodiak Island, who have been by themselves for so long that their skulls have a slightly different shape to them. (Taxonomists have declared them a subspecies.) You can tell a black from a brown bear by the brown bear's enormous shoulder hump, its longer face, and smaller ears (don't look at the color of the coat, though; just like the black bear, these bears come in a number of different shades). While there are expensive floatplane rides that allow tourists to view brown bears from above, the least expensive way to see one is from one of the shuttles in Denali National Park (where they're a fairly common sighting).

POLAR BEAR   For tourists, perhaps the most important things to know about polar bears are that they're curious, aggressive, and are the species most likely to view people as prey. They're also fast. If it came down to a foot race between you and a polar bear, the polar bear would win. They live along the Arctic coastline and upon the southern edge of the ice pack, preying mostly upon seals, walruses, birds, and fish. Though easily distinguishable by their white hue, their fur is actually translucent. It keeps them so well insulated that when viewed in the infrared, only their muzzles appear. If you want to see these impressiv beasts, you can head to Barrow in winter and sign up for a polar bear viewing tour.

Polar Bear

CARIBOU   Caribou are the undomesticated version of reindeer. They live in the Arctic and in the Interior, traveling through the mountains and across the tundra in huge herds that can number into the thousands (an awesome sight). Alaska has nearly a million caribou divided into 32 distinct herds, some of which have dual Alaskan-Canadian residency. You might see small groups of a few dozen in Denali National Park, but you're unlikely to see them at all unless you get off the beaten tourist path and above the treeline on the rural northern roads, such as the Dalton or Steese highways. Caribou are skittish and encounters with them are fleeting. If you happen to spot some while driving, pull over, stay very still, and enjoy the spectacle.

REINDEER   You're most likely to see caribou in the wild and reindeer on the plate (reindeer sausage is a standard breakfast item in Alaska). To see these domesticated animals alive, you can head to the Williams Reindeer Farm in Palmer, at the Alaska Zoo in Anchorage, the Alaska Wildlife Conservation Center near

Girdwood, or the Large Animal Research Station in Fairbanks. Reindeer on the hoof have shorter legs and weigh more than caribou.

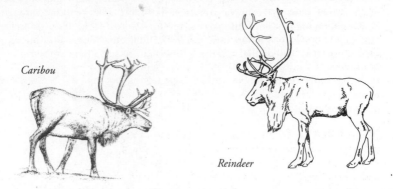

Caribou

Reindeer

MOOSE   Moose may look more like hunched-back horse-cow hybrids, but they're actually members of the deer family. Weighing in at up to 1,600 pounds, moose are found in most parts of Alaska. They're so common and they have such a propensity for getting hit by cars (and chowing down on gardens) that many Alaskans consider them a pest. They're usually peaceful creatures, but during the fall rutting season, males may grow aggressive enough to charge trains. And mothers with calves won't hesitate to try to trample a perceived threat. You can tell male from female, for part of the year at least, by their antlers: males have them, but females don't (though males shed them each year after mating season, when they're used to battle other moose for mates).

Dall Sheep

Moose

DALL SHEEP   Dall sheep inhabit sub-Arctic mountain ranges throughout Alaska. They occupy meadows, ridges, and steep slopes, never far from the safety of craggy mountain faces, which they can dash into if predators appear. Typically, you'll only get a good look at Dall sheep through a strong pair of binoculars, but there's a stretch of the Seward Highway south of Anchorage where you might get an unaided look at them cantering across the impossibly steep cliffs along the road.

MOUNTAIN GOAT   Mountain goats occupy similar terrain as Dall sheep and they're often mistaken for female Dall sheep, although they're distinguishable by their deeper chests, black horns, and longer hair, which stops suddenly before reaching their hooves, creating a pantaloon-like effect. They're found throughout Southeastern Alaska, along the coastal mountains to Cook Inlet, through the Chugach and Wrangell mountains, and in the Talkeetna Mountains, but as with Dall Sheep, they stay up high (so bring binoculars to get a look at them).

Mountain Goat

SEA OTTER   A square centimeter of sea otter fur can have 100,000 hairs in it, which makes sea otter fur the densest fur there is. It's also what nearly doomed them to extinction in the mid–18th century, a few decades after the Russians found out what lovely hats and stoles they could make from the fur. Sea otters have made a strong comeback since the hunting ended (going from fewer than 2,000 in 1911 to closer to 200,000 today), re-inhabiting most of their historic habitat in Alaska. You'll see them along rocky shores throughout the Southeast and Southcentral parts of the state. They can dive up to 250 feet to gather mussels, crabs, and other food, which they stuff into the pouches beneath their forepaws. They like to float on their backs while dining, sometimes using rocks to crack open shellfish. When they're not eating or mating (both of which they do prolifically and year-round), they're grooming. Sea otters take great pains to keep their insulating coats in top shape.

River Otter

Sea Otter

RIVER OTTERS   Endowed with broad hips and short legs, river otters are not only powerful in water but can travel overland for miles between bodies of water. While hiking, you may come across the well-defined trails that river otters develop for these treks. You might also come upon an otter territorial marker called a scent post, which consists of several yards of flattened, urine-sprayed vegetation or snow, littered with twisted tufts of grass, little piles of dirt, and scat. In terms of looks, river otters have a dense coat, similar to sea otters (it made them similarly popular with trappers). They live in groups with no apparent social leader, traveling together, though they don't hunt cooperatively or share what they catch. They spend about half their lives sleeping, and they enjoy horseplay—wrestling, dunking each other, playing hide-and-seek, tag, and whatnot. You'll find them in rivers through most of Alaska, but don't ever try and race one. They can run as fast as a human across snow, but they cheat, switching back and forth between running and sliding.

SEA LION   Sea lions are loud, cranky, foul smelling, and huge. They congregate in large groups, hauling their blubbery bodies—adult males can be more than 10 feet long and weigh up 1,250 pounds—onto the rocks, bellowing their disapproval at each other as they come and go. Historically, they have been a primary source of protein for the people of the Aleutian Islands, who depended on their skins for clothing, boots, and boat coverings. Natives around the Aleutians, Kodiak, and Pribilof Island still hunt them on a small scale today.

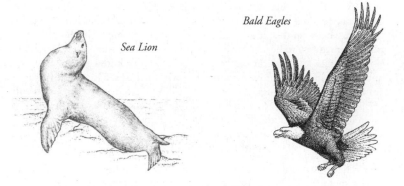

Bald Eagles

Sea Lion

BALD EAGLES   In the Lower 48, bald eagles, the United States' national bird, wound up on the federal endangered species list, following years of habitat destruction, poaching, pesticides, and poisoning. Bald eagles never had such troubles in Alaska, where they're seen in every fishing town, perched on branches, soaring on thermals, dive bombing fish, or just standing around on the beach. They're most common in Southeast Alaska, though they're also found on the state's offshore islands, and around lakes and rivers in the Interior. Contrary to a widespread but inaccurate theory, bald eagles don't screech as they swoop down upon their prey (the screech of the red-tailed hawk is sometimes dubbed over a diving bald eagle for dramatic effect). Bald eagles speak in squeaks and shrill cries mixed with grunts.

WHALE SPOTTING 101
by Charles Wohlforth

The waters near Petersburg, Sitka, and Gustavus are favored by whales as are those in Glacier Bay National Park, and near Seward and Kenai Fjords National Park. On cruises and sometimes even from shore, you're likely to spot the following massive mammals:

THE HUMPBACK WHALE   These migratory whales spend their summer in Alaska feeding, then swim to Mexican or Hawaiian waters for the winter, where they give birth to their young and then fast until going north again in spring. The cold northern waters produce the small fish and other tiny creatures that humpbacks filter through their baleen—the strips of stiff, fibrous material that humpbacks have instead of teeth. A humpback is easy to recognize by its huge, mottled tail; by the hump on its back, just forward of its dorsal fin; and by its armlike flippers, which can grow to be 14 feet long. Most humpback sightings are of the whales' humped backs as they cruise along the surface, resting, and of the flukes of their tails as they dive.

Humpbacks weave nets of bubbles around their prey, then swim upward through the schooled fish, mouths wide open, to eat them in a single swoop, sometimes finishing with a frothy lunge through the surface. Feeding dives can last a long time and often mean you won't see that particular whale again, but if you're lucky, the whale may just be dipping down for a few minutes to get ready to leap completely out of the water, a behavior called breaching. No one knows for sure why whales do this; it may simply be play. Breaching is thrilling for viewers and, if you happen to be in a small boat or kayak, a little scary (paddlers should group their boats and tap the decks to let the whales know where they are). Humpbacks are highly sensitive to noise, so keep quiet to see longer displays.

Humpbacks tend to congregate to feed, making certain spots with rich supplies of food reliable places to watch them. In Southeast Alaska, the best humpback-watching spots include the waters of Icy Strait, just outside Glacier Bay, Frederick Sound outside Petersburg, and Sitka Sound. In Southcentral Alaska, Resurrection Bay, outside Seward near Kenai Fjords National Park, has the most reliable sightings.

The Humpback Whale.
Maximum length: 53 ft.

THE ORCA (KILLER WHALE)   The starkly defined black-and-white patches of the orca, the ocean's top predator, recall the sharp, vivid look of the Native American art of the Pacific Northwest and Southeast Alaska. Moving like wolves in highly structured family groups called pods, and swimming at up to 25 knots (about 29 mph), orcas hunt salmon, porpoises, seals, sea lions, and even juvenile whales. There's never been a report of one attacking a human being. Like dolphins, orcas often pop above the surface in a flashing, graceful arc when they travel, giving viewers a glance at their sleek shape, markings, and tall dorsal fin.

Unlike humpbacks and other whales that rely on a predictable food supply, orcas' hunting patterns mean it's not easy to say exactly where you might find them—you need to be where their prey is that day. Resurrection Bay and Prince William Sound both have pods that are often sighted in the summer, and we saw a pod of orcas from the beach in Gustavus, but they could show up anywhere in Southeast Alaska waters. For cruisers coming to Alaska from Vancouver, a top spot to see orcas is Robson Bight, an area in Johnstone Strait (between Vancouver Island and mainland British Columbia).

The Orca, or Killer Whale.
Maximum length: 30 ft.

THE BELUGA WHALE   This small white whale with a cute rounded beak is one of only three types that spend all their lives in cold water rather than heading south for the winter. (The other two are the narwhale and bowhead.) Belugas are more likely to be mistaken for dolphin than any other whales are. However, the beluga is larger and fatter than a dolphin and lacks the dolphin's dorsal fin. Adults are all white, while juveniles are gray. Belugas swim in large packs that can number in the dozens. The beluga is the only whale that can turn its head, and it's one of a few species with good eyesight.

Belugas feed on salmon, making the mouths of rivers with salmon runs the best places to see them. Occasionally, a group will strand itself chasing salmon on a falling tide, swimming away when the water returns. The Cook Inlet group of belugas is the most often seen: If you're in Anchorage after your cruise, head out the Seward Highway, just south of town, and keep your eyes on the waters of Turnagain Arm, or watch from the beach near the mouth of the Kenai River in Kenai.

The Beluga Whale.
Maximum length: 16 ft.

THE MINKE WHALE   The smallest of the baleen whales, the minke is generally under 26 feet long and has a blackish-gray body with a white stomach; a narrow, triangular head; and white bands on its flippers. Along with the humpback and (occasionally) the gray whale, it is the only baleen whale commonly seen in Alaskan waters.

When breaching, minkes leap something like dolphins, gracefully reentering the water headfirst—unlike humpbacks, for instance, which smash down on their sides. Also unlike the humpbacks, they don't raise their flukes (the tips of their tails) clear of the water when they dive. Minkes are easy to confuse with dolphins: Watch for the dark skin color to tell the difference.

The Minke Whale. Maximum length: 26 ft.

THE GRAY WHALE   Here's one whale you'll probably see only if you take a shoulder-season cruise (in May or very late Sept), and then only if you're lucky. The grays spend their winter months off the coast of California and in the Sea of Cortez (between Baja and mainland Mexico) and their summer months off northern Alaska, meaning that cruise passengers sailing in the Inside Passage and Gulf of Alaska can only spot one while it's on its migration.

The Gray Whale.
Maximum length: 45 ft.

Like the humpback, grays are baleen whales. They're also about the same size as the humpback, though they lack the humpback's huge flippers. Their heads are pointed, and they have no dorsal fin. Grays will often smack the water with their flukes and are very friendly—it's not uncommon for them to swim right up to a small boat and allow their heads to be patted.

Index

See also Accommodations and Restaurant indexes, below.

GENERAL INDEX

Accommodations, saving money on, 371–372
Admiralty Island, 232–233
Air travel, 367–369
Alaska Aviation Heritage Museum (Anchorage), 49
Alaska Bald Eagle Festival (Haines), 364
Alaska Bound, 375–376
Alaska Candle Factory and Gift Shop (Girdwood), 69
Alaska Center for the Performing Arts (Anchorage), 56
Alaska Chilkat Bald Eagle Preserve (Haines), 254
Alaska Day Festival, 364
Alaska Discovery, 374–375
Alaska Folk Festival (Juneau), 223, 363
Alaska General Store (Juneau), 226
Alaska Gold Company Dredge (near Nome), 350
Alaska Heritage Library Museum (Anchorage), 46
Alaska Indian Arts (Haines), 257
Alaska Marine Highway System, 369
The Alaskan (Cordova), 105
Alaska Native Heritage Center (Anchorage), 7, 47
Alaska Native Medical Center (Anchorage), 49–50
Alaskan Brewing Company (Juneau), 224
Alaska.org, 376
Alaska Rag Company (Fairbanks), 287
Alaska Range Overlook (Fairbanks), 279
Alaska Raptor Center (Sitka), 199
Alaska River Expedition Campground (near Cordova), 102
Alaska Salmon Bake (Glitter Gulch), 328
Alaska SeaLife Center (Seward), 117

Alaska State Capitol (Juneau), 219
Alaska State Fair (near Anchorage), 77, 364
Alaska State Museum (Juneau), 6, 217
Alaska State Troopers Museum (Anchorage), 47
Alaska Tour & Travel, 376
Alaska Wild Berry Products (Anchorage), 55–56
Alaska Wildlife Conservation Center (near Portage Glacier), 61
Aleutian World War II National Historic Area (Dutch Harbor), 340–341
Alganik Slough, 106–107
Alutiiq Museum & Archeological Repository (Kodiak), 148
    gift shop, 150–151
Alutiiq Museum Community Archeology Program (Kodiak), 149
Alyeska Resort (Girdwood), 67–68
Alyeska Resort Spring Carnival and Slush Cup, 363
Alyeska Ski Resort, 8
American Bald Eagle Foundation Museum (Haines), 255
American Society of Travel Agents (ASTA), 20
America the Beautiful Pass, 375
Anan Creek Wildlife Observatory (Wrangell), 180
Anan Wildlife Observatory, 5
Anchorage, 28–78
    accommodations, 33–40
    getting to and around, 31–33
    guided tours and visitor help, 48
    history of, 29–30
    lay of the land, 30–31
    must-dos in, 29
    nightlife, 56–58
    outdoor activities, 51–54
    restaurants, 40–45
    shopping, 54–56
    side trips from, 58–78

    sights and attractions, 45–49
    taxis, 32
    visitor information, 31
The Anchorage Alaska Zoo, 48
Anchorage Bed-and-Breakfast Association, 33
Anchorage Convention and Visitors Bureau, 31
Anchorage Downtown Partnership Security Ambassadors, 48
The Anchorage Folk Festival, 361
The Anchorage Fur Rendezvous Winter Festival, 361
Anchorage Historic Properties, 48
Anchorage Market and Festival, 54
Anchorage Museum at Rasmuson Center, 6, 44–47
Angel Rocks Trail, 285
Arctic Brotherhood Hall (Skagway), 242
Arctic Circle, 300
Arctic Interagency Visitor Center (Coldfoot), 301
Arctic Region Supercomputing Center (Fairbanks), 279
Area codes, 385
Art galleries
    Homer, 139–140
    Ketchikan, 170
    Petersburg, 188
Art workshops (Homer), 138
The Ascending Path (Girdwood), 68
Atigun Pass, 303
Auke Village Campground, 214
Aurora borealis (northern lights), 278
Aurora Ice Museum, 291

Backcountry Information Center (Denali National Park), 319
Bald eagles, 106, 393
    Haines, 247, 254, 255
    Sitka, 199, 200
Ballyhoo, Mount, 340, 341
Baranov Museum (Kodiak), 148

Barnes & Noble (Anchorage), 50
Barrow, 7, 335, 351–358
Bartlett Cove, 230
The Bartlett Lecture Series
  (Anchorage), 50
Battery Point Trail, 256
Beach Sculpture Sunday
  (Homer), 138–139
Bears and bear-viewing, 389–390
  Admiralty Island, 232–233
  Anan Creek Wildlife
    Observatory (Wrangell),
    180
  best places to see, 5
  Kodiak Island, 150–151
  polar. See Polar bears
  safety tips, 377–378
Bear Tooth Theatrepub
  (Anchorage), 56–57
Beaver Sports (Fairbanks),
  286–287
Begich-Boggs Visitor Center
  (Portage Valley), 61–62
Beluga Point, 59
Benson, Benny, 109
Big Ray's (Fairbanks), 286
Biking and mountain biking, 107
  Anchorage, 51–53
  Denali National Park, 327
  Juneau, 208
  Seward, 110
  Wrangell, 174
Birch Hill Recreation Area, 286
Bird Creek, 60
Bird Creek Campground
  (Anchorage), 40
Bird Point Scenic Overlook, 61
Bird Ridge Trailhead, 60
Birds and bird-watching, 375.
  See also Bald eagles
  Anchorage, 51
  Copper River Delta,
    106, 363
  Juneau Raptor Center, 217
  Kachemak Bay, 363
  Sitka, 199
  Stikine Flats, 180
  Unalaska, 341–342
Bird-to-Gird Trail, 60–61
Birnirk Archaeological Site
  (Barrow), 356
The Blue Loon (Fairbanks), 289
Boating. See also Canoeing;
  Kayaking
  safety, 378
Boat tours and excursions. See
  also Cruise ships and lines
  Fairbanks, 276
  Glacier Bay, 229

Haines, 249, 250
Kenai Fjords National Park,
  120
Ketchikan, 167
Misty Fiords National
  Monument, 171
Prince William Sound, 96–97
Resurrection Bay, 117–118
  marine wildlife
    tours, 122
Sitka, 200
Skagway, 247
Valdez area, 93
Wrangell, 179
Books, recommended, 384–385
Borders (Anchorage), 56
Bore tides, Turnagain Arm, 62
Bunker Hill, 341
Bunnell Street Gallery (Homer),
  139–140
The Bush, 4, 333–358
  getting to and around, 335
  lay of the land, 334–335
  must-dos in, 334
Business hours, 385
Byron Glacier, 62–63

**Cabin Nite Dinner Theater
  (McKinley Village), 328**
Cabins, 373
  Fairbanks, 285
  near Girdwood, 65
  Juneau, 213
  Prince William Sound, 102
  Resurrection Bay area,
    114–115
  Skagway area, 239
  Wrangell area, 177
Caines Head State Recreation
  Area, 114, 117
Camping, 372
  Anchorage, 40
  Bartlett Cove, 230
  Cordova area, 102
  Denali National Park,
    310, 312
  Fairbanks area, 271
  Fort Abercrombie State
    Historic Park, 144
  Homer, 135
  Juneau, 213–214
  Kachemak Bay State Park
    and State Wilderness
    Park, 141
  Ketchikan area, 164
  Nome, 345
  Petersburg, 186
  Seward area, 113

Sitka, 194
Skagway area, 239
Soldotna, 126
Valdez area, 93
Wrangell area, 177
Canned Salmon Classic
  (Petersburg), 187
Canoeing, 107, 203, 283–284
Cape Fox Funicular (Ketchikan),
  168
Cape St. Elias Lighthouse, 102
Cape Smythe Whaling and
  Trading Station (Barrow), 356
Carlo Creek, 314–315, 318
Carnival Cruise Lines, 23
Caroline's Handmade in Homer,
  141–142
Carrie M. McClain Memorial
  Museum (Nome), 348
Car travel, 370
Castle Hill (Sitka), 198
Celebration (Juneau), 223
Celebrity Cruises, 23–24
Cellphones, 384
Centennial Park (Anchorage), 40
Centennial Park Campground
  (Soldotna), 126
Central, 295
Chatanika River, 283–284, 293
Chena Dome Trail, 285
Chena Hot Springs Resort,
  290–291
Chena Hot Springs Road, 260
Chena Hot Springs Trail, 285
Chena River, 283
  Recreation Area, 285
  State Recreation Site, 271
Chief Shakes Tribal House
  (Wrangell), 178
Childs Glacier, 4, 98, 105
Chilkat Dancers (Haines), 256
Chilkat River, 254
Chilkoot Charlie's (Anchorage),
  57–58
Chilkoot Trail, 244
Chugach National Forest
  Cordova Ranger District,
  99, 107
Chugach State Park, 59, 60
  Glen Alps Trailhead, 52
Circle, 295
Circle District Historical Museum
  (Central), 295
Circle Hot Springs, 295
Clausen Memorial Museum
  (Petersburg), 187
Cleary Summit scenic viewpoint,
  293

Climate change (global warming), 280, 303, 352, 357, 360, 382–383

Climbing, rock and ice
  Anchorage, 53–54
  Girdwood, 68
  Juneau, 225–226
  Valdez area, 92

Coldfoot, 300–301
  Services Truckstop, 301

Colony House Museum (Palmer), 73

Columbia Glacier, 92–93

Consulates, 386

Cooking classes (Homer), 138

Cook Inlet, Beluga whales, 60

Cook Inlet Book Co. (Anchorage), 56

Copper River Delta, 98, 99, 105–107
  Shorebird Festival, 363

Copper River Fleece (Cordova), 105

Copper River Highway, 98, 107

Cordova, 80–81, 97–107

Cordova Chamber of Commerce Visitor Center, 98–100

Cordova Historical Museum, 103–104

Council, 349–350

The Craft Market (Fairbanks), 287–288

Creamer's Field (Fairbanks), 284

Crime, 378

Cross-country skiing, Fairbanks, 285–286

Crow Creek Mine, 68–69

Crow Pass, 68

Cruise Lines International Association (CLIA), 20

Cruise ships and lines, 15–27, 369. *See also* Boat tours and excursions

Cruisetours, 17–18

Curling, 8, 280–281

Customs regulations, 366–367

Cyrano's Off-Center Playhouse (Anchorage), 57

Dalton Highway, 261, 297–305

Darwin's Theory (Anchorage), 57

Davidson Ditch, 293

"Days of 98" (Skagway), 246

Deadhorse, 303–304

Deer Mountain Tribal Hatchery and Eagle Center (Ketchikan), 167

Dejon Delights (Haines), 257

Denali National Park and Preserve, 5, 306–332
  accommodations, 310–316
  communities outside the park, 308
  entrance and reservation fees, 319
  getting to and around, 308–310
  history of, 307
  interpretive bus tours, 324–326
  lay of the land, 307–308
  nightlife, 328
  outdoor activities, 327–328
  sights and attractions, 319–327
  tours and transportation, 322–324
  wildlife, 324–325
  tours, 325–326

Denali Natural History Tour, 325

Denali Park Road, 322–323

Disabilities, travelers with, 380–381

Disaster Creek, 301

Dock Point Trail, 91

Dolly's House (Ketchikan), 168

Downhill skiing, 67, 286

Drinking laws, 385

Driving tours, 9–10
  Denali Park Road, 322–323
  the Interior, 291–305
  Matanuska-Susitna Valley, 70–71
  along Turnagain Arm, 58–63

Duggan's Waterfront Pub (Homer), 142

Dutch Harbor, 334, 335–342

Dyea, 246

Eagle Park (Petersburg), 187

Eagle River Campground (Anchorage), 40

Eagle Summit, 294

Earthquake Park (Anchorage), 51

Edgecumbe, Mount, 203

Eielson Visitor Center, 323

86-Mile Overlook, 299

Eklutna, 49

El Dorado Gold Mine (Fairbanks), 276

Electricity, 385–386

Elliott Highway, 260, 296

Embassies and consulates, 386

Emergencies, 386

Entry requirements, 365

Equinox Wilderness Expeditions, 375

Escorted package trips, 373–374

Evening at Egan (Juneau), 223–224

Evergreen Cemetery (Juneau), 220–221

Exit Glacier, 109, 118–119

Exit Glacier Campground (near Seward), 113

Exxon Valdez oil spill, 90

Fairbanks, 260–305
  accommodations, 266–271
  excursions out of town, 289–291
  festivals and events, 281, 283
  getting to and around, 263–264, 266
  history of, 261–262
  lay of the land, 262–263
  nightlife, 288–289
  outdoor activities, 283–286
  restaurants, 271–275
  shopping, 286–288
  sights and attractions, 275–281

Fairbanks Convention and Visitors Bureau, 266

Fairbanks Curling Club, 281

Fairbanks Golf and Country Club, 285

Fairbanks Ice Museum, 276–277

Families with children, 11–12, 384

The Far North, 334–335

Felix Creek, 292–293

Felix Pedro Monument, 293

Festivals and special events, 361–364

Finger Rock, 300

First Friday (Homer), 139

Fisherman's Trail, 107

Fishermen's Memorial Park (Petersburg), 186–187

Fishing, 375
  Anchorage, 53
  best, 5
  Homer, 138, 139
  Kenai, 127–128
  licenses, 386
  safety warning, 128
  Talkeetna, 331
  Unalaska, 341

The Fish Pirate's Daughter (Ketchikan), 170

Flattop Mountain, 52
Flightseeing, 172, 222, 326–327
Floathouses, Sitka, 194
Forest Service cabins and camp-
    grounds. *See* Cabins; Camping
Fort Abercrombie State Historic
    Park, 144
Fort Knox Gold Mine, 293
Fort Seward accommodations,
    250–252
Frederick Sound, 5
Friday Night Insight
    (Ketchikan), 169
Friends of the Alaska State
    Museum Store (Juneau), 226

Garnets, Wrangell, 181
Gavan Hill-Harbor Mountain
    Trail, 202
Gay and lesbian travelers, 383
    Anchorage nightlife, 58
Geophysical Institute
    (Fairbanks), 280
George Parks Highway, 260
Georgeson Botanical Garden
    (Fairbanks), 278–279
Girdwood, 63–69
Girdwood Junction, 61
Girdwood Market Place, 67
Glacier Bay National Park,
    4, 7, 227–231
Glacier Park (near Palmer), 74
Glaciers, 4, 153, 222. *See also*
    specific glaciers
Glacier Travel Clinic
    (Girdwood), 67
Glenn Highway, 70–71
Glitter Gulch (Nenana Canyon)
    accommodations, 313–314
    restaurants, 317–318
Global warming (climate
    change), 280, 303, 352, 357,
    360, 382–383
Gobblers Knob, 300
Goddard Hot Springs, 205
Goldberg Cigar Store (Skagway),
    243
Gold Creek (Juneau), 220
Gold Dredge Number 8 (near
    Fairbanks), 276, 292
Golden Heart Greeter Program
    (Fairbanks), 279
Golden Heart Park (Fairbanks),
    262
Golden Heart Revue (Fairbanks),
    288
Gold Rush Days (Juneau), 223

Golf, 179, 285
Governor's Mansion (Juneau),
    220
Granite Creek Trail, 224
Granite Tors Trail, 285
Grayling Lake Wayside, 300
Great Alaskan Bowl Company
    (Fairbanks), 287
Great Alaskan Lumberjack Show
    (Ketchikan), 168–169
Gustavus, 156, 230–231

Haines, 155–156, 247–257
Haines Brewing Company, 257
Halibut Point State Recreation
    Area, 199
Hammer Museum (Haines),
    255–256
Harding Icefield Trail, 119
Hatcher Pass, 75
Hatcher Pass Road, 71
Haystack Trail, 107
Health and safety, 377–379
Healy, 315–316, 318–319
Heney Ridge Trail, 104
High Lonesome BirdTours, 375
Highway Pass, 323
Hiking and trekking. *See also*
    *specific state and national
    parks and trails*
    Anchorage, 51–53
    Cordova area, 104
    Fairbanks, 284–285
    Juneau, 217, 224–225
    Kachemak Bay State Park
        and State Wilderness
        Park, 140–141
    Seward/Resurrection Bay
        area, 117, 119
    Sitka, 201, 202–203
    Unalaska, 341
    Valdez area, 91
    Wrangell area, 180–181
Holidays, 386
Holland America Line,
    24–25, 374
Holy Ascension Cathedral
    (Unalaska), 340
Homer, 5, 82, 128–142
    accommodations, 130–135
    getting to and around, 130
    history of, 129
    lay of the land, 129–130
    nightlife, 142
    outdoor activities, 139
    restaurants, 135–136
    shopping, 139–142
    sights and attractions,
        136–139

Homer Council on the Arts, 138
Howling Dog Saloon
    (Fairbanks), 289
Humpy's Great Alaskan Alehouse
    (Anchorage), 57
Hutliana Hot Springs, 296, 297
Hypothermia, 379

Ice climbing. *See* **Climbing,
    rock and ice**
Ice House (Skagway), 243
Ididaride Sled Dog Tours, 121
Iditarod Trail Sled Dog Race,
    75–77, 363
Iditarod Trail Store
    (Anchorage), 55
Igloo Campground, 312
The Imaginarium Science
    Discovery Center (Anchorage),
    47–48
Independence Day, 364
Independence Mine State
    Historical Park, 74–75
Indian River Trail, 202
Insect bites, 379
The Inside Passage, 16–17
Insurance, 376–377
The Interior, 4, 258–305
    driving tours, 291–305
    getting to and around, 261
    lay of the land, 259–261
    must-dos in, 259
International Arctic Research
    Center (Fairbanks), 280
Internet access, 384
Iñupiat Heritage Center
    (Barrow), 355–356
Isabel Miller Museum
    (Sitka), 198
The Islands and Ocean Visitor
    Center (Homer), 137
Itineraries, suggested, 8–14

**James Bernard Moore House
    (Skagway), 243**
Jesus Town, 281, 290
John Brown's Beach, 199
Juneau, 155, 206–227
    accommodations, 208–214
    getting to and around,
        207–208
    history of, 206–207
    lay of the land, 207
    Macaulay Salmon Hatchery,
        222–223
    nightlife, 227
    outdoor activities, 224–226
    restaurants, 214–216

shopping, 226–227
sights and attractions,
216–224
visitor information, 207
walking tour, 218–221
Juneau-Douglas City Museum,
217–220
Juneau Icefield, 222
Juneau Raptor Center, 217

Kachemak Bay, 118
Kachemak Bay Shorebird
Festival, 363
Kachemak Bay State Park and
State Wilderness Park,
7, 140–141
Kantishna Experience, 326
Kantishna Wilderness Trails, 326
Kantishsna accommodations, 312
Kayakers Cove, 115
Kayaking
Anchorage, 53
best places for, 7
Chatanika River, 293
Copper River Delta, 107
Glacier Bay, 230
Kachemak Bay, 141
Kenai Fjords National Park,
121–122
Misty Fiords, 171–172
Resurrection Bay, 115
Sitka area, 203
Unalaska, 342
Valdez area, 93
Whittier area, 97
Kenai, 81–82, 122–128
Kenai Fjords National Park,
4, 5–6, 82, 109, 114–115,
118, 120–122
Kenai Peninsula, 81
Kenai River, 5, 81
Ketchikan, 6, 154, 157–172
accommodations, 161–164
excursions out of town,
171–172
getting to and around,
160–161
history of, 158
lay of the land, 158, 160
nightlife, 170–171
restaurants, 164–165
shopping, 169–170
sights and attractions,
165–169
Kharacters (Homer), 142
Kivgiq (Barrow), 356
KJNP (Fairbanks), 281
Kodiak, 142–151

Kodiak Crab Festival, 363–364
Kodiak Fisheries Research Center
(Kodiak), 148–149
Kodiak Island, 5, 82
Kodiak Island Brewing Co.,
149–150
Kodiak Island Winery, 151
Kodiak National Wildlife Refuge,
143, 150
Kodiak Smoking and Processing
Plant, 149
Kodiak State Fair and Rodeo, 364
Kodiak WhaleFest, 363

**Large Animal Research Station
(Fairbanks), 277–278**
Gift Shop (Fairbanks), 287
Last Chance Campground, 164
Last Chance Mining Museum
(Juneau), 218
Last Chance State Wayside, 303
The Last Train to Nowhere,
349, 350
Laurence, Sydney, 46
Little Norway Festival
(Petersburg), 187, 363
Live at Five Concert Series
(Anchorage), 56
Llanka Cultural Center
(Cordova), 104
Log Cabin Visitor Information
Center (Anchorage), 31

**Macaulay Salmon Hatchery
(Juneau), 222–223**
McHugh Creek, 59
McHugh Trail, 59
McKinley, Mount, 320–322
Made In Alaska Gift Shop
(Sitka), 204
Mail, 387
Maksutov, Princess, grave
(Sitka), 198
Mammoth Creek, 295
Manley, 296
Manley Hot Springs, 296
Mantanuska Glacier State
Recreation Area, 74
Margaret Murie Science &
Learning Center (Denali
National Park), 322
Marine life. *See also* Whales and
whale-watching
Kodiak Fisheries Research
Center (Kodiak), 148–149
tours
Resurrection Bay, 122
Sitka, 200

The Marlin (Fairbanks), 288–289
Mascot Saloon (Skagway), 243
Matanuska Glacier, 73–74
Matanuska River, 74
Matanuska-Susitna Valley and
environs, 69–78
Meares Glacier, 93
The Mecca Bar (Fairbanks), 288
Medical requirements for entry,
366
Mendenhall Glacier, 221
Mendenhall Glacier Campground,
214
Mendenhall Glacier Visitor
Center, 221
Midnight Sun Baseball Game,
364
Midnight Sun Festival, 364
Miller's Landing (near Seward),
113
The Million Dollar Bridge, 106
Minto, 296
Misty Fiords National
Monument, 171
Money matters, 377
Monk's Rock (Kodiak), 150
The Monthly Grind (Ketchikan),
169
Moore Cabin (Skagway), 243
Moose Mountain, 286
Mosquito Cove Trail, 203
Mount Dewey Trail, 180–181
Mount Marathon Race, 364
Mount Ripinsky Trail, 256
Mount Roberts Trail, 225
Mount Roberts Tramway
(Juneau), 216–217
Mt Aurora/Skiland (near
Fairbanks), 286
Mud flats, Anchorage, 52
Museum of the Aleutians
(Unalaska), 342
Museum of the North
(Fairbanks), 6, 259, 277
Museums, best, 6
The Music of Denali, 328
Muskeg Meadows Golf Course
(Wrangell), 179
Musk Ox Farm (near Palmer), 72

**Naa Kahidi Dancers (Sitka),
197**
Nalukataq (Barrow), 356
National Association of Cruise
Oriented Agencies (NACOA),
20
National Park Service Dyea
Campground, 194, 239

Native Alaskans, 6–7, 54. *See also* Tlingits; Totem poles
  Anchorage area, 49–50
  Eklutna, 49
  Iñupiat Heritage Center (Barrow), 355–356
  Kodiak, 148, 149
  Ilanka Cultural Center (Cordova), 104
  Museum of the Aleutians (Unalaska), 340
  Ketchikan, 166–167, 170
  Sitka, 197, 198, 201, 202, 204
  World Eskimo Indian Olympics (Fairbanks), 282
  Wrangell, 178–179
Nenana Canyon (Glitter Gulch), 313
Nenana Ice Classic, 363
The New Archangel Dancers (Sitka), 197
Newspapers and magazines, 387
Niukluk River, 349
NOAA/NESDIS Command and Data Acquisition Station (Fairbanks), 292
Nolan Center Museum (Wrangell), 178
Nome, 334–335, 342–351
Nome-Council Road, 349
Nome-Taylor Road, 350
Nome-Teller Road, 350
Norovirus, 18
North American Open Sled Dog Championship (Fairbanks), 283
Northern lights (aurora borealis), 278
North Pole, 289
North Pole Post Office, 290
North Star Golf Club (Fairbanks), 285
Norwegian Cruise Line, 25–26
Nova, 74, 375

One People One World (Anchorage), 54–55
Oomingmak Musk Ox Producers Co-op (Anchorage), 54, 72
Outdoor adventures and tours, 373–376
Outfitters and outdoor package trips, 374–375
Outlook Park (Petersburg), 189
Out North Contemporary Art House (Anchorage), 57

Pack Creek, 5, 232–233
Packing tips, 379–380
Pack Train Building (Skagway), 243
Paragliding, 68
Parks Highway, 260
Passports, 365–366
Perseverance Theatre Company (Juneau), 227
Perseverance Trail, 224
Petersburg, 155, 181–189
Petroglyph Beach State Historic Park, 178–179
PhotoSymphony (Fairbanks), 288
Pier One Theatre (Homer), 142
Pilgrim Hot Springs, 350
Pinnell Mountain National Recreation Trail, 294
Pioneer Cemetery (Circle), 295
Pioneer Park (Fairbanks), 275–276
Piuraagiaqta (Barrow), 356
Planning your trip to Alaska, 359–388
Poker Flat Research Range (near Fairbanks), 293
Polar Bear Club (Barrow), 356
Polar bears, 8, 357, 390
Polychrome Pass, 323
Portage Glacier, 58, 61, 63
Potter Marsh, 58–59
Potter Section House (Potter Marsh), 59
The Pratt Museum (Homer), 6, 137
Primrose Campgrounds (near Seward), 113
Primrose Ridge, 322
Princess Cruises, 26–27
  Tours, 374
Princess Maksutov's grave (Sitka), 198
Prince William Sound, 4, 7, 80, 96–97
The Prospector (Valdez), 91–92
Prudhoe Bay, 303
Pullen Creek RV Park, 194
Pyramid Peak, 341

Rafting
  Copper River, 107
  Denali National Park, 327–328
  Haines, 254
  Matanuska Glacier, 74
  Talkeetna, 331
Rainbow Falls Trail, 181

Raspberries, Homer, 137
Red Light District (Skagway), 244
Red Onion Saloon & Brothel (Skagway), 242, 246
Regions of Alaska, 3–4
Resurrection Bay, 114–115, 117, 118, 120, 122
Richardson Highway, 260
Riley Creek Campground, 310
River rafting. *See* Rafting
Rock climbing. *See* Climbing, rock and ice
Royal Caribbean International, 27
Running of the Bulls at the Musk Ox Farm, 78
The Rushin' Tailor's Quilt Alaska (Skagway), 245
The Russian-American Company (Sitka), 203–204
Russian Bishop's House (Sitka), 196–198
Russian Blockhouse (Sitka), 196
Russian Orthodox cemetery (Eklutna), 49
RV travel and rentals, 370–371

Sable Pass, 323
Safety, 377–379
St. Lazaria Island National Wildlife Refuge, 200
St. Michael's Cathedral (Sitka), 198–199, 201
St. Nicholas Orthodox Church (Juneau), 218
St. Nicholas Russian Orthodox Church (Eklutna), 49
St. Nicholas Russian Orthodox Church (Juneau), 227
Saint Tikhon Russian Orthodox Church (Anchorage), 50
Salmon. *See also* Fishing
  Deer Mountain Tribal Hatchery and Eagle Center (Ketchikan), 167–168
  Juneau, 226
  types of, 127
Salmon Lake, 350
The Salty Dawg (Homer), 142
Sanctuary River Campground, 312
Sandy Beach Park (Petersburg), 189
Santa Claus House (North Pole), 289–290
Savage River Campground, 310

Saxman and the Saxman Arts Co-op Ketchikan (Ketchikan), 170
Saxman Native Village, 166–167
Scenic drives. See Driving tours
Science for Alaska (Anchorage), 50–51
Science for Alaska lecture series (Fairbanks), 280
Scuba diving, Resurrection Bay and Kachemak Bay, 118
Sea Life Discovery Tours (Sitka), 200
Seasickness, 120
Seaside Farms (Homer), 137
Seasons, 359, 361
    for cruises, 16, 21
Seniors, 382
    cruise discounts, 22
Service With a Smile (Fairbanks), 288
Settler's Cove State Park, 164
Seward, 81, 108–122
Seward Community Library, 109
Seward Museum, 116–117
Sheldon Jackson Museum (Sitka), 198
Sheldon Museum and Cultural Center (Haines), 255
Ship Creek, 53
Shoemaker Bay Recreation Area, 177
Shoup Glacier, 92
Shoup Glacier Trail, 91
Shrine of St. Therese (Juneau), 213, 221–222
Siberian-style prayer chapel (Eklutna), 49
Signal Creek Campground, 164
Sitka, 6–7, 155, 189–205
    accommodations, 191–194
    excursions from, 205
    getting to and around, 190–191
    history of, 189–190
    lay of the land, 190
    nightlife, 205
    outdoor activities, 202–203
    restaurants, 195
    shopping, 203–205
    wildlife, 199–200
Sitka Conservation Society, 201
Sitka Cross Trail, 202
Sitka National Historical Park, 195–196
Sitka Sound, 5

Sitka Spruce Park (Dutch Harbor), 340
Sitka State Pioneers' Home, 202
Sitka Summer Music Festival, 205, 364
The Sitka Symposium, 201
Sitka Tribal Bingo, 202
Sitka WhaleFest, 364
Skagway, 155, 233–247
Skagway Museum, 240–241
Skagway Streetcar Company, 241
Skookum Pass, 349
Sled dog racing
    Fairbanks, 283
    Iditarod Trail Sled Dog Race, 75–77, 363
    Yukon Quest International Sled Dog Race, 361
Sled dog tours, 121
Smith, Soapy, 234, 242
Smoking, 387
Snowboarding, Girdwood, 67
Soapy Smith's Parlor (Skagway), 242
Soho Coho Art Gallery (Ketchikan), 170
Soldotna, 81–82, 122–128
Solomon, 349
Solomon Gulch Trail, 91
Sons of Norway Hall (Petersburg), 186, 187
Southcentral Alaska, 3, 79–151
    lay of the land, 80–82
    must-dos in, 79–80
Southeast Alaska, 3, 152–257
    getting to and around, 156–157
    lay of the land, 154–156
    must-dos in, 153–154
Southeast Alaska Discovery Center (Ketchikan), 168
Southeast Alaska State Fair, 364
Southwest Alaska, 334
Special events and festivals, 361–364
Sport Fishing Alaska, 375
Stan Price State Wildlife Sanctuary, 232
State Office Building (Juneau), 220
Steamer Bay Cabin (Wrangell), 177
Steese Highway, 260
    driving tour, 291–295
Stikine Flats, 180
Stikine River, 179–180

Stikine River Delta, 172
Students, 382–383
Sukapak Mountain, 301
Swanberg Dredge (Nome), 348
Sycamore buoy tender (Cordova), 105

Talkeetna, 308, 328–332
Talkeetna RV, 329
Tanana Valley State Fair (Fairbanks), 281, 364
Taxes, 387
Ted Stevens Anchorage International Airport, 31
Teklanika Campground, 310, 312
Teklanika River, 322
Telephone, 387
Teller, 350
10th and M Seafoods (Anchorage), 55
Thumbs Cove State Marine Park, 114
Thunderbird Falls, 53
Tide pools, Sitka, 199
Time zones, 387–388
Tipping, 388
Tlingits, 187
    Haines, 256
    Sitka, 189, 195–198, 201, 204
    Wrangell, 172, 180
Tongass Historical Museum (Ketchikan), 167
Tongass Trading Company (Ketchikan), 169–170
Tony Knowles Coastal Trail (Anchorage), 51
Toolik Lake, 303
Totem Beach, 199
Totem Bight State Historical Park (Ketchikan), 166
Totem Heritage Center (Ketchikan), 165–166
Totem poles, 6
    Ketchikan, 165–167
    Sitka, 195–196
Totem Village Tribal House (Haines), 256
Tracy Arm-Fords Terror Wilderness, 231–232
Train travel, 369
Trans-Alaska Pipeline, 292
Transportation, 368–371
Travel agents, for cruises, 20
Traveling to Alaska, 367–371
Travel insurance, 376–377

Treadwell Ice Arena (Juneau), 224

Treadwell Mine Historic Trail, 225

Trekking. *See* Hiking and trekking

Tripod Mountain Trail, 104

Tsirku Canning Co. (Haines), 254–255

Tundra Wilderness Tour, 325–326

Turnagain Arm, driving tour along, 58–63

Twelvemile Summit, 294

Twentymile River, 61

Unalaska, 334, 335–342

Uniquely Alaskan Arts (Haines), 257

University of Alaska Fairbanks, 277–279, 285–286

Upper Chatanika River Campground, 293

Valdez, 80, 84–93

Valdez Museum, 90–91

Verstovia, Mt., 203

Victor Emanuel Nature Tours, 375

Visas, 365

Ward Lake Recreation Area, 164

Water, drinking, 379

Whale Park (Sitka), 200

Whales and whale-watching, 393–396

Cook Inlet, 60

Petersburg area, 188

Sitka WhaleFest, 364

Whale-watching, best places for, 5

The White Elephant (Sitka), 204

White Mountains National Recreational Area Nome Creek Valley, 293

White Mountains Recreation Area, 296, 297

White Mountains Summit Trail, 297

White Pass and Yukon Railroad Depot & Administration Building (Skagway), 241–242

White Pass & Yukon Route Railroad, 239, 240

White-water rafting. *See* Rafting

Whittier, 80, 94–97

Wickersham House State Historic Site (Juneau), 219

Wilderness Access Center (WAC; Denali National Park), 308, 319

Wildlife and wildlife viewing, 389–396. *See also* Bears and bear-viewing; Birds and bird-watching; Whales and whale-watching

Denali National Park, 324–325

tours out of Sitka, 200

William Sound Science Center (Cordova), 104–105

The Williams Reindeer Farm (near Palmer), 73

Windy Point, 59–60

Winner Creek Trail, 68

Winter, best things to do in, 8

Winterfest at Alyeska Resort (Girdwood), 361

Wiseman, 301

Wonder Lake, 323

Wonder Lake Campground, 312

World Eskimo Indian Olympics (Fairbanks), 282

World Ice Art Championships (Fairbanks), 363

Worthington Glacier, 92

Wrangell, 154–155, 172–181

Yoga, 226, 286

Yukon Quest International Sled Dog Race (Fairbanks), 283, 361

Yukon River, 298–299

Yukon River Bridge, 299

Yukon River Camp, 299

ACCOMMODATIONS

Aimee's Guest House (Gustavus), 231

AK Fireweed House Bed and Breakfast (Juneau), 212

Alaska Adventure Cabins (Homer), 133, 135

The Alaskan Hotel (Cordova), 100

The Alaskan Hotel (Juneau), 210

Alaska Ocean View Bed & Breakfast (Sitka), 192

Alaska Salmon Bake Cabins (Glitter Gulch), 313

Alaska's Capital Inn (Juneau), 212

All Seasons Inn (Fairbanks), 268

Alyeska Adventures (Girdwood), 65

Alyeska Hideaway (Girdwood), 65–66

The Amundsen House (Anchorage), 34

The Anchorage International Hostel, 34

Arctic Caribou Inn (Fairbanks), 304

The Arctic Getaway (Dalton Highway), 302

Aurora Express Bed and Breakfast (Fairbanks), 267–268

Aurora Inn Suites (Nome), 346

Bev's Bed & Make Your Own Darn Breakfast (Kodiak), 144–145

Blue Heron Bed and Breakfast at Glacier Bay (Gustavus), 231

Bridgewater Hotel (Fairbanks), 270

Brookside Inn B&B 55 (Valdez), 88

Camp Coogan Bay Hideaway (Sitka), 194

Captain's Choice Motel (Haines), 250

Caribou Inn Bed & Breakfast (Anchorage), 34

Carlo Creek Lodge, 315

Cascade Inn (Sitka), 192

Chilkat Eagle Bed and Breakfast (Fort Seward), 250–251

Chilkoot Trail Outpost (Skagway), 238

Cloudberry Lookout Bed & Breakfast (Fairbanks), 266–267

Colony Inn (Palmer), 72

Copper Whale Inn (Anchorage), 38

Crow Pass Cabin (near Girdwood), 65

Denali Crow's Nest (Glitter Gulch), 313–314

Denali River Cabins and Cedars Lodge (McKinley Village), 314

Denver Caboose (Skagway), 239

Driftwood Inn (Homer), 133

EarthSong Lodge (Healy), 316

Edgewater Grill (Valdez), 90

Eider House Bed & Breakfast (Kodiak), 146

Ester Gold Camp (Fairbanks), 269

Fairview Inn (Talkeetna), 329–330

Fort Seward Bed and Breakfast, 252
Fort Seward Condos, 252
Gilmore Hotel (Ketchikan), 163
Glacier Bay Lodge, 230
Golden North Motel (Fairbanks), 269
GoNorth Hostel (Fairbanks), 271
The Grand Aleutian Hotel (Unalaska), 338–339
Harborside Cottages (Kenai), 125–126
Harding's Old Sourdough Lodge (Wrangell), 176
Hatcher Pass Lodge (Matanuska-Susitna Valley), 71–72
Hermitage Cabin (Juneau), 213
Historic Anchorage Hotel, 39
Historic Chatanika Gold Camp (Fairbanks), 270–271
Hotel Alyeska (Girdwood), 64
Hotel Captain Cook (Anchorage), 39
Hotel Hälsingland (Fort Seward), 251–252
House of Seven Trees (Talkeetna), 329
The Inn at Creek Street (Ketchikan), 163–164
Jewel Lake B&B (Anchorage), 36
Jubilee Cabin (Juneau), 213
June's Whittier Condo Suites (Whittier), 96
Kenai Landing, 126
Keystone Hotel (Valdez), 88
King Eider Inn (Barrow), 354
Kodiak Bed & Breakfast (Kodiak), 146
Kodiak Island Winery Cottages, 146–147
Lake Hood Inn (Anchorage), 36
Lake House B&B (Valdez), 87–88
Laughton Glacier Cabin (Skagway), 239
Little Flower Cabin (Juneau), 213
Lucky Pierre Charters (Homer), 134
Madame's Manor (Ketchikan), 164
McKinley Trail Cabin (near Cordova), 102
Microtel Inn & Suites (Anchorage), 36
Mile Zero Bed and Breakfast (Skagway), 238
Minnie Street Bed & Breakfast Inn (Fairbanks), 268
Motel Nord Haven (Healy), 316

Mountain Morning Hostel & Lodge (Carlo Creek), 315
New York Hotel (Ketchikan), 163
Nome Nugget Inn, 346
The Northern Nights Inn 555 (Cordova), 100
Old Town Bed & Breakfast (Homer), 132–133
Orca Adventure Lodge (Cordova), 101–102
The Pipeline Club (Valdez), 90
Post Office Cabin (Juneau), 213
Prudhoe Bay Hotel (Deadhorse), 304
Rain Haven (Wrangell), 176
Reluctant Fisherman Inn (Cordova), 100
Ridgetop Cabins (Healy), 316
Rockwell Lighthouse (Sitka), 192, 194
Rooney's Roost Bed & Breakfast (Wrangell), 175–176
Russian Heritage Inn (Kodiak), 146
Sea Lion Cove (Homer), 134
Seaside Farms (Homer), 132
Sergeant Preston's Lodge (Skagway), 236–237
Seward Military Resort, 112
Sheep Mountain Lodge (Matanuska-Susitna Valley), 71
The Silverbow Inn (Juneau), 212
Sitka Hotel, 191–192
The Skagway Inn (Skagway), 237–238
Skyline Lodge (Kantishna), 312
Soundview Getaway Waterfront Condos (Whittier), 96
Spit Sisters Cafe B&B (Homer), 134
Sprucehaven B&B by the Sea (Kodiak), 145–146
Stikine Inn (Wrangell), 176
The Summer Inn Bed and Breakfast (Haines), 250
Susitna Place (Anchorage), 34
Sweet Dreams B&B (Nome), 345
Talkeetna Roadhouse, 330
Tanglewood Bed & Breakfast (Kenai), 125
Tides Inn Motel (Petersburg), 184–186
Top of the World Hotel (Barrow), 354
Totem Inn Hotel & Suites (Valdez), 88–89
Two Sisters Suites by the Beach (Homer), 133

The UniSea Inn (Unalaska), 338
The Valley Hotel (Palmer), 72
Van Gilder Hotel (Seward), 112–113
The Voyager Hotel (Anchorage), 38–39
Waterfront Bed & Breakfast (Petersburg), 184
Water's Edge Bed & Breakfast (Petersburg), 184
Wedgewood Resort (Fairbanks), 269–270
Westmark Baranof (Juneau), 210, 212
Whistle Stop Lodging (Seward), 112
At the White House (Skagway), 238
Wildflower Inn's (Anchorage), 40
Wiseman Gold Rush B&B (Dalton Highway), 302

RESTAURANTS

Airport Way Family Restaurant (Fairbanks), 271
Alaska Salmon Bake (Fairbanks), 274
Amelia's (Unalaska), 339
Arctic Pizza (Barrow), 355
Backdoor Café (Sitka), 195
Baja Taco (Cordova), 103
The Bakery Restaurant (Fairbanks), 271–272
The Bamboo Room (Haines), 253
Black Bear Coffee House (Glitter Gulch), 317
Brewsters (Fairbanks), 273
Bub's Subs (Glitter Gulch), 317
Café Savannah (Anchorage), 42–43
Capital Café (Juneau), 214–215
Channel Side Chowder House (Kodiak), 147
Chart Room (Unalaska), 339
Chilkat Restaurant and Bakery (Haines), 253
Chinook's Waterfront Restaurant (Seward), 115–116
Club Paris (Anchorage), 42
Commander's Room Restaurant (Haines), 253
The Cookie Jar (Fairbanks), 272
Costa's Diner (Juneau), 214
Crab Feast (Sitka), 195
Creekside Café (Carlo Creek), 318
Dancing Bear Salmon Bake (Talkeetna), 331

Diamond C Café (Wrangell), 177
Diaz Café (Ketchikan), 165
Eddie's Fast Food (Juneau), 215
Ester Gold Camp Dining Hall
    Buffet Dinner (Fairbanks), 274
Exit Glacier Salmon Bake
    (Seward), 116
Fat Freddies (Nome), 347
Fat Olive's (Homer), 136
Finn's Pizza (Homer), 136
Glacier Brewhouse
    (Anchorage), 42
Gwennie's Old Alaska Restaurant
    (Anchorage), 45
Harborside Coffee and Goods
    (Kodiak), 147
Harding's Old Sourdough Lodge
    Restaurant (Wrangell), 178
Henry's Coffee House, 318–319
Henry's Great Alaskan
    Restaurant and Sports Bar
    (Kodiak), 148
Hot Licks Homemade Ice Cream
    (Fairbanks), 273
Hot Spot Café (Mile 60 on
    Dalton Highway), 299
Hot Tamale (Fairbanks), 272
Jack Sprat (Girdwood), 66–67
Lemongrass (Fairbanks), 272
Little Saigon (Fairbanks), 272
Ludvig's Bistro (Sitka), 195
Margaret Bay Café (Unalaska),
    339
Marx Bros. Café (Anchorage), 44
Maxine's Glacier City Bistro
    (Girdwood), 66

McCafferty's (Fairbanks), 272
Milano's Pizzeria (Nome), 347
Mill Bay Coffee & Pastries
    (Kodiak), 147–148
Mountain Market (Haines),
    252–253
Orso (Anchorage), 42
Overlook Bar and Grill (Glitter
    Gulch), 317–318
Paco's Tacos (Fairbanks), 272
Papa Bear's Pizza (Petersburg),
    186
Parks (Carlo Creek), 318
The Peanut Farm
    (Anchorage), 44
Pel'meni (Merchants Wharf,
    (Juneau), 216
Pepe's North of the Border
    (Barrow), 354
Pioneer Café (Ketchikan),
    164–165
Pizzeria Roma (Juneau), 215
Polar Café (Nome), 347
Powder House Bar and
    Restaurant (Cordova), 103
Ray's Waterfront (Seward), 116
Rooney's Northern Lights
    Restaurant (Petersburg), 186
Salmon Bake Alaska (Glitter
    Gulch), 317
Sal's Klondike Diner (Soldotna),
    126
Sam's Sourdough Cafe
    (Fairbanks), 271

Shogun Teriyaki House (Barrow),
    354–355
The Silverbow Bakery (Juneau),
    214
The Smoke Shack (Seward), 113
Snow City Café (Anchorage), 41
Snow Goose Restaurant and
    Sleeping Lady Brewing
    Company (Anchorage), 41
Spit-Fire Grill (Homer), 136
Spit Sisters Cafe (Homer), 135
Steamers (Ketchikan), 165
Stikine Inn Restaurant
    (Wrangell), 178
Sweet Basil Café (Anchorage),
    40–41
Sweet Tooth Café (Skagway),
    236
Swiftwater Café (Whittier), 96
Thai House (Fairbanks), 273
The Turtle Club (Fairbanks), 275
Twin Dragons (Nome), 347
Two Sisters Bakery (Homer), 135
UniSea Inn Sports Bar
    (Unalaska), 339
Veronica's Cafe (Kenai),
    126–127
West Rib Café & Pub
    (Talkeetna), 330
Wild Spice (Juneau), 215–216
The Winter Thyme
    (Anchorage), 41
Wolf Run Restaurant
    (Fairbanks), 273–274
Yoly's Bistro (Seward), 113
Zen (Juneau), 216